Éditorial

Editorial

As we complete this issue, the war of invasion launched by Russia against Ukraine enters its second month. And as we in Western Europe and the rest of the world go about our daily lives, the relentless machine of destruction and death continues to grind out images of cities progressively reduced to rubble, of civilians maimed and killed, of millions, women, children and elderly, fleeing in terror. We also see the many thousands of young men and women, and others not so young, who remain behind, determined to defend their land and home, willing to pay any price.

Faced with horror on this scale, it is maybe derisory simply to continue with our professional lives as lawyers, practicing, studying or teaching international arbitration. And yet, there is perhaps no other branch of the law that so concretely reflects the necessity, for so many kinds of peaceful exchanges across borders, of the peaceable, just and sustainable resolution of conflicts. There is a sense in which what we do every day, usually without thinking of its more profound implications, is the clearest, most absolute opposite of what we have been seeing for the past month.

Admittedly, that is only one, small reason to carry on doing what we do, as conscientiously as we can. And as we do, we should have a special thought for our friends and colleagues in Ukraine. We hope, above all, for their safety; and we also hope that soon they will be able to resume their lives as lawyers and once again make their own, valued contribution to our community.

This issue includes a highly interesting study concerning a country which is particularly dear to your editors but sometimes a bit of an arbitration outlier, compared to its European neighbours. I am of course speaking of Italy. Our old friend Andrea Carlevaris has contributed his thoughts on the reform of Italian arbitration law and more particularly on the power of arbitrators under Italian law to grant interim relief, a power which has until now been reserved to the Italian State Courts.

In this issue we also announce the founding by the Journal's old friend and eminent contributor Thomas Clay, of "Sorbonne Arbitrage" described by him as an "unidentified academic object", clearly connected with the ancient university of that name and concerned with thinking, writing and speaking about international arbitration. For more thoughts about what this "thing" might actually develop into, please see the piece within by Kamalia Mehtiyeva who reports on its inaugural event.

Une autre contribution concerne, elle, l'exercice des pouvoirs effectivement conférés aux arbitres et surtout leur délégation. Il s'agit du rôle joué par les secrétaires de tribunaux arbitraux, dont l'usage se développe toujours plus dans notre pratique. Dans quelle mesure doivent-ils être bornés à des tâches administratives et de simple exécution ou peuvent-ils, au contraire, participer à la rédaction de la sentence et, si oui, doivent-ils lever leur plume dès que l'on en atteint les motifs décisoires ? Peuvent-ils participer ou même assister aux délibérations du tribunal ? Qu'en dit la jurisprudence ? La pratique autorisée ? Pour trouver la réponse à ces questions et bien d'autres, il suffit de consulter l'excellent article de José Rosell, qui nous fait profiter de toute son expérience.

Ce n'est donc pas tout à fait un hasard si la première décision commentée dans ce numéro, du Tribunal de première instance francophone de Bruxelles, concerne précisément le rôle joué par le secrétaire du Tribunal arbitral dans l'élaboration de sa décision et si celui-ci avait été de nature a en affecter la régularité. Le Tribunal de première instance répond heureusement par la négative à cette question. Nous remercions Marc Dal et Estelle Lévy pour leurs excellentes observations.

Nous faisons suite à nos précédents épisodes de la saga judiciaire franco-britannique (encore une) découlant de l'affaire *Kout Food*. On se souviendra que cette affaire met en relief la différence d'approche adoptée des deux côtés de la Manche, lorsqu'il s'agit de déterminer le droit applicable à la clause compromissoire, la France ayant développé des règles matérielles (i.e. du for judiciaire français) abandonnant ainsi la méthode conflictualiste, à laquelle la justice anglaise reste fermement attachée. Une fois de plus, cette différence méthodologique conduit à des solutions opposées, ce qui ne surprendra personne, comme nous l'expliquent très bien Peter Rosher (auteur du précédent épisode de ce feuilleton) et Mathilde Adant, que nous remercions chaleureusement.

L'inexorable campagne de l'Union européenne et de ses institutions contre tout arbitrage entre un investisseur ressortissant d'un État membre de l'Union et un État hôte, également membre de l'Union, poursuit son chemin. Il n'est donc pas surprenant de voir la Cour de justice sévir contre toute possibilité pour un État membre défendeur en tel cas de renoncer, fût-ce par inadvertance, à soulever une objection aussi fondamentale à la compétence du tribunal arbitral. Cette décision, contestable en elle-même, et potentiellement lourde de conséquences, dans l'affaire *PL Holding* c. *Pologne* nous est très habilement commentée par Benjamin Rémy.

Nous remercions tout particulièrement François de Bérard de ses judicieuses observations sur la nature particulière du contrôle par le juge français de la compétence de l'arbitre statuant dans le cadre d'un traité bilatéral d'investissement, à propos de l'arrêt de la Cour de cassation rendu dans l'affaire *Serafin Garcia*.

Enfin, merci à Bernard Hanotiau pour son panorama de jurisprudence belge et bien sûr à Priscille Pedone, l'âme de cette revue, pour ses panoramas français en matière d'arbitrage et de Règlements amiables. Et saluons au passage le travail de Romains effectué par Priscille et Bertrand Robert, pour la préparation des tables et index de 2020.

Charles Kaplan — Charles Nairac

Sommaire

2022-1

In memoriam Thierry Garby

Éditorial / Editorial

Charles KAPLAN et Charles NAIRAC 1

I. Doctrine – Débats / Articles – Debates

Towards a New Arbitration Law in Italy: Arbitrators' Power to Order Interim Relief Finally Recognized?
by Andrea CARLEVARIS 7

L'intervention des secrétaires des tribunaux arbitraux
par Jose ROSELL 29

II. Commentaires de jurisprudence – Case Law

Sous la direction de Christophe SERAGLINI

Quelles tâches le tribunal arbitral peut-il confier à son secrétaire ?
par Marc DAL et Estelle LEVY 61
[Tribunal de première instance francophone de Bruxelles du 17 juin 2021]

La saga Kabab-Ji c. Kout Food *continue : Zoom sur la décision de la Supreme Court du 27 octobre 2021*
par Peter ROSHER et Mathilde ADANT 71
[*Kabab-Ji SAL (Lebanon) (Appellant) v Kout Food Group (Kuwait) (Respondent)* [2021] UKSC 48]

La condamnation des arbitrages d'investissement internes à l'UE fondés sur l'accord des parties : l'inconséquence de la CJUE avérée
par Benjamin REMY 79
[CJUE, C-109/20, grande Chambre, 26 octobre 2021, *Pologne c. PL Holdings*]

Portée du Traité bilatéral d'investissement devant le juge français et contrôle de la compétence du tribunal arbitral : l'affaire Serafin Garcia
par François DE BÉRARD 85
[Cass.1re civ., 1er décembre 2021, n° 20-16714]

III. Panorama international de jurisprudence / Panorama Of World Case Law

Sous la direction de Michael POLKINGHORNE et Louis DEGOS

– *Belgique*
par Bernard HANOTIAU, Iris RAYNAUD et Arno JANSSENS.............. 95

– *France, partie I [arbitrage interne et international]*
par Priscille PEDONE 119

– *France, partie II [Règlements amiables]*
par Priscille PEDONE 259

IV. Tables de jurisprudence 2020-2021 / 2020-2021 Table of Cases

par Priscille PEDONE et Bertrand ROBERT 305

V. Index 2020-2021

par Bertrand ROBERT et Priscille PEDONE 325

VI. Événement / Event

Sous la direction de Priscille PEDONE

Sorbonne Arbitrage: a legal scientific pilgrimage
Kamalia MEHTIYEVA.. 339

Un encart « Lettre abonné » est joint à ce numéro.

Doctrine – Débats

Articles – Debates

Towards a New Arbitration Law in Italy: Arbitrators' Power to Order Interim Relief Finally Recognized?

Andrea CARLEVARIS
BonelliErede, Partner
Italian Association for Arbitration, President

RÉSUMÉ

En décembre 2021, une loi-cadre pour la réforme de la justice civile et de l'arbitrage a été adoptée en Italie. Outre des changements mineurs, la loi a pour objectif la réforme de trois aspects majeurs du droit de l'arbitrage. En premier lieu, elle reconnaît le pouvoir des parties d'attribuer aux arbitres le pouvoir d'ordonner des mesures provisoires et conservatoires, abrogeant ainsi l'interdiction prévue par l'Article 818 du Code de procédure civile, qui fait du droit italien une exception sur la scène internationale et qui est généralement indiquée comme l'obstacle principal à l'attrait de l'Italie comme siège d'arbitrages internationaux. Cependant, l'impact révolutionnaire de la réforme est limité par la condition que les parties attribuent ledit pouvoir aux arbitres de façon expresse. Le pouvoir des tribunaux étatiques d'ordonner des mesures provisoires et conservatoires lorsque les arbitres sont compétents sur le fond, qui est maintenant exclusif dans tous les états du processus, sera limité au stade précédant l'acceptation du mandat par les arbitres. Le deuxième principe majeur dont s'inspire la réforme concerne l'indépendance et l'impartialité des arbitres. La loi introduit un devoir de révélation de circonstances qui pourraient mettre en cause l'existence de ces conditions fondamentales. Le troisième principe-clé de la réforme consiste à reconnaître le pouvoir des parties de choisir le droit applicable au fond. Les décrets délégués devront clarifier d'autres aspects à cet égard, notamment : (a) les critères pour déterminer le droit applicable en l'absence d'accord des parties ; et (b) si les parties ou, en l'absence de clause de choix de loi, le tribunal arbitral, pourront choisir d'appliquer des règles de droit non étatiques.

ABSTRACT

In December 2021, a framework law to reform civil proceedings and arbitration was enacted in Italy. In addition to minor changes, the law aims to reform three main areas of arbitration law. First, it recognizes the parties' power to vest arbitrators with the power to order interim relief, thus removing the prohibition under Art. 818 of the Italian Civil Procedure Code, which keeps Italy isolated from the international scene and is commonly cited as the main obstacle to Italy's attractiveness as a seat for international arbitration proceedings.

However, the reform's revolutionary implications in this regard are somewhat curtailed by the requirement that arbitrators be expressly granted powers to order interim relief by the parties. The courts' power to issue interim measures when an arbitration agreement is in place, which is currently exclusive in all phases of the process, will be limited to the stage before the arbitrators accept their appointment. The second main principle underpinning the framework law concerns the independence and impartiality of arbitrators. Specifically, the law introduces a duty to disclose circumstances that could cast doubt on whether the arbitrators meet these fundamental requirements. The reform's third key principle consists in granting the parties the right to choose the applicable law. The implementing legislative decrees will clarify other important aspects, specifically: (a) the criteria to determine the applicable law when the parties do not make the choice; and (b) the extent to which the parties – or, in the absence of a choice-of-law clause, the arbitral tribunal – may apply non-national rules of law.

On 9 December 2021, a framework law (*legge delega*) to reform civil proceedings was published in the Italian Official Gazette (Law No. 206 of 2021). Para. 15 of the framework law's sole article deals with arbitration. It sets out the fundamental principles to be followed in the implementing legislation, which the government has now been instructed to adopt within 12 months.

Unlike prior arbitration reforms (the last two date back to 1994 and 2006), the framework law does not envisage an entirely new regime. Rather, it seeks to introduce a limited number of changes. This minimalistic and pragmatic approach – which can be appreciated – makes the prospect of fixing certain perceived defects in Italy's current regime within a reasonable timeframe realistic.

One of the proposed changes, i.e., granting arbitrators powers to order interim relief, is undoubtedly "historic", whereas the need for some of the others is questionable – although none (perhaps with one exception) can be viewed as entirely negative.

I. – Interim Relief

The infamous Art. 818 of the Civil Procedure Code ("CPC"), in its current version, stipulates as follows: "Arbitrators cannot order attachments or other interim measures unless otherwise provided by law".

Over the years, this provision – which, despite severe criticism, has survived several arbitration reforms[1] – has been described from opposing viewpoints as an expression of an "old and universally recognized"[2] principle, as a "genetic" limit that reflects the "incompatibility" of interim relief with "the arbitrator's nature

1. For the related legislative history, see A. Villa, "Arbitrato e tutela cautelare", in L. Salvaneschi and A. Graziosi (eds.), *L'Arbitrato*, Milano, 2020, pp. 518-519.
2. S. Satta, *Commentario al codice di procedura civile*, vol. IV, 2, Torino, 1971, pp. 282-283.

and characteristics"[3], and as "a diehard matter of fact"[4]. The framework law thus represents a unique opportunity to remove this anachronistic rule.

Of the novelties concerning arbitration in the framework law, the abolition of the prohibition on arbitrators to order interim relief is by far the most important. Point c) of para. 15 of the law's sole article requires the government to adopt legislation based on the following criteria: "provide for the recognition of formal arbitrators' [*arbitri rituali*] power to adopt interim measures in the case of express agreement of the parties set out in the arbitration agreement or in a subsequent written deed, unless otherwise provided by law; in such a case, confirm the courts' power only in the event that a request for interim relief is made before the arbitrators accept their appointment; regulate challenges against interim measures before the courts on the grounds provided by Art. 829, para. 1, of the Civil Procedure Code and for breach of public policy; regulate the implementation of interim measures under the courts' supervision"[5].

Italy is well known for being one of the very few jurisdictions in the world where arbitrators are still barred from granting provisional and conservatory measures (together with China, Thailand and a few other ones[6]). Given the growing importance of interim relief in international arbitration, the lack of arbitrators' powers to order protective measures is generally viewed as the main obstacle to Italy being more frequently chosen as a seat for international arbitration proceedings[7].

As far as the power to order interim relief is concerned, the framework law seeks to reverse the current rule: first, it recognizes arbitrators' power to do so "unless otherwise provided by law" and subject to the parties' express agreement; second, it excludes the courts' power to adopt provisional and conservatory measures – if an arbitration agreement is in place – from the arbitrators' acceptance of their appointment.

3. G. Arieta, "Le cautele. Il processo cautelare", in *Trattato di diritto processuale civile*, Padova, 2011, p. 819 ff.

4. G.F. Ricci, "Articolo 818", in F. Carpi (ed.), *Arbitrato*, Bologna, 2016, p. 589.

5. Author's translation. The original Italian of Art. 1, para. 15, point c) of the framework law reads as follows: "*prevedere l'attribuzione agli arbitri rituali del potere di emanare misure cautelari nell'ipotesi di espressa volontà delle parti in tal senso, manifestata nella convenzione di arbitrato o in atto scritto successivo, salva diversa disposizione di legge; mantenere per tali ipotesi in capo al giudice ordinario il potere cautelare nei soli casi di domanda anteriore all'accettazione degli arbitri; disciplinare il reclamo cautelare davanti al giudice ordinario per i motivi di cui all'articolo 829, primo comma, del codice di procedura civile e per contrarietà all'ordine pubblico; disciplinare le modalità di attuazione della misura cautelare sempre sotto il controllo del giudice ordinario*". On this point, the framework law, as approved by Parliament, follows the proposal of the commission ("Commissione per l'elaborazione di proposte di interventi in materia di processo civile e strumenti alternativi") chaired by Prof. Francesco Paolo Luiso ("Luiso Commission"), which served as a basis for the initial draft of the bill.

6. G. Born, *International Commercial Arbitration*, Alphen aan den Rjin, 2021, pp. 2619-2620.

7. Born, 2606 refers to the increased risks in international disputes that vital evidence be taken out of reach of the tribunal or that assets necessary to satisfy an award be removed to a jurisdiction where enforcement may be more difficult; P. Biavati, "Spunti critici sui poteri cautelari degli arbitri", in Rivista dell'arbitrato, 2013, p. 335; for references and an analysis of the various positions, see A. Carlevaris, *La tutela cautelare nell'arbitrato internazionale*, CEDAM, Padova, 2006, pp. 251 ff.

A. The Parties' Agreement to Vest Arbitrators with the Power to Order Interim Relief

Recognizing arbitrators' powers to grant interim relief unless otherwise provided by law is the exact opposite of the current situation. Indeed, Art. 818 CPC prohibits arbitrators from issuing provisional and conservatory measures "unless otherwise provided by law".

The words "unless otherwise provided by law" were introduced with the 2006 reform to take into account not only any subsequent legislative changes (which obviously would have been possible even without an express provision), but also – and especially – the exception that already existed at the time for corporate arbitration (*arbitrato societario*): namely, Art. 35, para. 5, of Legislative Decree No. 5 of 2003, which establishes that if an arbitration agreement allows disputes concerning the validity of shareholders' resolutions to be referred to arbitration, arbitrators are empowered to stay the effectiveness of the resolutions with an order that cannot be challenged[8].

Thus, under the new regime, a different legal provision may have the effect of excluding the arbitrators' powers. The inclusion of the wording "unless otherwise provided by law" does not appear justified and seems to confirm the persistent distrust in arbitrators when it comes to their making decisions considered particularly sensitive and intrusive on the parties' rights. Once this distrust is dispelled in general terms, it is difficult to understand what could justify excluding arbitrators' powers to order interim relief with respect to specific fields or legal relationships.

Arbitrators' prerogatives will be more seriously curtailed by the pre-condition that the power to order interim relief be expressly agreed by the parties. This requirement is unknown to the most developed arbitration laws, which tend to follow the opposite principle: arbitrators' powers are the rule, and the parties' express exclusion of powers is the exception. Most national arbitration laws provide – or national courts have held – that, absent clear indication to the contrary, the parties will be presumed to have agreed to authorize the arbitral tribunal to grant provisional measures (or at least certain types of provisional measures). For example, Art. 183(1) of the Swiss Private International Law Act ("PILA") provides as follows: "*Sauf convention contraire, le tribunal arbitral peut ordonner des mesures provisionnelles ou des mesures conservatoires à la demande d'une partie*"[9]. Likewise, in England, express recognition of arbitrators' powers is unnecessary for important categories of measures, such as security for costs, measures relating to any property that is the subject of the proceedings or is otherwise relevant to the proceedings, and measures relating to the taking and preservation of evidence; in these cases, arbitrators have the necessary powers unless expressly excluded by the parties[10].

8. Villa, p. 518 ff.

9. S. Berti *et al.* (eds.), *International Arbitration in Switzerland – An Introduction to and a Commentary on Articles 176-194 of the Swiss Private International Law Statute*, Basel, Geneva, Munich, 2000, p. 428 ff.

10. See Sect. 38 of the 1996 Arbitration Act: "(2) Unless otherwise agreed by the parties the tribunal has the following powers. (3) The tribunal may order a claimant to provide security for

The framework law states that the parties' will to vest arbitrators with interim powers can be expressed in the arbitration agreement "or in a subsequent written deed". The reference to "arbitration agreement" is certainly sufficient to encompass the three types of arbitration agreements known to Italian law, i.e., submission agreement (*compromesso*, Art. 807 CPC), arbitration clause (*clausola compromissoria*, Art. 808 CPC) and arbitration agreement relating to non-contractual relationships (*convenzione arbitrale relativa a rapporti non contrattuali*, Art. 808-*bis* CPC); however, one may wonder what the legislator had in mind when it referred to "a subsequent written deed". Parties are obviously free to vest arbitrators with the power to order interim relief through an *ad hoc* written agreement at any stage, including after the conclusion of the arbitration agreement – before or after a dispute arises and arbitration commences. However, from a practical viewpoint, such an agreement is unlikely to be reached when the parties are already in dispute and are likely to have diverging views on, among other things, the forms of relief that can be sought from the arbitrators. More realistically, one can envisage an agreement being reached while discussing the applicable procedural rules, to be reflected in a document such as the Terms of Reference in ICC arbitration (Art. 23 of the ICC Rules) or instruments with a similar function in other arbitration systems.

The real impact of this requirement will depend to a large extent on how it is construed in the implementing legislation (*decreti delegati*) or, failing any indication therein, how it is construed by those called on to interpret it. If reference to arbitration rules that provide for the power of arbitrators to adopt provisional and conservatory measures is considered sufficient to grant them those powers, there will be no significant impact on institutional arbitration, which represents a very significant part – if not the majority – of international arbitration proceedings seated in Italy. Virtually all arbitration rules most commonly used internationally, including those most frequently used in Italian-based proceedings, provide for arbitrators' power to grant interim relief (see, e.g., Art. 28(1) of the ICC Rules and Art. 26(1) of the Arbitration Rules of the Milan Chamber of Arbitration, the latter of which, in the version in force since 2020, recognizes these powers on condition they "are not barred by any mandatory provisions applicable to the proceedings"; recognition of the parties' power to vest arbitrators with these powers would certainly exclude the existence of a mandatory prohibition). Given the "express" nature of the choice of arbitration rules and the incorporation of chosen rules in arbitration agreements, considering the reference to arbitration rules sufficient for the purpose of this requirement would be compatible with the framework law's directives. This solution had been envisaged during a previous attempt at reforming

the costs of the arbitration [...] (4) The tribunal may give directions in relation to any property which is the subject of the proceedings or as to which any question arises in the proceedings, and which is owned by or is in the possession of a party to the proceedings: (a) for the inspection, photographing, preservation, custody or detention of the property by the tribunal, an expert or a party, or (b) ordering that samples be taken from, or any observation be made of or experiment conducted upon, the property. (5) The tribunal may direct that a party or witness shall be examined on oath or affirmation, and may for that purpose administer any necessary oath or take any necessary affirmation. (6) The tribunal may give directions to a party for the preservation for the purposes of the proceedings of any evidence in his custody or control". However, see Art. 24 of the Egyptian Law on Arbitration in Civil and Commercial Matters, which requires the parties' agreement for any provisional and conservatory measure to be adopted by an arbitral tribunal.

arbitration law, in 2017, when the proposed text confirmed the principle enshrined in Art. 818 CPC but permitted derogation therefrom by reference to arbitration rules[11].

However, one cannot exclude that an opposite interpretation will eventually prevail, based on the framework law's reference to an "express" agreement of the parties and on the text proposed by the Luiso Commission, which refers to the "free and conscious choice of the parties" (*"libera e consapevole scelta dei compromittenti"*). Therefore, if a mere reference to arbitration rules is not considered sufficient – and, in any event, for *ad hoc* arbitration – parties will have to keep the "express agreement" requirement in mind when entering into an arbitration agreement and will have to explicitly establish the arbitrators' power to grant interim relief if they so wish.

B. The Exclusion of Courts' Concurrent Power

While the recognition of arbitrators' power to order interim relief (*rectius*, the recognition of the parties' power to vest arbitrators with that power) has long been announced and wished for, much more surprising is the exclusion of state courts' concurrent power as of the arbitrators' acceptance of their appointment.

This development would represent a complete turnabout with respect to the current situation: Italy would shift from a system in which state courts have exclusive power at every stage to a system in which, after their appointment, arbitrators would have exclusive power. Though the courts' powers before the constitution of the arbitral tribunal would still be recognized, the concurrent jurisdiction of courts and tribunals after the arbitrators' acceptance of their appointment – which lies at the basis of most modern arbitration legislation[12] and rules[13] – would be excluded.

The possibility for parties to vest arbitrators with the power to grant interim relief after the commencement of an arbitration could cause the courts to lose their corresponding power while proceedings are under way. Therefore, this abrupt

11. See "Proposta in materia di provvedimenti cautelari nei procedimenti arbitrali amministrati", put forward by the "Commissione di studio per l'elaborazione di ipotesi di organica disciplina e riforma degli strumenti de degiurisdizionalizzazione, con particolare riguardo alla mediazione, alla negoziazione assistita e all'arbitrato", chaired by Prof. Guido Alpa ("Alpa Commission"). The proposal consisted in adding the following wording to Art. 832 CPC, which deals with administered arbitration: *"Il regolamento arbitrale può anche prevedere deroghe al divieto di cui all'art. 818. In tal caso, il provvedimento è richiesto e deliberato a norma del regolamento e il medesimo ricorso non può essere proposto al giudice. Il provvedimento cautelare non è soggetto a impugnazione e si applica l'art. 825 in quanto compatibile"* (Author's translation: "The arbitration rules may derogate from the prohibition under Art. 818. In that case, the interim measure is requested and ruled on based on the arbitration rules, and the same request may not be submitted to national courts. The interim measure is not subject to challenge, and Art. 825 applies to it to the extent compatible").

12. See, e.g., Art. 17J of the UNCITRAL Model Law on International Commercial Arbitration, as amended in 2006: "A court shall have the same power of issuing an interim measure in relation to arbitration proceedings, irrespective of whether their place is in the territory of this State, as it has in relation to proceedings in courts. The court shall exercise such power in accordance with its own procedures in consideration of the specific features of international arbitration".

13. See Art. 28 of the ICC Rules; Art. 26(3) of the UNCITRAL Rules; and Art. 37(5) of the Rules of the Arbitration Institute of the Stockholm Chamber of Commerce ("SCC Rules").

change of direction will also require at least an amendment of Art. 669-*quinquies* CPC, which establishes that, when an arbitration agreement is in place (including when arbitral proceedings are pending), the competent court is that which would otherwise have jurisdiction on the merits[14]. Specifically, this provision will have to take into account the fact that parties could, during the arbitration, agree to vest arbitrators with the power to grant provisional and conservatory measures, which would result in excluding the courts' power to grant those measures.

The reference to the "arbitrators' acceptance of their appointment" as the start date as of which the courts lose their power to order interim relief may give rise to doubts. Art. 820 CPC establishes that, for the purposes of determining the time limit for issuing an award, arbitration proceedings are considered to commence upon the arbitrators' acceptance of their appointment under Article 813 CPC. However, Article 820 can be – and is *de facto* – derogated from by referring to arbitration rules that set out additional requirements to be fulfilled subsequent to the arbitrators' acceptance of their appointment for the purpose of considering the arbitration proceedings effectively commenced[15]. It will therefore be appropriate for the implementing legislation to take this potential time gap into account. Alternatively, absent any express guidance in the rules to be adopted, reference to the acceptance of the appointment should be interpreted broadly to avoid a vacuum of interim relief after arbitrators accept their appointment but before they are effectively in a position to intervene.

If the legislative process did indeed result in the exclusion of state courts' power to grant interim measures as of the arbitral tribunal's constitution (in this respect, the framework law does not seem to leave room for doubt), Italian law would end up adopting a regime more favorable to arbitrators' powers than even that of the most arbitration-friendly jurisdictions. Although domestic legislation generally recognizes arbitrators' prominent role in deciding on applications for interim relief, the most progressive jurisdictions tend to let the parties choose the body – i.e., the courts or arbitral tribunal – to be seized after the arbitral tribunal's constitution. For instance, Swiss law provides for perfect equality between courts and arbitrators[16]. In English law, the power of courts to grant interim relief during the arbitration is limited to cases in which the arbitrators are unable to intervene or unable to do so in an effective manner[17].

In this respect, the *favor arbitrati* seems to have been interpreted in an extreme and inappropriate manner by the legislator. It is questionable that the exclusion of courts' power to grant provisional relief is in the parties' best interests. The

14. Art. 669-*quinquies* CPC: "If the dispute is subject to an arbitration clause or is referred to arbitration, even if informal [*irrituale*], *or if arbitration proceedings are pending* [emphasis added], the request shall be addressed to the judge that would have jurisdiction on the merits" ("*Se la controversia è oggetto di clausola compromissoria o è compromessa in arbitri, anche non rituali, o se è pendente il giudizio arbitrale, la domanda si propone al giudice che sarebbe competente a conoscere del merito*") (emphasis added).

15. See, e.g., Art. 16 of the ICC Rules, which stipulates that the arbitration file is to be transmitted to the arbitral tribunal upon its constitution, provided that the advance on costs requested by the ICC Court has been paid in its entirety by the parties.

16. P. Lalive, J.-F. Poudret, C. Reymond, *Le droit de l'arbitrage interne et international en Suisse*, Éditions Payot, Lausanne, 1990, p. 369.

17. See Sect. 44(5), of the Arbitration Act 1996; R. Merkin, L. Flannery, *Merkin Flannery on the Arbitration Act 1996*, London/Singapore, 2020, *sub* Sect. 44.

parties would in fact benefit more if they could choose between the two bodies based on the type of measure sought, the jurisdiction the measure is to be enforced in, urgency, and any other relevant circumstances. For example, when the effectiveness of the measure sought depends on its immediate enforceability, and enforcement presupposes the exercise of coercive powers that arbitrators lack (e.g., attachment), the requesting party may have an interest in seeking the measure from a judicial authority, thereby avoiding the need to obtain a judicial decision enforcing the arbitral measure. In this respect, it is significant that even in France, where arbitral tribunals have exclusive jurisdiction to order any type of interim relief as of their constitution, attachment orders are still reserved to the judiciary[18]. The inadequacy of arbitrators' powers is even more evident in relation to measures whose effectiveness depends on their producing effects on entities not bound by the arbitration agreement concerned; indeed, such measures are obviously unavailable to arbitrators because of the subjective limits of arbitration agreements whereas they are available to judicial authorities[19]. An arbitrator does not have the power to order attachment or the preservation of property held by third parties. Another good example can be found in one of the most common types of measures sought in international arbitration, i.e., orders to abstain from calling bank or insurance guarantees ancillary to the contractual relationship that contains the arbitration agreement. Any such measure may prove fully effective only if also issued against the guarantor bank or insurance company. As a third party, however, a guarantor bank or insurance company would not be bound by an arbitral measure but rather only by an order issued by a judicial authority.

One might wonder how the boundaries between the courts' and the arbitrators' respective powers will be determined in relation to "emergency arbitration" proceedings, i.e., the mechanisms introduced into the rules of numerous arbitral institutions over the last 15 years to remedy the absence of an arbitral body that can be seized before the constitution of an arbitral tribunal through the appointment of an emergency arbitrator for the granting of urgent relief[20]. Although proceedings before an emergency arbitrator are not unrelated to ordinary arbitral proceedings – quite the contrary, in several cases the continuing effectiveness of any emergency arbitrator decision presupposes the commencement of arbitral proceedings on the merits[21] – it is likely that the jurisdiction of state courts will be excluded as of the emergency arbitrator's acceptance of his/her appointment (or as of the moment any other procedural requirement under the applicable rules is satisfied), not as of the ordinary arbitral tribunal's constitution.

18. Art. 1468(1) of the French Civil Procedure Code; Th. Clay, "L'appui du juge à l'arbitrage", in Paris Journal of International Arbitration/Les Cahiers de l'arbitrage, 2011, No. 2, p. 85. Likewise, the power to order attachment is reserved to the judiciary in Belgium: Art. 1691(2) of the Belgian *Code Judiciaire*: *"Le tribunal arbitral ne peut toutefois autoriser une saisie conservatoire"*.

19. See Art. 17 of the UNCITRAL Model Law, which authorizes an arbitral tribunal to "order *any party* [emphasis added] to take such interim measures of protection" considered necessary. See P. Ortolani, Article 17: Power of Arbitral Tribunal to Order Interim Measures, in I. Bantekas et al. (eds.), *UNCITRAL Model Law on International Commercial Arbitration: A Commentary*, Cambridge, 2020, p. 338.

20. See Art. 29 and App. V to the ICC Rules; App. II to the SCC Rules; Article 9B of the Rules of the London Court of International Arbitration; and C. Sim, *Emergency Arbitration*, Oxford, 2021.

21. See, e.g., Art. 1(6) of App. V to the ICC Rules.

C. Recognition and Enforcement

The recognition of arbitrators' power to grant interim relief presupposes the adoption of rules on the implementation of the related orders, which the framework law envisages ("regulate the implementation of interim measures") without, however, providing any guidance as to how implementation is to occur, other than by stating the obvious, i.e., that it will be done "under the courts' supervision".

1. The Applicability of the New York Convention

The recognition and enforcement of arbitral interim measures is possible based on either ordinary legislative provisions or conventional instruments applicable in the jurisdiction where enforcement is sought. However, the best-known instrument for the recognition and enforcement of arbitral decisions – i.e., the 1958 New York Convention on the Recognition and Enforcement of Foreign Arbitral Awards – is not of assistance in this respect, for several reasons[22].

First, even though it were considered applicable to interim measures, the New York Convention deals only with the recognition and enforcement of decisions issued in foreign arbitral proceedings. Therefore, in no case could it be invoked for the enforcement of orders issued in the same jurisdiction where enforcement is sought.

Second, the New York Convention notoriously contains neither a provision specifically dealing with the recognition and enforcement of foreign provisional measures nor a definition of the notion of "arbitral award" that would allow one to precisely define its scope *ratione materiae*[23]. Irrespective of the methodological approach to the latter problem, interim measures can *prima facie* hardly be qualified as awards, given their provisional and unstable nature[24]. Despite some contrary views[25], the form in which an arbitrator adopts an interim measure is irrelevant for the purpose of determining whether it can be enforced under the New York Convention. A court in which recourse is sought for the enforcement of a measure would in fact be free to characterize the measure based on its substantive content, regardless of the form chosen by the arbitrator[26].

---

22. See A Carlevaris, *The Enforcement of Provisional Measures*, in F. Palombino, R. Virzo, G. Zarra (eds.), Provisional Measures Issued by International Courts and Tribunals, The Hague, 2021, p. 297 ff. ; for rare views favorable to the New York Convention's applicability, see T. Kojović, "Court Enforcement of Arbitral Decisions on Provisional Relief – How Final is Provisional", in Journal of Int. Arbitration, 2001, p. 511 ff.

23. The reference to the notion of "award" aims to ensure that the New York Convention's scope includes awards rendered both in institutional arbitrations and in *ad hoc* proceedings; it is therefore irrelevant for our present purposes: see Art. I(2) of the New York Convention. See also P. Bernardini, "Sentenze arbitrali e Convenzione di New York", in Rivista di diritto processuale, 2006, p. 89; A. Carlevaris, "La qualificazione delle decisioni arbitrali", in Rivista dell'arbitrato, 2002, p. 470 ff.

24. For a decision of the Swiss Federal Tribunal of 13 April 2010 on this point, see ATF 136 III 2010.

25. See Kojović, pp. 524 ff. The enforceability of foreign interim measures adopted in the form of an award based on domestic legislation or the New York Convention has been recognized also in jurisdictions in which arbitrators have no power to order interim measures, such as Italy: see F. Tommaseo, "Lex fori e tutela cutelare nell'arbitrato commerciale internazionale", in Rivista dell'arbitrato, 1999, pp. 14 ff.; and P. Bernardini, "Arbitrato internazionale e misure cautelari", in Rivista dell'arbitrato, 1993, pp. 24-25.

26. A. Carlevaris, La qualificazione, cit., p. 469 ff. (and arbitral practice and caselaw cited therein).

Third, the New York Convention specifically addresses the recognition of arbitration agreements and the recognition of arbitral awards made pursuant thereto. It would be inconsistent to consider interim measures excluded from the New York Convention's scope with respect to the former yet covered by it with respect to the latter. Admitting that interim measures can be recognized and enforced based on the New York Convention would necessarily lead one to admit that arbitrators have exclusive jurisdiction to adopt provisional measures under Art. II(3) of the New York Convention – which, on the contrary, and as stated above, is almost universally denied, and which not even the Italian reform would provide.

Finally, as described in greater detail below, several requirements for the recognition (*rectius*, grounds for refusing recognition and enforcement) of arbitral awards based on the New York Convention seem incompatible with the characteristics and nature of interim measures and instead presuppose awards on the merits. In one of the few reported cases on the New York Convention's applicability to interim orders, the Australian Supreme Court of Queensland, in a thoroughly motivated ruling in *RCI v. Bolwell*, resolutely denied that the New York Convention is applicable to interim orders[27].

2. *Domestic Legislation*

Turning to domestic legislation, numerous jurisdictions have adopted specific rules on the recognition of interim measures. Although the approach taken varies significantly, two main – and substantially homogeneous – models can be identified[28].

The more common approach is to allow enforcement of a measure by a declaration of enforceability, as in the case of awards. By means of an *exequatur*, the arbitral measure is introduced into the national legal system and produces the same effects as a decision of a state authority. This approach, which can be called the "*exequatur* model", does not presuppose the characterization of the arbitral decision as an award or its adoption in the form of an award. Certain jurisdictions require the measure to take the form of an award, whereas others simply put provisional orders on the same footing as awards *quoad effectum*, irrespective of their form.

The second model can be called the "court assistance model". It entails a state court order confirming the arbitrator's decision or forcing the recalcitrant party to comply with it.

In jurisdictions that use the *exequatur* model, court intervention is limited to ensuring that the arbitral decision meets certain basic, mandatory requirements and declaring it enforceable (or denying its enforceability), without reproduction or modification. In jurisdictions that use the court assistance model, the court issues a self-standing order following the arbitral measure. The court pursues the arbitral measure's aim, but the content of its order may vary – and courts

27. Supreme Court of Queensland, *Resort Condominiums International, Inc. v. Ray Bolwell and Resort Condominiums (Australasia) Pty. Ltd.*, 29 October 1993, in Yearbook Commercial Arbitration 1995, pp. 628 ff.

28. A. Carlevaris, "The Recognition and Enforcement of Interim Measures Ordered by International Arbitrators", Yearbook of Private International Law, 2007, 512 ff. ; *Id.*, La tutela cautelare, cit., 504 ff.

generally have limited power to adapt the measures to their procedural law. One of the first jurisdictions to adopt the *exequatur* approach was the Netherlands. The Dutch Civil Procedure Code provides that the rules applicable to awards are fully applicable also to arbitral decisions issued in "summary proceedings"[29]. The recognition of arbitral provisional measures through a mere declaration of enforceability is increasingly common in recent national legislation, which frequently simply extends the rules applicable to arbitral awards to cover orders for interim relief. This approach is particularly common in jurisdictions that have adopted the UNCITRAL Model Law, which in most cases have extended the scope of provisions on the recognition and enforcement of awards (Arts. 35 and 36 of the Model Law) to provisional measures. After the 2006 revision, the Model Law provides for a specific enforcement regime, which follows the *exequatur* model[30].

Among jurisdictions that adopt the *exequatur* model, only a few provide that the rules for awards apply also to foreign provisional orders. When no similar solution is provided, only provisional orders issued in arbitration proceedings with their seat in the same state can be recognized and enforced. The territorially limited scope of the applicable regime is thus unsuitable for ensuring transnational recognition and enforcement.

The paradigm of the court assistance model is represented by Art. 183(2) PILA, which provides as follows: *"Si la partie concernée ne s'y soumet pas volontairement, le tribunal arbitral peut requérir le concours du juge compétent. Celui-ci applique son propre droit"*. The judicial assistance provided by this norm is generally considered the only mechanism available to obtain implementation of an interim measure in Switzerland. A party seeking to enforce an order cannot avail itself of the possibility of obtaining the *exequatur* that Art. 193 of the same law reserves to awards on the merits[31]. In the court assistance model, the court has no discretion in its intervention[32]. Besides the case where the type of decision to be enforced is unknown to the jurisdiction of enforcement, courts can withhold their assistance only in cases of manifest invalidity or inapplicability of the arbitration agreement, irregular constitution of the arbitral tribunal or, according to some commentators, non-conformity with public policy or breach of due process[33].

A variant of the court assistance model can be found under German law. To avoid the risk of conflicting enforceable measures, Sect. 1041(2) of the *Zivilprozessordnung* allows the party that has obtained an order to apply to a court for its enforcement – on condition, however, that no similar request for interim measures has already been submitted to the courts. Moreover, the enforcement court is empowered to reclassify the arbitral order to adapt its content to the types of measures available under German law. German courts are thus not authorized to replace the arbitral order whenever the latter can be enforced as originally

29. Art. 1051(3) of the Dutch Code of Civil Procedure reads as follows: "A decision rendered in summary proceedings shall be regarded as an arbitral award to which the provisions of Sections Three to Five inclusive of this Title shall be applicable". The provisions referred to concern the formal and substantive requirements of awards, enforcement and recourses.

30. See Arts. 17H and 17I of the UNCITRAL Model Law, as amended in 2006.

31. Lalive, Poudret, Reymond, p. 362.

32. S. Besson, *Arbitrage international et mesures provisoires*, Zurich, 1998, p. 309.

33. See the authors referred to in Carlevaris, The Recognition, cit., p. 517.

formulated. However, they can deny their assistance whenever no corresponding measure exists under German law[34].

The *exequatur* of an arbitral order produces its effects only in the jurisdiction in which it is issued, whereas a court order in support of an arbitral measure is no different from any ordinary judicial decision and may circulate based on the applicable rules for recognition and enforcement of foreign judicial decisions.

English law features a mixed approach, i.e., one that combines elements of the *exequatur* model with elements of court assistance mechanisms – though it contains certain aspects that are manifestly different from either model. Sect. 42 of the Arbitration Act, which regulates the enforcement of arbitral "orders" in general, provides that English courts have no power to adopt a self-standing decision based on an arbitral order (as in court support mechanisms) or to revise or modify an arbitral order, but only the power to vest an arbitral order with the legal force it originally lacks. However, unlike jurisdictions that follow the *exequatur* model, English law does not put orders on the same footing as awards *tout court*; rather, it provides for a specific enforcement mechanism with different characteristics and effects. The court issues an order requiring a party to comply with an arbitral "peremptory order", which the arbitral tribunal is empowered to issue only after the party has failed to comply with a previous order "without showing sufficient cause". Therefore, in order for a party to obtain the courts' assistance in enforcing an arbitral measure, a double refusal by the other party is necessary: first with respect to the original order, and then with respect to the more coercive "peremptory order". Seeking court assistance is subject to a party's exhaustion of all available remedies for non-compliance before the arbitrators ("any available arbitral process"; see Sect. 42(3)) and to the expiration of any deadline set by the arbitrators to abide by the order. This provision is an expression of the "subsidiarity principle", on which English arbitration law is largely based.

An additional legislative model consists in the issuance of an autonomous court order based on a factual and legal assessment previously carried out by an arbitrator. However, in this case, the court order is not limited to the enforcement of the arbitral order but rather is based on the courts' concurrent jurisdiction to adopt provisional measures when an arbitration agreement is in place.

3. *The grounds for refusing enforcement*

One will therefore have to wait until the implementing legislation is enacted to see whether the Italian legislator opts for an *exequatur* model, a court assistance model, or a hybrid system such as the German or English one. If the legislator chooses the *exequatur* model – which is the prevailing one in domestic legislation worldwide – it will be appropriate for the legislator to take the specific characteristics of interim relief into account when establishing the grounds for refusal of recognition and enforcement of provisional and conservatory measures

34. F. Niggemann, "The New German Arbitration Law", in Revue du droit des affaires internationales, 1998, p. 656. For a case in which an order akin to a "Mareva Injunction" was reformulated as an injunction known to German law, see the decision of the Court of Appeal of Karlsruhe reported in Kojović, p. 517.

rather than sticking with the grounds for refusal applicable to awards under Arts. 839-840 CPC and Art. V of the New York Convention.

The grounds for refusal set out in Arts. 839-840 CPC and in Art. V of the New York Convention clearly aim to regulate the recognition of final decisions on the merits, not interim measures. This is particularly true with respect to Art. 840, No. 1, CPC and Art. V(1)(a) of the New York Convention, which allow the courts of the state in which recognition is sought to refuse the *exequatur* if the arbitration agreement is invalid or inapplicable, thus implying a previous – and positive – assessment of the arbitrator's jurisdiction on the merits. However, given their inherent urgency, interim measures are frequently ordered based on a mere summary assessment, before the tribunal's jurisdiction has been fully assessed[35]. A similar standard should be applied for the purpose of enforcement.

Another ground which is hardly compatible with interim relief is the respect of due process in the proceedings that resulted in the decision to be enforced (Art. 840, No. 2, CPC and Art. V(1)(b) of the New York Convention). In interim measure proceedings, the applicable procedural standards differ from those of proceedings on the merits. Although the power of tribunals to order provisional relief *ex parte* – i.e., without giving notice to the other party before an order is issued – is controversial and is even denied by some commentators[36], limited, temporary restrictions of the parties' right to be heard are considered acceptable in light of the urgent nature of interim measure applications and to ensure the measures' effectiveness. These different standards should also be reflected in the enforcement regime.

In addition to grounds for refusing enforcement that are not suitable for protective measures, additional requirements for the recognition of such measures should be considered. The legislator may look at some of the requirements introduced into the Model Law with the 2006 amendment. Art. 17 of the Model Law provides grounds for non-enforcement of provisional measures in addition to the grounds applicable to awards under Art. 36 of the Model Law. Art. 17I(1)(a)(ii) provides that recognition and enforcement is to be denied at the request of the party against which it is sought if the party seeking enforcement failed to comply with any order for security on which provisional measures were conditioned. Art. 17I(1)(a)(iii) permits non-enforcement if the provisional measures were terminated or suspended by the arbitral tribunal or by a court in "the State in which the arbitration takes place or under the law of which that interim measure was granted", although on condition that the court was "so empowered". Art. 17I(1)(b)(i), which seems to take inspiration from the abovementioned provision of German law, provides that enforcement may be refused, even *ex officio*, if the enforcing court finds that the interim measure is incompatible with the powers of the enforcing court itself, unless

35. S. Benz, "Strengthening Interim Measures in International Arbitration", in Georgia Journal of Int. Law, 2018, p. 143.

36. For references, see Born, p. 2696. Arts. 17B and 17C of the UNCITRAL Model Law, as amended in 2006, provide that *ex parte* preliminary orders (i.e., orders issued without giving prior notice to the recipient, the effects of which may be limited in time) may be issued when the arbitrators conclude that "prior disclosure of the request for the interim measure to the party against whom it is directed risks frustrating the purpose of the measure". However, Art. 17C also specifically requires the arbitral tribunal to give immediate notice of any decision it makes on an application for a preliminary order to all parties and establishes that any such decision is not enforceable.

such court decides to reformulate the interim measure to the extent necessary to adapt it to its own powers and procedures for the purposes of enforcing that interim measure and without modifying its substance.

These requirements – which differ from those applicable to awards and are instead specific to interim relief – deserve consideration as part of the new law's enforcement regime.

4. *The enforcement of emergency arbitrator orders*

It is probably too much to ask that the implementing legislation deal specifically with the recognition and enforcement of decisions made by emergency arbitrators based on the mechanisms referred to above, as is the case in some of the most progressive arbitration legislation[37].

Whatever mechanism is ultimately chosen to implement interim measures ordered by arbitrators in ordinary proceedings will also serve as the mechanism for enforcement of emergency arbitrators' decisions, regardless of the form they take[38].

5. *The scope of the enforcement regime and the modification or revocation of measures*

The implementation regime for arbitral interim measures should not be limited to measures adopted in proceedings seated in Italy – rather, it should be extended to foreign proceedings. Once arbitrators' powers are recognized as a matter of principle for arbitration proceedings seated in Italy, there will seemingly be no obstacle to the enforceability of foreign orders, which is in fact admitted by the Model Law (Art. 17H(1): "irrespective of the country in which it was issued").

Finally, an exhaustive enforcement regime should also contemplate the possibility of an arbitral decision – which by its very nature is provisional and unstable – being terminated, suspended or modified by the arbitral tribunal. In addition to constituting a ground for refusing enforcement of a measure, as stated above, the termination, suspension or modification of a given measure should affect an already recognized measure.

D. Challenges of Arbitral Interim Measures

The framework law contemplates a role for state courts not only in the implementation but also in the challenge of provisional and conservatory measures issued by arbitrators "on the grounds provided by Art. 829, para. 1, CPC and for breach of public policy". Art. 1, para. 15, point f), of the framework law, examined in greater detail below, provides that the abovementioned order staying the effects

37. See Sects. 22A e 22B of the *Hong Kong Arbitration Ordinance*; Sect. 2(1) of the *International Arbitration Act* and Sect. 2(1) of the *Arbitration Act* of Singapore; and Sect. 2(1) of the *Arbitration Act* of New Zealand.

38. Certain arbitration rules provide that emergency arbitrators' orders must be rendered in the form of orders (Art. 29(2) of the ICC Rules), whereas others leave emergency arbitrators free to decide whether to render the order as an order or as an award (Art. 8 of App. II to the SCC Rules).

of shareholders' resolutions – currently non-appealable be instead made subject to challenge (*reclamo*)[39].

It is unsurprising that the framework law provides that arbitral measures be appealable. Commentators have long advocated for the possibility of removing the effects of interim measures in the jurisdiction where they are issued to counterbalance their enforceability[40]. Moreover, it is to be expected that, in recognizing arbitrators' powers for the first time, the legislator wishes to reserve some form of judicial control over the arbitral measures. Nevertheless, this approach entails a risk of interference by the courts, which may be tempted to make up for the absence of an autonomous power to issue interim measures by interpreting their role at the appeal stage broadly. For the reasons stated above, it would have been preferable to provide for state courts' concurrent powers, with those powers being limited, when a tribunal has already issued its own order, to cases in which the circumstances existing at the time the order was issued subsequently change[41].

The reference to the grounds for appeal of awards limits the possibility of challenges to major flaws in the contested measure and thus constitutes, in this respect, a safeguard against the risk that an arbitral measure be set aside on grounds pertaining to its merits. However, as already observed with respect to enforcement, the reference to the grounds for annulment of arbitral awards is unconvincing. For the reasons stated above, for example, one may question the automatic application to interim relief of the grounds for setting aside awards under nos. 1, 2, 3, 4, 6 and 10 (on the validity and scope of arbitration agreements, the regularity of the constitution of arbitral tribunals, the capacity of arbitrators, expiry of the time limit to render the award and the erroneous dismissal of jurisdiction) and 9 (on breach of due process) of Art. 829 CPC. It will thus be appropriate for the legislator to consider, when implementing the framework law, the specific features of interim relief, or at least to adapt the grounds for setting aside awards under Art. 829(1) CPC.

II. – Independence, Impartiality and the Duty of Disclosure

The framework law's second key principle concerns the independence and impartiality of arbitrators and the transparency of circumstances that could cast doubt on whether the arbitrators meet these fundamental requirements. It is another topic of great importance for Italy's reputation in the international arbitration community, which has been tarnished by recent episodes[42].

---

39. Arbitral interim measures issued based on arbitration rules were not subject to appeal in the Alpa Commission's proposal. See Villa, p. 519.

40. S. Besson, pp. 343-344; K.P. Berger, *International Economic Arbitration*, Deventer/Boston, 1993, p. 589.

41. The Alpa Commission took a similar approach in its proposal, which, as stated above, excluded the courts' concurrent power whenever a measure has already been sought from arbitrators based on the applicable arbitration rules.

42. See, e.g., the judgment of the European Court of Human Rights of 20 May 2021, in which the Court held that Italy had breached Art. 6(1) of the European Convention on Human Rights by giving effect to an arbitral award issued by an arbitral tribunal that included an arbitrator who lacked the necessary independence: European Court of Human Rights (First Section), Judgment of 20 May 2021, Application No. 5312/11, *Case of BEG S.p.A. v. Italy*.

The reform's impact in this respect is much more limited than that in respect of arbitrators' power to order interim relief. Para. 15, point a), of the framework law directs the government to "strengthen the guarantees of impartiality and independence of arbitrators by reintroducing the right to challenge on serious grounds of convenience, establishing a duty [for arbitrators] to issue, upon acceptance of an appointment, a statement mentioning any factual circumstance relevant to the abovementioned guarantees, and providing for the invalidity of acceptance in the event of failure to disclose, in particular disqualification if, at the time an appointment is accepted, the arbitrator omits to declare circumstances that may be invoked as grounds for challenge under Art. 815 of the Civil Procedure Code"[43].

The introduction of a duty to disclose any circumstance relevant to the assessment of arbitrators' independence and impartiality is neither innovative nor surprising. Quite the contrary: one may find it surprising that a duty of disclosure had not been envisaged up to this point[44], given that it is part of the best practices of international arbitration[45] and is regularly set out in arbitration rules[46].

The duty notoriously exists for the entire duration of the arbitration and requires the disclosure of any circumstance that arises, or of which the arbitrator becomes aware, in the course of the proceedings. It will therefore be important for the legislator to bear in mind the ongoing nature of the duty of disclosure in adopting the implementing legislation. It will also be important to clarify that the duty does not encompass only circumstances that would disqualify the arbitrator, but any circumstance that may call the arbitrator's independence and impartiality into question from the parties' perspective. If an arbitrator is of the opinion that a circumstance exists that would justify his/her disqualification, he/she should decline the appointment, regardless of the chance of success of any challenge[47].

---

43. Author's translation. The original Italian of Art. 1, para. 15, point a), of the framework law reads as follows: "*rafforzare le garanzie di imparzialità e indipendenza dell'arbitro, reintroducendo la facoltà di ricusazione per gravi ragioni di convenienza nonché prevedendo l'obbligo di rilasciare, al momento dell'accettazione della nomina, una dichiarazione che contenga tutte le circostanze di fatto rilevanti ai fini delle sopra richiamate garanzie, prevedendo l'invalidità dell'accettazione nel caso di omessa dichiarazione, nonché in particolare la decadenza nel caso in cui, al momento dell'accettazione della nomina, l'arbitro abbia omesso di dichiarare le circostanze che, ai sensi dell'articolo 815 del codice di procedura civile, possono essere fatte valere come motivi di ricusazione*".

44. On the need for a duty of disclosure in Italian legislation, see G. Verde, "La posizione dell'arbitro dopo l'ultima riforma", in Rivista dell'arbitrato, 1997, p. 475, wherein the author expresses regret over the fact that such a duty was not introduced by the 1994 reform.

45. See IBA Guidelines on Conflicts of Interest in International Arbitration, General Standard 3. See also T. Clay, *L'arbitre*, Dalloz, Paris, 2001, p. 318.

46. See Art. 11(2), of the ICC Rules and Art. 20 of the Rules of the Milan Chamber of Arbitration.

47. See IBA Guidelines, General Standard 2(a) ("An arbitrator shall decline to accept an appointment or, if the arbitration has already been commenced, refuse to continue to act as an arbitrator, if he or she has any doubt as to his or her ability to be impartial or independent") and General Standard 3(c) ("an arbitrator who has made a disclosure considers himself or herself to be impartial and independent of the parties, despite the disclosed facts, and, therefore, capable of performing his or her duties as arbitrator. Otherwise, he or she would have declined the nomination or appointment at the outset, or resigned."). See also ICC Note to Parties and Arbitrators on the Conduct of Arbitration under the ICC Rules, para. 26: "A disclosure does not imply the existence of a conflict. On the contrary, arbitrators who make disclosures consider themselves to be impartial and independent, notwithstanding the disclosed facts, or else they would decline to serve" (available at:

The framework law aims to reintroduce "the right to challenge on serious grounds of convenience" (*gravi ragioni di convenienza*) provided by Art. 51 CPC for the recusal of judges[48]. Art. 51 is a residual provision, which requires judges to recuse themselves from a case when circumstances exist that make the continuing exercise of their functions inappropriate regardless of the existence of any of the listed grounds. Before the 2006 reform, in the absence of a specific provision on the challenge of arbitrators, Art. 815 CPC referred to the grounds for recusal of judges under Art. 51. However, it was doubtful whether that reference encompassed also Art. 51, para. 2 – i.e., precisely the one that permits the recusal of judges on grounds of convenience. It is therefore certain whether the reform's effect will be to "reintroduce" this rule, as the framework law states, or rather to "introduce" it anew.

The same goal of enhancing the quality of the appointment process for arbitrators is pursued by para. 15, point h), which directs the government to "provide that, in all cases, the appointments of arbitrators by a judicial authority be based on criteria of transparency, rotation and efficiency"[49]. The involvement of judicial bodies as appointing authorities is relatively frequent in domestic *ad hoc* arbitrations, whereas it is extremely rare in international proceedings and virtually non-existent in institutional arbitration, where the role of appointing authority is typically performed by the arbitral institution itself in the absence of agreements to the contrary between the parties. The intention to enhance the overall quality of the appointment process is, of course, to be commended. However, the wording used in the framework law is perplexing and can certainly be improved in the implementing legislation: first, the framework law omits fundamental criteria, such as competence and specific experience in the subject-matter of the dispute; second, the term "rotation" suggests a limited pool of candidates for the competent authority to choose from on a rotating basis, which is far from a commendable practice.

III. – Applicable Law

The framework law requires the government to adopt a provision on applicable law whereby party autonomy is recognized, namely a provision "that, in the event of a decision based on the law, the parties have the power to determine and choose the applicable law"[50].

This provision evidently constitutes a reconsideration by the legislator of the decision to abrogate, with the 2006 reform, the provision on applicable law introduced in 1994 (Art. 834 CPC, abrogated in 2006). Given that it eliminated almost all

---

https://iccwbo.org/content/uploads/sites/3/2020/12/icc-note-to-parties-and-arbitral-tribunals-on-the-conduct-of-arbitration-english-2021.pdf).

48. This part of para. 15, point a), was not in the original draft of the framework law approved by the Senate; it was added at a later stage, when the text was approved by the Chamber of Deputies.

49. Author's translation. The original Italian of para. 15, point h), of the framework law reads as follows: "*prevedere che, in tutti i casi, le nomine degli arbitri da parte dell'autorità giudiziaria siano improntate a criteri che assicurino trasparenza, rotazione ed efficienza*".

50. Author's translation. The original Italian of para. 15, point d), of the framework law reads as follows: "*prevedere, nel caso di decisione secondo diritto, il potere delle parti di indicazione e scelta della legge applicabile*".

distinctions between domestic and international arbitration, the 2006 legislator must have assumed that a provision on applicable law had become superfluous. Needless to say, the return to a "monistic" system and the abolition of a specific, separate regime applicable to international arbitration did not result in the elimination of international arbitration proceedings, i.e., proceedings seated in Italy but connected to more than one jurisdiction. Therefore, a provision on applicable law remains useful. Moreover, the problem of determining the applicable law can arise even in domestic arbitration proceedings in which the parties may agree on the applicability of a foreign law, subject to any mandatory rule of otherwise applicable law.

The reintroduction of a provision on the applicable law is therefore appropriate. However, as formulated, the provision in the framework law serves little purpose. It states the obvious by recognizing party autonomy in determining the applicable law. As far as contractual relationships (which constitute the basis of the vast majority of disputes referred to arbitration) are concerned, the parties' freedom to choose the applicable law is already recognized under Italian law by Art. 57 of the Private International Law Statute (Law No. 218 of 1995) and, within the European Union, by Art. 3(1) of the "Rome I" Regulation[51].

Conversely, the provision is silent on other important aspects of the choice of law, which will have to be clarified in the implementing legislation. First, no guidance is given as to the criteria to determine the applicable law in the frequent case in which the parties have not themselves chosen it (for example, "the law to which the relationship is most closely related", as provided by Art. 834 CPC, abrogated in 2006, or "the rules of law which [the arbitral tribunal] considers most appropriate", as provided by Art. 21 of the ICC Rules). Second, and more importantly, the framework law does not specify whether the parties – or, in the absence of agreement between them, the arbitral tribunal – will be empowered to determine that also non-state rules, or only a domestic legal system, apply. By referring to the notion of "rules" (*norme*), Art. 834 CPC in force between 1994 and 2006 empowered the parties to choose a-national rules of law ("The parties may agree on *the rules* [emphasis added] that arbitrators shall apply"), but limited the power of arbitrator to select a domestic legal system in the absence of an agreement between the parties ("If the parties do not agree, *the law* [emphasis added] to which the relationship is most closely related shall apply"). The reference to the notion of "law" in the framework agreement suggests that both the parties and the arbitral tribunal may choose only a domestic legal system as applicable law, but one may wonder whether this is the consequence of a conscious decision of the legislator or rather a mere oversight.

IV. – Other Minor Changes

In addition to the changes illustrated above, the framework law directs the government to implement other minor amendments, the purpose of which is

51. Regulation (EC) No. 593/2008 of the European Parliament and of the Council of 17 June 2008, Art. 3(1): "A contract shall be governed by the law chosen by the parties".

to clarify issues that are currently debated, rationalize and unify the arbitration regime, or fill in lacunae.

Clarifying a debated issue is the purpose of para. 15, point b), which requires the government to "provide expressly for the enforceability of decrees whereby the president of a court of appeal declares a foreign award containing an order [*lodo straniero con contenuto di condanna*] enforceable"[52]. This provision resolves in the affirmative a question that has proved controversial in the caselaw and in legal literature, i.e., whether a decision issued by the president of a court of appeal at the end of the first phase of the foreign award enforcement process is immediately enforceable[53]. When *ex parte* proceedings under Art. 839 CPC ascertain the enforceability of an award containing an order, it will thus not be necessary for the interested party to await the conclusion of the opposition phase under Art. 840 CPC or expiry of the time limit to appeal the *exequatur* decree before being able to proceed to enforcement.

Para. 15, point e) provides for the implementing legislation to "reduce the time limit under Art. 828, para. 2, of the Civil Procedure Code to request the setting aside of formal [*rituali*] awards to six months, equating it with the one under Art. 327 of the Civil Procedure Code"[54]. This would reduce what is known as the "long time limit", i.e., the time limit that runs from the date an award is issued in the absence of any formal notification by the interested party, which conversely would trigger a "short", 90-day time limit. The legislator's goal here is to shorten the overall period of uncertainty as to the fate of appealed awards and to make the time limit consistent with that for the appeal of court rulings[55].

The mere reorganization and unification of Italy's arbitration regime is the goal pursued by para. 15, point f), which requires the provisions on corporate arbitration – i.e., arbitration of internal disputes in trade companies (between shareholders, between shareholders and the company, or between the company and any of its organs) – to be moved from Legislative Decree No. 5 of 2003 (where it is currently) to the CPC[56]. As mentioned above, the only substantive change required by this provision consists in making stays of shareholders' resolutions

52. Author's translation. The original Italian of para. 15, point b), of the framework law reads as follows: "*prevedere in modo esplicito l'esecutività del decreto con il quale il presidente della corte d'appello dichiara l'efficacia del lodo straniero con contenuto di condanna*".

53. For a recent analysis of the debate and comments on a ruling denying the immediate enforceability of this kind of decree, see A. Carosi, "In tema di efficacia del lodo estero riconosciuto in pendenza di opposizione: in favore di una ragionevole (ma non ancora automatica) provvisoria esecutorietà", in Rivista dell'arbitrato, 2020, 85 ff. (case note to Court of Appeal of Genoa, 18 December 2019).

54. Author's translation. The original Italian of para. 15, point e), of the framework law reads as follows: "*ridurre a sei mesi il termine di cui all'articolo 828, secondo comma, del codice di procedura civile per la proposizione dell'impugnazione per nullità del lodo rituale, equiparandolo al termine di cui all'articolo 327, primo comma, del codice di procedura civile*".

55. The "long" time limit to request the setting aside of awards under Art. 828 CPC starts running from the date the award is signed. The analogous time limit for the appeal of court rulings starts running from the date the ruling is published.

56. Author's translation. The original Italian of para. 15, point f) reads as follows: "*prevedere, nella prospettiva di riordino organico della materia e di semplificazione della normativa di riferimento, l'inserimento nel codice di procedura civile delle norme relative all'arbitrato societario e la conseguente abrogazione del decreto legislativo 17 gennaio 2003, n. 5*". 'It goes on to state as follows: "*prevedere altresì la reclamabilità dell'ordinanza di cui all'articolo 35, comma 5, del decreto legislativo 17 gennaio 2003, n. 5, che decide sulla richiesta di sospensione della delibera*".

ordered by tribunals in corporate arbitration subject to appeal – consistent with the new general regime of arbitral provisional and conservatory measures under para. 15, point c) (commented on above).

Para. 15 closes with a perplexing provision, which instructs the government to: "regulate the *translatio iudicii* between arbitral proceedings and court proceedings and between court proceedings and arbitral proceedings". The "*translatio iudicii*" towards arbitration – i.e., shifting court proceedings to arbitration – was contemplated by Law No. 162 of 2014 to reduce the workload of courts, an eternal and intractable problem of civil justice in Italy[57]. This goal was not successfully pursued, probably in part due to the lack of clarity as to how exactly proceedings were to migrate to arbitration. One may therefore welcome the requirement to adopt a specific procedural regime in this respect. What is difficult to understand is the reference to the opposite process, i.e., the migration of arbitral proceedings to state courts. It is unclear why the legislator would want to encourage shifting arbitral proceedings to state courts, as that would undermine greater recourse to arbitration – which in all other respects seems to be one of the main principles underlying the reform. One can hope that the only goal pursued by the legislator in introducing a specific regime for the *translatio iudicii* from arbitration to court proceedings is not to encourage and regulate cases of willful transfer of proceedings from arbitration to courts, but rather to govern situations in which an arbitral tribunal has declined jurisdiction and the dispute has to resume before state courts. If this is indeed the *ratio legis*, the framework law could have been drafted in more explicit terms[58].

V. – Conclusion

The new arbitration regime outlined in Law No. 206 of 2021 is far from perfect. One may find it disappointing that arbitrators' power to order interim relief requires the parties' express agreement, which, in the absence of a broad interpretation in the implementing legislation, could seriously curtail the reform's innovative impact. The legislator's intention to exclude state courts' concurrent power to adopt provisional and conservatory measures is surprising – and not convincing. It would have been appropriate to take into account the specific features of interim measures when providing for the grounds for setting aside and enforcing arbitral interim measures. Suggesting that parties involved in arbitration proceedings may refer the dispute to state courts despite a prior agreement to arbitrate seems at odds with the reform's general goal.

---

57. Law No. 162 enacted Law Decree No. 132 of 2014, Art. 1(1) of which provides as follows: "*Nelle cause civili dinanzi al tribunale o in grado d'appello pendenti alla data di entrata in vigore del presente decreto, che non hanno ad oggetto diritti indisponibili e che non vertono in materia di lavoro, previdenza e assistenza sociale, nelle quali la causa non è stata assunta in decisione, le parti, con istanza congiunta, possono richiedere di promuovere un procedimento arbitrale a norma delle disposizioni contenute nel titolo VIII del libro IV del codice di procedura civile*".

58. By Ruling No. 223 of 2013, the Constitutional Court declared Art. 819-*ter* CPC unconstitutional to the extent it excludes the applicability, in the relationship between arbitral and court proceedings, of rules corresponding to those of Art. 50 CPC, i.e., rules governing the resumption of proceedings before the competent court. See C. Stefanetti, "La *translatio iudicii* tra giudizio ordinario e arbitrato", in Salvaneschi, Graziosi, cit., p. 495 ff.

That said, the removal of the "taboo" of arbitral provisional and conservatory measures is reason for great satisfaction for all those who have at heart the effectiveness of the arbitral process and Italy's appeal as a seat for international arbitration[59].

Given the framework law's terseness on several of the issues discussed above, the reform's quality will depend to a great extent on how the general principles set out in Law No. 206 will be enhanced and developed in the implementing legislation.

Given the reform's limited scope as far as arbitration is concerned, it is probably possible – and it would certainly be desirable – for the government to adopt legislation within a short timeframe that broadly interprets the principles underlying the Parliament's mandate yet remains within the boundaries of such mandate.

59. In the words of the Advocate General of the European Court of Justice, G. Tesauro: "Interim protection has precisely that objective purpose, namely to ensure that the time needed to establish the existence of the right does not in the end have the effect of irremediably depriving the right of substance, by eliminating any possibility of exercising it; in brief, the purpose of interim protection is to achieve that fundamental objective of every legal system, the effectiveness of judicial protection". See *The Queen v. Secretary of State for Transp., ex parte Factortame Ltd*, Case No. C-213/89, [1990] E.C.R. I-02433, ¶ 18 (E.C.J.).

L'intervention des secrétaires des tribunaux arbitraux[1]

José ROSELL[2]

RÉSUMÉ

Face au débat généré par les affaires Yukos et Gazprom v Naftogaz of Ukraine, puis, plus récemment, par le jugement de première instance francophone de Bruxelles rendu dans l'affaire Commission Européenne c/ Emek et WTE, en raison de la participation du secrétaire du tribunal arbitral lors de la rédaction de la sentence, plusieurs institutions d'arbitrage, qui ont récemment révisé leurs règlements d'arbitrage, ont décidé de réglementer l'intervention des secrétaires de tribunaux arbitraux. Malheureusement, cette codification n'a pas été effectuée de manière uniforme. Les avis de la doctrine et la pratique arbitrale sont également partagés. Tout cela est source d'incertitude et de contestation, qui ne peut être minimisée que par une concertation entre les parties et le tribunal arbitral dès le début de la procédure.

ABSTRACT

Due to the debate generated by the Yukos and Gazprom v Naftogaz of Ukraine cases, and then, more recently, by the Judgment of the French-speaking First Instance Court of Brussels in European Commission v. Emek and WTE, arising out of the participation of the secretary to the Arbitral Tribunal during the drafting of the award, several arbitration institutions, which have recently revised their arbitration rules, have decided to regulate the intervention of tribunal secretaries. Regrettably, this codification has not been carried out in a uniform manner. The opinions of legal commentators and arbitral practice are also divided. All this is a source of uncertainty and challenge, which can only be minimized by consultation between the parties and the arbitral tribunal at the outset of the proceedings.

1. Le présent article est une actualisation d'un article du même auteur publié au Spain Arbitration Review, N° 38/2020 sous le titre « *La redacción del laudo por el secretario del tribunal : Opiniones contrastadas* ».

2. Arbitre Indépendant, Avocat Honoraire du Barreau de Paris, Avocat au Barreau de Barcelone. Contact : jose.rosell@arb-intal.com.

Introduction

Nonobstant la volonté récente des principales institutions d'arbitrage de codifier l'institution des secrétaires de tribunaux arbitraux, dénommés aussi secrétaires administratifs, leur intervention ne va pas sans soulever certaines interrogations, parmi lesquelles figure la possibilité de rédiger tout ou partie de la sentence.

Plusieurs juridictions nationales ont eu à se prononcer sur ce sujet. Mais, force est de constater que les solutions adoptées par celles-ci ne sont guère uniformes.

L'affaire la plus retentissante a été l'affaire *Yukos*, sans doute en raison du montant de la condamnation prononcée par le tribunal arbitral à l'encontre de la Fédération de Russie[3].

Quelques années plus tard, la sentence arbitrale rendue dans l'affaire opposant Gazprom à la société d'état ukrainienne Naftogaz a également été attaquée devant la juridiction suédoise sur la base du même grief, à savoir la supposée rédaction de la sentence par le secrétaire du tribunal arbitral[4].

D'autres juridictions nationales, telles que la High Court d'Angleterre[5] et tout récemment, le Tribunal de première instance francophone de Bruxelles[6], ont aussi été sollicitées pour trancher cette même question. Au moment d'écrire cet article, nous restons attentifs au sort qui sera donné à la sentence confirmée en première instance par le Tribunal de Bruxelles, précité, dont le jugement a fait l'objet d'un recours devant la Cour de cassation belge[7].

En parallèle de ce contentieux arbitral, la position des principales institutions d'arbitrage a évolué, allant du silence de leurs règlements d'arbitrage vers la reconnaissance et la précision du rôle des secrétaires. Il sera ainsi intéressant d'examiner la tendance suivie par ces institutions d'arbitrage au moment de règlementer l'intervention des secrétaires du tribunal arbitral (**II**).

Un aperçu de la doctrine nous permettra aussi de vérifier que les avis sur le rôle des secrétaires de tribunaux arbitraux sont bien divergents (**III**).

Avant de comparer la position adoptée par les principales institutions d'arbitrage et d'observer quels sont les avis les plus significatifs de la doctrine sur l'intervention des secrétaires, nous examinerons les affaires les plus marquantes qui ont été portées devant les juridictions nationales (**I**).

I. Analyse du contentieux arbitral

Nous commencerons cette analyse par étudier d'abord l'affaire *Gazprom c/ Naftogaz* qui, bien que n'ayant pas abouti à une décision judiciaire, en raison

3. *Yukos Universal Limited (Isle of Man) c/ Fédération de Russie*, affaire CPA N° AA 227, sentence finale du 18 juillet de 2014.
4. *National Joint Stock Company Naftogaz d'Ukraine c/ Public Joint Stock Company Gazprom*, affaire SCC N° V2014/078/080, sentence finale du 22 décembre 2017.
5. *P v. Q, R, S, U* [2017] EWHC 148 et 194 (Comm).
6. Jugement du 17 juin 2021, 4e chambre, affaires civiles.
7. *Global Arbitration Review, News*, 2 février 2022.

de l'accord intervenu entretemps entre les parties, présente un intérêt particulier du fait des arguments qu'elles ont développés devant la cour d'appel de Svea (A). Ensuite nous nous attarderons sur les conclusions auxquelles sont arrivées d'autres juridictions nationales avant de terminer sur la position adoptée, à ce stade, par les juges néerlandais, dans l'affaire *Yukos* (B).

A. L'affaire *Gazprom c/ Naftogaz*

1) Le contexte de l'affaire

Gazprom et Naftogaz conclurent deux contrats en date du 19 janvier de 2009. Un premier portant sur l'achat de gaz pour la période 2009-2019 (le « Contrat d'approvisionnement »), puis un deuxième pour le transit de gaz naturel provenant de Russie et d'autres pays, à travers le territoire ukrainien pour la même période (le « Contrat de transit »).

En juin 2014 les deux parties initièrent des procédures d'arbitrage, à la suite de désaccords intervenus pendant l'exécution du Contrat d'approvisionnement, devant l'Institut d'arbitrage de la Chambre de commerce de Stockholm (SCC).

Naftogaz prit les devants en commençant le premier arbitrage dans lequel cette société d'État réclamait le paiement de la somme de 15 milliards de dollars, au regard des ristournes résultant de l'application de la formule de prix prévue au Contrat d'approvisionnement.

De son côté, la société Gazprom engagea une procédure d'arbitrage distincte à l'encontre de Naftogaz afin de lui réclamer un montant de 56 milliards, au titre de livraisons de gaz impayées.

Les deux arbitrages furent, par la suite, consolidés en un seul arbitrage, qui donna lieu, d'abord, à une sentence partielle, en date du 31 mai de 2017, puis à une sentence finale, en date du 22 décembre 2017[8].

Dans sa sentence partielle le tribunal arbitral faisait droit à la réclamation de Naftogaz tendant à réduire la révision du prix de gaz, à partir d'avril 2014 au lieu de 2011, en même temps qu'il rejetait la demande reconventionnelle de Gazprom, considérant que Naftogaz n'avait pas violé son engagement de « *take-or-pay* ». En vertu du Contrat d'approvisionnement. Dans sa sentence finale le tribunal arbitral condamnait Gazprom à payer à Naftogaz un montant de 2 milliards de dollars.

Par la suite, Naftogaz commença un autre arbitrage devant la SCC au titre du Contrat de transit, en vue de réclamer à Gazprom le paiement de la somme de 15 milliards de dollars, plus les intérêts, en raison du transit de volumes de gaz insuffisants et du défaut de paiement de droits de transit. Dans ce même arbitrage, Gazprom formula une demande reconventionnelle à hauteur de 50 milliards de dollars. En date du 28 février 2018, le tribunal arbitral rendit une sentence finale, par laquelle il condamna Gazprom à payer la somme de 4,630 milliards de dollars à Naftogaz, à défaut d'avoir respecté son obligation

8. *National Joint Stock Company Naftogaz d'Ukraine c/ Public Joint Stock Company Gazprom*, préc.

de faire transiter les volumes minimums convenus[9]. Cependant, le tribunal arbitral décida de compenser cette dernière somme avec le montant de la condamnation dans la sentence finale du 22 décembre 2017, précitée, laissant ainsi Gazprom débitrice de la somme nette de 2,560 milliards de dollars, plus les intérêts.

Le même tribunal arbitral fut désigné tout aussi bien pour l'arbitrage consolidé afférent au Contrat d'approvisionnement que pour celui concernant le Contrat de transit. Avec l'accord des parties la SCC nomma un secrétaire administratif. Le siège des arbitrages était fixé à Stockholm.

Le règlement d'arbitrage applicable aux arbitrages était celui de la SCC, dans sa version de 2010. Le droit applicable au fond était le droit suédois, conformément aux dispositions du Contrat d'approvisionnement et du Contrat de transit.

Les trois sentences furent l'objet d'un recours en annulation devant la cour d'appel de Svea[10]. Le recours formé à l'encontre de la sentence partielle du 31 mai 2017 fut rejeté le 27 novembre 2019[11].

Parallèlement aux arbitrages précités, Gazprom initia, en 2018, un arbitrage d'investissement à l'encontre de l'Ukraine, conformément au Règlement de la CNUDCI, en se basant sur l'Accord portant sur l'encouragement et la protection réciproques des investissements conclus entre la Russie et l'Ukraine, à la suite de la saisie des actions que Gazprom possédait dans une filiale commune avec Naftogaz. Cette saisie avait été sollicitée par le ministère de la justice ukrainien pour garantir le paiement d'une amende de 6,4 milliards de dollars que les autorités de la concurrence avaient imposée à Gazprom, au motif que Gazprom aurait abusé de sa position dominante dans le marché pour forcer Naftogaz à accepter des droits de transit de gaz vers l'Europe de faible niveau[12].

D'après les informations publiées par la presse en décembre 2019, Gazprom trouva un accord avec le gouvernement ukrainien et se désista des demandes formulées devant le tribunal d'investissement précité[13].

Par ailleurs, Gazprom et Naftogaz trouvèrent un accord au regard des deux arbitrages SCC, précités, d'après lequel Gazprom s'engagea à payer à Naftogaz la somme de 2,9 milliards de dollars et à se désister des deux recours en annulation pendants devant la cour d'appel de Svea[14].

En raison de cet accord transactionnel, nous ne connaîtrons pas la solution que la cour d'appel de Svea aurait pu donner aux arguments soutenus par les deux sociétés dans le cadre de la procédure d'annulation des sentences. Cependant, il nous paraît intéressant d'analyser tout particulièrement l'argument consistant à soutenir que la rédaction totale ou partielle des sentences par le secrétaire du tribunal arbitral constituait un motif d'annulation des sentences finales.

---

9. *National Joint Stock Company Naftogaz d'Ukraine c/ Public Joint Stock Company Gazprom*, affaire SCC N° V2014/129.
10. Cour d'appel de Svea, N° T 1019-17, T 2826-18 et T 3250-18.
11. Cour d'appel de Svea, N° T 1019-17.
12. Global Arbitration Review, 29 mai 2018.
13. https://en.interfax.com.ua/news/economic/633385.html.
14. www.rfi.fr/en/wires/20191221-russias-gazprom-pays-29-bn-settle-ukraine-dispute.

2) Les arguments développés devant la cour d'appel de Svea

À titre préliminaire, nous devons préciser que Gazprom n'a pas soutenu devant la cour d'appel de Svea que le secrétaire du tribunal arbitral avait rédigé la sentence partielle du 31 mai 2017. Ainsi, notre analyse ne portera que sur les deux sentences finales des 22 décembre 2017 et 28 février 2018.

Les recours en annulation introduits par Gazprom à l'encontre de ces deux sentences finales étaient basés sur la section 34, paragraphe 1, alinéas 3 et 7 de la nouvelle loi sur l'arbitrage suédoise, qui est entrée en vigueur le 1er mars 2019.

Sur la base de l'alinéa 3 le demandeur en annulation pouvait prétendre obtenir l'annulation d'une sentence « si les arbitres avaient excédé leur mandat, de sorte que probablement cela avait eu une influence sur le résultat ».

D'après l'alinéa 7, le recours en annulation est admis « si, sans faute de sa part [à savoir la demanderesse au recours], s'est produit une irrégularité au cours de la procédure qui avait probablement eu une influence sur le résultat du cas d'espèce ».

Nous nous limiterons ici à analyser le motif fondé sur la supposée délégation des devoirs, que les parties avaient confiés au tribunal arbitral, au profit du secrétaire administratif.

En principe, si la rédaction de la sentence par le secrétaire était assimilée à une délégation des devoirs du tribunal à son profit, cela pourrait constituer une violation des alinéas 3 et 7 du premier paragraphe de la section 34 de la loi d'arbitrage suédoise. La raison étant que le tribunal arbitral aurait, d'une part, excédé le mandat qui lui a été confié par les parties, ce qui serait contraire à l'alinéa 3, et, d'autre part, il aurait commis une irrégularité d'ordre procédural, ce qui serait sanctionné par l'alinéa 7, en ce que le secrétaire aurait accompli des devoirs confiés aux arbitres, pour autant que les tâches accomplies par le secrétaire auraient exercé une influence sur le résultat de l'affaire.

Au cours de la procédure d'annulation de la sentence, Gazprom avait allégué que, sauf accord des parties, le secrétaire ne pouvait accomplir que des tâches administratives, alors que le tribunal arbitral lui avait confié la rédaction de la partie de la sentence relative à la motivation de la décision du tribunal et lui avait permis d'assister aux délibérations. De ce fait, selon Gazprom, deux erreurs de procédure auraient été commises qui entachaient les sentences de nullité.

Selon Gazprom, la première erreur consistait à avoir délégué au secrétaire des fonctions qui correspondaient au mandat que les parties avaient octroyé au tribunal arbitral en vertu de la clause d'arbitrage. La deuxième résultait du fait d'avoir autorisé le secrétaire à exercer une influence sur l'issue de l'arbitrage. Ces deux erreurs avaient pour conséquence que le tribunal était allé au-delà de son mandat ainsi qu'une erreur de procédure qui affectait le résultat de l'arbitrage.

Au soutien de son argumentation, Gazprom avait présenté le rapport d'un expert en analyse linguistique et sémantique portant sur l'auteur de la partie de la sentence relative à la motivation. Cet expert arrivait à la conclusion qu'il était très probable que le secrétaire du tribunal arbitral avait rédigé une partie importante de la motivation de la sentence.

Dans ses écritures Gazprom faisait référence au Règlement d'arbitrage de la SCC et à ses « *Guidelines for Arbitrators* », ainsi qu'aux Notes de la CNUDCI sur l'Organisation de la procédure arbitrale, à la Note aux parties et au tribunal arbitral sur la conduite de l'arbitrage conformément au Règlement d'arbitrage de la CCI et au « *Young ICCA Guide on Arbitral Secretaries* ».

En outre, Gazprom avait fait état du débat sur les tâches confiées au secrétaire administratif, qui avait eu lieu dans le cadre du recours en annulation introduit par la Fédération de Russie à l'encontre de la sentence rendue dans l'affaire *Yukos*, qui se trouvait, en ce moment-là, dans l'attente d'une décision de la Cour suprême des Pays-Bas[15].

Il est intéressant de souligner que Gazprom s'est également référé à la décision de la cour d'appel de Svea du 24 novembre de 2017, bien que cette Cour se soit prononcée contre l'annulation d'une sentence après avoir considéré qu'il n'avait pas été prouvé que l'intervention du secrétaire du tribunal arbitral avait influencé la décision prise par le tribunal arbitral[16]. Dans la section B ci-dessous, nous examinerons plus extensivement le raisonnement suivi par la cour d'appel de Svea dans cette affaire.

Sans rentrer dans le détail des débats qui ont été menés lors de la modification de l'ancienne loi suédoise de l'arbitrage de 1999, il peut être utile de mettre en relief que les pouvoirs exécutif et législatif du Royaume de Suède n'avaient pas cru bon d'adopter la Loi Modèle de la CNUDCI, même si la nouvelle loi de 2019 comporte certaines similitudes avec la Loi Modèle.

Après de longs et intenses débats, en particulier au regard du motif d'annulation prévu à l'alinéa 7 du premier paragraphe de la Section 34, la nouvelle loi d'arbitrage de 2019 n'a pas inclus une définition de ce qu'il y avait lieu d'entendre par irrégularité de procédure.

Toutefois, dans les Travaux Préparatoires de la loi de 2019 il est précisé qu'il « est difficile d'évaluer la matérialité d'une erreur dans une procédure d'arbitrage sans en même temps réfléchir sur son importance au regard du résultat. Pour cela, une erreur de procédure qui a eu un impact sur le résultat doit, en principe, permettre que la sentence soit annulée en partie ou dans sa totalité »[17].

Ainsi, dans les cas où la loi suédoise de l'arbitrage aura vocation à s'appliquer, la difficulté résidera non seulement à établir qu'il y a eu une erreur de procédure, mais encore que celle-ci a eu un impact sur le résultat.

Comme on l'a vu, dans l'affaire *Gazprom*, le rapport de l'expert avait conclu à la forte probabilité que le secrétaire administratif avait largement contribué à la motivation de la sentence. Mais, il restait à déterminer si cela pouvait constituer une erreur de procédure et, dans l'affirmative, si l'intervention du secrétaire avait pu exercer une influence sur le résultat final. Étant donné que les parties sont arrivées à un accord transactionnel, nous ne saurons pas ce que la cour d'appel de Svea aurait pu conclure sur cette question.

Toutefois, nous examinerons ci-après ce que cette Cour avait décidé, le 24 novembre 2017, à la suite d'un recours en annulation d'une autre sentence, qui avait aussi été rédigée en partie par le secrétaire du tribunal arbitral, tout en notant que la décision de la cour d'appel de Svea avait été prise sur la base de la loi d'arbitrage de 1999.

---

15. https://globalarbitrationreview.com/article/1226901/will-yukos-now-go-before-the-ecj?
16. Cour d'appel de Svea, N° T 10896-16.
17. Projet du Gouvernement 1998/99 :35, p. 148.

B. Autres décisions judiciaires

Pour illustrer la position adoptée par les juges sur la question du rôle des secrétaires de tribunaux arbitraux, nous avons choisi quelques décisions rendues par diverses juridictions nationales qui nous paraissent intéressantes.

a) Jurisprudence suédoise

Dans l'affaire T 10896-16 de la cour d'appel de Svea qui a donné lieu à la décision, du 24 novembre 2017 les parties avaient, là aussi, accepté que le tribunal arbitral soit assisté par un secrétaire, comme cela avait été le cas dans l'affaire *Gazprom*[18].

La partie demanderesse au recours soutenait que le tribunal arbitral avait fait appel à un secrétaire non seulement pour effectuer des tâches administratives, mais aussi pour réaliser des tâches essentiellement juridiques, telles que la rédaction de plusieurs parties de la sentence, à savoir les faits, les arguments juridiques développés par les parties, ainsi que l'examen de la preuve apportée par ces dernières. En outre, la partie recourante avait prétendu que la sentence ne reprenait pas une grande partie de ses arguments, ce qui démontrait, selon elle, que le tribunal arbitral ne les avait pas pris en considération. Elle en concluait que si le tribunal arbitral n'avait pas confié au secrétaire administratif la tâche de rédiger la sentence, le tribunal arbitral aurait tenu compte des arguments omis.

Comme il est d'usage devant les juridictions suédoises dans les procédures de recours en annulation de sentences, le président du tribunal arbitral et le secrétaire ont comparu devant la cour d'appel de Svea, en qualité de témoin. Le secrétaire déclara qu'il avait effectivement rédigé les parties de la sentence qui lui avaient été confiées par le président du tribunal arbitral, mais que ce dernier avait revu et corrigé le projet qu'il lui avait présenté. Pour sa part, le président du tribunal arbitral déclara qu'il avait revu et contrôlé tout le travail effectué par le secrétaire.

La cour d'appel de Svea considéra que, même si les parties s'attendaient à ce que le tribunal arbitral rédige le texte définitif de la sentence, cela ne devait pas avoir pour effet d'interdire au secrétaire du tribunal arbitral de participer à cette rédaction.

La Cour décida, d'une part, qu'il avait été établi que le tribunal arbitral n'avait pas délégué au secrétaire la responsabilité de rédiger la version définitive de la sentence et, d'autre part, que la partie requérante n'avait pas apporté la preuve de ce que les tâches accomplies par le secrétaire avaient exercé une influence sur les décisions prises par le tribunal arbitral. En outre, la Cour considéra que le travail accompli par le secrétaire dans cette affaire, était conforme à la pratique, lorsqu'un secrétaire est désigné pour assister le tribunal arbitral.

En conclusion, la cour d'appel de Svea décida que le tribunal arbitral n'avait pas outrepassé son mandat et qu'il n'y avait pas eu d'erreur de procédure[19].

18. *Ibid.*

19. Finn Madsen, *"The Challenges of the Arbitral Awards in the Gas Sales and Gas Transit Arbitrations in Stockholm, Sweden"*, SÄRTRYCK UR JURIDISK TIDSKRIFT, 2019-20 NR 4, pp. 947-948.

Avant de quitter le paysage suédois, il est important de souligner que dans cette dernière affaire, la demanderesse au recours en annulation n'avait pas allégué que le secrétaire du tribunal arbitral avait rédigé les motifs de la décision, comme cela avait été le cas dans l'affaire *Gazprom*. Ainsi, il nous reste le doute de savoir quelle serait la position de la cour d'appel de Svea, dans les cas où le secrétaire rédige la motivation des décisions du tribunal arbitral.

b) Jurisprudence anglaise

Les juges anglais ont aussi eu à se prononcer sur le rôle du secrétaire du tribunal arbitral.

L'affaire *P* v. *Q, R, S, U* présente la particularité d'avoir été initiée par une partie qui tentait, devant la juridiction anglaise, de récuser les deux co-arbitres, après avoir failli d'obtenir gain de cause devant la Cour de la LCIA, alors qu'elle avait réussi à faire récuser le président du tribunal arbitral pour défaut d'impartialité.

Au cours de la procédure de récusation des trois arbitres devant la LCIA, la partie requérante avait soutenu que le tribunal arbitral avait délégué certaines tâches au secrétaire du tribunal arbitral, qui n'étaient autorisées, ni par son Règlement d'arbitrage, ni par le guide de la LCIA portant sur les secrétaires administratifs, argument repris devant le juge étatique.

La partie requérante soutenait également que le président du tribunal arbitral avait manqué à son mandat et à ses devoirs, en invitant le secrétaire à exprimer son avis sur des questions de procédure importantes, malgré le fait qu'il n'était ni partie à la procédure, ni membre du tribunal arbitral.

Au vu de la décision de la Cour de la LCIA de ne pas récuser les deux co-arbitres, la partie requérante engagea une procédure de récusation à leur encontre devant la Commercial Court (Queen's Bench Division) de la High Court. Dans le cadre de cette procédure, la partie requérante demanda la production forcée de certains documents échangés entre les arbitres et le secrétaire, ce qui amena le Juge Popplewell de la High Court à rendre deux décisions. La première, datée du 3 février 2017[20], était afférente à la production des documents et la deuxième, rendue le 9 février de la même année[21], portait sur la demande de récusation des co-arbitres.

Au soutien de ses arguments, la partie requérante produisit un courriel du président du tribunal arbitral adressé au secrétaire, malencontreusement envoyé, en copie, aux parties. Selon la partie requérante, le temps dédié par le secrétaire à cet arbitrage, comparé à celui passé par les co-arbitres démontrait qu'il y avait eu une délégation inappropriée de leurs fonctions. Elle demanda donc la production de l'ensemble des documents de travail du tribunal afin de confirmer ce point. Toutefois, le Juge Popplewell rejeta la demande de production des documents de travail du tribunal arbitral, au motif qu'ils formaient partie intégrante de la délibération des arbitres et, par conséquent étaient exclus de toute production forcée[22].

20. *P v. Q, R, S, U* [2017] EWHC 148 (Comm).
21. *P v. Q, R, S, U* [2017] EWHC 194 (Comm).
22. Cf. paragraphes 75-77 de la Décision du Juge Popplewell du 3 février 2017. *Ibid.*

Dans sa Décision du 9 février 2017, le Juge Popplewell décida également de rejeter la demande de récusation des deux co-arbitres, considérant que les tâches confiées au secrétaire par les co-arbitres étaient appropriées, sur la base des éléments de preuve apportés par la partie requérante.

Dans sa demande de récusation, la partie requérante s'était référée à la conduite des co-arbitres au regard de trois décisions d'ordre procédural prises par le tribunal arbitral au regard : (i) de la possibilité de communiquer des documents produits dans deux arbitrages distincts auxquels la partie requérante était partie, (ii) de la possibilité de suspendre le deuxième arbitrage jusqu'à ce que la sentence ne soit rendue dans le premier et (iii) de la production de documents en possession de tiers.

Il ressort de la décision du Juge Popplewell que le président du tribunal arbitral avait envoyé par erreur un courriel au conseil de la partie requérante, qui était destiné au secrétaire du tribunal arbitral. Dans ce courriel, le président du tribunal arbitral demandait au secrétaire son avis sur la demande de production de documents formulée par la partie requérante.

Sur la base de ce courriel la partie requérante demanda au tribunal arbitral de lui fournir le détail des tâches confiées au secrétaire, ainsi que de lui communiquer toute une série de documents échangés entre les arbitres et le secrétaire. Le tribunal arbitral refusa de faire droit à cette demande, mais accepta de fournir une relation des tâches confiées au secrétaire.

C'est dans ce contexte que la partie requérante décida de présenter, par la suite, une demande de récusation de l'ensemble du tribunal arbitral devant la LCIA. Comme on l'a vu, la LCIA n'accepta de récuser que le président du tribunal arbitral.

Une fois devant la High Court, la partie requérante développa essentiellement les mêmes arguments que ceux qu'elle avait formulés devant la LCIA. Toutefois, elle compléta sa demande en prétendant que le président du tribunal arbitral avait délégué de manière inappropriée ses pouvoirs au profit du secrétaire, en lui confiant la rédaction des projets de décisions à prendre sans les avoir portés, au préalable, à la connaissance des co-arbitres.

Dans sa décision, le Juge Popplewell ratifia les motifs par lesquels la LCIA avait décidé de rejeter la demande de récusation des co-arbitres, considérant que les heures consacrées à cette affaire, tant par les co-arbitres que par le secrétaire, étaient appropriées et proportionnelles.

S'agissant de la délégation des pouvoirs décisionnels au profit du secrétaire, le Juge Popplewell considéra que la partie requérante n'était pas en droit de demander la récusation des co-arbitres en se fondant sur le fait que le président du tribunal arbitral avait délégué son devoir de rédiger les décisions du tribunal arbitral au secrétaire, sans avoir informé les co-arbitres, même si cette délégation était inappropriée. En d'autres termes, selon le juge Popplewell, le comportement injustifié du président du tribunal arbitral ne pouvait être imputé aux co-arbitres.

De manière intéressante, le Juge Popplewell a pris soin de relever la divergence d'opinions existantes au sein de la communauté arbitrale, sur les tâches que peuvent accomplir les secrétaires des tribunaux arbitraux. Ainsi, il s'est référé, entre autres commentaires, aux « *Frequently Asked Questions* » du site web de la LCIA, dans lequel apparaît une description plus illustrative que limitative des fonctions du secrétaire. Il a par ailleurs reconnu que le « *Young ICCA Guide on Arbitral Secretaries* », de même que le guide de la LCIA sur les secrétaires administratifs, constituent davantage des bonnes pratiques, plutôt que des règles prescriptives.

Pour le Juge Popplewell, quelles que soient les divergences existantes sur ce qu'il convient de considérer comme étant des bonnes pratiques s'agissant de la participation des secrétaires à la rédaction des sentences, ce qui importe, dans la perspective de la Section 24 de la loi anglaise d'arbitrage de 1996[23], est que les arbitres ne délèguent pas leurs fonctions décisionnelles. Toutefois, le Juge Popplewell précise que le fait de ne pas respecter les bonnes pratiques ne peut être assimilé à une absence de gestion appropriée de la procédure, au sens de la Section 24(1)(d) de la loi de 1996.

Or, l'on peut observer, d'une part, que le Juge Popplewell considère que le fait de consulter le secrétaire ne signifie pas que l'arbitre ait renoncé à exercer sa fonction décisionnelle pleine et indépendante et que, par conséquent, en l'espèce il ne pouvait y avoir de délégation inappropriée de la fonction décisionnelle. Cependant, d'autre part, le juge anglais conclut que, pour s'assurer que les fonctions décisionnelles ont bien été exercées par les membres du tribunal arbitral, il est nécessaire de ne pas confier des tâches au secrétaire qui pourraient l'amener à exprimer son opinion sur le fond d'une question litigieuse.

À notre avis, la décision du Juge Popplewell est critiquable étant donné que le secrétaire n'est ni membre du tribunal arbitral, ni expert nommé par celui-ci. En effet, en demandant au secrétaire de donner son avis, l'arbitre procède, selon nous, à une délégation de ses fonctions essentielles, à savoir celle de prendre des décisions personnellement en toute indépendance.

Avant de nous tourner vers l'approche prise dans d'autres juridictions, il nous paraît important de citer une autre décision de la High Court du 2 avril 2014, antérieure donc à celle rendue par le Juge Popplewell, dans une affaire *Sonatrach c/ Statoil*. Dans cette affaire, la High Court décida de rejeter une demande d'annulation d'une sentence CCI, fondée sur l'argument selon lequel le fait d'avoir permis au secrétaire d'assister aux délibérations était une délégation inappropriée des pouvoirs du tribunal arbitral. Nous reviendrons brièvement sur cette question lorsque nous examinerons ultérieurement l'affaire *Yukos*[24].

c) Une décision italienne

Bien qu'elle soit déjà un peu ancienne, il nous paraît utile de citer un arrêt rendu par la Cour suprême d'Italie dans l'affaire *Sacheri c. Robotto*, en date du 7 juin 1989. Il est vrai que cette affaire était un peu particulière, dans la mesure où les arbitres qui constituaient le tribunal n'avaient aucune formation juridique. Pour cette raison, ils nommèrent un juriste pour rédiger la sentence. La Cour suprême

---

23. La Section 24 de la loi anglaise de 1996 permet aux parties de demander la récusation des arbitres dans les cas prévus dans cette section. Dans le cas qui nous occupe, il est d'application le paragraphe (1)(d) qui dispose ce qui suit : *"that he [the arbitrator] has refused or failed-*

(i) *properly to conduct the proceedings, or*

(ii) *to use all reasonable dispatch in conducting the proceedings or making an award, and that substantial injustice has been or will be caused to the applicant."*

24. *Sonatrach v. Statoil* [2014] EWHC 875 (Comm), paragraphs 46-50.

d'Italie considéra toutefois que la fonction de décider incombait exclusivement aux arbitres, lesquels ne pouvaient pas déléguer cette fonction à un tiers et décida d'annuler la sentence[25].

d) La position suisse

Dans la pratique suisse, il est habituel de désigner des secrétaires pour assister le tribunal arbitral. Pour cette raison, il nous a paru particulièrement intéressant de faire état de la position du Tribunal Fédéral en la matière, même brièvement.

Dans un arrêt du 21 mai de 2015[26], le Tribunal Fédéral a décidé qu'il n'y avait pas lieu à exclure la participation du secrétaire à la rédaction des sentences parmi les tâches que pouvait lui confier le tribunal arbitral, dans les termes suivants : « *...les tâches du secrétaire juridique...n'excluent pas une certaine assistance dans la rédaction de la sentence, sous le contrôle et conformément aux directives du tribunal arbitral.* (...) *sous la réserve* (...) *que le tribunal arbitral n'abandonne pas aux auxiliaires commis par lui les prérogatives inhérentes à sa mission, en particulier celle de trancher lui-même le différend qui lui a été soumis* ».

La position du Tribunal Fédéral est donc claire, il appartient au tribunal arbitral de décider, mais il n'empêche qu'il peut se faire assister par un secrétaire pour rédiger la sentence. Malgré, la position nuancée du Tribunal fédéral, cet arrêt ne permet pas de clarifier la question de savoir quelles sont les parties de la sentence qui peuvent être rédigées par le secrétaire, notamment celles relatives à la motivation. Souvenons-nous de l'argument développé par Gazprom devant la cour d'appel de la Svea, mais au regard duquel celle-ci n'a pas eu à se prononcer à cause de l'accord transactionnel intervenu entre les parties.

e) Les Pays Bas – l'affaire Yukos

Le propos de cet article étant d'examiner l'intervention des secrétaires de tribunaux arbitraux, notre regard sur l'affaire *Yukos* se limitera à cet aspect.

Tout récemment, le 5 novembre 2021[27], la Cour suprême des Pays-Bas a annulé l'arrêt rendu par la cour d'appel de La Haye le 18 février 2020[28], qui avait confirmé la validité des trois sentences rendues par le même tribunal arbitral, tout en renvoyant l'affaire devant la cour d'appel d'Amsterdam. Ainsi faisant, la Cour suprême a rejeté tous les griefs soulevés par la Fédération de Russie, à l'exception de celui relatif à la fraude qui aurait été commise par les actionnaires de Yukos pendant la procédure arbitrale. Selon la Cour suprême, la cour d'appel de La Haye aurait, à tort, rejeté ce dernier argument sans l'examiner. La cour d'appel d'Amsterdam aura donc à se prononcer sur ce point. Quant à la question qui nous intéresse plus particulièrement, à savoir la supposée rédaction de la sentence par le secrétaire du tribunal arbitral, la

25. Yearbook Commercial Arbitration, Volume 16, Kluwer Law International [1991], pp. 156-157 ; Julian D. M. Lew, Loukas A. Mistelis, et. Al., « *Comparative International Commercial Arbitration* », Kluwer Law International [2013], pp. 234 et 637.

26. Tribunal Fédéral, 21 mai 2015, 4A_709/214.

27. www.rechtspraak.nl.

28. Gerechtshof Den Haag, *Veteran Petroleum Limited, Yukos Universal Limited and Hulley Entreprises Limited v. Russian Federation*, No. 200.197.079/01, 18 février 2020.

Cour suprême de La Haye a sommairement écarté ce moyen, en décidant qu'il ne pouvait pas justifier l'annulation des sentences arbitrales[29].

Le 18 juillet 2014, le tribunal arbitral rendit trois sentences dans le différend qui opposait les anciens actionnaires majoritaires de OOO Yukos Oil Company (« Yukos ») à la Fédération de Russie, condamnant celle-ci à payer aux trois actionnaires de Yukos : Yukos Universal Limited (Isle of Man), Hulley Enterprises Limited et Veteran Petroleum Limited, une somme de plus de 50 milliards d'euros.

Le tribunal arbitral avait été constitué conformément à l'Article 26 du Traité de l'Énergie et au Règlement d'arbitrage de la CNUDCI de 1976. Il était assisté par un assistant, un secrétaire et un secrétaire adjoint. La procédure était administrée par la Cour Permanente d'Arbitrage de La Haye. Au cours de la première audience de procédure le président du tribunal arbitral informa les parties de la désignation d'un assistant pour exercer les fonctions administratives et de liaison.

La Fédération de Russie introduisit un recours en annulation à l'encontre des trois sentences devant la Cour du District de La Haye. En 2016, cette Cour décida d'annuler les trois sentences, estimant que la convention d'arbitrage n'était pas valable.

Les trois actionnaires majoritaires de Yukos interjetèrent appel de ce jugement devant la cour d'appel de La Haye, qui décida d'annuler le jugement de la Cour du District. À la suite de cette décision, la Fédération de Russie introduisit un pourvoi devant la Cour de cassation des Pays-Bas[30].

Parmi les questions que la cour d'appel de La Haye avait eu à résoudre était celle de savoir si l'intervention de l'assistant du tribunal arbitral lors de la rédaction des sentences était un motif de nature à justifier leur annulation[31].

Selon la Fédération de Russie les membres du tribunal arbitral n'avaient pas respecté leur mandat d'exécuter personnellement leurs fonctions en permettant que l'assistant analyse en profondeur aussi bien les preuves produites que les arguments juridiques formulés par les parties, assiste aux délibérations et participe à la rédaction des sentences.

D'après la Fédération de Russie, la délégation inappropriée des pouvoirs du tribunal arbitral au profit de l'assistant était mise en évidence par la comparaison des honoraires de l'assistant du tribunal, dont le montant s'élevait à EUR 970 562, avec ceux des arbitres dont le montant oscillait entre EUR 1 513 880 et 2 011 092[32]. Compte tenu des tarifs horaires de l'assistant et des arbitres, la Fédération de Russie concluait que le nombre d'heures consacrées par l'assistant se situait entre 40 % et 70 % des heures passées par les arbitres.

En outre, la Fédération de Russie soutenait que le fait par le tribunal arbitral d'avoir déclaré qu'il ne pouvait pas, en réponse à sa demande d'informations,

---

29. IAReporter du 5 novembre de 2021 (www.iareporter.com/news-and-analysis/) ; Global Arbitration Review, 17 décembre 2021.

30. Global Arbitration Review, 18 février 2020, *"Russia reels as Yukos awards are* revived" ; Global Arbitration Review, Daily news & analysis,15 mai 2020, *"Will Yukos now go before the ECJ?"*; Global Arbitration Review, Volume 15, Issue 1, p. 2, *"Russia reels as Yukos awards are revived"*, Simon Rainey QC and Gaurav Sharma ; *"In search of certainty : the Dutch appeal court decision in Yukos"*, Quadrant Chambers, 15 avril 2020 ; Global Arbitration Review, 8 juin 2021, C.J. Carswell and L. Winnington-Ingram, *"Awards : Challenges Based on Misuse of Tribunal Secretaries"*.

31. http :arbitrationblog.kluwerarbitration.com/2015/02/27/the-challenge-of-the-yukos-award-an-award-written-by-some-one-else-a-violation-of-the-tribunals-mandate/.

32. Cf. paragraphes 1860-1863 de la sentence finale du 18 juillet 2014.

dévoiler la nature des tâches effectuées par son assistant parce que cela violerait « *la confidentialité des délibérations du tribunal* », constituait la preuve que l'assistant avait participé aux délibérations du tribunal.

Au soutien de ses allégations, la Fédération de Russie versa également le rapport d'un expert en linguistique qui arrivait à la conclusion que l'assistant du tribunal avait tenu la plume.

En conclusion, la Fédération de Russie soutenait que l'assistant du tribunal arbitral était un quatrième arbitre et, par conséquent, que le tribunal avait été irrégulièrement constitué.

Dans l'arrêt rendu en date du 18 février 2020, la cour d'appel de La Haye décida que le tribunal arbitral n'avait pas outrepassé son mandat, dès lors qu'il n'avait pas été établi que :

– L'assistant avait participé à la phase de prise des décisions ou que le tribunal lui avait délégué les fonctions afférentes à cette phase,

– Les parties du texte des sentences remises en question par la Fédération de Russie avaient été écrites avant que les arbitres ne prennent leurs décisions.

Par ailleurs, la cour d'appel rejeta l'argument fondé sur les conclusions de l'expert en linguistique et sémantique et considéra qu'il ne pouvait être déduit des heures passées par l'assistant que le tribunal lui avait délégué des fonctions décisionnelles.

De même, la cour d'appel déclara qu'elle n'était pas convaincue par l'argument développé par la Fédération de Russie tendant à établir que la rédaction des projets par l'assistant avait influencé la décision des arbitres, étant donné qu'il appartient aux arbitres de vérifier l'exactitude et l'intégrité du texte rédigé par leur assistant/secrétaire.

La cour d'appel considérait donc qu'en signant les sentences, les arbitres assumaient la responsabilité des projets rédigés par l'assistant, qu'ils aient été modifiés par les arbitres ou pas.

La cour d'appel écarta également l'argument selon lequel le rôle joué par l'assistant avait été contraire à la règle non écrite que les sentences devaient être rédigées par les arbitres, en raison de l'inexistence d'une telle règle.

En revanche, la cour d'appel reprocha au tribunal de ne pas avoir informé les parties, comme elles l'avaient sollicité, quant à la nature et l'étendue du rôle de l'assistant.

Il n'est pas certain que les juridictions françaises auraient pu arriver aux mêmes conclusions que la cour d'appel de La Haye, à partir du moment où il avait été établi que le secrétaire du tribunal arbitral avait participé aux délibérations, sans l'accord exprès des parties, dès lors que, en droit français, les délibérations du tribunal arbitral sont secrètes, en vertu de l'article 1479 du Code de procédure civile[33].

f) La tendance belge

Tout récemment, le Tribunal de première instance francophone de Bruxelles a eu à se prononcer pour la première fois, en Belgique, sur la problématique de la rédaction des sentences par le secrétaire du tribunal arbitral.

33. En effet, l'article 1479 du Code de procédure civile français dispose que : « *Les délibérations du tribunal arbitral sont secrètes* ».

Par jugement du 17 juin 2021, ce Tribunal a déclaré non fondé une demande d'annulation d'une sentence CCI rendue en Belgique[34], dans une affaire opposant les sociétés Emek et WTE à la Commission européenne[35].

Compte tenu du fait que ce jugement fait l'objet d'une note très complète, publiée dans ce même numéro de la revue, nous nous limiterons à relever quelques points intéressants du jugement, en vue d'alimenter la réflexion sur le sujet qui nous préoccupe.

Il convient, tout d'abord, de préciser qu'après la signature de l'acte de mission, les parties avaient accepté que le tribunal arbitral se fasse assister par une secrétaire administrative. Sur la base de cet accord, la secrétaire administrative s'était engagée à agir conformément à la « *Note aux parties et aux tribunaux arbitraux sur la conduite de l'arbitrage selon le Règlement d'arbitrage de la CCI* », en vigueur en 2019. Le tribunal arbitral s'est également engagé à respecter cette Note de la CCI.

À la suite d'une sentence partielle rendue par le tribunal arbitral, l'une des parties a posé deux questions à chaque membre du tribunal arbitral, dans le cadre d'une demande d'interprétation de cette sentence, tendant à connaître (i) qui avait préparé les questions posées par le président du tribunal arbitral aux experts, lors de l'audience et (ii) quel était le rôle joué par la secrétaire dans la préparation d'une partie de la sentence.

Dans leurs réponses, les membres du tribunal arbitral avaient mentionné que le tribunal arbitral avait travaillé de manière collégiale. En outre, le président du tribunal arbitral avait précisé le rôle joué par la secrétaire administrative pendant l'arbitrage. Ainsi, il avait confirmé, d'une part, que la secrétaire avait participé aux délibérations, sans participer aux discussions et, d'autre part, qu'elle l'avait assisté dans le processus de rédaction de la sentence, tout en soulignant qu'il avait revu, vérifié et si, nécessaire, corrigé le texte à la lumière des délibérations du tribunal arbitral.

Après avoir reçu la réponse à ces questions de la part de chaque membre du tribunal arbitral, ces mêmes parties ont demandé au président du tribunal arbitral de préciser si l'une des questions posées aux experts et l'élément correspondant de la sentence avaient été préparés par la secrétaire administrative.

Malgré le fait que le président du tribunal arbitral avait répondu par la négative à ces deux questions, les parties défenderesses à l'arbitrage ont adressé un courrier au président du tribunal arbitral, à la secrétaire administrative et à la conseillère de la Cour de la CCI, affirmant que la préparation des questions aux experts et la rédaction de la partie décisionnelle de la sentence constitueraient une violation de la Note de la CCI. Les défenderesses demandaient également la communication (i) des textes préparés par la secrétaire administrative, y compris la liste des questions aux experts et les projets relatifs aux parties de la sentence pour lesquelles elle avait assisté le président, ainsi que (ii) les fiches relatives au temps passé par la secrétaire depuis sa désignation.

Le secrétariat de la Cour de la CCI s'est refusé de communiquer le temps passé par la secrétaire administrative, en soulignant que cela était confidentiel, tout en invitant les parties à s'adresser, à ce sujet, au tribunal arbitral.

34. Tribunal de première instance francophone de Bruxelles, Section civile, 4e chambre.
35. Global Arbitration Review, des 30 juin 2021 et 2 février 2022.

Quelques jours après, le président du tribunal arbitral a présenté sa démission à la CCI, en indiquant, notamment, que plutôt qu'une demande de correction ou d'interprétation de la sentence les parties défenderesses formulaient des critiques sur certaines décisions contenues dans la sentence, dans des termes « *agressifs, voire vexatoires* » et qu'il ne se sentait plus impartial à l'égard des parties.

La Cour de la CCI a accepté la démission du président du tribunal arbitral et a désigné un autre président.

La sentence partielle a ensuite fait l'objet d'une demande d'annulation des parties défenderesses, invoquant quatre moyens, dont celui de « *L'irrégularité de la procédure arbitrale, et plus particulièrement la délégation du pouvoir décisionnel à la secrétaire administrative* » que le Tribunal bruxellois a déclaré infondé.

Nous résumerons ci-après le raisonnement suivi par le Tribunal pour écarter le moyen soulevé par les parties demanderesses à l'annulation.

Pour le Tribunal : « *L'un des principes cardinaux de l'arbitrage est le caractère intuitu personae de la désignation d'un arbitre... Les arbitres désignés s'engagent donc à trancher personnellement le litige qui leur est soumis par les parties, ce qui exclut toute délégation* ».

Les juges bruxellois n'ont pas hésité à se référer à la pratique arbitrale, dans les termes suivants :

« *La doctrine enseigne néanmoins qu'en pratique, le Tribunal arbitral a recours de plus en plus fréquemment à l'assistance d'un(e) secrétaire administratif(ve)*[[36]] *dont les tâches peuvent dépasser le cadre purement administratif et organisationnel* ».

Ensuite, le Tribunal a examiné les paragraphes 184, 185 et 187 de la Note de la CCI, en vue de déterminer les fonctions du secrétaire du tribunal arbitral. Ce qui l'a amené à interpréter le paragraphe 187 de la Note, qui prévoit :

« *Le fait pour un Tribunal arbitral de demander au Secrétaire administratif de préparer des notes écrites ou des mémorandums ne pourra en aucun cas dispenser le Tribunal arbitral de son obligation de revoir personnellement le dossier et/ou de rédiger lui-même toute décision du Tribunal arbitral.* »

Selon le Tribunal bruxellois, « ... *en utilisant les termes "et/ou", l'article 187 précité autorise implicitement mais certainement le secrétaire administratif à rédiger tout ou partie d'un projet de sentence...* »

Il convient de noter que la version de la Note que le Tribunal bruxellois a eue à examiner a été modifiée par la CCI en date du 1er janvier 2021. Dans cette dernière version, les parties relatives au secrétaire du tribunal arbitral sont davantage précisées. Nous examinerons en plus de détail les nouvelles modifications introduites dans la version du 1er janvier 2021 dans la Section II ci-dessous.

Toutefois, nous pouvons préciser d'ores et déjà que l'équivalent du paragraphe 187 dans la dernière version a été modifié comme suit[37] :

« ... *De même, les tâches confiées à un secrétaire administratif, comme la préparation de notes écrites ou d'un mémorandum, ne déchargeront pas le tribunal*

36. Voir not. M. FONTAINE, « l'arbitre et ses collaborateurs », b-Arbitra, 2013/1, pp. 30-36 ; C. PARTASIDES, « *Secretaries to the Arbitral tribunal* », in *Player's interaction in International Arbitration*, ICC Institute Dossiers, 2012, pp. 87-91.

37. #223 de la Note de la CCI, version du 1er janvier 2021.

arbitral de son obligation d'effectuer personnellement un examen du dossier et/ou de rédiger lui-même un projet de décision du tribunal arbitral. »

Nous constatons, ainsi, que dans le nouveau paragraphe 223, l'expression « un projet de décision » a été préférée à celle de « toute décision ».

De manière plus spécifique, dans le nouveau paragraphe 224 de la Note, nous retrouvons parmi les attributions du secrétaire administratif les précisions suivantes[38] :

« *Un secrétaire administratif peut, conformément à ce qui précède, accomplir les tâches relatives à l'organisation et à la gestion telles que :*

(...)

«

- *la préparation de projets d'ordonnances de procédure ainsi que la rédaction des parties factuelles d'une sentence (p. ex. résumé de la procédure, chronologie des faits, synthèse des positions des parties) qui seront soumis à l'examen du tribunal arbitral, sous réserve que ces ordonnances de procédure ainsi que ces parties d'une sentence fasse par la suite l'objet d'un examen par le tribunal arbitral lui-même* ; »

(...)

La CCI a voulu, ainsi, lever les doutes existants quant aux parties de la sentence que le secrétaire du tribunal arbitral pouvait rédiger.

Pour en revenir au jugement rendu par le Tribunal de Bruxelles, celui-ci a constaté que dans la sentence « *la section VI fait près de 200 pages et contient tant des données factuelles que les positions réciproques des parties et l'appréciation du Tribunal arbitral. Rien ne permet au tribunal de céans de déterminer précisément les passages de ladite section écris de la plume de* [la secrétaire du tribunal arbitral] *et ceux qui furent rédigés ou corrigés par* [le président du tribunal arbitral].

En outre, le fait que le président du tribunal ait confirmé qu'« *il n'y a pas une seule phrase dans la sentence et pas une seule note en bas de page qui n'aurait pas été au moins revue, vérifiée et si nécessaire corrigée par moi à la lumière de mon point de vue et des délibérations du Tribunal arbitral* » a amené les juges bruxellois à conclure que le projet de sentence rédigé par la secrétaire du tribunal arbitral respectait le cadre d'intervention posé par la Note de la CCI et ne témoignait pas d'une délégation du pouvoir décisionnel.

Pour ce qui est de la rédaction des questions à l'expert lors de l'audience, le Tribunal de Bruxelles a constaté qu'à la lecture des retranscriptions de l'audience rien ne permettait d'observer une méconnaissance de ces questions par le président du tribunal arbitral. Ainsi, le Tribunal a considéré que la seule rédaction de la liste des questions posées à l'expert « *ne suffit pas, en soi, pour établir une délégation de pouvoir décisionnel, alors que* [le président du tribunal arbitral] *a confirmé avoir revu le projet de liste, c'est-à-dire relu et le cas échéant corrigé ledit projet* ».

En conclusion sur cette affaire, il pourrait être conclu que le Tribunal a adopté, au vu des preuves apportées par les parties et à l'interprétation qu'il a fait de la Note de la CCI applicable en l'espèce, une attitude permissive s'agissant des fonctions rédactionnelles pouvant être exercées par le secrétaire du tribunal arbitral. Il sera

38. #224 de la Note de la CCI, version du 1er janvier 2021.

intéressant de savoir ce que la Cour de cassation belge décidera finalement, à la suite du recours formé par la société chypriote Emek à l'encontre du jugement du Tribunal de Bruxelles[39].

Après avoir parcouru les décisions prises par les juridictions nationales, ayant eu à se prononcer sur le rôle des secrétaires de tribunaux arbitraux, notamment en ce qui concerne leur participation dans les délibérations et dans la rédaction des sentences, nous examinerons maintenant la position adoptée par les principales institutions arbitrales à cet égard.

II. La position des institutions d'arbitrage

De manière progressive, les institutions d'arbitrage ont adopté des règles spécifiques sur les secrétaires de tribunaux arbitraux, soit dans leurs règlements d'arbitrage, soit par la voie de notes ou encore dans les deux.

Une distinction importante est à faire entre les institutions qui désignent un secrétaire, dès le commencement de tout arbitrage, sans que le tribunal arbitral ait à solliciter leur assistance et celles qui permettent la désignation d'un secrétaire, si le tribunal arbitral souhaite se faire assister en fonction de la nature de l'affaire, avec ou sans l'accord des parties, eu égard au règlement d'arbitrage applicable.

Dans le premier groupe, nous retrouvons, notamment, le CIRDI et le Centre d'arbitrage de la Chambre de Commerce de Lima, alors que la plupart des principales institutions d'arbitrage appartiennent au deuxième groupe.

A. Les secrétaires nommées par l'institution dès le début de l'arbitrage

a) Le cas du CIRDI

Le Centre International pour le Règlement des Différends Relatifs aux Investissements (CIRDI) a été un pionnier en la matière. Il convient de noter que les références aux secrétaires de tribunaux ne se trouvent pas dans son Règlement d'arbitrage, mais dans le Règlement Administratif et Financier, dont l'Article 25 dispose ce qui suit :

« *Le Secrétaire général désigne pour chaque Commission, Tribunal et Comité un secrétaire qui peut appartenir au Secrétariat du Centre et sera considéré en tout cas, dans l'exercice de cette fonction, comme un membre du personnel du Centre…* »

Ce même article énumère les différentes fonctions du secrétaire. Toutefois, aucune référence n'est faite aux tâches relatives à la rédaction des ordonnances de procédure ou des sentences. Par ailleurs, l'Article 25(c) ne fait qu'autoriser implicitement le secrétaire à assister aux audiences, dans la mesure où il prévoit

39. Global Arbitral Review, 2 février 2022.

qu'il « *établit des procès-verbaux sommaires des audiences, sauf accord entre les parties et la Commission, le Tribunal ou le Comité sur une autre manière de prendre acte des audiences ;* ».

Néanmoins, la possibilité que le secrétaire assiste personnellement aux audiences était déjà confirmée dans la Note C de l'Article 31 de la version de 1968 du Règlement d'arbitrage du CIRDI, laquelle faisait référence à l'Article 25(c) du Règlement Administratif et Financier.

Par ailleurs, il y a lieu de remarquer que l'Article 25(d) permet au secrétaire d'« *exerce*(r) *toutes autres fonctions relatives à l'instance à la demande du Président de la Commission, du Tribunal ou du Comité, ou sur les instructions du Secrétaire général* ».

Au regard des délibérations, l'Article 15(2) du Règlement d'arbitrage du CIRDI dispose que « [S]*euls les membres du Tribunal prennent part aux délibérations. Aucune autre personne n'est admise sauf si le Tribunal en décide autrement* ». Il ne fait pas de doute que cette règle octroie la faculté aux tribunaux de décider si le secrétaire et/ou l'assistant du tribunal arbitral peuvent assister aux délibérations.

Il convient de souligner qu'il existe une différence entre le secrétaire et l'assistant sans que, pour autant il y ait une définition de leurs rôles respectifs. Il est habituel dans les arbitrages d'investissement que les tribunaux désignent des assistants, outre le secrétaire désigné par le Secrétaire Général du CIRDI[40], ou encore, par la Cour Permanente d'Arbitrage (CPA) quand il lui appartient d'administrer l'arbitrage[41].

En effet, ainsi que nous l'avons mentionné précédemment, dans l'affaire *Yukos* le règlement d'arbitrage applicable était celui de la CNUDCI, mais l'arbitrage était administré par la CPA. Dans cette affaire, deux fonctionnaires du Bureau International de la CPA furent nommés, l'un en tant que secrétaire administratif et l'autre en tant que secrétaire administratif adjoint, pour effectuer des tâches administratives sous la direction du tribunal, comme il est d'usage dans les arbitrages administrés par la CPA. En outre, comme cela a déjà été mentionné, le tribunal nomma un assistant pour exercer des fonctions administratives et de liaison. En réalité, dans l'affaire *Yukos* les tâches accomplies par l'assistant du tribunal ne correspondaient pas à de simples tâches administratives et de liaison, comme indiqué par le président du tribunal aux parties.

Parmi les arbitrages CIRDI dans lesquels la question de la participation du secrétaire du tribunal dans la rédaction de la sentence a été soulevée, il y a lieu de mentionner l'affaire *Compañía de Aguas del Aconquija S.A. & Vivendi Universal S.A. c/ République d'Argentine*[42], en raison de l'Opinion établie par le Professeur Jan Hendrik Dalhuisen. Selon cette Opinion, le secrétaire d'un tribunal CIRDI ne doit rédiger aucune partie de la sentence, sans quoi le texte de la sentence perdrait toute légitimité. Pour le Professeur Dalhuisen, le secrétaire ne doit pas être le quatrième membre d'un tribunal CIRDI.

---

40. *Caratube International Oil Company LLP c/ République du Kazakhstan*, CIRDI No. ARB/08/12, Sentence finale du 5 juin 2012. Dans cette affaire, l'assistant devait fournir une « assistance logistique », sans qu'il ne soit définit en quoi elle devait consister.

41. https://pca-cpa.org/fr/services/arbitration-services/case-administration/

42. CIRDI No. ARB/97/3 : www.italaw.com/sites/default/files/case-documents/ita0221.pdf.

b) Le Centre d'arbitrage de Lima

Dans la catégorie des institutions où le secrétaire du tribunal arbitral est nommé sans que ce dernier le demande, nous pouvons également citer le cas du Centre national et international d'arbitrage de la Chambre de Commerce de Lima (le « Centre d'arbitrage de Lima »). Celui-ci est l'institution d'arbitrage plus importante du Pérou, par le nombre d'affaires administrées. Le Centre d'arbitrage de Lima exerce ses fonctions à travers le Conseil Supérieur d'Arbitrage et le Secrétariat Général, indépendamment de la Chambre de Commerce de Lima et de ses autres organes[43].

La principale fonction du Conseil Supérieur d'Arbitrage est de veiller à l'application de ses règlements, dont le Règlement d'arbitrage du Centre d'arbitrage de Lima.[44] L'organisation et l'administration des arbitrages sont la responsabilité du Conseil Supérieur d'Arbitrage. De même, il nomme, confirme, remplace et décide s'il y a lieu de récuser les arbitres.[45] Pour l'exercice de ses fonctions, il est assisté par le Secrétariat Général. Ce dernier est composé du Secrétaire Général et des secrétaires de tribunaux arbitraux[46].

Les secrétaires de tribunaux contribuent à l'exercice des fonctions du Secrétariat Général, sous le contrôle du Conseil Supérieur d'Arbitrage.

Toutefois, le Règlement d'arbitrage du Centre d'Arbitrage de Lima du 1er janvier 2017 ne comporte aucune règle particulière concernant l'intervention ou les fonctions des secrétaires de tribunaux arbitraux[47]. Il y a lieu de se reporter à l'Article 10 des Statuts du Centro de Arbitraje de la CCL, qui dispose que « *les secrétaires arbitraux ont pour fonction d'assister les Tribunaux Arbitraux dans la procédure d'arbitrage et, en général, de contribuer à l'exercice des fonctions du Secrétaire Général, sous le contrôle du Conseil* ». Les secrétaires de tribunaux arbitraux sont choisis parmi les membres du Secrétariat Général du Centre d'Arbitrage de Lima, contrairement aux arbitrages CCI où les membres du Secrétariat de la Cour ne peuvent agir comme secrétaire du tribunal arbitral[48].

Quant aux frais et honoraires des secrétaires, ils font partie des frais administratifs du Centre d'Arbitrage de Lima. Ainsi, lorsque le Conseil Supérieur d'Arbitrage fixe les frais de l'arbitrage, ainsi que les provisions, conformément aux Articles 41 et 42 du Règlement d'arbitrage, il inclut les frais administratifs.

Dans le cas d'arbitrages qui ne sont pas administrés par la Centre d'Arbitrage de Lima, il est fait application de l'article 70 de la loi d'arbitrage péruvienne de 2008, modifiée en 2015,[49] lequel dispose qu'il appartient au tribunal arbitral de fixer les frais d'arbitrage dans la sentence et définit les éléments inclus dans ces frais, parmi lesquels figurent les frais et honoraires du secrétaire du tribunal arbitral.

43. Article 1 des Statuts du Centre d'arbitrage de Lima.
44. Article 1 du Règlement d'Arbitrage ; Article 3 des Statuts.
45. Article 3 des Statuts du Centre d'arbitrage de Lima.
46. Article 7 des Statuts du Centre d'arbitrage de Lima.
47. L'article 22(1) du Règlement d'arbitrage de 2008, en vigueur jusqu'en 2016, prévoyait, quant à lui : « Le Secrétaire Général pourra désigner un Secrétaire Arbitral, qui prendra en charge l'arbitrage. De même, il pourra le remplacer par un autre Secrétaire Arbitral, de manière discrétionnaire ».
48. Paragraphe 219 de la Note de la CCI, version du 1er janvier 2021.
49. Décret législatif No. 1071, publié au Journal Officiel péruvien le 28 juin 2008, modifié par le Décret législatif No. 1231 du 26 septembre 2015.

Il en résulte que les frais et honoraires des secrétaires de tribunaux arbitraux sont à la charge des parties, soit directement, en l'absence de disposition contraire d'un règlement d'arbitrage applicable, soit indirectement, lorsque la rémunération des secrétaires est comprise dans les frais administratifs de l'institution d'arbitrage concernée. En tout cas, cela démontre la reconnaissance de l'intervention des secrétaires dans les arbitrages se déroulant au Pérou.

B. Les secrétaires nommés à l'initiative du tribunal arbitral

Actuellement, la plupart des principales institutions d'arbitrage font une référence expresse aux secrétaires de tribunaux arbitraux, dans leurs règlements d'arbitrage, et/ou dans les notes ou lignes directrices qu'elles émettent.

Dans cette catégorie d'arbitrages institutionnels, la nomination des secrétaires est généralement faite par les tribunaux arbitraux, sauf quelques rares exceptions, comme c'est le cas de la SCC. Dans tous les cas, l'initiative de nommer un secrétaire revient au tribunal arbitral.

a) Les Règlements d'arbitrage comportant des dispositions relatives aux secrétaires

Parmi les institutions d'arbitrage qui ont opté pour ne faire référence aux secrétaires que dans leurs règlements d'arbitrage, nous pouvons citer, entre autres, le London Court of International Arbitration, le Danish Institute of Arbitration, l'Institut d'Arbitrage de la Chambre de Commerce de Stockholm (SCC), le Singapore International Arbitration Centre (SIAC), l'Institut d'Arbitrage Finlandais (FAI), le Hong Kong International Arbitration Centre (HKIAC), le Nordic Arbitration Centre for Commercial Arbitration de la Chambre de Commerce d'Islande, le Cairo Regional Centre for International Commercial Arbitration (CRCICA), la Swiss Chambers Arbitration Institution, le Netherlands Arbitration Institute (NAI), la Corte Civil y Mercantil de Madrid (CIMA) et le Centro Internacional de Arbitraje de Madrid (CIAM).

Dans cette catégorie nous pouvons observer que certaines de ces institutions ont choisi de ne pas émettre de notes ou de lignes directrices traitant du secrétaire du tribunal arbitral, en complément des dispositions de leur règlement d'arbitrage. Néanmoins, on peut aussi observer que leurs approches sur cette question sont bien différentes. En guise d'illustration, nous avons choisi trois institutions arbitrales, dont deux situées dans le même pays, à savoir l'Espagne.

Dans ces trois exemples, tant celui de la CIMA, comme celui du CIAM ou le Danish Arbitration Institute disposent de règlements d'arbitrage dans lesquels les fonctions des secrétaires sont définies.

Dans son nouveau Règlement d'arbitrage du 13 avril 2021, le Danish Arbitration Institute réglemente l'institution du secrétaire du tribunal arbitral en imposant que le secrétaire soit impartial et indépendant et qu'il communique son CV aux parties. Cependant, le Règlement d'arbitrage ne requiert pas l'accord des parties avant qu'il ne soit nommé par le tribunal arbitral. En revanche, la rémunération du secrétaire ne fait pas partie des frais de l'arbitrage, qui ne couvrent que ses dépenses. La rémunération est une question à régler entre les membres du tribunal arbitral et leur secrétaire. Quant aux fonctions du secrétaire, ce règlement ne prévoit que l'interdiction d'assister aux délibérations, sauf accord des membres du tribunal arbitral.

De son côté, le Règlement d'arbitrage de la CIMA est encore plus laconique au sujet des fonctions du secrétaire, en se bornant à disposer que :

« *Le tribunal arbitral ne peut, en aucun cas, déléguer ses fonctions décisionnelles ou l'accomplissement de l'une quelconque de ses fonctions essentielles à son secrétaire administratif, qui ne participe pas aux délibérations du tribunal arbitral.* »[50]

Selon ce règlement, la désignation du secrétaire doit être approuvée au préalable par les parties, mais il passe sous silence son obligation d'indépendance et impartialité. Quant à sa rémunération, le règlement de la CIMA présente une légère différence par rapport à celui du Danish Arbitration Institute, dans la mesure où il dispose que l'intervention d'un secrétaire ne doit générer aucun frais supplémentaire pour les parties.

Le Règlement d'arbitrage du CIAM quant à lui, est plus explicite au sujet des fonctions du secrétaire et admet, sans réserve, que le secrétaire puisse participer aux délibérations du tribunal arbitral. Toutefois, il requiert que le tribunal arbitral rédige toute décision et décrit les différentes tâches permises au secrétaire, dans les termes suivants[51] :

« *Les arbitres ne pourront déléguer aux secrétaires les prises de décision. Sauf convention contraire des parties, le secrétaire administratif exécute les tâches administratives, organisationnelles et de soutien qui lui sont confiées par les arbitres, telles que la transmission des communications au nom des arbitres, l'organisation et la conservation de la copie du dossier arbitral jusqu'à l'achèvement de la procédure, l'organisation des audiences et des réunions du tribunal, la participation aux audiences, réunions et délibérations, la préparation de notes écrites ou mémorandums ou les corrections formelles des ordonnances de procédure et des sentences. La préparation par le secrétaire administratif de notes écrites ou de mémorandums ne libèrera pas les arbitres de leur devoir personnel d'examiner le dossier et de rédiger toute décision.* »

Tout comme le règlement de la CIMA, celui du CIAM requiert l'accord des parties avant qu'un secrétaire ne puisse être nommé par le tribunal arbitral. À propos de sa rémunération, les deux règlements contiennent des dispositions très similaires. En effet, il prévoit, lui aussi, que les parties ne doivent supporter aucun frais résultant de la désignation d'un secrétaire. Cependant, il se rapproche de celui du Danish Arbitration Institute en ce qu'il prévoit l'obligation d'indépendance et d'impartialité et la communication du CV du secrétaire aux parties.

b) Les notes ou lignes directrices des institutions qui traitent des secrétaires de tribunaux

Parmi les institutions d'arbitrage qui ont opté pour l'établissement de notes ou de lignes directrices qui traitent des secrétaires de tribunaux arbitraux, sans inclure

50. Article 22.3.
51. Article 15.4.

de dispositions particulières à cet égard dans leurs règlements d'arbitrage, on peut notamment citer le HKIAC, le FAI et la CCI.

Les "*Guidelines on the Use of a Secretary to the Arbitral Tribunal*" du HKIAC de 2014 sont particulièrement détaillées. En ce qui concerne les tâches rédactionnelles et la présence du secrétaire aux délibérations, nous observons qu'elles interdisent au tribunal arbitral de déléguer toute fonction décisionnelle. Néanmoins, elles permettent au secrétaire d'assister aux délibérations, et de rédiger, sous forme de projet, les parties non essentielles des lettres, des ordonnances de procédure, des décisions du tribunal et des sentences, à moins que les parties ou les arbitres n'en décident autrement. Toutefois, ces *Guidelines* précisent, à propos des parties non essentielles des sentences, « *such as procedural histories and chronologies of events* », ce qui, à notre avis, exclut les parties décisionnelles des sentences[52].

Les dispositions relatives à la rémunération des secrétaires, de ces lignes directrices sont très exhaustives. Elles prévoient, notamment, une rémunération calculée sur la base d'un taux horaire si les arbitres sont rémunérés sur cette même base. Dans les cas où la rémunération des arbitres est déterminée en fonction du montant en litige, celle des secrétaires fait partie de la rémunération des arbitres, qui doivent supporter, à parts égales, le montant de la compensation allouée au secrétaire, à moins que les arbitres n'en décident autrement[53].

Dans le cas du FAI, dont le Règlement d'arbitrage est entré en vigueur le 1er janvier 2020, la « *Note on the Use of a Secretary* » est moins explicite que celle du HKIAC. Toutefois, il est intéressant de noter qu'avant de nommer un secrétaire, le tribunal doit consulter les parties. Mais, si l'une des parties s'oppose à sa nomination, le tribunal arbitral peut néanmoins y procéder, s'il est convaincu que cela permettra d'économiser des frais et de réduire la durée de la procédure.

Sur le plan des tâches que le secrétaire peut effectuer, le tribunal arbitral ne peut pas déléguer sa fonction décisionnelle, qui lui est personnelle. Le tribunal peut se faire assister pour la correction de ses projets par le secrétaire, qui peut aussi rédiger des mémorandums sur les positions des parties et les éléments de preuve produits, sans que le tribunal puisse s'appuyer uniquement sur le travail effectué par le secrétaire. En outre, il incombe aux arbitres d'étudier le dossier, en ce y compris les sources juridiques citées par les parties. La Note de la FAI établi comme principe que la désignation d'un secrétaire ne doit entraîner aucune charge financière pour les parties. La rémunération du secrétaire vient en déduction de celle perçue par le président du tribunal arbitral, à moins que les membres du tribunal arbitral n'en décident autrement.

Pour sa part, la CCI, n'a pas non plus estimé opportun d'inclure des dispositions spécifiques visant le secrétaire du tribunal arbitral, lors de la révision de son Règlement d'arbitrage en janvier 2021. En revanche, la version du 1er janvier 2021 de la « *Note aux parties et aux tribunaux arbitraux sur la conduite de l'arbitrage selon le règlement d'arbitrage CCI* » consacre une longue section au secrétaire du tribunal arbitral[54].

Selon la Note, les secrétaires doivent satisfaire aux conditions d'indépendance et d'impartialité requises des arbitres, conformément au Règlement d'arbitrage CCI.

52. Section 3 des Guidelines on the Use of a Secretary to the Arbitral Tribunal du HKIAC.
53. Section 4 des Guidelines on the Use of a Secretary to the Arbitral Tribunal du HKIAC.
54. Section XX, paragraphes 216-230.

Les membres du Secrétariat de la Cour internationale d'arbitrage de la CCI ne peuvent être désignés en qualité de secrétaire d'un tribunal arbitral.

Avant de nommer un secrétaire le tribunal arbitral doit demander l'accord de l'ensemble des parties. Ce faisant, il doit leur communiquer le CV du candidat, accompagné d'une déclaration d'indépendance et d'impartialité, ainsi que deux attestations, l'une émanant du Secrétariat de la Cour attestant que le secrétaire s'engage à se conformer à la Note et l'autre du tribunal arbitral indiquant qu'il s'engage à assurer le respect de cette obligation par le secrétaire[55].

S'agissant des fonctions du secrétaire, la Note souligne, notamment, que le tribunal ne doit pas déléguer ses fonctions décisionnelles et qu'il a l'obligation « *d'effectuer personnellement un examen du dossier et/ou de rédiger lui-même un projet de décision du tribunal arbitral* »[56].

Comme nous l'avons évoqué antérieurement à propos du jugement du Tribunal de première instance francophone de Bruxelles du 17 juin 2021, celui-ci a considéré que les termes de l'ancien paragraphe 187 de la Note de la CCI, rédigé en des termes très proches de ceux du nouveau paragraphe 223, devaient être interprétés comme permettant au secrétaire du tribunal arbitral de « *rédiger tout ou partie d'un projet de sentence* »[57].

Même s'il aurait été souhaitable que le nouveau paragraphe 223 soit moins ambigü, l'ajout du terme « *projet* » avant celui de « *décision* » n'ayant pas apporté la clarté nécessaire, nous sommes loin de partager l'interprétation faite de la Note par le Tribunal de Bruxelles. En effet, l'utilisation de l'expression « *et/ou* » à la fin de la phrase ne permet pas, grammaticalement, de rattacher la tâche de rédiger la partie décisionnelle à celle de « la préparation de notes écrites ou un mémorandum » envisagée au début de la phrase. D'autant plus, que la permission octroyée au secrétaire de rédiger des notes écrites ou des mémorandums devrait être comprise, comme étant une exception au principe rappelé ensuite, dans la même phrase, selon lequel le tribunal arbitral a l'obligation d'examiner le dossier et/ou de rédiger lui-même le projet de décision, s'il y a lieu.

Cette interprétation est renforcée par le nouveau paragraphe 224, selon lequel le secrétaire du tribunal arbitral peut préparer des projets d'ordonnance de procédure et rédiger « *des parties factuelles d'une sentence (p. ex. résumé de la procédure, chronologie des faits, synthèse des positions des parties)* », sous réserve « *que ces ordonnances de procédure ainsi que ces parties d'une sentence fasse par la suite l'objet d'un examen par le tribunal lui-même* ». Comme nous pouvons l'observer les parties décisionnelles de la sentence ne sont pas envisagées.

Outre la rédaction des diverses décisions du *tribunal* arbitral, la Note énumère en détail les « *tâches relatives à l'organisation et à la gestion* » qui peuvent être confiées à un secrétaire[58]. Parmi celles-ci, il est indiqué que le secrétaire peut participer aux délibérations du tribunal arbitral.

55. Paragraphe 220 de la Note de la CCI.
56. Paragraphe 223 de la Note de la CCI.
57. Page 14 du jugement du 17 juin de 2021.
58. Paragraphe 224 de la Note de la CCI.

En cas de doute sur la détermination des tâches pouvant être accomplies par le secrétaire, la Note requiert que le tribunal arbitral ou son secrétaire, s'il y a lieu, consultent le Secrétariat de la Cour de la CCI[59].

Sur la question de la rémunération, la Note précise que l'intervention du secrétaire ne doit imposer aucune charge financière supplémentaire aux parties. Sa rémunération doit être prélevée sur les honoraires alloués aux arbitres[60].

c) La réglementation de l'intervcention des secrétaires de tribunaux dans les règlements d'arbitrage et les textes annexes des institutions

Il nous reste maintenant à examiner le groupe d'institutions qui règlementent l'intervention du secrétaire de tribunal, aussi bien dans leur règlement d'arbitrage que dans leurs notes ou lignes directrices.

Dans ce groupe nous trouvons, notamment, la LCIA, la SCC et le ICDR (International Centre for Dispute Resolution).

L'arbitrage SCC présente la particularité que le secrétaire du tribunal arbitral doit être nommé par l'institution elle-même, si le tribunal en fait la demande, lui propose le candidat et les parties l'acceptent[61].

Avant toute nomination, le Règlement d'arbitrage de la SCC requiert que le tribunal arbitral consulte les parties au regard des tâches à accomplir, sans que le tribunal arbitral puisse déléguer ses fonctions décisionnelles[62]. Sur ce point le Règlement d'arbitrage diffère des « *Guidelines for Arbitrators* » de la SCC, dans la mesure où celles-ci prévoient, en outre, que le secrétaire ne peut pas rédiger les parties substantielles des décisions ou des sentences. Son rôle doit se limiter à exercer des fonctions d'ordre organisationnel, bureaucratique et administratif[63].

Le secrétaire se doit d'être impartial et indépendant et doit aussi signer une déclaration à cet effet[64].

La rémunération du secrétaire doit être prélevée sur les honoraires perçus par le tribunal arbitral, mais ses frais peuvent être remboursés par les parties[65].

Outre les questions relatives aux fonctions du secrétaire et à sa rémunération, où il existe des différences entre le règlement d'arbitrage et les lignes directrices, les autres questions sont traitées de manière cohérente entre les deux textes.

Lors de la révision de son Règlement d'arbitrage, en vigueur depuis le 1er octobre 2020, la LCIAa décidé d'inclure un nouvel article 14A dédié au secrétaire du tribunal arbitral. Toutefois, au moment de finaliser le présent article, la « *Note for Arbitrators* » de la LCIA du 26 octobre 2017, dans laquelle figurent des dispositions complémentaires concernant le secrétaire du tribunal arbitral, n'a toujours pas été modifiée en vue de l'adapter au nouveau Règlement d'arbitrage. Il y a donc, pour l'instant, un certain décalage entre ces deux textes.

59. Paragraphe 225 de la Note de la CCI.
60. Paragraphes 228-230 de la Note de la CCI.
61. Article 24(1) du Règlement d'arbitrage de la SCC, entré en vigueur le 1er janvier 2017.
62. Article 24(2).
63. Guidelines for Arbitrators, p. 8, version de juin 2020.
64. Articles 24(3) et 24(4).
65. Article 24(6). Guidelines for Arbitrators, p. 8, version de juin 2020.

Le nouvel Article 14A autorise désormais les arbitres à se faire assister par un secrétaire qui exerce ses fonctions sous le contrôle du tribunal arbitral. Comme dans les autres règlements d'arbitrage examiné dans cet article, le Règlement d'arbitrage de la LCIA ne permet pas aux arbitres de déléguer leurs fonctions décisionnelles au secrétaire et requiert que celui-ci déclare par écrit qu'il est indépendant et impartial[66].

Avant qu'il ne soit nommé par le tribunal arbitral les parties doivent donner leur accord sur le secrétaire, les tâches qu'il pourra accomplir, ainsi que sur son taux horaire et les frais pouvant lui être remboursés[67]. Une fois le secrétaire approuvé, il doit remplir sa mission jusqu'à la fin de l'arbitrage, à moins qu'il ne soit démis de ses fonctions par le tribunal arbitral, pour quelque motif que ce soit[68].

Étant donné que les *Notes for Arbitrators* de 2017 sont toujours en vigueur, il convient de s'y référer dans l'attente dans l'attente de leur actualisation par la LCIA. Les tâches du secrétaire, telles que définies au paragraphe 71 des Notes, doivent non seulement être portées à la connaissance des parties, mais encore les parties doivent donner leur accord pour que le secrétaire puisse accomplir les tâches que le tribunal souhaite lui confier, conformément à l'Article 14.10 du Règlement d'arbitrage et au paragraphe 70 a. des Notes.

Parmi les tâches autorisées dans les *Notes for Arbitrators*, il est prévu que le secrétaire puisse assister aux délibérations et rédiger les projets des sentences et des ordonnances de procédure, sous le contrôle du tribunal arbitral[69].

Quant à ICDR, son Règlement d'arbitrage international, qui a été modifié le 1er mars 2021, incorpore un nouvel article, très succinct, dédié au secrétaire du tribunal arbitral[70] :

« *The tribunal may, with the consent of the parties, appoint an arbitral tribunal secretary, who will serve in accordance with ICDR guidelines"*

Aucune « *ICDR guidelines* » relative aux secrétaires de tribunaux arbitraux n'a été publiée à ce jour. Toutefois, dans la mesure où le Règlement d'arbitrage international de l'ICDR requiert désormais que les arbitres respectent le « *Code of Ethics for Arbitrators in Commercial Disputes* », dont la dernière version date du 1er mars 2004, il convient de se référer, en particulier, au Canon V C., lequel fait interdiction aux arbitres de déléguer leur devoir de décider au profit d'une autre personne, à savoir un secrétaire du tribunal.

d) Les textes adoptés par d'autres organismes et associations professionnelles

Pour compléter cette analyse des différents règlements d'arbitrage, il est nécessaire de considérer également le point de vue de la CNUDCI sur cette question. Le nouveau Règlement d'arbitrage CNUDCI de 2010 ne contient aucune disposition concernant les secrétaires de tribunaux. Toutefois, il est on trouve une référence aux secrétaires dans les Notes de la CNUDCI sur l'organisation des

66. Articles 14.8 et 14.9.
67. Articles 14.10-14.13
68. Article 14.15.
69. Paragraphes 69 et 71 des Notes for Arbitrators.
70. Article 17.

procédures arbitrales de 2016. En effet, celles-ci comportent une définition de leurs fonctions, selon laquelle les secrétaires peuvent rédiger le résumé des faits de l'affaire litigieuse, ainsi que l'historique de la procédure suivie, mais ils ne peuvent pas participer aux prises de décision des tribunaux arbitraux[71].

Par ailleurs, la version de 2014 des « *Guidelines on Conflict of Interest in International Arbitration* » de la International Bar Association reconnaît la possibilité pour les arbitres de nommer un secrétaire ou un assistant, en précisant que ceux-ci sont tenus par la même obligation d'indépendance et d'impartialité que les arbitres[72].

D'autres associations ou organismes dédiés à l'arbitrage se sont également intéressés à l'intervention des secrétaires dans les procédures d'arbitrage.

De son côté, le Club Español del Arbitraje (CEA) a aussi apporté sa contribution dans ce domaine, en incluant dans son « *Código de Buenas Prácticas* » de 2019 une référence aux secrétaires de tribunaux arbitraux.

D'après ce code, les arbitres ont la faculté de nommer des secrétaires, avec le consentement des parties, afin d'effectuer des tâches d'ordre administratif, organisationnel et d'appui[73].

Bien que le Code du CEA n'inclue aucune précision s'agissant de la rédaction de la sentence par le secrétaire du tribunal, il spécifie néanmoins que les arbitres ne peuvent déléguer aucune fonction décisionnelle ni l'évaluation des positions factuelles ou juridiques des parties[74].

Il est aussi intéressant de citer les conclusions auxquelles sont arrivés les comités de la New York City Bar Association en 2006 sur cette question[75] :

« *The role of the arbitrator is characterised by its* intuitu personae *nature. The appointment of a secretary may be reconciled with its fundamental principle so long as the arbitral tribunal exercises both close supervision of and has ultimate authority over the decision-making process*[76].

(...)

There is concern that a secretary permitted substantial involvement may exercise undue influence over the arbitral tribunal and, as a result, affect the disposition. This concern is best addressed by disclosure, transparency and informed consent of the parties."[77]

Le groupe des jeunes de l'International Council for Commercial Arbitration (ICCA), à la suite de l'enquête qu'il avait menée en 2012 et 2013, a décidé d'élaborer le « Young ICCA Guide on Arbitral Secretaries ». Selon cette enquête 60 % des participants avaient exprimé leur intérêt pour que les tâches des secrétaires soient plus réglementées. En outre, 67 % des participants à cette enquête s'étaient déclarés contraires à ce que les secrétaires rédigent le premier projet de la sentence. Nonobstant, les rédacteurs de ce Guide ont préféré prévoir que les secrétaires pourraient rédiger les parties appropriées d'une sentence et participer aux délibérations.

71. Paragraphe 36.
72. Standard 5(b) des IBA Guidelines on Conflicts of Interest in International Arbitration.
73. Paragraphe 95.
74. Paragraphe 97.
75. The American Review of International Arbitration [2006], Vol. 17, No. 4.
76. Page 586.
77. Page 591.

Plus récemment, l'ICCA a publié, en 2021, les « Guidelines on Standards of Practice in International Arbitration » dans lesquelles il est question du comportement des secrétaires de tribunaux arbitraux. Cet aspect est abordé dans la « Guideline IV C. » dans les termes suivants :[78]

« *Tribunal secretaries and personnel of arbitral institutions involved in a particular international arbitration shall address all participants in a courteous and impartial manner.*

Explanation to Guideline IV.C

Guideline IV.C derives from Guideline III.A applicable to arbitrators, and describes the manner in which tribunal secretaries (including assistants) – under the supervision and direction of the arbitral tribunal – and the staff of arbitral institutions who participate in any aspect of administering the case should address all participants during the course of the arbitration. »

Pour conclure brièvement sur ce chapitre, il convient de noter les différentes approches adoptées par les institutions d'arbitrage pour traiter la question des secrétaires de tribunaux arbitraux, tant en ce qui concerne leur rôle que de leur rémunération. Cette absence de cohérence est, malgré tout, le reflet de la pratique, qui demeure divisée sur ces questions. Cette constatation se verra confirmée lorsque nous considérerons, ci-dessous, quelques opinions divergentes exprimées par la doctrine.

III. Le point de vue de la doctrine

Devant la disparité des points de vue sur l'intervention des secrétaires de tribunaux et le résultat obtenu à travers les enquêtes menées conjointement par White & Case et la Queen Mary University de Londres,[79] d'une part, et par l'ICCA,[80] de l'autre, certains praticiens ont appelé à une plus grande uniformisation du rôle des secrétaires.[81] Nonobstant cet appel, l'examen des réformes intervenues, ces dernières années, dans les règlements d'arbitrage des principales institutions, nous a montré que les institutions sont loin de partager l'idée qu'une certaine uniformisation est nécessaire, si ce n'est que sur les aspects purement formels. En effet, toutes les institutions ne considèrent pas qu'il soit opportun d'inclure une référence aux secrétaires dans leur règlement d'arbitrage et préfèrent traiter cette question par le moyen de notes ou des lignes directrices.

La doctrine est partagée entre ceux qui ont une attitude plus favorable à une intervention des secrétaires dans les arbitrages, et ceux qui le sont moins.

Ainsi, d'un côté, on peut observer que certains auteurs considèrent l'intervention du secrétaire comme étant un moyen d'améliorer l'efficacité les procédures

78. https://cdn.arbitration-icca.org/s3fs-public/document/media_document/ICCA_Guidelines_on_Standards_of_Practice_in_International_Arbitration.pdf.

79. www.whitecase.com/files/Uploads/Documents/Arbitration/Queen-Mary-University-London-International-Arbitration-Survey-2012.pdf.

80. *Ibid.*

81. Michael Polkinghorne and Charles B. Rosenberg, *"The Role of the Tribunal Secretary in International Arbitration : A Call for a Uniform Standard"* : www.ibanet.org/Article/NewDetail.aspx?ArticleUid=987d1cfc-3bc2-48d3-959e-e18d7935f542.

d'arbitrage, car cela permettrait aux arbitres de se concentrer sur le fond de l'affaire et de rendre leurs sentences plus rapidement[82].

Un autre groupe d'auteurs, parmi lesquels nous pouvons citer Gary B. Born, est plus réticent à l'intervention des secrétaires, estimant qu'il ne doit pas influencer la décision du tribunal arbitral :[83]

"An arbitrator's obligations include the duty not to delegate his or her responsibilities or tasks to third parties. This duty is widely reflected in ethical guidelines, national court decisions and commentary. Most fundamentally, an arbitrator cannot delegate the duty of deciding a case, attending hearings or deliberations, or evaluating the parties' submissions and evidence to others : these are the essence of the arbitrator's adjudicative function and they are personal, non-delegable duties.

It is nevertheless common for arbitrators to obtain a range of assistance in connection with the arbitral proceedings from third parties. Arbitrators obviously use clerical assistance, which can readily extend beyond typing, organizing files and the like, to dealing with administrative matters ; these tasks will often be conducted either by secretarial or similar staff, but sometimes by junior lawyers or interns. As discussed below, in some instances arbitrators will appoint a "secretary" to assist the tribunal, being a younger lawyer (often from the presiding arbitrator's law firm).

(...)

A central premise of the role of the secretary is that he or she may not assume the tribunal's (or an arbitrator's) functions and may not influence the tribunal's decision. In the words of the ICC Secretariat's Note Concerning the Appointment of Administrative Secretaries "Under no circumstances may the Arbitral Tribunal delegate decision-making functions to an Administrative Secretary. Nor should the Arbitral Tribunal rely on the Administrative Secretary to perform any essential duties of an arbitrator."

D'autres auteurs, comme Yves Derains, adoptent une position plus tranchée en faveur d'une conception plus large de l'intervention des secrétaires :[84]

« *L'arbitre n'est pas un scribe et rédiger n'est pas sa fonction essentielle. Il doit décider en connaissance de cause. Pour cela, il doit avoir une connaissance personnelle du dossier... Les conditions de la rédaction ultérieure du projet de sentence sont des circonstances purement matérielles qui dépendent du mode de travail du président du tribunal arbitral.* »

Le professeur Pierre Tercier s'est prononcé à plus d'une reprise sur cette question. Dans un article qu'il a consacré au rôle des secrétaires du tribunal arbitral il a exprimé l'opinion suivante :[85]

« *The very essence of this function is that arbitrators – whom the parties have entrusted with this competence- must render their decisions personally. A violation*

82. Constantine Partasides, "*Secretaries to Arbitral Tribunals*", Dossier du ICC Institute of World Business Law : "*Players' interaction in International Arbitration*" [2012].

83. Gary B. Born, "*International Commercial Arbitration*" [2014].

84. Yves Derains, « *Le professionnalisme des arbitres internationaux* », Revue de l'arbitrage, 2019, pp. 671-672, paragraphe 28.

85. Pierre Tercier, "*The Role of the Secretary to the Arbitral Tribunal*", in Lawrence W. Newman and Richard D. Hill, "*The leading Arbitrator's Guide to International Arbitration*", Juris Publishing [2014], p. 537.

of this principle could endanger the effectiveness of the award and lead to a refusal to recognize it."

Dans un autre article, il s'est exprimé ainsi :[86]

« *J'ai travaillé toute ma vie avec des assistants, à l'Université, à la Commission fédérale de la concurrence, à la Cour de la CCI, et maintenant dans les procédures que je mène. Or, il n'est pas une décision, pas une ligne couverte par ma signature que je n'aie écrite, adaptée ou approuvée.* »

En somme, le professeur Tercier laisse entrevoir que la rédaction du projet de sentence pourrait être confiée à un secrétaire, pour autant que le président du tribunal arbitral supervise de près le projet rédigé par le secrétaire.

Sur cette question, nous sommes plutôt de l'avis exprimé par Constantine Partasides dans l'un de ses articles :[87]

« *Even a careful review by an arbitrator of a secretary's draft does not entirely remove the scope given to the secretary to make judgments as to what to emphasize and what to omit, judgments that the arbitrator reviewing the draft may not even be able to identify never mind control. The act of writing is the ultimate safeguard of intellectual control. An arbitrator should be reluctant to relinquish it.* »

Il n'est pas contesté que les arbitres doivent décider. Mais, il est tout aussi souhaitable que les arbitres ne se laissent pas influencer du fait du rôle joué par leur secrétaire.

Le secrétaire peut être amené à intervenir à différents stades : les plus critiques se situent au moment de la rédaction des décisions et de la participation aux délibérations. Mais, comme nous l'avons aussi constaté, à la lecture du jugement du Tribunal de première instance francophone de Bruxelles[88], la préparation des audiences peut également créer des difficultés.

A chacun de ces stades, se présentera le dilemme de savoir quel est le rôle que doit jouer le secrétaire, en fonction de ce qui a été accepté par les parties au moment de définir avec elles les tâches pouvant lui être confiées. Ainsi, si les parties décident, par exemple, que le secrétaire ne doit pas assister aux délibérations, le problème ne se poserait pas. Mais, si le secrétaire est autorisé à y assister, encore faudra-t-il savoir s'il aura le droit de s'exprimer sur un point du dossier, autre que l'identification matérielle des pièces auxquelles les arbitres veulent faire référence, bien évidemment.

Le sujet le plus délicat est sans doute la nature du rôle du secrétaire dans la rédaction des décisions prises par le tribunal arbitral, notamment du projet de sentence. En effet, l'incorporation des éléments de fait ou de droit sélectionnés par un secrétaire au moment de rédiger le projet de sentence viendra influencer, nécessairement, la pensée des arbitres. Nous savons que, même si, lors des délibérations, les arbitres ont pris des décisions sur certains points litigieux, lors de la rédaction et de la lecture du projet de sentence, il se peut que les arbitres changent d'avis. Par ailleurs, laisser au secrétaire du tribunal le soin de rédiger les

---

86. Pierre Tercier, « *Entre nous à propos des relations entre arbitres* », Revue de l'arbitrage, 2016, p. 1078.

87. Constantine Partasides, « *The Fourth Arbitrator? The Role of Secretaries to Tribunals in International Arbitration* », Arbitration International [2002], Vol. 18, No. 2, p. 158.

88. *Ibid.*

parties relatives à la motivation de la sentence ne fait qu'aggraver le risque que les arbitres soient influencés par les seuls éléments retenus par le secrétaire et ne considèrent pas ceux qu'il a omis de mentionner, volontairement ou pas.

Conclusion

L'intervention des secrétaires de tribunaux arbitraux, nous l'avons constaté, est une question controversée. Néanmoins, leur intervention est devenue plus fréquente ces dernières années ; la preuve en est qu'un bon nombre d'institutions arbitrales ont décidé « d'institutionnaliser » les secrétaires en y consacrant des dispositions spécifiques dans leurs nouveaux règlements d'arbitrage ou, à tout le moins dans les notes ou lignes directrices. Toutefois, ce faisant, les institutions ont choisi de se distinguer plutôt que de tendre à une certaine uniformisation.

Le manque de cohérence est générateur de tensions, qui peuvent mener jusqu'à des demandes de récusation d'arbitres ou, pire encore, d'annulation de sentences. Ces tensions peuvent aussi se manifester au sein du tribunal arbitral[89], lorsque les arbitres n'arrivent pas à trouver un accord sur la nécessité de désigner un secrétaire ou bien sur les tâches à lui confier, mais aussi, dans certains cas, sur la contribution financière des arbitres au regard de la rémunération des secrétaires. S'il y a bien, on peut le dire sans hésiter, une unanimité quant à l'interdiction de toute délégation de la fonction décisionnelle des arbitres au profit des secrétaires, il en va autrement de deux des questions les plus épineuses, à savoir les tâches qui peuvent être confiées aux secrétaires de tribunaux arbitraux et leur rémunération.

C'est en raison de la sensibilité existante autour de ces points, qu'il ne faut pas ignorer le rôle que doivent avoir les parties lors de la désignation et de la définition des fonctions d'un secrétaire.

En effet, l'intention du tribunal arbitral de désigner un secrétaire devrait être portée à la connaissance des parties aussitôt que possible, en toute transparence, en identifiant le candidat présumé, les fonctions qu'il envisage de lui confier, ainsi que son mode de rémunération, si le règlement d'arbitrage applicable permet que les parties en supportent directement la charge. Un accord entre parties et le tribunal arbitral sur chacun de ces points, dès que l'intérêt de désigner d'un secrétaire a été identifié, permettra de minimiser le risque de tensions et de contestation par la suite.

89. Voir dans ce sens, l'opinion dissidente dans l'affaire *Compañía de Aguas del Aconquija S.A. & Vivendi Universal S.A. c/ République d'Argentine*, précitée.

Commentaires de jurisprudence

Case Law

Quelles tâches le tribunal arbitral peut-il confier à son secrétaire ?

Marc DAL et Estelle LEVY
Avocats, DALDEWOLF, Bruxelles

RÉFÉRENCE :

– Commentaire du jugement du tribunal de première instance francophone de Bruxelles du 17 juin 2021

I. – Introduction

1. S'agissant du rôle du secrétaire ou de l'assistant du tribunal arbitral, chacun garde en mémoire la sentence rendue dans l'affaire Yukos qui avait à l'époque défrayé la chronique. La décision avait été attaquée en annulation au motif notamment que les arbitres n'avaient pas personnellement exécuté leur mission parce qu'ils avaient délégué leur pouvoir décisionnel à un « *assistant du tribunal* ». Selon les experts linguistiques mandatés par la partie demanderesse en annulation, entre 41 % et 70 % de trois chapitres décisionnels de la sentence arbitrale finale avaient été rédigés par l'assistant du tribunal. Cette partie avait comparé le rôle de l'assistant du tribunal arbitral à celui de secrétaire qui, selon elle, devait se limiter à un soutien administratif au tribunal arbitral[1]. Dans un arrêt du 18 février 2020, la cour d'appel de La Haye, réformant le jugement rendu en première instance qui n'avait pas tranché ce moyen, a décidé que, sauf accord contraire des parties, le tribunal arbitral pouvait faire appel à un assistant pour rédiger un projet de sentence, l'important étant que le tribunal arbitral endosse la responsabilité dudit projet[2]. La cour d'appel de La Haye n'a pas retenu le motif d'annulation selon lequel le tribunal arbitral n'aurait pas été valablement constitué. La cour a jugé que le tribunal arbitral n'avait pas commis de violation grave dans le cadre de son mandat en insérant dans la sentence finale des textes rédigés par l'assistant après les avoir acceptés[3]. Elle a néanmoins précisé que le tribunal arbitral avait failli en n'informant pas les parties sur la nature et l'étendue du rôle joué par son assistant[4].

1. Gerechtshof Den Haag, Veteran Petroleum Limited, *Yukos Universal Limited and Hulley Enterprises Limited v. Russian Federation*, No. 200.197.079/01, 18 février 2020, n° 6.6.9.
2. Gerechtshof Den Haag, Veteran Petroleum Limited, *Yukos Universal Limited and Hulley Enterprises Limited v. Russian Federation*, No. 200.197.079/01, 18 février 2020, n° 6.6.10 et n° 6.6.14.1.
3. *Ibidem*, n° 6.6.14.1
4. Gerechtshof Den Haag, Veteran Petroleum Limited, *Yukos Universal Limited and Hulley Enterprises Limited v. Russian Federation*, No. 200.197.079/01, 18 février 2020, n°6.6.14.2,

2. Dans un jugement rendu le 17 juin 2021, le tribunal de première instance francophone de Bruxelles s'est prononcé sur le rôle exercé par le secrétaire du tribunal arbitral dans un arbitrage organisé conformément au règlement de la CCI en vigueur en 2019. Ce jugement fait l'objet d'un pourvoi en cassation.

3. La question est importante : la sentence arbitrale ne doit pas être susceptible d'être annulée en raison de l'intervention d'un secrétaire qui ne se serait pas limité à l'accomplissement de tâches administratives mais qui aurait exercé la fonction juridictionnelle confiée par essence aux arbitres, de telle sorte qu'il serait *de facto* devenu un quatrième arbitre[5].

4. Quelles tâches le secrétaire peut-il exercer ? Doit-il se limiter à des tâches strictement administratives ? Son intervention doit-elle se borner à des questions d'organisation ? Peut-il rédiger tout ou partie du projet de la sentence arbitrale ? Si oui, peut-il écrire autre chose que le récapitulatif de la procédure et l'exposé des faits ? La partie décisionnelle du projet de sentence peut-elle être de sa plume ?

5. Les enseignements qui peuvent être tirés de ce jugement sont utiles pour répondre à ces questions.

6. La doctrine belge commentant le rôle du secrétaire du tribunal arbitral est rare[6] [7]. À notre connaissance, aucune décision de justice belge ne s'était à ce jour prononcée sur cette question. La décision commentée constitue donc une première en Belgique. Elle est intéressante pour les praticiens de l'arbitrage international car elle porte sur le rôle du secrétaire administratif dans les procédures organisées conformément aux règles de la CCI.

II. – Le jugement du tribunal de première instance francophone de Bruxelles du 17 juin 2021

A. Les faits

7. Après la signature de l'acte de mission, le tribunal arbitral avait proposé aux parties de s'adjoindre l'aide d'une secrétaire administrative, par ailleurs collaboratrice au sein du cabinet d'avocats du président du tribunal arbitral.

8. Celle-ci et le tribunal s'étaient engagés à agir conformément à la « *Note aux parties et aux tribunaux arbitraux sur la conduite de l'arbitrage selon le Règlement d'arbitrage CCI* » en vigueur en 2019.

---

voy. également C.J. Carswell and L. Winnington-Ingram, "Awards: Challenges Based on Misuse of Tribunal Secretaries", *GAR*, 8 juin 2021.

5. C. Partasides, "The Fourth Arbitrator ? The Role of Secretaries to Tribunals in International Arbitration", in W.W. Park (ed), *Arbitration International*, 2002, pp. 147-164.

6. M. Fontaine, « L'arbitre et ses collaborateurs », *b-Arbitra*, 2013, issue 1, p. 34.

7. Le jugement commenté fait l'objet d'une note de J. Kolber, Belgian Court settles long-standing controversy : arbitral secretaries may draft awards (Brussel Court of First Instance), Practical Law UK, Thomson Reuters, 16 juillet 2021 ; N. Bassiri et M. Draye, *Arbitration in Belgium – A Practioner's Guide*, The Netherlands, Wolters Kluwer, 2016, pp. 145-146 ; G. Keutgen, G.-A. Dal (avec la collaboration de M. Dal et D. Matray), *L'arbitrage en droit belge et international*, Bruxelles, 2015, p. 265.

9. Les parties avaient marqué leur accord sur la désignation de la secrétaire administrative.

10. Le tribunal arbitral a rendu une sentence partielle attribuant environ 60 % de la responsabilité aux défendeurs. Ceux-ci ont posé deux questions aux membres du tribunal arbitral : quel fut le rôle tenu par la secrétaire administrative au cours de la procédure dans la préparation des questions posées par le tribunal au témoin expert au cours de l'audience ? Quel rôle la secrétaire avait-elle joué dans la préparation d'une partie (décisionnelle) de la sentence ?

11. L'une des co-arbitres a répondu qu'elle ne connaissait pas la réponse à la première question. Concernant la seconde, elle a précisé que les trois arbitres avaient « *travaillé de manière collégiale à la préparation du projet par le biais d'échanges continus et intenses de sections du projet et de commentaires sur ces projets et quand nécessaire de discussions téléphoniques* »[8].

12. L'autre co-arbitre a indiqué que chaque membre du tribunal avait préparé sa propre liste de questions à l'expert en précisant que « *la présence de la secrétaire durant les délibérations (...) avait été annoncée et acceptée par les membres du tribunal* ». Il a ajouté que la secrétaire administrative n'était pas intervenue au cours des discussions. Il a conclu que la sentence était « *un travail réalisé en trio, exclusivement de manière conjointe et commune, où chaque arbitre a rédigé, discuté et pris des décisions de façon collégiale* »[9].

13. Le président du tribunal arbitral a précisé le rôle tenu par la secrétaire : elle avait « *préparé un projet de liste de questions à poser au témoin expert* » (projet qu'il avait revu) ; elle avait participé aux conférences téléphoniques entre les arbitres, sans prendre part à la discussion ; enfin, elle l'avait assisté dans le processus de rédaction de la sentence. Le président indiquait : « (...) *il n'y a pas une seule phrase dans la sentence et pas une seule note de bas de page qui n'aurait pas été au moins revue, vérifiée et si nécessaire corrigée par moi à la lumière de mon point de vue et des délibérations du Tribunal arbitral* »[10].

14. Les défendeurs ont ensuite écrit au président du tribunal qu'ils pensaient que la question posée au témoin expert et que l'élément correspondant de la sentence avaient été préparés par la secrétaire administrative.

15. Le président a répondu par la négative.

16. Les défendeurs ont ensuite fait part au président du tribunal arbitral, à la secrétaire administrative et à la conseillère de la CCI de leurs préoccupations concernant le respect par le tribunal et par la secrétaire de leurs engagements pris au moment de la désignation de cette dernière. La préparation des questions à poser à l'expert par la secrétaire ainsi que son assistance dans la rédaction de la partie décisionnelle de la sentence constituaient selon eux des violations de la note de la CCI que le tribunal arbitral et la secrétaire s'était engagés à respecter. Ils ont alors demandé la production de divers documents : les fiches d'entrée de temps de la secrétaire administrative, les listes de questions préparées par la secrétaire et le tribunal et les projets préparés par la secrétaire. Le demandeur s'est opposé à ces demandes « *considérant que la pêche aux informations initiée (par les défendeurs) était illégitime et futile* »[11].

---

8. Page 6 du jugement.
9. Pages 6 et 7 du jugement.
10. Page 7 du jugement.
11. Page 9 du jugement.

17. Face aux critiques des défendeurs dont il a dénoncé les termes « *assez agressifs, voire vexatoires* », le président du tribunal a présenté sa démission à la CCI. Dans sa lettre démission, le président du tribunal arbitral précisait qu'« *à aucun moment, Mme (X) n'a excédé son rôle et ses fonctions de secrétaire administrative* »[12].

B. L'action en annulation

18. Les défendeurs à l'arbitrage ont introduit une action devant le tribunal de première instance francophone de Bruxelles afin d'obtenir l'annulation de la sentence partielle rendue notamment[13] en raison de « *l'irrégularité de la procédure arbitrale, et plus particulièrement la délégation du pouvoir décisionnel à la secrétaire administrative* ».

19. Ils ont fondé leur demande sur l'article 1717, §3, v) du Code judiciaire qui dispose que :

« *§ 3. La sentence arbitrale ne peut être annulée que si :*

a. La partie en faisant la demande apporte la preuve :

(…)

v) que *la constitution du tribunal arbitral, ou la procédure arbitrale, n'a pas été conforme à la convention des parties, à condition que cette convention ne soit pas contraire à une disposition de la sixième partie du présent Code à laquelle les parties ne peuvent déroger, ou, à défaut d'une telle convention, qu'elle n'a pas été conforme à la sixième partie du présent Code ; à l'exception de l'irrégularité touchant à la constitution du tribunal arbitral, ces irrégularités ne peuvent toutefois donner lieu à annulation de la sentence arbitrale s'il est établi qu'elles n'ont pas eu d'incidence sur la sentence* »[14].

C. La décision

20. Selon la thèse défendue par les parties qui ont intenté le recours en annulation, en rédigeant la liste des questions posées par le président à l'expert durant l'audience et une partie décisionnelle de la sentence partielle, la secrétaire administrative aurait commis un excès de pouvoir qui « *a vicié tant la constitution du tribunal arbitral que la procédure arbitrale* ». Cet excès de pouvoir constituerait un motif d'annulation conformément à l'article 1717, §3, v) du Code judiciaire[15].

---

12. Page 10 du jugement.

13. Ce seul moyen d'annulation fait l'objet de la présente note. D'autres moyens d'annulation ont été invoqués. Le tribunal les a rejetés.

14. O. Caprasse, « Recours en annulation et exequatur des sentences : questions diverses », *b-Arbitra*, 2015, p. 367 ; M. Dal, « Les recours contre les sentences arbitrales en droit belge », in *L'arbitre et le juge étatique. Études de droit comparé à la mémoire de Giuseppe Tarzia*, Bruxelles, Bruylant, 2014 ; M. Dal, « De quelques causes – anciennes et nouvelles – d'annulation des sentences arbitrales », *b-Arbitra*, 2015, n° 2, p. 389 ; P. de Bournonville, *L'arbitrage*, Bruxelles, Larcier, 2017, p. 193 ; B. Hanotiau et O. Caprasse, « L'annulation des sentences arbitrales », *J.T.*, 2004, p. 413 ; G. Keutgen et G.-A. Dal (avec la collaboration de M. Dal et D. Matray), *L'arbitrage en droit belge et international, t. I, Le droit belge*, Bruxelles, Bruylant, 2015, p. 531.

15. Page 12 du jugement.

21. Le tribunal constate que le président a confirmé que la secrétaire administrative a effectivement rédigé la liste des questions posées à l'expert ainsi qu'une partie de la sentence comprenant notamment les motifs décisionnels.

22. Le tribunal relève ensuite que l'un des « *principes cardinaux de l'arbitrage est le caractère intuitu personae de la désignation d'un arbitre* » ce qui a pour conséquence que les arbitres désignés s'engagent à trancher personnellement le litige qui leur est soumis par les parties, ce qui exclut en principe donc toute délégation[16].

23. Concernant les tâches du secrétaire administratif, le tribunal souligne ensuite l'évolution dans la pratique qui admet que ces tâches « *peuvent dépasser le cadre purement administratif et organisationnel* »[17].

24. Le tribunal poursuit en examinant l'article 185 de la note de la CCI qui précise les tâches relatives à l'organisation et à la gestion que peut accomplir le secrétaire administratif[18]. Conformément à cette disposition, il relève que le secrétaire est autorisé à mener des recherches ou à rédiger des parties factuelles de la sentence et « *peut être amené à effectuer un travail intellectuel dont l'impact est susceptible d'affecter la prise de décision* »[19].

25. Il relève ensuite que la note de la CCI pose plusieurs balises afin de « *prévenir le risque de délégation du pouvoir de juger au secrétaire administratif* »[20]. Ces balises sont consacrées par les articles 184[21] et 187 de la note de la CCI.

26. Le tribunal va principalement fonder sa décision sur l'article 187 de la note de la CCI qui disposait que « *(l)e fait pour un Tribunal arbitral de demander au Secrétaire administratif de préparer des notes écrites ou des mémorandums ne pourra en aucun cas dispenser le Tribunal arbitral de son obligation de revoir personnellement le dossier et/ou de rédiger lui-même toute décision du Tribunal arbitral* »[22].

---

16. Page 12 du jugement.
17. Page 13 du jugement.
18. L'article 185 de la note de la CCI (actuel article 224 de la note CCI 2021) disposait que : « *Nonobstant ce qui précède, un Secrétaire administratif peut accomplir des tâches relatives à l'organisation et à la gestion telles que :*
- *La transmission de documents et de documents au nom du Tribunal arbitral ;*
- *L'organisation et la tenue du dossier du Tribunal arbitral ainsi que la localisation de documents ;*
- *L'organisation d'audiences et de réunions, et servir de liaison avec les parties à cet égard ;*
- *La rédaction de correspondance à l'intention des parties et son envoi pour compte du tribunal arbitral ;*
- *La préparation de projets d'ordonnances de procédure ainsi que la rédaction des parties factuelles d'une sentence (p. ex. résumé de la procédure, chronologie des faits, synthèse des positions des parties) qui seront soumis à l'examen du Tribunal arbitral ;*
- *La participation aux audiences, réunions et délibérations du Tribunal arbitral ; la prise de notes, la réalisation de procès-verbaux, le chronométrage ;*
- *Les recherches juridiques ou autres ; et*
- *La relecture et la vérification de citations, dates, références dans les ordonnances de procédure et sentences ainsi que la correction d'erreurs typographiques, de grammaire ou de calcul.* »

19. Page 13 du jugement.
20. Page 13 du jugement.
21. L'article 184 de la note de la CCI (actuel article 223 de la note CCI 2021) disposait que « *(l)es tâches confiées au Secrétaire administratif ne sauraient en aucune circonstance décharger le Tribunal arbitral de son obligation d'examiner personnellement le dossier. Le Tribunal arbitral ne saurait en aucun cas déléguer ses fonctions décisionnelles à un Secrétaire administratif pas plus que qu'un Tribunal arbitral ne doit s'appuyer sur un Secrétaire administratif afin qu'il exerce pour son compte les attributions essentielles d'un arbitre.* »
22. Actuel article 223 de la note CCI 2021.

27. Le juge en conclut « *qu'en utilisant les termes* "et/ou", [la note] *autorise implicitement mais certainement le secrétaire administratif à rédiger tout ou partie d'un projet de sentence, à charge pour le Tribunal arbitral de revoir personnellement le dossier et valider ou corriger ledit projet à la lumière de son examen du dossier. Autrement dit, la CCI n'aurait pas utilisé ces termes alternatifs* "et/ou" *si elle avait voulu exclure la rédaction de tout ou partie de la sentence par le secrétaire administratif* »[23].

28. Il ajoute que, puisque la secrétaire administrative a suivi la formation organisée par la CCI à la rédaction de sentences arbitrales, les parties, en soumettant leur litige à la CCI, ont « *souscrit au type d'intervention des secrétaires administratifs tel que prévu par la CCI* »[24].

29. Le tribunal juge qu'en tout état de cause, le seul fait de confier au secrétaire administratif la rédaction d'une liste de questions à l'expert ne suffit pas, en soi, à démontrer une délégation du pouvoir décisionnel dans la mesure où le président a confirmé avoir relu et corrigé le projet de liste. Il poursuit : « *Tout dépend en réalité de la manière avec laquelle l'arbitre exerce et conçoit sa mission. Pour certains,* "l'acte d'écrire est la sauvegarde ultime du contrôle intellectuel". *Pour d'autres, le même degré de contrôle sur l'acte décisionnel peut être atteint sans avoir rédigé le premier projet. Il est question en définitive de l'intégrité et de la conscience professionnelle de l'arbitre lui-même que les parties ont précisément choisi pour ses qualités. Par ailleurs, le choix du secrétaire administratif se portera généralement sur un jeune juriste dont le manque d'expérience sera le gage du peu, voire de l'absence, d'influence sur le processus décisionnel. En ce sens, la Cour internationale d'arbitrage a refusé la désignation comme secrétaire d'un arbitre renommé qui faisait autorité, le danger étant manifeste que ce secrétaire ne limite pas son rôle à la réalisation de tâches administratives et au contraire influence la décision du Tribunal arbitral. Enfin, le secrétaire administratif ne peut être désigné qu'avec l'accord des parties et l'article 180 de la Note CCI précise qu'il doit satisfaire aux mêmes conditions d'indépendance et d'impartialité que les arbitres* »[25].

30. Après avoir relevé que rien dans les retranscriptions d'audience ne permet d'observer la moindre méconnaissance des questions à poser aux experts dans le chef du président du tribunal arbitral, le tribunal décide que la seule rédaction de cette liste de questions ne permet pas « *en soi* » d'établir une délégation du pouvoir décisionnel. S'agissant de la participation de la secrétaire administrative à la partie litigieuse de la sentence attaquée, le tribunal relève que ladite partie « *fait près de 200 pages et contient tant des données factuelles que les positions réciproques des parties et l'appréciation du Tribunal arbitral. Rien ne permet au tribunal de céans de déterminer précisément les passages de ladite section écrits de la plume* (de la secrétaire administrative) *et ceux rédigés ou corrigés par* (le président) »[26].

31. Le juge en conclut que « *la relecture et la révision par (le président) du projet de sentence rédigé par (la secrétaire administrative) respectent le cadre de*

23. Page 14 du jugement.
24. Page 14 du jugement.
25. Page 25 du jugement.
26. Page 16 du jugement.

l'intervention de la secrétaire administrative posée par la Note CCI et ne témoigne pas d'une délégation du pouvoir décisionnel »[27].

32. En définitive, le tribunal juge que le moyen pris de l'irrégularité de la constitution du tribunal arbitral et de la procédure arbitrale n'est pas fondé dès lors que rien ne permet de constater que la secrétaire administrative « *aurait outrepassé les compétences que lui reconnait la Note CCI ni qu'elle se serait vu déléguer un pouvoir décisionnel [par le président]* »[28].

III. – Observations

33. Certes, le tribunal de première instance francophone de Bruxelles fonde sa décision sur le fait qu'aucun élément factuel ne lui permet de conclure que la secrétaire administrative aurait outrepassé ses pouvoirs en préparant la liste des questions aux experts ou en rédigeant des parties dites décisionnelles du projet de sentence.

34. À cet égard, deux éléments de ce jugement nous semblent importants : les parties avaient marqué leur accord sur la désignation de la secrétaire administrative ainsi que sur l'application de la note de la CCI qui définit les missions pouvant être accomplies par cette dernière.

35. Restait à décider si la secrétaire administrative pouvait rédiger des parties décisionnelles du projet de sentence. Les termes du jugement sont clairs : « *la relecture et la révision par (le président) du projet de sentence rédigé par (la secrétaire administrative) respectent le cadre de l'intervention de la secrétaire administrative posée par la Note CCI et ne témoigne pas d'une délégation du pouvoir décisionnel* »[29].

36. Comme nous l'avons écrit dans l'introduction, le jugement du 17 juin 2021 s'inscrit donc dans la tendance actuelle selon laquelle le secrétaire peut participer à la rédaction de toute partie de la sentence.

37. En 2015, le tribunal fédéral Suisse avait ainsi jugé que « *les tâches du secrétaire juridique (...) n'excluent pas une certaine assistance dans la rédaction de la sentence, sous le contrôle et conformément aux directives du tribunal arbitral. (...) sous la réserve [...] que le tribunal arbitral n'abandonne pas aux auxiliaires commis par lui les prérogatives inhérentes à sa mission, en particulier celle de trancher lui-même le différend qui lui a été soumis* »[30].

38. Quelques années plus tard, la cour d'appel de La Haye, dans l'arrêt précité, avait décidé qu'aucune règle d'arbitrage international n'interdisait à l'assistant du tribunal d'écrire des parties de la sentence[31]. Par conséquent, en l'absence d'une convention contraire entre les parties, tant que les décisions sont prises par les arbitres sans l'influence de tiers, ceux-ci peuvent décider la mesure dans laquelle

27. Page 16 du jugement.
28. Page 16 du jugement.
29. Page 16 du jugement.
30. Tribunal fédéral, 21 mai 2015, 4A_709/214, Consid. 3.2.2.
31. Gerechtshof Den Haag, Veteran Petroleum Limited, Yukos Universal Limited and Hulley Enterprises Limited v. Russian Federation, No. 200.197.079/01, 18 février 2020, n° 6.6.14.1.

ils souhaitent faire appel à un assistant ou à un secrétaire pour la rédaction de la sentence[32].

39. L'English High Court a toutefois adopté une position plus prudente. Après avoir constaté que les règles de la LCIA permettaient de confier un rôle étendu au secrétaire administratif, la cour a jugé que, conformément aux meilleures pratiques de l'arbitrage international, le tribunal devrait éviter de déléguer à un secrétaire toute tâche qui impliquerait l'expression du point de vue de ce dernier sur le litige que le tribunal arbitral doit trancher[33].

40. Le jugement commenté présente un intérêt particulier en ce qu'il interprète la note de la CCI comme autorisant « *implicitement mais certainement le secrétaire administratif à rédiger tout ou partie d'un projet de sentence, à charge pour le tribunal arbitral de revoir personnellement le dossier et valider ou corriger ledit projet à la lumière de son examen du dossier* »[34,35].

41. Ceci nous semble conforme à l'article 223 de l'actuelle note de la CCI qui reprend en substance les anciens articles 184 et 187 et dispose que : « *(l)e tribunal arbitral ne saurait en aucun cas déléguer ses fonctions décisionnelles à un secrétaire administratif ni s'appuyer sur un secrétaire administratif afin qu'il exerce pour son compte les attributions essentielles d'un arbitre. De même, les tâches confiées à un secrétaire administratif, comme la préparation de notes écrites ou d'un mémorandum, ne déchargeront pas le tribunal arbitral de son obligation d'effectuer personnellement un examen du dossier et/ou de rédiger lui-même un projet de décision du tribunal arbitral* »[36].

42. Pour consacrer le caractère *intuitu personae* de la décision des arbitres, la CCI a d'ailleurs procédé à un ajout dans le nouvel article 224 de l'actuelle note[37]. Il y est prévu que le secrétaire peut participer à « *la préparation des projets d'ordonnances de procédure ainsi que de la rédaction des parties factuelles d'une sentence qui seront soumis à l'examen du tribunal arbitral* ». Il y est désormais ajouté : « *sous réserve que ces ordonnances de procédure ainsi que ces parties d'une sentence fassent par la suite l'objet d'un examen par le tribunal arbitral lui-même* ».

43. Ceci ne fait que confirmer ce qu'avaient écrit deux éminents praticiens de l'arbitrage international. Ainsi le professeur Pierre Tercier a écrit : « *J'ai travaillé toute ma vie avec des assistants, à l'université, à la Commission fédérale de la concurrence, à la cour de la CCI, et maintenant dans les procédures que je mène. Or, il n'est pas une décision, pas une ligne couverte par ma signature que je n'aie écrite, adaptée ou approuvée* »[38]. Pour Yves Derains, « *Pour beaucoup, le rôle du secrétaire administratif ne saurait aller jusqu'à la rédaction de la sentence. C'est*

32. *Ibidem*, par. 6.6.14

33. P v. Q and Ors [2017], EWHC 194 (Comm).

34. Page 14 du jugement.

35. Comme cela a été relevé par J. Kolber, Belgian Court Settles long-standing controversy : arbitral secretaries may draft awards (Brussels Court of First Instance), Practical Law UK, Thomson Reuters, 16 juillet 2021.

36. J. Ole Jensen, « 5. Permissible Tasks », *Tribunal Secretaries in International Arbitration*, Oxford International Arbitration series, 2019, n° 5.117.

37. Correspondant à l'ancien article 185 de la note en vigueur en 2019.

38. P. Tercier, « Entre nous à propos des relations entre arbitres », Revue de l'arbitrage, 2016, p. 1078.

un faux débat sur lequel on s'est excessivement focalisé car il n'est pas précisé ce que l'on entend par "rédaction". L'arbitre n'est pas un scribe et rédiger n'est pas sa fonction essentielle. Il doit décider en connaissance de cause. Pour cela, il doit avoir une connaissance personnelle du dossier. C'est à partir de cette connaissance qu'il doit prendre ses décisions. D'ailleurs les parties l'y aident en faisant vivre devant lui, avec le concours de témoins et de façon contradictoire, les documents principaux du dossier, pendant de longues audiences. De plus, dans un tribunal de trois membres, les décisions sont collégiales et prises à l'occasion d'un délibéré. Les conditions de la rédaction ultérieure du projet de sentence sont des circonstances purement matérielles qui dépendent du mode de travail du président du tribunal arbitral »[39].

44. Quelles tâches peut donc accomplir le secrétaire administratif ? La réponse est apportée par les fondements intrinsèques de l'arbitrage : le caractère *intuitu personae* de la mission de l'arbitre et le caractère conventionnel de l'arbitrage. Au moment de la proposition de désignation du secrétaire administratif, le tribunal arbitral communiquera aux parties l'étendue précise des missions qui lui seront confiées. Cela évitera toute difficulté par la suite. En tout état de cause, si les parties acceptent que le secrétaire administratif rédige, à l'état de projet, des parties décisionnelles de la sentence arbitrale, celle-ci sera nécessairement et exclusivement le résultat de la décision collégiale des arbitres qui seuls en endosseront la responsabilité.

⁂

39. Y. Derains, « Le professionnalisme des arbitres internationaux », Revue de l'arbitrage, 2019, pp. 659 et suivantes, par. 28.

La saga *Kabab-Ji c. Kout Food* continue Zoom sur la décision de la *Supreme Court* du 27 octobre 2021

Peter ROSHER et Mathilde ADANT
Avocat associé, Reed Smith
Avocate collaboratrice, Reed Smith

– RÉFÉRENCE : [Kabab-Ji SAL (Lebanon) (Appellant) v Kout Food Group (Kuwait) (Respondent) [2021] UKSC 48]

ABSTRACT

The English Supreme Court has confirmed the English law position on the thorny question of the applicable law of an arbitration agreement: the law applicable to the contract will, in general, be deemed to apply to the arbitration agreement. This solution, much more complex to apply in practice than it initially appears, is irreconcilable with the French solution based on substantive rules of international arbitration. This confirmation serves to highlight the real need for parties to specify the applicable law to their arbitration agreement in their contract.

RÉSUMÉ

La Supreme Court *anglaise a confirmé la position anglaise sur la question épineuse du droit applicable à la clause compromissoire : le droit applicable au contrat sera, en général, jugé applicable à la clause compromissoire. Cette solution, d'application plus complexe qu'il n'y paraît, apparaît irréconciliable avec la solution française fondée sur les règles matérielles, ce qui ajoute à la nécessité pour les parties de clarifier le droit applicable à la clause compromissoire dans leur contrat.*

Introduction

Du nouveau dans l'affaire *Kabab-Ji c. Kout Food* : la *Supreme Court* anglaise a rendu le 27 octobre 2021 sa décision[1], très attendue, qui vient apporter un point final à la saga – côté anglais uniquement, puisque la décision de la Cour de cassation française se fait toujours attendre.

On se souvient[2] que cette affaire avait donné lieu à deux décisions contradictoires de la *Court of Appeal* anglaise[3] et de la cour d'appel de Paris[4] sur la question du droit applicable à la convention d'arbitrage : la *Court of Appeal* anglaise avait favorisé le droit anglais, applicable au contrat principal, tandis que la cour d'appel de Paris avait appliqué la méthode française des règles matérielles pour étendre la clause compromissoire à un non-signataire.

La récente décision de la *Supreme Court* confirme celle de la *Court of Appeal*, portant un coup au peu d'espoir qui pouvait subsister de voir les deux positions réconciliées. Cette décision était attendue sans beaucoup de suspense, car il était peu probable qu'elle modifierait la position anglaise. Au demeurant, elle a le mérite de confirmer la solution anglaise sur le sujet épineux du droit applicable à la convention d'arbitrage – même si, comme on le verra, cette position claire en théorie n'est pas dénuée de complexité dans son application.

I. – La saga Kabab-Ji / Kout Food, ou l'opposition des méthodes anglaise et française de détermination de la loi applicable à la convention d'arbitrage

Pour rappel, l'affaire avait débuté par un contrat de franchise (*Franchise Development Agreement*), signé en 2001 entre la société de droit koweitien AHFC (Al-Homaizi) et la société de droit libanais Kabab-Ji. Ce contrat donnait le droit à AHFC de développer le concept de restauration de Kabab-Ji sur le territoire du Koweït pendant dix ans. Il contenait une clause désignant le droit anglais comme applicable au contrat, ainsi qu'une clause compromissoire prévoyant un arbitrage CCI avec un siège fixé à Paris, sans préciser le droit applicable à la procédure d'arbitrage. Enfin, le contrat contenait également une clause d'intégralité (« *Entire Agreement* »), stipulant que les documents contractuels formaient un ensemble indivisible et que toute modification contractuelle serait soumise à un écrit signé par un représentant dûment habilité.

En 2005, le franchiseur AHFC est devenu filiale du groupe Kout Food (KFG), également situé au Koweït.

1. Kabab-Ji SAL (Lebanon) (Appellant) v Kout Food Group (Kuwait) (Respondent) [2021] UKSC 48 (« ***Kabab-Ji*** »).

2. P. Rosher, « Conflits de culture sur les limites de la séparabilité de la clause compromissoire et incidence de la volonté des parties sur les règles régissant l'extension de la clause compromissoire », 1er janvier 2020, Cahiers de l'arbitrage n° 1, p. 61.

3. Kabab-Ji S.A.L. v. Kout Food Group [2020] EWCA Civ. 6.

4. Cour d'appel de Paris, 23 juin 2020, n° 17/22943.

Dans la mesure où, en dépit de l'expiration du terme du contrat, le groupe KFG avait poursuivi l'utilisation de la franchise Kabab-Ji sur le territoire du Koweït, le franchisé Kabab-Ji a initié une procédure d'arbitrage à l'encontre de la holding du groupe, sans attraire son cocontractant formel, AHFC. Dans l'arbitrage, la société mère KFG soutenait qu'elle n'était pas partie au contrat de franchise et a contesté la compétence du tribunal arbitral.

La sentence arbitrale a été rendue en 2017. Par une décision majoritaire, les arbitres ont décidé que la clause compromissoire devait être étendue à KFG et l'ont condamnée à indemniser le franchisé Kabab-Ji pour un montant de l'ordre de 6 millions de dollars. La sentence était accompagnée d'une opinion dissidente de l'un des arbitres, avocat anglais, selon laquelle le droit anglais, applicable en l'espèce, ne permettait pas l'extension du contrat à la société mère car cette solution contredirait les stipulations du contrat.

Le franchisé Kabab-Ji a alors engagé une procédure de reconnaissance et d'exécution de la sentence devant la *Commercial Court*, tandis que la société mère KFG demandait l'annulation de la sentence devant la cour d'appel de Paris. Par décision du 29 mars 2019, la *Commercial Court* a sursis à statuer dans l'attente de la décision de la cour d'appel de Paris sur l'annulation de la sentence.

Les deux parties ont interjeté appel de la décision de la *Commercial Court*, ce qui a donné lieu à l'arrêt de la *Court of Appeal* du 20 janvier 2020[5]. La *Court of Appeal* a infirmé le jugement de première instance et jugé que la convention d'arbitrage était soumise au droit anglais, lequel ne permettait pas l'extension de la clause compromissoire à la société mère, au motif que le contrat, qui constituait un ensemble indivisible en vertu de la clause d'intégralité, ne limitait pas le droit applicable choisi à la seule *lex contractus*, mais l'étendait à toutes les clauses du contrat, y compris la convention d'arbitrage.

Quelques mois plus tard, la cour d'appel de Paris a rejeté le recours en annulation formé contre la sentence[6]. De manière diamétralement opposée à la solution adoptée par la *Court of Appeal*, la cour d'appel a appliqué la règle matérielle du droit français de l'arbitrage international selon laquelle une convention d'arbitrage peut être étendue à des parties non-signataires lorsque leur implication dans l'exécution du contrat fait présumer qu'elles ont accepté cette clause.

Ces décisions contradictoires ont fait couler beaucoup d'encre et ont toutes deux été contestées, devant la *Supreme Court* anglaise, d'une part, et la Cour de cassation d'autre part.

II. – Confirmation de la position anglaise par la *Supreme Court*

Sans surprise, la *Supreme Court* confirme la décision de la *Court of Appeal*, sur trois questions : (i) la loi applicable à l'extension de la convention d'arbitrage ; (ii) la possibilité d'extension de la clause d'arbitrage *ratione personae* en droit anglais ; et (iii) l'absence d'obligation pour la *Court of Appeal* de surseoir à statuer dans l'attente de la décision des juridictions françaises.

5. Kabab-Ji S.A.L. v. Kout Food Group [2020] EWCA Civ. 6.
6. Cour d'appel de Paris, 23 juin 2020, n° 17/22943.

Le droit anglais, applicable à l'extension de la convention d'arbitrage à une partie non-signataire

En premier lieu, la *Supreme Court* décide que la loi régissant l'extension de la clause d'arbitrage à un tiers est la loi anglaise.

Le point de départ du raisonnement de la *Supreme Court* est la Convention de New York de 1958[7], ainsi que l'*Arbitration Act* de 1996 qui l'a transposée en droit anglais, lesquels prévoient[8] que la convention d'arbitrage est régie par le droit auquel les parties ont choisi de la soumettre ; en l'absence d'un tel choix, le droit de l'État dans lequel la sentence est rendue, c'est-à-dire le droit du siège de l'arbitrage[9], est applicable.

Les parties avaient-elles, au cas d'espèce, choisi le droit applicable à la convention d'arbitrage ?

La *Supreme Court* répond en plusieurs temps.

D'abord, elle relève qu'il n'existe aucun consensus au niveau international sur la question de savoir si le choix du droit applicable au contrat constitue une indication suffisante de la volonté des parties d'y soumettre également la convention d'arbitrage. En conséquence, il appartient aux juridictions anglaises de former leur propre opinion[10].

Ensuite, elle interprète la Convention de New York pour conclure que celle-ci n'exige pas que le choix du droit applicable à la convention d'arbitrage soit exprès. Par ailleurs, le choix d'un droit applicable au contrat constitue généralement une indication suffisante que les parties ont également souhaité y soumettre la convention d'arbitrage[11], conformément à la jurisprudence *Enka v Chubb*[12] d'octobre 2020.

Passant à l'application de cette solution aux faits de l'espèce, la *Supreme Court* constate que la clause de droit applicable prévoit que « *ce Contrat sera régi par et interprété selon le droit anglais* » (« [t]*his Agreement shall be governed by and construed in accordance with the laws of England* »)[13], formulation qui englobe selon elle la convention d'arbitrage, notamment au motif que le contrat définissait le terme « Contrat » comme « *les termes du contrat énoncés ci-dessous* » (« [t]*his Agreement consists of… the terms of agreement set forth herein below* »)[14].

Enfin, la *Supreme Court* rejette les arguments de la partie demanderesse, pour conclure que le choix du droit anglais par les parties s'applique à la convention d'arbitrage[15] :

– la partie demanderesse avait mis en avant que la clause de choix de droit applicable, au-delà de sa désignation du droit anglais, prévoit que « *les*

7. Convention pour la reconnaissance et l'exécution des sentences arbitrales étrangères signée à New York le 10 juin 1958 (la « **Convention de New York** »).
8. Convention de New York de 1958, Article V(1)(a) ; *Arbitration Act* 1996, Section 103(2)(b).
9. *Arbitration Act* 1996, Section 100(2)(b).
10. *Kabab-Ji*, para. 32.
11. *Kabab-Ji*, paras. 28, 35.
12. Enka Insaat Ve Sanayi AS v OOO "Insurance Company Chubb" [2020] USKC 38 (« ***Enka*** »).
13. *Kabab-Ji*, para. 37.
14. *Kabab-Ji*, para. 37.
15. *Kabab-Ji*, para. 53.

arbitres appliqueront aussi les principes de droit généralement reconnus dans les transactions internationales » – ce que la cour reconnaît être une référence aux principes UNIDROIT – pour soutenir qu'il n'y avait pas suffisamment d'indications du droit choisi par les parties et qu'il fallait donc recourir au droit du siège. La cour rejette cet argument en jugeant que l'objectif des principes UNIDROIT est d'interpréter ou de compléter le droit applicable mais non de le contredire, et qu'en vertu de la clause, ces principes sont applicables uniquement aux questions de fond, décidées par les arbitres, et ne constituent ni le droit applicable au contrat ni celui applicable à la convention d'arbitrage[16] ;

– la partie demanderesse se prévalait également du « principe de validation », selon lequel les stipulations contractuelles, et notamment la clause de choix de droit applicable, doivent être interprétées pour donner effet à l'intention présumée que la convention d'arbitrage sera valide et effective. La cour rejette cet argument en jugeant que le principe de validation est un principe d'interprétation contractuelle qui ne s'applique qu'aux parties ayant donné leur accord à la convention d'arbitrage, et qu'il ne saurait donc s'appliquer à la question de savoir si un tel accord existe[17].

Le droit anglais, obstacle à l'extension de la clause d'arbitrage ratione personae

Une fois le droit – anglais – applicable à la clause compromissoire déterminé, la *Supreme Court* se penche sur la question de son extension à une partie non-signataire.

La *Supreme Court* relève qu'au cas d'espèce, le contrat comprend plusieurs clauses selon lesquelles toute modification de ses stipulations est soumise à la forme écrite. Ce formalisme n'ayant pas été respecté, la clause compromissoire ne pouvait être étendue à la société mère KFG[18] et ce, malgré les arguments de la partie défenderesse, qu'elle rejette. En effet, selon la cour :

– aucune novation ne saurait être invoquée par le franchisé, en l'absence de document écrit et signé démontrant que les parties l'avaient acceptée[19] ;

– la règle de l'estoppel ne trouvait pas à s'appliquer en l'absence de comportement contradictoire de la partie défenderesse[20] ;

– les principes UNIDROIT ne pouvaient être invoqués que pour interpréter ou compléter le droit anglais, et non pour le contredire[21] ; enfin,

– le manquement au principe de bonne foi prévu au contrat n'était pas applicable à la question de l'extension du contrat à une partie non-signataire[22].

---

16. *Kabab-Ji*, paras. 40-48.
17. *Kabab-Ji*, paras. 49-52.
18. *Kabab-Ji*, para. 75.
19. *Kabab-Ji*, para. 65.
20. *Kabab-Ji*, para. 67.
21. *Kabab-Ji*, para. 72
22. *Kabab-Ji*, para. 73.

Absence de nécessité de surseoir à statuer dans l'attente de la décision des juridictions françaises

En troisième et dernier lieu, la *Supreme Court* juge que la *Court of Appeal* n'a pas fait d'erreur en décidant qu'il était inutile de suspendre la procédure dans l'attente de l'arrêt de la cour d'appel de Paris[23].

La cour indique dans ce sens que ni l'Article VI de la Convention de New York, ni l'Article 103(5) de l'*Arbitration Act* invoqués n'obligent le juge saisi d'une demande d'exequatur à surseoir à statuer en attendant la décision du juge du siège sur l'annulation, mais leur en donnent seulement la possibilité. La cour aborde ensuite la question du risque de décisions contradictoires en indiquant qu'il est raisonnable de surseoir à statuer lorsque les fondements invoqués pour demander l'annulation de la sentence sont identiques à ceux invoqués pour en contester l'exequatur, en application du droit du siège. En l'espèce, ajoute la cour, ce cas de figure ne se présentait pas dans la mesure où le droit anglais, et non le droit du siège, était applicable à la convention d'arbitrage[24], et que la position française fondée sur des règles matérielles de l'arbitrage international est essentiellement différente de la position anglaise fondée sur une approche conflictualiste[25]. Dès lors, la cour en conclut qu'une décision française appliquant la méthode des règles matérielles ne pourrait donner lieu à un *issue estoppel*[26]. La cour termine son raisonnement en indiquant que le risque de décisions contradictoires ne peut pas être évité, et que ce risque ne peut justifier un sursis à statuer[27].

III. – Les positions anglaise et française, irréconciliables ?

La décision *Kabab-Ji* de la *Supreme Court* confirme sans surprise la position anglaise sur la question du droit applicable à la convention d'arbitrage.

Dans la droite lignée de sa décision récente *Enka v. Chubb*, la *Supreme Court* confirme qu'en présence d'un choix de droit applicable au contrat, ce choix est généralement considéré s'appliquer également à la convention d'arbitrage[28]. Dans l'affaire *Enka*, la *Supreme Court* avait rappelé ce principe, avant de se pencher sur la deuxième branche de l'hypothèse : l'absence de choix, exprès ou implicite, de droit applicable. Dans ce cas, avait jugé la cour, la convention d'arbitrage serait régie par la loi avec laquelle elle présente le lien le plus étroit – généralement la loi du siège.

La position anglaise, clarifiée par ces décisions récentes, semble donc claire sur le principe : le droit applicable à la convention d'arbitrage sera (i) le droit

23. *Kabab-Ji*, para. 92.
24. *Kabab-Ji*, para. 87.
25. *Kabab-Ji*, para. 88.
26. *Kabab-Ji*, para. 89. L'*issue estoppel* interdit à une partie de soulever une question une seconde fois, lorsque cette question a déjà été tranchée et est considérée comme « fondamentale » pour une décision.
27. *Kabab-Ji*, para. 90.
28. *Enka*, paras. 43-52.

choisi par les parties, ou, à défaut de choix, (ii) le droit le plus étroitement lié à la convention d'arbitrage.

Cependant, l'application de la règle aux faits d'espèce peut s'avérer bien plus complexe que l'apparente clarté de son énoncé ne le laisse présumer. En effet, il peut exister d'importantes différences d'appréciation sur ce qui constitue un « choix de droit » par les parties.

Cela est parfaitement illustré par les opinions dissidentes dans l'affaire *Enka*.

Si dans l'affaire *Kabab-Ji*, les parties avaient expressément choisi le droit anglais comme droit applicable à leur contrat, les choses étaient moins claires dans l'affaire *Enka*, dans laquelle le contrat en cause ne comportait pas de choix de droit applicable. Pour cette raison, les juges de la *Supreme Court* ont majoritairement décidé que les parties n'avaient pas choisi de droit applicable et qu'il fallait donc prendre en considération le droit le plus étroîtement lié avec la convention d'arbitrage, c'est-à-dire en l'espèce le droit du siège de l'arbitrage, qui se trouvait être le droit anglais[29]. Mais dans leurs opinions dissidentes, les juges Lord Burrows et Lord Sales ont exprimé leur désaccord, notamment sur la question de savoir si les parties avaient effectivement choisi le droit applicable : contrairement à l'opinion majoritaire, ils ont considéré que les parties avaient implicitement choisi le droit russe comme droit applicable au contrat, et donc à la convention d'arbitrage[30] – ce en raison de nombreuses références au droit russe dans le contrat et des nombreux éléments rattachant le contrat à la Russie.

On voit que l'application des principes dégagés par la jurisprudence anglaise n'est pas sans poser problème, puisque même au sein de la *Supreme Court*, l'application de la règle est susceptible de donner lieu à des solutions radicalement opposées. On peut donc légitimement s'interroger sur la prévisibilité juridique découlant de cette règle. Il faut également noter que son application, une fois en faveur du droit du contrat dans *Kabab-Ji*, l'autre fois en faveur du droit du siège dans *Enka*, a conduit à deux reprises à l'application… du droit anglais. Dès lors, l'affirmation de la *Supreme Court* selon laquelle la solution anglaise « *encourage la prévisibilité juridique, l'uniformité et la cohérence en évitant la complexité et l'artifice* »[31] laisse particulièrement songeur… D'aucuns pourraient même être tentés d'y voir l'expression d'une certaine hypocrisie[32] !

Nous attendons désormais la décision de la Cour de cassation qui viendra a priori apporter un (autre) point final à la saga *Kabab-Ji* (côté français). Il est très probable qu'elle confirmera la position de la cour d'appel de Paris, et qu'elle ne comblera donc pas le fossé créé entre les solutions française et anglaise, qui semblent bel et bien irréconciliables. Ce risque de décisions contradictoires a des conséquences réelles pour les usagers de l'arbitrage, notamment lorsque la sentence est appelée à avoir des effets dans plusieurs pays. Ainsi, une partie désirant obtenir une sentence valable en France et au Royaume-Uni devra anticiper les solutions apportées par

29. *Enka*, paras. 118-119.

30. *Enka*, para. 228, 274.

31. Communiqué de presse de la *Supreme Court* sur l'affaire *Enka*, 9 octobre 2020.

32. E. Gaillard, « Les vertus de la méthode des règles matérielles appliquées à la convention d'arbitrage (les enseignements de l'affaire Kout Food) », Revue de l'arbitrage, 2020, Issue 3, p. 708 : « *Il est* […] *permis de penser que, dans la délicate balance créée par les situations dans lesquelles le siège et le droit applicable au fond du contrat sont dissociés, un siège à Londres aurait, pour le juge anglais, plus de poids qu'un siège fixé ailleurs.* […] *Au total, la méthode conflictuelle se montre à la fois peu prévisible et passablement hypocrite* ».

les deux pays aux questions de droit en jeu, et, si possible, s'y conformer. Par exemple, une partie non-signataire qui ne souhaite pas se voir opposer la clause d'arbitrage devra en tout état de cause, si la décision risque d'être exécutée en France, s'assurer qu'elle ne pourra se voir appliquer les conditions d'extension de la clause compromissoire établies par la jurisprudence française, systématiquement appliquées par les tribunaux français[33]. Une autre complexité vient s'ajouter à ce risque, liée au sort réservé aux sentences annulées au siège de l'arbitrage. Par exemple, l'Angleterre reconnaît généralement les décisions d'annulation rendues au siège et, sauf circonstances particulières, refuse généralement d'accorder l'exequatur à des sentences annulées au siège[34]. La France, au contraire, considère que la sentence internationale n'est rattachée à aucun ordre juridique et que son annulation par les juridictions du siège ne fait pas obstacle à sa reconnaissance ou à son exequatur en France[35].

Face à de telles incertitudes, le principal enseignement de la saga *Kabab-Ji* reste à destination des usagers de l'arbitrage : pour éviter une telle situation de conflit entre deux systèmes juridiques, la clarté est la clé et il est essentiel de préciser spécifiquement dans le contrat le droit applicable à la convention d'arbitrage. En l'absence d'une telle précision, l'incertitude demeurera sur ce droit, qui a pourtant d'importants impacts juridiques sur la possibilité d'exécuter la sentence. Le droit applicable à la convention d'arbitrage est encore trop peu souvent précisé dans les contrats, tant par manque d'habitude que par manque de connaissance par les parties des conséquences de cette omission. Une avancée dans ce domaine pourrait être la modification de certaines conventions d'arbitrage types, afin d'y inclure la mention du droit applicable[36]. En tout état de cause, il est déconseillé aux parties de désigner plusieurs lois nationales dans leur contrat, dont les solutions risqueraient d'être divergentes.

Il est tout de même à noter que même lorsque le droit applicable à la convention d'arbitrage est clair, il existe un risque de décisions contradictoires quand deux tribunaux différents interprètent les mêmes faits selon le même droit. Cela est parfaitement illustré par l'affaire *Dallah*, dans laquelle, on s'en souvient, la *Supreme Court* et la cour d'appel de Paris avaient rendu, là encore, deux décisions diamétralement opposées, alors qu'elles appliquaient pourtant le même droit (le droit français). Si les deux cours étaient d'accord sur les principes applicables à l'extension de la clause compromissoire en droit français, leur application de ces principes aux faits a conduit à des résultats opposés : la cour d'appel de Paris a approuvé l'extension de la clause d'arbitrage à la partie non-signataire, tandis que la *Supreme Court* l'a écartée. Un exemple de plus que les tribunaux étatiques ont tendance à juger d'après les réflexes juridiques propres à leur pays, qui, eux, ne sauraient faire l'objet d'un accord des parties...

33. Une illustration récente de la position constante des tribunaux français sur les critères applicables à l'extension de la clause compromissoire a été donnée par la cour d'appel de Paris dans son arrêt *Damietta* (cour d'appel de Paris, 23 novembre 2021, n° 18/22323).

34. Voir *Kabab-Ji*, para. 91.

35. Cour de cassation, Chambre civile 1, 29 juin 2007, n° 05-18.053.

36. Par exemple, la clause d'arbitrage CCI standard ne prévoit pas la précision du droit applicable : ce n'est que dans le texte d'accompagnement qu'il est précisé que les parties peuvent la modifier notamment en ajoutant le droit applicable. Il est à noter que les clauses standard proposées par le centre d'arbitrage de Hong Kong (HKIAC) prévoient cette mention.

La condamnation des arbitrages d'investissement internes à l'Union européenne fondés sur l'accord des parties : l'inconséquence de la CJUE avérée

Benjamin REMY
Professeur à CY Cergy Paris Université
Directeur du LEJEP

RÉFÉRENCE :

– CJUE, Grande Chambre, 26 octobre 2021 dans l'affaire *Pologne c. PL Holdings Sàrl* (C-109/20)

RÉSUMÉ

À l'occasion de l'arrêt rendu le 26 octobre 2021 dans l'affaire PL Holdings, *la CJUE est invitée à se prononcer sur la portée de la jurisprudence* Achmea. *Plus précisément, les juges suédois souhaitaient s'assurer de la pertinence de la distinction entre les arbitrages dont « l'origine » est un traité bilatéral d'investissement (TBI) et ceux fondés sur un accord de volontés des parties, distinction introduite dans un* obiter dictum *de la décision du 6 mars 2018. C'est dans ce contexte que la CJUE a révélé l'inconséquence de sa jurisprudence dans la mesure où elle condamne une procédure d'arbitrage d'investissement interne à l'Union européenne alors qu'elle trouvait son « origine » dans un accord de volontés des parties.*

ABSTRACT

In its decision rendered on 26th October 2021 in PL Holdings, *the CJEU was faced with defining the scope of its findings in* Achmea. *More precisely, Swedish judges raised the issue of whether the distinction made in* Achmea *between arbitration proceedings deriving from the freely expressed wish of the parties as opposed to arbitration proceedings deriving from a Bilateral Investment Treaty (BIT) could lead to the conclusion that investment arbitration proceedings under a BIT but deriving from a freely expressed wish of the parties was valid. Unfortunately, the CJEU has exposed the inconsistency in* Achmea's *reasoning and found such arbitration proceedings to be contrary to EU law.*

La Guerre de Troie a bien eu lieu en dépit des efforts déployés par Busiris, « plus grand expert vivant du droit des peuples », pour réinterpréter les faits sous un jour plus favorable à la paix. L'oublier ne permet pas de saisir l'exacte portée des mots que Jean Giraudoux place dans la bouche d'Hector s'adressant au jurisconsulte : le droit serait « la plus puissante des écoles de l'imagination. Jamais poète n'a interprété la nature aussi librement qu'un juriste la réalité » (La Guerre de Troie n'aura pas lieu, Acte II, Scène 5). À en croire Hector, ce pouvoir prêté au juriste ne trouverait de limite que dans l'imagination ; il est en fait borné par la fatalité chez Giraudoux et par la Raison en démocratie. Le juriste en démocratie se doit de formuler un discours susceptible d'entraîner l'adhésion du Peuple. Il ne peut le faire durablement qu'en abandonnant le terrain des passions et en situant ses motifs sur les lieux communs qu'offre la Raison, en s'assurant, notamment, de la cohérence de ses propositions.

C'est pour avoir méconnu ces limites essentielles de l'activité du juriste en démocratie dans son arrêt *Achmea* du 6 mars 2018 que la Cour de Justice a été amenée à se dédire dans un arrêt rendu le 26 octobre 2021 par la grande Chambre de la CJUE dans l'affaire *PL Holdings* (C-109/20). Commenter l'arrêt *PL Holdings* suppose donc de rappeler sommairement l'arrêt *Achmea*, qui lui sert de prétexte.

Le contexte : la jurisprudence Achmea

Dans l'arrêt *Achmea*, la CJUE a décidé qu'une clause de règlement des différends contenue dans un traité bilatéral d'investissement (TBI) conclu entre deux État membres de l'UE était contraire au droit de l'Union européenne. Cette clause de règlement des différends offrait la possibilité à tout investisseur ressortissant de l'un des États contractants d'engager une action en responsabilité contre l'autre État contractant dès lors qu'il estimait que l'État n'avait pas respecté ses obligations de protection des investissements telles que définies dans le TBI.

Pour l'essentiel, la CJUE est parvenue à cette conclusion en soulignant, d'une part, que le tribunal arbitral institué en application d'un TBI est susceptible d'interpréter ou d'appliquer des dispositions du droit de l'UE, et d'autre part, que ni les juridictions des États membres, ni la CJUE ne sont en mesure de s'assurer systématiquement de ce que l'interprétation ou l'application du droit de l'UE par le tribunal arbitral assure sa « pleine efficacité ». Cette situation serait, d'après la CJUE, contraire à « l'autonomie du droit de l'Union ». En d'autres termes, ce qui était problématique était l'activité du tribunal arbitral, et plus spécifiquement l'application et l'interprétation éventuelle du droit de l'UE ; c'est ce qui avait permis à la Cour d'invoquer les articles 267 et 344 du TFUE et, partant, d'offrir un fondement textuel à sa décision[1].

1. Rappelons que l'article 267 TFUE dispose que la CJUE est compétente pour statuer sur l'interprétation des traités ainsi que sur la validité et l'interprétation des actes issus des organes de l'Union européenne. Le même article impose également aux juridictions nationales dont les décisions ne sont pas susceptibles de recours de soumettre une question préjudicielle à la CJUE lorsqu'elles sont confrontées à ce type de difficulté. Pour sa part, l'article 344 TFUE impose aux États membres de ne pas soumettre un différend relatif à l'interprétation ou à l'application des traités instituant l'Union européenne à un mode de règlement autre que ceux prévus par le TFUE.

Cette motivation, fruit de l'imagination de la Cour pour satisfaire les passions de la Commission, est néanmoins problématique du point de vue de la Raison. Sa portée dépasse de beaucoup le seul arbitrage d'investissement. À prendre cette motivation au sérieux, il faudrait conclure que n'importe quel arbitrage, y compris commercial, mais aussi n'importe quelle procédure devant le juge d'un État non-membre de l'UE ou d'une juridiction internationale peut constituer une atteinte à « l'autonomie du droit de l'UE ». En effet, chacune de ces procédures peut être l'occasion d'une interprétation ou d'une application d'une disposition du droit de l'UE sans pour autant que cette interprétation ou cette application soit systématiquement contrôlée par les juridictions des États membres ou par la CJUE. Ne conviendrait-il pas pour cette raison, de refuser systématiquement de tenir compte de ces procédures, de refuser de reconnaître les décisions qui en résultent ? On le perçoit aisément, la pente de la motivation développée par la CJUE au soutien de sa décision *Achmea* est glissante car elle conduit à des résultats inopportuns et non souhaités.

Ce constat et les exigences de la Raison auraient dû conduire la CJUE soit à rechercher une autre motivation susceptible de justifier la condamnation du seul arbitrage d'investissement intra-UE, soit à ne pas condamner l'arbitrage d'investissement intra-UE. La CJUE a cependant pris au mot le Hector de Giraudoux en considérant que son imagination suffisait et qu'elle lui offrait la « liberté » de se plier au souhait de la Commission. C'est en effet par un *obiter dictum* que la CJUE a tenté de soustraire l'arbitrage commercial à la portée dévastatrice de son raisonnement. Selon elle, les articles 267 et 344 du TFUE ne s'opposeraient pas aux procédures d'arbitrage commercial car celles-ci trouvent leur « origine » dans « l'autonomie de la volonté des parties en cause » et non dans un « traité » international (*Achmea*, § 55).

Une telle distinction n'est cependant pas susceptible de justifier la différence de traitement opérée par la Cour entre les deux types d'arbitrage. Dès lors que la décision de la Cour à l'égard de l'arbitrage d'investissement est motivée par l'absence d'un contrôle sérieux de la sentence permettant de s'assurer de l'efficacité du droit de l'Union, qu'importe que cette sentence trouve son « origine » dans un accord de volontés ou dans un traité.

Du reste, l'inconséquence de cette motivation est établie par la CJUE elle-même dans l'affaire *PL Holdings*.

L'affaire PL Holdings

Dans cette affaire, une société luxembourgeoise, *PL Holdings Sarl*, reprochait à la Pologne d'avoir méconnu ses obligations découlant du TBI conclu le 19 mai 1987 entre le Luxembourg et la Belgique, d'une part, et la Pologne d'autre part. Aussi a-t-elle porté ses prétentions le 28 novembre 2014 devant un tribunal arbitral en se fondant sur l'article 9 du TBI, stipulation correspondant en tous points au type de stipulation que la CJUE allait déclarer contraire au droit de l'UE le 6 mars 2018 dans son arrêt *Achmea*. Au cours de la procédure arbitrale, ce n'est que très tardivement – deux ans après son premier mémoire – que l'État défendeur a soutenu que le TBI était contraire au droit de l'UE. Une première sentence partielle a été rendue le 28 juin 2017, par laquelle le tribunal arbitral se reconnaissait compétent sur le fondement de l'article 9 du TBI et retenait le principe de la responsabilité de l'État. La sentence finale a été rendue le 28 septembre 2017, soit plus de cinq mois avant l'arrêt *Achmea*.

Toutefois, le recours en annulation formé contre cette sentence était encore pendant le 6 mars 2018. Or, les conséquences des procédures d'arbitrage d'investissement internes à l'UE sont désormais fixées par l'Accord du 5 mai 2020 portant extinction des traités bilatéraux d'investissement entre États membres. Selon l'article 1er, 4) de cet accord, une procédure arbitrale ne peut être qualifiée d'« achevée » qu'à la condition qu'aucun recours ne soit encore en cours au 6 mai 2018. Faute d'être « achevée » au sens de l'Accord du 5 mai 2020, la sentence rendue dans l'affaire *PL Holdings* est soumise à l'article 7 du même Accord selon lequel les juridictions des États membres doivent l'annuler ou refuser de la reconnaître.

Pourtant, tout en admettant la nullité du TBI et de son article 9, les juges suédois de première instance ont rejeté la demande d'annulation de la sentence. Leur raisonnement sollicitait autant le droit suédois de l'arbitrage que l'*obiter dictum* que la CJUE avait formulé dans son arrêt *Achmea*.

Les juges suédois ont tout d'abord sollicité l'article 34 de la loi suédoise sur l'arbitrage et les travaux préparatoires de cette loi, pour retenir qu'une partie qui participe à un arbitrage sans contester la compétence du tribunal est réputée avoir « accepté » l'arbitrage sur la base du droit des contrats. En l'espèce et en dépit du fait que la requête d'arbitrage se fondait sur l'article 9 du TBI, les juges suédois ont estimé qu'en application de l'article 34, la Pologne devait être considérée comme ayant accepté l'offre d'arbitrage émise par l'investisseur dans sa requête d'arbitrage.

Le caractère artificiel du raisonnement développé par les juges suédois sous couvert de volonté tacite est difficilement contestable. Il permet cependant, ensuite, d'invoquer l'*obiter dictum* inscrit dans l'arrêt *Achmea*. Tacitement acceptée par l'État, la procédure d'arbitrage semblait trouver son « origine » dans la volonté des parties et non plus dans le TBI.

Question de droit et solution

L'« origine » de la procédure n'étant plus le TBI mais la volonté des parties à la procédure, la sentence ne devait-elle pas être soustraite à la jurisprudence *Achmea* comme semblait le dire la Cour dans la motivation de cet arrêt ?

C'est à cette question préjudicielle soumise à la CJUE par la Cour suprême suédoise que les juges de Luxembourg apportent une réponse négative dans les termes suivants : « *Les articles 267 et 344 TFUE doivent être interprétés en ce sens qu'ils s'opposent à une législation nationale permettant à un État membre de conclure avec un investisseur d'un autre État membre une convention d'arbitrage ad hoc rendant possible la poursuite d'une procédure d'arbitrage engagée sur le fondement d'une clause d'arbitrage de contenu identique à cette convention, figurant dans un accord international conclu entre ces deux États membres et nulle en raison de sa contrariété avec ces mêmes articles.* »

L'appréciation

On sait gré à la CJUE d'avoir évité d'affirmer que la volonté supposée de l'État telle que conçue dans les travaux préparatoires de la loi suédoise de l'arbitrage ne correspond pas à la volonté des parties évoquée dans l'arrêt *Achmea*. Bien entendu, cette volonté tacite est généralement une fiction, et ce tout particulièrement en l'espèce : d'une part, la requête d'arbitrage de l'investisseur se référait très clairement à l'article 9 du TBI et, d'autre part, si l'État a tardé à soutenir que la compétence du tribunal arbitral sur le fondement de cet article 9 était contraire au droit de l'UE, ce n'est pas tant parce qu'elle y avait renoncé – et qu'elle avait implicitement accepté l'offre d'arbitrage qu'exprimerait la requête d'arbitrage – mais davantage parce qu'elle n'avait pas conscience de la portée potentielle de cet argument quatre années avant l'arrêt *Achmea*. L'artifice du raisonnement des juges suédois est patent et la CJUE laisse entendre qu'elle n'est pas convaincue par l'existence, en l'espèce, d'une volonté de l'État d'accepter l'arbitrage (§§ 38 à 43). Tout en faisant comprendre qu'elle n'est pas dupe de cette requalification des faits par les juges suédois, la CJUE a eu le courage d'affronter le problème qui découle de la motivation de l'arrêt *Achmea*.

La CJUE n'a en revanche pas eu le courage de régler le problème, dès lors que cela aurait supposé, nous l'avons dit, qu'elle dégage une autre motivation à la solution de l'arrêt *Achmea* ou qu'elle opère un revirement de jurisprudence. Confrontée au problème mais n'osant le résoudre, la CJUE n'a pu que rendre évidente l'incohérence de son propos. Qu'importe donc l'« origine » de la procédure arbitrale, qu'importe que l'État ait pu accepter l'arbitrage, dès lors que le tribunal arbitral peut avoir l'occasion d'interpréter ou d'appliquer le droit de l'UE, activité qui porterait atteinte à l'autonomie du droit de l'UE et, plus spécifiquement, aux articles 267 et 344 TFUE.

En d'autres termes, cet arrêt est un aveu d'impuissance.

La CJUE n'ose pas s'opposer au désir de la Commission de mettre un terme à toutes les procédures d'arbitrage d'investissement internes à l'UE. Pour autant, elle n'arrive pas à justifier juridiquement un tel dessein sans menacer d'autres pans de sa jurisprudence relatifs, notamment, à l'arbitrage commercial. Elle ne peut donc que rendre une décision dont le dispositif révèle l'opposition du droit de l'UE aux procédures d'arbitrage d'investissement internes à l'UE. Les termes très circonstanciés de son dispositif – celui-ci concerne la poursuite d'une procédure engagée sur le fondement d'un TBI – doivent être perçus comme l'expression maladroite de la volonté de la CJUE de contenir la portée de sa jurisprudence aux seules procédures d'arbitrage d'investissement.

Faute de proposer des justifications convaincantes à ses décisions, la CJUE sape les fondements de son autorité et laisse les justiciables dans l'expectative, incapables de déterminer avec un degré de certitude satisfaisant quels enseignements tirer de sa jurisprudence. À une heure où il peut paraître légitime de rappeler à chacun des États membres les exigences de l'État de droit, il est regrettable de voir la Cour suprême de l'Union européenne ne pas être suffisamment exigeante avec elle-même. Le pouvoir de l'imagination de la CJUE n'est pas sans limite. Si elle n'apprend pas à s'astreindre à la discipline de la Raison, elle ne pourra empêcher, à terme, la défaite de la démocratie. Il serait alors souhaitable que la Cour européenne des droits de l'homme, dernière gardienne de l'État de droit, rappelle à leurs obligations les États membres qui déjouent les légitimes prévisions des parties.

Portée du Traité bilatéral d'investissement devant le juge français et contrôle de la compétence du tribunal arbitral : l'affaire *Serafin Garcia*

François de BÉRARD
Maître de conférences Paris Nanterre
Membre du CEDIN
Avocat à la Cour

RÉFÉRENCE :

– Civ. 1re civ., 1er décembre 2021, n° 20-16714 (reproduit à la fin)

RÉSUMÉ

L'arrêt du 1er décembre 2021 rendu dans l'affaire Serafin Garcia *par la Cour de cassation soulève plus de questions qu'il n'apporte de réponse à la lecture de la motivation très courte relative à l'interprétation et à l'application devant le juge français d'un traité bilatéral d'investissement auquel la France n'est pas partie.*
La question de l'étendue du contrôle d'un tel traité, à valeur de fait, par la Cour de cassation mérite d'être posée dans ce litige.

ABSTRACT

The December 1, 2021 French Cour de cassation decision rendered in the Serafin Garcia *case raises more questions than it answers on reading the very short reasons relating to the interpretation and application before French judge of a bilateral investment treaty to which France is not a party.*
The question of the extent of the review of such a treaty by the Cour de cassation deserves to be raised in this dispute.

L'affaire *Serafin Garcia/Venezuela* franchit, avec l'arrêt ici commenté, une nouvelle étape judiciaire sans pour autant toucher à sa fin : la première chambre civile ayant cassé l'arrêt de la cour d'appel de Paris du 3 juin 2020 (Paris, 3 juin 2020, n° 19/03588, *Garcia*, Dalloz actualité, 15 janvier 2021, obs. J. Jourdan-Marques, Gaz. Pal. 13 juillet 2020, n° 382, p. 30, D. Bensaude ; Rev. arb. 2020, 1158, note I. Fadlallah) avec renvoi devant la Cour d'appel de Paris autrement composée.

Au demeurant la Cour de cassation avait déjà eu l'occasion de se prononcer, et de casser avec renvoi, un premier arrêt de la Cour d'appel de Paris du 25 avril 2017 (CA Paris, 25 avril 2017, n° 15/01040, Gaz. Pal. 18 juillet 2017, n° 299, p. 31, n. D. Bensaude, et Civ. 1re, 13 février 2019, N17-25851, Gaz. Pal. 2 juillet 2019, n° 354, p. 21, note D. Bensaude, Dalloz actualité, 28 janvier 2020, obs. J. Jourdan-Marques).

Ce serpent de mer processuel apporte, avec l'arrêt du 1er décembre 2021 (Recueil Dalloz 2021, p. 2272, Th. Clay, Dalloz actualité, 21 janvier 2022, J. Jourdan-Marques), une contribution intéressante au pouvoir de contrôle de la Cour de cassation en matière de compétence arbitrale dans l'arbitrage international, en particulier en présence d'un Traité bilatéral d'investissement non signé par la France.

Très clairement, la position adoptée par la Cour de cassation consiste à une lecture stricte du Traité bilatéral d'investissement (**I**) qui soulève néanmoins une véritable interrogation quant à l'étendue du pouvoir de la Cour dans ce contexte (**II**).

I. – Du contrôle strict de la Cour de cassation...

L'affaire *Serafin Garcia / Venezuela* débute par la sentence arbitrale internationale rendue le 15 décembre 2014, sous le contrôle de la Cour permanente d'arbitrage, aux termes de laquelle le tribunal arbitral s'estime compétent pour statuer dans un litige opposant le Venezuela à des associés de sociétés vénézuéliennes lesquels étaient de nationalité vénézuélienne mais avaient, depuis, acquis la nationalité espagnole faisant d'eux des binationaux.

La compétence du tribunal arbitral procédait de l'application du Traité bilatéral d'investissement conclu entre l'Espagne et le Venezuela le 2 novembre 1995. La France n'est pas partie à ce Traité, on le verra la précision évidente est d'importance.

Selon l'article 1er du Traité, sont des investisseurs « *les personnes physiques qui ont la nationalité d'une des Parties contractante en vertu de leur loi nationale et qui réalisent l'investissement sur le territoire de l'autre Partie contractante.* » Le même texte définit les investissements comme « *tout type d'actifs, investis par des investisseurs d'une Partie contractante sur le territoire de l'autre Partie contractante* ».

En l'espèce, les acquisitions litigieuses avaient été réalisées en 2001 et 2006 et les associés avaient acquis leur double nationalité espagnole en 2003 et 2004.

Compte tenu tout à la fois de cette évolution et de cette double nationalité, le tribunal arbitral saisi du litige avait considéré, pour retenir sa compétence, que l'application du Traité bilatéral d'investissement conduisait à vérifier la nationalité de l'investisseur au moment où ce dernier avait accordé son consentement ou lors du début de l'arbitrage. Le tribunal arbitral écartait, en revanche, la possibilité de se fixer sur la date de réalisation de l'investissement soumis au Traité, considérant qu'il « *n'était pas pertinent de s'enquérir de la nationalité des demandeurs aux dates auxquelles ils ont effectué leur investissement au Venezuela, du fait que ces dates ne constituent pas un facteur déterminant pour décider de l'application* » du TBI.

C'est cette condition et la lecture qui peut être faite du TBI entre l'Espagne et le Venezuela qui est à la source des nombreux recours devant les juridictions françaises dans cette affaire.

En 2017 la Cour d'appel annulait partiellement la sentence de 2014 en considérant que le tribunal arbitral n'était pas compétent pour statuer au fond dès lors que la notion d'investissement, au sens du Traité en cause, supposait « *nécessairement* » que la nationalité de l'investisseur soit appréciée « *à la date de l'investissement* » (*arrêt précité*). Cet arrêt sera cassé pour un motif procédural (Cass. 1re civ., 13 février 2019, *précité*).

C'est en cet état que l'affaire a été portée une seconde fois devant la cour de renvoi de la cour d'appel de Paris qui, par une décision du 3 juin 2020, annule intégralement la sentence de 2014. Statuant, de nouveau, sur la condition de la qualité d'investisseur au sens du Traité, la Cour considère que le tribunal arbitral aurait dû s'assurer que la condition de nationalité dans la personne des investisseurs devait être appréciée à la date de l'investissement comme au jour de l'arbitrage, non sans prendre la peine de préciser « *qu'il n'est pas nécessaire d'interpréter* » le Traité.

Dit autrement, selon la cour d'appel de Paris, qui maintient, on le voit, son analyse, la notion d'investisseur est intimement liée à celle d'investissement. Dès lors, ne peut être un investisseur au sens du Traité que celui qui dispose de la nationalité d'un des États partie au Traité au jour où il réalise son investissement, à défaut de quoi l'opération économique en question n'est pas soumise au TBI de 1995. La sentence est annulée puisque, selon la Cour d'appel, le tribunal arbitral aurait dû s'assurer de la condition de nationalité des investisseurs en 2001 au jour de l'investissement.

Cette solution, discutée (*voir obs. J. Jourdan-Marques et note I. Fadlallah précitées*), est cassée par l'arrêt aujourd'hui commenté. Visant l'article 1520, 1°, selon lequel le recours en annulation est ouvert si « *le tribunal arbitral s'est déclaré à tort compétent ou incompétent* », la Cour de cassation casse l'arrêt du juge du fond pour violation de la loi.

Loin des nouveaux canons de l'exercice, selon lesquels il conviendrait de procéder par une « *motivation développée* » qui doit notamment mettre en évidence « *la méthode d'interprétation des textes pertinents retenue par la Cour* » (voir site internet de la Cour de cassation accueil/décisions/ le nouveau mode de rédaction...), la Cour de cassation se contente d'une formule extrêmement brève et radicale en jugeant qu'« *en statuant ainsi, la cour d'appel, qui a ajouté au Traité une condition qu'il ne prévoit pas, a violé le texte susvisé* ».

Ce faisant on comprend que la Cour de cassation retient une interprétation à l'exact opposé de la position de la cour d'appel de Paris qui relève du sens et de l'objet du Traité bilatéral d'investissement. En effet, la lecture stricte de seuls termes de l'article 1er du TBI en cause peut laisser penser que l'application du Traité ne tiendrait pas compte de la réalité de l'investissement réalisé sur le territoire de l'autre État partie et qu'il suffirait, comme semble le soutenir la première chambre civile, qu'à un moment donné – qui coïncide probablement avec celui de la naissance du différend – l'investisseur ait eu la nationalité de l'autre État partie pour que la compétence du tribunal arbitral en application de ce Traité soit vérifiée.

Pourtant, à bien lire le Traité en question, une autre approche est envisageable comme le montre la solution retenue à deux reprises par la cour d'appel de Paris.

On rappellera, au demeurant, que les conditions d'interprétation d'un Traité international sont fixées par la Convention de Vienne sur le droit des traités qui dispose, dans son article 31,1° notamment qu'« *un traité doit être interprété de bonne foi suivant le sens ordinaire à attribuer aux termes du traité dans leur contexte et à la lumière de son objet et de son but* », le texte poursuivant à l'article 31,2° le détail de ce que le « *contexte* » du traité désigne. De sorte que lorsque le juge français interprète un traité le contexte, l'objet et le but de ce traité doivent être pris en compte pour le mettre en œuvre.

Sous un tel prisme, la solution de la Cour d'appel paraît plus logique et plus conforme aux termes du TBI. En effet aux termes de ce Traité est-il question de protéger tout investissement au sens large quand bien même les investisseurs lors de l'investissement n'avaient pas la nationalité de l'un des États parties, ou est-il question de s'assurer que l'investissement effectivement réalisé l'était par des nationaux de l'un des États parties lors de la réalisation de l'opération ? La Cour d'appel semble adopter la seconde branche de l'alternative et, outre qu'elle semble conforme à l'objet même des traités bilatéraux d'investissements, elle bénéficie d'autres indices du texte lui-même pour retenir une telle approche.

Ainsi, par exemple l'article XI du TBI de 1995 entre l'Espagne et le Venezuela précise, concernant les litiges entre une partie contractante et les investisseurs de l'autre partie contractante, que le différend peut être soumis notamment « *aux tribunaux compétents de la partie contractante sur le territoire de laquelle l'investissement a été réalisé* ». Une telle précision conforte l'idée selon laquelle ce qui compte fondamentalement pour les parties au Traité c'est la réalisation de l'investissement et dès lors, il peut être soutenu qu'un tel objectif suppose qu'au jour de l'investissement celui-ci soit réalisé par un national de l'autre État partie au Traité.

Ce n'est pas l'approche retenue par la Cour de cassation qui, au cas d'espèce, fait une lecture stricte du texte et considère que la Cour d'appel ajoute une condition au Traité. Ce faisant l'arrêt soulève la question ancienne de la portée d'un Traité international devant le juge français, lorsque la France n'y est pas partie.

II. – ... à la portée d'un Traité international devant le juge français

La radicalité de la solution de l'arrêt du 1er décembre 2021 ouvre, de façon sous-jacente, une réflexion de fond essentielle et dont on voit les conséquences directes au cas d'espèce. La question posée est celle de la portée devant le juge français d'un Traité international et l'étendue du contrôle réalisé par la Cour de cassation dans un tel contexte.

Le laconisme de la motivation de la Cour de cassation ne facilite pas l'interprétation de sa solution.

Assurément la Cour de cassation n'opère pas un contrôle de la dénaturation d'un droit étranger. On se souvient en effet des termes que la Cour retenait dans son arrêt *Montefiore* de principe sur le sujet jugeant, pour casser une décision d'appel qui méconnaissait les termes d'un droit étranger, que l'arrêt attaqué « *a méconnu et dénaturé le sens clair et précis* » d'un document législatif étranger (Cass. 1re civ.,

21 novembre 1961, *Montefiore*, Rev. crit. 1962. 329, note P. Lagarde, Clunet 1962.686, note Goldman, GADIP, n° 36). Tel était encore le cas dans son arrêt de 2014 au sujet du droit marocain, la Cour de cassation cassant la décision de la Cour d'appel qui « *a dénaturé la loi étrangère* » (Cass. 1re civ., 24 septembre 2014, n° 13-20049, D. 2015.1056, obs. Gaudemet-Tallon et Jault-Seseke, JDI 2015.114, note Mélin).

Rien de tel au cas d'espèce, ce qui conduit à considérer que la Cour n'a pas opéré un simple contrôle de la dénaturation mais un contrôle plein du traité étranger.

Une telle analogie avec le contrôle du droit étranger en droit international privé paraît d'autant plus pertinente que, parmi les autres éléments du puzzle, la jurisprudence la plus classique du droit international privé considère que relève de l'interprétation et l'appréciation souveraine des juges du fond, à l'instar des éléments de faits, le traité international conclu entre deux États étrangers, et auquel la France n'est pas partie, comme en l'espèce.

Dans son arrêt *Rougeron* du 1er février 1972, la Cour indiquait en des termes très clairs que « *le sens et la portée d'un traité passé entre deux puissances étrangères* » relevaient de l'appréciation souveraine des juges du fond, ledit traité devant « *être considéré comme une loi étrangère* ». Ce contrôle souverain était limité, rappelle la Cour dans la même solution, par le contrôle de la « *dénaturation* » (Cass. 1re civ., 1er février 1972, *Rougeron*, D. 1973, p. 59, note P. Lagarde). Le commentateur approuvait alors sans réserve l'assimilation entre le traité conclu entre des pays étrangers et la loi étrangère.

Aussi, à suivre ce raisonnement et à rebours de la décision commentée, la Cour de cassation n'aurait pas le pouvoir d'apprécier le sens et la portée d'un tel traité, sous réserve de la dénaturation du texte par le juge du fond.

Les termes généraux et incisifs de la solution commentée laissent, au contraire, penser que la Cour de cassation a opéré un véritable contrôle plein d'un TBI auquel la France n'est pas partie. À la lecture des précédents évoqués ici, une telle approche soulève pourtant une véritable difficulté relative au pouvoir de contrôle de la Cour qui s'arroge la capacité d'opérer un contrôle plein de fait et de droit dans le litige.

Certes, à l'occasion de sa jurisprudence *Abela* la Cour de cassation avait dans un attendu remarqué fait état des constatations factuelles de la Cour d'appel au sujet de l'extension de la clause compromissoire à des tiers, conduisant certains observateurs à considérer que la haute juridiction opérait ici un contrôle en fait et en droit de la sentence arbitrale relative à la compétence (Civ. 1re, 6 octobre 2010, n° 08-20563, JCP G, 2010, p. 1028, note P. Chevalier, JCP G, 2010, n° 54, 1286, p. 2403, note J. Ortscheidt).

Cependant, le sujet se pose d'une façon différente dans l'espèce du 1er décembre 2021 alors que le contrôle porte sur la portée d'un instrument législatif étranger, dont on sait que le statut est discuté de longue date tant dans la doctrine que dans la jurisprudence du droit international privé (P. Mayer, V. Heuzé, B. Remy, *Droit international privé,* 12e éd., LGDJ, n° 184 et s., M.-L. Niboyet, G. de Geouffre de La Pradelle, *Droit international privé,* 7e éd, LGDJ, n° 699 et s., B. Audit et L. d'Avout, *Droit international privé,* Economica, 1re éd., spéc. n° 345 et s.).

A minima, la Cour de cassation aurait dû être plus précise dans ses intentions connaissance prise, notamment, de la jurisprudence Rougeron de la Cour et de la valeur usuelle en droit international privé français des traités internationaux auxquels la France n'est pas partie.

Dans une telle perspective, l'alternative qui s'offrait à la Cour de cassation devait se poser différemment de la solution retenue. Soit, comme elle semble le faire ici, la Cour considérait que son pouvoir de contrôle en la matière s'étend aux faits comme au droit, et alors elle aurait dû procéder à une interprétation globale du contexte du TBI en analysant l'ensemble de ses dispositions, dans le cadre de la Convention de Vienne rappelée ci-dessus, ce qui devait la conduire à suivre la position de la Cour d'appel. Soit, la haute juridiction s'inscrivait dans la suite de la jurisprudence *Rougeron* et, considérant le traité auquel la France n'est pas partie comme un élément de fait, elle ne pouvait que rejeter le pourvoi sauf dénaturation. Ce qu'elle n'a pas fait.

On peut imaginer assez aisément que, dans cette affaire *Serafin Garcia c/ Venezuela*, la résistance de la Cour d'appel de Paris s'explique par la volonté de cette dernière de conserver son pouvoir souverain d'apprécier et d'interpréter le traité. Pour autant, et à notre connaissance, la question de la valeur et de la portée d'un traité entre États étrangers devant le juge français n'a pas été développée à ce jour dans les méandres de ce contentieux.

Peut-être le second procès de renvoi donnera à la Cour d'appel de Paris l'occasion de discuter ce point.

À la condition, bien entendu, que cette dernière « *compte suffisamment de membres pour examiner à nouveau l'affaire* » comme le souligne non sans une certaine malice un commentateur (obs. J. Jourdan-Marques, précitées, sous Cass. 1re civ., 1er décembre 2021).

On guettera alors avec intérêt la solution retenue par la Cour d'appel et celle de la Cour de cassation qui, manifestement, ne manquera pas d'être à nouveau saisie. Affaire à suivre...

Extrait arrêt

Faits et procédure

1. Selon l'arrêt attaqué (Paris, 3 juin 2020), rendu sur renvoi après cassation (Civ. 1re, 13 février 2019, pourvoi n° 17-25.851), M. [K] [P] et sa fille, Mme [K] [L] (les consorts [K]), ont, en 2001 et 2006, acquis de Mmes [W] et [G] [K] les parts de deux sociétés vénézuéliennes, Transporte Dole et Alimentos Frisa.

2. Les consorts [K], qui n'ont respectivement retrouvé et acquis la nationalité espagnole qu'en 2004 et 2003, ont introduit en 2012 une procédure d'arbitrage à l'encontre de la République bolivarienne du Venezuela sur le fondement des dispositions concernant le règlement des différends du Traité bilatéral pour la promotion et la protection réciproque des investissements, conclu entre le Royaume d'Espagne et la République bolivarienne du Venezuela le 2 novembre 1995 (TBI).

3. La sentence sur la compétence rendue à [Localité 3] le 15 décembre 2014 a fait l'objet d'un recours en annulation par la République bolivarienne du Venezuela.

Examen des moyens

Sur le premier moyen

(...)

6. Le moyen n'est donc pas fondé.

Mais sur le second moyen, pris en sa première branche

Énoncé du moyen

7. Les consorts [K] font grief à l'arrêt d'annuler la sentence, alors « que selon l'article XI (1) du Traité bilatéral de promotion et de protection réciproques des investissements hispano-vénézuéliens du 2 novembre 1995, peut être soumis à l'arbitrage « tout différend survenant entre un investisseur d'une Partie contractante et l'autre Partie contractante concernant l'exécution par celles-ci des obligations établies dans le présent Accord » ; que, selon l'article I (1) du même Traité, le terme investisseur désigne « les personnes physiques qui ont la nationalité d'une des Parties contractantes en vertu de leur loi nationale et qui réalisent l'investissement sur le territoire de l'autre Partie contractante » ; que l'article I (2) du Traité définit les investissements comme « tout type d'actifs, investis par des investisseurs d'une Partie contractante sur le territoire de l'autre Partie contractante » et énumère, de manière non limitative, des actifs considérés comme des investissements ; qu'en statuant comme elle l'a fait, motif pris qu'il résulte des termes « du TBI suivant leur sens ordinaire, sans qu'il soit nécessaire de les interpréter, que l'investissement protégé par le Traité est un actif investi par l'investisseur de l'autre Partie contractante, de sorte que l'investissement justifiant la compétence rationae materiae du tribunal est celui réalisé par l'investisseur qui détient la nationalité de l'autre Partie contractante, en vertu de sa législation, à la date à laquelle il réalise cet investissement sur le territoire de l'autre Partie », la cour d'appel, qui a ajouté une condition que le Traité ne prévoit pas, a violé l'article 1520,1°, du Code de procédure civile. »

Réponse de la Cour

Vu l'article 1520, 1°, du Code de procédure civile :

8. Selon ce texte, le recours en annulation n'est ouvert que si le tribunal arbitral s'est déclaré à tort compétent ou incompétent.

9. Pour annuler la sentence, l'arrêt relève, d'abord, que l'article XI du TBI prévoit que peut être soumis à l'arbitrage « tout différend survenant entre un investisseur d'une Partie contractante et l'autre Partie contractante concernant l'exécution par celles-ci des obligations établies dans le présent Accord » et que, selon l'article I du même Traité, le terme investisseur désigne « les personnes physiques qui ont la nationalité d'une des Parties contractantes en vertu de leur loi nationale et qui réalisent l'investissement sur le territoire de l'autre Partie contractante » et le terme investissements, « tout type d'actifs, investis par des investisseurs d'une Partie contractante sur le territoire de l'autre Partie contractante ». Il retient, ensuite, qu'en ne vérifiant pas que la condition de nationalité des investisseurs était remplie au jour où les investissements étaient réalisés en 2001, le tribunal s'est déclaré à tort compétent pour connaître de toutes les demandes des consorts [K].

10. En statuant ainsi, la cour d'appel, qui a ajouté au Traité une condition qu'il ne prévoit pas, a violé le texte susvisé.

PAR CES MOTIFS, et sans qu'il y ait lieu de statuer sur les autres griefs, la Cour :

CASSE ET ANNULE, mais seulement en ce qu'il annule dans son intégralité la sentence rendue à Paris le 15 décembre 2004, l'arrêt rendu le 3 juin 2020, entre les parties, par la cour d'appel de Paris ;

Remet l'affaire et les parties dans l'état où elles se trouvaient avant cet arrêt et les renvoie devant la cour d'appel de Paris autrement composée ;

Panorama international de jurisprudence

Panorama of World Case Law

Belgique | Belgium

Prof. Bernard HANOTIAU
Avocat aux Barreaux de Bruxelles et de Paris,
Hanotiau & van den Berg

Iris RAYNAUD
Avocat aux Barreaux de Bruxelles (Liste E) et de Paris,
Hanotiau & van den Berg

Arno JANSSENS
Avocat aux Barreaux de Bruxelles et de New York,
Hanotiau & van den Berg

2020-2021 (octobre 2021)

1/

Recevabilité d'une intervention volontaire à titre conservatoire – Immunité de juridiction des États – Renonciation à l'immunité par un État – Reconnaissance et exécution des sentences arbitrales CIRDI – Articles 53 et 54 Convention de Washington – Recours en annulation – Saisie-arrêt exécution – Titre exécutoire – Effet de la procédure en annulation d'une sentence arbitrale – Exécution d'une sentence arbitrale – Fait du prince – Obstacle à l'exécution – Art. 288 TFUE – Aide d'État – Question préjudicielle CJUE

L'arrêt de la Cour d'appel de Bruxelles (la « **Cour** ») du 12 mars 2019 fait suite à un jugement du 25 janvier 2016 de la chambre des saisies du Tribunal de première instance francophone de Bruxelles (le « **Tribunal** »), qui s'est prononcé sur une tierce-opposition formée par la Roumanie et ROMASTA contre une saisie-arrêt exécution pratiquée le 9 septembre 2015 entre les mains d'EUROCONTROL sur la base d'une sentence arbitrale du 11 décembre 2013.

Cet arrêt est rendu dans l'affaire dite *Micula contre Roumanie*. Dans cette affaire, un tribunal arbitral constitué en vertu des règles du Centre international pour le règlement des différends relatifs aux investissements (« **CIRDI** ») a rendu une sentence le 11 décembre 2013 condamnant la Roumanie à indemniser D.A., F.C., et les S.C. European Food S.A., Starmill S.R.L., et Multipack S.R.L., à hauteur d'environ 376 millions de Lei roumains (RON) pour violation du Traité bilatéral d'investissement Suède-Roumanie. Le 18 avril 2014, la Roumanie a introduit un recours en annulation devant le Comité *ad hoc* du CIRDI. Le 30 mars 2015, la Commission européenne (la « **Commission** ») a rendu une décision qualifiant l'indemnisation due en vertu de la sentence arbitrale d'aide d'État incompatible avec le Traité sur le fonctionnement de l'Union européenne (« **TFUE** »). La Commission a interdit à la Roumanie de verser les sommes dues aux bénéficiaires de la sentence, et a enjoint la Roumanie à récupérer les sommes déjà versées. Le 9 septembre 2015, D.A. a fait pratiquer une saisie-arrêt exécution entre les mains d'EUROCONTROL sur le fondement de la sentence. Le 6 novembre 2015, D.A., F.C. et les S.C. European Food, Starmill, S.R.L. et Multipack S.R.L. ont introduit un recours en annulation devant les juridictions communautaires contre la décision de la Commission du 30 mars 2015. Le 26 février 2016, le recours en annulation de la sentence arbitrale a été rejeté par le Comité *ad hoc* du CIRDI.

Dans son arrêt du 12 mars 2019, la Cour se prononce (i) sur l'intervention volontaire à titre conservatoire de F.C., et des S.C. European Food, Starmill, S.R.L. et Multipack S.R.L., (ii) sur la saisie-arrêt exécution du 9 septembre 2015, et (iii) sur l'invocation de la décision de la Commission du 30 mars 2015 comme « fait du prince ».

Sur l'intervention volontaire à titre conservatoire

La Cour confirme le jugement du Tribunal en ce qu'il a déclaré l'intervention volontaire des entités précitées irrecevable devant le premier juge pour cause de tardiveté. La Cour déclare l'intervention volontaire formulée pour la première fois en degré d'appel recevable. La partie qui fait une intervention volontaire à titre purement conservatoire peut intervenir à la cause même pour la première fois en degré d'appel. La Cour retient que l'immunité de juridiction invoquée par la Roumanie ne remet pas en question la recevabilité de l'intervention volontaire. L'immunité de juridiction invoquée par un État dans le cadre d'une procédure introduite devant le tribunal d'un autre État porte sur le litige à trancher dans sa globalité, elle ne se limite pas à une action spécifique ou à une partie spécifique et ne peut être opposée avec succès à l'intervenant volontaire conservatoire qui ne demande pas pour lui-même mais se borne à se rallier à la thèse d'une autre partie à la cause. En l'espèce, le litige a été soumis à l'appréciation du Tribunal et de la Cour, à l'initiative de la Roumanie, qui, de ce fait, a accepté de faire juger le différend par les juges belges, renonçant ainsi à son immunité de juridiction. La Roumanie a accepté la procédure d'arbitrage et est à l'origine de la tierce-opposition formée devant le Tribunal. Il s'ensuit que la décision de la Roumanie de soumettre le litige aux juridictions belges vaut tant pour les parties défenderesses initiales que pour les intervenants volontaires conservatoires.

Sur la saisie-arrêt exécution

La Cour retient que la procédure en annulation de la sentence introduite par la Roumanie le 18 avril 2014 n'a pas de caractère suspensif, elle n'empêche pas le titulaire d'une créance de prendre des mesures d'exécution, fût-ce qu'il agit alors à son propre risque. Par ailleurs, la demande en annulation n'a pas abouti et la sentence est dès lors définitive, n'étant plus susceptible de recours. La sentence constitue un titre exécutoire régulier en soi. La saisie a été pratiquée sur la base d'une sentence dûment revêtue de la formule exécutoire, qui en vertu de l'article 54 de la convention du 18 mars 1965 pour le règlement des différends relatifs aux investissements entre États et ressortissants d'autres États (la « **Convention de**

Washington ») impose la reconnaissance et l'exécution des sentences arbitrales à chaque État contractant, en ce compris la Belgique. La Cour en conclut que la saisie a été pratiquée sur la base d'un titre qui, même étant frappé d'un recours, était exécutoire en application des articles 53 et 54 de la Convention de Washington (article 53 : « *(1) La sentence est obligatoire à l'égard des parties et ne peut être l'objet d'aucun appel ou autre recours, à l'exception de ceux prévus à la présente Convention. Chaque partie doit donner effet à la sentence conformément à ses termes, sauf si l'exécution en est suspendue en vertu des dispositions de la présente Convention.* [...] » article 54 : « *(1) Chaque État contractant reconnaît toute sentence rendue dans le cadre de la présente Convention comme obligatoire et assure l'exécution sur son territoire des obligations pécuniaires que la sentence impose comme s'il s'agissait d'un jugement définitif d'un tribunal fonctionnant sur le territoire dudit État. Un État contractant ayant une constitution fédérale peut assurer l'exécution de la sentence par l'entremise de ses tribunaux fédéraux et prévoir que ceux-ci devront considérer une telle sentence comme un jugement définitif des tribunaux de l'un des États fédérés.* [...] *(3) L'exécution est régie par la législation concernant l'exécution de jugements en vigueur dans l'État sur le territoire duquel on cherche à y procéder* »).

Sur le fait du prince

La Cour rappelle que le fait du prince constitue une cause étrangère, libératoire qui peut justifier qu'un débiteur, agissant comme toute personne normalement prudente et raisonnable placée dans la même situation, ne paie pas son créancier muni d'un titre exécutoire régulier. En l'espèce, la décision de la Commission du 30 mars 2015 est présentée comme un obstacle majeur à l'exécution de la sentence arbitrale. Cette décision crée un conflit entre l'obligation de respecter une sentence CIRDI exécutoire, en vertu des articles 53 et 54 de la Convention de Washington précités, et celle de se conformer à une décision de la Commission en vertu de l'article 288 TFUE (qui dispose : « *Pour exercer les compétences de l'Union, les institutions adoptent des règlements, des directives, des décisions, des recommandations et des avis.* [...] *La décision est obligatoire dans tous ses éléments. Lorsqu'elle désigne des destinataires, elle n'est obligatoire que pour ceux-ci.* [...] »). La Cour constate que la décision de la Commission du 30 mars 2015 n'existait pas au moment où le tribunal CIRDI a rendu sa sentence qui constitue un titre exécutoire, et que cette décision fait l'objet d'un recours devant les juridictions communautaires. Il existe ainsi un risque réel de conflit entre une décision d'une juridiction nationale et celle de l'Union européenne, la décision de la Commission étant invoquée comme « fait du prince » dans le cadre du litige portant sur l'exécution forcée d'une sentence arbitrale CIRDI. La position de D.A., selon laquelle la décision de la Commission n'interdirait pas, en tant que telle, une exécution forcée de la sentence en Belgique, est sérieusement contestée. Il est dès lors décidé de surseoir à statuer dans l'attente de la réponse de la Cour de justice de l'Union européenne (« **CJUE** ») aux trois questions préjudicielles suivantes :

« *1. Est-ce que la décision (UE) 2015/1470 de la Commission européenne du 30 mars 2015 (...) concernant l'aide d'État SA.38517 (2014/C) (ex 2014/NN) doit être comprise comme visant les paiements dus par la Roumanie même dans le cas où les paiements seront recouvrés à son encontre à la suite d'une procédure d'exécution forcée de la sentence arbitrale CIRDI du 11 décembre 2013, entamée devant les juridictions d'un État membre autre que la Roumanie ?*

2. Est-ce que le droit de l'Union exige en soi et d'office qu'une juridiction d'un État membre (autre que la Roumanie), saisie d'un recours à l'encontre d'une procédure d'exécution forcée d'une sentence arbitrale CIRDI qui a force de chose jugée selon les règles de procédures nationales propres à cet État membre, écarte cette sentence, au seul motif qu'une décision non définitive de la Commission européenne adoptée postérieurement à la sentence considère que cette exécution forcée de la sentence est contraire au régime européen des aides d'État ?

3. Est-ce que le droit de l'Union, notamment le principe de coopération loyale ou le principe d'autorité de chose jugée, permet qu'une juridiction nationale d'un État membre (autre que la Roumanie) ne respecte pas ses obligations internationales découlant de la Convention du CIRDI dans l'hypothèse où la Commission européenne a adopté une décision postérieurement à la sentence, qui considère que l'exécution forcée de la sentence serait contraire au régime européen des aides d'État et ce même si la Commission européenne a participé à la procédure d'arbitrage (en ce compris le recours en annulation à l'encontre de la sentence) et a fait valoir ses moyens relatifs au régime européen des aides d'État ? ».

Dans un souci du respect de la sécurité juridique et du droit communautaire et des décisions rendues par les juridictions européennes, et agissant dans un esprit de coopération loyale entre les juridictions de l'Union européenne et les juridictions nationales, et en vue d'éviter le risque de décisions incohérentes, la Cour dit qu'il y a également lieu de surseoir à statuer dans l'attente d'une décision définitive des juridictions européennes sur les recours en annulations de la décision de la Commission du 30 mars 2015.

- C.A. Bruxelles (17e ch.), 2016/AR/393 et 2016/AR/394, 12 mars 2019, « *D.A., F.C., S.C. European Food S.A., S.C. Starmill S.R.L., S.C. Multipack S.R.L. / Romanian Air Traffic Services Administration, La Roumanie, La Commission européenne, L'Organisation européenne pour la sécurité de la navigation aérienne* », b-Arbitra 2020/2, pp. 433-456.

2/

Articles 1680, § 4 et 1708 du Code judiciaire – Mesures d'instruction pendant la procédure arbitrale – Obtention de preuves – Tiers à la procédure arbitrale – Autonomie du tribunal arbitral – Effet de l'accord préalable du tribunal arbitral

Dans son ordonnance du 12 juin 2019, le président du tribunal de première instance néerlandophone de Bruxelles (le « **Tribunal** »), statuant en référé, se prononce sur une requête en mesure d'instruction formée par K en vertu des articles 1680, § 4 et 1708 du Code judiciaire, au soutien d'une procédure arbitrale en cours l'opposant à SA-V.

L'objet de la procédure arbitrale sous-jacente concerne des dysfonctionnements afférents à un système de chauffage et de refroidissement suite à des travaux de rénovation. Dans sa requête devant le Tribunal, K demande qu'il soit ordonné à

SA-B, SCRL-D et SA-C, tiers à la procédure arbitrale, de (i) fournir des explications techniques sur le fonctionnement du système litigieux, objet de l'arbitrage, (ii) donner une estimation des coûts liés à des travaux de réparation, (iii) donner leur avis sur un point technique, (iv) coopérer pleinement à l'obtention de la preuve par K dans l'arbitrage, notamment en formulant des commentaires sur le rapport préliminaire de l'expert nommé dans l'arbitrage, (iv) fournir plusieurs documents, et (v) payer des dommages-intérêts dans l'hypothèse où elles ne coopéreraient pas à la bonne administration de la preuve pour les besoins de l'arbitrage.

Le Tribunal rappelle que les articles 1680, § 4 (« *Le président du tribunal de première instance statuant comme en référé prend toutes les mesures nécessaires en vue de l'obtention de la preuve conformément à l'article 1708. Sa décision n'est susceptible d'aucun recours* ») et 1708 (« *Une partie peut avec l'accord du tribunal arbitral, demander au président du tribunal de première instance statuant comme en référé d'ordonner toutes les mesures nécessaires en vue de l'obtention de preuves conformément à l'article 1680, § 4* ») du Code judiciaire doivent être interprétés de manière stricte et restrictive, afin de ne pas porter atteinte à l'autonomie du tribunal arbitral et respecter le fait que le litige au fond ait été soustrait du pouvoir judiciaire. Le Tribunal en déduit deux limitations. D'une part, une limitation de fond : les mesures provisoires sollicitées qui ne concernent pas la collecte de la preuve ou n'ont pas pour objet de faciliter une telle collecte ne relèvent pas du pouvoir décisionnel du Tribunal. D'autre part, une limitation procédurale : une partie à la procédure arbitrale ne peut saisir le président du tribunal de première instance sans avoir obtenu l'accord préalable du tribunal arbitral, cet accord n'ayant, toutefois, pas d'effet prescriptif ou restrictif à l'égard du président du tribunal saisi des demandes en mesures provisoires.

Le Tribunal rejette la demande en dommages-intérêts de K qui constitue une réclamation sur le fond, sortant de ce fait du champ des demandes pouvant être formées sur la base des articles 1680, § 4 et 1708 du Code judiciaire. Le Tribunal rejette également les mesures visant à obtenir de SA-B, D et C leur pleine coopération dans l'administration de la preuve, des explications techniques, une estimation de coûts de réparation, et un avis technique. Ces mesures ne visent pas à obtenir des preuves directes et sortent de ce fait du champ des articles 1680, § 4 et 1708 du Code judiciaire. Le Tribunal précise que ces mesures ne sauraient non plus être accordées sur la base d'une obligation générale de prudence ou du principe d'interdiction de l'abus de droit.

Enfin, le Tribunal estime que, pour obtenir les documents dont la production est sollicitée, il revient à K de démontrer l'existence de ces documents, l'identité du détenteur des documents, et leur rôle utile pour l'expertise arbitrale. Le Tribunal constate qu'il n'est pas démontré en l'espèce que les documents sollicités existent, à savoir la version mise à jour d'un rapport, et qu'il n'y a pas lieu d'ordonner l'établissement d'une telle mise à jour dans la mesure où K ne démontre pas le rôle utile d'une telle mesure.

La requête de K est rejetée dans son ensemble.

- **Voorz. Rb. Brussel (10 k.), 2019/28/C, 12 juin 2019, « *NV K, NV P, TV KP / NV B, CVBA D, NV C* » (décision en langue néerlandaise), b-Arbitra 2021/1, pp. 189-204.**

3/

Intérêt à agir – Recours en annulation d'une sentence exequaturée – Article 1717, § 7 du Code judiciaire – Délai de recours en annulation – Obtention de la sentence par fraude – Conformité de l'Article 1717, § 4 du Code judiciaire à la Constitution – Requête civile – Question préjudicielle – Tierce opposition – Article 1122, al. 2, 3° du Code judiciaire – Intérêt à agir du tiers créancier qui se prétend préjudicié par une sentence arbitrale obtenue par fraude

Dans son jugement du 19 juin 2019, le Tribunal de première instance francophone de Bruxelles (le « **Tribunal** ») se prononce sur plusieurs questions procédurales afférentes aux recours en annulation formés par Monsieur P.J., Madame B.M. et Messieurs V. contre quatre sentences arbitrales rendues en 2015 et 2016 en faveur de B., et exequaturées.

Recevabilité de la demande principale de Monsieur P.J.

Le Tribunal confirme l'intérêt de Monsieur P.J. à agir en annulation des sentences, quand bien même B. aurait déjà obtenu une ordonnance d'exequatur lui permettant d'en poursuivre l'exécution. Le Tribunal rappelle qu'une annulation des sentences ferait perdre son actualité exécutoire à l'ordonnance d'exequatur. Le titre exécutoire étant indissociablement constitué de la sentence arbitrale et de l'ordonnance d'exequatur, un éventuel jugement d'annulation de la sentence aurait pour effet d'anéantir l'une des composantes essentielles du titre exécutoire, l'atteignant dans sa substance même. Par conséquent, Monsieur P.J. peut se prévaloir d'un intérêt à poursuivre l'annulation des sentences litigieuses.

Le Tribunal ajoute que l'article 1717, § 7 du Code judiciaire n'impose pas à Monsieur P.J. d'introduire simultanément à sa demande d'annulation une tierce opposition à l'ordonnance d'exequatur. L'article 1717, § 7 du Code judiciaire dispose que « *la partie qui fait tierce opposition contre une décision par laquelle la sentence a été revêtue de la force exécutoire et qui prétend obtenir l'annulation de la sentence sans avoir précédemment introduit une demande à cet effet doit former sa demande d'annulation, à peine de déchéance, dans la même procédure pour autant que le délai prévu au §4 ne soit expiré* ». L'article 1717, § 7 du Code judiciaire ne vise que l'hypothèse où une tierce opposition est introduite avant toute procédure d'annulation, auquel cas le demandeur en annulation doit obligatoirement former sa demande dans la même procédure que celle traitant de la tierce opposition. Cette disposition ne vise pas l'hypothèse où, comme en l'espèce, un recours en annulation a bien été introduit sans qu'il ne soit précédé ou suivi d'une tierce opposition à l'exéquatur.

Le Tribunal sursoit à statuer sur la question de savoir si l'action en annulation de Monsieur P.J. est forclose en application de l'article 1717, § 4 du Code judiciaire (qui dispose que « [...] *une demande d'annulation ne peut être introduite après l'expiration d'un délai de trois mois à compter de la date à laquelle la sentence a été communiquée, conformément à l'article 1678, à la partie introduisant cette demande* »). Le Tribunal souligne que le délai de recours en annulation est fixé à trois mois à compter de la notification de la sentence, quels que soient les moyens d'annulation invoqués à l'appui du recours, en ce compris lorsqu'il s'agit, comme en l'espèce, de l'obtention de la sentence par fraude. L'article 1717, § 4 du Code judiciaire ne prévoit aucun autre délai pour l'introduction d'une demande en annulation d'une sentence arbitrale, à la différence de l'ancien régime qui prévoyait expressément un délai particulier prescrit en cas de fraude (article 1707.3 ancien du Code judiciaire). Monsieur P.J. considère qu'il y a une discrimination entre, d'une part, les préjudiciés par une sentence arbitrale obtenue par fraude ou sur la base de faux documents, et d'autre part, les préjudiciés par une décision judiciaire obtenue suite à un dol commis par l'autre partie ou la découverte ultérieure de pièces retenues par celle-ci ; la seconde catégorie de préjudiciés bénéficiant d'un délai de 6 mois à partir de la découverte de la cause alléguée pour déposer une requête civile (en application des articles 1133 et 1136 du Code judiciaire), alors que la partie préjudiciée par une sentence arbitrale obtenue par fraude ne bénéficie que d'un délai de 3 mois à dater de la notification de ladite sentence pour introduire son recours en annulation.

Le Tribunal fait droit à la demande de Monsieur P.J. de renvoi préjudiciel à la Cour constitutionnelle sur la conformité de l'article 1717, § 4 du Code judiciaire aux articles 10 et 11 de la Constitution. Le Tribunal note que l'objet du recours en annulation prévu par l'article 1717, § 3, b), iii) du Code judiciaire est comparable à celui prévu à l'article 1133 du Code judiciaire, à savoir la mise à néant d'une décision de justice obtenue par fraude. Le Tribunal note que, jusqu'en 1972, la loi belge permettait le recours en requête civile contre une sentence arbitrale, la loi du 4 juillet 1972 ayant par la suite remplacé ce recours par un recours en annulation tout en lui appliquant des causes d'annulation similaires à celles reprises pour la requête civile. L'article 1713, § 9 du Code judiciaire indique par ailleurs que « *la sentence arbitrale a, dans les relations entre les parties, les mêmes effets qu'une décision d'un tribunal* ». Le Tribunal en conclut qu'il existe, à première vue, suffisamment d'éléments comparables entre ces deux catégories de préjudiciés pour soumettre la question préjudicielle suivante à la Cour constitutionnelle : « *L'article 1717 § 4 du Code judiciaire viole-t-il les articles 10 et 11 de la Constitution, le cas échéant combinés à l'article 6 de la Convention européenne de sauvegarde des droits de l'homme et des libertés fondamentales, en ce qu'il instaure un délai de déchéance qui ne permet plus à une partie à une procédure arbitrale de remettre en cause la sentence lorsqu'elle découvre plus de trois mois après la communication de celle-ci qu'elle a été obtenue par fraude alors qu'en vertu des articles 1132 et suivants du Code judiciaire, une partie à une procédure judiciaire dispose d'un délai de six mois à dater de la découverte de la fraude pour introduire une requête civile ?* » (v. pour une réponse à cette question préjudicielle l'arrêt de la Cour constitutionnelle n° 14/2021 du 28 janvier 2021 dont la synthèse est présentée *infra* dans les présents *Cahiers de l'Arbitrage*).

Recevabilité de la demande incidente de Messieurs V.

Le Tribunal retient que Messieurs V. ne sont pas recevables à attaquer les sentences litigieuses par la voie du recours en annulation, ni par celle de la tierce opposition. Le Tribunal rappelle que, suite à l'arrêt du 16 février 2017 de la Cour constitutionnelle (voir *Les Cahiers de l'Arbitrage*, 2018/2, pp. 336-339), le tiers qui se prétend préjudicié par une sentence arbitrale obtenue par fraude a le choix d'introduire soit un recours en annulation sur la base de l'article 1717, § 3, b) iii) du Code judiciaire, soit un recours en tierce opposition sur la base des articles 1122 et s. du Code judiciaire. Dans la mesure où il n'a ni été plaidé ni *a fortiori* démontré que les sentences litigieuses auraient été obtenues par la fraude dans le seul but de porter atteinte aux droits de Messieurs V., le Tribunal juge que ces derniers ne peuvent se prévaloir de l'intérêt à agir requis pour le recours en annulation prévu par l'article 1717, § 3.

S'agissant de la tierce opposition introduite à titre subsidiaire par Messieurs V., le Tribunal rappelle que pareille tierce opposition est admissible si elle remplit les conditions prescrites par les articles 1122 et s. du Code judiciaire. L'article 1122, al. 2, 3° du Code judiciaire dispose que « *toute personne qui n'a point été dûment appelée ou n'est pas intervenue à la cause en la même qualité, peut former tierce opposition à la décision, même provisoire, qui préjudicie à ses droits [...]. Néanmoins, le recours n'est ouvert : [...] 3° aux créanciers, qu'en cas de fraude de leur débiteur ou s'ils peuvent invoquer une hypothèque, un privilège ou tout autre droit distinct de leur droit de créance* ». En l'espèce, Monsieur P.J. est le seul débiteur de Messieurs V. dont les droits de créances ont été lésés par les sentences arbitrales prétendument obtenues par la fraude de B. Or, Messieurs V. ne formulent pas de reproche à l'encontre de Monsieur P.J., et n'indiquent pas quel autre droit, distinct de leur droit de créance, aurait été lésé par les sentences litigieuses. Le Tribunal en conclut qu'à défaut d'invoquer une fraude de leur débiteur ou un droit distinct de leur droit de créance, Messieurs V. ne sont pas recevables à attaquer les sentences litigieuses par la voie de la tierce opposition.

- **Civ. Bruxelles (4e ch.), 18/26/A, 19 juin 2019, « *P.J. / SA Belle Roche Sablar* », b-Arbitra 2020/2, pp. 485-499.**

4/

Exéquatur d'une sentence arbitrale – Article V de la Convention de New York – Existence d'une sentence arbitrale

Dans son arrêt du 12 novembre 2019, la Cour d'appel de Bruxelles (la « **Cour** ») infirme le jugement du tribunal de première instance néerlandophone de Bruxelles (le « **Tribunal** ») du 6 juin 2016, ayant annulé l'ordonnance d'exéquatur d'une sentence finale rendue le 4 août 2008.

La procédure arbitrale sous-jacente oppose la société Diag Human à la République tchèque. Une sentence partielle a été rendue en faveur de Diag Human le 25 juin 2002 (la « **Sentence Partielle** »), puis une sentence finale le 4 août 2008 (la « **Sentence Finale** »), qui a elle-même fait l'objet d'un examen devant un Comité de révision (« *Review Panel* » prévu par la convention d'arbitrage) ayant rendu une « *Review Resolution* » le 23 juillet 2014 (la « **Résolution de 2014** »).

Dans son arrêt du 12 novembre 2019, la Cour examine (i) si la Sentence Finale est une sentence arbitrale au sens de la Convention pour la reconnaissance et l'exécution des sentences arbitrales étrangères de 1958 (la « **Convention de New York** »), et (ii) s'il existe un motif de refus de reconnaissance et d'exécution.

L'existence d'une sentence arbitrale

La Cour estime que la Sentence Finale est une sentence arbitrale au sens de la Convention de New York. La Cour rappelle que les tribunaux belges ne sont pas liés par les décisions judiciaires étrangères rendues dans des procédures d'exequatur parallèles. Ces décisions étrangères n'ont pas valeur de précédent et ne produisent d'effets que dans le pays où l'exéquatur est demandée.

La Cour estime que la Sentence Finale a définitivement réglé le litige entre Diag Human et la République tchèque, la Résolution de 2014 n'ayant aucun impact puisqu'il ne s'agit pas d'une sentence arbitrale au sens strict du terme. Le fait qu'une procédure de révision puisse aboutir à la confirmation, la modification ou l'annulation d'une sentence arbitrale antérieure n'implique pas que la sentence arbitrale antérieure n'existe plus lorsque, comme en l'espèce, la procédure de révision est terminée. La seule procédure à laquelle la Résolution de 2014 a mis fin est la procédure de révision elle-même, la Sentence Finale ayant déjà été rendue longtemps auparavant. La Cour observe, par ailleurs, que la Résolution de 2014 n'a jamais été exéquaturée en Belgique, et n'a donc aucun effet dans l'ordre juridique belge. Une décision de nature procédurale non reconnue en Belgique, mettant fin à la procédure de révision ne se substitue pas à une sentence arbitrale au fond, et ce, quelle que soit la motivation qui sous-tend cette décision.

La Cour retient, enfin, que ni le texte de la Convention de New York ni aucune autre source juridique ne requièrent que la « légalité » de la sentence arbitrale soit examinée et établie pour que la Convention de New York s'applique. Le texte de la Convention de New York n'impose, en outre, aucune exigence particulière lorsqu'un État est impliqué dans le litige à résoudre, et il est admis que la Convention de New York s'applique aux litiges concernant les actes *jure gestionis* d'un État, comme en l'espèce.

L'existence des motifs de refus de reconnaissance et d'exécution

La Cour rejette l'ensemble des motifs invoqués par la République tchèque contre la reconnaissance du caractère exécutoire de la Sentence Finale.

La Cour considère que la Sentence Finale n'a pas été annulée, mise de côté ou remplacée par la Résolution de 2014. La possibilité de révision prévue par les parties dans leur convention d'arbitrage n'a pas empêché la Sentence Finale de devenir contraignante. La Cour rejette également l'argument selon lequel la procédure d'arbitrage n'a pas été menée conformément à la convention d'arbitrage ou au droit de la République tchèque. La Cour n'est pas convaincue que la Sentence Partielle a octroyé des dommages-intérêts provisoires en violation du droit tchèque, comme le soutient la République tchèque. La Cour estime au contraire que la Sentence Partielle est une décision finale sur une partie des pertes subies par Diag Human, qui envisage une décision ultérieure et finale sur le reste des dommages.

Enfin, la Cour n'estime pas que la Sentence Finale ait été rendue en violation de l'autorité de la chose jugée de la Sentence Partielle, et que son exécution violerait de ce fait l'ordre public belge. La Cour retient que l'ordre public international est un concept plus étroit que l'ordre public national, la violation du principe de l'autorité de la chose jugée en matière civile ne portant pas atteinte à l'ordre public

« interne » de la Belgique. En tout état de cause, la Cour n'est pas convaincue que la Sentence Finale a violé l'autorité de la chose jugée de la Sentence Partielle antérieure. Elle considère au contraire, que la Sentence Finale a traité des questions qui n'avaient pas encore été tranchées dans la Sentence Partielle.

La Cour infirme le jugement de première instance.

– **HvB Brussel (17e k.), 2016/AR/1596, 12 novembre 2019, « *Diag Human SE / De Tsjechische Republiek* » (décision en langue néerlandaise), b-Arbitra 2020/2, pp. 357-373.**

5/

Articles 1680, § 4 et 1708 du Code judiciaire – Mesures d'instruction pendant la procédure arbitrale – Obtention de preuves – Effet de l'autorisation préalable du tribunal arbitral – Secret professionnel des réviseurs d'entreprise – Secret d'affaires

Dans son ordonnance du 4 décembre 2019, le président du tribunal de première instance néerlandophone de Bruxelles (le « **Tribunal** »), statuant en référé, se prononce sur une requête en mesure d'instruction formée par B en vertu des articles 1680, § 4 et 1708 du Code judiciaire, au soutien d'une procédure arbitrale en cours l'opposant à P.

B. sollicite qu'il soit ordonné à P. de produire toute la correspondance échangée entre la société O, tiers à l'arbitrage, et son réviseur d'entreprise, également tiers à l'arbitrage. P. s'y oppose au motif que cette correspondance est couverte par le secret professionnel applicable entre les réviseurs d'entreprise et leurs clients. Par une décision du 31 mai 2019, le tribunal arbitral a retenu que le secret professionnel empêche la production de la correspondance échangée entre la société O et son réviseur d'entreprise, à l'exception de la correspondance en possession de P. Le Tribunal a ainsi donné son accord pour que B. demande au Tribunal la production par P. de la correspondance sollicitée « *préparée par, adressée ou copiée à, ou transmise à P, ou autrement en possession de P* ».

Le Tribunal s'estime lié par la décision du 31 mai 2019 et déclare irrecevables les demandes formées par P. qui ne rentrent pas dans le champ de l'accord donné par le tribunal arbitral. Le Tribunal refuse, par ailleurs, de revenir sur l'examen conduit par le tribunal arbitral sur la portée du secret professionnel liant les réviseurs de sociétés. Revenir sur cette décision reviendrait à former un recours inapproprié contre la décision du tribunal arbitral. En vertu de l'autonomie de la procédure arbitrale et de l'autorité de la chose jugée, le Tribunal rejette cette partie de la requête.

Le Tribunal juge la demande en production de documents suffisamment précise. Le Tribunal se réfère à l'article 877 du Code judiciaire (« *Lorsqu'il existe des indices sérieux et précis de la détention par une partie ou un tiers, d'un document contenant la preuve d'un fait pertinent, le juge peut ordonner que ce document ou une copie de celui-ci certifiée conforme, soit déposé au dossier de la procédure* »), et à la jurisprudence relative à cette disposition, qui autorise non seulement la production de documents spécifiques, mais également la production d'un ensemble de documents. En l'espèce, la catégorie de documents demandés est suffisamment précise, il s'agit de correspondances entre deux entités déterminées, sur une période donnée, portant sur un sujet spécifique délimité. S'agissant de la pertinence des documents demandés, le Tribunal se réfère à la décision du tribunal arbitral, qui a lui-même jugé ces documents pertinents ; et considère qu'il ne lui revient pas de revenir sur cette décision.

Le Tribunal estime qu'il n'est pas démontré que la production des documents sollicités enfreindrait le secret d'affaires au sens de l'article I.17/1 du Code de droit économique (« *1° secret d'affaires: information qui répond à toutes les conditions suivantes : a) elle est secrète en ce sens que, dans sa globalité ou dans la configuration et l'assemblage exacts de ses éléments, elle n'est pas généralement connue des personnes appartenant aux milieux qui s'occupent normalement du genre d'information en question, ou ne leur est pas aisément accessible ; b) elle a une valeur commerciale parce qu'elle est secrète ; c) elle a fait l'objet, de la part de la personne qui en a le contrôle de façon licite, de dispositions raisonnables, compte tenu des circonstances, destinées à la garder secrète* »). Le Tribunal retient que l'article I.17/1 du Code économique et l'article 871 *bis*, §1 du Code judiciaire (« *Les parties, leurs avocats ou autres représentants, les magistrats et le personnel judiciaire, les témoins, les experts et toute autre personne qui ont eu, en raison de leur participation à une procédure judiciaire, ou de leur accès à des documents faisant partie d'une telle procédure judiciaire, connaissance d'un secret d'affaires ou d'un secret d'affaires allégué au sens de l'article I.17/1, 1°, du Code de droit économique, que le juge a, en réponse à la demande dûment motivée d'une partie intéressée ou d'office, qualifié de confidentiel, ne sont pas autorisés à utiliser ou divulguer ce secret d'affaires ou secret d'affaires allégué.* [...] ») protègent toutefois les secrets d'affaires allégués. Le Tribunal limite ainsi l'accès aux documents aux seuls acteurs de la procédure arbitral, (tribunal arbitral, avocats et assistants).

– Voorz. Rb. Brussel (10e k.), 19/2282/A, 4 décembre 2019, « *NV H / NV P, NV O* » (décision en langue néerlandaise), b-Arbitra 2021/1, pp. 205-221.

6/

Tribunal arbitral du sport (TAS) – Fédération internationale de football association (FIFA) – Third Party Ownership (TPO) – Article 1713, § 9 du Code judiciaire – Articles 24 et 28 du Code judiciaire – Effet d'une sentence arbitrale entre les parties – Autorité de la chose jugée d'une sentence arbitrale – Force de chose jugée d'une sentence arbitrale – Effet du rejet d'une exception d'arbitrage sur une procédure arbitrale parallèle – Article 22, § 1 du Code de droit international privé – Reconnaissance et autorité de chose jugée d'un jugement en annulation d'une sentence étranger en Belgique – Opposabilité de la sentence arbitrale – Force probante – Charge de la preuve

L'arrêt de la Cour d'appel de Bruxelles (la « **Cour** ») du 12 décembre 2019 fait suite à l'arrêt interlocutoire du 29 août 2018 rendu par la même Cour (voir *Les Cahiers de l'Arbitrage*, 2019/3, pp. 478-481), sur appel du jugement du 17 novembre 2016 du tribunal de commerce francophone de Bruxelles (le « **Tribunal** »), dans l'affaire opposant, d'une part, Doyen Sports Investment Limited (« **DS** »), le Royal Football Club Seraing (le « **RFCS** ») (demanderesses originaires), l'ancien président du club hollandais de première division FC Twente et dix personnes se présentant comme des supporters du FC Twente (intervenants volontaires originaires, à titre conservatoire) (les « **Intervenants Volontaires de Twente** ») et, d'autre part, l'Union royale belge des sociétés de football association (« **URBSFA** »), la Fédération internationale de football association (la « **FIFA** »), l'Union des associations européennes de football (l'« **UEFA** ») (défenderesses originaires), et la Fédération internationale des footballeurs professionnels (la « **FIFPRO** ») (intervenant volontaire, à titre conservatoire).

La Cour rappelle que DS et RFCS recherchent la responsabilité de la FIFA, de l'UEFA et de l'URBSFA sur la base des articles 1382 et s. du Code civil. Dans le cadre de cette action en responsabilité, DS et RFCS contestent la légalité, au regard du droit de l'Union européenne (« **UE** »), des règles de la FIFA interdisant, sous peine de sanctions disciplinaires, la pratique de la cession à un tiers des droits économiques attachés à un joueur, pratique dite du « Third Party Ownership » (« **TPO** »). La Cour rappelle que (i) DS et le RFCS ont demandé au Tribunal de poser à la Cour de justice de l'Union européenne (« **CJUE** ») cinq questions préjudicielles sur la conformité de l'interdiction de la pratique du TPO avec le droit de l'UE et, au vu de la réponse de la CJUE, de constater l'illégalité énoncée ; (ii) dans son jugement du 17 novembre 2016, le Tribunal s'est déclaré incompétent pour connaître de ces demandes, faisant droit à l'exception d'arbitrage opposée par les défen eresses ; et (iii) ce jugement a été infirmé par l'arrêt interlocutoire du 29 août 2018, qui a rejeté l'exception d'incompétence (voir *Les Cahiers de l'Arbitrage*, 2019/3, pp. 478-481).

Dans son arrêt du 12 décembre 2019, la Cour statue sur (i) les moyens de procédure et d'irrecevabilité qui n'ont pas été définitivement tranchés dans les arrêts interlocutoires précédents et (ii) le fond du litige.

Pour rappel, l'interdiction des contrats de TPO a été prononcée par la FIFA en 2015. DS et le RFCS ayant conclu, au cours de cette même année, plusieurs TPO, la FIFA a initié une procédure d'investigation contre le RFCS et DS. Le 4 septembre 2015, le Comité de discipline de la FIFA a sanctionné le RFCS en imposant plusieurs interdictions de transferts et une amende de 150 000 CHF pour violation de l'interdiction contre les TPO. La décision a été partiellement confirmée par le Comité d'appel de la FIFA en 2016 et par une sentence du Tribunal arbitral du sport (« **TAS** ») du 9 mars 2017, contre laquelle un recours en annulation a été formé devant le Tribunal fédéral suisse qui, dans un arrêt du 20 février 2018, a rejeté ce recours.

Devant la Cour, le RFCS et les Intervenants Volontaires de Twente demandent, à titre principal, de poser une série de questions préjudicielles à la CJUE, et, à titre subsidiaire, de constater l'illégalité des dispositions du règlement de la FIFA interdisant la pratique des TPO (le « **Règlement** »), soulevant 13 moyens à l'appui de leurs demandes.

Les moyens dirigés contre la FIFA

Les moyens 1 à 6 et 8 concernent la violation de plusieurs dispositions du Traité sur le fonctionnement de l'Union européenne (« **TFUE** ») et de la Convention européenne des droits de l'Homme (« **CEDH** »), portant sur plusieurs libertés fondamentales, le droit de la concurrence, le droit de propriété garanti par la CEDH et la légalité des sanctions disciplinaires. La Cour estime ces moyens irrecevables en raison de l'autorité de la chose jugée de la sentence du TAS du 9 mars 2017. La Cour se réfère à l'article 1713, § 9 du Code judiciaire (« *La sentence, a, dans les* *relations entre les parties, les mêmes effets qu'une décision d'un tribunal* »), et aux articles 24 et 28 du Code judiciaire, selon lesquels toute décision définitive a, dès son prononcé, autorité de chose jugée (article 24) et toute décision passe en force de chose jugée dès qu'elle n'est plus susceptible d'opposition ou d'appel, sauf les exceptions prévues par la loi et sans préjudice des effets des recours extraordinaires (article 28). Il résulte de ces dispositions qu'une sentence arbitrale a autorité de la chose jugée dès la date à laquelle elle est rendue sans qu'une procédure d'exequatur doive être préalablement diligentée, sous réserve d'une réformation en appel devant d'autres arbitres ou d'une annulation par le juge étatique. En l'espèce, la sentence du TAS du 9 mars 2017 est définitive et coulée en force de chose jugée suite au rejet du recours en annulation par le Tribunal fédéral suisse le 20 février 2018. Cette sentence tranche la question litigieuse de la compatibilité des dispositions du Règlement de la FIFA avec le droit de l'UE, posée dans des termes identiques devant la Cour. La Cour déclare les moyens 1 à 6 et 8 dès lors irrecevables.

Les moyens 9 à 13 ont trait à la légalité au regard du droit de l'UE (i) des sanctions disciplinaires infligées au RFCS par la FIFA et (ii) de la sentence du TAS du 9 mars 2017. La Cour juge le moyen d'illégalité des sanctions disciplinaires déduit du caractère prétendument forcé de l'arbitrage (moyen 12) non fondé dans la mesure où l'arrêt interlocutoire du 29 août 2018, par lequel la Cour a rejeté l'exception d'arbitrage opposée par la FIFA, n'a pas pour effet d'invalider *ipso facto* la procédure disciplinaire arbitrale, et par répercussion, la sentence du TAS, le RFCS n'ayant pas non plus contesté la compétence du TAS au moment de l'arbitrage.

S'agissant des moyens 9 et 11 sur la qualité de juridiction impartiale et indépendante du TAS et la validité de la sentence, la Cour constate que ces moyens ont déjà été soulevés, à l'identique, devant le Tribunal fédéral suisse qui, dans son arrêt du 20 février 2018, les a rejetés. En vertu de l'article 22, § 1 du Code de droit international privé belge, tout jugement étranger est reconnu de plein dBelgiqueBelgique sans aucune procédure, cette reconnaissance ayant pour effeBelgiquettre en Belgique l'autorité de chose jugée de la décision étrangère. L'effet positif de la chose jugée qui s'attache à l'arrêt du Tribunal fédéral suisse du 20 février 2018 fait donc obstacle à ce que ces mêmes moyens puissent être à nouveau tranchés par la Cour.

Enfin, la Cour juge le moyen d'illégalité des sanctions déduit de l'absence d'exequatur de la sentence du TAS (moyen 13), lui aussi, non-fondé. Une sentence arbitrale n'est pas invalidée du seul fait qu'elle n'a pas fait l'objet d'une exéquatur. Le fait qu'une sentence puisse, comme en l'espèce, être mise en œuvre sans recourir à la contrainte n'implique pas en soi une violation de l'article 47 de la Charte des droits fondamentaux de l'UE relatif au droit d'accès à un tribunal et au droit à un recours effectif.

La Cour rejette également le moyen selon lequel les sanctions disciplinaires imposées par le TAS seraient illégales au regard du principe de la personnalité des peines (moyen 10). La Cour retient que ces sanctions sont imposées par le TAS en application du Règlement de la FIFA et non aux tiers qui restent libres de pratiquer le football.

Les moyens dirigés contre l'URBSFA

S'agissant des moyens 1 à 6 et 8, 9 et 11, la Cour les estime infondés. La Cour rappelle que l'opposabilité d'un jugement aux tiers signifie que la force probante de ce qui a été jugé sur une question litigieuse peut être invoquée contre et par les tiers, sous réserve de la preuve contraire, et que cette règle vaut également pour les sentences arbitrales. URBSFA peut ainsi opposer aux moyens soulevés par RFCS devant la Cour, la sentence du TAS du 8 mars 2017 et l'arrêt du Tribunal fédéral suisse du 20 février 2018. Il revient au RFCS de rapporter la preuve contraire des faits et des actes admis par le TAS dans sa sentence et par le Tribunal fédéral suisse dans son arrêt du 20 février 2018. Le TAS a déjà examiné dans sa sentence la compatibilité du Règlement de la FIFA avec le droit de l'UE (moyens 1 à 6 et 8). La Cour constate que le RFCS ne fait pas valoir d'éléments ou de moyens convaincants de nature à remettre en cause la chose jugée par le TAS en ce qui concerne la légitimité des objectifs poursuivis par la FIFA et la proportionnalité de l'interdiction totale de la pratique du TPO pour atteindre ces objectifs, alors que la charge de la preuve lui incombe. La Cour en conclut qu'il n'est pas nécessaire pour elle d'examiner si les restrictions aux libertés de circulation et au droit de la concurrence, alléguées par le RFCS, sont établies, et qu'il n'y a donc pas lieu de poser des questions préjudicielles à la CJUE.

En ce qui concerne l'indépendance et l'impartialité du TAS et la proportionnalité des sanctions disciplinaires (moyens 11 et 9), la Cour retient que le RFCS n'invoque pas d'éléments ou de moyens convaincants de nature à remettre en cause la chose jugée par le Tribunal fédéral suisse alors que la charge de la preuve lui incombe, en raison de la force probante qui s'attache à la chose jugée par le Tribunal fédéral suisse à son égard sur ces questions. Il n'y a donc pas lieu de poser des questions préjudicielles à la CJUE.

Par identité avec les motifs exposés lors de l'examen de la demande du RFCS dirigée contre le FIFA, la Cour rejette comme infondés les moyens 11, 12 et 13. Quant au moyen 7, déduit de l'illégalité de la règle UEFA sur le Fair Play Financier au regard du droit de l'UE, la Cour constate que l'URBSFA n'est pas l'auteur de cette règle qui est en outre étrangère à la procédure disciplinaire de la FIFA et sans rapport avec le préjudice allégué par le RFCS. La Cour juge qu'il n'y a là encore pas lieu de poser des questions préjudicielles à la CJUE sur ces points.

La Cour en conclut que la demande d'indemnisation du RFCS dirigée contre la FIFA, l'UEFA et l'URBSFA n'est pas fondée.

- C.A. Bruxelles (18ᵉ ch. F), 2016/AR/2048, 12 décembre 2019, « *Doyen Sports Investments Ltd (D.S.), asbl R.F.C. Seraing United (R.F.C.S.) et al. / URBSFA, FIFA, UEFA, FIFPRO* », b-Arbitra 2020/2, pp. 457-482.

7/

Articles 1713, § 2 et 1717 § 3 (a) (vi) du Code judiciaire – Recours en annulation – Délai pour rendre la sentence arbitrale – Accord implicite pour prolonger le délai – Excès de pouvoir – Défaut de motivation – Droit de la défense – Absence d'audience

Dans son jugement du 27 janvier 2020, le Tribunal de première instance de Gand (le « **Tribunal** ») se prononce sur le recours en annulation formé par la SPRL-D contre une sentence arbitrale rendue le 31 décembre 2018 contre la SPRL-P.

La SPRL-D invoque (i) un excès de pouvoir de l'arbitre, (ii) divers défauts de motivation, (iii) et une violation du droit de la défense. Le Tribunal écarte ces moyens et rejette le recours.

Sur l'excès de pouvoir, le Tribunal se réfère à l'article 1713, § 2 du Code judiciaire (« *Les parties peuvent fixer le délai dans lequel la sentence doit être rendue ou prévoir les modalités selon lesquelles ce délai sera fixé et le cas échéant, prolongé. Faute de l'avoir fait, si le tribunal arbitral tarde à rendre sa sentence et qu'un délai de six mois s'est écoulé à compter de la désignation du dernier arbitre, le président du tribunal de première instance peut impartir un délai au tribunal arbitral conformément à l'article 1680, §3. La mission des arbitres prend fin de plein droit lorsque le tribunal arbitral n'a pas rendu sa sentence à l'expiration du délai imparti.* »), et à l'article 23 du règlement d'arbitrage applicable (« *Le tribunal arbitral doit rendre sa sentence dans un délai de trois mois après la prise en considération de l'affaire. Ce délai peut être prolongé une fois du même temps à la demande du tribunal arbitral ou d'office par une décision du Président de l'ASBL OVAR.* »). Le Tribunal constate que le délai de trois mois prévu par le règlement d'arbitrage a commencé à courir le jour du dépôt du dernier mémoire, le 9 juillet 2018, et devait donc expirer le 8 octobre 2018. Quand bien même la SPRL-D a exhorté l'arbitre à rendre sa sentence le 25 octobre 2018 et le 17 novembre 2018, l'arbitre a indiqué qu'il rendrait sa sentence en décembre 2018, ce à quoi ni la SPRL-D ni la SPRL-P ne se sont opposées. Le Tribunal en déduit que les parties se sont accordées, au moins implicitement, à prolonger le délai, l'arbitre n'ayant, dès lors, pas excédé son pouvoir.

Sur les défauts de motivation, le Tribunal se réfère à l'article 1717, § 3, a), iv) du Code judiciaire (« *§ 3. La sentence arbitrale ne peut être annulée que si : a) la partie en faisant la demande apporte la preuve : [...] iv) que la sentence n'est pas motivée ; [...]* »). Le Tribunal rappelle que le juge ne peut se substituer à l'arbitre, son pouvoir se limitant à vérifier si l'arbitre a répondu formellement à tous les moyens soulevés. Le Tribunal considère qu'en l'espèce l'arbitre a correctement motivé sa décision.

Sur la violation du droit de la défense, le Tribunal constate que les parties à l'arbitrage n'ont pas répondu à la correspondance de l'arbitre du 13 juin 2018 qui interrogeait les parties sur le format de l'audience (physique ou virtuelle) et sur les dates potentielles d'audience. Le Tribunal juge que les parties ont ainsi implicitement accepté que la procédure soit écrite. L'arbitre a dès lors agi légalement, sans violer les droits de la défense, en rendant une sentence sans organiser d'audience.

– **Rb. Gent (1er k.), 19/1132/A, 27 janvier 2020, « *BVBA D / BVBA P* » (décision en langue néerlandaise), b-Arbitra 2020/2, pp. 501-508.**

8/

Recours en annulation – Ordre public – Droit de défense – Article 6 de la Convention européenne des droits de l'homme – Effet de la nullité d'une sentence intermédiaire sur la validité de la sentence finale

Les deux arrêts de la Cour d'appel de Bruxelles (la « **Cour** ») du 16 juin 2020 et du 20 octobre 2020 font suite à deux jugements du 12 octobre 2016 et du

22 février 2018 du tribunal de première instance néerlandophone de Bruxelles (le « **Tribunal** ») ayant rejeté les recours en annulation formés contre une sentence intermédiaire de 2014 et une sentence finale de 2016 rendues dans un arbitrage assurantiel opposant Agfa Finance NV (« **Agfa** ») à Euler Hermes NV.

Arrêt du 16 juin 2020 (sur le recours formé contre la sentence intermédiaire)

Devant la Cour, Agfa affirme que (i) les sentences intermédiaire et finale sont contraires à l'ordre public, (ii) le tribunal arbitral a excédé ses pouvoirs, (iii) les droits de la défense d'Agfa ont été violés, et (iv) les sentences sont entachées d'un défaut de motivation.

Sur la violation de l'ordre public, Afga fait valoir que le tribunal arbitral n'aurait pas dû suivre l'article 72 de Loi sur le contrat d'assurance terrestre du 25 juin 1992, cet article étant contraire au droit européen et à la Constitution belge. La Cour retient que le tribunal arbitral a pris une décision motivée et qu'il n'appartient pas au pouvoir judiciaire de vérifier le fond de la décision arbitrale. La sentence arbitrale ne viole pas non plus l'ordre public du fait d'un délai de procédure déraisonnable au sens de l'article 6 de la Convention européenne des droits de l'homme. Le règlement d'arbitrage applicable ne fixe aucun délai pour le rendu de la sentence. Quand bien même la procédure arbitrale a été longue, le délai n'a pas été déraisonnable ou excessivement long, compte tenu du fait, notamment, que les débats ont été rouverts à plusieurs reprises.

Sur l'excès de pouvoir, la Cour rappelle qu'en l'absence de délai formel pour rendre une sentence, un tribunal arbitral ne perd pas sa compétence ou sa juridiction par un simple écoulement du temps. Le moyen tiré d'une durée déraisonnable de la procédure pour établir un excès de pouvoir du tribunal arbitral est rejeté.

Sur la violation des droits de la défense, la Cour se réfère à l'article 1704, §2, g) (ancien) du Code judiciaire (« *§2. La sentence arbitrale peut être annulée: [...] g) s'il n'a pas été donné aux parties la possibilité de faire valoir leurs droits et moyens ou s'il y a eu méconnaissance de toute autre règle impérative de la procédure arbitrale, pour autant que cette méconnaissance ait une influence sur la sentence arbitrale* »). L'approche majoritaire de la jurisprudence et de la doctrine considère qu'il découle de cette disposition que l'impact sur la sentence arbitrale du non-respect des droits de la défense ne doit pas être examiné, et qu'il suffit d'établir une violation des droits de la défense pour annuler la sentence arbitrale. En l'espèce, avant le prononcé de la sentence intermédiaire, une audience a eu lieu, préalablement à laquelle Agfa a explicitement demandé au tribunal arbitral si l'objet de l'audience serait limité aux questions de recevabilité et de compétence, ou si le fond de l'affaire serait également abordé. Rien ne permet de déduire que le fond de l'affaire ait été plaidé à l'audience. Or, la sentence intermédiaire contient une section « *IV. L'évaluation sur le fond* », dans laquelle les arbitres se prononcent sur des points relatifs au fond du litige non discutés à l'audience. La Cour estime que le tribunal arbitral a de ce fait violé les droits de la défense d'Agfa, et annule la sentence intermédiaire.

Le moyen tiré du défaut de motivation n'est pas examiné.

Arrêt du 20 octobre 2020 (sur le recours formé contre la sentence finale)

La Cour juge l'appel formé contre les trois arbitres irrecevable. L'implication des arbitres dans la procédure d'appel est inutile, puisqu'une décision d'annulation est en tout état de cause opposable aux arbitres dans le cadre d'une procédure en dommages et intérêts, qu'ils aient été ou non parties au recours en annulation. De plus, une demande d'annulation est une demande entre les parties à l'arbitrage, dont les arbitres ne font pas partie.

S'agissant de l'effet de la nullité de la sentence intermédiaire sur la sentence finale, la Cour relève que la sentence intermédiaire a statué sur le droit applicable, et que c'est à la lumière de ce droit que la sentence finale a évalué les questions en litige ; de sorte que la question tranchée dans la sentence finale est « *indissociablement lié*[e] » à ce qui a été décidé dans la sentence intermédiaire annulée. Une annulation partielle est de ce fait impossible, la sentence finale ne pouvant avoir une existence distincte sans la détermination de la loi applicable tranchée dans la sentence intermédiaire. La sentence finale est de ce fait entièrement annulée.

- HvB Brussel (17e k.), 2017/AR/369 et 2018/AR/823, 16 juin 2020 et 20 octobre 2020, « *Agfa Finance NV / Euler Hermes NV* » (décisions en langue néerlandaise), b-Arbitra 2020/2, pp. 397-421.

9/

Litiges en matière de baux pour résidence principale et pour logement d'étudiants – Exclusion de la voie d'arbitrage – Obstacle financier à la résolution de litiges locatifs – Compétence exclusive du juge de paix – Article 44 du décret flamand du 9 novembre 2018 – Article 10 de la loi spéciale du 8 août 1980 de réformes institutionnelles – Articles 10 et 11 de la Constitution

L'arrêt de la Cour constitutionnelle (la « **Cour** ») du 12 novembre 2020 se prononce sur un recours en annulation formé contre l'article 44 du décret flamand du 9 novembre 2018 « contenant des dispositions relatives à la location de biens destinés à l'habitation ou de parties de ceux-ci », publié au Moniteur belge du 7 décembre 2018 (le « **Décret** »), excluant l'arbitrage dans le cadre de litiges en matière de baux pour résidence principale et pour le logement d'étudiants, dont la compétence exclusive est accordée au juge de paix (l'article 44 du Décret dispose : « *Exclusion de la possibilité d'arbitrage. Toute convention d'arbitrage conclue avant la naissance d'un litige ou à l'occasion d'un litige, dont le juge prend connaissance en application de l'article 43, est nulle de plein droit* »).

La Cour retient que l'article 44 du Décret ne viole pas l'article 10 de la loi spéciale du 8 août 1980 de réformes institutionnelles. L'article 10 de la loi spéciale du 8 août 1980 de réformes institutionnelles permet à la Région flamande d'adopter des dispositions décrétales dans une matière, comme en l'espèce, qui relève de la compétence de l'autorité fédérale, à condition que ces dispositions soient nécessaires à l'exercice des compétences de la région, que cette matière se prête à un régime différencié et que l'incidence de ces dispositions sur la matière fédérale ne soit que marginale. La Cour constate que le législateur décrétal a adopté l'article 44 du Décret dans le but d'éviter que des conventions d'arbitrage puissent constituer un obstacle financier à la résolution de litiges locatifs. Cette disposition cadre donc avec l'objectif de simplifier et de faciliter au maximum l'accès au juge dans les litiges relatifs à des baux de résidence principale et à des baux pour le logement d'étudiants. Eu égard à cet objectif, le législateur décrétal a pu estimer, dans l'exercice de la compétence qui lui a été attribuée, qu'il était nécessaire d'éviter que l'impact financier éventuel d'une procédure d'arbitrage puisse constituer un obstacle à la résolution de conflits locatifs. Ce choix est conforme à celui qui consiste, à la lumière de ce même objectif, à confier exclusivement au juge de paix la compétence relative aux litiges locatifs. La Cour constate par ailleurs que, dès lors que le législateur fédéral permet explicitement d'exclure certains litiges de l'arbitrage en vertu de l'article 1676, § 4 du Code judiciaire, il apparaît que la matière réglée se prête à un règlement différencié. L'article 44 du Décret s'appliquant uniquement aux litiges en matière de baux de résidence principale et/ou de baux pour le logement d'étudiants, l'incidence sur la matière fédérale est en outre marginale, de sorte que l'article 44 du Décret satisfait aux conditions d'application de l'article 10 de la loi spéciale du 8 août 1980 de réformes institutionnelles.

La Cour examine également si l'article 44 du Décret viole les articles 10 et 11 de la Constitution en ce qu'elle fait naître une différence de traitement, sans qu'il existe une justification raisonnable à cet égard, entre les justiciables impliqués dans les litiges auxquels s'applique la disposition attaquée et dans lesquels un arbitrage est exclu, d'une part, et les justiciables impliqués dans des litiges qui peuvent faire l'objet d'un arbitrage, d'autre part. La Cour rappelle que le principe d'égalité et de non-discrimination n'exclut pas qu'une différence de traitement soit établie entre des catégories de personnes, pour autant qu'elle repose sur un critère objectif et qu'elle soit raisonnablement justifiée. L'existence d'une telle justification doit s'apprécier en tenant compte du but et des effets de la mesure critiquée ainsi que de la nature des principes en cause. Le principe d'égalité et de non-discrimination est violé lorsqu'il est établi qu'il n'existe pas de rapport raisonnable de proportionnalité entre les moyens employés et le but visé. La Cour rappelle que le législateur décrétal est, conformément aux conditions de l'article 10 de la loi spéciale du 8 août 1980 de réformes institutionnelles, compétent pour exclure toute forme d'arbitrage dans le cadre de litiges en matière de baux de résidence principale et de baux pour le logement d'étudiants. Les différences de traitement critiquées résultent de l'autonomie qui a été attribuée aux régions et à l'autorité fédérale par ou en vertu de la Constitution, dans les matières qui relèvent de leurs compétences respectives. Sans préjudice de l'application éventuelle du principe de proportionnalité dans l'exercice des compétences, cette autonomie serait dépourvue de signification si le seul fait qu'il existe une différence de traitement entre des destinataires de règles fédérales, d'une part, et les destinataires de règles régionales, d'autre part, dans des matières analogues, était jugé contraire au principe d'égalité et de non-discrimination. La Cour conclut en l'absence de violation des articles 10 et 11 de la Constitution.

- **C. const., n° 145/2020, 12 novembre 2020, «** ***Vzw Kamer van Arbitrage en Bemiddeling / Chambre d'Arbitrage et de Médiation, O.D., D.G., de Ministerraad, de Vlaamse Regering*** **», b-Arbitra 2021/1, pp. 59-68, Moniteur belge 03.05.2021, pp. 41999-42004, Jura.**

10/

Litiges en matière de baux pour résidence principale et pour logement d'étudiants – Clause d'arbitrage réputée non écrite avant la naissance du différend – Obstacle financier à la résolution de litiges locatifs – Article 233, § 2 du Code bruxellois du Logement — Article 10 de la loi spéciale du 8 août 1980 de réformes institutionnelles

L'arrêt de la Cour constitutionnelle (la « **Cour** ») du 26 novembre 2020 se prononce sur un recours en annulation formé contre l'article 233, § 2 du Code bruxellois du Logement, inséré par l'article 15 de l'ordonnance de la Région de Bruxelles-Capitale du 27 juillet 2017 « visant la régionalisation du bail d'habitation » publiée au Moniteur belge du 30 octobre 2017, réputant non écrite toute clause d'arbitrage convenue entre les parties à un bail d'habitation avant la naissance du différend (l'article 233, § 2 du Code bruxellois du Logement dispose : « *§ 1er. Sans préjudice de la saisine d'une juridiction, les parties peuvent régler leur différend à l'amiable en recourant aux services d'un médiateur agréé ou à tout autre processus alternatif auquel il est fait référence dans l'annexe visée à l'article 218, § 5. § 2. Les parties peuvent convenir de soumettre leur différend à un arbitre après la naissance du différend. Toute clause d'arbitrage convenue avant la naissance du différend est réputée non écrite* »).

La Cour retient que l'article 233, § 2 du Code bruxellois du Logement ne viole pas l'article 10 de la loi spéciale du 8 août 1980 de réformes institutionnelles. L'article 10 de la loi spéciale du 8 août 1980, lu en combinaison avec l'article 4, al. 1er de la loi spéciale du 12 janvier 1989, permet à la Région de Bruxelles-Capitale d'adopter des dispositions ordonnancielles dans une matière, comme en l'espèce, qui relève de la compétence de l'autorité fédérale, à condition que ces dispositions soient nécessaires à l'exercice des compétences de la région, que cette matière se prête à un règlement différencié et que l'incidence de ces dispositions sur la matière fédérale ne soit que marginale. La Cour constate que le législateur ordonnanciel a adopté l'article 233, § 2 dans le but d'éviter que des conventions d'arbitrage puissent constituer un obstacle financier à la résolution de conflits locatifs. Cette disposition cadre donc avec l'objectif de rendre l'accès au juge le plus simple et le moins coûteux possible dans des différends relatifs à des baux conclus pour des résidences principales et pour des logements d'étudiants. À la lumière de cet objectif, dans le cadre de l'exercice de la compétence relative à la location de biens ou de parties de biens destinés à l'habitation qui lui a été attribuée, le législateur ordonnanciel a pu estimer qu'il était nécessaire d'éviter que l'impact financier éventuel d'une procédure d'arbitrage puisse constituer un obstacle à la résolution des conflits locatifs. La Cour constate par ailleurs que, dès lors que le législateur fédéral permet explicitement d'exclure certains litiges de l'arbitrage en vertu de l'article 1676, § 4 du Code judiciaire, il apparaît que la matière réglée se prête à un règlement différencié. L'article 233, § 2 du Code bruxellois du Logement s'appliquant uniquement aux différends relatifs aux baux d'habitation, l'incidence sur la matière fédérale est en outre marginale, de sorte que l'article 233, § 2 du Code bruxellois du Logement satisfait aux conditions d'application de l'article 10 de la loi spéciale du 8 août 1980 de réformes institutionnelles.

– **C. const., n° 156/2020, 26 novembre 2020, « *Vzw Kamer van Arbitrage en Bemiddeling / Chambre d'arbitrage et de Médiation, O.D., de***

Ministerraad, de Vlaamse Regering, de Brusselse Hoofdstedelijke Regering », b-Arbitra 2021/1, pp. 69-75, Moniteur belge 26.01.2021, pp. 5302-5304, Jura.

11/

Litiges en matière de baux d'habitation – Clause d'arbitrage réputée non écrite avant la naissance du différend – Obstacle financier à la résolution de litiges locatifs – Articles 16 et 18 du décret de la Région wallonne du 2 mai 2019 -- Article 10 de la loi spéciale du 8 août 1980 de réformes institutionnelles – Articles 10 et 11 de la Constitution – Effet rétroactif sans justification

L'arrêt de la Cour constitutionnelle (la « **Cour** ») du 4 mars 2021 se prononce sur un recours en annulation formé contre les articles 16 et 18 du décret de la Région wallonne du 2 mai 2019 « modifiant le Code wallon du Logement et de l'Habitat durable et le décret du 15 mars 2018 relatif au bail d'habitation » publié au Moniteur belge du 28 mai 2019 (le « **Décret** »), réputant non écrite toute clause d'arbitrage convenue entre les parties à un bail d'habitation avant la naissance du différend, avec effet rétroactif (l'article 16 du Décret dispose : « *§ 1er. Sans préjudice de la saisine d'une juridiction, les parties peuvent régler leur différend à l'amiable en recourant à des processus de règlements alternatifs tels que la médiation, l'arbitrage ou la conciliation. § 2. Les parties peuvent convenir de soumettre leur différend à un arbitre après la naissance du différend. Toute clause d'arbitrage convenue avant la naissance du différend est réputée non écrite* » ; l'article 18 du Décret dispose : « *Le présent décret entre en vigueur le 1er mars 2019, à l'exception de l'article 17 qui produit ses effets le 1er septembre 2018* » ; l'article 18 du Décret dispose : « *Le présent décret entre en vigueur le 1er mars 2019, à l'exception de l'article 17 qui produit ses effets le 1er septembre 2018*).

La Cour retient que l'article 16 du Décret ne viole pas l'article 10 de la loi spéciale du 8 août 1980 de réformes institutionnelles. L'article 10 de la loi spéciale du 8 août 1980 permet à la Région wallonne d'adopter des dispositions décrétales dans une matière, comme en l'espèce, qui relève de la compétence de l'autorité fédérale, à condition que ces dispositions soient nécessaires à l'exercice des compétences de la région, que cette matière se prête à un règlement différencié et que l'incidence de ces dispositions sur la matière fédérale ne soit que marginale. La Cour constate que le législateur décrétal a adopté l'article 16 dans le but d'éviter que des conventions d'arbitrage puissent constituer un obstacle financier à la résolution des conflits locatifs. Cette disposition cadre donc avec l'objectif de rendre l'accès au juge le plus simple et le moins coûteux possible dans des différends relatifs à des baux d'habitation. À la lumière de cet objectif, dans le cadre de l'exercice de la compétence relative à la location de biens ou de parties de biens destinés à l'habitation qui lui a été attribuée, le législateur décrétal a pu estimer qu'il était nécessaire d'éviter que l'incidence financière éventuelle d'une procédure d'arbitrage puisse constituer un obstacle à la résolution des conflits locatifs. La Cour constate par ailleurs que, dès lors que le législateur fédéral permet explicitement d'exclure certains litiges de l'arbitrage en vertu de l'article 1676, § 4 du Code judiciaire, il apparaît que la matière réglée se prête à un règlement différencié. L'article 16 du Décret s'appliquant uniquement aux différends relatifs aux baux d'habitation, l'incidence sur la matière fédérale est en outre marginale, de sorte que l'article 16 du Décret satisfait aux conditions d'application de l'article 10 de la loi spéciale du 8 août 1980 de réformes institutionnelles.

La Cour conclut également en l'absence de violation de l'article 16 du Décret aux articles 10 et 11 de la Constitution, en ce que la différence de traitement créée par cette disposition n'est pas dénuée de justification raisonnable.

La Cour dit, toutefois, que l'article 18 du Décret viole les articles 10 et 11 de la Constitution, lus en combinaison avec le principe de la sécurité juridique, en ce qu'il confère un effet rétroactif à l'article 16 du Décret sans justification.

– **C. const., n° 37/2021, 4 mars 2021, « *L'ASBL Chambre d'arbitrage et de Médiation / Kamer van Arbitrage en Bemiddeling, O.D., le Conseil des ministres, la Région wallonne* », b-Arbitra 2021/1, pp. 76-88, Jura.**

12/

Tierce opposition – Compétence – Régime transitoire – Article 59 de la Loi du 24 juin 2013 – Application *ratione temporis* de la Loi du 24 juin 2013 – Distinction entre les arbitrages belges et internationaux

L'arrêt de la Cour d'appel de Bruxelles (la « **Cour** ») du 17 novembre 2020 se prononce sur le jugement du tribunal de première instance francophone de Bruxelles (le « **Tribunal** ») du 20 décembre 2019 ayant déclaré non fondée la tierce-opposition formée par la République du Kazakhstan (le « **Kazakhstan** ») contre l'ordonnance d'exéquatur de deux sentences arbitrales rendues par le tribunal de première instance francophone de Bruxelles le 11 décembre 2017 (voir *Les Cahiers de l'Arbitrage*, 2020/3, p. 650).

La Cour déclare l'appel formé par le Kazakhstan recevable. La Cour rappelle que la loi du 24 juin 2013 modifiant la sixième partie du Code judiciaire relative à l'arbitrage (la « **Loi du 24 juin 2013** ») est une loi de procédure entrée en vigueur le 1er septembre 2013 qui devait, en principe, s'appliquer immédiatement aux procès en cours conformément à l'article 3 du Code judiciaire (établissant le principe d'entrée en vigueur immédiate d'une nouvelle loi de procédure sauf disposition contraire). En vue de tempérer le principe de l'application immédiate, le législateur a toutefois inséré une disposition transitoire à l'article 59 de la Loi du 24 juin 2013, qui prévoit que cette loi s'applique aux arbitrages ayant commencé après le 1er septembre 2013, date d'entrée en vigueur de la loi, ainsi qu'aux procédures judiciaires en annulation ou en exécution de sentences arbitrales rendues dans des arbitrages ayant commencé après cette date. À l'inverse, en vertu de l'article 59 al. 2 et 4 de la loi, les anciennes dispositions de la sixième partie du Code judiciaire demeurent d'application à tous les arbitrages – nationaux ou étrangers – entamés avant le 1er septembre 2013, ainsi qu'à toutes les procédures judiciaires en annulation ou en exécution de sentences arbitrales – nationales ou étrangères – qui portent sur des arbitrages entamés avant le 1er septembre 2013, que ces procédures judiciaires soient pendantes ou non à la date du 1er septembre 2013. La Cour retient que cette interprétation est la seule possible sur la base du texte clair de la loi, et qu'elle est confirmée par la doctrine. L'arbitrage litigieux ayant débuté avant le 1er septembre 2013, la Cour en déduit que ce sont les dispositions de la sixième partie du Code judiciaire, avant leur modification par la Loi du 24 juin 2013, qui s'appliquent en l'espèce, et en conclut que le jugement du Tribunal est bien susceptible d'appel.

La Cour rejette l'argument selon lequel la disposition transitoire ne concernerait que les sentences arbitrales rendues dans des procédures d'arbitrage dont le siège est situé en Belgique. La Cour estime ce raisonnement contraire aux termes de l'article 59 de la Loi du 24 juin 2013. L'article 59 n'introduit aucune distinction entre les procédures d'exequatur de sentences belges et de sentences étrangères. Si le législateur avait voulu limiter le champ d'application de la règle transitoire aux sentences belges ou rendues en Belgique, il l'aurait évidemment précisé dans la loi. Le choix du législateur de rendre applicables aux procédures judiciaires concernant les sentences les mêmes dispositions que celles qui étaient applicables *ratione temporis* au moment de la procédure arbitrale, et le souci de sécurité juridique qui justifie ce choix, sont pertinents pour les sentences étrangères également. C'est donc à tort que le Tribunal a retenu que les dispositions du régime transitoire de la Loi du 24 juin 2013 nécessitent d'être interprétées, alors que le régime d'entrée en vigueur de ladite loi, tel que prévu par les articles 59 et 34, clairs et limpides, notamment en ce qu'ils n'introduisent pas de distinction entre les arbitrages belges et internationaux. La Cour confirme donc que l'appel formé par le Kazakhstan sur le fondement de la sixième partie du Code judiciaire telle qu'en vigueur avant l'adoption de la Loi du 24 juin 2013 est recevable.

Quant à la compétence du tribunal ayant rendu l'ordonnance d'exequatur du 11 décembre 2017, la Cour retient que le tribunal a fondé sa décision en matière de compétence sur des dispositions légales non applicables (à savoir, les articles 1680, § 6, et 1719 à 1721 du Code judiciaire), et que cette décision est la conséquence logique de l'application erronée des nouvelles dispositions de la sixième partie du Code judiciaire. La Cour juge toutefois qu'il n'y a pas lieu de procéder à la rétractation de l'ordonnance d'exequatur du chef de défaut de compétence du juge dans la mesure où la Cour, confrontée à un déclinatoire de compétence portant sur la compétence du premier juge, est elle-même compétente, et prend connaissance du litige, exerçant les pouvoirs revenant au juge d'appel, tout comme elle l'aurait fait au cas où l'appel aurait été dirigé contre une décision sur tierce opposition à une ordonnance d'exequatur rendue par le tribunal compétent, à savoir en l'occurrence, le Président près le tribunal de première instance. Le moyen d'incompétence du Kazakhstan est ainsi rejeté pour défaut d'intérêt.

La Cour renvoie à une étape ultérieure les autres points en litige, en ce compris les autres griefs du Kazakhstan.

– C.A. Bruxelles (17e ch.), 17 novembre 2020, « *République du Kazakhstan/A.S., G.S., la société de droit étranger A., la société de droit étranger T.* », b-Arbitra 2021/1, pp. 148-159.

13/

Recours en annulation d'une sentence pour fraude – Délai de recours – Point de départ du délai de recours – Constitutionnalité de l'Article 1717, § 4 du Code judiciaire – Articles 10 et 11 de la Constitution – Article 6 de la Convention européenne des droits de l'homme

Dans son arrêt du 28 janvier 2021, la Cour constitutionnelle (la « **Cour** ») répond à la question préjudicielle posée le 19 juin 2019 par le Tribunal de première instance francophone de Bruxelles (voir Civ. Bruxelles (4e ch.), 18/26/A, 19 juin 2019 dont la synthèse est présentée *supra* dans les présents *Cahiers de l'Arbitrage*).

La Cour dit pour droit que l'article 1717, § 4 du Code judiciaire (« *§ 2. [...] La sentence ne peut être annulée que dans les cas énumérés au présent article. § 3. La sentence arbitrale ne peut être annulée que si : [...] b) le tribunal de première instance constate : [...] iii) que la sentence a été obtenue par fraude. § 4. Hormis dans le cas visé à l'article 1690, § 4, alinéa 1er, une demande d'annulation ne peut être introduite après l'expiration d'un délai de trois mois à compter de la date à laquelle la sentence a été communiquée, conformément à l'article 1678, à la partie introduisant cette demande, ou, si une demande a été introduite en vertu de l'article 1715, à compter de la date à laquelle la décision du tribunal arbitral sur la demande introduite en vertu de l'article 1715 a été communiquée, conformément à l'article 1678, à la partie introduisant la demande d'annulation* ») viole les articles 10 et 11 de la Constitution, lus en combinaison avec l'article 6 de la Convention européenne des droits de l'homme, en ce qu'il ne permet pas à une partie à une procédure arbitrale de demander l'annulation d'une sentence lorsque cette partie découvre, plus de trois mois après la communication de la sentence, que celle-ci a été obtenue par fraude. Dès lors que l'article 1717 du Code judiciaire permet aux parties de demander l'annulation d'une sentence arbitrale au motif que celle-ci aurait été obtenue par fraude, ces parties doivent disposer d'un délai utile pour introduire une telle demande, sous peine d'être privées d'un recours auquel elles ont en principe droit.

La Cour retient qu'il appartient au législateur de mettre un terme à l'inconstitutionnalité constatée.

- C. const., n° 14/2021, 28 janvier 2021, « *P.J. / nv « Belle Roche Sablar », Conseil des ministres* », b-Arbitra 2021/1, pp. 103-115, Revue de droit commercial belge (R.D.C.), 2021-1, pp. 52-55, Journal des tribunaux (J.T.), 2021/6864, pp. 507-509, Jura.

14/

Recours en annulation – Ordre public – Liberté d'entreprendre – Article II.3 du Code de droit économique – Clause de non-concurrence

Dans son arrêt du 26 février 2021, la Cour de cassation (la « **Cour** ») rejette le pourvoi formé contre le jugement du 6 mars 2020 rendu par le tribunal de première instance d'Anvers (le « **Tribunal** ») ayant lui-même rejeté un recours en annulation formé par JVDB et JPL contre une sentence arbitrale du 25 octobre 2018, rendue dans un arbitrage opposant ces dernières aux sociétés P&V.

JVDB et JPL reprochent à la sentence d'avoir retenu que leur contrat avec P&V a été résolu illégalement, tout en déclarant P&V fondées à se prévaloir de l'effet post-contractuel de la clause de non-concurrence prévue au dit contrat. En donnant effet à une clause de non-concurrence qui restreint de manière abusive la liberté d'entreprendre au sens de l'article II.3 du Code économique (« *Chacun est libre d'exercer l'activité économique de son choix* »), JVDB et JPL estiment que la sentence viole l'ordre public.

Dans son jugement du 6 mars 2020, le Tribunal a retenu que l'applicabilité de la clause de non-concurrence, qui a fait l'objet de débats approfondis devant le tribunal arbitral, relève exclusivement de la discrétion de l'arbitre. En tout état de cause, la jurisprudence actuelle confirme que la résiliation est sans effet sur les clauses destinées à continuer à s'appliquer après la fin du contrat, et le Tribunal ne constate aucune violation de l'article II.3 du Code de droit économique.

La Cour confirme ce jugement. Le tribunal n'est pas tenu de réévaluer le litige à la lumière des dispositions d'ordre public appliquées dans la sentence arbitrale, mais seulement de vérifier si la sentence arbitrale, ou sa reconnaissance ou exécution, est contraire à l'ordre public. Bien que l'article II.3 du Code économique dispose que chacun est libre d'exercer l'activité économique de son choix, il ne s'ensuit pas que l'exécution d'une clause de non-concurrence limitée dans le temps, l'espace et en termes d'activités, restreindra toujours de manière disproportionnée la liberté d'entreprendre si le contrat contenant la clause est illégalement résilié par la partie en faveur de laquelle la clause de non-concurrence a été stipulée.

- **C. Cass., C.20.0331.N, 26 février 2021, « *J. V. D. B., JPK CONSULT bv / P&V ELEKTROTECHNIEK nv, P&V IMMO nv* » (décision en langue néerlandaise), Jura.**

France Arbitrage | France Abitration

Priscille PEDONE
Avocat

Arbitrage institutionnel – Clause d'arbitrage – Règlement ICC – Arbitrage multipartite – Tribunal arbitral – Constitution – Cinq arbitres – Nomination – Déséquilibre dans la nomination – Centre chargé d'organiser l'arbitrage – Volonté des parties – Irrégularité – Principe d'ordre public – Égalité des parties – Respect des intérêts – Adéquation – Principe de compétence compétence – Moyen tardif – Contrôle du juge – Ordre public international – Nouveaux griefs – Nouveaux moyens – Contrôle en fait et en droit – Portée de la convention d'arbitrage – Mission – Désignation d'arbitre – Institution – Pouvoir de discrétion – Arbitre – Indépendance et impartialité – Déclaration – Obligation de divulgation – Révélations – Conflits d'intérêts – Faits notoires – Principe de célérité et de loyauté – Guidance Note on conflict disclosures by arbitrators – Guide ICC – Doute raisonnable dans l'esprit des parties – Définition – Pièces – Production

Sur le grief tiré de la violation de la clause d'arbitrage et de l'article 12 (8) du Règlement CCI

47 – La clause d'arbitrage figurant à l'article 16 du pacte d'actionnaires est rédigée comme suit : Version originale : « *16.1 Any claim, dispute or other matter in question between the Parties with respect to or arising under this Agreement or the breach thereof, shall be decided by arbitration, by a panel of five [5] arbitrators, one to be designated by each Party, and the fifth one to be designated by the other four arbitrators, provided, however, that if no agreement between the arbitrators designated by the Parties is reached, the independent arbitrator shall be designated by the President for the time being of the International Chamber of Commerce. Such arbitration shall be in accordance with [the] Rules of the International Chamber of Commerce. Any such arbitration shall be conducted in English in Paris* ». Version française : « *16.1. Toute demande, tout différend ou autre question survenant entre les Parties en ce qui concerne ou découlant du présent Pacte ou de sa violation, sera tranché par voie d'arbitrage, par un groupe de cinq [5] arbitres, chaque Partie devant en désigner un et le cinquième devant être désigné par les quatre autres arbitres, sous réserve, toutefois, que si les arbitres désignés par les Parties ne trouvent pas d'accord, l'arbitre indépendant devra être désigné par le président en exercice de la Chambre de commerce internationale. Ledit arbitrage se déroulera conformément au Règlement de la Chambre de commerce internationale. Tout arbitrage se déroulera en anglais à Paris* ».

[...]

54 – Il ressort de l'article 1453 du Code de procédure civile, rendu applicable en arbitrage international, par l'article 1506, et en la cause la loi du siège de l'arbitrage, que « *Lorsque le litige oppose plus de deux parties et que celles-ci ne s'accordent pas sur les modalités de constitution du tribunal arbitral, la personne chargée d'organiser l'arbitrage ou, à défaut, le juge d'appui, désigne le ou les arbitres* ».

55 – En l'espèce, les parties ont entendu expressément soumettre l'arbitrage au règlement CCI de sorte que, conformément à cette volonté, il appartenait bien à la CCI, en tant que centre d'arbitrage institutionnel chargé d'organiser l'arbitrage, de régler cette difficulté, en veillant à ce que l'arbitrage rendu sous son égide le soit conformément à son Règlement.

56 – Il ressort à cet égard de l'article 11 (6) du Règlement CCI que « *Sous réserve des conventions particulières des parties, le tribunal arbitral est constitué conformément aux dispositions des articles 12 et 13* ».

57 – En outre l'article 12 (8) de ce Règlement (version CCI 2012) dispose qu'à « *défaut d'une désignation conjointe conformément à l'article 12, paragraphe 6 ou 7, et de tout autre accord entre les parties sur les modalités de constitution du tribunal arbitral, la Cour peut nommer chacun des membres du tribunal arbitral et désigne l'un d'entre eux en qualité de président. Dans ce cas, la Cour est libre de choisir toute personne qu'elle juge adéquate pour agir en qualité d'arbitre, en appliquant l'article 13 lorsqu'elle l'estime approprié.* ».

58 – Une partie ne peut soutenir que cet article est inapplicable aux motifs que l'article 12 (8) renvoie expressément aux modalités de constitution prévues à l'article 12, lequel n'envisage que les hypothèses d'un différend tranché par « *un arbitre unique ou par trois arbitres* » et non par cinq arbitres.

59 – En effet, l'article 41 du Règlement CCI dispose que « *Dans tous les cas non visés expressément au Règlement, la Cour et le tribunal arbitral procèdent en s'inspirant du Règlement et en faisant tous les efforts pour que la sentence soit susceptible de sanction légale* ». Ce texte autorise ainsi une interprétation utile de ce Règlement, c'est-à-dire une interprétation qui lui confère un effet plutôt que celle qui ne lui en fait produire aucun.

60 – L'article 41 précité autorisait donc la Cour d'arbitrage de la CCI à faire application de l'article 12 (8) pour un tribunal arbitral composé par cinq arbitres.

61 – De même, il ne résulte pas non plus de la mise en œuvre de ces modalités de désignation par la CCI, une violation de la clause d'arbitrage dès lors que ces modalités ont été appliquées conformément au Règlement de la CCI, auquel les parties ont entendu expressément se soumettre.

62 – En outre, ces dispositions ont permis la mise en place d'un tribunal arbitral et ainsi de respecter la volonté des parties de voir trancher leur différend selon cette voie et de surmonter l'obstacle résultant de l'opposition des parties quant aux modalités de désignation des arbitres telles que prévues par cette clause.

63 – Il incombait donc bien à la CCI, en tant que centre chargé d'organiser l'arbitrage, compte tenu de l'opposition des parties, d'organiser les modalités de désignation des arbitres conformément à son Règlement, et ce dans des conditions telles qu'elles permettaient de satisfaire au principe d'ordre public de l'égalité des parties dans la désignation des arbitres, qui suppose la possibilité

pour chaque partie de pouvoir participer de manière égale à la constitution d'un tribunal arbitral.

64 – À cet égard, si au jour de la conclusion de la clause compromissoire, il était conforme audit principe de prévoir que chacune des parties au pacte d'actionnaires puisse effectivement être en mesure de désigner un arbitre, au jour où le litige est né, ce principe de l'égalité doit s'apprécier non plus seulement au regard de la qualité des parties au contrat, mais aussi au regard des prétentions et des intérêts de chacune des parties au litige. Ce faisant, si plusieurs d'entre elles sont susceptibles de défendre des intérêts communs et partagés contre une seule autre, il convient de veiller à constituer un tribunal arbitral permettant d'en garantir le respect.

65 – Ainsi, dans la configuration telle que celle de la présente cause, au terme de laquelle le litige oppose l'un des actionnaires aux trois autres, le premier mettant en cause l'action conjointe de ces derniers dans son éviction et le non-respect dudit pacte, le respect du principe de l'égalité des parties dans la désignation des arbitres justifiait, en l'absence de meilleur accord des parties, de s'assurer d'une modalité de désignation compatible avec le respect dudit principe, qui s'impose aux parties nonobstant les dispositions de la convention d'arbitrage.

66 – Au regard de ces éléments, le grief sera rejeté.

Sur le grief tiré de la violation du principe compétence compétence

[...]

70 – En application de l'article 1466 du Code de procédure civile, la partie qui, en connaissance de cause et sans motif légitime, s'abstient d'invoquer en temps utile une irrégularité devant le tribunal arbitral est réputée avoir renoncé à s'en prévaloir.

71 – Cette disposition ne vise pas les seules irrégularités procédurales mais tous les griefs qui constituent des cas d'ouverture du recours en annulation des sentences, à l'exception des moyens fondés sur l'article 1520, 5° du Code de procédure civile tirés de ce que la reconnaissance ou l'exécution de la sentence violerait l'ordre public international.

72 – En outre, la renonciation présumée par l'article 1466 précité du Code de procédure civile vise des griefs précisément et concrètement articulés et non des catégories de moyens.

73 – S'il a été admis que lorsque la compétence a été débattue devant les arbitres, les parties ne sont pas privées du droit d'invoquer sur cette question, devant le juge de l'annulation, de nouveaux moyens et arguments relatifs à la compétence et à faire état, à cet effet, de nouveaux éléments de preuve, une telle option résulte de la faculté pour le juge de l'annulation de contrôler la décision du tribunal arbitral statuant sur la compétence, qu'il se soit déclaré compétent ou incompétent, en recherchant tous les éléments de droit ou de fait permettant d'apprécier la portée de la convention d'arbitrage et d'en déduire les conséquences sur le respect de la mission confiée aux arbitres.

74 – Tel n'est pas le cas lorsque le juge de l'annulation statue sur le moyen tiré de l'irrégularité de la constitution du tribunal arbitral de sorte que pour ce moyen il appartient à la partie de soulever préalablement durant l'instance arbitrale, tous les griefs qui justifient l'irrégularité de cette constitution, et à défaut, elle n'est plus recevable à s'en prévaloir devant le juge de l'annulation.

[...]

77 – Pour l'ensemble de ces motifs, le grief sera rejeté.

Sur le grief tiré du refus de la CCI de confirmer les arbitres déjà désignés par les parties et qui avaient accepté leur mission ;

[...]

Sur l'examen au fond de ce grief

82 – Il ressort de l'article 13 du Règlement CCI, intitulé « *Nomination et confirmation des arbitres* », que la CCI dispose d'une large discrétion pour confirmer ou rejeter la désignation d'un arbitre par les parties puisqu'il est prévu qu'il est tenu « *compte de sa nationalité, de son lieu de résidence et de tout lien avec les pays auxquels ressortissent les parties et les autres arbitres ainsi que de la disponibilité et de l'aptitude de l'arbitre à conduire l'arbitrage conformément au Règlement* » et qu'il ressort du guide du secrétariat de la CCI (Secretariat's Guide to ICC Arbitration), que la liste des éléments de l'article 13(1) n'est pas exhaustive. La Cour peut prendre en considération tout autre élément qu'elle considère pertinent.

83 – Dans cette perspective, et alors que, comme il a été indiqué ci-dessus, compte tenu des divergences survenues entre les parties à l'occasion de la constitution du tribunal arbitral, il appartenait à la Cour d'arbitrage de la CCI, en application du Règlement CCI de procéder à cette désignation, elle n'était en aucun cas tenue de confirmer les arbitres désignés par les parties selon les modalités contestées de la clause d'arbitrage et susceptibles de remettre en cause le principe d'ordre public d'égalité des parties dans la constitution du tribunal arbitral.

84 – Ce grief n'est donc pas fondé.

Sur le grief tiré de l'impossibilité pour le président de la Cour d'arbitrage de la CCI de nommer le président du tribunal arbitral

[...]

Sur le bien-fondé de ce grief

88 – Il convient d'observer que la désignation par le président de la CCI du président du Tribunal n'était envisagée que si les co-arbitres nommés par les Parties ne parvenaient pas à s'accorder sur la nomination du président, condition qui ne s'est pas réalisée en l'espèce, puisqu'en l'état de la divergence entre les parties, la désignation de tous les arbitres a été faite par la Cour d'arbitrage de la CCI.

89 – En outre, ainsi qu'il l'a été indiqué ci-dessus, compte tenu des divergences survenues entre les parties à l'occasion de la constitution du tribunal arbitral, il appartenait à la Cour d'arbitrage de la CCI de procéder à cette désignation, de sorte que conformément à son règlement, elle pouvait s'écarter de la convention d'arbitrage pour procéder à la désignation des cinq arbitres, en ce compris son président.

90 – Ce grief sera en conséquence rejeté.

2 – Sur le grief tiré du défaut d'indépendance de deux membres du tribunal arbitral

[...]

104 – En application de l'article 11 du Règlement CCI 2012, il incombe à l'arbitre de divulguer par écrit au Secrétariat tout fait ou circonstance qui pourrait être de nature à remettre en cause son indépendance aux yeux des parties, ainsi que toute circonstance pouvant donner lieu à des doutes raisonnables quant à son impartialité. L'arbitre doit en outre immédiatement divulguer par écrit au Secrétariat et aux parties tout fait ou circonstance de nature similaire à ceux visés

à l'article 11(2) concernant son impartialité ou son indépendance qui peuvent survenir au cours de l'arbitrage.

105 – Aux termes de l'article 1456 al. 2 du Code de procédure civile, applicable à l'arbitrage international en vertu de l'article 1506 du même code, « *Il appartient à l'arbitre, avant d'accepter sa mission, de révéler toute circonstance susceptible d'affecter son indépendance ou son impartialité. Il lui est également fait obligation de révéler sans délai toute circonstance de même nature qui pourrait naître après l'acceptation de sa mission* ».

106 – Il ressort de ces textes que l'arbitre est tenu de révéler toute circonstance qui pourrait être de nature à remettre en cause son indépendance ou son impartialité aux yeux des parties ou qui pourrait être susceptible de l'affecter et ce, avant ou après l'acceptation de sa mission.

Sur la fin de non-recevoir opposée

107 – En application de l'article 1466 du Code de procédure civile, la partie qui, en connaissance de cause et sans motif légitime, s'abstient d'invoquer en temps utile une irrégularité devant le tribunal arbitral est réputée avoir renoncé à s'en prévaloir.

108 – À cet égard, en vertu de l'article 14(2) du Règlement CCI, une demande de récusation « *doit être soumise par une partie, à peine de forclusion, soit dans les trente jours suivant la réception par celle-ci de la notification de la nomination ou de la confirmation de l'arbitre, soit dans les trente jours suivant la date à laquelle la partie introduisant la récusation a été informée des faits et circonstances qu'elle invoque à l'appui de sa demande de récusation, si cette date est postérieure à la réception de la notification susvisée.* ».

[...]

111 – Cependant, si avant d'accepter sa mission, l'arbitre, qui est tenu de révéler toutes circonstances susceptibles d'affecter son indépendance, est dispensé de révéler les faits notoires, entendus comme ceux qui recouvrent les informations publiques aisément accessibles que les parties ne pouvaient manquer de consulter avant le début de l'arbitrage, cette dispense cesse une fois que l'instance arbitrale est en cours.

112 – En effet, lorsque l'arbitre a communiqué sa déclaration d'indépendance, et qu'il a accepté sa mission, il lui appartient de faire état de toutes circonstances de même nature qui sont nées après cette acceptation de sorte que même la notoriété des faits révélés en cours d'instance arbitrale n'est pas de nature à l'en dispenser et ne saurait être opposée à une partie à l'appui de la fin de non-recevoir précitée, sans préjudice de l'obligation qui demeure pour les parties, en application de l'alinéa 3 de l'article 1464 du Code de procédure civile, rendu applicable à l'arbitrage international par l'article 1506, de satisfaire au principe de célérité et de loyauté dans la conduite de la procédure.

113 – La fin de non-recevoir sera en conséquence écartée.

Sur l'obligation de révélation incombant aux arbitres et son incidence sur leur indépendance

114 – Le contenu de l'obligation de révélation n'est pas précisé par l'article 1456 du Code de procédure civile.

115 – Toutefois, s'agissant en l'espèce d'un arbitrage rendu sous l'égide de la CCI, l'arbitre peut notamment se référer aux recommandations émises en cette matière par ce centre d'arbitrage.

116 – À cet égard, il ressort des recommandations émises par la CCI du 23 février 2016 (« Guidance Note on conflict disclosures by arbitrators ») que les circonstances qui doivent particulièrement être considérées par l'arbitre sont celles par lesquelles cet arbitre, ou le cabinet d'avocats auquel il appartient : – représente ou conseille, ou a représenté ou conseillé, l'une des parties ou l'une de ses filiales ; – intervient ou est intervenu à l'encontre de l'une des parties ou de l'une de ses filiales ; – entretient une relation commerciale avec l'une des parties ou l'une de ses filiales, ou a un intérêt personnel, de quelque nature qu'il soit, dans l'issue du litige ; – appartient, intervient ou est intervenu au nom de l'une des parties ou de l'une de ses filiales, en qualité d'administrateur, de membre du conseil, de dirigeant ou autrement ; – a été impliqué dans le litige, ou a exprimé une opinion sur le litige d'une manière susceptible d'affecter son impartialité ; – entretient une relation professionnelle ou personnelle étroite avec le conseil de l'une des parties ou le cabinet d'avocats de ce conseil ; – intervient ou est intervenu en qualité d'arbitre dans une affaire impliquant l'une des parties ou l'une de ses filiales ; – intervient ou est intervenu en qualité d'arbitre dans une affaire connexe ; – a précédemment été nommé en tant qu'arbitre par l'une des parties ou l'une de ses filiales, ou par le conseil de l'une des parties ou le cabinet d'avocats de ce conseil.

117 – Il ressort de ces recommandations qu'elles concernent des circonstances mettant l'arbitre ou le cabinet d'avocats auquel il appartient en lien direct, soit avec l'une des parties, soit avec une société filiale de cette partie.

118 – En dehors de ces cas caractérisant des causes réputées objectives, l'arbitre est dispensé de déclaration sauf à devoir révéler les circonstances qui, bien que non visées dans cette liste, peuvent être de nature à créer, dans l'esprit des parties, un doute raisonnable sur son indépendance, c'est-à-dire un doute qui peut naître chez une personne placée dans la même situation et ayant accès aux mêmes éléments d'information raisonnablement accessibles.

119 – Pour être caractérisé ce doute raisonnable doit résulter d'un potentiel conflit d'intérêts dans la personne de l'arbitre, qui peut être soit direct parce qu'il concerne un lien avec une partie, soit indirect parce qu'il vise un lien d'un arbitre avec un tiers intéressé à l'arbitrage. À cet égard, lorsque le potentiel conflit d'intérêts est seulement indirect, l'appréciation du doute raisonnable dépendra notamment de l'intensité et la proximité du lien entre l'arbitre, le tiers intéressé et l'une des parties à l'arbitrage.

120 – C'est à la lumière de ces considérations qu'il convient d'apprécier en l'espèce, si les arbitres pouvaient se dispenser de compléter leur déclaration d'indépendance et si le défaut de complément était susceptible de créer dans l'esprit d'une partie un doute raisonnable sur leur indépendance.

Sur le cas du premier arbitre

121 – La partie reproche à l'un des arbitres de ne pas avoir révélé « *une multitude de liens, anciens et continus, directs et indirects* » avec la société (J) faisant ainsi valoir avoir découvert après que la sentence fut rendue que M. (D), ainsi que son cabinet, étaient les « conseils habituels de M. (U) », actionnaire de la société (J) au moment de l'arbitrage, et de ses sociétés ainsi que d'autres sociétés détenues à 100 % par M. (U), la société (XX), la société (XY), la société (XZ) et avec la société (O), qui a agi comme fiduciaire, registraire et agent payeur de la société (J), estimant que l'ensemble de ces liens caractérise un manque d'indépendance vis-à-vis de la société (G).

[...]

128 – À cet égard, il convient de rappeler qu'en application de l'alinéa 3 de l'article 1464 du Code de procédure civile, les parties sont tenues de satisfaire au principe de célérité et de loyauté dans la conduite de la procédure, en vertu duquel notamment en cas de doute sur l'incidence d'une circonstance dont elles ont pu avoir connaissance sur l'indépendance d'un arbitre, elles doivent l'en aviser ou en aviser l'institution chargée de l'arbitrage pour recueillir des observations complémentaires, sans attendre l'issue de l'arbitrage pour s'en prévaloir, selon que cette issue lui est favorable ou non. À défaut, ces parties sont présumées avoir considéré que cette circonstance n'était pas de nature à créer dans leur esprit un doute raisonnable quant à l'indépendance de l'arbitre.

129 – Il ressort de ces éléments, dont la partie ne pouvait pas ne pas avoir eu connaissance, et du principe de loyauté procédurale, que si celle-ci n'a pas souhaité en faire état ou sollicité des explications complémentaires auprès de l'arbitre ou du centre chargé de l'organiser, c'est que ces circonstances n'étaient pas non plus de nature à créer, dans son esprit, comme dans celui d'une personne placée dans une même situation ayant eu accès aux mêmes éléments d'information raisonnablement accessibles, un doute raisonnable sur l'indépendance de l'arbitre.

[...]

161 – Au regard de ces éléments, la seule circonstance qu'un cabinet membre du même réseau que celui d'un arbitre ait eu des liens d'affaires avec une société faisant partie du même groupe qui en comprend plus de 40 que celui auquel appartient l'une des parties, les cabinets étant situés dans deux pays distincts et étant indépendants juridiquement et financièrement, n'oblige pas un arbitre à en faire la déclaration de sorte que l'arbitre n'était pas tenu de compléter sa déclaration du fait de cette circonstance intervenue en cours d'arbitrage.

162 – En outre, il convient d'observer que la partie ne pouvait ignorer cette circonstance alors qu'elle a elle-même produit au cours de la procédure arbitrale deux pièces qui mentionnent expressément la désignation de M. (R) dans la procédure néerlandaise précitée.

163 – À cet égard, la partie ne peut se retrancher derrière le volume de ces documents (respectivement de 75 et 371 pages) qu'elle a pourtant elle-même produit devant le tribunal arbitral et dont elle avait dès lors nécessairement une connaissance précise et complète pour les estimer suffisamment utiles à cette procédure.

164 – Ayant eu connaissance de cette information et n'ayant pas estimé utile de le signaler lors de l'instance arbitrale, il doit être considéré que cette information, comme les éléments rappelés ci-dessus, n'étaient pas de nature à créer un doute raisonnable dans son esprit sur l'indépendance de cet arbitre, comme elle ne l'aurait pas été aux yeux d'une personne raisonnable placée dans la même situation.

165 – Ce grief sera en conséquence rejeté.

166 – Il convient en conséquence de rejeter le recours en annulation.

– Paris, Pôle 5 – Chambre 16, Chambre commerciale internationale, 26 janvier 2021, n° 19/10666, *F c. G, H et I*

Recours en annulation – Sentence arbitrale – Notion – Sentence intérimaire – Addendum – Exequatur – Procédure – Appel de l'ordonnance – Tribunal arbitral – Mission – Étendue – Ordre public international – Notion

– Conception française – Règles et valeurs – Fraude à la loi – Suspicions – Loi étrangère

1. Sur la recevabilité de la demande d'annulation de la sentence intérimaire et de l'addendum

18-Il résulte de l'article 1527 du Code de procédure civile applicable en matière d'arbitrage international que l'appel de l'ordonnance ayant statué sur l'exequatur et le recours en annulation sont formés, instruits et jugés selon les règles relatives à la procédure contentieuse prévues aux articles 900 à 930-1 du Code de procédure civile.

19-Sont ainsi applicables aux recours en annulation les dispositions régissant la procédure avec représentation obligatoire devant la cour d'appel.

20-Aux termes de l'article 901 du Code de procédure civile, l'indication de la décision attaquée est requise à peine de nullité dans la déclaration valant recours. Il en résulte qu'en cas de pluralité de décisions attaquées par la voie de l'annulation, il doit être fait mention de toutes les décisions visées par ledit recours ou il doit être fait autant de recours que de décisions contestées.

21-En conséquence, le recours en annulation formé contre la sentence visée dans la déclaration de recours n'emporte pas implicitement recours en annulation contre une autre sentence, non indiquée dans le recours.

[...]

26-De même, concernant la sentence intérimaire rendue le 8 avril 2016 notifiée le 30 septembre 2016, le fait que ladite sentence soit qualifiée d'intérimaire et qu'elle ordonne un paiement par provision, assorti d'une astreinte, ne lui ôte pas sa qualité de sentence, même partielle, dès lors qu'elle tranche, même à titre provisoire, une partie du litige et qu'elle est dès lors susceptible de faire l'objet d'un recours en annulation, dans les conditions fixées par le Code de procédure civile.

27-Or, il résulte des éléments de la procédure que la société n'a pas formé de recours contre ladite sentence, ni de façon autonome, ni conjointement avec le recours en annulation qu'elle a formé le 19 mars 2018 contre la seule sentence finale du 2 novembre 2017.

28-Par conséquent, elle est irrecevable à solliciter l'annulation de la sentence intérimaire.

29-La cour d'appel n'est dès lors saisie que du recours en annulation de la sentence finale.

2. Sur l'annulation de la sentence finale pour défaut de conformité du Tribunal à sa mission (Art. 1520(3) CPC)

[...]

36-Aux termes de l'article 1520, 3° du Code de procédure civile, le recours en annulation n'est ouvert que si le tribunal arbitral a statué sans se conformer à la mission qui lui avait été confiée.

37-À ce titre, il appartient au tribunal arbitral de statuer dans les limites des demandes formulées de sorte que s'il accorde plus que ce qui avait été demandé, sa sentence est susceptible d'être annulée pour méconnaissance de sa mission.

38-Pour apprécier l'existence de ce vice, le juge doit se pencher sur les demandes des parties et non sur les pièces de la procédure, qui ne fixent pas l'étendue du litige.

[...]

47-Le dépassement de mission allégué n'est dès lors pas établi, le tribunal arbitral ayant statué dans les limites de sa saisine.

48 – Il y a lieu par conséquent de rejeter la demande d'annulation sur ce motif.

3. Sur l'annulation de la sentence finale pour contrariété à l'ordre public international (Art. 1520(5) CPC)

[...]

58-Aux termes de l'article 1520, 5° du Code de procédure civile, une sentence ne peut être reconnue ou exécutée en France « *si la reconnaissance ou l'exécution de la sentence sont contraires à l'ordre public international* ».

59-L'ordre public international s'entend de la conception française de l'ordre public, c'est-à-dire de l'ensemble des règles et des valeurs dont l'ordre juridique français ne peut souffrir la méconnaissance, même dans des matières internationales.

60-A cet égard, une sentence qui donnerait effet à une opération constitutive d'une fraude à la loi caractérisée violerait l'ordre public international français et encourrait la nullité.

[...]

62 – Il appartient dès lors à la cour de rechercher en droit et en fait les éléments permettant de vérifier que la solution résultant de la sentence ne permet pas de donner effet à une telle opération constitutive d'une fraude à la loi caractérisée.

63-Ce faisant, il convient de considérer que la société ne peut se contenter, pour s'opposer à la demande d'annulation, de faire valoir que la fraude alléguée par la partie adverse ne concernerait ni le contrat litigieux, ni les parties à la présente procédure, mais des contrats distincts, conclus exclusivement par des tiers alors que la fraude alléguée en l'espèce résulterait précisément du lien d'interdépendance entre ces contrats qui constitueraient une seule et même opération unique frauduleuse.

64 – Il convient de relever en revanche que le tribunal arbitral a examiné la question de l'interdépendance entre le contrat d'escompte et les contrats de souscription, et qu'il ne l'a pas retenue, estimant après analyse des pièces du dossier que « *le Contrat d'escompte et les contrats de Rio Forte ne constituent pas une seule et même opération économique* ».

[...]

67-En outre, la simple suspicion tirée de la condamnation de Monsieur X pour violation des mesures de cantonnement, et ses poursuites dans d'autres affaires pour blanchiment, ne permettent pas d'établir qu'il était le concepteur de l'opération alléguée, en faisant un montage pour contourner l'interdiction de transfert de capitaux de la partie financière à la partie non financière du groupe dont il était le dirigeant.

68-De même le fait que la BES ait fait faillite n'est pas un indice suffisant pour établir une dissimulation d'opérations illégales dont le groupe serait le bénéficiaire.

69-En conséquence, à supposer même que la loi portugaise sur les règles prudentielles puisse relever de l'ordre public international français, l'existence d'une opération économique unique n'étant pas établie, la fraude à la loi alléguée n'est pas caractérisée.

70-Dès lors, le grief de violation de l'ordre public international n'est pas caractérisé et sera par conséquent rejeté.

– Paris, Pôle 5 – Chambre 16, Chambre commerciale international, 11 mai 2021, n° 18/06076, *Asperbras Limited c. Groupe A B*

Tribunal arbitral – Constitution – Arbitrage multipartite – Moyen tardif – Indépendance et impartialité – Notions – Définition – Approche objective – Obligation de révélation – Doute raisonnable – Preuve – Mission – Ultra petita – Annulation partielle – Évocation – Principe de la contradiction – Relever d'office – Violation – Annulation partielle – Compétence – Évocation

a) Sur le premier moyen d'annulation tiré de ce que le tribunal a été irrégulièrement constitué (art. 1492, 2°, du Code de procédure civile) Moyens des parties

[...]

En premier lieu, l'article 1466 du Code de procédure civile dispose que « *la partie qui, en connaissance de cause et sans motif légitime, s'abstient d'invoquer en temps utile une irrégularité devant le tribunal est réputée avoir renoncé à s'en prévaloir* ».

[...]

Le moyen d'annulation est donc recevable.

En second lieu, la société soulève le défaut d'indépendance et d'impartialité de deux des arbitres.

À ce sujet, il y a lieu de rappeler, d'une part, que l'appréciation d'un défaut d'indépendance d'un arbitre procède d'une approche objective consistant à caractériser des facteurs précis et vérifiables externes à l'arbitre susceptibles d'affecter sa liberté de jugement, tels que des liens personnels, professionnels ou économiques avec l'une des parties. Or, la société n'invoque aucun élément factuel précis et vérifiable caractérisant l'existence d'un lien quelconque entre ces arbitres et MM. X, Y et B G et permettant de mettre en cause leur indépendance. [...] Il n'est donc pas établi que les arbitres auraient manqué à leur obligation de révélation.

D'autre part, l'impartialité de l'arbitre suppose l'absence de préjugés ou de partis pris susceptibles d'affecter le jugement de l'arbitre. Toutefois, le défaut d'impartialité doit résulter d'éléments qui pour être pris en compte, doivent créer, dans l'esprit des parties, un doute raisonnable sur son impartialité. L'appréciation de ce défaut doit donc procéder d'une démarche objective. [...] En outre, si la société fait état d'un doute sur l'indépendance « *face aux violations multiples et flagrantes par le tribunal arbitral de l'article 1492 du Code de procédure civile* », elle ne fait état d'aucun élément précis qui serait révélateur d'un manque d'indépendance.

Le premier moyen d'annulation soutenu doit donc être rejeté.

b) Sur le deuxième moyen d'annulation tiré de ce que le tribunal ne s'est pas conformé à sa mission (art. 1492, 3°, du Code de procédure civile)

[...]

En premier lieu, concernant l'allégation selon laquelle le tribunal aurait statué ultra petita à l'égard du contrat [...]

Contrairement à ce qu'a retenu le tribunal arbitral, elle n'a pas formulé de demandes tendant à son inscription en qualité d'obtenteur et au paiement d'une redevance, de sorte que le tribunal ne pouvait pas condamner la société à ces titres.

Ainsi que le soutient cette dernière, le tribunal arbitral a statué ultra petita en jugeant de la sorte.

La sentence est donc partiellement annulée, sans qu'il y ait lieu de rouvrir les débats sur ce point et d'inviter les parties à conclure sur le fond, dès lors que la sentence arbitrale a rejeté la demande formée et que la cour n'a pas à se prononcer sur ce qui a été jugé ultra petita puisqu'aux termes de l'article 1493 du Code de procédure civile, lorsque la juridiction annule la sentence arbitrale, elle statue sur le fond dans les limites de la mission de l'arbitre, sauf volonté contraire des parties.

En second lieu, concernant l'allégation selon laquelle le tribunal arbitral aurait statué ultra petita à l'égard du contrat [...]

Or, le tribunal arbitral n'a pas, de la sorte, statué ultra petita à propos du paiement de redevances et de la communication de livres de comptes mais s'est borné à répondre aux demandes. [...]

c) Sur le troisième moyen d'annulation tiré de ce que le tribunal n'a pas respecté le principe de la contradiction (art. 1492, 3°, du Code de procédure civile)

[...]

L'article 16 du Code de procédure civile dispose que « *le juge doit, en toutes circonstances, faire observer et observer lui-même le principe de la contradiction* ».

Il n'est pas contesté que les parties n'ont pas invoqué devant le tribunal arbitral la notion de perte de chance, que le tribunal arbitral a relevé d'office l'existence d'une perte de chance et qu'il n'a pas invité les parties à s'expliquer sur ce point.

Le tribunal arbitral a dès lors violé le principe de la contradiction.

La sentence est donc partiellement annulée. La réouverture des débats doit être ordonnée, la cour devant statuer sur le fond de la demande, en application de l'article 1493, précité, du Code de procédure civile.

d) Sur le quatrième moyen d'annulation tiré de ce que le tribunal s'est déclaré à tort compétent (art. 1492, 1°, du Code de procédure civile)

[...]

La cour a déjà jugé qu'en ordonnant à la société d'inscrire la partie adverse en qualité d'obtenteur, alors qu'il n'avait pas été saisi d'une telle demande, le tribunal arbitral a excédé sa mission. En conséquence, la cour a annulé ces dispositions contestées de la sentence arbitrale, sans qu'il y ait lieu d'examiner la compétence du tribunal arbitral pour se prononcer sur cette demande dont il n'était pas saisi.

– Paris, Pôle 5 – Chambre 16, 18 mai 2021, n° 18/28526, *Phycomat c. Établissements André G*

Arbitrage ICC – Règlement ICC – Principe de la contradiction – Notion – Calendrier de procédure – Hors délai – Clôture des débats – Égalité des armes – Définition – Loyauté des débats – Soulever d'office – Procès équitable – Preuve supplémentaire – Ordre public international – dimension procédurale – Tribunal arbitral – Constitution – Récusation – Forclusion – Moyen tardif – Révélation – GAR – Informations – Post sentence

– Sur le moyen d'annulation tiré de ce que le principe de la contradiction n'a pas été respecté (article 1520, 4° du Code de procédure civile)

33-Le principe de la contradiction exige seulement que les parties aient pu faire connaître leurs prétentions de fait et de droit et discuter celles de leur adversaire de telle sorte que rien de ce qui a servi à fonder la décision des arbitres n'ait échappé à leur débat contradictoire.

34-Le principe de la contradiction permet d'assurer la loyauté des débats et le caractère équitable du procès. Il interdit qu'une décision soit rendue sans que chaque partie ait été en mesure de faire valoir ses prétentions de fait et de droit, de connaître les prétentions de son adversaire et de les discuter. Il interdit également que des écritures ou des documents soient portés à la connaissance du tribunal arbitral sans être également communiqués à l'autre partie, et que des moyens de fait ou de droit soient soulevés d'office sans que les parties aient été appelées à les commenter.

35-Il incombe aux arbitres de rechercher, au cas par cas, un juste équilibre entre le droit de la partie demanderesse de voir examiner ses prétentions dans un délai raisonnable et le droit de la partie défenderesse d'organiser utilement sa défense.

36-L'article 22.1 du règlement d'arbitrage CCI auquel les parties ont accepté de se soumettre prévoit également que « *Le tribunal arbitral et les parties font tous leurs efforts pour conduire la procédure d'arbitrage avec célérité et efficacité en termes de coût, eu égard à la complexité et à l'enjeu du litige.* ».

37-Selon l'article 22.4 du règlement « *Dans tous les cas, le tribunal arbitral conduit la procédure de manière équitable et impartiale et veille à ce que chaque partie ait eu la possibilité d'être suffisamment entendue* ».

38-Selon l'article 25 du même règlement « *Le tribunal arbitral instruit la cause dans les plus brefs délais par tous moyens appropriés.* »

– Sur le moyen d'annulation pris en sa première branche ;

[...]

[...]

41-Il n'est pas contesté que le calendrier de procédure prévoyait sur un pied d'égalité 4 échanges distincts sur la demande principale et sur la demande reconventionnelle dont le principe et le calendrier avaient été entérinés dans le document Règles de procédure signé par les parties le 8 novembre 2016 devant les conduire à une audience de plaidoirie à Paris début novembre 2017.

42-Par une communication n° 15 en date du 24 avril 2017 le président du tribunal a accordé à chacune des parties à leur demande un délai supplémentaire pour soumettre leurs mémoires sans changer les règles prévues ni modifier la durée de la procédure ni la date des plaidoiries.

[...]

56-I1 résulte de ce qui précède que c'est sans manquer au principe de la contradiction que le président du tribunal a dit irrecevable et écarté des débats les paragraphes du dernier mémoire d'une partie se rattachant à la demande principale et le rapport d'expertise produit à son soutien qui avaient été produits en dehors du délai prévu par le calendrier procédural qu'aucune circonstance ne justifiait de remettre en cause.

Sur le même moyen d'annulation pris en sa deuxième branche

57-Selon l'article 25.5 du règlement d'arbitrage CCI, à tout moment de la procédure, le tribunal arbitral peut demander aux parties de produire des éléments de preuve supplémentaires.

[...]

64-Il ressort de ces éléments que la production de la pièce demandée fût-elle établie, a été incontestablement effectuée par la société en dehors du délai fixé par le tribunal de sorte qu'elle ne peut reprocher au tribunal de ne pas en avoir tenu compte et dès lors invoquer une violation de la contradiction.

Sur le moyen d'annulation pris en sa troisième branche

65-Selon l'article 27 du règlement d'arbitrage CCI : Dès que possible après la dernière audience relative aux questions à résoudre dans une sentence, ou la présentation des dernières écritures autorisées concernant ces questions si celle-ci est postérieure, le tribunal arbitral : a) prononce la clôture des débats relativement aux questions à trancher dans la sentence et b) informe le Secrétariat et les parties de la date à laquelle il entend soumettre son projet de sentence à la Cour pour approbation conformément à l'article 33.

66-Après la clôture des débats, aucun argument, ni aucunes écritures, ne peuvent être présentés ni aucune preuve supplémentaire produite relativement aux questions à trancher dans la sentence, sauf à la demande ou avec l'autorisation du tribunal arbitral. [...]

71-Il résulte de ce qui précède que la société ne peut utilement tirer de cette production de pièces soumise au débat contradictoire la preuve d'une violation de la contradiction par le tribunal.

Sur le moyen d'annulation tiré de la méconnaissance de l'ordre public international dans sa dimension procédurale (article 1520, 5° du Code de procédure civile)

72-L'égalité des armes qui représente un élément du procès équitable protégé par l'ordre public international, implique l'obligation d'offrir à chaque partie une possibilité raisonnable de présenter sa cause, dans des conditions qui ne la placent pas dans une situation ou substantiellement désavantageuse par rapport à son adversaire.

[...]

74-Pour les motifs exposés plus haut, il ne ressort pas du fait des évènements déjà mentionnés qu'une partie ait été avantagée ni bénéficié de délais supplémentaires.

75-Ce moyen sera en conséquence écarté.

Sur le moyen d'annulation tiré de ce que le tribunal arbitral a été irrégulièrement constitué (article 1520, 2° du Code de procédure civile)

Sur la forclusion

76-Suivant l'article 14 (2) du règlement d'arbitrage de la Chambre de commerce internationale, la demande de récusation « *doit être soumise par une partie, à peine de forclusion, soit dans les trente jours suivant la réception par celle-ci de la notification de la nomination ou de la confirmation de l'arbitre, soit dans les trente jours suivant la date à laquelle la partie introduisant la récusation a été informée des faits et circonstances qu'elle invoque à l'appui de sa demande de récusation si cette date est postérieure à la réception de la notification susvisée* ».

77-La partie qui, en connaissance de cause, s'abstient d'exercer, dans le délai prévu par le règlement d'arbitrage applicable, son droit de récusation, en se fondant sur toute circonstance de nature à mettre en cause l'indépendance ou l'impartialité d'un arbitre, est réputée avoir renoncé à s'en prévaloir devant le juge de l'annulation.

[...]

84-Dès lors, l'information apportée par la revue du GAR, en ce qu'elle porte sur une affaire dont l'existence avait été révélée par l'arbitre dès sa déclaration d'indépendance, n'était pas de nature à aggraver de manière significative les doutes de la société sur l'indépendance de l'arbitre et à faire renaître au bénéfice de celle-ci un nouveau délai pour solliciter la récusation de cet arbitre, de sorte que faute de l'avoir engagé initialement, elle était forclose et ne peut plus se prévaloir de cette circonstance devant le juge de l'annulation.

85-Enfin la recourante n'établit pas non plus en quoi l'arbitre a manqué à son obligation de révéler ses prétendus liens avec le cabinet.

86-En effet le seul refus de répondre à un courrier, plus d'un an après la reddition de la sentence, lui demandant des précisions sur ses liens avec ce cabinet ne suffit pas en soi à soupçonner une proximité susceptible de créer un doute qui jusqu'alors était inexistant, dans l'esprit de la société recourante quant à l'indépendance et l'impartialité de l'arbitre.

87-Pour ces motifs il n'y a pas lieu de faire droit à sa demande subsidiaire d'instruction.

88-Le moyen sera en conséquence écarté.

89-I1 résulte de ce qui précède que le recours en annulation doit être rejeté.

– Paris, Pôle 5 – Chambre 16, chambre commerciale internationale, 18 mai 2021, n° 18/10511 *Zakhem International Construction Ltd c. À (Société Nationale pour la Recherche, la Production, le Transport, la Transformation, et la Commercialisation des Hydrocarbure)*

Sentence arbitrale – Exequatur – Tierce opposition – Procédure – Ouverture – Voie de recours de droit commun

Vu les articles 1525, alinéa 1, et 585 du Code de procédure civile :

6. Selon le premier de ces textes, la décision qui statue sur une demande d'exequatur d'une sentence arbitrale rendue à l'étranger est susceptible d'appel.

7. Aux termes du second, tout jugement est susceptible de tierce opposition si la loi n'en dispose autrement.

8. Pour déclarer irrecevable, l'arrêt retient que l'article 1506 du Code de procédure civile n'ouvre pas la voie de la tierce opposition à l'encontre des sentences rendues en France en matière internationale ou à l'étranger. Il ajoute que le seul recours contre l'ordonnance d'exequatur est l'appel prévu à l'article 1525 de ce même code, dans les cas d'ouverture énumérés à l'article 1520 qui visent la sentence elle-même et non l'ordonnance d'exequatur.

9. En statuant ainsi, alors que la tierce opposition contre l'arrêt de la cour d'appel ayant accordé l'exequatur constituait une voie de recours de droit commun à l'encontre, non de la sentence arbitrale, mais de la seule décision d'exequatur de la sentence rendue à l'étranger, la cour d'appel a violé les textes susvisés.

– Cass. 1re civ., 26 mai 2021, n° A 19-23.996, *Central Bank of Libya c. Libyan Investment Authority,* contre Ordonnance du 5 octobre 2017 et Arrêts Paris (pôle 1, chambre 1), 6 mars 2018 et 28 mai 2019, Déchéance partielle

Fins de non-recevoir – Conseiller de la mise en état – Pouvoirs – Décrets n° 2019-1333 du 11 décembre 2019 et n° 2020-1452 du 27 novembre 2020 – Réforme – Procédure – Déféré – Cour de cassation – Avis – Autorité de la chose jugée

2. Le conseiller de la mise en état, magistrat de la cour d'appel, chargé de l'instruction de l'appel, dispose de pouvoirs spécifiques, notamment définis par référence à ceux du juge de la mise en état du tribunal judiciaire à l'article 907 du Code de procédure civile. Ce texte dispose : « *à moins qu'il ne soit fait application de l'article 905, l'affaire est instruite sous le contrôle d'un magistrat de la chambre*

à laquelle elle est distribuée, dans les conditions prévues par les articles 780 à 807 et sous réserve des dispositions qui suivent ». Ces dernières dispositions comportent, aux articles 914 et 916, des règles particulières en matière de fins de non-recevoir.

3. Dès lors, la réforme issue du décret n° 2019-1333 du 11 décembre 2019, qui a conféré au juge de la mise en état la compétence, énoncée à l'article 789, 6° du Code de procédure civile, pour « statuer sur les fins de non-recevoir », s'applique également au conseiller de la mise en état.

4. La réforme issue de ce décret du 11 décembre 2019 s'inscrit, en outre, dans le cadre fixé par le Code de l'organisation judiciaire, notamment dans son livre III relatif aux juridictions du second degré. L'article L. 311-1 de ce code donne ainsi compétence à la cour d'appel, sous réserve des compétences attribuées à d'autres juridictions, pour connaître des décisions judiciaires, civiles et pénales, rendues en premier ressort, et précise qu'elle statue souverainement sur le fond des affaires. Selon les articles L. 312-1 et L. 312-2 du même code, la cour d'appel statue en formation collégiale, sa formation de jugement se composant d'un président et de plusieurs conseillers. Le Code de procédure civile complète cet ordonnancement juridique par son article 542, selon lequel l'appel, tend, par la critique du jugement rendu par une juridiction du premier degré, à sa réformation ou à son annulation par la cour d'appel.

5. L'appel engageant, au terme d'une jurisprudence constante, une nouvelle instance (Ass. plén., 3 avril 1962, pourvoi n° 61-10.142, Bull. 1962, Ass. plén., n° 1), il résulte de la seconde phrase du II de l'article 55 du décret du 11 décembre 2019 que le nouveau renvoi opéré à l'article 789, 6°, par l'article 907, est applicable aux appels formés à compter du 1er janvier 2020.

6. Pour autant, il résulte de ce qui est dit aux paragraphes 3 et 5 que les nouvelles attributions conférées par le décret du 11 décembre 2019 au conseiller de la mise en état s'exercent sous réserve que soit ouvert contre ses décisions un déféré devant la cour d'appel, organe juridictionnel appelé à trancher en dernier ressort les affaires dont elle est saisie. À cette fin, le décret n° 2020-1452 du 27 novembre 2020 a complété l'article 916 du Code de procédure civile pour étendre le déféré aux ordonnances du conseiller de la mise en état statuant sur toutes fins de non-recevoir. Dans la rédaction antérieure de ce texte, le déféré n'était ouvert qu'à l'encontre des ordonnances par lesquelles ce conseiller tranchait les fins de non-recevoir tirées de l'irrecevabilité de l'appel et celles tirées de l'irrecevabilité des conclusions et des actes de procédure en application des articles 909, 910 et 930-1 de ce code, dont la connaissance lui était déjà confiée par l'article 914, dans des conditions spécifiquement fixées par ce texte.

7. Ce décret du 27 novembre 2020 étant, aux termes de son article 12, alinéa 2, entré en vigueur le 1er janvier 2021, pour s'appliquer aux instances d'appel en cours, le conseiller de la mise en état ne peut donc statuer sur les autres fins de non-recevoir qui lui sont soumises ou qu'il relève d'office qu'à compter de cette date.

8. Sous cette réserve, la détermination par l'article 907 du Code de procédure civile des pouvoirs du conseiller de la mise en état par renvoi à ceux du juge de la mise en état ne saurait avoir pour conséquence de méconnaître les effets de l'appel et les règles de compétence définies par la loi. Seule la cour d'appel dispose, à l'exclusion du conseiller de la mise en état, du pouvoir d'infirmer ou d'annuler la décision frappée d'appel, revêtue, dès son prononcé, de l'autorité de la chose jugée.

9. Il en résulte que le conseiller de la mise en état ne peut connaître ni des fins de non-recevoir qui ont été tranchées par le juge de la mise en état, ou par le tribunal, ni de celles qui, bien que n'ayant pas été tranchées en première instance, auraient pour conséquence, si elles étaient accueillies, de remettre en cause ce qui a été jugé au fond par le premier juge.

La Cour est d'avis que : Le conseiller de la mise en état ne peut connaître ni des fins de non-recevoir qui ont été tranchées par le juge de la mise en état, ou par le tribunal, ni de celles qui, bien que n'ayant pas été tranchées en première instance, auraient pour conséquence, si elles étaient accueillies, de remettre en cause ce qui a été jugé au fond par le premier juge.

– Cass. 2e civ., avis, 3 juin 2021, N° 21-70.006

Article 1449 CPC – Clause compromissoire – Référé – Conditions – Mesures provisoires ou conservatoires – Urgence – Critères – Irrémédiablement compromis

Sur la compétence de la juridiction des référés

[...]

L'article 1449, alinéa 1er du Code de procédure civile dispose : « *L'existence d'une convention d'arbitrage ne fait pas obstacle, tant que le tribunal arbitral n'est pas constitué, à ce qu'une partie saisisse une juridiction de l'État aux fins d'obtenir une mesure d'instruction ou une mesure provisoire.* »

En application de l'article 1449 du Code de procédure civile, si la clause compromissoire n'exclut pas, tant que le tribunal arbitral n'est pas constitué, la faculté de saisir le juge des référés aux fins de mesures provisoires ou conservatoires, cette compétence exceptionnelle reconnue au juge des référés est soumise à la condition de l'urgence.

L'appelante échoue à caractériser l'urgence, alors que : – le litige est ancien, apparu il y a près de quatre années, avec la présentation par l'intimée à l'appelante d'une contre-proposition de décompte général définitif, étant observé que l'ancienneté de la créance alléguée par le sous-traitant est, en tout état de cause, insuffisante à caractériser l'urgence ; – l'appelante ne soutient pas être en procédure collective, ni ne rapporte la preuve que ses difficultés financières résulteraient à l'évidence du seul non-paiement de la créance alléguée ; si, en effet, son bilan 2018 révèle un résultat négatif [...], le résultat 2017 ayant été positif [...] – ce seul élément est insuffisant à caractériser une situation irrémédiablement compromise de la société appelante qui, au surplus, ne produit aucun bilan au titre des années 2019 et 2020 et n'établit pas une dégradation de sa situation de nature à mettre en péril sa pérennité, situation qui ne ressort pas davantage de l'attestation de l'expert-comptable de la société. – il n'apparaît pas que la société puisse, dans ces conditions, se prévaloir d'une urgence telle qu'elle ne permettrait pas d'attendre la constitution du tribunal arbitral.

Il convient dès lors pour la cour, par infirmation de la décision entreprise, de dire que le juge des référés est incompétent pour connaître du litige.

– Paris, Pôle 1 – Chambre 3, 9 juin 2021, n° 20/15172, *Pasquinelli c. Bouygues Bâtiment Île-de-France*

Fin de non-recevoir – Nul ne peut se contredire au détriment d'autrui – Attitude procédurale – Définition – Déni de justice – Principe de compétence compétence – Contrats – Effet relatif – Clause compromissoire – Autonomie – Validité – Signataire de la clause – Partie au contrat – Non signataire – Tiers – Participation – Unité économique – Opposabilité – Article 1448 du code de procédure – Applicabilité – Manifestement inapplicable – Personne physique – Dirigeant – Article L. 225-251 du Code de commerce – Connaissance de la clause – Étendue – Champ – Sursis à statuer

Sur la recevabilité de l'exception d'incompétence

[...]

La fin de non-recevoir tirée du principe selon lequel nul ne peut se contredire au détriment d'autrui sanctionne l'attitude procédurale consistant pour une partie, au cours d'une même instance, à adopter des positions contraires ou incompatibles entre elles dans des conditions qui induisent en erreur son adversaire sur ses intentions.

[...]

L'existence d'un déni de justice ne peut être retenue dans la mesure où la voie arbitrale restera ouverte si l'exception d'incompétence est fondée.

Sur l'applicabilité de la clause compromissoire au présent litige

[...]

En principe, conformément à l'effet relatif des contrats et à l'autonomie de la personne morale, la clause compromissoire signée par une société n'engage que celle-ci. Conformément aux usages du commerce, la clause compromissoire insérée dans un contrat a une validité et une efficacité propres qui commandent d'en étendre l'application aux parties directement impliquées dans l'exécution du contrat et les litiges qui peuvent en résulter, dès lors qu'il est établi que leur situation contractuelle, leurs activités et les relations commerciales habituelles existant entre les parties font présumer qu'elles ont accepté la clause d'arbitrage, dont elles connaissaient l'existence et la portée, bien qu'elles n'aient pas été signataires du contrat qui la stipulait.

L'unité économique entre plusieurs sociétés permet également d'étendre la clause arbitrage aux entités du groupe non-signataires dès lors qu'elles ont pris part à la conclusion, l'exécution ou la résolution du contrat.

Le contrat de partenariat du 22 juillet 2011 signé entre les sociétés l'intimée et GP prévoit en sa section 11 que « *Tous les litiges, controverses et réclamations nés ou impliquant la présente convention ou se rapportant à celle-ci doivent être renvoyés, réglés et finalement résolus exclusivement par arbitrage conformément au règlement de la CCI pour l'arbitrage par un ou plusieurs arbitres nommés conformément à ces règles.* »

La société appelante n'étant pas partie à ce contrat, elle n'est pas signataire de ladite clause qui ne lui est donc normalement pas opposable.

[...]

L'appelante a nécessairement eu connaissance de l'existence et de la portée de la clause compromissoire dès lors que ses fondateurs et dirigeants en sont les signataires.

[...]

Il sera fait application du principe compétence compétence prévu à l'article 1448 du Code de procédure civile qui impose, dans le cas où la clause compromissoire n'est ni manifestement nulle ni manifestement inapplicable, de renvoyer l'appelante à mieux se pourvoir.

Sur la compétence pour statuer sur les demandes à l'égard de Monsieur C

[...]

L'article 21 des statuts de la société au 13 mai 2013, stipule que : « *[t]ous différends susceptibles de surgir pendant la durée de la société, ou après sa dissolution pendant le cours des opérations de liquidation, soit entre les associés, le président et la société, soit entre les associés eux-mêmes, relativement aux affaires sociales ou à l'exécution des dispositions statutaires, seront soumis à l'arbitrage.* »

Le fait que les actionnaires de la société puissent supprimer à tout moment cette clause ne signifie pas qu'elle aurait été stipulée dans l'intérêt exclusif de la société et que celle-ci pourrait y renoncer unilatéralement. Le tribunal de commerce a, à juste titre précisé, que cela ne résultait d'aucune clause des statuts.

M. C, non-actionnaire de l'appelante, n'a pas adhéré à la clause compromissoire, et celle-ci ne lui est pas d'emblée applicable. Cependant, l'application de la clause compromissoire peut être étendue aux parties directement impliquées dans l'exécution du contrat et dans le litige pouvant en résulter. La clause prévue dans les statuts peut également s'appliquer à une partie du fait de son implication directe dans le fonctionnement de la société même si elle est n'est ni actionnaire ni associée.

[...] En sa qualité de dirigeant de la société, Monsieur C a pu prendre connaissance de l'existence de cette clause.

Il résulte de l'article 21 des statuts de la société que les litiges devant être soumis à l'arbitrage sont notamment ceux susceptibles de surgir entre le président et la société relativement aux affaires sociales ou à l'exécution des dispositions statutaires.

Il ressort de l'assignation devant le tribunal de commerce délivrée le 13 mars 2019 que l'action à l'égard de M. C est fondée sur l'article L. 225-251 du code de commerce, en vue d'engager sa responsabilité en qualité de dirigeant de la société, des fautes lui étant reprochées en qualité de président de celle-ci, en ce qu'il aurait utilisé cette qualité pour faire prévaloir les intérêts des autres sociétés dans lesquelles il occupait également des fonctions de direction.

Ce litige est en lien avec la nature du contentieux visé par la clause compromissoire et concerne directement M. C, alors qu'il était dirigeant de la société appelante.

Dans ces conditions, la clause compromissoire n'étant pas manifestement inapplicable à M. C, il sera fait application du principe compétence compétence prévu à l'article 1448 du Code de procédure civile qui impose, dans le cas où la clause compromissoire n'est ni manifestement nulle ni manifestement inapplicable, de renvoyer la société à mieux se pourvoir.

Le jugement sera confirmé en ce que le tribunal de commerce, conformément aux dispositions de l'article 81 du Code de procédure civile, a renvoyé la société à mieux se pourvoir quant à ses demandes relatives à la société et à M. C.

[...]

Sur le sursis à statuer prononcé par le jugement

Aux termes de l'article 378 du Code de procédure civile : « *La décision de sursis suspend le cours de l'instance pour le temps ou jusqu'à la survenance de l'évènement qu'elle détermine* ».

[...]

La procédure en principal et notamment quant à la compétence relevant des juridictions arbitrales, le jugement sera confirmé en ce qu'il a sursis à statuer sur les demandes de l'appelante à l'égard de M. B.

Ce sursis à statuer sera ordonné jusqu'à ce que les juridictions arbitrales aient statué sur leur compétence.

– Paris, Pôle 5 – Chambre 5, 10 juin 2021, n° 20/07754, *Middle Fast Petroleum Investors c. C, B, et X*

Arbitrage sportif – Arbitrage interne – Arbitrage international – Caractère international – Critères – Définition économique – Volonté des parties – Article 6 CESDH – Heurte des garanties – Tribunal arbitral – Composition – Impartialité et indépendance – Moyen tardif – Contrôle – Périmètre – Doute raisonnable dans l'esprit des parties – Recherche objective – Critères – Règlement applicable – Liste d'arbitres – Avocat conseil – Arbitre – Droit de choisir son avocat

22. Aux termes de l'article 1504 du Code de procédure civile, « *est international l'arbitrage qui met en cause des intérêts du commerce international* ».

23. Il résulte de cette définition exclusivement économique que l'arbitrage revêt un caractère international lorsque le différend soumis à l'arbitre porte sur une opération qui ne se dénoue pas économiquement dans un seul État, peu important la qualité ou la nationalité des parties, la loi applicable au fond du litige ou à la procédure, ainsi que le siège du tribunal arbitral. Cette qualification ne dépend pas de la volonté des parties.

24. En l'espèce, l'opération économique qui est à l'origine du litige a été formalisée par le contrat d'agent sportif signé entre les parties le 25 novembre 2015, contrat dont l'objet était pour l'agent, moyennant commissions sur le salaire brut du joueur, de négocier avec un club l'ensemble des dispositions relatives à un contrat de travail de joueur de football professionnel homologué par la Ligue de Football Professionnel, le contrat d'agent lui-même devant être dûment déposé à la Fédération française de football, cette condition étant déterminante de l'engagement des parties, le joueur ayant été embauché successivement par le Toulouse Football Club le 26 janvier 2012 renouvelé le 28 juin 2013 puis par le PSG le 23 juillet 2014.

25. Nonobstant la nationalité étrangère des parties qui est sans effet sur l'internationalité du litige, il résulte des éléments versés aux débats que le litige est né de la rupture du contrat d'agent par le défendeur alors qu'il était joueur du PSG, la rupture anticipée du contrat ainsi que son caractère fautif constituant l'objet du litige, donnant lieu à une demande d'indemnisation par la demanderesse d'un préjudice financier lié à sa perte de commissions et d'un préjudice d'image à l'égard des supporters et de sa réputation vis-à-vis de la FFF, conséquence de la rupture entre ledit joueur et son agent, sans que le litige n'emporte aucun transfert de biens ni de personnes ni de flux financiers transfrontaliers, la seule localisation en Suisse du compte bancaire de la société et le fait que le défendeur ait signé

un nouveau contrat de travail avec un club étranger en quittant le PSG étant insuffisants pour caractériser l'internationalité du litige.

[...]

27. Il ne résulte en outre d'aucun autre élément que le litige aurait vocation à se dénouer économiquement dans un autre pays que la France à la date de la rupture, le contrat d'agent soumis au droit français ayant été dûment enregistré à la Fédération Française de Football, ce que le défendeur au recours lui-même a demandé au tribunal arbitral de vérifier, et le joueur étant sous contrat avec le PSG, club français de football, après avoir été au Racing Club de Lens depuis 2009 et au Toulouse Football Club depuis 2012.

28. Il y a lieu par conséquent d'appliquer les règles relatives à l'arbitrage interne et de rejeter la fin de non-recevoir soulevée à ce titre.

Sur la recevabilité du moyen d'annulation tiré de l'irrégularité de la composition du tribunal arbitral du fait de la méconnaissance des principes d'impartialité et d'indépendance (article 1492, 2° du CPC et article 6§1 CESDH),

Sur la fin de non-recevoir tirée de l'absence de contestation lors de la procédure arbitrale

[...]

32. Selon l'article 1466 du Code de procédure civile, la partie qui, en connaissance de cause et sans motif légitime, s'abstient d'invoquer en temps utile une irrégularité devant le tribunal arbitral est réputée avoir renoncé à s'en prévaloir.

[...]

Sur la fin de non-recevoir tirée de la renonciation à se prévaloir de l'article 6-1 de la CESDH ;

35. Si la Convention européenne des droits de l'homme engage les États et ne s'impose pas directement aux arbitres, il appartient au juge de l'annulation dans le cadre du périmètre de son contrôle, de veiller à ce que la sentence rendue par un tribunal arbitral ne heurte pas, parmi les garanties protégées par l'article 6-1 de cette Convention, celles auxquelles les parties n'ont pas valablement renoncé.

36. À cet égard, le seul fait de soumettre le litige à un tribunal arbitral en vertu d'une clause compromissoire et de saisir la CAS ne saurait être regardé comme emportant une renonciation à contester l'impartialité ou l'indépendance d'un arbitre.

37. Ce grief sera également rejeté.

38. Il y a lieu en conséquence d'écarter les moyens d'irrecevabilité soulevés.

Sur le bien-fondé du moyen d'annulation relatif à la composition du tribunal

[...]

43. En l'espèce, la question qui se pose est celle de savoir si le simple fait pour l'avocate de l'une des parties, d'être inscrite sur la liste des arbitres de la CAS constitue une circonstance qui est de nature à créer un doute raisonnable dans l'esprit des parties quant à l'indépendance ou l'impartialité du tribunal arbitral.

44. Il convient de rappeler que l'appréciation d'un défaut d'indépendance d'un arbitre procède d'une approche objective consistant à caractériser des facteurs précis et vérifiables externes à l'arbitre susceptibles d'affecter sa liberté de jugement, tels que des liens personnels, professionnels et/ou économiques avec l'une des parties.

45. L'impartialité de l'arbitre suppose l'absence de préjugés ou de partis pris susceptibles d'affecter le jugement de l'arbitre, lesquels peuvent résulter de multiples

facteurs tels que la nationalité de l'arbitre, son environnement social, culturel ou juridique.

46. En l'espèce, il convient de relever d'une part que le règlement d'arbitrage auquel la société a consenti ne prévoyait pas de règles interdisant à un conseil d'être inscrit sur la liste des arbitres de la chambre arbitrale du sport et que c'est la raison pour laquelle la demande de la société de voir interdire à Maître M d'intervenir comme avocate pour assister une partie dans le cadre de la présente procédure d'arbitrage a été rejetée, outre le fait qu'il convient d'ajouter qu'une telle décision touchait aussi au droit d'une partie de son choisir son avocat.

47. D'autre part, le tribunal arbitral a été composé de trois arbitres et non d'un seul.

48. En outre, se prévalant de cette seule circonstance, la société ne justifie d'aucun élément complémentaire qui pourrait accréditer l'existence d'un lien de dépendance entre les membres du tribunal arbitral et l'avocat.

49. De même, il n'est fait état d'aucun élément permettant de considérer que cette seule circonstance ait emporté des préjugés ou un parti pris susceptibles d'affecter le jugement des arbitres.

50. Il convient dès lors de considérer que cette seule circonstance n'est pas en soi de nature à créer un doute raisonnable des parties quant à l'impartialité et/ou l'indépendance du tribunal arbitral.

Ce moyen sera en conséquence rejeté.

– Paris, Chambre commerciale internationale, Pôle 5 – Chambre 16, 8 juin 2021, n° 19/02245, *Sports Management International c. X*

Arbitrage international – Règlement ICC – Acceptation des parties – Articles 12 et 33 du Règlement – Tribunal arbitral – Constitution – Impartialité et indépendance – Récusation – Délai – Article 1466 du Code de procédure civile – Moyen tardif – Institution – Décisions de récusation – Doute raisonnable – Absence de recours – Autorité de la chose jugée – Instance arbitrale – Clause compromissoire – Compétence – Contrôle en droit et en fait – Portée – Validité – Droit applicable – Règle matérielle du droit international de l'arbitrage – Principe d'autonomie – Règles impératives du droit français – Ordre public international – Commune volonté des parties – Non référence à une loi étatique – Conflit de lois – Loi étrangère – Loi du siège – Convention de New York – Licéité – Partie non signataire – Extension – Participation – Compensation – Compétence – Qualité à agir et/ou de fond – Absence de contrôle du juge de l'annulation – Demande non formulée – Principe de la contradiction – Notion – Audition de témoins – Amiable composition – Mission – Délimitation par l'objet du litige – Ordre public international – Violation manifeste effective et concrète – Lien professionnel – Proximité géographique

S*ur le moyen d'annulation tiré de la constitution irrégulière du tribunal arbitral (article 1520 (2°) du Code de procédure civile)*

Sur la recevabilité du moyen

Sur la recevabilité des griefs ayant fait l'objet des deux demandes de récusation ;

[...]

26-En application de l'article 11.2 du règlement CCI (version 1998) la demande de récusation, fondée sur une allégation de défaut d'indépendance ou sur tout autre motif, est introduite, à peine de forclusion, soit dans les trente jours suivant la réception par celle-ci de la notification de la nomination ou de la confirmation de l'arbitre, soit dans les trente jours suivant la date à laquelle la partie introduisant la récusation a été informée des faits et circonstances qu'elle invoque à l'appui de sa demande de récusation, si cette date est postérieure à la réception de la notification susvisée.

27-De même, en application de l'article 33 de ce même règlement, « *Toute partie qui poursuit l'arbitrage sans soulever des objections sur le non-respect de toute disposition du Règlement, de toute autre règle applicable à la procédure, de toute instruction du tribunal arbitral, ou de toute stipulation contenue dans la convention d'arbitrage relative à la constitution du tribunal arbitral ou à la conduite de la procédure est réputée avoir renoncé à ces objections* ».

28-La partie qui, en connaissance de cause, s'abstient d'exercer, dans le délai prévu par le règlement d'arbitrage applicable, son droit de récusation, en se fondant sur toute circonstance de nature à mettre en cause l'indépendance ou l'impartialité d'un arbitre, est réputée avoir renoncé à s'en prévaloir devant le juge de l'annulation.

29-Il convient en conséquence de déclarer la société irrecevable en son moyen fondé sur les griefs relatifs à la phase de constitution du tribunal.

[...]

32-En application de l'article 1466 du Code de procédure civile, la partie qui, en connaissance de cause et sans motif légitime, s'abstient d'invoquer en temps utile une irrégularité devant le tribunal arbitral est réputée avoir renoncé à s'en prévaloir.

33-Il ressort de cet article que l'irrégularité doit être invoquée « *devant le tribunal arbitral* », lequel ne se confond pas avec l'institution en charge de l'organisation de l'arbitrage, en l'espèce la Cour de la CCI.

34-Le fait que les décisions de récusation rendues par la Cour de la CCI ne soient pas susceptibles de recours aux termes de son règlement d'arbitrage, ce que les parties ont au demeurant accepté en soumettant leur arbitrage à ce règlement et que les décisions rendues par ce centre ne soient pas revêtues de l'autorité de chose jugée et ne lient pas le juge de l'annulation, ne dispensent pas la partie qui entend maintenir sa contestation de formuler expressément une objection ou à tout le moins des réserves devant le tribunal arbitral, dès lors que si elle s'abstient de le faire, elle doit être réputée avoir pris acte des décisions de récusation et accepté de se soumettre au tribunal arbitral ainsi constitué.

35-Aussi, le fait de se défendre au fond devant un tribunal arbitral sans avoir pris soin de soulever préalablement devant ce même tribunal l'irrégularité de sa constitution emporte ainsi renonciation à se prévaloir de cette irrégularité devant le juge de l'annulation.

36-Le moyen est en conséquence irrecevable.

Sur la recevabilité des griefs portant sur le déroulement de la procédure arbitrale

[...]

38-Force est de constater cependant que l'ensemble de ces points, qui visent non pas à remettre en cause l'indépendance de l'arbitre mais cette fois plus précisément son impartialité, entendue comme l'absence de préjugés ou de partis pris susceptibles d'affecter le jugement de l'arbitre, a trait à la procédure d'arbitrage avant la clôture des débats de sorte que les sociétés, qui n'ont émis aucune réserve sur l'attitude de l'arbitre avant l'exercice du recours en annulation, et ont ainsi considéré que ces circonstances n'étaient pas de nature à leurs yeux à créer un doute raisonnable sur l'indépendance ou l'impartialité de l'arbitre, doivent être réputées y avoir renoncé.

39-Les sociétés sont donc également irrecevables à soulever ces griefs devant le juge de l'annulation.

Sur le moyen d'annulation tiré de ce que le Tribunal arbitral s'est déclaré à tort compétent à l'égard de la société (article 1520 (1) du Code de procédure civile)

[...]

47-Selon l'article 1520, 1°, du Code de procédure civile, le recours en annulation est ouvert si le tribunal s'est déclaré à tort compétent ou incompétent.

Sur la recevabilité de ce moyen ;

48-Aux termes de l'article 1466 du Code de procédure civile « *La partie qui, en connaissance de cause et sans motif légitime, s'abstient d'invoquer en temps utile une irrégularité devant le tribunal arbitral est réputée avoir renoncé à s'en prévaloir* ».

49-En l'espèce, la compétence du tribunal arbitral à son égard a été soulevée par la société ainsi que cela est repris par le tribunal arbitral dans la sentence attaquée en vertu de laquelle le tribunal retient sa compétence pour « *connaître des actions dirigées contre la société ainsi que de celles que cette dernière a présentées contre les autres parties* ».

50-Ces seules constatations suffisent à considérer que la société est bien recevable à se prévaloir de ce moyen devant le juge de l'annulation.

51-La fin de non-recevoir sera en conséquence rejetée.

Sur le bien fondé du moyen

52-Dans le cadre d'un recours en annulation fondé sur l'article 1520, 1° du Code de procédure civile, il appartient au juge de l'annulation de contrôler la décision du tribunal arbitral sur sa compétence, qu'il se soit déclaré compétent ou incompétent, en recherchant tous les éléments de droit ou de fait permettant d'apprécier la portée de la convention d'arbitrage.

53-Nonobstant le fait que l'article 11 du contrat de cession d'actions de 2007 contenant la clause compromissoire stipule que « *la loi applicable à la validité, à l'interprétation et à l'exécution du présent contrat est la loi algérienne* » et s'agissant de la procédure d'arbitrage que « *la loi applicable à l'arbitrage sera la loi algérienne, le siège étant fixé à Paris (France)* », il convient de rappeler qu'en vertu d'une règle matérielle du droit international de l'arbitrage, la clause compromissoire est indépendante juridiquement du contrat principal qui la contient directement ou par référence, et que son existence et son efficacité s'apprécient, sous réserve des règles impératives du droit français et de l'ordre public international, d'après la commune volonté des parties, sans qu'il soit nécessaire de se référer à une loi étatique.

54-Ainsi, le principe de l'autonomie de la clause compromissoire est d'application générale en matière d'arbitrage international, en tant que règle matérielle internationale consacrant la licéité de la convention d'arbitrage, hors de toute référence à un système de conflit de lois, la validité de la convention devant être contrôlée au regard des seules exigences de l'ordre public international, abstraction faite de toute loi étatique fût-elle celle régissant la forme ou le fond du contrat qui la contient.

55-En l'espèce, les parties n'ont pas soumis la validité et les effets de la clause compromissoire à la loi algérienne.

56-En outre, il n'est rapporté la preuve d'aucune circonstance de nature à établir de manière non équivoque la volonté commune des parties de désigner le droit algérien comme régissant l'efficacité, le transfert et l'extension de la clause compromissoire, et dont le régime est indépendant de l'acte qui la contient.

57-En conséquence, il est inopérant d'invoquer la loi algérienne applicable au contrat de cession d'actions pour s'opposer à l'extension de la clause compromissoire, de même que la Convention de New York, qui ne régit pas cette question.

58-En outre, une clause compromissoire insérée dans un contrat international peut être étendue aux parties directement impliquées dans l'exécution du contrat et dans les litiges qui peuvent en résulter, cette situation contractuelle et leurs activités présumant qu'elles l'ont acceptée et qu'elles ne pouvaient en ignorer l'existence et la portée, bien qu'elles n'aient pas été signataires du contrat qui la stipulait.

[...]

66-Il résulte de l'ensemble de ces éléments que nonobstant l'absence de signature du contrat de cession, la société, directement impliquée dans l'exécution du contrat et dans les litiges qui en sont résultés, est tenue par la clause compromissoire qui y est stipulée.

67-Il convient en conséquence de considérer que le tribunal arbitral s'est à raison déclaré compétent pour statuer sur les demandes à l'encontre de la société.

Sur le moyen d'annulation tiré de ce que le Tribunal arbitral s'est déclaré à tort compétent à raison de la matière (article 1520 (1) du Code de procédure civile)

[...]

Sur le grief tiré de l'absence de demande de compensation ;

75-Le grief qui tend à reprocher au tribunal arbitral d'avoir statué sur une demande qui n'avait pas été formulée ne relève pas d'une question de compétence du tribunal arbitral de sorte qu'il ne saurait être opérant pour fonder une annulation sur le moyen tiré de non-respect de l'article 1520, 1° du Code de procédure civile.

76-Il sera en conséquence rejeté.

Sur le grief tiré de l'incompétence du tribunal pour statuer sur les frais de réparation et prononcer une compensation

[...]

80-Sur ce point, il convient de considérer que le tribunal arbitral est compétent pour prononcer une compensation entre deux créances s'il est compétent pour statuer sur l'une et l'autre des créances alléguées qui ont fait l'objet de la compensation.

[...]

86-Il résulte de l'ensemble de ces éléments que ces deux créances trouvant leur source dans le contrat de cession comportant la clause compromissoire, le tribunal arbitral a pu considérer qu'il avait compétence pour statuer sur leur compensation étant ajouté que la question de savoir si ces frais ont été avancés par les sociétés filiales de la société, pour le compte de cette dernière ou non, et les conditions dans lesquelles cette dernière peut s'en prévaloir pour solliciter une compensation avec la créance due à son égard par les sociétés, relève non pas d'une question de compétence mais d'une question de qualité à agir et/ou de fond, que le juge de l'annulation ne peut examiner.

87-Le moyen tiré de l'incompétence du tribunal arbitral sera en conséquence rejeté.

Sur le moyen d'annulation tiré de ce que le tribunal arbitral n'a pas respecté le principe de la contradiction (article 1520 3° du Code de procédure civile)

[...]

Sur la recevabilité du moyen

95-S'agissant d'une part de l'audition des témoins des parties au litige, il convient de constater que la société avait bien émis des contestations sur ces auditions devant le tribunal arbitral ainsi que cela ressort de la transcription des propos lors de l'audience.

96-S'agissant d'autre part des autres griefs, ceux-ci s'appuient plus précisément sur les motifs de la sentence dont les sociétés ne pouvaient avoir connaissance qu'au moment où celle-ci a été rendue.

97-En l'état de ces éléments, les sociétés ne peuvent être réputées y avoir renoncé et sont donc recevables à s'en prévaloir devant le juge de l'annulation.

Sur le fond :

[...]

105-Il ressort de ces éléments que le débat sur les frais de réparation et leur montant n'a pas été découvert par les sociétés lors des plaidoiries et qu'elles étaient en mesure d'en critiquer le montant sans qu'elles puissent aujourd'hui se prévaloir d'un défaut de respect de la contradiction.

Sur la fixation du taux d'intérêt

[...] trancher ce point en fixant comme suit ce taux d'intérêt sans méconnaître le principe de la contradiction qui ne l'oblige pas à soumettre aux parties le détail de son argumentation.

[...]

Sur l'audition des témoins

[...].

112-Cependant d'une part, il est constant que cette question a fait l'objet d'un débat contradictoire devant le tribunal arbitral à la suite de la contestation émise par les sociétés dans leurs mémoires et lors de l'audience de plaidoiries.

113-D'autre part, il ressort de la clause compromissoire que l'arbitrage était soumis au règlement de la CCI et que l'acte de mission précise que « *Le Tribunal arbitral appliquera le Règlement d'arbitrage de la CCI en vigueur depuis le 1er janvier 1998* ».

114-L'article 20.3 de ce règlement autorise le tribunal arbitral à entendre des témoins ou des experts commis par les parties, ou « *toute autre personne* » de sorte qu'il pouvait ainsi entendre ces deux personnes, dont au demeurant le tribunal arbitral précise dans sa sentence qu'il lui appartiendra « *d'évaluer le poids, le sens et la valeur de leurs déclarations* ».

115-Il ne ressort en conséquence de ces éléments aucun grief de nature à caractériser une violation du principe de la contradiction par le tribunal arbitral.

[...]

Sur le moyen d'annulation tiré de ce que le tribunal arbitral ne s'est pas conformé à sa mission (article 1520 4° du Code de procédure civile) ;

[...]

128-Selon l'article 1520, 3°, du Code de procédure civile, le recours en annulation est ouvert si le tribunal a statué sans se conformer à la mission qui lui avait été confiée.

129-La mission des arbitres, définie par la convention d'arbitrage, est délimitée principalement par l'objet du litige, tel qu'il est déterminé par les prétentions des parties sans s'attacher uniquement à l'énoncé des questions dans l'acte de mission.

130-Comme indiqué ci-dessus, il a été demandé au tribunal arbitral de procéder à la compensation querellée de même qu'à l'évaluation des actions de la société de sorte que ce grief manque en fait.

131-De même, s'il est constant que le tribunal arbitral s'écarte de sa mission s'il ne respecte pas les règles procédurales qui ont été arrêtées par les parties, en l'espèce, comme indiqué ci-dessus, les parties ont soumis l'arbitrage au règlement CCI (version 1998). Celui-ci permet en son article 20 l'audition par le tribunal de toute personne qu'il estime utile pour l'éclairer sur la solution du litige de sorte qu'en procédant à l'audition des deux témoins, quand bien même ils seraient assimilés à des parties, le tribunal arbitral n'a pas méconnu sa mission.

132 – Enfin, comme amiables compositeurs, les arbitres reçoivent le pouvoir de modifier ou de modérer les conséquences des stipulations contractuelles selon ce que l'équité l'exige ou l'intérêt bien compris des parties.

[...]

133-Au regard de l'ensemble de ces éléments, le moyen sera rejeté.

Sur le moyen d'annulation tiré de la contrariété de la sentence à l'ordre public international (article 1520 5° du Code de procédure civile)

[...]

139-Il résulte de l'article 1520, 5° du Code de procédure civile que le recours en annulation est ouvert si la reconnaissance ou l'exécution de la sentence est contraire à l'ordre public international.

140-L'ordre public international au regard duquel s'effectue le contrôle du juge de l'annulation s'entend de la conception qu'en a l'ordre juridique français, c'est-à-dire des valeurs et des principes dont celui-ci ne saurait souffrir la méconnaissance même dans un contexte international.

141-Le contrôle exercé par le juge de l'annulation pour la défense de l'ordre public international s'attache seulement à examiner si l'exécution des dispositions prises par le tribunal arbitral heurte de manière manifeste, effective et concrète les principes et valeurs compris dans l'ordre public international.

Sur le grief tiré du défaut d'indépendance de l'arbitre ;

142-En ce qu'il serait ainsi porté atteinte au principe d'égalité entre les parties et aux droits de la défense, une sentence rendue par un arbitre dont le défaut d'indépendance serait établi, heurterait l'ordre public international.

143-A cet égard, au titre de ce moyen d'annulation, il convient d'observer que les sociétés mettent en cause, non plus précisément l'impartialité de l'arbitre, mais spécialement son "indépendance", laquelle était fondée sur les griefs tirés de la proximité géographique et du lien professionnel avec le conseil de l'une des parties, qu'il convient donc d'examiner.

Sur le grief lié à la proximité géographique entre le domicile de l'arbitre et les dirigeants d'une des sociétés

[...]

145-Cependant, la seule circonstance que le domicile de l'un des arbitres se situe fortuitement à la même adresse qu'un logement appartenant à des dirigeants de la société, ne peut être suffisant en soi à caractériser un défaut d'indépendance de l'arbitre et à rendre la sentence rendue contraire à l'ordre public international alors qu'il n'est justifié par ailleurs, fût-ce par de simples allégations purement hypothétiques, d'aucune relation professionnelle et personnelle entre ces personnes et qu'il résulte des déclarations données par l'arbitre qu'il « n'a aucune relation d'aucune sorte, même de simple voisinage » avec ces personnes ainsi que des informations non contredites données par ces derniers que les consorts P ne résident pas dans ce logement depuis plusieurs années, qui est désormais occupé par une société qui n'est pas une filiale de la société Pharaon.

146-Ce grief sera en conséquence rejeté.

Sur le grief lié au lien professionnel entre l'arbitre et le conseil de l'une des parties ;

[...]

148-Il en résulte que les relations professionnelles entre l'arbitre et le cabinet ne revêtent pas un caractère systématique de nature à créer les conditions d'un courant d'affaires entre eux, lui-même de nature à créer un lien de dépendance de l'arbitre et ainsi atteindre la sentence rendue d'une méconnaissance de l'ordre public international.

149-Ce grief, non fondé, sera en conséquence rejeté.

Sur le grief de méconnaissance du principe de la contradiction ;

150-Si le non-respect par le tribunal arbitral du principe de la contradiction et/ou des droits de la défense est susceptible de heurter l'ordre public international et emporter de ce chef également l'annulation d'une sentence rendue au mépris de ces principes il a été relevé dans les motifs ci-dessus exposés dans la présente décision que la méconnaissance de ces principes par le tribunal arbitral n'était nullement caractérisée de telle sorte que la reconnaissance ou l'exécution de la sentence qu'il a rendue ne peut être considérée comme contraire à l'ordre public international.

Sur le grief lié aux obstacles légaux de la compensation

151-Il convient de rappeler que la méconnaissance éventuelle par un tribunal arbitral d'une règle d'ordre public ne suffit pas à caractériser une méconnaissance de l'ordre public international français.

[...]

Sur le grief tiré de la méconnaissance de la Convention de New York du 10 juin 1958 s'agissant de la compétence à l'égard d'une partie

154-Loin de heurter l'ordre public international, la sentence qui, après avoir considéré en l'espèce que la société bien que non-signataire du contrat de cession d'action dans lequel est insérée la clause compromissoire pouvait se voir opposer cette clause et justifier la compétence du tribunal arbitral à son égard dès lors qu'elle avait signé les annexes 6 et 7 de ce contrat qui en font « parties intégrantes » et que ce contrat a fait bénéficier la société de « certains droits » et qu'elle a « assumé des obligations dérivant du contrat de cession : prêt, loyers du fret des navires, prise en charge des frais des réparations, etc. », ne fait que consacrer une règle matérielle du droit international de l'arbitrage, selon laquelle la clause compromissoire est indépendante juridiquement du contrat principal qui la contient directement ou par référence, et son existence et son efficacité s'apprécient d'après la commune volonté des parties.

155-Ce grief ne peut donc conduire à annuler ladite sentence dont le résultat ne heurte en conséquence aucunement l'ordre public international.

156-Le moyen tiré de la contrariété à l'ordre public international sera en conséquence rejeté.

– Paris, Chambre commerciale internationale, Pôle 5 – Chambre 16, 15 juin 2021, n° 20/07999, *CNAN Group et IBC c. CTI Group Inc. et Pharaon Commercial Investment Group Limited*

Sentence annulée – Contrat d'arbitre – Nature – Nature juridictionnelle – Responsabilité contractuelle – Prestation de service – Obligation de révélation – Manquement – Tribunal arbitral – Constitution – Conduite – Mission – Juridiction compétente – Règlement (UE) n° 1215/2012 du 12 décembre 2012 – Champ d'application – Arbitrage exclu – Juridiction compétente – Lieu de la prestation de service – Siège de l'arbitrage

Sur l'application du Règlement (UE) n° 1215/2012 du 12 décembre 2012 pour déterminer la juridiction compétente ;

22 – Le présent litige ayant pour objet une action en responsabilité exercée par une société de droit qatari, partie à une procédure d'arbitrage dont le siège était fixé à Paris, contre l'un des arbitres, résidant en Allemagne, auquel sont reprochés des manquements à ses obligations contractuelles découlant d'un contrat d'arbitre, la cour est en présence d'un litige à caractère international qui pose la question de l'application du Règlement (UE) n° 1215/2012 du Parlement européen et du Conseil du 12 décembre 2012 concernant la compétence judiciaire, la reconnaissance et l'exécution des décisions en matière civile et commerciale.

23-En effet, en application de l'article 1.2 (d) du règlement Bruxelles I Bis, « *sont exclus de son application : (...) d) l'arbitrage* (...) ».

24-Selon le considérant 12 de ce règlement, dont la liste qu'il comporte n'est pas exhaustive, « *Le présent règlement ne devrait pas s'appliquer à une action ou demande accessoire portant, en particulier, sur la constitution d'un tribunal arbitral, les compétences des arbitres, le déroulement d'une procédure arbitrale ou tout autre aspect de cette procédure ni à une action ou une décision concernant l'annulation, la révision, la reconnaissance ou l'exécution d'une sentence arbitrale, ou l'appel formé contre celle-ci.* ».

25-Il ressort en outre de la Cour de justice de l'Union européenne, interprétant la disposition de la convention de Bruxelles du 27 septembre 1968, équivalente à cet article 1er.2 (d) du règlement n° 1215/2012, qu'« *en excluant du champ d'application de la convention la matière de l'arbitrage au motif que celle-ci faisait déjà l'objet de conventions internationales, les parties contractantes ont entendu exclure l'arbitrage en tant que matière dans son ensemble, y compris les procédures introduites devant les juridictions étatiques* » (CJCE, C-190/89, aff. Rich arrêt du 25 juillet 1991 point 18 et aussi CJCE, arrêt Van Uden du 17 novembre 1998, paragraphe 31).

26-L'action visant à mettre en cause la responsabilité d'un arbitre après l'annulation d'une sentence arbitrale fondée sur le manquement de ce dernier son obligation de révélation est étroitement liée à la constitution du tribunal arbitral et à la conduite de l'arbitrage puisqu'elle vise à apprécier si l'arbitre a exercé, conformément à ses obligations découlant de son contrat d'arbitre, sa mission, laquelle participe de la mise en œuvre de l'arbitrage.

27-Cette action relève ainsi, quand bien même au fond elle serait régie par le droit commun de la responsabilité civile, de la matière de l'arbitrage.

28-En conséquence, il convient de considérer que cette action entre dans le champ de l'exclusion posée par l'article 1.2 (d) du règlement, qui dès lors n'est pas applicable pour désigner la juridiction compétente.

Sur la désignation de la juridiction compétente ;

29-En application de l'article 46 du Code de procédure civile, étendu à l'ordre international, le demandeur peut saisir à son choix, outre la juridiction du lieu où demeure le défendeur, en matière contractuelle, la juridiction « *du lieu de l'exécution de la prestation de service* ».

30-En matière d'arbitrage international, sauf volonté contraire des parties, le juge étatique du lieu de la prestation de service pour statuer sur une action en responsabilité dirigée contre l'arbitre dans l'exécution du contrat d'arbitre est celui dans le ressort duquel se situe le siège de l'arbitrage.

31-En effet, le contrat d'arbitre participe de la nature mixte de l'arbitrage, contractuelle par sa source et juridictionnelle par son objet, et dérive de la convention d'arbitrage à laquelle il est étroitement lié.

32-Ainsi, la prestation de service d'un arbitre consiste en l'accomplissement de sa mission de trancher le litige qui lui est soumis par les parties et comprend celle de rendre une sentence au siège de l'arbitrage choisi par les parties ou en accord avec elles.

33-Il y a lieu en conséquence, eu égard à la nature particulière du contrat d'arbitre étroitement lié à la convention d'arbitrage, de considérer que le lieu de l'exécution de la prestation de l'arbitre se situe audit siège, quand bien même la procédure d'arbitrage et les travaux de réflexion des arbitres, ont pu, en accord entre les parties, se dérouler en d'autres lieux.

34-En l'espèce, il est constant que le siège de l'arbitrage litigieux a été fixé à Paris, France.

35 – Il convient en conséquence de considérer que le tribunal judiciaire de Paris est compétent pour statuer sur l'action et d'infirmer le jugement.

- Paris, Chambre commerciale internationale, Pôle 5 – Chambre 16, 22 juin 2021, n° 21/07623, *Saad Buzwair Automotive Co c. X* (Voir commentaire de l'arrêt de S. Akhouad Barriga dans les Cahiers de l'arbitrage / the Paris Journal of International Arbitration 2020/4)

Clause compromissoire – Contrats – Étendue – Indivisibilité – Champ – Inapplicabilité – Volonté des parties

À hauteur de cour, la société appelante ne soutient plus que l'indivisibilité des contrats a pour effet d'étendre la clause compromissoire existant dans l'un des contrats à l'ensemble des contrats concernés. Il s'en évince que la juridiction étatique saisie est bien compétente pour statuer sur les demandes.

- Paris, Pôle 1 – Chambre 3, 23 juin 2021, n° 20/18057, *Daly Ker c. Carrefour proximité France*

Clause compromissoire – Article 1449 CPC – Référé – Mesure d'instruction – Mesure provisoire ou conservatoire – Mesure *in futurum* – Urgence – Compétence – Territorialité – Siège du tribunal – Juge d'appui – Lien

avec la mesure – Tribunal judiciaire – Tribunal de commerce – Président du Tribunal

5. Aux termes de l'article 1449 du Code de procédure civile, l'existence d'une convention d'arbitrage ne fait pas obstacle, tant que le tribunal arbitral n'est pas constitué, à ce qu'une partie saisisse une juridiction de l'État aux fins d'obtenir une mesure d'instruction ou une mesure provisoire ou conservatoire. Sous réserve des dispositions régissant les saisies conservatoires et les sûretés judiciaires, la demande est portée devant le président du tribunal judiciaire ou de commerce, qui statue sur les mesures d'instruction dans les conditions prévues à l'article 145 et, en cas d'urgence, sur les mesures provisoires ou conservatoires sollicitées par les parties à la convention d'arbitrage.

6. Il résulte des articles 42, 46, 145 et 493 du Code de procédure civile que le juge territorialement compétent pour statuer sur une requête fondée sur le troisième de ces textes est le président du tribunal susceptible de connaître de l'instance au fond ou celui du tribunal dans le ressort duquel les mesures d'instruction sollicitées doivent, même partiellement, être exécutées (2° Civ., 18 novembre 1992, pourvoi n° 91-16447, Ab. 1992, II, n° 266 ; 2° Civ., 15 octobre 2015, pourvois n° 14-17.564 et 14-25.654, Bull. 2015, II, n° 233), sans que la partie requérante puisse se prévaloir d'une clause compromissoire.

7. En présence d'une telle clause, le tribunal étatique susceptible de connaître de l'instance au fond est celui auquel le différend serait soumis si les parties, comme elles en ont la faculté, ne se prévalaient pas de la convention d'arbitrage.

8. Ayant relevé que les quatre sociétés défenderesses au litige potentiel étaient domiciliées à Dives-sur-Mer (Calvados) et qu'aucune mesure d'instruction ne devait être effectuée dans le ressort de la juridiction parisienne, c'est à bon droit que la cour d'appel, qui n'a pas statué sur la compétence du tribunal arbitral, a jugé que le président du tribunal de commerce de Paris n'était pas territorialement compétent pour ordonner les mesures demandées, peu important que le siège du tribunal arbitral ait été fixé à Paris, avec comme juge d'appui le président de ce tribunal de commerce.

– **Cass. 1re civ., 23 juin 2021, n° 19-13.350, FS-B, *Système U centrale régionale Nord-Ouest et société coopérative U enseigne c. Valma distribution, Dives distribution, Stadis et C3B,* contre l'arrêt rendu le 10 janvier 2019 par la cour d'appel de Paris (pôle 1, chambre 2), Rejet**

Garantie de passif – Acte de cession – Clause compromissoire – Droit applicable – Principe de compétence compétence – Sursis à statuer – Événement – Saisine d'un tribunal arbitral – Attitude des parties – Révocation du sursis – Incompétence Juridiction prud'homale – Inapplicabilité manifeste – Nullité manifeste

Le premier juge a fait un juste rappel du droit applicable en matière d'arbitrage, à savoir les dispositions de l'article 1465 du Code de procédure civile auxquelles renvoie l'article 1506 du même code relatif à l'arbitrage international qui prévoient que lorsqu'un litige relève d'une convention d'arbitrage devant une juridiction de l'État, celle-ci doit se déclarer incompétente sauf si la convention est manifestement nulle ou manifestement inapplicable. Il est admis qu'il appartient à l'arbitre de statuer par priorité sur sa propre compétence et de déterminer les parties intéressées par la procédure d'arbitrage.

Dans sa décision du 8 novembre 2016, le premier juge a donc logiquement ordonné un sursis à statuer afin que les parties saisissent la juridiction arbitrale.

Dans sa décision du 5 février 2019, le juge départiteur dans le cadre du suivi de ses dossiers a interrogé les parties sur l'avancée de leurs démarches auprès de la juridiction arbitrale et a pu constater qu'aucune des parties ne l'avait saisie ni exprimé l'intention de saisir prochainement cette juridiction.

La cour considère que c'est à bon droit que le premier juge a ordonné la révocation du sursis à statuer en l'absence de survenue de l'événement qui avait motivé cette décision qui est une mesure d'administration judiciaire.

L'examen de la demande de garantie se présente devant la juridiction prud'homale dans les mêmes termes à savoir que la juridiction arbitrale n'est pas saisie, plus encore les deux sociétés ne l'ont pas fait au jour de l'audience d'appel pour des choix stratégiques qui leur appartiennent.

Or la juridiction étatique ne peut retenir sa compétence en écartant celle de la juridiction arbitrale dont la compétence est revendiquée que dans deux cas limitativement énumérés à savoir la nullité de la clause compromissoire ou son inapplicabilité manifeste.

Or tel n'est pas le cas en l'espèce puisqu'une discussion sérieuse s'élève entre les parties sur la portée du Purchase Agreement qui la contient, son opposabilité aux seules parties signataires ou son rattachement indivisible à un accord-cadre à savoir le traité d'apport d'actif partiel conclu le même jour, d'apport d'actif partiel conclu avec la société G.

La cour observe que lorsqu'elle avait retenu sa compétence en procédant à une analyse des deux traités, sa décision avait été cassée par la Cour de cassation, étant observé que l'une des sociétés intimées qui avait pourtant obtenu gain de cause, s'est désistée de son action devant la juridiction de renvoi.

La cour considère que la clause compromissoire dont l'application est demandée par l'une des parties ne lui apparaît pas manifestement inapplicable au litige ce qui ne lui permet pas de retenir sa compétence en écartant celle de l'arbitre pour statuer sur la demande de mise en œuvre de la garantie par la société intimée.

Il n'y a cependant pas lieu d'ordonner un nouveau sursis à statuer, les deux sociétés n'ayant pas mis à profit le précédent sursis à statuer pour saisir la juridiction arbitrale et n'ayant pas manifesté l'intention de le faire à hauteur d'appel.

[...]

Vu l'absence d'inapplicabilité manifeste de la clause compromissoire, dit n'y avoir lieu à écarter la compétence de la juridiction arbitrale pour statuer sur la demande de recours en garantie.

– Caen, Chambre sociale, Section 1, 24 juin 2021, n° 17/00129 et suivants, *X c. Honey Well Matériaux de Friction devenue Garret Motion France B et Valeo* (21 arrêts)

Clause compromissoire – Principe de compétence compétence – Exception d'incompétence – Procédure – JME – CME – Tardif – Irrecevabilité – Inapplicabilité manifeste – Nullité manifeste – Révélation postérieure

Aux termes de l'article 1448 du Code de procédure civile, lorsqu'un litige relevant d'une convention d'arbitrage est porté devant une juridiction de l'État, celle-ci se déclare incompétente sauf si le tribunal arbitral n'est pas encore saisi et si la convention d'arbitrage est manifestement nulle ou manifestement inapplicable.

Il est constant que l'exception tirée de l'existence d'une clause compromissoire est régie par les dispositions qui gouvernent les exceptions de procédure et doit être soulevée avant toute défense au fond ou fin de non-recevoir.

Aux termes de l'article 771 du même code, lorsque la demande est présentée postérieurement à sa désignation, le juge de la mise en état est, jusqu'à son dessaisissement, seul compétent, à l'exclusion de toute autre formation du tribunal, pour statuer sur les exceptions de procédure, les demandes formées en application de l'article 47 et sur les incidents mettant fin à l'instance. Les parties ne sont plus recevables à soulever ces exceptions et incidents ultérieurement à moins qu'ils ne surviennent ou soient révélés postérieurement au dessaisissement du juge.

En l'espèce, l'intimée ne conteste aucunement être liée à l'appelante par une convention d'arbitrage entre assureurs applicables aux sinistres survenus à compter du 1er janvier 2006, laquelle a pour objet de favoriser le règlement des litiges entre assureurs en évitant les procédures judiciaires.

Si l'appelante fait valoir que cette convention prévoit l'obligation pour toute compagnie d'assurance y ayant souscrit de faire application d'une procédure d'arbitrage définie dans celle-ci, la cour constate qu'elle n'a aucunement soulevé cette exception de procédure devant le juge de la mise en état dans le cadre de la procédure de première instance ou devant le conseiller de la mise en état dans le cadre de la procédure d'appel, de sorte que l'exception de procédure soulevée doit être rejetée.

– Douai, 3e Chambre, 24 juin 2021, n° 20/00582, *Swiss Life Assurances de Biens c. Macif et a.*

Sentence arbitrale – Arbitrage interne – Appel – Loi dans le temps – Volonté des parties – Renonciation expresse

28-En application de l'article 1489 du Code de procédure civile la sentence n'est pas susceptible d'appel sauf volonté contraire des parties. Ce texte issu du décret n° 2011-48 du 13 janvier 2011 n'est cependant applicable, comme le dispose son article 3-1°, que lorsque la convention d'arbitrage a été conclue après le 1er mai 2011.

29-La convention d'arbitrage conclue avant le 1er mai 2011 demeure régie par l'ancien article 1482 du Code de procédure civile selon lequel « *La sentence arbitrale est susceptible d'appel à moins que les parties n'aient renoncé à l'appel dans la convention d'arbitrage* ».

30-En l'espèce, la clause d'arbitrage est incluse dans les statuts de la société depuis l'origine de cette société constituée le 10 avril 1995 dont l'article 37 était rédigé comme suit : « *sauf organisation par l'autorité disciplinaire à laquelle sont soumis les associés professionnels, les contestations qui pourraient survenir entre les actionnaires pour raison de leur société seront résolues par voie d'arbitrage. L'arbitrage sera effectué par un seul arbitre si les parties s'entendent sur sa désignation. Si les parties ne peuvent se mettre d'accord sur le nom d'un seul arbitre, il sera constitué un Tribunal Arbitral composé de trois arbitres. Deux des trois arbitres seront nommés par chacune des parties. Si sur la désignation de son arbitre par l'une des parties et la notification qui en aura été faite à l'autre par lettre recommandée avec accusé de réception, celle-ci ne désignait pas son arbitre dans la quinzaine qui suit la réception de cette lettre, il y sera pourvu par Monsieur le Président du Tribunal de Grande Instance d'Hazebrouck. Le troisième arbitre sera désigné par les deux arbitres nommés ainsi qu'il vient d'être dit, pour constituer avec eux un Tribunal Arbitral statuant à la majorité. À défaut par les deux premiers arbitres de s'entendre sur le nom du troisième, celui-ci sera désigné par Monsieur le Président du Tribunal de Grande Instance d'Hazebrouck et saisi par la partie la plus diligente* ».

31 – Il n'est pas contesté que si les statuts ont été modifiés par la suite à plusieurs reprises depuis 1995, le contenu de cette clause n'a pas été modifié, seule sa numérotation ayant changé, la clause compromissoire figurant dans la version modifiée des statuts du 29 juin 2015 à l'article 30.

32-Il ressort des échanges produits que c'est sur le fondement de cette clause compromissoire prévue par les parties en cas de contentieux futur que la procédure a été engagée devant le tribunal arbitral et non sur le fondement d'un compromis d'arbitrage qui aurait été élaboré une fois le litige né qui serait donc régi par les nouvelles dispositions issues du décret n° 2011-48 du 13 janvier 2011 s'agissant de l'appel des sentences.

[...]

36-En d'autres termes aucune présomption d'une volonté des parties de tenir compte du nouveau régime n'est exprimée par la clause d'arbitrage.

37-A cet égard, la clause compromissoire litigieuse ne comporte aucune renonciation à l'appel, une telle renonciation devant être expresse.

– **Paris, Chambre commerciale internationale, Pôle 5 – Chambre 16, 29 juin 2021, n° 21/05838 et 21/05848, (déférée : Ord. sur incident, 16 mars 2021 – 20/07845),** ***X c. Y***

Sentence arbitrale – Contrôle – Ordre public international – Ordre juridique français – Valeurs et principes – Violation manifeste, effective et concrète – Applicabilité – Accès au juge – Clause de conciliation – Mise en œuvre – Révision au fond – Recours en annulation – Ouverture – Égalité des parties – Principe de la contradiction – Égalité des armes – Définition – Procès équitable – Expertise contradictoire – Sentence partielle – Recevabilité – Règlement ICC – Article 25.4 du Règlement CCI

Sur le moyen d'annulation tiré de la violation de l'ordre public international (art. 1520 (5) du CPC)

24-Il résulte de l'article 1520, 5° du Code de procédure civile que le recours en annulation est ouvert si la reconnaissance ou l'exécution de la sentence est contraire à l'ordre public international.

25-L'ordre public international au regard duquel s'effectue le contrôle du juge de l'annulation s'entend de la conception qu'en a l'ordre juridique français, c'est-à-dire des valeurs et des principes dont celui-ci ne saurait souffrir la méconnaissance même dans un contexte international.

26-Le contrôle exercé par le juge de l'annulation pour la défense de l'ordre public international s'attache seulement à examiner si l'exécution des dispositions prises par le tribunal arbitral heurte de manière manifeste, effective et concrète les principes et valeurs compris dans l'ordre public international.

Sur le grief tiré de la violation de la clause de conciliation stipulée à l'article 20 du contrat pour l'exécution des travaux de réparation

[...]

38-Le tribunal arbitral a écarté la mise en œuvre de cette clause, en rappelant la nécessité d'interpréter strictement les clauses de conciliation préalable en raison de la restriction qu'elles imposent au droit fondamental d'accès au juge. Il a estimé que la rédaction ne prévoit pas clairement comment les paragraphes s'articulent ni la fonction exacte que remplit l'intervention du Bureau Veritas.

39-Sous couvert d'une violation de l'ordre public international et du principe d'exécution des contrats de bonne foi, la partie reproche au tribunal d'avoir procédé à une interprétation de la clause de conciliation nonobstant son caractère clair et précis et d'en avoir écarté son application, invitant ce faisant la cour d'appel à une révision au fond de la sentence partielle, ce qui est prohibé, même à l'occasion de l'examen d'un moyen tiré de la méconnaissance de l'ordre public international.

40-Il convient dès lors de rejeter ce grief.

• *Sur le grief tiré du non-respect du principe d'égalité des armes*

[...]

43-En vertu de l'article 1510 du Code de procédure civile, le tribunal arbitral doit garantir l'égalité des parties et le principe de la contradiction. L'égalité des armes est un élément du procès équitable protégé par l'ordre public international et qui implique l'obligation d'offrir à chaque partie une possibilité raisonnable de présenter sa cause – y compris les preuves – dans des conditions qui ne la placent pas dans une situation substantiellement désavantageuse par rapport à son adversaire.

[...]

45-L'examen de ce grief par le juge de l'annulation suppose que la Cour se prononce sur le bien-fondé de la décision du tribunal arbitral relativement à la mise en œuvre de la clause de conciliation, ce qui revient à solliciter la révision de la sentence partielle sur ce point, ce qui est prohibé.

[...]

47-Toutefois, la sentence partielle entreprise ne tranche que la question de la recevabilité de l'action engagée, au regard notamment de la mise en œuvre de la clause de conciliation, sans se prononcer sur les éléments de preuve de nature à fonder les demandes. Dans le cadre de l'interprétation de cette clause de conciliation, le tribunal arbitral a retenu qu'une partie n'a pas fait suite aux propositions de l'autre de soumettre le différend au Bureau Veritas comme le prévoit la clause litigieuse.

48-Par ailleurs, la demanderesse ne prétend ni ne démontre avoir sollicité du tribunal arbitral l'organisation d'une expertise contradictoire, tel que permis par l'article 25.4 du règlement de la Cour Internationale d'Arbitrage de la Chambre de Commerce Internationale (CCI), selon lequel « *le tribunal arbitral peut, après avoir consulté les parties, nommer un ou plusieurs experts, définir leurs missions et recevoir leurs rapports. Si l'une des parties le demande, celles-ci doivent avoir la possibilité d'interroger lors d'une audience tout expert ainsi nommé.* ».

49-Il s'infère de ce qui précède que le grief n'est pas fondé et doit être rejeté.

– Paris, Chambre commerciale internationale, Pôle 5 – Chambre 16, 29 juin 2021, n° 20/01304, *C.M.R.T c. Sofema*

Contrat de franchise – Contrats – Ensemble contractuel – Indivisibilité – Clauses compromissoires – Principe de compétence compétence – Volonté des parties – Champ d'application – Étendue – Pratiques anticoncurrentielles ou restrictives de concurrence – Ordre public – Déni de justice – Compétence prioritaire – Moyens financiers – Impécuniosité – Incidence – Rôle des acteurs de l'arbitrage – Risque de déni de justice – Coûts de l'arbitrage – Production de pièces – Refus

Le tribunal, par le jugement entrepris, a estimé que les conventions d'arbitrage opposées étaient manifestement inapplicables au litige sur le fondement de l'article 1448 du Code de procédure civile, en ce que le litige nécessitait d'appréhender un ensemble contractuel indivisible dont l'acte fondateur, les statuts, ne contient pas de clause compromissoire.

Aux termes de l'article 1448 du Code de procédure civile, « *lorsqu'un litige relevant d'une convention d'arbitrage est porté devant une juridiction de l'État, celle-ci se déclare incompétente sauf si le tribunal arbitral n'est pas encore saisi et si la convention d'arbitrage est manifestement nulle ou inapplicable* ».

En l'espèce, tant le contrat de franchise, en son article 12, que le contrat d'approvisionnement en son article 8 liant les parties, contiennent une clause compromissoire aux termes de laquelle : – article 12 du contrat de franchise : « *Toutes contestations auxquelles pourront donner lieu la conclusion, l'interprétation et l'exécution du présent accord, seront soumises à trois arbitres.(..)* », – article 8 du contrat d'approvisionnement : « *Toutes contestations auxquelles pourront donner lieu l'exécution ou l'interprétation du présent accord, seront soumises à trois arbitres* ».

Sur la nullité manifeste des deux clauses compromissoires

[...]

Mais, dans la mesure où les parties sont libres de définir contractuellement le champ d'application matériel de la clause compromissoire, il ne saurait leur être fait grief d'avoir « restreint » l'objet de la clause compromissoire et aucune nullité manifeste au sens de l'article 1448 du Code de procédure civile ne saurait en résulter de nature à faire exception à l'application du principe compétence compétence qui veut que l'arbitre se prononce par priorité sur sa compétence.

En outre, il importe peu que le fond du litige concerne des dispositions relatives à des pratiques anticoncurrentielles ou restrictives de concurrence qui seraient d'ordre public, au regard de la compétence prioritaire dont bénéficie l'arbitre pour statuer sur sa propre compétence.

[...]

Mais, l'indivisibilité d'une convention ne peut conduire à écarter la compétence de l'arbitre en application du principe compétence compétence, alors que selon ce principe couplé aux dispositions de l'article 1448 du Code de procédure civile, l'arbitre est seul compétent pour statuer sur sa propre compétence de sorte que le juge étatique doit décliner sa compétence.

Ainsi, il n'appartient pas à la Cour de rechercher si les contrats du groupe forment un ensemble contractuel indivisible, cette question n'étant pas de nature à caractériser l'inapplicabilité manifeste de la clause au sens de l'article 1448 du Code de procédure civile.

Il sera ajouté que la seule circonstance que les statuts ne contiennent pas de clause d'arbitrage ne suffit pas à rendre manifestement inapplicables au sens de l'article 1448 du Code de procédure civile, les clauses d'arbitrage stipulées dans les autres contrats du groupe.

– Sur l'impécuniosité d'une partie

[...]

Mais, l'impécuniosité d'une partie n'est pas de nature à faire échec à l'application du principe compétence compétence. L'impécuniosité ne constitue, en effet, pas un critère de nature à caractériser l'inapplicabilité manifeste d'une clause compromissoire et il revient aux acteurs de l'arbitrage d'écarter tout risque de déni de justice face à un plaideur aux moyens financiers limités.

Dès lors, la demande de condamnation sous astreinte des sociétés à produire toutes factures, pièces comptables ou attestation d'expert-comptable, permettant de connaître le coût moyen des procédures d'arbitrage opposant les sociétés du Groupe à ses franchisés au cours des 10 dernières années, ne peut qu'être rejetée.

Il en est de même de la demande des sociétés tendant à voir écarter des débats les attestations de l'ancien salarié du groupe pour son manque d'impartialité, dans la mesure où cette attestation qui tend à établir le coût de la procédure d'arbitrage, est indifférente à l'issue de l'exception d'incompétence soulevée, l'impécuniosité d'une partie étant impropre à faire échec au principe compétence compétence, ainsi qu'il a été dit.

Pour ce même motif, la demande tendant à voir écarter des débats des pièces qui ont trait à une affaire ayant opposé une des parties à un franchisé doit être rejetée.

N'étant pas établi que les clauses compromissoires liant les parties seraient manifestement nulles ou inapplicables au sens de l'article 1448 du Code de procédure civile, le jugement du tribunal de commerce de Rennes qui a débouté les sociétés de leur exception d'incompétence et s'est déclaré compétent pour connaître du litige en cause, est infirmé.

Il convient de recevoir les sociétés en leur exception d'incompétence, de déclarer le tribunal de commerce de Rennes incompétent pour connaître du litige en cause, de renvoyer les parties à mieux se pourvoir en application de la clause compromissoire stipulée au contrat de franchise signé et de celle stipulée au contrat d'approvisionnement.

– Paris, Pôle 5 – Chambre 4, 30 juin 2021, n° 21/02568, ***Carrefour Proximité France et CSF c. CPP Le Mans Distribution, Selima et a.***

Clause compromissoire – Clause à étages – Modes de résolution successifs – Notion – Tiers – Consentement – Confidentialité – Opposabilité – Clause attributive de juridiction – Groupe – Acceptation – Brexit

Sous le titre Governing law et arbitration (loi applicable et arbitrage), les conventions intitulées par la première McLaren Dealer Agreement et pour la seconde McLaren Maintenance and repair agreement, signées entre la société McLaren Automobile Ltd et la société NDBMI (qualifiée de subsidairy of groupe Neubaueur SA), vient préciser selon la traduction libre de l'appelante : *– 28-2 (...) Tout différent découlant du présent contrat ou en relation avec celui-ci y compris toute question concernant son existence, sa validité ou sa résiliation (un différend)* *doit d'abord être soumis à la procédure d'escalade suivante : (a) chaque partie désignera un individu, ces individus se réuniront pour tenter de bonne foi de résoudre le litige dans le cours normal des affaires ; (b) si les personnes désignées conformément à la clause 28.2 (a) ne résolvent pas le différend, chaque partie peut demander l'escalade des négociations à un dirigeant cadre supérieur ayant le pouvoir de régler le différend, en donnant à l'autre partie un avis écrit du différend non résolu (l'Avis de Contestation). L'Avis de Contestation comprendra (i) un bref énoncé de la position de cette partie et un résumé des arguments à l'appui de cette position, et (ii) le nom et le titre du ou des dirigeants qui représenteront cette partie dans la négociation ; (c) dans les cinq (5) jours ouvrables suivant la remise de l'Avis de Contestation, la partie réceptrice peut soumettre une réponse écrite à l'Avis de Contestation à la partie contestante (la Réponse). La Réponse doit comprendre (i) un bref énoncé de la position de la partie réceptrice et un résumé des arguments à l'appui de cette position, et (ii) le nom et le titre du ou des dirigeants qui représenteront cette partie dans la négociation. Dans les dix (10) Jours Ouvrables après la remise de l'Avis de Contestation et par la suite aussi souvent qu'ils le jugent raisonnablement nécessaire, les dirigeants désignés de chacune des parties se réuniront pour tenter de résoudre le différend par voie de négociation. Si aucune réponse n'a été signifiée par la partie destinataire après l'expiration du délai spécifié dans la présente clause 28.2 (c), l'une ou l'autre des parties peut renvoyer le différend à l'arbitrage LCIA ou à la compétence exclusive des tribunaux anglais en vertu de la clause 28.3 ou de la clause 28.4 ci-dessous (le cas échéant) ; (d) Si le différend n'a pas été résolu par la négociation dans les vingt-cinq (25) jours ouvrables suivant la livraison de l'Avis de Contestation, chaque partie peut soumettre le Différend à l'arbitrage LCIA ou à la juridiction exclusive des tribunaux d'Angleterre, et sous l'article 28-3 ou l'article 28-4 ci-dessous (comme applicable) ; et (e) dans le calcul du délai de prescription pour toute réclamation qui est finalement poursuivie par voie de litige ou d'arbitrage, la période entre la date de signification de l'Avis de Contestation et la date à laquelle les parties sont libres de soumettre le différend à un litige ou à l'arbitrage sera exclu. 28-3 Tout Différend qui n'est pas résolu conformément à la clause 28.2 peut être renvoyé par l'une ou l'autre des parties à l'arbitrage en vertu du règlement de la Cour d'arbitrage international de Londres (LCIA), lequel règlement est réputé incorporé par renvoi dans la présente clause.. Le nombre d'arbitres sera d'un (1). Le siège ou le lieu légal de l'arbitrage sera Londres, Angleterre. La langue à utiliser dans la procédure arbitrale est l'anglais. Si un Différend est renvoyé par l'une des parties à l'arbitrage en vertu de la présente Clause, il sera finalement résolu par un tel arbitrage. McLaren peut, à tout moment après la Date d'Expiration du MVBER, sur préavis écrit d'au moins deux (2) semaines au Concessionnaire, retirer au Concessionnaire le droit de renvoyer les Différends à l'arbitrage. 28-4 Rien dans la clause 27.3 n'empêche l'une ou l'autre partie d'avoir recours aux tribunaux pour tout différend (sauf que ce droit ne s'applique pas si une partie a déjà notifié à l'autre partie que le différend doit être renvoyé à l'arbitrage conformément à Article 27.3). Dans le cas où l'une des parties recourt à un litige, chaque partie s'engage irrévocablement à se soumettre à la juridiction exclusive des tribunaux d'Angleterre. Toute décision des tribunaux est définitive et exécutoire.* »

Rien dans la présente clause 27 ou autrement dans le présent Contrat n'empêchera une partie d'engager des poursuites judiciaires dans un forum pour protéger ou faire respecter les DPI.

Il en ressort de ce texte la soumission du litige à des modes de résolution successifs avec en dernier lieu une alternative : l'arbitrage ou la saisine de juridictions étatiques et dans cette dernière hypothèse, la désignation de ces dernières (les tribunaux d'Angleterre).

Dès lors que ce choix était ouvert à l'une et l'autre des parties, sous la condition qu'elle soit la plus diligente, la clause litigieuse ne constitue pas une clause compromissoire au sens de l'article 1442 du Code de procédure civile. Par conséquent, est inopérante l'invocation des règles et principes de l'arbitrage, dont le principe compétence compétence qui réserve à l'arbitre l'interprétation de la clause compromissoire (et donc son opposabilité) qui ferait échec à la compétence des juridictions françaises.

Il appartient à l'appelante, qui revendique l'application de la clause attributive de juridiction, d'établir qu'elle a été acceptée au moment de la formation du contrat. Or en l'espèce, la société intimée est tiers aux conventions invoquées signées l'une et l'autre par la société NDBM1. De stipulations expresses, les conventions limitent leurs effets aux parties entendues comme les signataires et leur cessionnaire, successeurs ou ayants droit autorisés, et excluent qu'un tiers puisse acquérir un droit quelconque. Elles contiennent également une clause de confidentialité qui s'étend à l'existence et aux termes du contrat et qui ne peut être levée qu'avec l'accord écrit de la société appelante, incompatible avec l'allégation d'une acceptation de la convention pour l'ensemble des sociétés d'un groupe qui ne pourraient e prendre connaissance.

De surcroît, aucune référence n'est faite à la convention de concessionnaire (non exclusif) dans les documents relatifs à la vente entre les sociétés, qui plus est, renvoie aux incoterms 2010. Les autres éléments retenus par l'appelante ne viennent que caractériser l'appartenance à un même groupe – communauté de dirigeant, livraison aux dires de l'appelante au siège social de la société mère – mais sont inopérants pour justifier de l'acceptation de la société en question de la clause de juridiction signée par une société tierce.

Enfin, en application de l'article 67-1 de l'accord sur le retrait du Royaume-Uni de Grande-Bretagne et d'Irlande du nord de l'Union européenne, les dispositions relatives à la compétence du règlement (UE) n° 1215/2012 du 12 décembre 2012 continuent à s'appliquer aux actions judiciaires, comme en l'espèce, intentées avant la fin de la période de transition et les procédures ou demandes liées à de telles actions judiciaires.

– Paris, Pôle 4 – Chambre 10, 1er juillet 2021, n° 21/01799, *Mclaren Automotive c. Ndl Paris*

•

Clause compromissoire – Parties – Signataire – Partie prenante – Liens étroits – Caractère indivisible – Inapplicabilité manifeste – Article 1448 CPC – Nullité manifeste – Responsabilité délictuelle – Principe de compétence compétence

30-Le tribunal de commerce a ensuite considéré, répondant au moyen soulevé, que la société, « *bien que non-signataire du SPA* » était « *partie prenante à l'opération de transfert* », ajoutant par ailleurs que cette société était aussi « *favorable au traitement du litige dans le cadre compromissoire prévu par le SPA* ».

31-Ainsi, après avoir constaté les liens étroits entre « *les éléments du litige* » et l'opération de transfert d'activité, le tribunal a pu écarter les arguments tirés de ce que les produits d'excavations ne « *puissent ne pas être en lien direct avec les activités transférées, le fait que la motivation de l'action porte sur la responsabilité quasi-délictuelle des défenderesses et non sur l'application directe du contrat SPA, le fait enfin que la société ne soit pas directement partie au SPA* ».

32-Enfin, il ne résulte pas du jugement une contradiction entre les motifs et le dispositif, le tribunal ayant simplement tiré les conséquences du caractère indivisible de l'opération qu'il a constaté, pour considérer dans son dispositif que la clause compromissoire n'était pas manifestement inapplicable pour statuer sur « les demandes » formulées.

33-Au regard de ces éléments, le jugement du tribunal de commerce n'encourt pas le grief de défaut ou de contradiction de motifs de telle sorte que la demande tendant à voir annuler ce jugement sera rejetée.

Sur le forum compétent pour connaître du litige ;

43-En application des articles 1448 du Code de procédure civile « *Lorsqu'un litige relevant d'une convention d'arbitrage est porté devant une juridiction de l'État, celle-ci se déclare incompétente sauf si le tribunal arbitral n'est pas encore saisi et si la convention d'arbitrage est manifestement nulle ou manifestement inapplicable* ».

44-En l'espèce, l'action engagée devant le tribunal de commerce de Paris vise à engager la responsabilité délictuelle des sociétés défenderesses au recours au titre de la pollution du carreau J1 situé sur la plateforme chimique de Pont de Claix et obtenir la réparation des dommages subis qu'elles indiquent avoir subis.

[...]

54-Au regard de l'ensemble de ces éléments, dont il ne ressort pas de manière manifeste, une inapplicabilité de la convention d'arbitrage tant à raison de la matière qu'à raison des parties au litige, il appartient prioritairement au tribunal arbitral de se prononcer sur sa compétence.

55-En conséquence, le jugement du tribunal de commerce de Paris sera confirmé.

– Paris, Chambre commerciale internationale, Pôle 5 – Chambre 16, 6 juillet 2021, n° 21/03597, *Novacid, Seqens, c. Rhodia Operations et Rhodia Chimie*

Sentence arbitrale – Exequatur – Procédure – Cas d'ouverture – Ordre public international – Violation – Heurte de manière manifeste, effective et concrète – Principes et valeurs – Motivation – Procès équitable – Conception française – Révision au fond – Dommages et intérêts – Contrôle – Mission – Étendue – Préjudices – Dommages et intérêts punitifs – Disproportion – Violation manifeste, effective et concrète

18-En application de l'article 1525 du Code de procédure civile, « *La décision qui statue sur une demande de reconnaissance ou d'exequatur d'une sentence arbitrale rendue à l'étranger est susceptible d'appel (...) La cour d'appel ne peut refuser la reconnaissance ou l'exequatur de la sentence arbitrale que dans les cas prévus à l'article 1520* ».

19-Selon l'article 1520 de ce même code, le recours en annulation n'est ouvert que si : 1° Le tribunal arbitral s'est déclaré à tort compétent ou incompétent ; ou 2° Le tribunal arbitral a été irrégulièrement constitué ; ou 3° Le tribunal arbitral a statué sans se conformer à la mission qui lui avait été confiée ; ou 4° Le principe de la contradiction n'a pas été respecté ; ou 5° La reconnaissance ou l'exécution de la sentence est contraire à l'ordre public international.

Sur le seul moyen tiré de la violation de l'ordre public international (article 1520, 5° du Code de procédure civile)

20-Le contrôle exercé par le juge de l'annulation pour la défense de l'ordre public international s'attache seulement à examiner si l'exécution des dispositions prises par le tribunal arbitral heurte de manière manifeste, effective et concrète les principes et valeurs compris dans l'ordre public international.

Sur le non-respect de l'obligation de motivation

21-L'exigence de motivation des décisions de justice est un élément du droit à un procès équitable.

22-Les arbitres qui s'abstiennent de motiver leur décision méconnaissent l'étendue de leur mission et la reconnaissance d'une sentence dépourvue de motif heurte la conception française de l'ordre public international.

[...]

27-En conséquence au terme de son raisonnement sur lequel il n'appartient pas à la cour de porter une appréciation, il a fait entièrement droit à la demande de la banque BDK pour ce qui concerne sa réclamation au titre des engagements contractuels comme indiqué dans son dispositif.

28-Il résulte de ce qui précède que la condamnation est motivée.

29-Les critiques de l'appelant dont il sera souligné qu'il n'a formé aucune observation devant le tribunal arbitral « *n'ayant jamais transmis au tribunal de demandes et prétentions* » portent en réalité sur le fond et sur ce qui a été jugé par le tribunal arbitral dont la révision par le juge de l'annulation est interdite.

[...]

36-Le principe d'une condamnation au paiement de dommages-intérêts punitifs, n'est pas, en soi, contraire à l'ordre public international français.

37-Il en est autrement lorsque le montant alloué est disproportionné au regard du préjudice subi et des manquements aux obligations contractuelles du débiteur.

[...]

42-En tout état de cause, il ne ressort pas de ces éléments une violation manifeste effective et concrète de l'ordre public international français.

43-Ce moyen sera en conséquence écarté.

– Paris, Chambre commerciale internationale, Pôle 5 – Chambre 16, 6 juillet 2021, n° 21/21216, *X c. BDK Financial Group*

Recours en annulation – Sentence rendue à l'étranger – Appel nullité – Ordonnance d'exequatur – Fin de non-recevoir – Cas d'ouverture – Ordre public international – Définition – Contrôle – Violation manifeste, effective et concrète – Principes et valeurs – Transaction – Autorité de la chose jugée – Décisions inconciliables – Définition – Annulation dans le pays d'origine – Décision de justice internationale – Sentence internationale – Détachée de tout ordre juridique – Révision au fond – Instance arbitrale – Impartialité

et indépendance – Obligation de révélation – Doute raisonnable – FINRA – Recommandation – Institution arbitrale – Règlement – Centre d'arbitrage – Obligation de divulgation – Intérêts financiers ou personnels – Obligation renforcée – Faits antérieurs – Connaissance – Omission Principe d'égalité – Droits de la défense – Fraude – Anti-suit – Juridictions américaines – Juridiction française – Contrôle

24. Il convient de rappeler que le seul recours ouvert contre une ordonnance d'exequatur d'une sentence rendue à l'étranger est l'appel prévu par l'article 1525 du Code de procédure civile, et la cour ne peut refuser la reconnaissance ou l'exequatur que dans les cas prévus à l'article 1520 de ce code qui vise la sentence elle-même et non l'ordonnance qui accorde l'exequatur, laquelle n'est donc susceptible, en tant que telle, d'aucun recours.

25. Il en résulte que sauf appel-nullité pour excès de pouvoir ou violation d'un principe essentiel de procédure, ce qui n'est pas soutenu en l'espèce, l'appel de l'ordonnance d'exequatur n'est ouvert que dans les cas limitativement énumérés à l'article 1520 du même code à savoir si : – Le tribunal arbitral s'est déclaré à tort compétent ou incompétent ou – Le tribunal arbitral a été irrégulièrement constitué ou – Le tribunal arbitral a statué sans se conformer à la mission qui lui avait été confiée ou – Le principe de la contradiction n'a pas été respecté, ou – La reconnaissance ou l'exécution de la sentence est contraire à l'ordre public international.

26. En l'espèce, les fins de non-recevoir soulevées ne portant que sur la recevabilité de la requête aux fins d'exequatur ne constituent pas un des cas d'ouverture de l'appel contre une ordonnance d'exequatur.

27. Il y a lieu par conséquent de rejeter la demande d'annulation sur ce fondement.

Sur l'infirmation de l'ordonnance d'exequatur au regard de l'article 1520 du Code de procédure civile

• *Sur le moyen tiré de la contrariété de la sentence à l'ordre public international (article 1520, 5° du Code de procédure civile)*

30. Il résulte par renvoi de l'article 1525 du Code de procédure civile rappelé ci-dessus que l'appel des ordonnances d'exequatur est limité aux moyens de recours prévus à l'article 1520, et qu'aux termes de l'article 1520, 5° du même code le recours en annulation est ouvert si la reconnaissance ou l'exécution de la sentence est contraire à l'ordre public international.

31. L'ordre public international au regard duquel s'effectue le contrôle du juge de l'annulation s'entend de la conception qu'en a l'ordre juridique français, c'est-à-dire des valeurs et des principes dont celui-ci ne saurait souffrir la méconnaissance même dans un contexte international.

32. Le contrôle exercé par le juge de l'annulation ou le juge de l'appel de l'ordonnance d'exequatur pour la défense de l'ordre public international s'attache seulement à examiner si l'exécution des dispositions prises par le tribunal arbitral heurte de manière manifeste, effective et concrète les principes et valeurs compris dans l'ordre public international.

[...]

34. Cependant, une méconnaissance de l'autorité de chose jugée par une sentence, ne constitue pas en soi une violation de l'ordre public international.

35. Seule la reconnaissance ou l'exécution d'une sentence inconciliable avec une décision de justice interne ou étrangère précédemment revêtue en France de l'exequatur est susceptible de violer de manière manifeste, effective et concrète l'ordre public international étant précisé que sont inconciliables des décisions de justice entraînant des conséquences juridiques qui s'excluent mutuellement.

36. À cet égard, en l'espèce, la sentence arbitrale litigieuse n'est inconciliable avec aucune décision rendue en France et aucune des décisions rendues par les juridictions américaines ayant constaté l'existence d'une transaction entre les parties n'a été revêtue de l'exequatur en France.

37. Par ailleurs, le fait que plusieurs juridictions américaines aient jugé qu'il y avait eu une transaction et aient annulé la sentence litigieuse est sans effet sur la présente procédure de reconnaissance de ladite sentence dans l'ordre juridique français.

38. En effet, les dispositions du droit français de l'arbitrage international ne prévoient pas comme cas de recours contre l'ordonnance d'exequatur que l'annulation de la sentence dans son pays d'origine constitue une cause de refus de reconnaissance et d'exécution de la sentence en France.

39. En outre, il est constant qu'une sentence internationale qui n'est rattachée à aucun ordre juridique étatique est une décision de justice internationale dont la régularité est examinée au regard des règles applicables dans le pays où sa reconnaissance et son exécution sont demandées et non au regard des règles du pays dans lequel elle a été rendue.

[…]

42. Or, il ne rentre pas dans les pouvoirs de la cour de rejuger le fond.

43. Dès lors le moyen tiré de la violation de l'article 1520-5° du Code de procédure civile doit être rejeté.

• *Sur le moyen tiré du défaut d'impartialité des arbitres (article 1520, 2° et 5° du Code de procédure civile)*

[...]

Sur le grief tiré du défaut d'impartialité au soutien d'un moyen fondé sur la constitution irrégulière du tribunal arbitral (article 1520, 2°).

51. Selon l'article 1520, 2° du Code de procédure civile, le recours en annulation est ouvert si le tribunal arbitral a été irrégulièrement constitué.

52. Aux termes de l'article 1456 al 2 du Code de procédure civile, applicable à l'arbitrage international en vertu de l'article 1506 du même code « *Il appartient à l'arbitre, avant d'accepter sa mission, de révéler toute circonstance susceptible d'affecter son indépendance ou son impartialité. Il lui est également fait obligation de révéler sans délai toute circonstance de même nature qui pourrait naître après l'acceptation de sa mission.* »

53. Il convient de rappeler que si dans le cadre de l'examen de ce moyen, il est utile de déterminer le contenu de l'obligation de révélation imposée à un arbitre, le non-respect de cette obligation ne suffit pas en soi à caractériser un défaut d'indépendance ou d'impartialité.

Encore faut-il que ce défaut soit de nature à provoquer dans l'esprit des parties un doute raisonnable quant à l'impartialité et à l'indépendance de l'arbitre, c'est-à-dire un doute qui peut naître chez une personne placée dans la même situation et ayant accès aux mêmes éléments d'information raisonnablement accessibles.

54. En l'espèce, l'arbitrage ayant été rendu sous l'égide de la FINRA, il convient notamment de se référer aux recommandations émises sur cette question par ce centre d'arbitrage pour préciser le contenu de l'obligation de révélation imposée aux arbitres.

55. À cet égard, il ressort de Règlement applicable pour les arbitrages FINRA (Financial Industry Regulatory Authorithy) ayant régi l'arbitrage qui a donné lieu à la sentence querellée du 30 juillet 2013, et du guide élaboré par cet organisme (FINRA Dispute resolution Arbitrator'Guide) qu'il appartient à l'arbitre désigné d'être « impartial *en apparence et dans les faits* » et que plusieurs diligences sont imposées à l'arbitre et notamment celles prévoyant que « *Les arbitres soumettent des informations biographiques détaillées au moment où ils soumettent une demande pour faire partie de la liste des arbitres de la FINRA. Les informations recueillies à partir de la demande sont compilées pour créer un rapport de divulgation de l'arbitre (rapport de divulgation). Pendant le processus de sélection de la liste, les parties ont la possibilité d'examiner le rapport de divulgation des arbitres sélectionnés au hasard pour un service potentiel. Le rapport de divulgation énumère les sentences antérieures de la FINRA rendues par l'arbitre, ainsi que les affaires actuelles auxquels l'arbitre est désigné* » (« *submit detailed biographical information at the time they submit an application to join FINRA's arbitrator roster. The information collected from the application is compiled to create an Arbitrator Disclosure Report (Disclosure Report). During the list selection process, the parties are given the opportunity to review the Disclosure Report of the arbitrators randomly listed for potential service. The Disclosure Report lists previous FINRA awards rendered by the arbitrator, and also lists the current cases to which the arbitrator is assigned* »).

56. De même ce guide mentionne que : « *Afin de s'assurer que les rapports de divulgation des arbitres sont exacts et à jour, la FINRA enverra aux arbitres leur rapport de divulgation chaque fois que l'arbitre sera, nommé pour une affaire. Il est extrêmement important que les arbitres mettent à jour leurs, rapports de divulgation fréquemment. « La divulgation de l'arbitre est la pierre angulaire de l'arbitrage de la FINRA, et l'obligation de divulgation de l'arbitre est continue et impérative. La divulgation comprend toute relation, expérience et information de base qui peut affecter – ou même sembler affecter – la capacité de l'arbitre à être impartial et la conviction des parties que l'arbitre sera capable de rendre une décision équitable. Lorsqu'ils font des divulgations, les arbitres doivent prendre en compte tous les aspects de leur vie professionnelle et personnelle et divulguer tous les liens entre l'arbitre, les parties et la question en litige, aussi éloignés qu'ils puissent paraître. Si vous devez vous demander si une divulgation est appropriée alors elle l'est : faites la divulgation (...)* ». (« *In order to ensure that the arbitrators' Disclosure Reports are accurate and up-to-date, FINRA will send the arbitrators their Disclosure Report each time the arbitrator is appointed to a case. It is extremely important that arbitrators update their Disclosure Reports frequently. « Arbitrator disclosure is the cornerstone of FINRA arbitration, and the arbitrator's duty to disclose is continuous and imperative. Disclosure includes any relationship, experience and background information that may affect – or even appear to affect – the arbitrator's ability to be impartial and the parties' belief that the arbitrator will be able to render a fair decision. When making disclosures, arbitrators should consider all aspects of their professional and personal lives and disclose all ties between the arbitrator, the parties and the matter in dispute, no matter how remote they may*

seem. If you need to think about whether a disclosure is appropriate, then it is : make the disclosure (…) »).

57. À cet égard, il est aussi rappelé dans le guide précité que « *la règle 12405 de la FINRA exige que les arbitres divulguent tout intérêt financier ou personnel, direct ou indirect, dans l'issue de l'arbitrage, ainsi que toute relation existante ou passée, directe ou indirecte, financière, commerciale, professionnelle, familiale, sociale ou autre, avec l'une des parties, les représentants, les témoins ou les co-arbitres. L'obligation de divulgation est permanente. Par conséquent, les arbitres sont également tenus de faire continuellement des efforts raisonnables pour s'informer des relations et des intérêts, y compris des changements dans leur emploi, leurs fonctions ou leurs clients, ou ceux des membres de leur famille immédiate, car ces faits peuvent entraîner un changement de leur classification en tant qu'arbitre public ou non public* » (« *FINRA Rule 12405 requires arbitrators to disclose any direct or indirect financial or personal interest in the outcome of the arbitration, as well as any existing or past, direct or indirect, financial, business, professional, family, social or other relationships with any of the parties, representatives, witnesses or co-panelists. The duty to disclose is ongoing. Therefore, arbitrators are also required to continually make reasonable efforts to inform themselves of relationships andinterests including changes in their or their immediate family member's3 employment, job functions or clients since these facts can result in a change to their classification as a public or non-public arbitrator* »).

58. Enfin, il ressort de ce même Guide qu'une « *fois qu'un arbitre a accepté sa nomination, la FINRA lui envoie le serment d'arbitre (serment), qui comprend la liste de contrôle de la divulgation de l'arbitre (liste de contrôle)* ». Cette liste comprenait dans sa version de 2010 une série de 33 questions auxquelles l'arbitre était tenu de répondre par oui ou par non.

59. Parmi plusieurs autres, figuraient notamment les questions suivantes :

60. Question n°4 : « Avez-vous eu des relations professionnelles ou sociales avec les avocats de l'une des parties à cette procédure ou avec le cabinet pour lequel ils travaillent ? » (*Have you had any profesionnel or social relationships with counsel for any party in this proceeding or the firm for which they work ?*).

61. Question n° 5 : « *Avez-vous eu des relations professionnelles ou sociales avec l'une des parties à cette procédure ou avec l'entreprise pour laquelle elle travaille ?* » (« *Have you had any profesionnel or social relationships with any party in this proceeding or the firm for which they work ?* »).

62. Question n° 7 : « *avez-vous servi d'arbitre dans une procédure dans laquelle l'un des témoins identifiés ou l'une des parties nommées a témoigné ?* » (« *Have you served as an arbitrator in a proceeding in which any of the identified witnesses or named parties gave testimony ?* »).

63. Question n°8 : « *Est-ce que vous, votre conjoint ou un membre de votre famille immédiate avez tenu un compte individuellement, conjointement ou à titre bénéficiaire auprès d'une société de courtage nommée dans cette procédure ?* » (« *Have you, your spouse, or any member of your immediate family maintained an account individually, jointly, or beneficially with a brockerage firm named in this proceeding ?* »).

64. Question n° 12 : « *Avez-vous déjà été nommé comme partie par un investisseur dans un procès civil ou une procédure d'arbitrage ?* » (« *Have you ever been named as a party by an investor in any civil lawsuit or arbitration proceeding ?* »).

65. Question 19 : « *Votre conduite a-t-elle été mise en cause dans une procédure d'arbitrage ou de litige (autre qu'une procédure dans laquelle vous avez servi d'arbitre) ?* (« *Has your conduct been an issue in an arbitration or litigation proceeding (other than a proceeeding in which you served as an arbitrator) ?* »).

66. Question n° 26 : « *Faites-vous actuellement office d'arbitre dans une autre affaire impliquant une partie ou un avocat dans cette procédure ou le cabinet pour lequel ils travaillent ? » (Are you presently serving as an arbitrator in another matter involving any party or counsel in this proceeding or the firm for which they work ?)*

67. Il ressort de ces recommandations que l'obligation de divulgation de l'arbitre dans le cadre d'un arbitrage FINRA est très large puisqu'elle porte, s'agissant de ses rapports avec l'une des parties, leurs représentants, les témoins ou les co-arbitres, sur tout intérêt ou toute relation directe ou indirecte existante ou passée, avec ces derniers, mais vise aussi, hors les rapports avec ces personnes, à connaître les situations et/ou comportement de chaque arbitre dans le passé et notamment les éventuels litiges et procédures dans lesquels ils ont été impliqués (autres que celles pour lesquelles ils étaient arbitres).

68. C'est à la lumière de ces considérations qu'il convient d'apprécier en l'espèce, si les arbitres ont satisfait à leur obligation de divulgation selon les règles FINRA et, si en cas de non-respect de cette obligation, ce manquement était susceptible de créer dans l'esprit des recourants un doute raisonnable sur leur impartialité.

S'agissant de la remise en cause de l'impartialité d'un arbitre ;

[...]

70. Il convient d'observer en premier lieu que tous les faits allégués susceptibles d'être la cause d'un manque d'impartialité allégué sont antérieurs à la déclaration qu'il a déposée le 12 juin 2010 accompagnée de la réponse au questionnaire qu'il a complété conformément au règlement FINRA.

71. En outre, il ressort du questionnaire évoqué ci-dessus qu'à la question n° 12 précitée, l'arbitre a bien répondu par l'affirmative de sorte que les recourants connaissaient cette information et pouvaient dès lors solliciter de l'arbitre des compléments et précisions si elles l'avaient jugé nécessaires au regard de doute qu'elle pouvait nourrir quant à son impartialité.

[...]

81. En l'état de ces éléments, qui ne permettent pas de caractériser un doute raisonnable sur l'existence de préjugés ou de partis pris susceptibles d'affecter le jugement de l'arbitre et ainsi son impartialité, le grief sera rejeté.

S'agissant de la remise en cause de l'impartialité de Mme l'arbitre ;

[...]

En l'état de l'absence de tout élément précis et vérifiable, cette seule omission, à la supposer établie, n'est pas de nature à créer un doute raisonnable sur le défaut d'impartialité de Mme l'arbitre.

[...]

89. Ces deux plaintes antérieures à sa déclaration, auraient pu justifier de la part de Mme l'arbitre une divulgation dans le cadre de cet arbitrage ou à tout le moins une réponse positive à la question n° 19 précitée qui pouvait laisser place à des précisions complémentaires suscitées par les parties.

90. Cependant, l'omission n'est pas de nature à créer un doute raisonnable sur son impartialité.

[...]

94. En l'état de ces éléments, qui ne permettent de caractériser un doute raisonnable sur l'existence de préjugés ou de partis pris susceptibles d'affecter le jugement de Mme l'arbitre et ainsi son impartialité, le grief sera rejeté.

Sur le grief tiré du défaut d'impartialité au soutien d'un moyen fondé sur la contrariété à l'ordre public international (article 1520, 5°).

95. Selon l'article 1520-5° du Code de procédure civile, le recours en annulation est ouvert si la reconnaissance ou l'exécution de la sentence est contraire à l'ordre public international.

96. En cas de défaut d'impartialité d'un arbitre, l'exécution de la sentence en France peut être refusée sur le fondement de la contrariété à l'ordre public international, dès lors qu'une sentence rendue par un arbitre dont le défaut d'impartialité serait établi porterait atteinte au principe d'égalité entre les parties et aux droits de la défense, et ce faisant heurterait l'ordre public international.

97. Il appartient au juge d'apprécier l'impartialité de l'arbitre en relevant toute circonstance de nature à affecter le jugement de celui-ci et à provoquer dans l'esprit des parties un doute raisonnable sur cette qualité qui est de l'essence de la fonction arbitrale.

98. À la lumière des éléments relevés ci-dessus, il convient de considérer que les circonstances relevées par les recourants ne permettent pas de caractériser un défaut d'impartialité des arbitres et ni d'établir que la sentence rendue porte une atteinte au principe d'égalité entre les parties et aux droits de la défense.

99. Ce moyen sera en conséquence rejeté.

Sur les demandes indemnitaires

[...]

Sur la demande de dommages-intérêts

[...]

106. Il n'est pas démontré que les voies de droit utilisées procèdent d'une fraude ou d'une intention dolosive, quand bien même les effets d'une « *anti-suit injunction* » obtenue légalement devant les juridictions américaines auraient eu des effets extra-territoriaux qui lui auraient porté préjudice.

107. De même, il n'appartient pas à la juridiction française de se prononcer sur la validité ou l'abus des procédures de « contempt of court » américaines dont il a été l'objet devant les juridictions de l'État de New York, sa stratégie de défense aux États-Unis n'étant pas soumise à l'appréciation des tribunaux français, seules les juridictions américaines pouvant rétracter ou maintenir les effets d'une telle décision.

– Paris, Chambre commerciale internationale, Pôle 5 – Chambre 16, 12 juillet 2021, n° 19/11413, *Citigroup global markets inc. c. X*

Conseil d'État – Sentence arbitrale rendue en France – Recours en annulation – Personne morale de droit public – Commerce international – Cas d'ouverture – Intérêts du commerce international – Contrôle – Contrôle d'office – Convention d'arbitrage – Licéité – Régularité de la procédure – Ordre public – Tribunal arbitral – Compétence – Mission – Principe du caractère contradictoire

– Motivation – Droit administratif – Vice d'une particulière gravité – Contrôle au fond – Objet illicite – Personnes publiques – Prérogatives – Intérêt général – Règles d'ordre public du droit de l'Union européenne – Exequatur

3. Lorsqu'il est saisi d'un recours dirigé contre une sentence arbitrale rendue en France dans un litige né de l'exécution ou de la rupture d'un contrat conclu entre une personne morale de droit public française et une personne de droit étranger, exécuté sur le territoire français mais mettant en jeu les intérêts du commerce international, il appartient au Conseil d'État de s'assurer, le cas échéant d'office, de la licéité de la convention d'arbitrage, qu'il s'agisse d'une clause compromissoire ou d'un compromis. Ne peuvent en outre être utilement soulevés devant lui que des moyens tirés, d'une part, de ce que la sentence a été rendue dans des conditions irrégulières et, d'autre part, de ce qu'elle est contraire à l'ordre public. S'agissant de la régularité de la procédure, en l'absence de règles procédurales applicables aux instances arbitrales relevant de la compétence de la juridiction administrative, une sentence arbitrale ne peut être regardée comme rendue dans des conditions irrégulières que si le tribunal arbitral s'est déclaré à tort compétent ou incompétent, s'il a été irrégulièrement composé, notamment au regard des principes d'indépendance et d'impartialité, s'il n'a pas statué conformément à la mission qui lui avait été confiée, s'il a méconnu le principe du caractère contradictoire de la procédure ou s'il n'a pas motivé sa sentence. S'agissant du contrôle sur le fond, une sentence arbitrale est contraire à l'ordre public lorsqu'elle fait application d'un contrat dont l'objet est illicite ou entaché d'un vice d'une particulière gravité relatif notamment aux conditions dans lesquelles les parties ont donné leur consentement, lorsqu'elle méconnaît des règles auxquelles les personnes publiques ne peuvent déroger, telles que notamment l'interdiction de consentir des libéralités, d'aliéner le domaine public ou de renoncer aux prérogatives dont ces personnes disposent dans l'intérêt général au cours de l'exécution du contrat, ou lorsqu'elle méconnaît les règles d'ordre public du droit de l'Union européenne.

[...]

7. Il résulte de tout ce qui précède que les sociétés requérantes ne sont pas fondées à demander l'annulation de la sentence qu'elles attaquent.

8. Par dérogation aux dispositions de l'article L. 311-1 du Code de justice administrative, le rejet par le Conseil d'État d'une demande d'annulation d'une sentence arbitrale rendue en France dans un litige né de l'exécution ou de la rupture d'un contrat exécuté sur le territoire français mais mettant en jeu les intérêts du commerce international confère l'exequatur à cette sentence.

9. Par suite, le rejet, par la présente décision, de la demande tendant à l'annulation de la sentence arbitrale du 24 juin 2020 a pour effet de conférer l'exequatur à cette sentence.

– Conseil d'État, (Section du contentieux, 7e et 2e chambres réunies), 20 juillet 2021, n° 443342, *Tecnimont SpA et TCM Fr c. Fosmax*

Arbitrage Federation of Cocoa Commerce – Clause compromissoire – Compétence – Sursis à statuer – Autonomie de la clause – Caractère manifestement inapplicable ou nul – Principe de compétence compétence

– Socle contractuel – Étendue – Question de fond – Arbitres – Liste – Règles de la FCC – Indépendance et impartialité – Parties – Renonciation – Valeur

Sur la demande de sursis à statuer

De manière très laconique, les appelantes font valoir qu'elles contestent la compétence de la Federation of Cocoa Commerce mais qu'elles ont néanmoins saisi cette institution. Elles en déduisent qu'il serait d'une bonne administration de la justice d'apprécier le litige en tenant compte de cette décision à intervenir.

S'il n'est pas contesté qu'elles ont saisi l'instance arbitrale, l'acte de saisine n'est pas produit. Il n'est donné aucun élément sur ses termes, puisque les appelantes maintiennent contester le principe même de cette compétence arbitrale, sur la date de saisine et sur le déroulement de la procédure en cours. Ceci constitue une première difficulté pour apprécier la pertinence d'un sursis à statuer.

Mais surtout, la cour est saisie de l'appel compétence de la décision du tribunal de commerce s'étant déclaré incompétent, une clause compromissoire ayant été invoquée. Il appartient à la cour de statuer uniquement dans les limites de l'appel compétence et la cour ne peut s'en remettre à la décision de l'instance arbitrale qui obéit à d'autres règles. La demande de sursis à statuer sera donc rejetée.

[…]

Mais surtout, la cour ne peut que rappeler le principe d'autonomie de la clause compromissoire. Cette autonomie juridique exclut, sauf stipulation contraire, qu'elle puisse être affectée par l'inefficacité de l'acte dans lequel elle est insérée.

La cour ne peut ainsi que constater que les appelantes entendent se prévaloir d'un contrat qui contient une clause compromissoire par laquelle les parties, en cas de litige, entendaient recourir à l'arbitrage conformément aux règles d'arbitrage et d'appel de la FCC. Si elles soutiennent qu'elles fondent leurs demandes sur des courriers postérieurs, le socle contractuel initial ainsi qu'il résulte de leur propre argumentation était bien les contrats incluant la clause compromissoire. Or, l'existence, la validité ou le maintien en vigueur de la convention d'arbitrage ne dépendent pas du sort du contrat principal auquel cette convention se réfère. Seule la juridiction qui sera compétente pourra envisager la validité ou même l'existence de la convention entre les parties mais la cour, au stade de la compétence, ne peut que constater qu'il existe une clause compromissoire.

Le seul élément qui puisse dès lors y faire obstacle serait son caractère manifestement nul ou inapplicable au sens de l'article 1448 du Code de procédure civile.

Le point de savoir si l'opération litigieuse portait sur une vente ou sur une opération de spéculation relève du fond et non pas de la compétence et ne saurait rendre la clause manifestement inapplicable, la cour n'ayant pas à apprécier si la compétence de la Federation of Cocoa Commerce s'étend à une opération spéculative.

La seule question qui subsiste est celle de l'absence d'indépendance et de la partialité invoquée de l'ensemble des arbitres de la Federation of Cocoa Commerce. Les appelantes considèrent ainsi qu'aucun des arbitres de la dite Federation ne pourrait accepter la mission de sorte qu'il ne peut y avoir d'arbitre impartial de désigné.

Mais alors que les appelantes doivent établir le caractère manifestement inapplicable de la clause, elles procèdent très largement par affirmations. Si elles font valoir que le dirigeant de la société intimée est membre de la section commerce de la Federation of Cocoa Commerce, elles indiquent également qu'il existe 44 arbitres élus. Dès lors, les liens qui peuvent exister avec 2 ou 3 des arbitres, comme invoqué dans les écritures, ne sont pas de nature à paralyser la mise en œuvre de la clause et par là même de la rendre manifestement inapplicable.

[...] Au-delà des observations de l'intimée sur la rédaction des courriers par un non-juriste, qui sont sans portée à ce stade, il apparaît que la question de savoir si le contrat pouvait être annulé, résilié ou même s'il pouvait s'appliquer relève du fond et que l'absence de toute référence à la clause compromissoire dans les courriers de 2018 ne saurait s'analyser comme une renonciation à son bénéfice. Il s'agit là encore de l'application du principe d'autonomie de la clause compromissoire.

C'est ainsi à juste titre que les premiers juges, faisant application de la clause compromissoire, se sont déclarés incompétents et ont renvoyé les parties à mieux se pourvoir.

Le jugement sera confirmé.

– Bordeaux, 4e Chambre civile, 27 juillet 2021, n° 21/00806, *société Africa Sourcing Côte d'Ivoire et société Africa Sourcing Cameroun limited c. Lbms*

Clause compromissoire – Contrat d'agent – Contrat d'adhésion – FIFA – Loi dans le temps – Contrat type – Caractère international – Critère – Fait générateur – Champ d'application –

Le litige étant né avant l'entrée en vigueur du nouveau règlement, le contrat de médiation ayant en effet été résilié par M. A le 8 décembre 2014, il demeure régi par le règlement adopté par le comité exécutif de la FIFA le 29 octobre 2007, entré en vigueur le 1er janvier 2008, alors applicable.

Le contrat type constituant l'annexe 3 dudit règlement prévoit, in fine, que « *les parties acceptent de soumettre toute demande à la juridiction de l'association compétente ou de la FIFA. Le recours devant les tribunaux ordinaires est interdit sauf disposition spéciale expresse contenue dans la réglementation de la FIFA* ».

Il résulte des dispositions précitées que le contrat type est impératif et s'impose aux parties qui ont seulement la possibilité de le compléter par un accord spécial supplémentaire conforme aux principes énoncés dans le Règlement (cf. article 4 du contrat type intitulé « accords supplémentaires ») mais non pas d'y déroger, les dispositions qu'il prévoit ayant ainsi nécessairement vocation à s'appliquer en cas de silence des parties.

En application tant de la clause ci-dessus rappelée, que de l'article 7 du code de déontologie que l'agent de joueur est tenu de respecter, qui énonce : « *conformément aux statuts de la FIFA, l'agent de joueurs ne peut pas porter de litige devant un tribunal ordinaire et il est tenu de soumettre toute demande à la juridiction de l'association ou de la FIFA* », le litige ne pouvait être porté par l'appelante devant le tribunal de grande instance de Strasbourg, sauf disposition spéciale expresse contenue dans la réglementation de la FIFA.

À cet égard, la société invoque la jurisprudence du tribunal arbitral de Lausanne, de la Chambre de résolution des litiges de la FIFA et de la commission de discipline qui déclinent leur compétence en cas de litige relatif au paiement d'une commission d'agent dans un contexte national.

Si la dimension internationale du litige apparaît en l'espèce faire défaut, M. A ayant en effet la nationalité française, le contrat ayant été conclu à Strasbourg avec une société alors établie en France, et M. étant agent licencié en France, la société demanderesse admet cependant qu'un litige entre un agent licencié et un joueur français peut être porté devant la Fédération française de football. C'est toutefois à tort qu'elle considère, en l'espèce, que la compétence de l'association nationale serait exclue s'agissant d'un litige ayant pour fait générateur la signature d'un contrat de travail avec un club néerlandais, le litige concernant non pas le contrat de travail liant le joueur professionnel au club qui est son employeur, mais l'exécution et les conditions de la rupture du contrat de médiation liant le joueur à son agent.

Le tribunal de grande instance étant, en l'état des dispositions applicables, non pas incompétent mais dépourvu du pouvoir juridictionnel de connaître du litige qui devait être soumis aux instances de l'association compétente ou le cas échéant de la FIFA, les demandes de la société doivent donc être déclarées irrecevables et le jugement confirmé sur ce point, par ces motifs substitués à ceux du premier juge.

– Colmar, 2e Chambre civile, 3 août 2021, n° 2 A 19/03374, *FLM et a. c. X*

Clause compromissoire – Recours en annulation – Tribunal arbitral – Compétence – Contrôle entier – Règle matérielle de droit international de l'arbitrage – Autonomie de la clause – Volonté des parties – Règle impérative – Ordre public international – Loi étrangère – Règlement ICC – Compétence ratione materiae – Compétence ratione personae – Bénéficiaire – Instance arbitrale – Constitution – Moyen tardif – Corruption – Agent public – Définition – Violation – Consensus international – Violation manifeste effective et concrète – Indices – Faisceau d'indices – Graves, précis et concordants – Accumulation – Fraude fiscale – Preuve matérielle – Climat général – Autorité publique – Inaction – Principe de la contradiction – Définition – Mission – Cas d'ouverture – Article 1509 CPC – Article 31 ICC Règlement – Motivation – Contrôle de la Cour – Argumentation – Pertinence – Juge de l'annulation – Pouvoirs

27 – Selon l'article 1520, 1°, du Code de procédure civile, le recours en annulation est ouvert si le tribunal s'est déclaré à tort compétent ou incompétent.

28 – Le juge de l'annulation contrôle la décision du tribunal arbitral sur sa compétence, qu'il se soit déclaré compétent ou incompétent, en recherchant tous les éléments de droit ou de fait permettant d'apprécier la portée de la convention d'arbitrage.

29 – En l'espèce, l'article 17 de l'accord de partenariat conclu en 2009 est ainsi rédigé : « *À défaut d'accord amiable entre les Parties dans un délai de six (6) mois suivant la date de survenance du litige, tout différend de toute nature, y incluant les Annexes et les éventuels avenants, susceptibles de s'élever entre elles, sera soumis à la compétence exclusive du Règlement d'arbitrage de la Chambre de Commerce Internationale de Paris par un ou plusieurs arbitres nommés conformément à ce Règlement* ».

30 – L'article 17.1 stipule en outre que « le *présent Contrat est soumis aux lois de la République de Guinée* ».

31 – En vertu d'une règle matérielle du droit international de l'arbitrage, la clause compromissoire est indépendante juridiquement du contrat principal qui la contient directement ou par référence, et son existence et son efficacité s'apprécient, sous réserve des règles impératives du droit français et de l'ordre public international, d'après la commune volonté des parties, sans qu'il soit nécessaire de se référer à une loi étatique.

32 – En l'espèce, l'existence et la validité de la clause d'arbitrage insérée dans l'accord précité ne sont pas contestées et il n'existe aucune règle impérative du droit français et tirée de la conception française de l'ordre public international faisant obstacle à celle-ci.

33 – Ainsi, la désignation du droit guinéen comme régissant de manière générale l'accord ne saurait suffire, à elle seule, à établir la volonté commune des parties de soumettre la clause compromissoire au droit Guinéen et de déroger ainsi à la règle matérielle précitée.

34 – À cet égard, le fait que l'article 77 du code de marchés publics guinéen, dont les recourants réclament l'application, à supposer même qu'il soit impératif en Guinée, prévoit le recours à un arbitrage pour trancher les litiges « dans le cadre des grands marchés publics » n'est pas de nature à caractériser un tel choix exprès alors que précisément, c'est en parfaite connaissance de l'existence de ces règles que l'ARPT, placée sous la tutelle du ministre chargé des télécommunications de la Guinée, a choisi avec la société GVG, non de renvoyer à l'arbitrage tel que prévu par l'article 77 du CMP mais au contraire d'insérer une clause d'arbitrage spécifique dans l'accord soumettant celui-ci au règlement CCI.

35 – Ainsi, le tribunal arbitral, comme il l'a retenu, était bien compétent ratione materiae.

36 – Il convient en conséquence de rejeter ce grief.

1-2 Sur l'incompétence ratione personæ

[...]

40 – Il convient de rappeler qu'une clause compromissoire insérée dans un contrat international est dotée d'une validité et d'une efficacité propres qui commandent d'en étendre l'application à une personne, qui bien que non expressément mentionnée comme « partie » au contrat dans lequel la clause d'arbitrage est incluse, est, selon la volonté commune des parties et les circonstances de la cause, directement impliquée dans l'exécution du contrat et intéressée aux bénéfices de ce contrat.

41 – En l'espèce, il ressort des pièces versées que si la République de Guinée n'apparaît pas en première page de l'accord de partenariat conclu entre l'ARPT et la société GVG, il n'est pas contesté que celle-ci a apposé sa signature sur cet accord en dernière page, de même que sur l'avenant du 6 juillet 2009.

42 – En outre, plusieurs paragraphes de l'accord renvoient directement et expressément aux attentes de la République de Guinée en en faisant ainsi un bénéficiaire direct.

[...]

49 – Il ressort de ces stipulations et éléments que la République de Guinée a été directement impliquée dans la détermination du contenu obligationnel de l'accord de partenariat.

[...]

52 – Il résulte de l'ensemble de ces éléments que la République de Guinée a également été, selon la volonté commune des parties, directement intéressée aux bénéfices de ce contrat et impliquée dans l'exécution de l'accord de partenariat, endossant un rôle allant au-delà de celui d'une autorité de tutelle de l'ARPT.

53 – En conséquence, le tribunal arbitral a pu ainsi retenir sa compétence également à l'égard de la République de Guinée.

54 – Le moyen tiré de l'incompétence du tribunal arbitral sera en conséquence rejeté.

2 – Sur le moyen d'annulation tiré de la constitution irrégulière du tribunal arbitral (article 1520 2° du Code de procédure civile)

[...]

57 – Selon l'article 1520, 2° du Code de procédure civile, le recours en annulation est ouvert si le tribunal a été irrégulièrement constitué.

Sur la recevabilité du moyen ;

58 – Aux termes de l'article 1466 du Code de procédure civile, la partie qui, en connaissance de cause et sans motif légitime, s'abstient d'invoquer en temps utile une irrégularité devant le tribunal arbitral est réputée avoir renoncé à s'en prévaloir.

[...]

Sur le bien-fondé du moyen ;

62 – Il convient de relever que ce moyen est uniquement articulé sur la méconnaissance par le tribunal arbitral de l'article 77 du code des marchés publics pour régir la constitution du tribunal arbitral.

63 – Ainsi qu'il a été jugé par la présente cour ci-dessus, ce moyen est inopérant dès lors que la constitution du tribunal arbitral a été faite selon le règlement de la CCI auquel renvoyait la clause d'arbitrage, excluant ainsi l'application de l'article 77 du CMP.

64 – Ce moyen sera en conséquence rejeté.

3-Sur le moyen d'annulation tiré de la contrariété de la sentence à l'ordre public international (article 1520 5° du Code de procédure civile)

3-1 Sur le grief tiré de la corruption

[...]

70 – La lutte contre la corruption est un objectif poursuivi, notamment, par la Convention de l'OCDE sur la lutte contre la corruption du 17 décembre 1997, entrée en vigueur le 15 février 1999, et par la Convention des Nations Unies contre la corruption faite à Merida le 9 décembre 2003, entrée en vigueur le 14 décembre 2005.

71 – Suivant le consensus international exprimé par ces textes, la corruption d'agent public, qu'il soit national ou étranger, consiste à offrir à celui-ci, directement ou indirectement, un avantage indu, pour lui-même ou pour une autre personne ou entité, afin qu'il accomplisse ou s'abstienne d'accomplir un acte dans l'exercice de ses fonctions officielles, en vue d'obtenir ou de conserver un marché ou un autre avantage indu, en liaison avec des activités de commerce international.

72 – La prohibition de la corruption d'agents publics est au nombre des principes dont l'ordre juridique français ne saurait souffrir la violation même dans un contexte international. Elle relève par conséquent de l'ordre public international.

73 – Le juge de l'annulation n'est cependant pas le juge du contrat, mais de l'insertion de la sentence dans l'ordre juridique national.

74 – Son contrôle vise seulement à s'assurer qu'il ne résulte pas de la reconnaissance ou de l'exécution de la sentence une violation manifeste, effective et concrète de l'ordre public international.

[...]

80 – En conséquence, l'insertion de la sentence dans l'ordre juridique français qui ne donne aucun effet à cet avenant n° 3, dont les parties soutiennent qu'il participerait d'une fraude liée à une corruption, ne viole pas de manière manifeste, effective et concrète l'ordre public international.

81 – Il en résulte que tous les indices de corruption allégués au titre du « second temps » [...] ne sont pas pertinents et ne peuvent venir utilement au soutien du moyen d'annulation contre la sentence qui ne donne en tout état de cause pas d'effet à cet avenant.

82 – Il en est de même du procès-verbal d'audition par la police de Conakry de M. [...] qui, bien que datant du 12 avril 2011, n'a été produit que dans le cadre du présent recours en annulation, et dont les déclarations, qui n'ont donné lieu à l'époque à aucune suite judiciaire, sont au surplus contestées par ce dernier et en tout état de cause portent sur des faits en lien avec la signature de l'avenant n° 3 sur le trafic national et les relations contractuelles [...] et donc sur des relations contractuelles non soumises au tribunal arbitral auxquelles la sentence ne donne par conséquent aucun effet.

83 – Il appartient dès lors à la cour d'apprécier si les indices allégués au titre du « premier temps », qui concernent les seuls accords auxquels la sentence donne un effet, constituent un faisceau d'indices graves précis et concordants de corruption, ce qui suppose de les examiner à la fois isolément mais aussi ensemble, la preuve d'une corruption pouvant résulter de leur accumulation.

84 – Parmi ces indices pertinents au regard du contrôle de la sentence litigieuse à l'ordre public international, ceux qui portent sur des faits en lien avec la société et l'objet du litige sont relatifs aux allégations de contournement des règles de passation des marchés publics, de prédation sur les deniers publics guinéens et de fraude fiscale reprochée à la société en Guinée.

85 – Le défaut de recours à un appel d'offres pour la conclusion d'un marché public peut constituer un indice opérant. Il n'est cependant pas acquis qu'en l'espèce, le marché litigieux nécessitait systématiquement de recourir à une procédure d'appel d'offres quand bien même il restait soumis au code des marchés publics.

86 – En effet, il ressort du code des marchés publics guinéen que certains contrats relevant de son champ peuvent aussi être passés « de gré à gré » (cf. article 27. 2) et ce notamment si « l'urgence impérieuse motivée par des circonstances imprévisibles et de force majeure, ne permet pas, pour la livraison des fournitures, l'exécution des prestations de travaux ou marchés industriels ».

[...]

92 – Il ressort de ces éléments, justement contrôlés par le tribunal arbitral, que le caractère abusif du modèle économique résultant de ce contrat n'est pas démontré quand bien même il a pu être particulièrement favorable à la société, au moins dans la première partie de son exécution.

[...]

94 – Ainsi, en toute hypothèse, la sentence ne s'appuie pas sur le modèle économique qualifié de déséquilibré par l'ARPT et la République de Guinée pour

les condamner mais a pris en compte une diminution significative du tarif telle que celle résultant de l'Addendum.

95 – Le caractère abusivement déséquilibré du contrat, auquel en tout état de cause la sentence ne donne aucun effet, n'est en conséquence pas suffisamment étayé pour constituer un indice grave susceptible d'être pris en compte pour caractériser une corruption.

96 – S'agissant de l'accusation de fraude fiscale, force est de constater que celle-ci n'est étayée par aucun document. Si s'agissant de la corruption, une preuve matérielle directe est complexe, de telle sorte que le recours à des indices est possible, tel n'est pas le cas de la fraude fiscale dont la preuve matérielle peut être rapportée, ce qui n'est pas le cas en l'espèce de sorte qu'il ne s'agit ici pas d'un indice recevable.

[...]

98 – Ainsi, l'invocation du climat général de corruption en Guinée en 2009, même ajouté aux autres indices précédemment allégués, n'est pas de nature à leur conférer un caractère grave, précis et concordant.

99 – En effet, d'une part, un État ne peut se dégager de ses engagements contractuels en se bornant à alléguer un tel climat général de corruption au sein de son administration.

100 – D'autre part, s'il n'est pas requis pour l'annulation d'une sentence que des poursuites contre les auteurs présumés et des sanctions pénales aient été prononcées, cette situation ne peut conduire non plus le juge de l'annulation à ignorer l'inaction manifeste des autorités publiques avant ou lors de la procédure arbitrale pour contester devant le tribunal arbitral, juge naturel du contrat, la licéité du contrat sur lequel porte le litige qui lui est soumis.

101 – En l'espèce, aucune action visant à poursuivre des faits de corruption n'a été engagée avant la procédure arbitrale alors même que devant la cour d'appel l'ARPT et la République de Guinée produisent un procès-verbal d'audition devant les services de police daté du 12 avril 2011 et dont les recourantes devaient ou pouvaient manifestement avoir connaissance bien avant l'introduction du litige.

[...]

104 – Il ressort ainsi tant du contrôle auquel le tribunal arbitral s'est livré, comme il lui incombait à juste titre de le faire, que de l'analyse de chacun des indices pris séparément et dans leur ensemble, que les agissements allégués ne caractérisent pas des indices graves, précis et concordants susceptibles de conduire à une annulation de la sentence pour méconnaissance de l'ordre public international.

105 – Ce grief sera en conséquence rejeté.

3-2 Sur le grief tiré de la méconnaissance du principe de la contradiction :

[...]

108 – Le principe de la contradiction exige seulement que les parties aient pu faire connaître leurs prétentions de fait et de droit et discuter celles de leur adversaire de telle sorte que rien de ce qui a servi à fonder la décision des arbitres n'ait échappé à leur débat contradictoire.

109 – Le principe de la contradiction interdit ainsi que des moyens de fait ou de droit soient soulevés d'office sans que les parties aient été appelées à les commenter.

110 – En revanche, ce principe de la contradiction n'emporte pas obligation pour le tribunal arbitral de soumettre en préalable l'argumentation juridique qui étaye sa motivation à la discussion des parties.

[...]

114 – Il ressort de ces éléments que le grief tiré du défaut de respect du principe de la contradiction sera rejeté.

115 – En conséquence, le moyen tiré de la violation de l'ordre public international sera rejeté.

4 – Sur le moyen d'annulation tiré de ce que le tribunal arbitral ne s'est pas conformé à sa mission (article 1520 4° du Code de procédure civile)

[...]

118 – Selon l'article 1520, 3°, du Code de procédure civile, le recours en annulation est ouvert si le tribunal a statué sans se conformer à la mission qui lui avait été confiée.

119 – En application de l'article 1509 du Code de procédure civile, « *la convention d'arbitrage peut, directement ou par référence à un règlement d'arbitrage ou à des règles de procédure, régler la procédure à suivre dans l'instance arbitrale. / Dans le silence de la convention d'arbitrage, le tribunal arbitral règle la procédure autant qu'il est besoin, soit directement, soit par référence à un règlement d'arbitrage ou à des règles de procédure* ».

120 – En l'espèce, l'article 31 du règlement CCI (version 2012), applicable à l'instance arbitrale, dispose que « la sentence doit être motivée ».

121 – Il relevait donc bien en l'espèce de la mission du tribunal arbitral de motiver sa sentence.

[...]

123 – Cependant, il résulte sur ce point de la sentence que le tribunal a expressément écarté l'application de l'article 77 du CMP au profit de la clause d'arbitrage prévu dans l'accord de partenariat comme rappelé ci-dessus à l'occasion de l'examen du moyen sur la compétence et il n'appartient pas à la cour d'apporter une appréciation sur la suffisance et les motifs adoptés par le tribunal.

[...]

125 – Cependant, d'une part, les arbitres ne sont pas tenus de répondre à la totalité de l'argumentation des parties.

126 – D'autre part, cet argument était invoqué au soutien du moyen tiré de la corruption du contrat, que le tribunal a considéré comme non établie dans sa sentence reprochant notamment aux parties de ne pas étayer suffisamment la preuve des allégations sur le caractère économiquement abusif du modèle économique du partenariat.

[...]

128 – Cependant le tribunal a rejeté dans leur ensemble ces arguments dans le $ 233 de sa sentence et la cour ne peut sous couvert du contrôle du respect de la mission, opérer un contrôle de la pertinence de la motivation.

[...]

130 – Enfin, s'agissant des motifs du tribunal arbitral selon lesquels l'arbitrage CCI ne serait pas contraire à l'ordre public guinéen en raison de la réforme du règlement des litiges dans les marchés publics réalisée par l'article 134 du Nouveau CMP, ou encore les motifs du tribunal arbitral concernant les dons et cadeaux, les parties, qui indiquent que ces cas couvrent une « motivation défaillante »,

critiquent ce faisant, non l'inexistence de ces motifs, mais leur pertinence ou leur suffisance, ce qui échappe au contrôle du juge de l'annulation.

131 – Il résulte de ces éléments que, sous couvert d'un défaut de motivation, les parties reprochent au tribunal une insuffisance de motivation, insusceptible de conduire à l'annulation d'une sentence.

132 – Ce moyen sera en conséquence rejeté.

– Paris, Pôle 5 – Chambre 16, Chambre commerciale internationale, 7 septembre 2021, n° 19/17531, *Organisme République de Guinée, Télécommunications et de l'Économie Numérique de la République de Guinée – Ministère des Postes – Télécommunications et de l'Économie – Conakry Guinée, Organisme Autorité de Régulation des Postes et Télécommunications de la Guinée c. Global Voice Group*

Clause compromissoire – Validité – Inopposabilité – Art 2061 du Code civil – Activité professionnelle – Principe de compétence compétence – Article L. 721-3 du Code de commerce – Acte commercial – Définition – Opération économique – Contrats – Indivision

Aux termes de l'article 1448 du Code de procédure civile, lorsqu'un litige relevant d'une convention d'arbitrage est porté devant une juridiction de l'État, celle-ci se déclare incompétente sauf si le tribunal arbitral n'est pas encore saisi et si la convention d'arbitrage est manifestement nulle ou manifestement inapplicable.

Sur la nullité ou l'inopposabilité de la clause compromissoire :

[...]

L'article 2061 du Code civil, dans sa rédaction applicable en l'espèce et issue de la loi du 15 mai 2001, dispose que « *sous réserve des dispositions législatives particulières, la clause compromissoire est valable dans les contrats conclus à raison d'une activité professionnelle* ».

L'article L. 721-3 du Code de commerce prévoit, d'une part, que les tribunaux de commerce connaissent des contestations relatives aux engagements entre commerçants, entre établissements de crédit, entre sociétés de financement ou entre eux, de celles relatives aux sociétés commerciales et de celles relatives aux actes de commerce entre toutes personnes, et, d'autre part, que les parties peuvent, au moment où elles contractent, convenir de soumettre à l'arbitrage les contestations ainsi énumérées.

L'article L. 721-3 du Code de commerce comprend ainsi des dispositions législatives particulières figurant au nombre de celles visées par l'article 2061 du Code civil. Il s'ensuit que la société invoque à bon droit les dispositions de l'article L. 721-3 du Code de commerce au soutien de la validité de la clause compromissoire insérée dans la convention de participation litigieuse.

Cette convention de participation a pour objet la réalisation de l'acquisition des parts sociales de la SARL T et de la SCI détenues par M. Ac et représentant 50 % du capital social de chacune de ces deux sociétés, ces titres faisant l'objet d'une promesse de cession préalablement conclue au bénéfice des époux B, et la réalisation de l'acquisition des autres parts sociales des mêmes sociétés propriétés d'autres associés. Dès lors qu'elle porte ainsi notamment sur l'acquisition de la totalité des parts sociales composant la SARL T et a pour objet la prise de contrôle de cette société, cette convention est un acte commercial et les contestations relatives à cet acte entrent dans les prévisions de l'article L. 721-3 du Code de commerce.

Il s'ensuit que, sans qu'il soit nécessaire de rechercher si la convention litigieuse a été conclue à raison de l'activité professionnelle de M. B dès lors que l'application de l'article 2061 du Code civil est écartée, la clause compromissoire n'est pas manifestement nulle et que la juridiction étatique n'est pas compétente pour connaître du litige.

Sur l'inopposabilité de la clause compromissoire à Mme B et, par voie de conséquence en raison de l'indivisibilité, à M. B :

[...]

Mme B est partie au protocole de cession des parts sociales de M. Ac du 11 février 2008 qui comprend une clause compromissoire. Elle n'a pas signé la convention de participation litigieuse, alors même qu'elle est désignée comme partie à la convention agissant avec son époux, ensemble et solidairement et que la convention stipule que la société en participation, occulte, est constituée entre la société et les époux B, que les époux B apportent la genèse de l'opération et les démarches aux fins d'obtention de la promesse de cession consentie par M. Ac et que le chiffre d'affaires est partagé entre les associés, soit 50 % pour les époux B. Dès lors que la convention de participation a notamment pour but la réalisation de l'acquisition des parts sociales des deux sociétés objet de la promesse de cession préalablement consentie par M. Ac à M. et Mme B, les deux contrats concourent à une même opération économique et Mme B est directement impliquée dans l'exécution de la convention de participation et les litiges pouvant en résulter. Il s'ensuit que la clause compromissoire est opposable à Mme B et qu'elle n'est pas manifestement inapplicable.

Le litige élevé relevant de l'arbitrage, le tribunal judiciaire de Paris est incompétent.

– Paris, Pôle 5 – Chambre 8, 14 septembre 2021, n° 21/03556, *B c. Buildinvest*

Arbitrage interne – Sentence arbitrale – Tribunal arbitral – Compétence – Contrôle étendu – Cession de créance – Règlement ISF (*International Seed Federation*) – CAIP – Changement de statut – Incidence – Révision au fond – Volonté des parties – Constitution du Tribunal – Règlement applicable

23 – En application de l'article 1520, 1° du Code de procédure civile le recours en annulation est ouvert si le tribunal arbitral s'est déclaré à tort compétent ou incompétent.

24 – En l'espèce, la CAIP a été saisie sur le fondement de la clause compromissoire des contrats de production ainsi libellée « *Tout litige survenant à l'occasion du présent contrat sera réglé par la Chambre Arbitrale de Paris suivant les règles ISF* » ;

25 – L'opposabilité de cette clause à la banque par l'effet de la cession des créances et le règlement par arbitrage du litige ne sont pas discutés.

26 – Les parties sont en désaccord sur la désignation de la CAIP, depuis qu'elle n'est plus membre de l'ISF, pour organiser l'arbitrage.

27 – Ce changement de situation crée une ambiguïté sur la portée de la clause qui a nécessité une interprétation de la part du tribunal arbitral statuant sur sa compétence.

28 – À cet égard, le juge de l'annulation n'étant pas le juge de révision de la sentence, il ne lui appartient pas d'infirmer ou de confirmer les motifs de la

sentence rendue sur cette question, mais d'apprécier au regard de la volonté des parties et de la convention d'arbitrage si le tribunal était compétent.

29 – Il est constant que la perte de l'affiliation ISF par la CAIP a eu pour conséquence de priver la chambre du pouvoir d'organiser l'arbitrage selon les règles de procédure ISF dénommées « *Règles de procédure pour le règlement de litiges dans le domaine du commerce des semences végétales et pour la gestion de la propriété intellectuelle de l'International Seed Federation* » et notamment de celles relatives à la désignation des arbitres figurant sur une liste nominative de professionnels dans le secteur des semences végétales.

30 – En l'occurrence l'arbitrage a été organisé conformément au règlement de la CAIP.

31 – Le tribunal arbitral a appliqué les règles de fond ISF au litige.

32 – Selon l'appelant dès lors que les parties ont fait référence dans leurs échanges aux normes ISF, tout litige doit être soumis à l'arbitrage professionnel tel que défini par les règles ISF de procédure et de fond à l'exclusion de toute autre forme d'arbitrage.

33 – Toutefois en matière d'arbitrage la clause compromissoire présente une complète autonomie par rapport au contrat.

34 – En outre en visant nommément la CAIP dans la clause compromissoire alors qu'elles n'y étaient pas tenues puisqu'une simple référence aux règles ISF, sans autre précision, aurait pu suffire comme cela a été le cas pour d'autres contrats pour l'examen desquels le tribunal arbitral constitué sous l'égide de la CAIP n'a pas retenu sa compétence, les parties ont sans équivoque possible exprimé leur intention de confier à cette institution en France le soin d'être l'organisateur de l'arbitrage pour régler les difficultés qui naîtraient de l'exécution de leurs conventions.

35 – Le choix par les parties d'une institution nécessairement identifiée a pour effet qu'elles acceptent, sauf volonté expresse contraire, de se soumettre à son règlement sans qu'il y ait lieu de le stipuler expressément.

36 – À ce titre aucune volonté contraire n'a été exprimée par les parties.

37 – Les règles de procédure ISF ne sont pas désignées explicitement et le prétendu caractère indissociable des règles de fond et de procédure ISF allégué au soutien du recours ne ressort pas des règlements ISF ni d'aucune pièce produite au débat.

38 – Il résulte ainsi de ce qui précède qu'en dépit de l'ambiguïté créée par le fait que la CAIP n'est plus membre de l'ISF et que les règles de procédure ISF ne peuvent plus s'appliquer, la CAIP est bien l'institution désignée par les parties pour organiser l'arbitrage.

39 – En faisant application de son règlement qui était à cette date le seul qui rendait possible l'arbitrage sous son égide en application de la clause compromissoire la désignant, la CAIP a fait prévaloir le choix de parties qui était de manière évidente de retenir sa compétence pour régler le litige.

40 – Ce moyen d'annulation sera en conséquence rejeté.

2. Sur le moyen d'annulation tiré de l'irrégularité de la constitution du tribunal arbitral

41 – En application de l'article 1520, 2° du Code de procédure civile le recours en annulation est ouvert si le tribunal arbitral a été irrégulièrement constitué.

[...]

43 – Dans la mesure où précisément la cour rejette le grief d'incompétence invoqué à tort il en résulte pour les mêmes motifs que le tribunal arbitral, dont il n'est pas contesté qu'il ait été constitué dans les formes et conditions prévues par le règlement de la CAIP, n'est pas susceptible d'encourir le grief qui lui est fait par la recourante.

44 – Ce moyen doit encore être écarté.

45 – En l'état de l'ensemble de ces éléments, il convient de rejeter le recours en annulation.

– Paris, Pôle 5 – chambre 16, Chambre commerciale internationale, 14 septembre 2021, n° 19/23063, *Feldsaaten Freudenberger GmbH & Co c. Banque Delubac*

Clause compromissoire – Article 48 du Code de procédure civile – Règlement UE 1215/2012 du Parlement européen et du conseil du 12 décembre 2012 concernant la compétence judiciaire, la reconnaissance et l'exécution des décisions en matière civile et commerciale (dit Bruxelles I *bis*) Inapplicabilité manifeste – Exclusion – Article 1448 du Code de procédure civile – Opposabilité – Contrat d'assurance – Qualité d'assurée – Non signataire – Caractère manifeste de l'inapplicabilité – Obstacle – Principe de compétence compétence

L'article 20 du document intitulé Informations relatives au contrat (détails relatifs à l'exposition et à l'assurance) et constituant les conditions particulières du contrat d'assurance souscrit par la société D avec la société A stipule que : « *Il est convenu que A. est le lieu de juridiction pour tous les litiges découlant de la présente police. 1. Tous les litiges relatifs au présent contrat d'assurance ou à sa validité qui ne peuvent être tranchés à l'amiable, sont de la compétence d'un tribunal arbitral appelé à trancher définitivement, les voies de droit ordinaires étant exclues. 5. Le lieu fixé pour la procédure d'arbitrage est Francfort, les parties peuvent déterminer un autre lieu en Allemagne. La Cour supérieure régionale de Francfort (Oberslandesgericht Frankfurt) est compétente pour les demandes portant sur la procédure d'arbitrage.* »

Les parties s'accordent pour considérer que ces dispositions constituent une clause compromissoire. Les dispositions de l'article 48 du Code de procédure civile relatives aux clauses attributives de compétence sont inapplicables aux clauses compromissoires.

De la même façon, l'arbitrage est exclu du règlement (UE) n° 1215/2012 du Parlement européen et du conseil du 12 décembre 2012 concernant la compétence judiciaire, la reconnaissance et l'exécution des décisions en matière civile et commerciale (dit Bruxelles I *bis*).

L'article 1448 du Code de procédure civile énonce que : « *Lorsqu'un litige relevant d'une convention d'arbitrage est porté devant une juridiction de l'État, celle-ci se déclare incompétente sauf si le tribunal arbitral n'est pas encore saisi et si la convention d'arbitrage est manifestement nulle ou manifestement inapplicable* ».

Mme A revendique sa qualité d'assurée même si elle n'est pas signataire du contrat d'assurance. Dès lors, le caractère manifeste de l'inapplicabilité de la clause d'arbitrage du fait qu'elle serait inopposable à Mme A, seule de nature à faire obstacle à la compétence prioritaire de l'arbitre pour statuer sur l'existence, la validité et l'étendue de la convention d'arbitrage n'est pas établi et la cour doit se déclarer incompétente, en confirmation de l'ordonnance déférée, par substitution de motifs.

– Paris, Pôle 4 – Chambre 13, 21 septembre 2021, n° 21/00569 et 21/01271, *A c. XL Insurance Company* (deux arrêts)

Pactes d'associés – Parties – Clause d'arbitrage – Étendue – Opposabilité – Groupe – Entité économique – Inapplicabilité manifeste – Nullité manifeste – Exception de procédure – Tribunal de commerce

Sur l'application de la clause compromissoire

L'article 1448 du Code de procédure civile dispose que : « *Lorsqu'un litige relevant d'une convention d'arbitrage est porté devant une juridiction de l'État, celle-ci se déclare incompétente sauf si le tribunal arbitral n'est pas encore saisi et si la convention d'arbitrage est manifestement nulle ou manifestement inapplicable. La juridiction de l'État ne peut relever d'office son incompétence. Toute stipulation contraire au présent article est réputée non écrite.* »

[...]

Or il ressort de la lecture du pacte d'associé du 30 septembre 2016 d'une part que ce ne sont pas les mêmes associés qui sont concernés par ce pacte, puisqu'il y en a deux de plus, Messieurs Ad A et Ad Z, et d'autre part qu'il ne concerne pas la même société. De plus ce premier pacte ne comporte aucune clause identique à celle de l'article 19 prévoyant une sanction financière en cas de non-respect du pacte par les associés, de telle sorte que là demande de M. Aa A, si elle était fondée sur le pacte du 30 septembre 2016, serait rigoureusement infondée et manifestement vouée à l'échec.

Enfin l'article 21 du pacte du 2 octobre 2017 stipule que : « *Le pacte représente l'intégralité des accords des parties quant à son objet et remplace, annule et prévaut sur toutes conventions ou documents antérieurs ayant un objet identique* ».

En conséquence, et sans qu'il y ait lieu de faire application de la notion de « groupe » ou « d'entité économique », il y a lieu de constater que le présent litige relève uniquement du pacte d'associé du 2 octobre 2017, de telle sorte qu'il ne relève pas de la clause d'arbitrage prévue dans l'autre pacte d'associé, à savoir celui du 30 septembre 2016.

Dès lors la clause arbitrale contenue dans le pacte du 30 septembre 2016 est manifestement nulle ou inapplicable.

Le pacte d'associé ne contenant aucune clause d'arbitrage mais au contraire donnant expressément compétence aux juridictions de la cour d'appel d'Aix-en-Provence en cas de litige, le tribunal de commerce d'Aix-en-Provence saisi par M. Aa A est bien compétent pour statuer sur le litige.

Le jugement est infirmé.

En ce qui concerne le régime de l'exception tirée de l'existence d'une clause compromissoire, il est constant qu'il s'agit d'une exception de procédure régie par les dispositions des articles 73 et 74 du Code de procédure civile, en ce qu'elle doit être soulevée avant toute défense, et ce par opposition aux défenses au fond ou fin de non-recevoir (article 122 et suivants du Code de procédure civile).

Cependant, il s'agit bien d'une exception d'incompétence régie par les articles 75 et suivants du Code de procédure civile, les exceptions d'incompétence étant une catégorie spécifique d'exceptions de procédure, puisque comprises dans la Section I du Chapitre relatif auxdites exceptions. L'article 80 vise d'ailleurs expressément le cas de l'incompétence au profit d'une juridiction arbitrale.

En conséquence, en application de l'article 78 a contrario du Code de procédure civile, et afin de ne pas priver les parties du double degré de juridiction, étant précisé que les défendeurs/intimés n'ont pas conclu au fond sur les demandes de M. Aa A puisque le tribunal de commerce a demandé que l'affaire soit plaidée uniquement sur l'exception d'incompétence, il convient de renvoyer les parties devant le tribunal de commerce au fond.

– Aix-en-Provence, Chambre 3-4, 23 septembre 2021, n° 21/01407, *A c. Pacte Provence Lbs et a.*

Investissement – TBI – Ratification – Tribunal arbitral – Compétence – Contrôle – Étendue – Compétence rationae materiae – Théorie de l'apparence – Convention de Vienne sur le droit des traités – Volonté de parties – Champ d'application – Révision – Fraude – Corruption – Révision au fond – Offre permanente d'arbitrage – Autonomie de l'offre – Investissement – Qualification – Droit international coutumier – Rationae temporis – Ordre public international – Définition – Heurte de manière manifeste, effective et concrètes – Principes et valeurs – Conception française – Mission – Définition – Conception permissive – Motivation

1. Sur le moyen principal d'annulation tiré de ce que le tribunal arbitral s'est reconnu à tort compétent (article 1520-1° du Code de procédure civile)

21 – Selon l'article 1520, 1° du Code de procédure civile, le recours en annulation est ouvert si le tribunal s'est déclaré à tort compétent ou incompétent.

22 – Le juge de l'annulation contrôle la décision du tribunal arbitral sur sa compétence, qu'il se soit déclaré compétent ou incompétent, en recherchant tous les éléments de droit ou de fait permettant d'apprécier la portée de la convention d'arbitrage. Il n'en va pas différemment lorsque les arbitres sont saisis sur le fondement d'un traité.

• *Sur l'incompétence du tribunal arbitral pour défaut d'entrée en vigueur du TBI*

[...]

30 – Le 25 novembre 2009 l'État de Libye a signé un accord concernant l'encouragement et la protection réciproque des investissements avec la Turquie (ci-après le TBI ou le Traité), les parties signataires étant The Republic of Turkey, représentée par le ministre d'État et « *The great socialist people's Libyan Arab Jamahiriya* » représentée par le secrétaire du « *General As's Committee for Industry, Economy and Trade* » (le Foreign Committee). Le 23 août 2010, le Foreign Committee a notifié la ratification du Traité par la Jamahiriya arabe libyenne à la Turquie. Le 14 avril 2011, la Turquie a ratifié le Traité. Le 22 avril 2011, la Turquie a notifié la ratification du Traité bilatéral d'investissement au Foreign Committee.

31 – S'il n'est pas contesté que le TBI a été signé entre la Turquie et la Libye le 25 novembre 2009 et que la Libye a notifié la ratification du TBI à la Turquie dès le 23 août 2010 par une note verbale du ministre des affaires étrangères libyen adressée à l'ambassade de Turquie à Tripoli, il est contesté par l'État de Libye que la notification de la ratification faite par la Turquie le 22 avril 2011 au Foreign Committee soit valable.

32 – Or, selon l'article 12(1) du TBI, relatif à l'entrée en vigueur du Traité, « *chaque partie contractante informe l'autre par écrit de l'accomplissement des formalités constitutionnelles requises sur son territoire pour l'entrée en vigueur du présent Accord. Le présent accord entre en vigueur à la date de la dernière des deux notifications. Il restera en vigueur pendant une période de 10 ans et continue de s'appliquer par la suite, sauf dénonciation dans les conditions énoncées au §2 du présent article* ».

33 – Il en résulte tout d'abord que l'information à l'autre partie contractante des formalités de ratification doit être faite à chaque partie contractante sans que le texte du Traité ne mentionne une ou plusieurs entités ou autorités au sein de chaque partie contractante à laquelle aurait dû être adressée la notification de la ratification. Selon les termes du Traité, la simple notification est suffisante pour l'entrée en vigueur du TBI, sans qu'aucune autre diligence ne doive être accomplie par l'une des parties contractantes notamment l'envoi de la notification à une entité ou une adresse spécifiée.

34 – En soutenant que la notification de la ratification par la Turquie dont la matérialité n'est pas mise en cause, aurait dû être faite au Conseil National de Transition (le CNT) à compter de la déclaration de fondation du CNT du 2 mars 2011, et non au Foreign Committee, comme l'a fait la Turquie, l'État de Libye ajoute une condition au Traité que le texte ne contient pas.

35 – Le TBI prévoit simplement que la partie contractante informe l'autre de sa propre ratification, ce qui ne nécessite pas d'interprétation, sauf à ce que le terme *partie contractante* puisse avoir plusieurs sens, ce qui n'est pas le cas, le traité désignant simplement comme *parties contractantes* les signataires du traité.

36 – Il résulte des éléments versés aux débats que la notification est intervenue le 22 avril 2011, l'Ambassade de Turquie à Tripoli étant restée en fonction jusqu'au 2 mai 2011 et la Turquie n'ayant reconnu le CNT que le 19 septembre 2011. L'État de Libye ne conteste pas avoir reçu ladite notification le 22 avril 2011.

37 – De plus, l'État de Libye avait déjà valablement de son côté ratifié et notifié sa ratification à la Turquie depuis le 23 août 2010 et la validité de la décision de la Turquie de ratifier ledit TBI et de notifier sa ratification ne dépendait plus de la volonté de la Libye, mais du choix autonome de la Turquie.

38 – La légitimité de la ratification faite par la Turquie au Foreign Committee est d'autant moins contestable que le CNT n'a été reconnu par la communauté internationale qu'en septembre 2011, soit postérieurement au 22 avril 2011, date de la notification. L'État de Libye, représenté par son Premier ministre, dirigeant du CNT, a en outre signé à Istanbul le 3 janvier 2014 une déclaration de politique commune pour la création du Haut Conseil de la coopération stratégique entre la République de Turquie et l'État de Libye, faisant expressément référence en son paragraphe 8 à l'Accord concernant la promotion et la protection réciproques des investissements (Agreement concerning the Reciprocal Promotion and Protection of Investments), reconnaissant ainsi cet Accord existant. Le tribunal arbitral a, pour se déclarer compétent, pris en considération ladite déclaration commune pour considérer que le TBI était bien entré en vigueur le 22 avril 2011.

39 – Enfin, la mise en œuvre du TBI a été admise dans plusieurs arbitrages opposant des sociétés de droit turc et l'État de Libye, notamment dans une sentence du 7 novembre 2018 soumise à la cour d'appel de Paris qui a rejeté le recours en

annulation par un arrêt du 25 mai 2021, dans le cadre duquel l'État de Libye n'a pas saisi la cour d'une contestation sur son entrée en vigueur.

40 – Il résulte de l'ensemble de ces éléments, et sans qu'il soit nécessaire de se référer à la théorie de l'apparence issue de la règle coutumière transposée à l'article 46 de la convention de Vienne sur le droit des traités, que le tribunal arbitral s'est à juste titre déclaré compétent rationae personae.

* *Sur l'incompétence rationae materiae du tribunal arbitral à raison de la corruption entachant l'investissement*

[...]

52 – Il est constant que seule la volonté commune des parties a le pouvoir d'investir l'arbitre de son pouvoir juridictionnel, lequel se confond en matière d'arbitrage avec sa compétence.

53 – Lorsque la clause d'arbitrage résulte d'un Traité bilatéral d'investissement, il convient d'apprécier cette volonté commune au regard de l'ensemble des dispositions du traité de sorte que le tribunal arbitral n'est compétent pour connaître d'un litige que s'il entre dans le champ d'application dudit traité et qu'il est satisfait à l'ensemble de ses conditions d'application.

54 – Cependant, sous couvert d'un contrôle de la compétence, le juge de l'annulation ne peut se substituer à l'arbitre pour trancher un litige portant sur la licéité de l'investissement du contrat qui concrétise cet investissement, qui ne relève que du seul fond du litige et non de l'appréciation de la compétence du tribunal arbitral.

55 – S'agissant de l'allégation de corruption au visa de l'article 1520, 1° du Code de procédure civile sur la compétence du tribunal arbitral dont la cour est saisie, le contrôle opéré par le juge de l'annulation sur ce moyen ne saurait priver les parties en amont et avant toute décision des arbitres sur le fond, du droit de soumettre leur litige à l'arbitrage, sauf si le vice allégué porte sur la seule compétence du tribunal arbitral lui-même, ce qui n'est pas le cas en l'espèce.

56 – À cet égard, si un État est fondé à refuser d'accorder sa protection à un investissement illégal, en signant un traité bilatéral d'investissement comportant une offre permanente d'arbitrage, il accepte toutefois par avance de se soumettre à un tribunal arbitral pour statuer sur les litiges liés aux investissements réalisés par un ressortissant de l'autre partie contractante sur son territoire.

57 – Il convient dès lors de considérer que cette offre permanente d'arbitre est autonome et indépendante de la validité de l'opération qui a donné naissance à l'investissement ou qui la soutient, de sorte que l'acceptation de l'arbitrage qui résulte de la notification de la requête d'arbitrage suffit à justifier la compétence du tribunal arbitral pour statuer sur la licéité de cet investissement et la demande en réparation.

58 – En l'espèce, l'article 8 du TBI porte sur le « *Règlement des différends entre une Partie contractante et les investisseurs de l'autre Partie contractante* » et stipule : 1. *En cas de différends surgissant entre l'une des Parties contractantes et un investisseur de l'autre Partie contractante concernant un investissement de ce dernier, l'investisseur notifie par écrit et de manière détaillée la Partie contractante sur le territoire de laquelle l'investissement a été réalisé. Dans la mesure du possible, l'investisseur et la Partie contractante concernée s'efforcent de régler ces différends par voie de consultations et de négociations, menées de bonne foi. 2. Si le différend*

ne peut être réglé de cette manière dans les 90 jours qui suivent la date de la notification écrite mentionnée au paragraphe 1 ci-dessus, le différend peut être soumis, si l'investisseur le décide, au tribunal compétent de la Partie contractante sur le territoire de laquelle l'investissement a été réalisé ou à l'arbitrage international, soit : a) Au Centre international pour le règlement des différends relatifs aux investissements (CIRDI) (le « Centre »), créé en vertu de la Convention pour le règlement des différends relatifs aux investissements entre États et ressortissants d'autres États, si les deux Parties contractantes sont signataires de la Convention ; b) À un tribunal d'arbitrage ad hoc constitué conformément aux Règles d'arbitrage de la Commission des Nations Unies pour le droit commercial international (CNUDCI) ; c) Au tribunal d'arbitrage de la Chambre de commerce internationale de Paris. 3. Dès que l'investisseur a soumis le différend à l'une des procédures de règlement stipulées au paragraphe 2 ci-dessus, le choix de la procédure est définitif. 4. Nonobstant les dispositions du paragraphe 2 du présent article, a) Seuls les différends découlant directement des activités d'investissement ayant obtenu les autorisations requises, le cas échéant, conformément à la législation pertinente des deux Parties contractantes sur les capitaux étrangers, et qui ont effectivement commencé, sont soumises à la juridiction du Centre, au cas où les deux Parties contractantes en viendraient à être signataires de la Convention, ou de tout autre mécanisme international de règlement des différends qui sera convenu entre les Parties ; b) Les différends relatifs aux droits de propriété et aux droits réels sur des biens immobiliers relèvent entièrement de la compétence de la Partie contractante sur le territoire de laquelle l'investissement est réalisé et ne sont pas soumis à la juridiction du Centre ou de tout autre mécanisme international de règlement des différends ; et c) En ce qui concerne l'article 64 de la Convention pour le règlement des différends relatifs aux investissements entre États et ressortissants d'autres États. La République turque n'accepte pas qu'un différend quel qu'il soit surgi entre la République turque et tout autre État contractant concernant l'interprétation ou l'application de la Convention pour le règlement des différends relatifs aux investissements entre États et ressortissants d'autres États, qui n'est pas réglé par voie de négociation, soit renvoyé à la Cour internationale de justice. 5. Les sentences arbitrales sont définitives et ont force obligatoire pour toutes les parties au différend. Chaque Partie contractante s'engage à exécuter une sentence conformément à sa législation interne ».

59 – Il ressort de cet article que le champ de l'offre d'arbitrage est très large puisqu'il porte sur tous « *différends surgissant entre l'une des Parties contractantes et un investisseur de l'autre Partie contractante concernant un investissement de ce dernier* ».

60 – En notifiant sa requête en arbitrage à l'État de Libye les 17 juin et 11 juillet 2016 concernant le Road Contract et les University Contracts sur le fondement de l'article 8 du Traité Bilatéral d'Investissement conclu entre l'État de Libye et la Turquie comprenant une clause compromissoire, et l'État de Libye ayant soulevé l'incompétence du tribunal et sollicité la disjonction du fond, les parties ont accepté de soumettre leur litige à l'arbitrage, à charge pour le tribunal arbitral de statuer tout d'abord sur sa seule compétence, ce qu'il a fait.

61 – S'agissant du fond du litige, dès lors que le tribunal arbitral s'est déclaré compétent et investi de ce pouvoir, il lui appartiendra de statuer au fond sur la corruption alléguée.

62 – C'est au demeurant en ce sens qu'a statué le tribunal arbitral qui a renvoyé les parties à une sentence future et finale sur le fond de l'affaire.

63 – Il n'est en outre pas soutenu, ni établi, qu'il existerait un vice lié à la corruption, susceptible d'invalider la compétence même du tribunal arbitral, l'État de Libye soutenant uniquement que l'investissement réalisé serait entaché de corruption, en raison de « pots-de-vin » versés ultérieurement, une fois les contrats signés, au bénéfice de la société du fils du colonel, ce qui relève du fond du litige.

64 – Le moyen tiré de l'incompétence rationae materiae du tribunal arbitral pour des faits de fraude ou de corruption au visa de l'article 1520, 1° du Code de procédure civile sera en conséquence rejeté, sans préjuger de la décision au fond que rendront les arbitres sur lesdites allégations de corruption.

• *Sur l'incompétence du Tribunal à raison de l'absence d'investissement au sens du TBI et du droit international coutumier (compétence ratione materiae)*

• *S'agissant de la qualification d'investissement au sens du TBI et du droit libyen.*

• *Sur la définition de l'existence d'investissements au sens du TBI*

70 – Selon l'article 31 de la Convention de Vienne, « *un traité doit être interprété de bonne foi selon le sens habituellement attribué à ses termes, dans leur contexte et en tenant compte de leur objet et de leur but* ».

71 – Le grief énoncé par l'État de Libye consiste à considérer que le TBI ne peut porter que sur des investissements tels que définis par la loi interne Libyenne. Or l'article 1(2) du Traité définit l'investissement : « *The term "investment", in conformity with the hosting Contracting party's laws and regulations, shall include every kind of asset in particular, but not exclusively :*» (Le terme "investissement", conformément aux lois et règlements de la partie contractante hôte, comprend tout type d'actif en particulier mais pas exclusivement).

72 – Il en résulte que le TBI ne subordonne pas son application à la définition de l'investissement par renvoi à la loi Libyenne, mais pose simplement une condition de légalité de l'investissement pour le bénéfice de la protection accordée par le traité.

73 – Cette interprétation est d'ailleurs celle qui résulte des articles 8 (4) et 10 de ce même traité.

74 – En effet, l'article 8 (4) stipule que « *a) Seuls les différends découlant directement des activités d'investissement ayant obtenu les autorisations requises, le cas échéant, conformément à la législation pertinente des deux Parties contractantes sur les capitaux étrangers, et qui ont effectivement commencé, sont soumises à la juridiction du Centre, au cas où les deux Parties contractantes en viendraient à être signataires de la Convention, ou de tout autre mécanisme international de règlement des différends qui sera convenu entre les Parties* ».

75 – De même l'article 10 stipule que : « *Le présent Accord s'applique aux investissements effectués sur le territoire d'une Partie contractants conformément à sa législation et à sa réglementation avant ou après son entrée en vigueur, par les investisseurs de l'autre Partie contractante. Toutefois, il ne s'applique pas aux différends qui sont nés avant son entrée en vigueur* ».

76 – Il en résulte qu'un investissement doit être réalisé en respectant les lois et règlements de l'État hôte, et non que l'investissement doit être défini par les lois et règlements de l'État hôte. La volonté des parties est bien de soumettre l'investissement à une exigence de légalité et non de conformité.

77 – En outre, une telle interprétation est conforme à l'objet d'un TBI, qui ne peut faire dépendre le bénéfice de la protection qu'il consacre d'une définition de la notion d'investissements qui serait dépendante de la seule volonté unilatérale de chacune des parties et qui pourrait ainsi unilatéralement modifier le champ d'application du traité.

78 – Tel ne peut être le cas de l'exigence alléguée en l'espèce de l'absence d'approbation par le Secrétariat du Congrès Général du Peuple libyen (conformément à l'article 3(8) de la loi n° 5), ou d'enregistrement au Registre des investissements en Libye (conformément à l'article 13 al 2 et 3 de la loi n° 5) dès lors qu'à supposer même établis, ces manquements ne sont pas de nature à remettre en cause l'existence de l'investissement mais sa seule régularité.

79 – En conséquence ce grief ne peut prospérer, les contrats A constituant bien des investissements au sens du Traité.

* *Sur l'absence d'investissements au sens du droit international coutumier*

80 – Dans le cadre de son contrôle de la compétence, la cour doit vérifier que l'opération qui sert de base à la demande entre dans le cadre des prévisions du TBI pour vérifier si elle peut effectivement bénéficier de l'offre d'arbitrage du traité.

81 – En l'espèce, le TBI ne comporte aucune exigence au titre de l'investissement telle que celles alléguées par l'État de Libye en termes d'apports, de durée et ou de risque, qui ont été dégagées dans le cadre d'investissements soumis à la convention CIRDI, ce qui n'est pas le cas en l'espèce.

82 – Au contraire la référence à l'investissement est très large puisqu'il ressort du TBI que la définition des investissements à l'article 1(2) comprend « *toute classe de biens, notamment mais non exclusivement (...)* » et que la liste dressée n'est pas exhaustive.

83 – En conséquence les critères invoqués ne résultant pas du Traité, il convient de considérer que ce grief pour justifier de l'incompétence du tribunal n'est pas fondé. En tout état de cause, le recourant ne justifie pas que les Contrats A ne satisfont pas le critère économique de l'investissement, à le supposer applicable, ces contrats portant sur des projets de constructions et de rénovation, justifiant le déploiement d'actifs importants, des équipements et du personnel, ainsi qu'une expertise et un savoir-faire permettant de répondre aux critères d'apport, de durée et de risque, à les supposer applicables.

84 – Le moyen tiré de l'incompétence du tribunal arbitral à raison de l'investissement allégué sera en conséquence rejeté.

– *Sur la compétence ratione temporis du Tribunal arbitral*

[...]

90 – L'article 10 du TBI stipule que : « *Le présent Accord s'applique aux investissements effectués sur le territoire d'une Partie contractants conformément à sa législation et à sa réglementation avant ou après son entrée en vigueur, par les investisseurs de l'autre Partie contractante. Toutefois, il ne s'applique pas aux différends qui sont nés avant son entrée en vigueur* ».

91 – Il en résulte clairement qu'il s'applique aux investissements effectués avant ou après son entrée en vigueur et qu'il ne s'applique qu'aux différends nés après son entrée en vigueur.

92 – C'est en application de ce texte que le tribunal arbitral a rejeté sa compétence ratione temporis pour une partie des demandes dont la naissance du différend a été considérée par le tribunal antérieure à l'entrée en vigueur du Traité.

[...]

94 – Tous ces éléments ont eu lieu postérieurement à l'entrée en vigueur du Traité fixée au 22 avril 2011, que ce soit le non-respect des accords de reprise, la résiliation des Contrats A, ou les conséquences de la guerre civile sur l'exécution des contrats et la sécurité des parties, quand bien même une partie de ces demandes nécessitent de prendre en compte des faits antérieurs, afin de tenir compte du contexte des différends.

95 – C'est donc à juste titre que le tribunal arbitral s'est déclaré compétent ratione temporis sur les différends mentionnés dans la Sentence.

96 – Le moyen tiré de l'incompétence du tribunal arbitral sera en conséquence rejeté en l'ensemble de ses moyens.

1. Sur le moyen (subsidiaire) d'annulation tiré de la contrariété de la reconnaissance et l'exécution de la sentence arbitrale du 22 novembre 2018 à l'ordre public international : article 1520 5° du Code de procédure civile.

[...]

101 – Il résulte de l'article 1520, 5° du Code de procédure civile que le recours en annulation est ouvert si la reconnaissance ou l'exécution de la sentence est contraire à l'ordre public international.

102 – L'ordre public international au regard duquel s'effectue le contrôle du juge de l'annulation s'entend de la conception qu'en a l'ordre juridique français, c'est-à-dire des valeurs et des principes dont celui-ci ne saurait souffrir la méconnaissance même dans un contexte international.

103 – Le contrôle exercé par le juge de l'annulation pour la défense de l'ordre public international s'attache seulement à examiner si l'exécution des dispositions prises par le tribunal arbitral heurte de manière manifeste, effective et concrète les principes et valeurs compris dans l'ordre public international.

104 – S'agissant d'une sentence statuant uniquement sur la compétence, et non sur le fond, le contrôle du juge porte uniquement sur les conséquences que l'exécution de cette sentence pourrait avoir au regard de la conception française de l'ordre public international lié à l'exercice de ladite compétence, c'est-à-dire la tenue du tribunal arbitral pour trancher le litige au fond opposant les parties.

105 – Or l'annulation d'une décision sur la compétence a pour effet de priver les parties du droit de soumettre leur litige au tribunal arbitral choisi, résultant de l'offre d'arbitrage du TBI, et non de prendre une décision sur l'issue du litige, qui pourrait être affectée au regard de la corruption alléguée, dont ni le tribunal arbitral à ce stade, ni la cour d'appel ne sont saisis.

[...]

108 – En conséquence, la demande d'annulation formulée sur le fondement de l'article 1520, 5° du Code de procédure civile, porte sur des faits dont seul le tribunal arbitral sera saisi au fond et ne saurait dès lors prospérer au stade de la seule compétence du tribunal arbitral, la demande d'annulation de la sentence du 22 novembre 2018 étant rejetée sur ce fondement.

Mission

[...]

112 – La mission des arbitres, définie par la convention d'arbitrage, est délimitée principalement par l'objet du litige, tel qu'il est déterminé par les prétentions des parties.

113 – Il résulte des écritures du recourant que celui-ci reproche au tribunal d'avoir écarté l'hypothèse de la corruption au titre des University Contracts

en se fondant sur une conception permissive et manifestement erronée de la corruption.

114 – Il ressort de cette critique que sous couvert de l'absence de motivation, le recourant entend en réalité contester la suffisance de celle-ci et donc sa pertinence, ce que la cour ne peut contrôler.

115 – Il en est de même sur la clause 10 dite de légalité, sur laquelle les arbitres ont appuyé leur décision sur la compétence, le recourant entendant faire rejuger cette appréciation sous couvert d'un non-respect de la mission des arbitres, ce qui ne saurait prospérer.

116 – Ce moyen sera en conséquence rejeté.

– Paris, Chambre commerciale internationale, Pôle 5 – chambre 16, 28 septembre 2021, n° 19/19834, *État de Libye c. À Insaat Ve Ticaret Anonim Sirketi*

Sentence arbitrale – Tribunal arbitral – Mission – Amiable composition – Notion – Équité – Motivation – Définition – Contrôle du juge – Révision au fond – Principe du contradictoire – Notion – Motifs

Sur le moyen d'annulation de la sentence tiré ce que le tribunal arbitral a statué sans se conformer à sa mission (article 1492-3° du Code de procédure civile)

[...]

L'article 14 du contrat du 13 décembre 2006 stipule que « [T]*ous les litiges auxquels le contrat pourra donner lieu, notamment au sujet de sa validité, de son interprétation, de son exécution et de sa résiliation seront résolus par voie d'arbitrage [...] Les arbitres [...] statueront en amiables compositeurs* ».

L'acte de mission signé par les parties et les arbitres rappelle en son article 2 qu'en application de la convention des parties, les arbitres statueront en amiable composition.

La clause d'amiable composition est une renonciation conventionnelle aux effets et au bénéfice de la règle de droit, les parties perdant la prérogative d'en exiger la stricte application et les arbitres recevant corrélativement le pouvoir de modifier ou de modérer les conséquences des stipulations contractuelles dès lors que l'équité ou l'intérêt commun bien compris des parties l'exige, sauf lorsqu'est en cause une disposition d'ordre public au bénéfice de laquelle une partie ne peut renoncer.

Lorsque les arbitres ont reçu mission de statuer comme amiables compositeurs, il doit ressortir de leur décision qu'ils ont pris en compte l'équité en la confrontant à la solution en droit. Il suffit qu'il ressorte de la sentence que l'arbitre a effectivement pris en compte l'équité, le juge du contrôle n'ayant pas à s'assurer que la solution donnée au litige par les arbitres, est équitable mais uniquement de vérifier que la motivation fait apparaître ou, à tout le moins, témoigne de la recherche d'une solution équitable.

Contrairement à ce que prétendent les demandeurs, pour évaluer le préjudice subi, le tribunal arbitral n'a pas fait une simple application d'une formule mathématique ou d'un simple calcul arithmétique.

[...]

Ainsi, à chaque étape de son raisonnement, le tribunal arbitral a fait ressortir les principes juridiques et comptables qu'il appliquait ou écartait ainsi que les considérations de droit et de fait qui le conduisaient à proposer en équité les éléments de calcul qu'il retenait, pour aboutir à l'indemnisation du préjudice subi qu'il a chiffré au titre de la réparation de la perte de chance, et à exclure le préjudice résultant de la perte de rémunération alléguée du mandataire social. Il ressort ainsi de la sentence que l'arbitre a effectivement pris en compte l'équité pour apprécier l'étendue de l'assiette du préjudice qu'il convenait de prendre en compte et motiver sa décision sur le montant du préjudice réparable.

[...]

Contrairement à ce que soutiennent les demandeurs, les arbitres n'ont ainsi pas manqué à leur mission d'amiables compositeurs alors qu'ils ont jugé en équité que la somme réparait l'entier préjudice subi.

Sur le moyen d'annulation de la sentence tiré ce que le tribunal arbitral a statué en violation du contradictoire (article 1492-4° du Code de procédure civile)

[...]

Le principe de la contradiction exige seulement que les parties aient pu faire connaître leurs prétentions de fait et de droit et discuter celles de leur adversaire de telle sorte que rien de ce qui a servi à fonder la décision des arbitres n'ait échappé à leur débat contradictoire. Le tribunal arbitral n'a pas l'obligation de soumettre au préalable l'argumentation juridique qui étaye sa motivation, à la discussion des parties.

[...]

La qualification du préjudice subi, en gain manqué ou en perte de chance, a donc été mise dans le débat contradictoire entre les parties par les sociétés devant les arbitres, sans que les demandeurs ne prétendent ne pas avoir été mis en mesure d'y répondre. En jugeant que le préjudice subi par les demandeurs consistait en une perte de chance, le tribunal arbitral n'a donc pas violé le principe du contradictoire et n'a fait que statuer en droit et en fait sur la question qui lui était soumise par les parties.

En second lieu, il en a été de même pour l'ensemble des éléments soumis au tribunal arbitral, pour déterminer le préjudice réellement subi tant par la société que par M. B. [...]

[...]

Le moyen doit en conséquence être écarté.

Sur le moyen tiré du non-respect de l'obligation de motivation (1482 et 1492-6° du Code de procédure civile)

[...]

Le contrôle du juge de l'annulation ne saurait porter que sur l'existence et non la pertinence des motifs de la sentence. La contestation de la pertinence de la motivation constitue nécessairement une critique au fond de la sentence qui échappe au juge de l'annulation.

– **Paris, Chambre commerciale internationale, Pôle 5 – chambre 16, 28 septembre 2021, n° 18/09530, *Clausylen et Lijak c. ITM Entreprises***

Sentence arbitrale – Arbitrage interne – Critère économique – Tribunal arbitral – Mission – Amiable composition – Notion – Équité – Contrôle – Révision au fond

L'article 1504 du Code de procédure civile dispose qu'est international l'arbitrage qui met en cause des intérêts du commerce international. Ainsi, l'internationalité de l'arbitrage fait appel à une définition économique selon laquelle il suffit que le litige soumis à l'arbitre porte sur une opération qui ne se dénoue pas économiquement dans un seul État, et ce, indépendamment de la qualité ou de la nationalité des parties, de la loi applicable au fond ou à l'arbitrage, ou encore du siège du tribunal arbitral.

En l'espèce, le contrat de 2014 porte sur la cession d'actions de la société de droit français, ayant son siège dans la commune de La Seauve-sur-Semene, à une autre société de droit français, le groupe, ayant son siège à Perigny. L'opération économique s'est donc dénouée uniquement en France, peu important que les cédants soient de nationalité espagnole et domiciliés en Espagne et peu important que les chèques, émis en France et tirés sur une banque française, aient été encaissés en Espagne.

L'arbitrage a donc un caractère interne.

Sur le moyen de nullité tiré de l'article 1492, 3°du Code de procédure civile

[...]

Les règles applicables

L'article 1478 du Code de procédure civile dispose que « *le tribunal arbitral tranche le litige conformément aux règles de droit, à moins que les parties lui aient confié la mission de statuer en amiable composition* » Le tribunal arbitral, auquel les parties ont conféré la mission de statuer comme amiable compositeur, doit faire ressortir dans sa sentence qu'il a pris en compte l'équité.

Par ailleurs, la clause d'amiable composition constitue une renonciation conventionnelle aux effets et au bénéfice de la règle de droit, les parties perdant la prérogative d'en exiger la stricte application et les arbitres recevant corrélativement le pouvoir de modifier ou de modérer les conséquences des stipulations contractuelles dès lors que l'équité ou l'intérêt bien compris des parties l'exige.

L'article 1492, 3°, du même code énonce, notamment et en substance, que le recours en annulation contre une sentence est ouvert si le tribunal arbitral a statué sans se conformer à la mission qui lui avait été confiée.

Ce recours ne conduit pas au contrôle de la pertinence du raisonnement du tribunal arbitral statuant comme amiable compositeur, compte tenu du principe de prohibition de la révision au fond de la sentence.

[...]

Étant rappelé qu'il n'appartient pas à la cour d'appel de contrôler l'équité de la solution donnée au litige par les arbitres.

– Paris, Pôle 5 – Chambre 16, 28 septembre 2021, n° 19/05842, *Groupe Lea Nature c. X*

Contrat de franchise – Clause compromissoire – Juge d'appui – Désignation – Choix des parties

Nous lisons à l'article 1459 du Code de procédure civile : « *Le juge d'appui compétent est le président du tribunal judiciaire. Toutefois, si la convention d'arbitrage le prévoit expressément, le président du tribunal de commerce est compétent pour connaître des demandes formées en application des articles 1451 à 1454. Dans ce cas, il peut faire application de l'article 1455. Le juge territorialement compétent est celui désigné par la convention d'arbitrage ou, à défaut, celui dans le ressort duquel le siège du tribunal arbitral a été fixé. En l'absence de toute stipulation de la convention d'arbitrage, le juge territorialement compétent est celui du lieu où demeure le ou l'un des défendeurs à l'incident ou, si le défendeur ne demeure pas en France, du lieu où demeure le demandeur.* » ; et à l'article 1461 du même code : « *Sous réserve des dispositions du premier alinéa de l'article 1456, toute stipulation contraire aux règles édictées au présent chapitre est réputée non écrite.* »

Nous relevons que l'article 11 « Clause de médiation et d'arbitrage » de l'accord de franchise conclu le 1° mars 2013 entre les parties stipule : « *Avant toute action contentieuse, les parties chercheront de bonne foi, à régler à l'amiable leurs différends relatifs à la validité, l'exécution et à l'interprétation du présent contrat. Les parties devront se réunir afin de confronter leurs points de vue et effectuer toutes constatations utiles pour leur permettre de trouver une solution au conflit qui les oppose. Les parties s'efforceront de trouver un accord amiable dans un délai de 30 jours à compter de la notification par l'une d'elles de la nécessité d'un accord amiable, par lettre recommandée avec avis de réception. À défaut d'accord amiable, les parties conviennent de soumettre leur différend sous l'égide du Centre de Médiation et d'Arbitrage de la Chambre de Commerce et d'Industrie de Paris. Les parties organiseront la médiation selon le règlement de médiation en vigueur. Les parties s'engagent à partager à frais égal les frais de ladite médiation tout en conservant à leur charge du frais et honoraires de leurs avocats respectifs. Les parties entendent conférer à cette procédure, prévue aux alinéas ci-dessus, une pleine force contractuelle. De commune volonté des parties, l'action en justice engagée par l'une d'elles en inobservation de cette procédure sera irrecevable. Il est convenu que, nonobstant les stipulations des paragraphes ci-dessus, les parties conservent en toutes circonstances la faculté d'agir par-devant la juridiction des référés sur le fondement notamment des articles 145, 872 et 873 du Code de procédure civile. En cas d'échec de la médiation, toute contestation auquel pourront donner lieu à la conclusion, l'interprétation et l'exécution du présent accord seront soumises à trois arbitres. La partie désirant recourir à l'arbitrage adressera à l'autre partie une notification, par lettre recommandée avec accusé de réception, de son intention de recourir à l'arbitrage en lui indiquant le nom de son arbitre. L'autre partie devra, dans les mêmes formes et dans le délai maximum de 15 jours à compter de la notification, indiquer à l'autre partie le nom de l'arbitre qu'elle aura désigné. À défaut de cette désignation, son arbitre pourrait être désigné par simple ordonnance de Monsieur le Président du tribunal de commerce de Paris statuant comme en matière de référé à la demande de la partie la plus diligente. Les arbitres désignés par les parties ou, le cas échéant par Monsieur le Président du tribunal de commerce, seront à se mettre d'accord sur le choix du troisième arbitre. S'ils n'y parvenaient pas, ce troisième arbitre serait désigné par ordonnance de Monsieur le Président du tribunal de commerce de Paris statuant comme en matière de référé. Ces arbitres, dont la durée de la mission est limitée à 6 mois, ne seront soumis à aucune règle ni aucun délai prévu au Code de procédure civile et ce conformément à l'article 1464 du Code de procédure civile. Ils agiront comme amiables compositeurs et statueront en dernier ressort, leur décision n'étant susceptible d'aucun recours à l'exception du recours en annulation. Dans l'hypothèse où la sentence arbitrale serait annulée, le différend sera soumis à nouveau à trois arbitres qui seront désignés et agiront dans les conditions ci-dessus fixées. L'arbitrage aura lieu à Paris.* » ;

Les parties n'ayant pas désigné, dans la convention d'arbitrage, le président du tribunal de commerce de Paris comme juge d'appui, nous nous déclarons incompétent au profit du président du tribunal judiciaire de Paris.

Sur l'irrecevabilité

[...]

Nous constatons que l'article 1459 du Code de procédure civile, qui désigne le président du tribunal judiciaire comme juge d'appui, laisse ouverte la possibilité pour les parties, dans la convention d'arbitrage, de désigner comme juge d'appui le président du tribunal de commerce. Il n'est donc pas exclu, pour les parties, de déroger conventionnellement à la compétence du président du tribunal judiciaire.

La partie échoue à démontrer cette exclusion totale qu'elle affirme ; en conséquence, nous la débouterons de sa demande en irrecevabilité.

– **TC Paris, Ord., 29 septembre 2021, n° 2021034991, *CSF c. Fadis* (voir arrêt du 14 décembre 2021 reproduit ci-dessous)**

Rupture de relations commerciales – Clause de conciliation – Fin de non-recevoir – Attitude des parties – Clause compromissoire – Examen prima facie – Évidence – Principe de compétence compétence – Portée – Applicabilité ou nullité manifeste

L'article 17-1 des CGA dispose : « *La présente commande est régie et interprétée et prend effet conformément au droit français à l'exclusion de l'application de la "Convention des Nations Unies sur les contrats de vente internationale de marchandises de 1980"* ». L'article 17-2 dispose : « *Règlement à l'amiable. En cas de litige, controverse ou réclamation (un litige) découlant de ou en relation avec la présente commande, y compris toute question concernant son existence, sa validité ou sa résiliation, les Parties feront tous les efforts nécessaires pour résoudre le Litige à l'amiable dans un délai de trois (3) mois suivant la notification écrite d'un Litige par l'une à l'autre* ». L'article 17-3 dispose : « *Arbitrage. Si les parties ne parviennent pas à résoudre le Différend à l'amiable dans le délai de trois (3) mois susmentionné, ce Différend sera définitivement réglé par arbitrage conformément au Règlement d'arbitrage de la Chambre de commerce internationale. Le nombre d'arbitres sera de trois (3) et le lieu de l'arbitrage sera Paris. La langue à utiliser dans la procédure est l'anglais* ».

S'agissant du règlement amiable, la Cour retient qu'une tentative de rapprochement a bien eu lieu entre les parties notamment le 22 novembre 2019 à l'initiative d'une partie. La fin de non-recevoir opposée est donc rejetée.

S'agissant de la clause d'arbitrage, le contentieux né de la rupture brutale d'une relation commerciale établie peut être soumis à l'arbitrage. Les parties divergent sur la portée de la clause.

[...]

En vertu du principe compétence compétence, il appartient à l'arbitre de se prononcer sur les contestations relatives à sa compétence sauf si le tribunal arbitral n'est pas encore saisi et si la clause d'arbitrage lui apparaît manifestement nulle ou manifestement inapplicable.

Sur ce dernier point, seule une nullité ou une inapplicabilité s'imposant avec la force de l'évidence, sans nécessité pour le juge de procéder à un examen factuel autre que superficiel, est susceptible de satisfaire ce caractère manifeste.

En l'espèce, la clause compromissoire vise un litige « *découlant ou en relation avec la commande* ». Un simple examen prima facie de cette clause ne permet pas de dire celle-ci manifestement inapplicable au litige.

Il appartient à l'arbitre de dire si une telle clause est suffisamment large pour s'appliquer au contentieux né de la rupture brutale de la relation commerciale établie alléguée. Il convient dès lors d'infirmer le jugement en ce que le tribunal s'est déclaré compétent et de renvoyer les parties à mieux se pourvoir.

– Paris, Pôle 5 – Chambre 4, 29 septembre 2021, n° 20/18243, *Agoranet c. Airbus*

Arbitrage CNUDCI – Tribunal arbitral – Compétence – Capacité à agir – Recevabilité – Investissement – Champ d'application – TBI – Volonté commune – Condition d'application – Compétence ratione personae – Investisseur – Notion – Contrôle – Convention de Vienne sur le droit des traités du 23 mai 1969 – Convention de Washington du 18 mars 1965 créant le CIRDI – Compétence ratione materiae – Recevabilité – Nationalité – Moyen tardif – Nouveaux arguments – Révision au fond – Champ d'application du traité – Pouvoir juridictionnel – Offre permanente d'arbitrage – Autonomie et indépendance – Validité de l'opération – Arbitre – Indépendance et impartialité – Règlement CNUDCI – Délai – Demande de récusation – Doute raisonnable – Démarche objective – Ordre public international – Corruption – Déni de justice substantiel par le tribunal arbitral – Contrôle de la motivation – Juridiction d'appel des décisions de justice internes – Lois internes – Souveraineté – Atteinte – Convention européenne de sauvegarde des droits de l'Homme et des libertés fondamentales – Applicabilité – Mission – Traitement juste et équitable – Charte africaine des droits de l'homme et des peuples – Principe de la contradiction – Défaut de qualification

Sur le non-respect de sa mission

1-Sur les demandes tendant à l'annulation totale de la sentence arbitrale

1-1 Sur le moyen d'annulation tiré de l'incompétence du tribunal arbitral (article 1520, 1° du Code de procédure civile)

[...]

20-Selon l'article 1520, 1°, du Code de procédure civile, le recours en annulation est ouvert si le tribunal s'est déclaré à tort compétent ou incompétent.

21-Dans le cadre d'un recours en annulation fondé sur l'article 1520, 1° du Code de procédure civile, il appartient au juge de l'annulation de contrôler la décision du tribunal arbitral sur sa compétence, qu'il se soit déclaré compétent ou incompétent, en recherchant tous les éléments de droit ou de fait permettant d'apprécier la portée de la convention d'arbitrage.

Sur la fin de non-recevoir soulevée

22-S'il est exact que la capacité à agir relève d'une question de recevabilité de l'action et non d'une question de compétence du tribunal arbitral qui a à en connaître, et qu'une telle contestation ne constitue pas un des cas d'ouverture du recours en annulation limitativement énumérés à l'article 1520 du Code de procédure civile, tel n'est pas le cas d'un moyen qui tend à contester l'aptitude d'un tribunal arbitral à connaître d'un litige au regard du champ d'application d'un traité bilatéral d'investissements, qui relève bien d'une question de compétence et non de recevabilité.

[...]

24-La fin de non-recevoir, qui repose sur une qualification erronée du moyen invoqué, sera en conséquence écartée.

Sur la compétence ratione personae du tribunal arbitral ;

25-Lorsque la clause d'arbitrage résulte d'un Traité bilatéral d'investissements, il convient d'apprécier la volonté commune des parties contractantes de recourir à l'arbitrage au regard de l'ensemble des dispositions du traité de sorte que le tribunal arbitral n'est compétent pour connaître d'un litige que s'il entre dans le champ d'application du traité et qu'il est satisfait à l'ensemble de ses conditions d'application.

26-En l'espèce, l'article 8 intitulé « *Règlement des différends entre un investisseur et une Partie contractante* » du TBI est ainsi rédigé : « *Tout différend relatif aux investissements entre l'une des Parties contractantes et un investisseur de l'autre Partie contractante est réglé à l'amiable entre les deux parties concernées. Si un tel différend n'a pas pu être réglé dans un délai de six mois à partir de la date à laquelle un règlement amiable a été demandé par l'une ou l'autre des parties au différend, il est soumis à la demande de l'investisseur concerné à l'arbitrage : – d'un tribunal arbitral ad hoc constitué selon les règles d'arbitrage de la Commission des Nations Unies pour le droit commercial international (CNUDCI), ou ; – du Centre international pour le règlement des différends relatifs aux investissements (CIRDI), créé par la Convention pour le règlement des différends relatifs aux investissements entre États et ressortissants d'autres États, signée à Washington le 18 mars 1965, ou ; – de la Cour commune de justice et d'arbitrage créée par le Traité de l'Organisation pour l'harmonisation du droit des affaires en Afrique du 17 octobre 1993 (OHADA), lorsque les parties aux différends relèvent de ce Traité. Dans le cas où le différend est de nature à engager la responsabilité pour les actions ou omissions de collectivités publiques ou d'organismes dépendants de l'une des deux Parties contractantes, au sens de l'article 2 du présent accord, ladite collectivité publique ou ledit organisme sont tenus de donner leur consentement de manière inconditionnelle au recours à l'arbitrage du Centre international pour le règlement des différends relatifs aux investissements (CIRDI), au sens de l'article 25 de la Convention pour le règlement des différends relatifs aux investissements entre États et ressortissants d'autres États, signée à Washington le 18 mars 1965* ».

27-Il ressort en outre de l'article 1 (2) (a) du TBI que les « *investisseurs* » sont définis comme « *Les nationaux, c'est-à-dire les personnes physiques possédant la nationalité de l'une des Parties contractantes* ».

28-Pour retenir sa compétence, le tribunal arbitral, à la majorité, a considéré dans le paragraphe 144 de sa sentence qu'un « *binational est une personne qui a pleinement et cumulativement deux nationalités. L'article 1.2 du TBI ne rencontre donc pas d'obstacle objectif à son application. Seule la volonté de traiter les binationaux comme différents de ceux qui n'ont qu'une nationalité justifierait qu'on les exclue de la catégorie générale de ceux qui possèdent la nationalité de l'une des Parties contractantes. Cela nécessiterait que l'on introduise au sein de cette dernière catégorie une distinction qui ne figure pas dans le TBI et qui ne s'impose pas rationnellement. Or, précisément, l'une des règles essentielles de l'interprétation est l'interdiction de distinguer là où le texte ne distingue pas. Le Tribunal arbitral ne saurait donc considérer, pour l'application du TBI, les binationaux sénégalo-français comme une catégorie distincte des Français, alors que le TBI ne comporte pas une telle distinction et que celle-ci serait injustifiée au regard du statut du binational. Le Tribunal arbitral statuant à la majorité de ses membres est donc d'avis que le silence du TBI à l'égard des binationaux sénégalo-français n'est pas une lacune : les binationaux sénégalo-français répondent pleinement à la condition posée à l'article 1.2 du TBI, à savoir la possession de la nationalité de l'une des Parties contractantes* ».

29-Il convient en effet de relever que le TBI ne contient aucune disposition concernant les binationaux.

30-Si, en application de l'article 31 intitulé « *Règle générale d'interprétation* » de la Convention de Vienne sur le droit des traités du 23 mai 1969 « *1. Un traité doit être interprété de bonne foi suivant le sens ordinaire à attribuer aux termes du traité dans leur contexte et à la lumière de son objet et de son but* » et que « *2. Aux fins de l'interprétation d'un traité, le contexte comprend, outre le texte, préambule et annexes inclus : a) Tout accord ayant rapport au traité et qui est intervenu entre toutes les parties à l'occasion de la conclusion du traité ; b) Tout instrument établi par une ou plusieurs parties à l'occasion de la conclusion du traité et accepté par les autres parties en tant qu'instrument ayant rapport au traité* », il ne résulte pas de ces règles qu'il conviendrait de distinguer là où le traité ne distingue pas.

31-De même, il ressort de l'article 32 de ce traité intitulé « *Moyen complémentaire d'interprétation* » qu'il « *peut être fait appel à des moyens complémentaires d'interprétation, et notamment aux travaux préparatoires et aux circonstances dans lesquelles le traité a été conclu, en vue, soit de confirmer le sens résultant de l'application de l'article 31, soit de déterminer le sens lorsque l'interprétation donnée conformément à l'article 31 : a) Laisse le sens ambigu ou obscur ; ou b) Conduit à un résultat qui est manifestement absurde ou déraisonnable* ».

32-En l'occurrence, le sens ordinaire des termes du traité, sans qu'il ne soit utile de se livrer à une interprétation de ce texte, de se référer aux règles propres à la protection diplomatique, ou encore de se livrer à une appréciation sur la nationalité dominante et effective de l'investisseur, ne peut conduire à exclure les binationaux de l'application du TBI, au risque d'ajouter une condition qui n'a pas été stipulée.

33-Une telle interprétation n'est au demeurant pas contraire à l'objet et au but du traité qui vise à « renforcer la coopération économique entre les deux États et de créer des conditions favorables pour les investissements français au Sénégal et sénégalais en France ; persuadés que l'encouragement et la protection de ces investissements sont de nature à stimuler les transferts de capitaux et de technologie entre les deux pays, dans l'intérêt de leur développement économique », de même qu'au regard de l'histoire des relations entre la France et la République du Sénégal et du nombre très important de binationaux des deux pays, évalué par les parties entre 3,3 et 5 millions, considération qui ne peut pas avoir échappé aux États signataires.

[...]

35-A cet égard, le fait que la Convention de Washington du 18 mars 1965 créant le CIRDI, rappelle expressément dans son article 25(2)(a) que le « *Ressortissant d'un autre État contractant* » signifie « *(a) toute personne physique qui possède la nationalité d'un État contractant autre que l'État partie au différend à la date à laquelle les parties ont consenti à soumettre le différend à la conciliation ou à l'arbitrage (...), à l'exclusion de toute personne qui, à l'une ou à l'autre de ces dates, possède également la nationalité de l'État contractant partie au différend* », est inopérant en l'espèce, dès lors qu'il est constant que les parties n'ont pas opté pour un arbitrage CIRDI mais, comme le TBI le leur permettait aux termes de son article 8 leur offrant une option, pour un arbitrage constitué sous l'égide de la CNUDCI, qui, précisément, ne reprend pas une telle règle.

36-De même, le fait que certains articles du TBI renvoient à la notion « d'investisseur étranger » (article 1.5) ou à celle d'investisseur « de l'autre partie contractante » (article 5, 6, et 8) n'est pas de nature à exclure la compétence du tribunal arbitral pour connaître d'un litige en faveur d'un binational ; outre le fait que cette question relève d'une appréciation au fond portant sur l'étendue de la protection substantielle (et non procédurale) à accorder effectivement à l'investisseur qui se prévaut des dispositions du TBI sans que cette circonstance puisse exclure la compétence du tribunal arbitral pour en connaître et décider du bénéfice possible de telle ou telle disposition protectrice en fonction de son champ d'application.

37-Il ressort de ces éléments que le TBI, contrairement à d'autres instruments internationaux, ne fait pas un sort particulier aux binationaux, de sorte qu'il n'y a pas lieu d'ajouter au texte une distinction que les parties contractantes n'ont pas entendu y insérer.

38-En l'état de ces éléments, ce grief sera rejeté.

Sur la compétence ratione materiae du tribunal arbitral ;

Sur la recevabilité du grief tiré d'une condition de nationalité de l'investisseur au moment de la constitution de l'investissement,

39-Aux termes de l'article 1466 du même code, la partie qui, en connaissance de cause et sans motif légitime, s'abstient d'invoquer en temps utile une irrégularité devant le tribunal arbitral est réputée avoir renoncé à s'en prévaloir.

40-Lorsque la compétence a été débattue devant les arbitres, les parties ne sont pas privées du droit d'invoquer sur cette question, devant le juge de l'annulation, de nouveaux moyens et arguments et à faire état, à cet effet, de nouveaux éléments de preuve.

[...]

Sur le bien-fondé du grief tiré d'une condition de nationalité de l'investisseur au moment de la constitution de l'investissement

42-Aux termes de l'article 1.1 du TBI, « *Le terme « investissement » désigne tous les avoirs, tels que les biens, droits et intérêts de toutes natures et plus particulièrement mais non exclusivement : (...). Il est entendu que lesdits avoirs doivent être ou avoir été investis conformément à la législation de la Partie contractante sur le territoire ou dans la zone maritime de laquelle l'investissement est effectué, avant ou après l'entrée en vigueur du présent accord* ».

43-Aucune condition supplémentaire n'est requise en lien avec la date à laquelle celui qui investit est titulaire la nationalité de l'autre partie contractante.

44-En tout état de cause, la partie étant française par filiation depuis sa naissance, cette condition à supposer exiger par le TBI serait satisfaite de sorte que le grief tiré de l'incompétence du tribunal arbitral n'est pas fondé.

Sur la notion d'investissement protégé

[...]

46-A cet égard, il convient de relever qu'une telle condition relative au « flux », qui devrait conduire à n'accorder une protection qu'aux seuls investissements réalisés sur le territoire sénégalais avec des capitaux transférés depuis la France, ne résulte pas de l'article 1.1 du TBI sur la définition du terme « investissement » qui ne comporte nullement une telle restriction, et qui précise en outre que ce terme peut couvrir aussi les « *participations, même minoritaires ou indirectes, aux sociétés constituées sur le territoire de l'une des Parties contractantes* ».

47-Elle ne résulte pas non plus du préambule de ce traité qui précise seulement que les deux pays sont « *désireux de renforcer la coopération économique entre les deux États et de créer des conditions favorables pour les investissements français au Sénégal et sénégalais en France* ».

48-Ainsi, il convient de considérer d'une part, que l'investissement peut mobiliser des ressources générées sur n'importe quel territoire et d'autre part, qu'il peut entrer dans le champ du TBI dès lors qu'il émane d'une personne ayant la nationalité française, ce qui est le cas en l'espèce, la partie ayant acquis cette nationalité dès sa naissance.

49-Enfin, l'article 8 du TBI relative à la protection procédurale (clause d'arbitrage) ne comporte pas non plus de conditions liées à la nécessité d'un « flux » tel qu'allégué par la République du Sénégal. Ce faisant, sous couvert d'un moyen tiré de l'incompétence du tribunal, la République du Sénégal entend remettre en cause la décision visant à accorder à l'investissement de M. A. la protection substantielle prévue par le TBI, laquelle est distincte de la protection procédurale.

[...]

51-Ce grief sera en conséquence rejeté.

Sur l'illégalité alléguée de l'investissement ;

52-En présence d'un traité bilatéral d'investissements, dès lors que la compétence du tribunal arbitral est la condition du consentement de l'État au recours à l'arbitrage, le tribunal arbitral ne peut connaître d'un litige que s'il entre dans le champ d'application du traité et qu'il est satisfait à l'ensemble de ses conditions d'application temporelle, personnelle et matérielle qui a trait à l'existence du pouvoir juridictionnel du tribunal.

53-Cependant, ces conditions ne doivent pas conduire à priver l'exercice par le tribunal arbitral de son pouvoir juridictionnel et ainsi faire dépendre la compétence du tribunal ni de la recevabilité des demandes portées devant lui, ni de l'examen du bénéfice effectif de la protection substantielle à l'investissement litigieux, dont l'appréciation dépend uniquement d'une analyse au fond du litige.

54-Ainsi, sous couvert d'un contrôle de la compétence, le juge de l'annulation ne peut, se substituer à l'arbitre pour apprécier la validité ou la régularité de l'investissement litigieux, qui ne relève que du seul fond du litige et non de l'appréciation de la compétence du tribunal arbitral pour en connaître.

55-En outre, lorsque la clause d'arbitrage résulte d'un Traité bilatéral d'investissements, l'offre permanente d'arbitre est autonome et indépendante de la validité de l'opération qui a donné naissance à l'investissement ou qui la soutient.

[...]

58-Ainsi, sous couvert d'un moyen d'annulation tiré de l'incompétence du tribunal arbitral, la partie ne peut conduire la cour à réapprécier la légalité de l'investissement qui suppose de procéder à un nouvel examen des procédures et décisions qui ont été rendues à l'encontre de l'intéressé par la CREI qui a conclu à l'établissement d'un comportement délictueux de ce dernier, lesquelles participent de la violation par la partie de ses engagements pris au titre du TBI, et constituent précisément l'objet principal du litige qui a été soumis au tribunal arbitral.

59-Ce grief, inopérant, sera en conséquence rejeté.

Sur le grief tiré de l'incompétence du Tribunal arbitral pour connaître des agissements imputés au cabinet et engager la responsabilité la République du Sénégal ;

60-En l'espèce, il ressort de l'article 2 du TBI que « *Pour l'application du présent Accord, il est entendu que les Parties contractantes sont responsables des actions et omissions de leurs collectivités publiques, et notamment de leurs États fédérés, régions, collectivités locales ou de toute autre entité sur lesquels la Partie contractante exerce une tutelle, la représentation ou la responsabilité de ses relations internationales ou sa souveraineté* ».

[...]

64-Il ressort de cette critique que sous couvert d'un moyen sur la compétence, la République du Sénégal demande à la cour de déterminer si les agissements du cabinet Auditex pouvaient être imputés à la République du Sénégal et engager sa responsabilité internationale de sorte qu'elle entend ainsi revenir sur l'imputabilité d'un comportement à la République du Sénégal et sa responsabilité internationale reconnue par le tribunal arbitral, ce qui relève d'une question touchant au fond du litige, dont ne dépend pas la compétence du tribunal arbitral pour en connaître.

[...]

66-Ce grief sera en conséquence rejeté.

[...]

1-2 Sur le moyen d'annulation tiré du défaut d'impartialité du président du tribunal arbitral (article 1520, 2° du Code de procédure civile)

[...]

Sur la recevabilité du moyen ;

72-En l'espèce, l'article 11 du Règlement CNUDCI (version 1976) applicable à la procédure arbitrale prévoit que « *Toute partie qui souhaite récuser un arbitre doit notifier sa décision dans les quinze jours suivant la date à laquelle la nomination de cet arbitre lui a été notifiée ou dans les quinze jours suivant la date à laquelle elle a eu connaissance des circonstances visées aux articles 9 et 10* ».

73-En outre, en application de l'article 30 de ce Règlement, « *Toute partie qui, bien qu'elle sache que l'une des dispositions ou des conditions énoncées dans le présent Règlement n'a pas été respectée, poursuit néanmoins l'arbitrage sans formuler d'objection est réputée avoir renoncé à son droit de faire objection.* ».

74-De même, en application de l'article 1466 du Code de procédure civile, la partie qui, en connaissance de cause, s'abstient d'exercer, dans le délai prévu par le règlement d'arbitrage applicable, son droit de récusation, en se fondant sur toute circonstance de nature à mettre en cause l'indépendance ou l'impartialité d'un arbitre, est réputée avoir renoncé à s'en prévaloir devant le juge de l'annulation.

75-Au regard de ces textes, il incombe à la cour de rechercher si, relativement à chacun des faits et circonstances allégués comme constitutifs d'un manquement à l'obligation d'impartialité de l'arbitre, le délai imparti par le règlement d'arbitrage pour exercer le droit de récusation a, ou non, été respecté.

[...]

82-Dès lors que ces circonstances sont postérieures à la clôture des débats et ont été révélées qu'une fois la sentence arbitrale rendue, la partie ne peut être réputée y avoir renoncé de telle sorte que, pour ces circonstances, le moyen doit être déclaré recevable devant le juge de l'annulation.

Sur le bien-fondé du moyen

83-L'impartialité de l'arbitre suppose l'absence de préjugés ou de partis pris susceptibles d'affecter le jugement de l'arbitre, lesquels peuvent résulter de multiples facteurs tels que la nationalité de l'arbitre, son environnement social, culturel ou juridique.

84-Toutefois pour être pris en compte ces éléments doivent créer, dans l'esprit des parties, un doute raisonnable sur son impartialité de telle sorte que l'appréciation de ce défaut doit procéder d'une démarche objective.

85-Si un tel doute peut le cas échéant résulter de la sentence elle-même, encore faut-il, dès lors que le contenu de la motivation de la sentence arbitrale échappe au contrôle du juge de l'annulation, que ce doute soit fondé sur des éléments précis quant à la structure de la sentence ou ses termes mêmes, qui laisseraient supposer que l'attitude de l'arbitre a été partiale ou à tout le moins serait de nature à donner le sentiment qu'elle l'a été.

[...]

87-Il résulte de ces griefs que, sous couvert d'un défaut d'impartialité que ces seules énonciations sont impropres à caractériser, la critique de la partie porte en réalité sur la motivation du tribunal arbitral que celle-ci considère comme insuffisante pour fonder sa décision.

88-Il convient au regard de ces éléments de rejeter ce grief qui n'est nullement caractérisé et en conséquence ce moyen d'annulation.

1-3 Sur le moyen d'annulation tiré de la contrariété de la sentence à l'ordre public international (article 1520, 5° du Code de procédure civile)

103-Il résulte de l'article 1520, 5° du Code de procédure civile que le recours en annulation est ouvert si la reconnaissance ou l'exécution de la sentence est contraire à l'ordre public international.

104-L'ordre public international au regard duquel s'effectue le contrôle du juge de l'annulation s'entend de la conception qu'en a l'ordre juridique français, c'est-à-dire des valeurs et des principes dont celui-ci ne saurait souffrir la méconnaissance même dans un contexte international.

105-Le contrôle exercé par le juge de l'annulation pour la défense de l'ordre public international s'attache seulement à examiner si l'exécution des dispositions prises par le tribunal arbitral heurte de manière manifeste, effective et concrète les principes et valeurs compris dans l'ordre public international.

Sur le grief tiré de ce que la sentence donnerait effet à un investissement illégal ;

[...]

109-Il convient de rappeler qu'il appartient à la cour, dans le cadre de son contrôle, de vérifier que la reconnaissance ou l'exécution de cette sentence en France ne peut avoir pour effet de faire bénéficier M. A. du produit d'une activité de corruption ou de blanchiment, dont l'investissement protégé aurait été l'instrument et/ou le produit.

110-Sur ce point, il convient de relever que le tribunal arbitral s'est précisément penché sur cette question pour en réfuter la pertinence.

[...]

119-Ainsi, il ressort de ces éléments précis et concordants d'une part, que bien que des poursuites pénales ont été engagées contre lui, M. A. n'a pas été reconnu coupable de corruption et/ou de blanchiment à l'occasion des investissements qu'il a réalisés au Sénégal et d'autre part, que les juridictions françaises ont refusé l'exécution en France des mesures de confiscations prononcées contre ce dernier au titre de sa condamnation pour complicité d'enrichissement illicite, faute pour la France de connaître une telle infraction pénale et pour les faits litigieux d'être susceptibles de recevoir une autre qualification pénale en France.

120-Ce faisant, la sentence, dont l'effet est de sanctionner le non-respect par la République du Sénégal de son engagement international visant à assurer un traitement juste et équitable à l'investissement de M. A. et de réparer le préjudice subi par ce dernier du fait de cette violation, ne viole pas de manière manifeste effective et concrète l'ordre public international, sans qu'il soit nécessaire de reprendre un à un les indices alléguées par la République du Sénégal qui seraient de nature à conduire le juge de l'annulation à procéder à une nouvelle instruction pénale des faits qui ont été reprochés à l'intéressé et qui ont donné lieu à la décision de la CREI.

121-Ce moyen sera en conséquence rejeté.

Sur le grief tiré de la reconnaissance d'un déni de justice substantiel par le tribunal arbitral

122-En substance, la République du Sénégal reproche au tribunal arbitral d'avoir, en effectuant un contrôle de la motivation des décisions de la CREI et de la Cour suprême, outrepassé ses pouvoirs en se comportant comme une véritable juridiction d'appel des décisions de justice internes à l'État du Sénégal et, ce faisant, en portant atteinte à sa souveraineté.

123-Cependant, sous couvert de l'ordre public international, la partie critique en réalité ainsi les motifs par lesquels le tribunal arbitral a considéré qu'une décision de justice pouvait constituer un déni de justice « *non seulement lorsque les garanties essentielles d'un procès équitable ont été refusées à l'investisseur, mais encore lorsque la décision porte elle-même clairement le discrédit sur la juridiction qui l'a rendue (déni de justice substantiel)* ».

124-Ce grief est donc impropre à emporter l'annulation de la sentence et ce d'autant que d'une part, il ressort expressément de la sentence que l'examen par le tribunal arbitral d'un déni de justice substantiel l'a été à « titre surabondant », le tribunal ayant pris soin de préciser que le déni de justice procédural ayant été caractérisé, c'était « *donc à titre surabondant [qu'il] va examiner à présent les imputations du demandeur relatives au déni de justice substantiel* ».

125-D'autre part, le tribunal arbitral s'est attaché à bien délimiter son appréciation en précisant qu'il « *ne saurait se comporter en juridiction d'appel ou de cassation de la décision et substituer sa propre appréciation des faits et des règles applicables à celle du jugement interne* » et en s'attachant à préciser que « *son contrôle s'exercera sur la motivation des décisions de la CREI et de la Cour suprême, laquelle ne doit être ni sommaire, ni obscure, ni manifestement erronée, ni inacceptable. Dans le cas contraire, la décision judiciaire serait considérée comme constitutive d'un déni de justice, étant rappelé que, pour atteindre ce seuil, une décision judiciaire doit manifester un caractère fondamentalement injuste ou inique* » (§ 478) et ajoutant s'agissant du contrôle de la motivation, qu'il doit « seulement vérifier que celle qu'ont portée les juridictions sénégalaises n'est pas manifestement entachée d'arbitraire, en examinant la motivation de leurs décisions » (§ 479).

126-En l'état de ces éléments, ce grief sera rejeté.

Sur le grief tiré de l'ingérence dans le système judiciaire sénégalais

[...]

130-En l'état de ces éléments, aucune violation manifeste, effective et concrète d'une règle relevant de l'ordre public international n'est caractérisée.

131-Ce grief sera en conséquence rejeté.

2-Sur les demandes tendant à l'annulation partielle de la sentence arbitrale

2-1 Sur l'incompétence du tribunal arbitral pour ordonner l'indemnisation de la perte d'un investissement réalisé par le biais des sociétés de droit panaméen (article 1520, 1° du Code de procédure civile)

[...]

136-Selon l'article 1520, 1°, du Code de procédure civile, le recours en annulation est ouvert si le tribunal s'est déclaré à tort compétent ou incompétent.

137-Dans le cadre d'un recours en annulation fondé sur l'article 1520, 1° du Code de procédure civile, il appartient au juge de l'annulation de contrôler la décision du tribunal arbitral sur sa compétence, qu'il se soit déclaré compétent ou incompétent, en recherchant tous les éléments de droit ou de fait permettant d'apprécier la portée de la convention d'arbitrage.

138-Cependant, d'une part, s'agissant de la compétence ratione materiae, au regard de la définition donnée par l'article 1.1 du TBI qui couvre « tous avoirs, [...] biens, droits et intérêts de toutes natures », et comprend « les actions, primes d'émission et autres formes de participation, même minoritaires ou indirectes, aux sociétés constituées sur le territoire de l'une des Parties contractantes », le tribunal arbitral était bien compétent pour statuer.

[...]

141-Ainsi, il entrait dans la compétence du tribunal arbitral de prononcer l'indemnisation à raison des participations indirectes de M. A. dans les SCP de droit sénégalais.

[...]

143-Ainsi, la critique portant sur l'évaluation du préjudice de M. A. par le tribunal du fait de sa participation via des sociétés de droit panaméennes dans des SCP de droit sénégalais, relève d'une appréciation au fond du tribunal dont le contrôle échappe au juge de l'annulation.

144-Ce moyen sera en conséquence rejeté.

2 2 Sur la méconnaissance par le tribunal arbitral de sa mission à raison de la référence à la Convention européenne des droits de l'Homme (article 1520, 3° du Code de procédure civile)

[....]

148-Selon l'article 1520, 3°, du Code de procédure civile, le recours en annulation est ouvert si le tribunal a statué sans se conformer à la mission qui lui avait été confié.

149-En l'espèce, l'article 4 al. 1er du TBI stipule que « *Chacune des parties contractantes s'engage à assurer, sur son territoire et dans sa zone maritime un traitement juste et équitable, conformément aux principes du droit international, aux investissements des investisseurs de l'autre partie et à faire en sorte que l'exercice du droit ainsi reconnu ne soit entravé ni en droit, ni en fait* ».

150-Il rentrait donc dans la mission du tribunal arbitral d'apprécier le respect de l'engagement de la République du Sénégal d'assurer un traitement juste et équitable à M. A., et ce « *conformément aux principes du droit international* ».

[…]

156-Cependant, ces références sont purement illustratives et sont accompagnées d'un renvoi à d'autres instruments internationaux ne permettent pas de conclure que le tribunal a tranché le litige en faisant application de Conv. EDH en méconnaissance de sa mission.

157-Il ressort au contraire de la sentence que le tribunal s'est conformé à cette mission puisque pour décider que la partie avait été victime d'un déni de justice procédural de la part des autorités sénégalaises, le tribunal a considéré « *qu'il a été porté gravement et clairement atteinte aux droits de la défense internationalement reconnus dont il pouvait bénéficier par la négation : (1) de son droit à comparaître devant ses juges et à participer à son procès, (2) de son droit à l'assistance d'un avocat, (3) des garanties fondamentales de composition régulière des juridictions et (4) par l'application à sa personne de traitements inhumains et dégradants* ».

[…]

C'est bien par référence aux « droits de la défense internationalement reconnus » et à l'engagement tiré de l'article 4 du TBI que la partie a été condamnée, et non comme cette dernière le soutient en application des dispositions de la Convention européenne de sauvegarde des droits de l'Homme et des libertés fondamentales (ci-après la Conv. EDH).

160-Au demeurant, il ressort de la sentence que la question du champ de la référence aux « *principes du droit international* » pour apprécier le standard du traitement juste et équitable a été « *abondamment débattu* » par les parties, une partie soutenant que le standard du traitement juste et équitable devait se limiter au standard minimum reconnu par la coutume internationale tandis que l'autre soutenait que ce standard devait être recherché non seulement dans la coutume internationale mais au-delà dans les principes du droit international.

[…]

162-De même, bien que non directement applicable au présent litige, la Conv. EDH et la jurisprudence de la Cour européenne des droits de l'homme contribuent à l'émergence des standards de protection en droit international et participent ainsi à l'élaboration des principes du droit international auxquels fait référence le TBI précité. Le fait que l'État partie n'ait pas ratifié la Conv. EDH n'interdisait donc pas au tribunal arbitral de faire référence à ce texte dans sa sentence pour se livrer à une appréciation du contenu du standard du traitement juste et équitable à la lumière des principes du droit international, voire même à la jurisprudence de la Cour européenne des droits de l'homme, dès lors qu'il ne s'appuie pas précisément et exclusivement sur ce texte pour caractériser la violation de l'engagement pris par la RS, mais uniquement sur les « principes du droit international » et l'article 4 du TBI.

163-En l'état de ces éléments, le moyen n'est pas fondé et sera rejeté.

2-3 Sur la violation du principe de la contradiction et de la mission tiré du défaut de qualification de la nature du préjudice subi (article 1520, 3° et 4° du Code de procédure civile)

Sur le non-respect de sa mission par le tribunal arbitral

166-La mission des arbitres, définie par la convention d'arbitrage, est délimitée principalement par l'objet du litige, tel qu'il est déterminé par les prétentions des parties sans s'attacher uniquement à l'énoncé des questions dans l'acte de mission.

[...]

170-Ce faisant, le tribunal arbitral a statué dans le cadre des demandes formées à titre subsidiaire et le seul fait que le tribunal arbitral n'ait pas qualifié expressément ce dommage, ne constitue pas une méconnaissance de sa mission.

171-Ce grief sera en conséquence rejeté.

Sur le non-respect du principe de la contradiction

172-Il résulte de l'article 1520, 4° du Code de procédure civile que le recours en annulation est ouvert si le principe de la contradiction n'a pas été respecté.

173-Le principe de la contradiction exige seulement que les parties aient pu faire connaître leurs prétentions de fait et de droit et discuter celles de leur adversaire de telle sorte que rien de ce qui a servi à fonder la décision des arbitres n'ait échappé à leur débat contradictoire.

[...]

176-Il ressort de ces éléments que la sentence n'encourt pas davantage une annulation partielle de sorte que la demande relative à la répartition définitive des frais de l'arbitrage sera également rejetée.

– Paris, Chambre commerciale internationale, Pôle 5 – Chambre 16, 12 octobre 2021, n° 19/21625 et 21/18882 (rectification d'erreur matérielle), *République du Sénégal c. A*

Clause compromissoire – Référé – Conditions – Article 1449 CPC – Accord amiable préalable – Demande provisoire – Trouble – Urgence

Il est constant que le règlement intérieur et les statuts comportent une clause de conciliation et d'arbitrage (article 9 du règlement intérieur et article 44 des statuts intitulé « contestation ») qui s'impose aux parties conformément à la jurisprudence actuelle de la Cour de cassation. Que cette procédure de conciliation obligatoire et préalable à la saisine du juge constitue une fin de non-recevoir qui s'impose au juge si les parties l'invoquent.

Qu'en l'espèce il est bien reproché de ne pas avoir recherché un accord amiable préalable conformément à l'article 9 du règlement intérieur.

S'agissant de la procédure arbitrale prévue à l'article 44 des statuts, l'article 1449 du Code de procédure civile dispose que : « *L'existence d'une convention d'arbitrage ne fait pas obstacle, tant que le tribunal arbitral n'est pas constitué, à ce qu'une partie saisisse une juridiction de l'État aux fins d'obtenir une mesure d'instruction ou une mesure provisoire ou conservatoire. Sous réserve des dispositions régissant les saisies conservatoires et les sûretés judiciaires, la demande est portée devant le président du tribunal judiciaire ou de commerce, qui statue sur les mesures d'instruction dans les conditions prévues à l'article 145 et, en cas d'urgence, sur les mesures provisoires ou conservatoires sollicitées par les parties à la convention d'arbitrage.* »

Il convient de constater d'une part que la demanderesse n'a soulevé aucune contestation relative à sa décision d'exclusion auprès du tribunal arbitral. D'autre part la demanderesse sans établir l'urgence de sa demande provisoire, se contente d'expliquer qu'elle n'a plus été en mesure de satisfaire les commandes d'un grand nombre de ses clients dont certains ont annulé leurs commandes, ou qu'elle n'a nullement été en mesure de pouvoir réorganiser son approvisionnement, sans en démontrer la réalité, ni même démontrer que le trouble dont elle se prévaut est toujours présent.

Il en ressort ainsi que les conditions de l'article 1449 du Code de procédure civile permettant de déroger à la clause compromissoire précitée ne sont nullement réunies.

Qu'en conséquence, il convient de constater que les demandes soulevées par là sont irrecevables.

– T. com. Dijon, 13 octobre 2021, n° 2021004566, *Prest'hyg c. Gafic*

Clause compromissoire – Validité – Applicabilité ou nullité manifeste – Article 1448 CPC – Clause attributive de compétence – Clauses contradictoires – Sanction – Intention commune des parties – Validité – Action directe – Sous-traitant – Loi n° 75-1334 du 13 décembre 1975 – Document type – Annexe – Article 2060 du Code civil – Parties impliquées – Inapplicabilité manifeste

L'article 1448 al.1er du Code de procédure civile prévoit que lorsqu'un litige relevant d'une convention d'arbitrage est porté devant une juridiction de l'État, celle-ci se déclare incompétente sauf si le tribunal arbitral n'est pas encore saisi et si la convention d'arbitrage est manifestement nulle ou manifestement inapplicable.

Il est constant qu'aucune partie n'avait saisi l'arbitre à la date de la délivrance de l'assignation introductive d'instance, le débat porte donc en premier lieu sur la validité de la clause d'arbitrage, en second lieu sur la possibilité de l'appliquer au présent litige.

Sur la validité de la clause d'arbitrage

En son article 14 intitulé « Règlement des contestations », le contrat passé entre la société R et la société C prévoit ce qui suit : « *Tous les litiges auxquels la présente convention pourra donner lieu, notamment au sujet de sa validité, de son interprétation, de son exécution seront résolus par voie d'arbitrage. Dans ce cadre, les parties conviennent d'une manière formelle et irrévocable de soumettre le règlement de leur différend à P, expert près la cour d'appel de Paris* [...]. *Chacune des parties pourra saisir l'arbitre du désaccord existant par simple lettre recommandée avec demande d'avis de réception. Cette lettre sera accompagnée d'un mémoire d'arbitrage valant exposé des demandes. L'arbitre entendra les parties et pourra se faire assister de tous spécialistes qu'il jugera bon de s'adjoindre, après avoir défini le calendrier de ses opérations. La partie perdante est condamnée au paiement de tous les frais et dépens comprenant les frais et honoraires de l'arbitre.*

L'arbitre statuera en amiable composition. Sa décision est sans appel. »

Il est annexé au contrat de sous-traitance des conditions générales d'achat comportant en leur article 14 intitulé « Règlement des contestations » la clause suivante : « *Toutes contestations relatives à l'interprétation ou à l'exécution de nos commandes seront tranchées par le tribunal de commerce du siège de l'entreprise ou de l'établissement secondaire dans la stricte application de la jurisprudence des gares principales.* ».

La régularité formelle de la clause compromissoire n'est pas critiquée au regard des dispositions des articles 1443 et 1444 du Code de procédure civile, en ce qu'elle est écrite et désigne l'arbitre, mais la société appelante infère de la confrontation de ces clauses contradictoires que la clause compromissoire est nulle et doit être réputée non écrite.

L'article 01.2 du contrat distingue, parmi les pièces contractuelles, les documents particuliers et les documents généraux, faisant spécifiquement prévaloir les premiers sur les seconds en cas de contradiction. Le premier juge a relevé que la clause compromissoire est contenue dans les conditions particulières comprises dans les documents particuliers en vertu de l'article 01.2.1.1 et considéré qu'elles prévalent sur les conditions générales.

Sur ce, les conditions générales d'achat sont établies dans un document type, anonyme et, de surcroît, destiné à la fourniture de marchandises et non à la prestation de sous-traitance. Pour autant, il n'est pas prétendu ni démontré qu'elles soient issues de l'un des documents généraux listés dans les articles 01.2.2.1 et 01.2.2.2, à savoir les conditions générales du contrat de sous-traitance du BTP édition 2014 et les documents généraux à caractère technique.

En présence de clauses contradictoires, il appartient au juge de rechercher l'intention commune des parties par application de l'article 1188 du Code civil. La clause compromissoire, de par sa précision et son intégration au contrat de sous-traitance stricto sensu, prévaut sur la clause des conditions générales d'achat contenues dans une simple annexe constituant un document type aux dispositions inadaptées à l'objet du contrat.

L'existence de ces conditions générales ne remet donc pas en cause la validité de la clause compromissoire.

Sur l'application de la clause d'arbitrage

Une partie rappelle que l'article 2060 du Code civil interdit de compromettre sur les matières qui intéressent l'ordre public. Elle soutient que la clause compromissoire, en ce qu'elle impose le recours à l'arbitrage pour « tous les litiges », emporte négation de la règle d'ordre public, issue de la loi du 31 décembre 1975, autorisant l'action directe du sous-traitant à l'encontre du maître de l'ouvrage.

L'article 15 de la loi n° 75-1334 du 13 décembre 1975, relative à la sous-traitance, édicte en effet une nullité d'ordre public affectant les clauses, stipulations et arrangements qui auraient pour effet de faire échec aux dispositions de la présente loi.

Le premier juge, en sa motivation critiquée par l'appelante, a considéré que le recours à l'arbitrage n'est pas exclu du seul fait que des règles impératives d'ordre public sont applicables. Relevant qu'il ne s'applique qu'aux relations entre la société et son sous-traitant, il a estimé qu'il n'affecte pas l'action directe de celle-ci à l'encontre du maître de l'ouvrage, exercée devant le tribunal judiciaire de Lyon.

Il a ajouté que la clause compromissoire résiste au caractère indivisible des demandes de la société dirigées contre les deux sociétés.

Ce faisant, le juge a fait une analyse théorique de la portée de la clause compromissoire, qui se limite, en principe, aux litiges opposant l'entreprise principale et le sous-traitant, sans empêcher l'exercice de l'action judiciaire directe de celui-ci contre le maître de l'ouvrage.

La société fait valoir avec pertinence que l'application de la clause compromissoire aurait ainsi pour effet d'évincer le maître de l'ouvrage du débat alors que sa présence est essentielle et même impérative dans le cadre d'une action directe du sous-traitant.

L'article 12 de la loi du 31 décembre 2015 prévoit ce qui suit : « *Le sous-traitant a une action directe contre le maître de l'ouvrage si l'entrepreneur principal ne paie pas, un mois après en avoir été mis en demeure, les sommes qui sont dues en vertu du contrat de sous-traitance ; copie de cette mise en demeure est adressée au maître de l'ouvrage. Toute renonciation à l'action directe est réputée non écrite. Cette action directe subsiste même si l'entrepreneur principal est en état de liquidation des biens, de règlement judiciaire ou de suspension provisoire des poursuites [...].* »

L'article 13 de la même loi précise que « *l'action directe ne peut viser que le paiement correspondant aux prestations prévues par le contrat de sous-traitance et dont le maître de l'ouvrage est effectivement bénéficiaire. Les obligations du maître de l'ouvrage sont limitées à ce qu'il doit encore à l'entrepreneur principal à la date de la réception de la copie de la mise en demeure prévue à l'article précédent.* »

Il s'en déduit que l'action directe du sous-traitant à l'encontre du maître de l'ouvrage vise au paiement des sommes dues par l'entrepreneur principal au sous-traitant, dans la limite prévue à l'article 13 al. 2 précité. Si aucune disposition légale n'impose que l'entrepreneur principal soit appelé dans la cause, le sous-traitant pouvant notamment faire choix de ne pas agir contre un entrepreneur principal insolvable, l'action exercée conjointement contre l'entrepreneur principal et le maître de l'ouvrage est indissociable.

[...]

L'application de la clause compromissoire priverait donc le sous-traitant de l'effectivité de son action directe contre le maître d'ouvrage qu'elle tient d'une règle d'ordre public.

La clause compromissoire doit être écartée comme étant manifestement inapplicable au litige, au sens de l'article 1448 du Code de procédure civile et, en conséquence, le tribunal judiciaire de Lyon est compétent pour connaître de l'ensemble du litige.

– **Lyon, 14 octobre 2021, n° 21/01459,** ***Entreprise A c. Roux Cabrero et Aix Bord du Lac 4***

Clause compromissoire – Référé – Mesure provisoire ou conservatoire – Conditions

Nous relevons que le contrat liant les parties prévoit une clause compromissoire, mais que | le tribunal arbitral n'est pas constitué.

Nous rappelons les dispositions de l'article 1449 ne fait pas obstacle, tant que le tribunal arbitral n'est pas constitué, à ce qu'une partie saisisse une juridiction de l'État aux fins d'obtenir une mesure d'instruction ou une mesure provisoire ou conservatoire.

La demande est portée devant le président du tribunal judiciaire ou de commerce, qui statue sur les mesures d'instruction dans les conditions prévues à l'article 145 et, en cas d'urgence, sur les mesures provisoires ou conservatoires sollicitées par les parties à la convention.

Nous nous déclarerons, en conséquence, compétent.

– T. com. Paris, 15 octobre 2021, n° 2021024971, *Udaipur Fze c. Hartford International Group Ltd*

Sentence arbitrale – Recours en annulation – Procédure – CME – Liquidation judiciaire – Qualité à agir – Article L. 641-9 du Code de commerce

Il n'y a pas lieu de statuer à nouveau sur les demandes aux fins de nullité de la déclaration de saisine en annulation de la sentence arbitrale et de caducité de la déclaration de saisine, qui ont été rejetées par l'ordonnance du conseiller de la mise en état en date du 11 septembre 2019 confirmée par l'arrêt de cette cour du 15 septembre 2020.

Aux termes du I de l'article L. 641-9 du Code de commerce : « *Le jugement qui ouvre ou prononce la liquidation judiciaire emporte de plein droit, à partir de sa date, dessaisissement pour le débiteur de l'administration et de la disposition de ses biens mêmes de ceux qu'il a acquis à quelque titre que ce soit tant que la liquidation judiciaire n'est pas clôturée. Les droits et actions du débiteur concernant son patrimoine sont exercés pendant toute la durée de la liquidation judiciaire par le liquidateur* ». [...]

Conformément à l'article 1498, alinéa 2, du Code de procédure civile, le rejet de l'appel ou du recours en annulation confère l'exequatur à la sentence arbitrale ou à celles de ses dispositions qui ne sont pas atteintes par la censure de la cour ; il y a donc lieu, en vertu de ce texte, de conférer l'exequatur à la sentence arbitrale du 31 octobre 2018.

La créance de la société, qui a été régulièrement déclarée entre les mains du mandataire judiciaire dans le délai de deux mois suivant la publication au Bodacc, le 1er octobre 2020, du jugement d'ouverture, doit, par ailleurs, être fixée, à titre chirographaire, à hauteur des sommes retenues dans la sentence arbitrale du 31 octobre 2018.

– Montpellier, Chambre commerciale, 19 octobre 2021, n° 18/06223, *Coxco Capestang c. Aecg Finexcom*

Contrat de distribution – Recours en annulation – Compétence – Contrôle en fait et en droit – contrôle étendu – Règle matérielle du droit international de l'arbitrage – Clause compromissoire – Indépendante – Autonomie – Validité – Règles impératives du droit français – Ordre public international – Connaissance – Coûts – Impécuniosité – Commune volonté des parties – Absence de référence à une loi étatique – Article 1112-1 du Code civil – Ordonnance du 10 février 2016 – Contrat antérieur – Loi dans le temps – Devoir pré-contractuel d'information – Vice consentement – Accès à la justice – Notion – Restrictions – But légitime et proportionné – Coûts raisonnables – Principe de la contradiction – Production de pièces – Bonne administration de la justice – Procédure américaine – Convention de La Haye 1965 – Ordre public international – Contrôle – Conception française – Valeurs et principes – Violation – Heurte de manière manifeste, effective et concrète – Loi Lurel – Loi de police – Application dans le temps – Loi étrangère – Annulation –

Article L. 420-2-1 Code de commerce – Refus de prêter le secours des voies de droit

16-Selon l'article 1520, 1°, du Code de procédure civile, le recours en annulation est ouvert si le tribunal s'est déclaré à tort compétent ou incompétent.

17-Dans le cadre d'un recours en annulation fondé sur l'article 1520, 1° du Code de procédure civile, il appartient au juge de l'annulation de contrôler la décision du tribunal arbitral sur sa compétence, qu'il se soit déclaré compétent ou incompétent, en recherchant tous les éléments de droit ou de fait permettant d'apprécier la portée de la convention d'arbitrage.

18-A cet égard, il convient de rappeler qu'en vertu d'une règle matérielle du droit international de l'arbitrage, la clause compromissoire est indépendante juridiquement du contrat principal qui la contient directement ou par référence, et son existence et son efficacité s'apprécient, sous réserve des règles impératives du droit français et de l'ordre public international, d'après la commune volonté des parties, sans qu'il soit nécessaire de se référer à une loi étatique.

19-En l'espèce, l'article 26 du contrat de distribution conclu entre les parties comporte une clause compromissoire ainsi rédigée : « *26. Arbitrage : Tous litiges, controverses ou réclamations nés du présent Contrat, incluant sans limitation, la formation, l'interprétation, la violation ou la résiliation de ce Contrat, ou si les réclamations portées sont de nature arbitrale, doivent être soumises et instruites par une procédure arbitrale obligatoire, menée par JAMS/Endispute ("JAMS") en accord avec les Règles Internationales de l'Arbitrage des JAMS, et dès lors qu'elle a vocation à s'appliquer, la Convention sur la Reconnaissance et l'Exécution des Sentences Arbitrales Étrangères (ci-après collectivement "Les Règles"). L'arbitrage doit être entendu par un arbitre sélectionné en accord avec les Règles, dans le Comté d'Orange, en Californie. La langue utilisée dans le cadre de la procédure arbitrale doit être l'anglais. La sentence arbitrale rendue peut être homologuée par le tribunal qui a compétence en la matière. Dans les sept (7) jours calendaires après sa nomination, l'arbitre doit fixer la date de l'audience, laquelle doit avoir lieu dans les quatre-vingt-dix (90) jours calendaires après la date de saisine du tribunal arbitral, à moins qu'une date ultérieure ne soit requise pour un motif légitime. L'arbitre doit ordonner l'échange mutuel de ce qu'il/elle considère être des pièces pertinentes et chaque partie peut prendre jusqu'à cinq (5) dépositions au total qui devront être soumises dans un délai de deux (2) jours calendaires. Les deux parties renoncent au droit, s'il en existe, de solliciter d'un autre tribunal arbitral ou d'une juridiction une pénalité à l'encontre de l'autre partie condamnée au paiement de dommages et intérêts exemplaires ou punitifs en raison de ce Contrat ou d'une violation de ses obligations contractuelles, ou une réclamation considérée comme étant invalide ; illégal ou nulle au regard des stipulations du Contrat. L'arbitre peut également ordonner la prise en charge des frais d'avocats de la partie gagnante au titre des mesures de réparations. L'arbitre doit rendre sa sentence dans les sept (7) jours calendaires à l'issue de la clôture de la communication des pièces ou du dépôt des derniers mémoires, si cette date est postérieure. La décision de l'arbitre est définitive et sans appel à l'encontre de l'ensemble des parties.* ». (en version originale : « *26. Arbitration : Any dispute controversy or claim arising out of or relating to this Agreement including without limitation, the formation, interpretation, or the breach or termination of this Agreement or whether the claims asserted are arbitral, shall be referred to and finally determined by binding arbitration conducted by JAMS / Endispute ("JAMS") in accordance with JAMS International Arbitration Rules, and to the extent applicable, the Convention on the Recognition and Enforcement of Foreign Arbitration Awards (collectively the Rules). The arbitration shall be heard by one arbitrator to be selected in accordance with the Rules, in Orange Ae A. The language to be used in the arbitration proceedings shall be English Judgement upon any award rendered may be entered in any court having jurisdiction thereof. Within seven (7) calendar days after appointment, the arbitrator shall set the hearing date, which shall be within ninety (90) calendar days after the filing date of the demand for arbitration unless a later date is required for good cause shown and shall order a mutual exchange of what he/she determines to be relevant documents and the dates hereafter for the taking of up to a maximum of five (5) depositions by each party to last no more than two (2) calendar days in aggregate for each party. Both parties waive the right, if any, to obtain any award for exemplary or punitive damages or any other amount for the purpose of imposing a penalty from the other in any arbitration or judicial proceeding or other adjudication arising out of or with respect to this Agreement, or any breach hereof, including any claim that said Agreement, or any part hereof is invalid, illegal or otherwise voidable or void. In addition to all other relief, the arbitrator shall have the power to award reasonable attorney's fees and costs to the prevailing party. The arbitrator shall make his or her award no later than seven (7) calendar days after the choice of evidence or submissions of final briefs, whichever occurs later. The decision of the arbitrator shall be final and conclusive upon all parties* ».).

20-Cette clause renferme la commune intention des parties de recourir en cas de litige à un arbitrage, ce que la société l'appelante ne peut raisonnablement contester étant en outre observé qu'il résulte des pièces versées que son attention avait même été attirée sur cette modalité de résolution dans un courrier qui lui a été adressé par la société adverse le 8 avril 2011, soit avant la signature de ce contrat.

Sur la nullité de la convention d'arbitrage sur le fondement de l'article 1112-1 du Code civil

21-En l'espèce, le contrat litigieux contenant la convention d'arbitrage ayant été conclu le 22 avril 2011, la société ne peut se prévaloir de l'article 1112-1 du Code civil, lequel est issu de l'ordonnance du 10 février 2016, entrée en vigueur le 1er octobre 2016, et dont l'article 9 indique qu'elle n'est pas applicable aux contrats conclus antérieurement.

22-Si cet article a consacré un devoir pré-contractuel d'information qui avait été antérieurement dégagé par la jurisprudence française, l'annulation du contrat suppose en tout état de cause de rechercher si le non-respect de ce devoir a eu pour effet de vicier le consentement du cocontractant de celui qui ignore légitimement cette information.

23-En matière d'arbitrage international cependant ce devoir repose sur chacune des parties à qui il incombe de s'informer sur les modalités de l'arbitrage étant en outre observé que le consentement à une convention d'arbitrage emporte nécessairement renonciation à soumettre un litige à une justice étatique.

24-De surcroît lorsque la convention d'arbitrage renvoie à un règlement existant, ses modalités sont aisément accessibles par chacune des parties et exclusives de toute ignorance légitime pour l'une ou l'autre des parties.

25-Tel est le cas en l'espèce de telle sorte que la nullité de la convention d'arbitrage litigieuse ne peut être encourue.

26 – I1 convient en conséquence de rejeter ce grief.

Sur la nullité de la convention d'arbitrage à raison du déni de justice qu'elle engendrerait

27-L'accès à la justice, en ce qu'il permet de garantir l'effectivité des droits, relève de l'ordre public international. Dès lors une convention d'arbitrage qui ferait obstacle à cet accès, serait contraire à l'ordre public international et donc nulle.

28-Cependant, si le droit d'accès à la justice implique qu'une personne ne puisse être privée de la faculté concrète de faire trancher ses prétentions par un juge, ce droit n'est pas inconditionnel. Des restrictions peuvent être apportées à l'exercice de ce droit, sous réserve de répondre à un but légitime et d'être proportionnées aux nécessités d'une bonne administration de la justice.

29-Ainsi, une convention d'arbitrage, par laquelle les parties consentent à soumettre leur litige à un arbitre et qui emporte nécessairement renonciation à la justice étatique et, en France, à la gratuité du service public de la justice, ne saurait en elle-même porter atteinte à l'accès à la justice.

30-Seules ses modalités doivent être examinées afin de vérifier qu'elles ne privent pas, dans leur mise en œuvre, une partie d'un accès à la justice et ne portent ainsi pas une atteinte effective au droit fondamental d'accès à la justice.

31-En l'espèce, il convient de relever qu'en signant le contrat contenant la clause d'arbitrage, la société appelante ne pouvait ignorer qu'elle renonçait à la gratuité du service de la justice et ce d'autant que cette clause renvoie aux « *Règles Internationales de l'Arbitrage des JAMS* », accessibles par toutes les parties, lesquelles prévoient que des frais d'arbitrage sont dus.

32-L'appelante ne pouvait ainsi l'ignorer avant de consentir à la convention d'arbitrage et en tout état de cause ne pouvait faire reposer cette information sur la seule société adverse.

33-A cet égard, il ressort des pièces versées que la provision qui a été demandée aux parties par le JAMS a été fixée en novembre 2016 à la somme de 5000 dollars, dont 2500 à la charge de chacune des parties.

34-La société appelante ne justifie par aucun élément avoir été dans l'impossibilité de faire l'avance d'une telle provision de 2 500 dollars, qui ne caractérise nullement un montant disproportionné susceptible d'empêcher une société commerciale de faire entendre sa position, étant observé que les frais d'arbitrage ont été finalement fixés aux termes de la sentence à la somme de 5 264,61 dollars.

35-S'agissant du montant des honoraires d'avocat mis à la charge de la société appelante, à hauteur de 133 701,50 €, il convient d'observer d'une part, que cette dernière était parfaitement informée de ce risque dès lors que la convention d'arbitrage mentionne expressément que « *L'arbitre peut également ordonner la prise en charge des frais d'avocats de la partie gagnante au titre des mesures de réparations* ».

36-D'autre part, ce montant qui résulte d'une évaluation par l'arbitre des frais « raisonnables » qui ont été supportés par la partie gagnante pouvant être mis à la charge du perdant après avoir tranché le litige au fond, n'est pas de nature à emporter la nullité de la convention d'arbitrage et être invoqué au soutien d'un moyen fondé sur l'incompétence du tribunal arbitral.

37-La société sera en conséquence déboutée de ce chef également.

Sur le moyen tiré de la violation du principe de la contradiction (articles 1520, 4°)

[...]

Sur la production d'un courrier confidentiel ;

43-En l'espèce, il ressort des éléments du dossier que le courrier prétendument confidentiel a été produit, non dans le cadre de l'instance arbitrale, mais dans le cadre de la procédure engagée devant la District Court de Californie afin de contraindre la société à se soumettre à la procédure arbitrale et ayant donné lieu à une décision en ce sens de cette juridiction californienne en date du 31 mars 2017.

44-Le juge de l'annulation de la sentence arbitrale n'est pas juge de la régularité d'une procédure suivie devant une juridiction californienne.

Ce grief inopérant sera en conséquence rejeté.

Sur le non-respect des règles de notification selon la convention de La Haye du 15 novembre 1965

45 – Il ressort des écritures de l'appelante que celle-ci se plaint du non-respect des règles de notification prévues par la Convention de La Haye dans le cadre de l'instance qui a été engagée devant la District Court de Californie, et non devant l'arbitre.

46-Ce grief, qui ne concerne pas la procédure arbitrale, est inopérant devant le juge de l'annulation de la sentence rendue au terme de cette procédure arbitrale et sera en conséquence rejeté.

Sur l'irrégularité des actes de procédure devant la District Court of Californie

47-Il ressort des écritures de la société que celle-ci se plaint de l'irrégularité de la notification de certains actes de procédure dans le cadre de l'instance qui s'est déroulée devant la District Court de Californie, et non devant l'arbitre.

48-Ce grief, qui ne concerne pas la procédure arbitrale, est lui aussi inopérant devant le juge de l'annulation de la sentence rendue au terme de cette procédure arbitrale et sera en conséquence rejeté.

Sur le moyen tiré de la violation de l'ordre public international

[...]

51-Il résulte de l'article 1520, 5° du Code de procédure civile que le recours en annulation est ouvert si la reconnaissance ou l'exécution de la sentence est contraire à l'ordre public international.

52-L'ordre public international au regard duquel s'effectue le contrôle du juge de l'annulation s'entend de la conception qu'en a l'ordre juridique français, c'est-à-dire des valeurs et des principes dont celui-ci ne saurait souffrir la méconnaissance même dans un contexte international.

53-Le contrôle exercé par le juge de l'annulation pour la défense de l'ordre public international s'attache seulement à examiner si l'exécution des dispositions prises par le tribunal arbitral heurte de manière manifeste, effective et concrète les principes et valeurs compris dans l'ordre public international.

54-En l'espèce, la société soutient en substance que le contrat, auquel donne effet la sentence, serait nul en ce qu'il méconnaît les dispositions d'ordre public international issues de la loi n° 2012-1270 du 20 novembre 2012 relative à la régulation économique outre-mer et portant diverses dispositions relatives aux outre-mer, dite « loi Lurel ».

55-L'article L. 420-2-1 du Code de commerce, instauré par l'article 5 de cette loi prohibe, notamment dans la collectivité d'outre-mer de la Guyane, les accords ou pratiques concertées ayant pour objet ou pour effet d'accorder des droits exclusifs d'importation à une entreprise ou à un groupe d'entreprises. En outre, l'article L. 420-3 de ce même code dispose qu'est « nul tout engagement, convention ou clause contractuelle se rapportant à une pratique prohibée par les articles L. 420-1, L. 420-2, L. 420-2-1 et L. 420-2-2 ».

56-De tels accords octroyant des droits exclusifs d'importation au profit d'un importateur-grossiste sont objectivement de nature à entraver l'implantation ou le développement d'autres importateurs-grossistes et génèrent une situation préjudiciable à l'égard des consommateurs.

57-Cette disposition, qui participe de la sauvegarde d'une organisation économique et sociale pour un secteur de l'activité économique d'un pays, constitue ainsi une loi de police française, dont l'ignorance par un tribunal arbitral est susceptible de faire obstacle à l'exequatur de la sentence si celle-ci heurte de manière manifeste, effective et concrète l'ordre public international.

58-Tel est le cas lorsque le tribunal arbitral statue sans mettre en œuvre une loi de police française, en ignorant ainsi son applicabilité même au litige alors que le respect d'une telle loi est considéré comme crucial pour la sauvegarde des intérêts publics du pays tels que son organisation politique, sociale ou économique.

[...]

60-Au terme de sa sentence, l'arbitre, se référant à la loi désignée par les parties pour régir leur relation contractuelle, a considéré que seule la loi californienne était applicable au litige et que la loi française n'avait pas vocation à s'appliquer « *et dans l'hypothèse où elle serait applicable, elle opérerait un renvoi vers la loi californienne* ».

61-En statuant ainsi, sans même mettre en œuvre la prohibition impérative prévue à l'article L. 420-2 1 du Code de commerce, applicable en la cause, la sentence arbitrale heurte l'ordre public international français et ne peut être accueillie dans l'ordre juridique français.

62-A cet égard, il est indifférent que le contrat litigieux ait été conclu avant l'entrée en vigueur de cette prohibition dès lors qu'il résulte de l'article 5, II, de la loi précitée que la prohibition qu'elle édicte est applicable aux pratiques en cours et que les parties à ces accords ou pratiques disposaient d'un délai de quatre mois à compter de la promulgation de la loi pour se mettre en conformité. La loi ayant été publiée au Journal officiel le 21 novembre 2012, le délai prévu à l'article 5 précité expirait donc le 22 mars 2013.

63-De même, il est indifférent que la société appelante ait pu effectivement bénéficier de ce contrat, l'éventuelle mauvaise foi de celle-ci étant indifférente, dès lors qu'est seulement en cause le refus de l'ordre juridique français de prêter le secours des voies de droit au paiement de sommes ordonnées en vertu d'une sentence méconnaissant l'ordre public international français.

64-En l'état de l'ensemble de ces éléments, il convient de dire bien fondé le moyen d'annulation tiré du non-respect de l'article 1520-5° du Code de procédure civile et de refuser l'exequatur de la sentence litigieuse.

– Paris, Pôle 5 – chambre 16, Chambre commerciale internationale, 19 octobre 2021, n° 18/01254, *Sainte Claire c. Monster Energy Company*

Recours en annulation – Moyen tardif – Irrégularité procédurale – Principe d'égalité des armes Ordre public international de protection – Ordre public international de fond – Principe du contradictoire – Notion – Audience – Volonté des parties – Motifs – Critiques des motifs – Pouvoir de direction – Révision au fond – Droit de la défense – Amiable composition – Principe du contradictoire – Égalité des armes

À titre préliminaire, sur la recevabilité des moyens d'annulation

[...]

13 – Aux termes de l'article 1466 du Code de procédure civile, la partie qui, en connaissance de cause et sans motif légitime, s'abstient d'invoquer en temps utile une irrégularité devant le tribunal arbitral est réputée avoir renoncé à s'en prévaloir.

14 – Ce texte ne vise pas les seules irrégularités procédurales mais tous les griefs qui constituent des cas d'ouverture du recours en annulation des sentences, en ce compris le principe d'égalité des armes qui relève de l'ordre public international de protection, à l'exception des moyens tirés de ce que la reconnaissance ou l'exécution de la sentence violerait l'ordre public international de fond.

15 – Toutefois, aux termes de l'article 954, al 3 du Code de procédure civile, la cour ne statue que sur les prétentions énoncées au dispositif et n'examine les moyens au soutien de ces prétentions que s'ils sont invoqués dans la discussion.

[...]

Sur le moyen d'annulation tiré du non-respect du principe de la contradiction (1520-4° CPC)

[...]

Sur la tenue de l'audience hors la présence des sociétés recourantes

23 – Il résulte de l'article 1520, 4° du Code de procédure civile que le recours en annulation est ouvert si le principe de la contradiction n'a pas été respecté.

24 – Le principe de la contradiction exige seulement que les parties aient pu faire connaître leurs prétentions de fait et de droit et discuter celles de leur adversaire de telle sorte que rien de ce qui a servi à fonder la décision des arbitres n'ait échappé à leur débat contradictoire.

[...]

29 – Il résulte de ces éléments et des pièces versées que l'Arbitre a pris sa décision refusant le report après avoir entendu les observations de chacune des parties et que les parties ont pu échanger sur le fond leurs arguments et pièces, ainsi que les déclarations écrites des témoins selon un calendrier fixé en accord avec les parties.

30 – Le fait pour les sociétés recourantes de soutenir que le refus de l'arbitre de reporter l'audience et d'avoir rendu la sentence en l'absence d'une des parties n'était fondé sur aucun motif valable alors que l'arbitre a clairement retenu « l'absence délibérée » d'une partie, a en réalité pour objet de critiquer les motifs qui ont conduit l'arbitre à refuser le report de l'audience, et ce faisant, sous couvert d'une violation du principe de la contradiction, conduire le juge de l'annulation à réviser la décision rendue par l'arbitre.

31 – Ce grief sera en conséquence rejeté.

– Sur l'allégation du moyen soulevé d'office tiré du respect des droits de la défense ;

32 – Le principe de la contradiction permet d'assurer la loyauté des débats et le caractère équitable du procès. Il interdit que des moyens de fait ou de droit soient soulevés d'office sans que les parties aient été appelées à les commenter.

[...]

36 – Enfin, en arguant que l'Arbitre se serait saisi d'office de la question de l'amiable composition en statuant sur la demande d'échelonnement du paiement des factures, alors que l'arbitre a indiqué qu'il n'avait pas les pouvoirs pour statuer en amiable compositeur, répondant ainsi à la demande d'échelonnement dont il était saisi et qu'il a rejetée, ce qui ne constitue pas une saisine d'office mais une motivation pour répondre à une demande, les sociétés recourantes entendent en réalité critiquer le fond de la décision de l'arbitre et ce faisant demander la révision de la sentence, ce qui n'entre pas dans les pouvoirs du juge de l'annulation.

37 – Il ressort ainsi de l'ensemble de ces éléments, sans qu'il soit nécessaire de rechercher si la position procédurale adoptée était constitutive d'un estoppel, que l'Arbitre n'a pas méconnu le principe de la contradiction.

38 – Ce moyen en toutes ses branches sera en conséquence rejeté.

Sur le moyen tiré de la violation de l'ordre public international par la violation du principe du contradictoire, des droits de la défense et de l'égalité des armes (1520-5° du Code de procédure civile)

[...]

69 – C'est dès lors à tort que les sociétés considèrent qu'il s'est déclaré incompétent sur l'octroi d'un délai de grâce, alors qu'il l'a estimé infondé et l'a rejeté.

70 – Ce grief sera en conséquence rejeté.

– Paris, Chambre commerciale internationale, Pôle 5 – Chambre 16, 19 octobre 2021, n° 19/23071, *Magpower Soluções de Energia c. Heliotrop*

Contrat de franchise – Clause compromissoire – Principe de compétence compétence – Pratiques anticoncurrentielles – Compétence exclusives des tribunaux – Article 1448 CPC – Nullité ou inapplicabilité manifeste – Juge de l'évidence – Contrats indivisibles – Impécuniosité – Coûts – Accès au juge – Arbitrage volontaire – Déni de justice – Tribunal arbitral – Constitution – Honoraires – Mise en œuvre – Convention européenne des droits de l'homme

La circonstance alléguée que le litige concerne la validité et les conséquences des pratiques anticoncurrentielles des sociétés relevant de la compétence exclusive et d'ordre public du tribunal de commerce statuant dans sa formation spécialisée conformément aux articles L 420-7 et D 442-3 du code de commerce, ne peut faire obstacle lorsqu'un litige entre dans le champ d'application matériel d'une clause d'arbitrage liant les parties, au principe compétence compétence qui investit les seuls arbitres du pouvoir de statuer sur leur compétence, en vertu de la combinaison des articles 1448 et 1465 du Code de procédure civile.

Également, si par exception au principe compétence compétence, le juge étatique peut se reconnaître compétent en présence d'une clause compromissoire, c'est à la condition en vertu des dispositions de l'article 1448 du Code de procédure civile, que le tribunal arbitral ne soit pas encore saisi et que la convention d'arbitrage soit manifestement nulle ou manifestement inapplicable.

Or, seule une nullité ou une inapplicabilité s'imposant avec la force de l'évidence, sans nécessité pour le Juge de procéder à un examen factuel autre que superficiel, est susceptible de satisfaire ce caractère manifeste.

Ainsi, la circonstance alléguée de l'existence d'un ensemble contractuel indivisible comportant des contrats pourvus de clause d'arbitrage, en l'espèce le contrat de franchise et le contrat d'approvisionnement, et d'un autre n'en contenant pas, en l'espèce, le contrat de location-gérance, est impropre à caractériser l'inapplicabilité manifeste des clauses d'arbitrage. La primauté de la compétence arbitrale prévaut dans de telles situations. Il s'ensuit que la juridiction étatique est incompétente à cet égard.

Enfin, s'agissant de l'atteinte au droit d'accès au juge, le coût prohibitif d'une procédure d'arbitrage et l'impécuniosité des parties ne sont pas de nature à faire obstacle au principe compétence compétence. Outre qu'il s'agit d'un arbitrage volontaire, il revient aux acteurs de l'arbitrage d'écarter tout risque de déni de justice en permettant l'accès du justiciable au tribunal arbitral quels que soient ses moyens financiers.

Il sera observé à cet égard qu'en l'espèce la constitution du tribunal arbitral ne fait pas du paiement des honoraires des arbitres une condition de sa mise en œuvre. Dès lors le moyen pris de la violation de l'article 6.8.1 de la Convention européenne des droits de l'homme est rejeté.

Il y a lieu, infirmant le jugement entrepris en ce qu'il s'est déclaré compétent, d'accueillir l'exception d'incompétence soulevée par les sociétés CPF et CSF et de renvoyer les parties à mieux se pourvoir.

– Paris, Pôle 5 – Chambre 4, 20 octobre 2021, n° 21/06054, *Carrefour Proximité France c. CSF*

Clause compromissoire – Article 1449 CPC – Mesure provisoire et conservatoire – Demande d'expertise – Mesure d'instruction *in futurum* – Conditions – Saisie conservatoire – sûreté judiciaire – Urgence – Article 145 CPC

Il est acquis aux débats que la clause compromissoire insérée à l'article 23 du contrat du 24 avril 2007 demeure valable et opposable aux parties pour tout différend relatif aux conséquences de sa résiliation.

Toutefois, l'article 1449 du Code de procédure civile dispose que l'existence d'une convention d'arbitrage ne fait pas obstacle, tant que le tribunal arbitral n'est pas constitué, à ce qu'une partie saisisse une juridiction de l'État aux fins d'obtenir une mesure d'instruction ou une mesure provisoire ou conservatoire.

Sous réserve des dispositions régissant les saisies conservatoires et les sûretés judiciaires, la demande est portée devant le président du tribunal judiciaire ou de commerce, qui statue sur les mesures d'instruction dans les conditions prévues à l'article 145 et, en cas d'urgence, sur les mesures provisoires ou conservatoires sollicitées par les parties à la convention d'arbitrage.

Or, en l'espèce, il n'est pas prétendu, ni justifié qu'un tribunal arbitral serait déjà constitué.

En outre, si en application de ces dispositions, le juge des référés n'a le pouvoir d'ordonner des mesures provisoires ou conservatoires sollicitées par une partie à la convention d'arbitrage qu'en cas d'urgence, l'appelante souligne à bon droit que cette condition n'est pas exigée pour une demande de mesure d'instruction *in futurum*.

Il s'en déduit qu'en l'espèce, le juge des référés du tribunal de commerce de Versailles et cette cour à sa suite, est compétent pour connaître de la demande tendant à ordonner sur le fondement de l'article 145 du Code de procédure civile une mesure d'expertise.

Il convient en conséquence de rejeter l'exception d'incompétence.

– Versailles, 14e chambre, 21 octobre 2021, n° 20/06163, *Euro Herramientas c. The Stanley Works Limited*

Clause compromissoire – Référé – Conditions – Urgence –

Considérant que « *la compétence exceptionnelle reconnue au juge des référés en présence d'une convention d'arbitrage est soumise à la condition de l'urgence* », qu'en l'espèce l'urgence n'est pas démontrée, le besoin de trésorerie pour la prise en charge des frais de justice de Monsieur A n'étant pas une raison valable, et en conséquence nous dirons incompétents et renverrons vers le tribunal arbitral.

– T. com. Paris, 26 octobre 2021, n° 2021025262, *A c. Exane*

Clause compromissoire – Contrat de licence de marques – Article 2061 du Code civil – Opposabilité – Activité professionnelle – Article 721-3 du Code de commerce – Acte de commerce – Signataires – Qualités des signataires – Arbitrage – Coûts – Impécuniosité – Principe de compétence compétence

Le contrat de licence de marque conclu entre les parties contient un article 27 rédigé comme suit : « *Les parties conviennent de recourir à la procédure d'arbitrage pour trancher toutes les contestations pouvant s'élever, pour quelque cause que ce soit, à l'occasion du présent contrat. Il est convenu que l'arbitrage sera effectué à trois arbitres. La partie souhaitant mettre en œuvre la procédure d'arbitrage notifiera à l'autre partie, par lettre recommandée avec demande d'avis de réception, sa volonté de se prévaloir de la présente clause, et indiquera les noms, adresse et profession de l'arbitre qu'elle désigne. L'autre partie disposera alors d'un délai maximum de quinze jours, à compter de la première présentation de ladite lettre, pour indiquer au demandeur les noms, adresse et profession de l'arbitre qu'elle désigne. Cette information sera également effectuée par lettre recommandée avec demande d'avis de réception. Les deux arbitres ainsi désignés s'adjoindront un troisième arbitre, au plus tard dans le délai d'un mois à compter de la dernière désignation. À défaut, par le défendeur, de désigner un arbitre dans les délais ci-dessus, ou à défaut d'accord entre les parties sur la désignation du troisième arbitre, comme en cas de refus ou d'empêchement de l'un des arbitres, et plus généralement au cas où le tribunal arbitral ne pourrait se constituer, la désignation du ou des arbitres sera faite par le président du tribunal de commerce de Paris, lequel sera saisi, comme en matière de référé, par la partie la plus diligente. Les parties conviennent que les arbitres ainsi désignés devront préalablement tenter une conciliation. La phase de conciliation aura une durée de 60 jours, à compter de l'acceptation de sa mission par le dernier des arbitres ayant accepté. Dans leur mission de conciliation, les arbitres pourront facturer aux parties des provisions d'honoraires. Les frais de conciliation seront supportés à égalité par chacune des parties, sauf accord de ces dernières sur une autre répartition.*

Au terme du délai imparti pour la conciliation, les parties seront réputées ne pas être parvenues à se concilier sauf si la preuve contraire est rapportée. Dans ce cas, la phase d'arbitrage proprement dite prendra le relais de la phase de conciliation. Les arbitres devront rendre leur sentence dans un délai de six mois à compter du terme du délai imparti pour la conciliation. Ce délai pourra être prorogé par accord des parties. Les parties confèrent aux arbitres le pouvoir de statuer comme amiables compositeurs. Les arbitres statueront à la majorité des voix. La sentence ne sera pas susceptible d'appel. Les opérations d'arbitrage se dérouleront dans le ressort du tribunal de commerce de Paris.

À l'exception des honoraires de conciliation, le montant et les modalités de la provision sur frais et honoraires à verser aux arbitres seront fixés par eux, au fur et à mesure du déroulement des opérations d'arbitrage La répartition définitive entre les parties, des frais et honoraires afférents à la procédure sera faite, par les arbitres, dans la sentence arbitrale.

Le présent article ne fait pas obstacle à la saisine du Président du Tribunal de commerce afin qu'il statue en référé dans les conditions prévues aux articles 872 et 873 du Code de procédure civile. Les parties conviennent que seul le Tribunal de commerce de Paris est alors compétent ».

En vertu des dispositions de l'article 2061 alinéa 2 du Code civil, lorsque l'une des parties n'a pas contracté dans le cadre de son activité professionnelle, la clause ne peut lui être opposée.

Selon les dispositions de l'article 721-3 du Code de commerce, les tribunaux de commerce connaissent des contestations relatives aux actes de commerce entre toutes personnes. Toutefois, les parties peuvent, au moment où elles contractent, convenir de soumettre à l'arbitrage leurs contestations.

Les parties ont conclu le 10 février 2018 un contrat de licence de marque. Les parties ont signé à titre personnel mais aussi en qualité de co-gérants d'une société en cours d'immatriculation. Le contrat avait pour objet de concéder à la société en création la licence d'exploitation de la marque française, sur une zone de chalandise en vue de l'exploitation d'une salle de remise en forme et de la commercialisation de produits textiles et diététiques.

Le contrat était dès lors un acte de commerce par nature, et les parties l'ont signé dans le cadre d'une activité professionnelle puisqu'en qualité de co-gérant d'une société en formation.

La clause compromissoire leur est opposable.

Les recourants plaident ensuite que la rédaction de la clause, faisant appel à trois arbitres chargés d'une mission de conciliation de six mois avant de statuer, conduit à les priver d'un accès effectif à une juridiction compte tenu du coût prohibitif de la rémunération des arbitres, qui serait selon eux d'environ 20 000 euros.

Cette allégation ne repose sur aucune pièce, dans la mesure où aucune évaluation du coût de l'arbitrage n'a été demandée par écrit à une chambre d'arbitrage, tandis qu'aucun exemple de coût de l'arbitrage dans un dossier similaire n'est justifié.

Il s'agit donc d'une pétition de principe non validée par un fait précis, tandis que les pièces versées aux débats ne témoignent pas d'une impécuniosité leur interdisant de faire appel à la procédure d'arbitrage, alors même qu'ils estimaient pouvoir s'investir dans un projet nécessitant un financement de plusieurs centaines de milliers d'euros.

Enfin, la clause compromissoire, en ce qu'elle a vocation à « trancher toutes les contestations pouvant s'élever, pour quelque cause que ce soit, à l'occasion du présent contrat', est applicable au litige. En conséquence de ce qui précède, le jugement déféré est confirmé.

– Rennes, 26 octobre 2021, n° 21/02556, *M. A et Mme B c. Ob Reseaux (anciennement dénommée atlas forme)*

Arbitrage – Article 2061 du Code civil – Contrat de travail – Licenciement – Indemnité – Procédure parallèle – Incidence – Inopposabilité

La cour observe que le contrat de travail ne fait pas mention des règlements d'intéressement (Incentive Plan) et qu'il n'est pas justifié d'une acceptation écrite et signée par le salarié des clauses dont l'employeur se prévaut dans les présents débats visant la soumission du litige à une procédure spécifique impliquant l'institut néerlandais d'arbitrage, ce alors même qu'en vertu de l'article 2061 du Code civil, la clause compromissoire doit avoir été acceptée par la partie à laquelle on l'oppose.

Étant en tout état de cause rappelé que l'exercice du droit de lever les options se rattache à l'exécution du contrat de travail et qu'en vertu de l'article L. 1411-7 du Code du travail, la clause compromissoire est inopposable au salarié dans un tel cadre, l'exception d'incompétence opposée en premier lieu par l'employeur doit être écartée.

– Versailles, 6e chambre, 28 octobre 2021, *Airbus Defence and Space c. A*

Principe de la contradiction – Définition – Corruption – Red flags – Faisceau d'indices – Ordre public international – Conception française – Valeurs et principes – Heurte de manière manifeste, effective et concrète – Principes et valeurs – Égalité des armes – Définition – Témoins – Audition – Langue – Compréhension – Interprète

19 – Il résulte de l'article 1520, 4° du Code de procédure civile que le recours en annulation est ouvert si le principe de la contradiction n'a pas été respecté.

20 – Le principe de la contradiction exige seulement que les parties aient pu faire connaître leurs prétentions de fait et de droit et discuter celles de leur adversaire de telle sorte que rien de ce qui a servi à fonder la décision de l'arbitre n'ait échappé à leur débat contradictoire.

[...]

27 – Il résulte au contraire de la Sentence que l'arbitre ne s'est fondé que sur le faisceau d'indices (« red flags »), largement débattus par les parties pendant la procédure arbitrale, dont l'accumulation lui a permis de considérer qu'ils étaient suffisants pour fonder la suspicion de corruption et justifier le refus de paiement, méthode critiquée, ce qui revient en réalité à demander au juge de l'annulation de réviser la sentence sous couvert d'une violation du principe du contradictoire.

28 – Enfin, la violation du contradictoire ne peut résulter de la seule allégation, au demeurant non justifiée par le rappel détaillé du témoignage du dirigeant d'une partie dans le corps de la Sentence, qu'il ne comprenait pas les questions.

29 – Ce moyen sera par conséquent rejeté.

Sur la violation de l'ordre public international (article 1520 5° du Code de procédure civile)

[...]

34 – Il résulte de l'article 1520, 5° du Code de procédure civile que le recours en annulation est ouvert si la reconnaissance ou l'exécution de la sentence est contraire à l'ordre public international.

35 – L'ordre public international au regard duquel s'effectue le contrôle du juge de l'annulation s'entend de la conception qu'en a l'ordre juridique français, c'est-à-dire des valeurs et des principes dont celui-ci ne saurait souffrir la méconnaissance même dans un contexte international.

36 – Cependant, le contrôle exercé par le juge de l'annulation pour la défense de l'ordre public international s'attache seulement à examiner si l'exécution des dispositions prises par le tribunal arbitral heurte de manière manifeste, effective et concrète les principes et valeurs compris dans l'ordre public international.

Sur le grief tiré de la méconnaissance de l'égalité des armes

37 – L'égalité des armes, qui constitue un élément du procès équitable protégé par l'ordre public international, implique l'obligation d'offrir à chaque partie une possibilité raisonnable de présenter sa cause dans des conditions qui ne la placent pas dans une situation substantiellement désavantageuse par rapport à son adversaire.

[...]

42 – De plus, il convient d'observer que les arguments développés au soutien de ce moyen sont identiques à ceux développés sur le moyen tiré du non-respect de la contradiction.

43 – D'une part, la violation alléguée du principe de l'égalité des armes par l'arbitre repose d'après la demanderesse sur le non-respect du contradictoire qui n'est pas caractérisé en l'espèce. L'arbitre ne s'est à aucun moment fondé sur des éléments issus de l'audit ou des enquêtes pénales qui n'ont pas été versés aux débats mais en fonction des seuls éléments produits par chacune des parties, et des « red flags ».

44 – D'autre part, les difficultés alléguées de compréhension de M. Ac n'ont pas été démontrées au soutien du moyen tiré de la violation du contradictoire. De plus, à les supposer réelles, il résulte de ses auditions extensives rappelées dans la sentence qu'elles n'ont eu aucune incidence sur sa capacité à présenter sa cause, celui-ci étant assisté d'un interprète au cours de la procédure arbitrale et de conseils maîtrisant l'anglais.

45 – Au regard de l'ensemble de ces éléments, il ne résulte pas que la société ait été ainsi placée dans une situation substantiellement désavantageuse et que ce faisant l'insertion de la sentence dans l'ordre juridique interne contrevienne à l'ordre public international.

46 – Ce grief sera écarté.

47 – Par voie de conséquence, le moyen soulevé pour s'opposer à l'annulation, tiré de la conséquence que pourrait avoir une annulation de ladite sentence au regard de l'ordre public international est devenu sans objet et sera écarté.

– Paris, Pôle 5 – Chambre 16, Chambre commerciale internationale, 2 novembre 2021, n° 20/01980, *Golden Power International Creation Limited c. Airbus Helicopters*

Arbitrage CCI – Règlement ICC – Recours en annulation – Recevabilité – Moyen tardif – Découverte – Arbitre unique – Mission – Volonté des parties – Règles procédurales choisies par les parties – Principe du contradictoire – Témoignage – Valeur probante – Ordre public international – Contrôle du juge de l'annulation – Conception française – Valeurs et principes – Égalité des armes – Définition – Omission de statuer – Cas d'ouverture – Demande de révision au fond

Sur les moyens d'annulation tirés de la violation de la mission, du principe du contradictoire et de l'ordre public international (articles 1520-3°, 4° et 5° du Code de procédure civile)

Sur la recevabilité des moyens d'annulation

[...]

13-Aux termes de l'article 1466 du Code de procédure civile « *La partie qui, en connaissance de cause et sans motif légitime, s'abstient d'invoquer en temps utile une irrégularité devant le tribunal arbitral est réputée avoir renoncé à s'en prévaloir* ».

Sur la recevabilité du grief allégué au soutien du moyen tiré du non-respect par l'arbitre de sa mission

14-Le tribunal arbitral s'écarte de sa mission notamment s'il ne respecte pas les règles procédurales qui ont été arrêtées par les parties.

[...]

21-Au regard de ces éléments, la société ne peut être réputée avoir renoncé à se prévaloir de ce grief dont elle n'a pu prendre connaissance qu'une fois la sentence rendue.

Sur la recevabilité du grief allégué au soutien du moyen tiré d'une méconnaissance du principe de la contradiction

22-Le principe de la contradiction exige seulement que les parties aient pu faire connaître leurs prétentions de fait et de droit et discuter celles de leur adversaire de telle sorte que rien de ce qui a servi à fonder la décision des arbitres n'ait échappé à leur débat contradictoire.

[...]

Sur le non-respect par l'arbitre de sa mission

[...]

44-Selon l'article 1520, 3° du Code de procédure civile, le recours en annulation est ouvert si le tribunal a statué sans se conformer à la mission qui lui avait été confiée.

45-Comme rappelé ci-dessus, le tribunal arbitral s'écarte de sa mission notamment s'il ne respecte pas les règles procédurales qui ont été arrêtées par les parties.

[...]

47-En application de l'article 19 du Règlement CCI (version 2012), choisi par les parties dans la convention d'arbitrage, « *la procédure devant le tribunal est régie par le Règlement et, dans le silence de ce dernier, par les règles que les parties, ou à défaut le tribunal arbitral, déterminent, en se référant ou non à une loi nationale de procédure applicable à l'arbitrage* ». De même son article 22 dispose que « *Dans tous les cas, le tribunal arbitral conduit la procédure de manière équitable et impartiale et veille à ce que chaque partie ait eu la possibilité d'être suffisamment entendue. Les parties s'engagent à se conformer à toute ordonnance rendue par le tribunal arbitral* ».

[...]

52-Dès lors, en s'appuyant sur ces pièces, régulièrement produites, l'arbitre n'a nullement méconnu sa mission étant observé que sous couvert de ce moyen la société entend en réalité critiquer la valeur probante conférée à ces documents par l'arbitre, ce qui ne relève pas de l'appréciation du respect de sa mission.

53-Ce moyen sera en conséquence rejeté.

Sur le non-respect du principe de la contradiction

54 – Il résulte de l'article 1520, 4° du Code de procédure civile que le recours en annulation est ouvert si le principe de la contradiction n'a pas été respecté.

55-Le principe de la contradiction exige seulement que les parties aient pu faire connaître leurs prétentions de fait et de droit et discuter celles de leur adversaire de telle sorte que rien de ce qui a servi à fonder la décision des arbitres n'ait échappé à leur débat contradictoire.

[...]

61-Il ressort de ces éléments que le principe de la contradiction n'a nullement été méconnu par l'arbitre et que la critique émise porte en réalité sur la valeur probante que l'arbitre a conféré à ces témoignages, qui relève du fond du litige et échappe au juge de l'annulation.

62-Ce moyen sera en conséquence rejeté.

Sur le non-respect de l'ordre public international

63 – Il résulte de l'article 1520, 5° du Code de procédure civile que le recours en annulation est ouvert si la reconnaissance ou l'exécution de la sentence est contraire à l'ordre public international.

64-L'ordre public international au regard duquel s'effectue le contrôle du juge de l'annulation s'entend de la conception qu'en a l'ordre juridique français, c'est-à-dire des valeurs et des principes dont celui-ci ne saurait souffrir la méconnaissance même dans un contexte international.

65-Le contrôle exercé par le juge de l'annulation pour la défense de l'ordre public international s'attache seulement à examiner si l'exécution des dispositions prises par le tribunal arbitral heurte les principes et valeurs compris dans l'ordre public international.

66-L'égalité des armes, qui constitue un élément du procès équitable protégé par l'ordre public international, implique l'obligation d'offrir à chaque partie une possibilité raisonnable de présenter sa cause ' y compris les preuves ' dans des conditions qui ne la placent pas dans une situation substantiellement désavantageuse par rapport à son adversaire.

67-I1 convient d'observer qu'en l'espèce, les arguments développés au soutien de ce moyen sont identiques à ceux développés sur le moyen tiré du non-respect de la contradiction.

68-Pour les mêmes motifs ayant conduit la cour à considérer que le principe de la contradiction n'a pas été méconnu, il convient de relever que chacune des parties a pu, également, être entendue et discuter des éléments de preuve produits aux débats sans que la société ait été placée dans une situation substantiellement désavantageuse de telle sorte qu'aucune violation de l'ordre public international n'est caractérisée.

Sur les moyens d'annulation tirés du refus de l'arbitre de statuer sur une demande constitutifs d'une violation par l'arbitre unique de sa mission et de l'ordre public international (article 1520-3° et 5° du Code de procédure civile)

[...]

79 – Il convient de rappeler que l'omission de statuer n'est pas un cas d'ouverture du recours en annulation, la partie qui s'en prévaut ayant, en vertu de l'article 1485 du Code de procédure civile, applicable à l'arbitrage international par renvoi de l'article 1506, la faculté de ressaisir les arbitres.

80-Par ailleurs, ne constitue pas un déni de justice, le fait pour l'arbitre de considérer, après avoir examiné les écritures des parties, qu'aucune demande n'avait été formée devant lui.

[...] Le déni de justice n'est donc pas caractérisé sauf à vouloir sous couvert de ce moyen remettre en cause l'appréciation par l'arbitre des demandes formées devant lui.

82-En outre, en faisant observer que l'arbitre ne pouvait écarter ce qu'elle considérait comme une demande, au motif qu'elle n'avait pas été reprise dans le dispositif de ses écritures, règle non applicable en arbitrage international, la société entend faire sanctionner par le juge de l'annulation les motifs de la décision de l'arbitre, ce qui échappe de surcroît à son contrôle.

83-Il convient en conséquence de rejeter de ce moyen.

– Paris, Pôle 5 – Chambre 16, 2 novembre 2021, n° 18/21508, *Blow Pack c. Windmoller et Holscher Kg*

Principe de compétence compétence – Applicabilité et nullité manifeste – Conditions – Évidence – Pouvoir juridictionnel – Instance arbitrale – Clause compromissoire – Composition – Nombre – Juge d'appui – Arbitrage multipartite – Principe de l'imparité – Ordre public

Compte tenu de la nature du litige et des dispositions du pacte d'associés auxquelles M. B a adhéré, est acquise une compétence de principe du tribunal arbitral et ce d'autant plus que l'article 1465 du Code de procédure civile dispose que : « *Le tribunal arbitral est seul compétent pour statuer sur les contestations relatives à son pouvoir juridictionnel* ».

Toutefois, l'article 1448 alinéa 1 du Code de procédure civile prévoit que : « *Lorsqu'un litige relevant d'une convention d'arbitrage est porté devant une juridiction de l'État, celle-ci se déclare incompétente sauf si le tribunal arbitral n'est pas encore saisi et si la convention d'arbitrage est manifestement nulle ou manifestement inapplicable.* » Les deux conditions ainsi posées sont cumulatives : certes aucun le tribunal arbitral n'est encore saisi, se pose désormais la seule question de savoir si la convention d'arbitrage est manifestement nulle ou manifestement inapplicable.

Il convient de retenir qu'au regard de ces deux textes, la compétence du tribunal judiciaire est résiduelle ; elle n'est possible que dans l'hypothèse où est établi le caractère manifeste de la nullité ou de l'inapplicabilité de la clause compromissoire litigieuse. Seule une nullité ou une inapplicabilité s'imposant avec la force de l'évidence, sans nécessité pour la cour de procéder à un examen factuel autre que superficiel, est donc susceptible de satisfaire ce caractère manifeste. Faute d'en rapporter la preuve, seul le tribunal arbitral pourrait être amené à statuer, y compris sur son pouvoir juridictionnel, l'étendue de ses pouvoirs et donc sur la compétence. La charge de cette preuve repose sur celui qui allègue l'existence de ces vices de la clause compromissoire.

L'inapplicabilité alléguée tient au fait qu'aussi bien la société que MM. À et AJ n'ont pas signé le pacte d'associés. Cependant, au regard de la nature du litige, M. B contestant son exclusion et ayant lui-même signé le pacte d'associés, aucune inapplicabilité manifeste de la clause compromissoire litigieuse ne peut résulter de son propre choix de les attraire à la procédure. Il appartiendra à la juridiction valablement saisie de statuer sur la recevabilité et le bien-fondé des demandes qui seront éventuellement formulées à leur encontre. Sera en conséquence rejeté le moyen tenant à l'inopposabilité du pacte d'associé.

Sur la nullité ou les difficultés d'application alléguées de la clause compromissoire, il est indiqué qu'aux termes de l'article 2 du Pacte d'associés de 2015 : « *Les parties prennent l'engagement d'honneur de soumettre non seulement les problèmes évoqués ci-dessus, mais plus généralement toutes les difficultés qui pourraient survenir entre elles à l'occasion du présent acte ou de ses suites à un Tribunal arbitral composé, sous réserve de toute autre formule choisie d'un commun accord, de deux arbitres choisis sur la liste des architectes experts judiciaires, chaque partie désignant un arbitre. Les deux arbitres pourront, s'ils le jugent utile, compléter le collège arbitral en désignant un troisième arbitre choisi sur la même liste. Le Tribunal arbitral aura pouvoir d'amiable composition et statuera sur le partage ou l'attribution des frais d'arbitrage. Si une partie est composée de plusieurs associés, ils auront à s'entendre pour désigner en commun un arbitre.* ».

Cette dernière disposition garantit l'égalité des parties devant le tribunal arbitral, même dans l'hypothèse qui est celle du litige, où l'appelant se trouve confronté à la fois à la société et à tous les associés qui ne forment cependant qu'une seule partie, peu important à ce stade de la procédure où la cour n'est amenée à statuer que sur la compétence, que M. Al, non-architecte, soit potentiellement en conflit d'intérêts ou qu'avec M. Ai, il n'ait pas signé le pacte d'associés.

Par ailleurs, selon l'article 1451 du Code de procédure civile, dans sa version résultant du décret n° 2011-48 du 13 janvier 2011 : le tribunal arbitral est composé d'un ou de plusieurs arbitres en nombre impair.

Il est complété si la convention d'arbitrage prévoit la désignation d'arbitres en nombre pair.

Si les parties ne s'accordent pas sur la désignation d'un arbitre complémentaire, le tribunal arbitral est complété dans un délai d'un mois à compter de l'acceptation de leur désignation par les arbitres choisis ou, à défaut, par le juge d'appui mentionné à l'article 1459.

La possibilité prévue par la clause litigieuse, pour les deux arbitres choisis, « *s'ils le jugent utile, de compléter le collège arbitral en désignant un troisième arbitre choisi sur la même liste* » correspond exactement à la solution préconisée par le troisième alinéa de ce texte qui dit « *le tribunal arbitral est complété dans un délai d'un mois à compter de l'acceptation de leur désignation par les arbitres choisis* ». Aucune irrégularité manifeste ne peut donc résulter de la rédaction de la clause compromissoire au regard du principe d'imparité.

Dans ces conditions, l'ordonnance querellée sera confirmée sur ce qu'elle a jugé sur la compétence.

– Versailles, 14e chambre, 4 novembre 2021, n° 21/04943, *X c. Y*

Tribunal arbitral – Compétence – Contrôle étendu – Clause compromissoire – Autonomie – Applicabilité – Validité – Opposabilité – Transmission

Sur le moyen d'annulation tiré de l'incompétence du tribunal arbitral (article 1520 1° du Code de procédure civile)

20-Selon l'article 1520, 1°, du Code de procédure civile, le recours en annulation est ouvert si le tribunal s'est déclaré à tort compétent ou incompétent.

21-Dans le cadre d'un recours en annulation fondé sur l'article 1520, 1° du Code de procédure civile, il appartient au juge de l'annulation de contrôler la décision du tribunal arbitral sur sa compétence, qu'il se soit déclaré compétent ou incompétent, en recherchant tous les éléments de droit ou de fait permettant d'apprécier la portée de la convention d'arbitrage.

22-L'appréciation de la portée de la convention d'arbitrage peut ainsi conduire la cour à devoir analyser son applicabilité, sa validité ou son opposabilité aux parties au litige et donc à devoir apprécier dans le cadre du recours en annulation les circonstances du litige en fait et en droit, sans que cet examen puisse être, en dehors des causes prévues par les textes, constitutif d'une irrecevabilité.

Sur la compétence du tribunal arbitral à l'égard de la société U France

[...]

24-A cet égard, il convient de rappeler qu'en vertu d'une règle matérielle du droit international de l'arbitrage, applicable à un arbitrage dont le siège est fixé en France, la clause compromissoire est indépendante juridiquement du contrat principal qui la contient directement ou par référence. Elle n'est pas affectée par l'inefficacité de cet acte.

25-En l'espèce, il ressort de l'article 17 du contrat de distribution conclu le 7 juin 2005 que « *les Parties feront leurs meilleurs efforts pour régler tous différends nés de l'exécution ou de la rupture de leurs accords par la voie amiable, et à défaut d'y parvenir dans le délai d'un mois à compter de la notification d'une difficulté faite par l'une des parties à l'autre partie, elles la soumettront à la médiation puis le cas échéant à l'arbitrage, conformément aux Règlements de médiation et d'arbitrage de la chambre de commerce international à Genève. Le tribunal arbitral constitué de trois arbitres siègera à Genève et la langue de la procédure arbitrale sera le français. Les débats auront lieu en français. Les documents nécessaires à la conduite de la procédure d'arbitrage sont rédigés en français* ».

26-En l'état de cette clause insérée dans le contrat, le tribunal arbitral est ainsi, comme il a pu le considérer justement, compétent pour statuer sur le litige né de l'exécution du contrat entre ces deux sociétés et dans lequel elle est insérée et ce indépendamment de l'appréciation de la validité et/ou de la résiliation alléguée dudit contrat.

27-Il convient en conséquence de rejeter le moyen d'annulation tiré de l'incompétence du tribunal arbitral à l'égard de la société U France.

Sur la compétence du tribunal arbitral à l'égard des sociétés UT et UG

28-Il est constant que les deux sociétés n'ont pas signé matériellement le contrat du 7 décembre 2005, sur lequel seule la signature de la société UF apparaît.

29-Il n'est pas non plus contesté que les trois recourantes font partie du Groupe U que : – Le capital de la société UF est détenu à hauteur de 64,54 % par la société UNV et à hauteur de 35,44 % par la société UPlc ; – Le capital de la société UT est détenu à hauteur de 64,54 % par la société UNV et à hauteur de 35,44 % par la société UPlc ; – Le capital de la société UG est détenu à hauteur de 100 % par la société UPlc.

30-La question qui se pose est donc celle de savoir si le contrat du 7 décembre 2005 a pu être transféré aux sociétés UT et UG de sorte que la clause compromissoire qu'il contient leur soit devenue opposable.

[...]

32-Ainsi, le tribunal arbitral a pu, s'interrogeant sur la réalité de la résiliation de ce contrat dont se prévaut la société UF, à qui il appartenait selon le même tribunal « *d'apporter la preuve qu'elle a valablement résilié le Contrat en respectant les conditions convenues à l'article 8 du Contrat* » (sentence) estimer que cette preuve n'était pas rapportée et en déduire que « *l'absence de preuve de réception de la lettre de résiliation du 20 décembre 2013 a pour conséquence de priver la résiliation de tout effet* ».

33-La preuve de la résiliation n'ayant pas été rapportée, il convient d'apprécier, comme s'est attaché à le faire le tribunal arbitral, si le contrat du 7 juin 2005 contenant la clause compromissoire a pu être transféré à la société UT puis à la société UG.

34-Il convient en effet de rappeler qu'au regard de sa dimension contractuelle, la clause compromissoire est transmise de façon automatique en tant qu'accessoire du droit d'action, lui-même accessoire du droit substantiel transmis.

[...]

43-Ainsi, le tribunal arbitral a pu énoncer que « (...) *le Contrat a été valablement transféré, en partie, à UT puis à UG et que ce transfert a, en toute hypothèse, emporté automatiquement le transfert de la clause compromissoire qu'il contient, en tant qu'accessoire des droits substantiels ainsi transférés. Le Tribunal est par conséquent compétent pour trancher le différend entre les parties en lien avec ce Contrat* ».

[...] Le moyen tiré de l'incompétence du tribunal arbitral envers les sociétés UT et UG sera rejeté.

Sur le moyen d'annulation tiré du non-respect de sa mission par le tribunal arbitral (article 1520 3° du Code de procédure civile)

[...]

47-Selon l'article 1520, 3°, du Code de procédure civile, le recours en annulation est ouvert si le tribunal a statué sans se conformer à la mission qui lui avait été confiée.

48-La mission des arbitres, définie par la convention d'arbitrage, est délimitée principalement par l'objet du litige, tel qu'il est déterminé par les prétentions des parties sans s'attacher uniquement à l'énoncé des questions dans l'acte de mission.

[...]

59-Il résulte de ces éléments que le tribunal arbitral a bien statué dans le cadre de sa mission, l'objet du litige, délimité par les prétentions des parties, ici corroboré par l'acte de mission, ayant consisté à statuer sur les conséquences de la rupture du contrat de distribution entre les parties et le préjudice subi par la société à la suite du non respect du préavis, que la société UG avait elle-même proposé de fixer à six mois dans sa lettre de résiliation, soumise aux débats.

60-En l'état de ces éléments, dont il ne ressort pas que le tribunal arbitral a statué sur une demande qui n'avait pas été formée, nonobstant le moyen allégué au soutien de cette demande, le moyen d'annulation sera rejeté.

– Paris, Pôle 5 – Chambre 16, Chambre commerciale internationale, 9 novembre 2021, n° 20/05583, *Unilever et a. Usine Pingouin*

Arbitrage interne – Clause compromissoire – Notion – applicabilité et nullité manifeste – Contrat de sous-traitance – Documents contractuels – Principe de compétence compétence – Nullité du contrat – Autonomie de la clause

Aux termes de l'article 1148 du Code de procédure civile, lorsqu'un litige relevant d'une convention d'arbitrage est porté devant une juridiction de l'État, celle-ci se déclare incompétente sauf si le tribunal n'est pas encore saisi et si la convention d'arbitrage est manifestement nulle ou manifestement inapplicable.

Les « *conditions générales du contrat de sous-traitance* », rédigées en anglais, contiennent un article 21.4, dont la traduction libre n'est pas contestée par l'appelante, ainsi rédigé : « *21.4. Arbitrage : Tout différent qui ne peut être réglé à l'amiable par les parties en vertu de l'article 21.3. sera réglé définitivement conformément au Règlement d'arbitrage de la Chambre de Commerce Internationale par un ou plusieurs arbitres nommés conformément audit règlement. L'arbitrage aura lieu à Paris. La langue à utiliser dans la procédure arbitrale sera l'anglais* (...) »

Le présent litige porte sur la question de savoir si la convention d'arbitrage figurant dans les conditions générales du contrat de sous traitance est ou non manifestement nulle, ou manifestement inapplicable, ce point déterminant, conformément au texte précité, la compétence ou non du tribunal de commerce de Dunkerque.

L'article 1443 du Code de procédure civile prévoit que « *À peine de nullité la convention d'arbitrage est écrite. Elle peut résulter d'un échange d'écrits ou d'un document auquel il est fait référence dans la convention principale* ».

[...]

Ces éléments suffisent à constater que la convention d'arbitrage, incluse dans les conditions générales du contrat de sous-traitance, n'est pas manifestement inapplicable au sens de l'article 1448 précité.

S'agissant de la nullité du contrat de sous traitance invoquée par l'appelante, la cour rappelle que l'article 1447 du Code de procédure civile prévoit que la convention d'arbitrage est indépendante du contrat auquel elle se rapporte et qu'elle n'est pas affectée par l'inefficacité de celui-ci ; c'est donc de manière inopérante que l'appelante, qui ne soutient aucun moyen spécifique de nullité de la clause d'arbitrage en elle-même, conclut à la nullité du sous-traité au motif qu'aucun cautionnement valable n'aurait été souscrit par la société en violation des dispositions de la loi du 31 décembre 1975 sur la sous-traitance, pour en déduire que la clause d'arbitrage serait elle-même nulle.

Il résulte de tout ce qui précède que la convention d'arbitrage contenue dans les conditions générales du contrat de sous-traitance signé entre les sociétés n'est ni manifestement nulle, ni manifestement inapplicable, de sorte que par application de l'article 1448 du Code de procédure civile précité, c'est à bon droit que le tribunal de commerce de Dunkerque a renvoyé à mieux se pourvoir au motif que l'affaire doit être examinée par la juridiction arbitrale convenue.

– Douai, chambre 2, section 2, 10 novembre 2021, n° 21/02469, *Prezioso Linjebygg c. Techint Compagnia Tecnica Internazionale*

Sentence arbitrale – Principe de la contradiction – Motivation – Contrôle – Révision au fond – Ordre public international – Conception française – Égalité des armes – Production tardive – Mission – Siège de l'arbitrage – Loi de la procédure – Arbitrage ICC – Règlement ICC – Motivation – Cadre de la mission – Pertinence – Contrôle du juge de l'annulation – Révision au fond.

23-Le principe de la contradiction permet d'assurer la loyauté des débats et le caractère équitable du procès. Il interdit qu'une décision soit rendue sans que chaque partie ait été en mesure de faire valoir ses prétentions de fait et de droit, de connaître les prétentions de son adversaire et de les discuter. Il interdit également que des écritures ou des documents soient portés à la connaissance du tribunal arbitral sans être également communiqués à l'autre partie, et que des moyens de fait ou de droit soient soulevés d'office sans que les parties aient été appelées à les commenter.

[...]

46-Cette question a été discutée contradictoirement et tranchée par le tribunal arbitral [...] de sorte que le grief allégué de violation du principe du contradictoire n'est pas justifié, étant observé que par ce biais la société critique en réalité la motivation juridique de la décision ce qui ne relève pas de la mission du juge de l'annulation.

47-Le moyen sera intégralement rejeté.

Sur le non-respect du principe de l'égalité constitutif d'une violation du principe du contradictoire et l'ordre public international (1520,4° et 1520,5° du Code de procédure civile)

[...]

56-Il résulte de l'article 1520, 5° du Code de procédure civile que le recours en annulation est ouvert si la reconnaissance ou l'exécution de la sentence est contraire à l'ordre public international.

57-L'ordre public international au regard duquel s'effectue le contrôle du juge de l'annulation s'entend de la conception qu'en a l'ordre juridique français, c'est-à-dire des valeurs et des principes dont celui-ci ne saurait souffrir la méconnaissance même dans un contexte international.

58-Cependant, le contrôle exercé par le juge de l'annulation pour la défense de l'ordre public international s'attache seulement à examiner si l'exécution des dispositions prises par le tribunal arbitral heurte (de manière manifeste, effective et concrète) les principes et valeurs compris dans l'ordre public international.

59-L'égalité des armes, qui constitue un élément du procès équitable protégé par l'ordre public international, implique l'obligation d'offrir à chaque partie une possibilité raisonnable de présenter sa cause dans des conditions qui ne la placent pas dans une situation substantiellement désavantageuse par rapport à son adversaire.

[...]

75-Il résulte de ce qui précède que la société a bien été en mesure de discuter avant et pendant l'audience les pièces communiquées en toute transparence dans le cadre de la procédure arbitrale par la partie adverse comme des extraits des documents qu'au surplus la requérante connaissait et pouvait produire depuis le début de la procédure.

76-N'ayant formulé aucune critique ni demande en ce sens, c'est sans violer l'égalité des armes que le tribunal arbitral a écarté la communication tardive de l'ensemble des notes de calculs que la société a joint à ses conclusions postaudience en dehors des règles procédurales convenues.

[...]

79-Elle se contente de dire « *qu'elles ont également soulevé de nombreuses questions s'agissant du respect du principe d'égalité* » sans justifier de manière effective d'une situation créatrice d'un net désavantage à son préjudice ayant donné à son adversaire un avantage décisif caractérisant la violation du principe d'égalité.

80-Ce moyen sera en conséquence entièrement rejeté.

Sur le non-respect par le tribunal arbitral de sa mission

[...]

82-Selon l'article 1520, 3° du Code de procédure civile, le recours en annulation est ouvert si le tribunal a statué sans se conformer à la mission qui lui avait été confiée.

83-Les parties ayant choisi Paris (France) en tant que siège de l'arbitrage, la loi française est applicable à la procédure.

84-Selon l'article 1482 du Code de procédure civile, rendu applicable en matière d'arbitrage international par l'article 1506, 4° du même code, « *la sentence arbitrale expose succinctement les prétentions respectives des parties et leurs moyens. Elle est motivée* ».

85-De plus, l'article 32 du règlement CCI de 2012, applicable à l'instance arbitrale, stipule que « *la sentence doit être motivée* ».

86-Il appartenait donc en l'espèce au tribunal arbitral de motiver sa sentence dans le cadre de la mission qui lui a été confiée, laquelle est délimitée principalement par l'objet du litige, tel qu'il est déterminé par les prétentions des parties.

87-Toutefois le contrôle du juge de l'annulation ne porte que sur l'existence et non sur la pertinence des motifs de la sentence.

Sur la critique relative à la détermination de la date de réception du Projet

[...]

92-Contrairement à ce que soutient la société cet énoncé constitue clairement une motivation dès lors qu'il présente la raison ayant justifié la date de réception.

93-Le grief tiré du fait que le tribunal ait retenu le critère fonctionnel du projet sans qu'il n'y ait selon elle aucun lien logique avec le reste de la section relative à la Réception du Projet pour fixer la date de réception au 11 mai 2015 remet en cause non pas l'existence mais le contenu de la motivation qui ne relève pas du pouvoir du juge de l'annulation.

94-Il en est de même du manquement reproché [...] qui critique en réalité le caractère pertinent et convaincant de la motivation étant observé que les arbitres ne sont pas obligés de suivre les parties dans le détail de leur argumentation.

95-I1 ressort de ces constatations que le grief tiré de ce chef sera rejeté.

Sur la critique relative à la libération des Retenues de Garantie

[...]

99-Il se déduit de ces éléments que cette question a bien été soumise à la discussion des parties et que le tribunal a motivé sa décision en indiquant dans la sentence la raison pour laquelle il a décidé en ce sens.

100-Bien que la motivation ne soit pas spécialement détaillée, la justification de cette décision résulte expressément de la considération des demandes reconventionnelles sur lesquelles le tribunal avait statué en amont [...]

101-Le surplus reproché au Tribunal arbitral par la société dans ses écritures « *d'avoir adopté une position en contradiction flagrante avec les termes du Marché et outrepassé les termes des Retenues de Garanties elles-mêmes* » porte sur la pertinence du raisonnement du tribunal qui l'a conduit à sa décision dont le contrôle par le juge de l'annulation est interdit.

102-Il résulte de ce qui précède que le grief tiré de l'absence de motivation sur ce chef sera également rejeté.

– Paris, Chambre commerciale internationale, Pôle 5 – Chambre 16, 16 novembre 2021, n° 19/20295, *Afcons Infrastructure Limited c. Jordan Phosphate Mines Company Plc*

Article 145 CPC – Procédure non contradictoire – Clause compromissoire – Responsabilité délictuelle – Concurrence déloyale – Champ – Référé – Conditions – Article 1449 CPC

Une partie se prévaut pour sa part de la clause d'arbitrage figurant à l'article 14 du contrat d'enseigne aux termes de laquelle : « *Tous les litiges auxquels le contrat pourra donner lieu, notamment au sujet de sa validité, de son interprétation, de son exécution et de sa résiliation, seront résolus par voie d'arbitrage. Si les parties s'entendent sur la désignation d'un arbitre unique, elles s'en remettront à l'arbitrage de celui qu'elles auront désigné. Dans le cas contraire, il sera constitué un tribunal arbitral composé de trois arbitres.* » et dont elle déduit que seule la juridiction arbitrale est compétente pour statuer sur les litiges survenant entre les parties, que ce soit au cours ou à l'expiration du contrat d'enseigne, à l'exclusion des juridictions étatiques.

Aux termes de ses requêtes, une intimée se plaint de faits de concurrence déloyale et de pratiques anti-concurrentielles commis à son préjudice. L'action que la société se propose d'engager sur le fondement des pratiques anti-concurrentielles alléguées relève des juridictions lyonnaises selon les articles R.420-3 et R.420-4 du Code de commerce. L'action sanctionnant les pratiques anti-concurrentielles comme les actes de concurrence déloyale est une action en responsabilité délictuelle qui, au vu de la généralité des termes de la clause compromissoire susvisée (*tous les litiges auxquels le contrat pourra donner lieu*), ne sort pas du champ de ladite clause, contrairement à ce qu'a pu considérer le premier juge.

Toutefois, il résulte de l'article 1449 du Code de procédure civile que « *l'existence d'une convention d'arbitrage ne fait pas obstacle, tant que le tribunal arbitral n'est pas constitué, à ce qu'une partie saisisse une juridiction de l'État aux fins d'obtenir une mesure d'instruction ou une mesure provisoire ou conservatoire. (..) la demande est portée devant le président du tribunal judiciaire ou de commerce qui statue sur les mesures d'instruction dans les conditions prévues à l'article 145 et, en cas d'urgence, sur les mesures provisoires ou conservatoires sollicitées par les parties à la convention d'arbitrage* ». En l'espèce, un arbitre unique n'a pas été désigné d'un commun accord des parties pas plus qu'à défaut un tribunal arbitral n'a été constitué, de sorte que la société avait la faculté de saisir le juge des référés sur requête aux fins de mesures d'instruction sur le fondement de l'article 145 du Code de procédure civile, a fortiori lorsque les circonstances exigent qu'elles ne soient pas prises contradictoirement.

– Paris, Pôle 1 – Chambre 3, 17 novembre 2021, n° 21/03462, *ITM Alimentaire Centre Est et a. c. Domalane et a.*

Clause de conciliation – Préalable obligatoire – Fin de non-recevoir – A tout moment – Procédure d'appel – Contrat d'architecte – Rédaction – Responsabilité contractuelle – Clause d'arbitrage – Centre de médiation et d'arbitrage de Paris – Faculté – Champ – Tiers – Inapplication

Il ressort de l'article 123 du Code de procédure civile que les fins de non-recevoir peuvent être soulevées en tout état de cause, sauf exception.

Le moyen tiré du non-respect d'une clause de conciliation préalable obligatoire et préalable à la saisine du juge peut être proposé pour la première fois en cause d'appel.

Cette clause est pleinement opposable lorsque la responsabilité contractuelle de l'architecte est recherchée, à condition que son libellé soit dénué d'équivoque quant à la volonté des parties d'en faire un préalable obligatoire à l'introduction de l'instance.

Une des parties, dont la responsabilité contractuelle est recherchée, se prévaut d'une clause insérée au contrat conclu en 2011 selon laquelle : « *si les parties ou l'une d'elles n'ont pas le statut de commerçant, elles s'engagent, avant toute procédure judiciaire, à examiner ensemble, avec le centre de médiation et d'arbitrage de Paris, la possibilité de soumettre le litige à l'arbitrage, à condition que le litige n'implique aucun tiers* ».

Cette clause ne saurait constituer une fin de non-recevoir, puisqu'il s'agit simplement pour les parties d'examiner ensemble « la possibilité » de soumettre le litige à l'arbitrage, vocabulaire qui traduit l'existence d'une simple faculté et non d'une obligation de saisine préalable.

Par ailleurs, le litige opposant en l'espèce le maître de l'ouvrage à l'architecte implique également des tiers, en l'occurrence les constructeurs défaillants et leurs assureurs, si bien que la clause n'était pas applicable quant à son champ.

Il y a enfin lieu de relever que les époux justifient avoir saisi l'ordre des architectes d'Île-de-France aux fins de conciliation, mais que les parties concernées, et notamment l'architecte, n'ont pas pu se rendre disponibles pour participer à la mesure.

Cette fin de non-recevoir ne peut donc qu'être rejetée.

– Rouen, 17 novembre 2021, 20/00377, *X c. Y*

Compromis – Clause compromissoire – Notion – Parties – Acceptation – Validité – Autonomie de la clause – Tiers – Participation – Opposabilité – Principe de compétence compétence – Applicabilité et nullité manifeste – Institution arbitrale

En vertu de l'article 1442 du Code de procédure civile : La convention d'arbitrage prend la forme d'une clause compromissoire ou d'un compromis.

La clause compromissoire est la convention par laquelle les parties à un ou plusieurs contrats s'engagent à soumettre à l'arbitrage les litiges qui pourraient naître relativement à ce ou à ces contrats.

Le compromis est la convention par laquelle les parties à un litige né décident de soumettre celui-ci à l'arbitrage.

Et de l'article 1448 du même code : Lorsqu'un litige relevant d'une convention d'arbitrage est porté devant une juridiction de l'État, celle-ci se déclare incompétente sauf si le tribunal arbitral n'est pas encore saisi et si la convention d'arbitrage est manifestement nulle ou manifestement inapplicable. La juridiction de l'État ne peut relever d'office son incompétence. Toute stipulation contraire au présent article est réputée non écrite.

Aux termes de l'article 1465 du Code de procédure civile, le tribunal arbitral est seul compétent pour statuer sur les contestations relatives à son pouvoir juridictionnel.

Ainsi, il appartient à l'arbitre de se prononcer par priorité sur sa propre compétence et les limites de son investiture ainsi que sur la validité et l'étendue de la convention d'arbitrage.

Lorsqu'un litige relevant d'une convention d'arbitrage est porté devant une juridiction de l'État, celle-ci se déclare incompétente, sauf si le tribunal arbitral n'est pas encore saisi et si la convention d'arbitrage est manifestement nulle ou manifestement inapplicable.

Le juge étatique ne peut se livrer à un examen approfondi des relations contractuelles entre les parties.

En l'espèce, le second memorandum of agreement (d'accord), dont l'application est sollicitée par l'appelante, vise : – 1 nome dell'acquirente (nom de l'acquéreur) : intimée ; – 2 nome del venditore (nom du vendeur) : Mr A ; – 3 mediatore (courtiers) maritimo venditore e acquirente : B Al Ad Appelante

Il est précisé, selon la traduction libre non contestée, d'une part, que le vendeur paiera les commissions du courtier au moment de la vente comme convenu dans un accord privé séparé, autorisant dès à présent à retenir le montant relatif aux commissions directement sur le compte séquestre décrit dans l'article 6, et d'autre part, que l'acquéreur paiera directement la commission du courtier.

Il est mentionné la clause suivante : Controversie Contrattuali e Giurisdizione : Il presente accordo è regolato e interpretato in conformita con le leggi italiane, e qualsiasi controversia derivante à sottoposta alla giurisdizione exclusiva della Am An Ao C. Law & Juridiction : This Agreement shall be governed by and construed in accordance with Italian laws, and any dispute arising shall be submitted to the exclusive juridiction Maritime Arbitration Council, Genova-Italy. Traduction libre non contestée : litige Contractuel et Juridiction : Le présent accord est régi et interprété conformément au droit italien et tout litige en découlant doit être soumis à la compétence exclusive du Conseil d'arbitrage maritime, Gênes-Italie.

Cette clause, très claire, est dénuée de toute ambiguïté et concerne tout litige.

Par ailleurs, les conditions générales indiquent l'identité et les coordonnées de l'acquéreur, du vendeur, et des deux courtiers.

L'exemplaire du second memorandum of agreement remis à la cour comporte la signature de l'acquéreur et, le 12 mars 2018, du vendeur, en l'occurrence l'intimée, représentée par M. Ac.

L'appelante fait valoir, à juste titre, l'acceptation de la clause par l'intimée.

En toute hypothèse, il est rappelé que la clause compromissoire présente par rapport à la convention principale dans laquelle elle s'insère une autonomie juridique, de sorte qu'elle ne peut être affectée par l'inefficacité de cet acte.

[...]

Il est donc constant que l'appelante est intervenue dans les négociations contractuelles et l'élaboration des memorandum of agreement. Son implication ne fait nul doute.

Au regard de ces éléments, l'éviction de la clause compromissoire ne peut s'imposer d'emblée, de sorte que le principe compétence compétence a vocation à s'appliquer et qu'il appartient prioritairement au tribunal arbitral de se prononcer sur sa compétence. De plus fort, la volonté de la société appelante de se soumettre à l'arbitrage est de nature à exclure l'inapplicabilité manifeste de la clause d'arbitrage.

Par ailleurs, il n'y a pas lieu de constater la nullité manifeste de la clause en raison de la désignation de la chambre d'arbitrage maritime de Gênes compte tenu de l'accord intervenu à compter du 1er janvier 2018 entre la chambre de commerce de Gênes, la chambre d'arbitrage de Milan et le barreau de Gênes, ainsi que le fait valoir l'appelante.

En conséquence des développements qui précèdent, le jugement sera infirmé. Lorsque le juge estime que l'affaire relève de la compétence d'une juridiction arbitrale, il renvoie les parties à mieux se pourvoir.

– Aix-en-Provence, Chambre 3-3, 18 novembre 2021, n° 21/02977, *A Avenue c. MDB, Allianz, Ste Coopérative banque Pop. Banque Populaire Méditerranée*

Arbitrage interne – Centre de Médiation et d'Arbitrage de Paris – Règlements d'arbitrage et de médiation – Sentence arbitrale – Sentence partielle – Recours en annulation – Clause compromissoire – Clause de médiation – Compétence – Obligatoire – Mise en œuvre – Fin de non-recevoir – Application – Médiation antérieure – nouveau différend – Tribunal arbitral – Mission – Annulation

Règle applicable

L'article 1492, 1° et 3°, du Code de procédure civile dispose que le recours en annulation est ouvert si le tribunal arbitral s'est déclaré à tort compétent ou incompétent ou s'il a statué sans se conformer à la mission qui lui avait été confiée.

Réponse de la cour

L'article 12 du protocole prévoit que « *les différends qui viendraient à se produire à propos de la validité, de l'interprétation, de l'exécution ou de l'inexécution du présent accord seront soumis au règlement de médiation et en cas d'échec au règlement d'arbitrage du CMAP auquel les parties déclarent adhérer* ».

Il résulte de ces stipulations que les parties ont entendu conférer au préalable de la médiation un caractère obligatoire, le recours à l'arbitrage ne pouvant avoir lieu qu'en cas d'échec de la médiation, la médiation et l'arbitrage ne pouvant de surcroît être organisés que dans le cadre des règlements du Centre de Médiation et d'Arbitrage de Paris.

Il est constant qu'une médiation a été initiée et qu'à la suite de l'échec de cette médiation, une sentence définitive a été prononcée.

Il est également constant qu'aucune médiation n'est intervenue en application du règlement de médiation visé par l'article 12 avant la saisine du tribunal arbitral ayant prononcé la sentence partielle, objet du recours.

Or, cet article 12 prévoit la mise en œuvre d'une médiation pour « *les différends qui viendraient à se produire* », ce dont il faut déduire que le préalable de la médiation s'impose pour tous les différends successifs entre les parties.

Dès lors, la saisine de 2009 du Centre de médiation et d'arbitrage de Paris à propos du premier différend qui a conduit, en l'absence de succès de la médiation, à la sentence de 2014 ne dispensait pas les parties de recourir à une nouvelle médiation avant de solliciter, en 2017, un nouvel arbitrage.

La sentence partielle a d'ailleurs elle-même énoncé que « *la clause de médiation n'épuise pas ses effets de par sa première mise en œuvre* », qu'« *elle a vocation à jouer de manière générale dès lors qu'un litige, au besoin nouveau, survient et entre dans son champ d'application* » et qu'« *en l'espèce, le litige soumis au tribunal entre parfaitement dans le périmètre de la clause de médiation* ».

[...]

Toutefois, s'il est vrai, d'une manière générale, qu'une clause d'un contrat instituant une procédure de médiation obligatoire et préalable constitue une fin de non-recevoir, il n'en demeure pas moins qu'en l'espèce, le tribunal arbitral s'est déclaré compétent, alors pourtant que les demandeurs au recours en annulation ont soutenu devant lui qu'une médiation préalable et obligatoire s'imposait en vertu de l'article 12 du protocole, qu'il a lui-même relevé que le litige relevait du champ d'application de la clause de médiation et qu'il a de surcroît invité les parties à mettre en œuvre une procédure de médiation parallèle à la procédure d'arbitrage.

Or, le tribunal arbitral ne pouvait pas se reconnaître compétent, alors que la procédure de médiation préalable prévue par l'article 12 du protocole n'avait pas été mise en œuvre.

Le non-respect de la clause de médiation n'est donc pas en l'espèce une fin de non-recevoir ne relevant pas de l'appréciation de la cour d'appel mais constitue une circonstance de l'espèce qui doit être prise en compte pour apprécier la violation de l'article 1492, 1°, du Code de procédure civile.

La sentence partielle doit donc être annulée en application de l'article 1492, 1°, du Code de procédure civile. L'annulation de la sentence étant prononcée en raison de l'incompétence du tribunal arbitral, la cour doit s'abstenir de statuer au fond et les parties doivent être renvoyées à mieux se pourvoir sans qu'il y ait lieu à désigner la juridiction devant être saisie.

– Paris, Pôle 5 – Chambre 16, 23 novembre 2021, n° 18/22099 et 19/19007, *X c. HD Holding*

Recours en annulation – Exequatur – Procédure – Appel – Recevabilité – Ordre public international – Loi de police – Loi de police interne – Directive européenne – CJUE – Contrat d'agent – Liberté d'établissement – Articles L. 134-1 et suivants du Code de commerce – Applicabilité – Droit européen – Droit suisse applicable – Lois de police du for – Conception

française – Règles et valeurs – Ordre juridique français – Arbitrage – Accès à la justice – Déni de justice – Coûts – Volonté des parties – Révision au fond – Principe du contradictoire – Notion

Sur le caractère irrecevable et mal fondé de l'appel en ce qu'il critique la sentence arbitrale

[...]

17-Cependant, il ressort de l'article 1525 du Code de procédure civile que « *La décision qui statue sur une demande de reconnaissance ou d'exequatur d'une sentence arbitrale rendue à l'étranger est susceptible d'appel* » de telle sorte que l'appel interjeté contre l'ordonnance d'exequatur du 6 mai 2019 est bien recevable,

18-En outre, cet article disposant également que « *la cour d'appel ne peut refuser la reconnaissance ou l'exequatur de la sentence que dans les cas prévus à l'article 1520* », il appartient bien à l'appelant d'articuler des griefs à l'encontre de la sentence arbitrale et non de l'ordonnance d'exequatur afin de soutenir les cas d'annulation limitativement prévus par l'article 1520 du Code de procédure civile, ce qu'a fait la société.

19-Il appartiendra à la cour d'apprécier à l'occasion de l'examen de chacun des moyens d'annulation invoqué si, sous couvert de ces moyens, la société entend remettre en cause l'interdiction pour le juge de l'annulation de réviser la sentence arbitrale, sans que cet argument ne puisse caractériser une fin de non-recevoir.

20-Cette demande sera en conséquence rejetée.

Sur le moyen d'annulation tiré de la contrariété de la reconnaissance ou l'exécution de la sentence à l'ordre public international (article 1520, 5° du Code de procédure civile)

Sur la méconnaissance d'une loi de police relevant de l'ordre public international

[...]

29-Il convient de relever qu'une loi de police interne, fût-elle le fruit d'une transposition d'une directive européenne dont le caractère impératif a été rappelé par la Cour de justice de l'Union européenne, n'est susceptible de relever de la conception française l'ordre public international que si, après avoir vérifié son applicabilité au litige, sa méconnaissance heurte cette conception, c'est-à-dire l'ensemble des règles et des valeurs dont l'ordre juridique français ne peut souffrir la méconnaissance, même dans des matières internationales.

[...]

31-De même, la Cour de justice de l'Union européenne, dans la décision INGMAR du 9 novembre 2000 (C-381/98) a dit pour droit que « *les articles 17 et 18 de la directive 86/653/CEE du Conseil, du 18 décembre 1986, relative à la coordination des droits des États membres concernant les agents commerciaux indépendants garantissent certains droits à l'agent commercial après la cessation du contrat d'agence, doivent trouver application dès lors que l'agent commercial a exercé son activité dans un État membre et alors même que le commettant est établi dans un pays tiers et que, en vertu d'une clause du contrat, ce dernier est régi par la loi de ce pays* ».

32-Un tel lien de rattachement en l'espèce est également satisfait comme l'a d'ailleurs reconnu l'arbitre dans sa sentence, le lieu d'exercice de l'activité de l'agent commercial couvrant, aux termes du contrat conclu le territoire de la France.

33-Au regard de ces éléments, la condition d'applicabilité des articles L. 134-1 et suivants du code de commerce est satisfaite.

34-Les parties au contrat litigieux ayant cependant indiqué que celui-ci était régi par la loi Suisse, la société n'était fondée à solliciter l'éviction de cette loi devant l'arbitre que si celle-ci est susceptible d'être qualifiée de loi de police.

[...]

36-Devant le juge de l'annulation, le débat n'est pas tant de savoir si les dispositions des articles L. 34-1 et suivants constituent des lois de police du for, mais plus précisément, si ces articles, fussent-ils qualifiés de loi de police, relèvent au surplus de la conception française de l'ordre public international en ce sens que leur méconnaissance heurterait la conception française de l'ordre public international qui s'entend de l'ensemble des règles et des valeurs dont l'ordre juridique français ne peut souffrir la méconnaissance, même dans des matières internationales.

37-Au soutien de cette thèse, la société s'appuie sur la jurisprudence de la Cour de justice de l'Union européenne émanant de l'arrêt rendu le 9 novembre 2000, Affaire A c. Ac Ad Technologies Inc, au terme de laquelle, la Cour de justice a rappelé notamment qu'il : « *est essentiel pour l'ordre juridique communautaire qu'un commettant établi dans un pays tiers, dont l'agent commercial exerce son activité à l'intérieur de la Communauté, ne puisse éluder ces dispositions par le simple jeu d'une clause de choix de loi. La fonction que remplissent les dispositions en cause exige en effet qu'elles trouvent application dès lors que la situation présente un lien étroit avec la Communauté, notamment lorsque l'agent commercial exerce son activité sur le territoire d'un État membre, quelle que soit la loi à laquelle les parties ont entendu soumettre le contrat* ».

38-Cependant, il convient de relever, comme l'a fait l'arbitre, que la jurisprudence française émanant de la plus haute juridiction, n'a pas à ce jour considéré que les dispositions des articles L. 134-1 et suivants pouvaient relever de la conception française de l'ordre public international ayant au contraire écarté une telle qualification à au moins deux reprises (1re Civ., 21 octobre 2015, n° 1420924 ; Com., 5 janvier 2016, n° 1410628).

39-En effet, les dispositions émanant du droit de l'Union européenne, fussent-elles qualifiées d'impératives, ne poursuivent pas toutes des objectifs visant à garantir des principes ou valeurs essentiels dont les États membres ne sauraient souffrir la méconnaissance dans un contexte international.

40 – En l'espèce, l'objectif de la directive précitée et de sa transposition est essentiellement d'harmoniser et de rapprocher les législations des États membres quant à la protection des intérêts privés des agents commerciaux, sans que soit en jeu la défense d'intérêts vitaux de ces mêmes États membres, ni même qu'il ressortisse de manière évidente de telles dispositions qu'elles sont nécessaires à la mise en œuvre d'une politique impérieuse de défense de la liberté d'établissement ou d'une concurrence non faussée.

41-En l'état de ces éléments, aucune contrariété à l'ordre public international ne pouvant être tirée du choix de la loi suisse, la demande subsidiaire tendant à ce que soit posée une question préjudicielle, qui est sans objet, sera également rejetée.

Sur le non-respect du droit d'accès au juge

[...]

44-L'accès à la justice, en ce qu'il permet de garantir l'effectivité des droits, relève de l'ordre public international. Dès lors, une convention d'arbitrage qui ferait obstacle à cet accès, serait contraire à l'ordre public international et donc nulle.

45-Cependant, si le droit d'accès à la justice implique qu'une personne ne puisse être privée de la faculté concrète de faire trancher ses prétentions par un juge, ce droit n'est pas inconditionnel. Des restrictions peuvent être apportées à l'exercice de ce droit, sous réserve de répondre à un but légitime et d'être proportionnées aux nécessités d'une bonne administration de la justice.

46-Ainsi, une convention d'arbitrage, par laquelle les parties consentent à soumettre leur litige à un arbitre et qui emporte nécessairement renonciation à la justice étatique et, en France, à la gratuité du service public de la justice, ne saurait en elle-même porter atteinte à l'accès à la justice.

47-Seules ses modalités doivent être examinées afin de vérifier qu'elles ne privent pas, dans leur mise en œuvre, une partie d'un accès à la justice et ne portent ainsi pas une atteinte effective au droit fondamental d'accès à la justice.

48-En l'espèce, il convient de relever que la société n'a pas été privée de son droit d'accès au juge, fût-il arbitral, auquel elle a bien eu accès et pu présenter ses demandes quand bien même elle se plaint du montant des frais et honoraires que l'arbitre a mis à sa charge, après avoir entendu les parties et tranché le litige.

[...]

51-Ainsi, la société entend, sous couvert de ce grief, remettre en cause l'appréciation par l'arbitre de la charge et du montant des frais, ce que le juge de l'annulation ne peut contrôler.

54-Ce moyen sera en conséquence rejeté.

Sur le moyen d'annulation tiré de la violation du principe du contradictoire

57 – Il résulte de l'article 1520, 4° du Code de procédure civile que le recours en annulation est ouvert si le principe de la contradiction n'a pas été respecté.

58-Le principe de la contradiction exige seulement que les parties aient pu faire connaître leurs prétentions de fait et de droit et discuter celles de leur adversaire de telle sorte que rien de ce qui a servi à fonder la décision des arbitres n'ait échappé à leur débat contradictoire.

[...]

61-En l'état de ces éléments, le principe de la contradiction n'a pas été méconnu de sorte que ce moyen sera également rejeté.

– Paris, Chambre commerciale internationale Pôle 5 – Chambre 16, 23 novembre 2021, n° 19/15670, *Accessoires Company c. Guess Europe Sagl*

Clause d'arbitrage – Conciliation – Définition – Fin de non-recevoir – Renonciation – Référé – Demande d'expertise

« *En prévision des cas où des contestations s'élèveraient entre elles, à l'occasion de la présente convention, les parties prennent l'engagement de soumettre les contestations à deux arbitres qui, en cas de divergence, devront s'adjoindre un troisième pour les départager. En cas de refus de l'une des parties de désigner son arbitre, comme au cas où les arbitres désignés ne pourraient s'entendre pour le choix d'un troisième arbitre, il sera procédé à la nomination de l'arbitre par Monsieur le Président du tribunal à la requête de la partie la plus diligente* ».

Cette clause prévoyant le recours à l'arbitrage ne constitue pas une procédure de conciliation obligatoire préalable à la saisine du juge, sanctionnée par une fin de non-recevoir par application de l'article 122 du Code de procédure civile.

En toutes hypothèses, Mme Y a renoncé à l'application de cette clause en saisissant elle-même, par acte d'huissier de 2018, le juge des référés aux fins de désignation d'un expert judiciaire.

La demande en paiement est donc recevable.

– Pau, 1re Chambre, 23 novembre 2021, n° 19/00619, *X c. Y*

Arbitrage international – Critères – Cession de parts – Clause compromissoire – Compromis – Notion – Pouvoir juridictionnel – Applicabilité et nullité manifeste – Juge de l'évidence – Étendue – Ensemble contractuel – Arbitrabilité – Ordre public – Loi de police

Selon l'article 1442 du Code de procédure civile, la convention d'arbitrage prend la forme d'une clause compromissoire ou d'un compromis. La clause compromissoire est la convention par laquelle les parties à un ou plusieurs contrats s'engagent à soumettre à l'arbitrage les litiges qui pourraient naître relativement à ce ou à ces contrats.

La clause compromissoire de la promesse synallagmatique de cession de parts sociales, signée en 2019 entre les parties, stipule que : « *La présente promesse sera régie et interprété conformément à la législation de la République Française. Les Parties s'efforceront de résoudre à l'amiable tout litige découlant de la présente promesse dans un délai de trente (30) jours après réception du document écrit invoquant le litige. En cas d'échec, toutes les contestations de toute nature qui peuvent ou pourront s'élever à l'occasion soit de l'exécution, soit de l'interprétation de la présente promesse ou de la mise en œuvre de ses contrats accessoires, seront soumises en premier et dernier ressort à un collège arbitral de trois arbitres constitués de la manière suivante : Une des parties désignera son arbitre, l'autre désignera le sien dans le délai de 15 jours suivant la notification qui lui aura été faite de la désignation du premier arbitre. Les arbitres ainsi désignés choisiront le troisième dans un délai de 15 jours de la notification qui leur aura été faite de leur désignation. En cas de défaillance de l'une des parties à désigner un arbitre, comme en cas de défaut de désignation du troisième arbitre, huit jours après la mise en demeure qui lui aura été fait, il sera pourvu à cette désignation par ordonnance du Président du Tribunal de grande instance de Perpignan, non susceptible de recours, sur assignation de la partie la plus diligente. Le collège arbitral sera amiable compositeur et sera tenu de déposer sa sentence, non susceptible de recours, dans un délai de 6 mois. Il sera dispensé des formalités de la procédure et des délais ordinaires. Les sentences arbitrales seront prononcées à la majorité et exécutées par provision nonobstant opposition. Le collège arbitral décidera par qui et dans quelles proportions seront supportés les honoraires de l'arbitrage, ainsi que les frais, y compris le cas échéant, ceux d'enregistrement, les doubles droits et amendes. Le collège arbitral sera dispensé de déposer sa sentence.* »

La validité de cette clause n'est pas contestée.

L'article 1448 du même code précise que lorsqu'un litige relevant d'une convention d'arbitrage est porté devant une juridiction de l'État, celle-ci se déclare incompétente sauf si le tribunal arbitral n'est pas encore saisi et si la convention d'arbitrage est manifestement nulle ou manifestement inapplicable. La juridiction de l'État ne peut relever d'office son incompétence. Toute stipulation contraire au présent article est réputée non écrite.

Selon l'article 1465 de ce code, le tribunal arbitral est seul compétent pour statuer sur les contestations relatives à son pouvoir juridictionnel.

Ces dispositions s'appliquent à l'arbitrage international, à savoir l'arbitrage, en application des articles 1504 et 1506, qui met en cause des intérêts du commerce international, à défaut de convention contraire comme c'est le cas en l'espèce s'agissant d'une opération de cession de parts sociales d'une société de droit tunisien, ne se dénouant pas économiquement dans un seul État eu égard notamment à la nationalité italienne, française et tunisienne des parties à l'acte.

Ainsi, en application combinée des articles 1442 et 1465 du Code de procédure civile, le principe est celui de la compétence du tribunal arbitral et de l'incompétence de la juridiction étatique, que le tribunal arbitral soit saisi ou non, comme en l'espèce, ce dernier ayant été saisi, c'est-à-dire définitivement constitué lors de l'acceptation par le dernier arbitre de sa mission le 16 octobre 2020, alors que le tribunal de commerce de Perpignan a été saisi par actes d'huissier en date des 8 et 10 juillet 2020, remis au greffe le 13 juillet 2020.

Le juge étatique doit se déclarer incompétent dès lors que l'objet du litige a un lien, apprécié de façon extensive, avec la matière arbitrale. Il appartient ensuite aux arbitres d'apprécier si le lien existant entre le litige et la matière arbitrale définie par la convention d'arbitrage est suffisant.

Cependant, lorsque le tribunal arbitral n'est pas encore constitué, le juge étatique est compétent s'il juge que la convention d'arbitrage est manifestement nulle ou manifestement inapplicable, seules exceptions au principe de la compétence de la juridiction arbitrale.

La nullité manifeste est celle qui s'impose à l'évidence, elle ne peut être retenue que lorsqu'elle est décelable à la seule lecture de la clause et du contrat litigieux. En l'espèce, aucune nullité n'est même alléguée.

La convention d'arbitrage est inapplicable lorsque, quoique valable, elle n'intègre pas le litige dans son champ d'application ; l'inapplicabilité doit être évidente et ne susciter aucun doute.

En l'espèce, le champ d'application de la clause compromissoire est, de façon assez habituelle, très large puisqu'elle prévoit de soumettre au tribunal arbitral « *toutes les contestations de toute nature qui peuvent ou pourront s'élever à l'occasion soit de l'exécution, soit de l'interprétation de la présente promesse ou de la mise en œuvre de ses contrats accessoires* ».

[...]

Ainsi, indépendamment de la similitude des demandes formées auprès de chaque juridiction, qui est étrangère à la priorité de la compétence de l'une sur l'autre, les demandes des parties, relatives à l'appréciation de la responsabilité contractuelle, et délictuelle, respectives de chacune dans le cadre de l'opération de cession de parts sociales qui les lie, se rattachent dans une acception large à l'exécution de la promesse synallagmatique de cession de parts sociales du 9 décembre 2019 et du projet de promesse de cession ayant suivi, qui forment un ensemble contractuel, en ce compris les relations pré-contractuelles, et entrent dans le champ d'application de la clause compromissoire.

Par ailleurs, les articles 2059 et 2060 du Code civil déterminent les litiges inarbitrables, à savoir ceux qui ne peuvent être soustraits à la connaissance des juges étatiques, lorsque, d'une part, la compromission concerne des droits indisponibles et d'autre part, lorsque les causes du litige (outre des matières étrangères au présent litige) intéressent l'ordre public.

Aucune illicéité de la convention d'arbitrage elle-même, en ce qu'elle donnerait mission au tribunal arbitral de violer l'ordre public n'est soulevée tandis que l'éventuelle violation du règlement général de l'Autorité des marchés financiers se situe hors du champ d'application de la clause compromissoire et ne relève pas de l'office du tribunal arbitral, ne pouvant, dès lors, rendre inarbitrable le litige.

Des dispositions d'ordre public, applicables au litige, fussent-elles constitutives de lois de police, ne font pas obstacle à la priorité de la compétence du tribunal arbitral, sauf comme déjà indiqué, inapplicabilité manifeste, au demeurant non établie, de la clause compromissoire. Il appartiendra le cas échéant au tribunal arbitral de juger d'une éventuelle violation de l'ordre public applicable par les demandes dont il est saisi, y compris celles fondées sur les dispositions de l'article L. 442-1 du Code de commerce.

[...]

Au vu de l'ensemble de ces éléments, la clause compromissoire n'étant ni manifestement nulle, ni manifestement inapplicable et le litige n'étant pas inarbitrable, le tribunal de commerce de Perpignan, et partant la cour, ne sont pas compétents pour statuer sur le litige opposant les parties.

En conséquence, le jugement ne pourra qu'être infirmé et les parties seront renvoyées en application des dispositions de l'article 81 du Code de procédure civile à mieux se pourvoir, sans qu'il y ait lieu de statuer sur l'irrecevabilité, tirée de la fin de non-recevoir touchant les demandes formées devant le premier juge sur le fondement des dispositions de l'article L. 442-1 du Code de commerce.

– **Montpellier, Chambre commerciale, 23 novembre 2021, n° 21/03721,** *Catana groupe et a c. X*

Arbitrage international – Clause compromissoire – Effets – Autonomie – Validité – Parties – Implication – Connaissance – Tiers non signataire – Contrôle entier – Extension de la clause

21-En matière d'arbitrage international une jurisprudence constante retient que « *l'effet de la clause d'arbitrage international s'étend aux parties directement impliquées dans l'exécution du contrat et aux litiges qui peuvent en résulter* » (Cass. 1re civ., 21 mars 2007, n° 04-20.842).

22 – La clause compromissoire insérée dans un contrat international a une validité et une efficacité propre qui commandent d'en étendre l'application aux parties directement impliquées dans l'exécution du contrat et les litiges qui peuvent en résulter, dès lors qu'il est établi que leur situation contractuelle, leurs activités et les relations habituelles existant entre les parties font présumer qu'elles ont accepté la clause compromissoire dont elles connaissaient l'existence et la portée bien qu'elles n'aient pas été signataires du contrat qui la stipulait.

23 – Il est acquis que dans le cadre de ce recours en annulation fondé sur le grief d'incompétence invoqué, la cour exerce son pouvoir de contrôle en recherchant en droit et en fait, tous les éléments d'existence du cas d'ouverture ; dit autrement la cour dispose d'une liberté d'appréciation des circonstances de fait et de droit relatives au grief invoqué.

24-En l'occurrence l'arbitrage est international.

25-La société n'est pas signataire du contrat de fourniture de grues portiques signé dans lequel la clause compromissoire fondant le pouvoir juridictionnel du tribunal arbitral a été insérée.

26-Il s'agit pour la cour de trancher la question de l'extension tacite de la clause d'arbitrage au tiers non signataire.

[...]

40-La cour retient de ces éléments qu'ils établissent que la société a eu un rôle significatif et décisionnaire dans la négociation et le suivi du contrat de fournitures signé par sa filiale l'impliquant directement dans son exécution et les litiges qui pouvaient en résulter.

41-Ces circonstances démontrent sa connaissance et son acceptation implicite de la clause compromissoire dont elle n'a pu ignorer la teneur ni la portée.

42-Il s'en suit que les effets de la clause prévoyant que les différends seraient tranchés par un tribunal arbitral, pouvaient être étendus à la société bien qu'elle n'ait pas été signataire du contrat.

43-Le moyen tiré de l'incompétence du tribunal arbitral envers la société sera en conséquence rejeté, sans qu'il y ait lieu de statuer sur la demande d'exequatur qui est conférée de plein droit à la décision de rejet.

– Paris, Chambre commerciale internationale, pôle 5 – chambre 16, 23 novembre 2021, n° 18/22323, *Damietta International Port Company S.A.E. c. Société Doosan Heavy Industries & Construction Co, Ltd*

Arbitrage international – Exequatur – Procédure – Déféré – Voie de recours – CME – Ordonnance – Déféré nullité – Recevabilité

Sur la recevabilité du déféré

24 – En application de l'article 1527 du Code de procédure civile, applicable à l'arbitrage international, le recours en annulation contre une sentence internationale est formé, instruit et jugé selon les règles relatives à la procédure contentieuse prévues aux articles 900 à 930-1 du Code de procédure civile. Le rejet de l'appel ou du recours en annulation confère l'exequatur à la sentence arbitrale ou à celles de ses dispositions qui ne sont pas atteintes par la censure de la cour.

25 – Il résulte de l'article 916 du Code de procédure civile que les ordonnances du conseiller de la mise en état ne sont susceptibles d'aucun recours indépendamment de l'arrêt sur le fond, et que, par exception, elles peuvent seulement être déférées à la cour lorsqu'elles ont pour effet de mettre fin à l'instance, lorsqu'elles constatent son extinction ou lorsqu'elles ont trait à des mesures provisoires en matière de divorce ou de séparation de corps. Elles peuvent également être déférées lorsqu'elles statuent sur une exception de procédure, sur un incident mettant fin à l'instance, sur une fin de non-recevoir ou sur la caducité de l'appel.

26 – L'ordonnance du conseiller de la mise en état statuant sur une demande d'exequatur dans le cadre d'un recours en annulation d'une sentence arbitrale internationale n'entre ni dans la catégorie des exceptions de procédure ni dans celle des fins de non-recevoir, ni dans celles ayant trait à la caducité.

27 – Seul est en jeu l'effet extinctif ou non sur l'instance d'une ordonnance du conseiller de la mise en état statuant sur une demande d'exequatur.

28 – À cet égard, il y a lieu tout d'abord de rappeler que selon l'article 50 du Code de procédure civile, les incidents d'instance sont tranchés par la juridiction devant laquelle se déroule l'instance qu'ils affectent, l'unicité de l'instance n'étant pas affectée par l'attribution de numéros de RG distincts, ou liée aux décisions de jonction ou disjonction de demandes qui sont des mesures d'administration judiciaire.

29 – En outre, si la demande d'exequatur d'une sentence internationale peut être formée dans le cadre d'une instance propre, distincte de l'instance au fond, c'est uniquement devant le tribunal judiciaire statuant à juge unique, qui rend une ordonnance dans les conditions fixées aux articles 1516 et s. du Code de procédure civile.

30 – Lorsque la cour d'appel est saisie d'un recours concernant une sentence internationale (régi par le chapitre IV, articles 1518 à 1527 du Code de procédure civile), les demandes d'exequatur relatives à cette sentence peuvent également être formées selon l'article 1521 du Code de procédure civile, soit devant le premier Président de la cour d'appel soit, dès qu'il est saisi, devant le conseiller de la mise en état.

31 – Dans ce cas, la demande d'exequatur constitue un incident de l'instance au sens de l'article 50 sus-rappelé, de telle sorte qu'en tout état de cause l'instance se poursuit, quelle que soit la décision prise par le conseiller de la mise en état, l'exequatur restant dans le débat puisque selon les articles 1524 et 1527 du Code de procédure civile, le rejet du recours en annulation aura pour effet de revêtir la sentence de l'exequatur.

32 – Dès lors, la décision du conseiller de la mise en état statuant sur l'exequatur formée en application de l'article 1521 du Code de procédure civile ne met pas fin à l'instance, que le conseiller ordonne ou rejette l'exequatur.

33 – Le déféré d'une ordonnance du conseiller de la mise en état statuant sur l'exequatur n'est dès lors pas recevable sur le fondement de l'article 916 du Code de procédure civile.

Sur la recevabilité du déféré-nullité

[...]

35 – Cependant, la possibilité ouverte à titre exceptionnel par la voie prétorienne, en cas d'excès de pouvoir, de contester la décision rendue par un juge, par la voie de l'appel-nullité ou du déféré-nullité, n'est pas conditionnée par le caractère « immédiat » ou non du recours possible, mais uniquement par l'existence ou l'absence de tout recours.

36 – Il est constant qu'en l'espèce, il existe un recours contre la décision du conseiller de la mise en état qui a refusé l'exequatur partiel dès lors que le recours en annulation de la sentence finale, pendant devant la cour, emporte de plein droit, par application des articles 1524 et 1527 du Code de procédure civile, saisine de la cour sur l'exequatur et donc recours sur celle-ci, et que le rejet du recours en

annulation, s'il est prononcé, conférera de plein droit l'exequatur à la sentence arbitrale ou à celles de ses dispositions qui ne sont pas atteintes par la censure de la cour.

37 – À cet égard, l'article 1523 du Code de procédure civile qui permet d'interjeter appel contre la décision du juge du tribunal judiciaire qui refuse l'exequatur n'a pas pour effet de créer un régime distinct selon que l'exequatur a été accordée ou non, ni de modifier les effets prévus de plein droit par les articles 1524 et 1527, en cas de saisine de la cour d'un recours en annulation, ni de créer un recours « différé », ce qui en tout état de cause, ne constituerait pas une « absence » de recours possible.

38 – Il en résulte qu'un recours existe contre l'ordonnance du conseiller de la mise en état ayant statué sur la demande d'exequatur, qu'elle ait ou non été accordée, et que le déféré-nullité contre une telle ordonnance est par conséquent irrecevable, sans qu'il soit nécessaire de rechercher si le juge a commis un excès de pouvoir, la condition de l'absence de toute voie de recours faisant défaut.

39 – Il ne peut pas plus être soutenu qu'il devrait être distingué, selon les chefs de la sentence visés par le recours en annulation, pour en déduire que ceux qui n'en seraient pas l'objet ne seraient dès lors pas couverts par l'exequatur de plein droit résultant d'un rejet du recours en annulation, et qu'il n'existerait dès lors pas de recours contre l'ordonnance du conseiller de la mise en état en ce qui les concerne, alors que l'article 1527 n'exclut de l'exequatur que les chefs de la sentence qui seraient annulés et non ceux qui ne sont pas visés par l'annulation, sans distinction.

40 – La demande de déféré-nullité devra par conséquent être déclarée irrecevable.

Sur la demande de dommages et intérêts pour procédure abusive et sur la condamnation à une amende civile

[…]

43 – Il est constant que l'abus du droit d'agir en justice n'est caractérisé qu'en présence d'une faute dans l'exercice de ce droit.

Il n'est pas établi en l'espèce que la société aurait fait dégénérer en abus son droit d'agir en justice en formant un déféré alors que la discussion sur l'existence d'une voie de recours contre une ordonnance du conseiller de la mise en état statuant sur une demande d'exequatur et les éléments factuels du dossier pouvaient permettre de s'interroger sur l'existence d'un recours sans que cela ne constitue un abus.

– **Paris, Chambre commerciale internationale, pôle 5 – chambre 16, 23 novembre 2021, n° 21/03754, *Ixblue c. Safran Electronics & Defense***

Clause compromissoire – Référé – Mesure provisoire – Conditions – Urgence – Créance – Ancienneté – Trouble – Dommage imminent – Pouvoirs – Fond – Évidence

Sur la compétence du juge des référés en présence d'une clause compromissoire

[…]

L'article 1449 du Code de procédure civile dispose qu'une convention d'arbitrage n'exclut pas la saisine d'une juridiction judiciaire tant que le tribunal arbitral n'est pas saisi et notamment le juge des référés en cas d'urgence, lorsque la demande porte sur une mesure provisoire.

En l'espèce, il n'est pas justifié de la saisine préalable d'un tribunal arbitral, il est sollicité une demande en paiement provisionnel ; quant à l'urgence, elle relève de l'ancienneté de la créance issue du protocole d'accord datant du 17 mars 2017, soit il y a plus de quatre ans.

La décision qui a retenu sa compétence sera donc confirmée de ce chef.

Sur le fond

Le président du tribunal de commerce peut, dans les limites de la compétence du tribunal, et même en présence d'une contestation sérieuse, prescrire en référé les mesures conservatoires ou de remise en état qui s'imposent, soit pour prévenir un dommage imminent, soit pour faire cesser un trouble manifestement illicite.

Et dans les cas où l'existence de l'obligation n'est pas sérieusement contestable, il peut accorder une provision au créancier, ou ordonner l'exécution de l'obligation même s'il s'agit d'une obligation de faire.

S'il appartient au demandeur à une provision d'établir l'existence de la créance qu'il invoque, c'est au défendeur de prouver que cette créance est sérieusement contestable. Et la contestation de l'obligation du créancier est sérieuse dès lors qu'il existe une difficulté d'appréciation ou que le juge est contraint de procéder à un examen des pièces, preuves et arguments permettant d'apprécier la portée des engagements des parties et trancher une question dont dépend l'existence de l'obligation invoquée, ce qui relève d'un examen au fond.

– **Toulouse, 3e Chambre, 24 novembre 2021, n° 20/03772,** ***Paprec Sud Ouest c. Ed Master***

Arbitrage interne – Clause compromissoire – Recours en annulation – Cas d'ouverture – Ordre public – Réforme 2011 – Contrôle limité – Motivation – Juge de l'apparence – Loi dans le temps – Droit des sociétés – Société civile – Personnalité morale – Annulation partielle – Amiable composition – Mission de la Cour – Exequatur

Sur l'annulation de la sentence arbitrale

L'article 13 des statuts de la SEP stipule que toutes les contestations qui pourraient s'élever entre les participants relativement à la société en participation seront soumises à la décision d'un arbitre amiable désigné d'un commun accord entre les parties ou, à défaut par Monsieur le président du tribunal de commerce de Nîmes, à la requête de la partie la plus diligente. Le dernier alinéa de cet article précise que l'arbitre aura les pouvoirs les plus étendus pour trancher comme amiable compositeur les questions qui lui seront soumises ou dont il se sera saisi ainsi qu'il est dit ci-dessus, sans avoir à observer les règles du droit et les formes de la procédure. Il rendra sa sentence en dernier ressort.

[...]

L'article 1492 relatif au recours en annulation des sentences arbitrales, énonce que ce recours en annulation n'est ouvert que si : 1° le tribunal arbitral s'est déclaré à tort compétent ou incompétent ou 2° le tribunal arbitral a été irrégulièrement constitué ou 3° le tribunal arbitral à statuer sans se conformer à la mission qui lui avait été confiée ou 4° le principe de la contradiction n'a pas été respecté ou 5° la sentence est contraire à l'ordre public ou 6° la sentence n'est pas motivée ou n'indique pas la date à laquelle elle a été rendue le nom du ou des arbitres qui l'ont rendue ne comportent pas la ou les signatures requises ou n'a pas été rendue à la majorité des voix. Le recours en annulation ne doit pas permettre une révision de la sentence.

[...]

Sur la violation par la sentence arbitrale d'une règle d'ordre public.

Depuis la réforme de l'arbitrage en 2011, en ce qui concerne la violation d'une règle d'ordre public, le contrôle du juge de l'annulation a été limité. Le contrôle de la Cour doit porter non sur la motivation du tribunal arbitral même s'il y avait lieu de faire application de dispositions d'ordre public, mais sur la solution du litige, l'annulation n'étant encourue que dans la mesure où cette solution heurte l'ordre public. Le juge de l'annulation est devenu un juge de l'apparence.

[...]

Dans la mesure où les statuts de la société ont été signés en 1994, s'appliquent à la présente instance les dispositions de l'article 1134 du Code civil dans sa rédaction antérieure à l'ordonnance du 10 février 2016. Dès lors, dans la présente instance le principe d'exécution de bonne foi de la relation contractuelle n'est pas d'ordre public et la violation de ce principe n'est pas de nature à entraîner la nullité de la sentence arbitrale de 2018.

[...]

Aux termes de l'article 1871 du Code civil, la société en participation n'a pas de personnalité morale, et donc pas de patrimoine. Il est donc incorrect de parler de capital social d'une SEP, mais comme il est indiqué dans les statuts, les termes empruntés aux sociétés sont utilisés par commodité.

L'article 1871-1 du Code civil édicte qu'à moins qu'une organisation différente n'ait été prévue, les rapports des associés sont régis, en tant que de raison, soit par les dispositions applicables aux sociétés civiles, si la société un caractère civil, soit, si elle a un caractère commercial, par celles applicables aux sociétés en nom collectif.

Dans la mesure où le tribunal arbitral a retenu que la SEP avait un caractère civil, s'applique en l'espèce l'alinéa 2 de l'article 1836 qui énonce qu'en aucun cas, les engagements de l'associé ne peuvent être augmentés sans le consentement de celui-ci.

Cette disposition est d'ordre public.

Néanmoins, cette règle ne s'applique qu'à l'occasion d'une modification des statuts par les associés, ou d'une décision de l'assemblée générale des associés conduisant à une augmentation de leurs participations, telle l'obligation de faire un apport en compte courant.

Une décision judiciaire ou une décision arbitrale qui a pour conséquence de mettre à la charge des associés une dette de la société n'est pas une augmentation des engagements de l'associé, mais est le corollaire de son obligation de participer aux pertes édictées par l'article 1844-1 du Code civil.

L'autorisation de retrait et la condamnation des associés de la SEP au remboursement aux retrayants de la valeur des parts qu'ils détiennent n'est pas contraire à la règle d'ordre public selon laquelle les engagements d'un associé ne peuvent être augmentés sans son consentement.

Les appelants soutiennent en troisième lieu que cette condamnation porte atteinte au principe d'ordre public du libre consentement à l'acquisition de la propriété, le Conseil Constitutionnel ayant rappelé que ce principe était indissociable du droit de disposer librement de son patrimoine qui est un attribut essentiel du droit de la propriété.

Cependant, en matière de société civile, en cas de retrait d'un associé tout comme en cas du non-agrément des héritiers d'un des associés décédés, il s'offre aux associés deux possibilités : soit un ou des associés se portent acquéreur des parts sociales du retrayant ou du de cujus, soit la société indemnise le retrayant ou les héritiers de la valeur des parts sociales qu'ils détiennent et procèdent ensuite à une réduction du capital social. Le rachat des parts sociales du retrayant n'est pas imposé, seule est imposée l'indemnisation de la valeur desdites parts.

[...]

Il n'y a donc pas atteinte au droit de consentir librement à l'acquisition de la propriété.

En quatrième lieu, les appelantes arguent que leur condamnation solidaire est contraire à l'ordre public.

L'article 1310 du Code civil énonce que la solidarité est légale ou conventionnelle et qu'elle ne se présume pas.

Par application des dispositions de l'article 1869 du Code civil, le remboursement de la valeur des parts sociales qu'ils détiennent dans le capital social de la SEP [...] ensuite de leur retrait est une dette de la SEP.

Il est admis que l'associé qui est admis à se retirer d'une société civile pour justes motifs, ne perd sa qualité d'associé qu'après le remboursement de la valeur de ses droits sociaux.

Il ne s'agit donc pas d'une dette de la société à l'égard de tiers, et il n'y a lieu à application des dispositions de l'article 1872-1 du Code civil relatif aux relations des associés d'une SEP avec les tiers.

Selon l'article 1844-1 auquel renvoie l'article 1871-1 du Code civil, les associés de la SEP contribuent aux pertes à proportion de leurs parts dans le capital social. Cette disposition est reprise dans les statuts de la société au dernier alinéa de l'article 10. La solidarité des associés aux pertes de la SEP n'a donc pas été stipulée.

Ainsi en l'absence de personnalité morale de la SEP, c'est avec raison que le tribunal arbitral a prononcé la condamnation de la gérante la SARL en ce qu'elle représente la SEP, mais il ne pouvait pas prononcer la condamnation solidaire des associés non-retrayants avec celle-ci et/ou entre eux.

Comme il a été explicité ci-dessus, la raison qui a conduit le tribunal arbitral a prononcé cette solidarité, même recevable en équité, ne peut être prise en considération par la Cour pour écarter la violation de l'ordre public constituée par une condamnation solidaire qui ne pouvait pas être prononcée.

Suite à la violation de cette règle d'ordre public, la décision arbitrale du 17 juillet 2018 encourt une annulation partielle uniquement en ce qu'elle condamne solidairement les parties au paiement des sommes auquel a été condamnée la SARL en son nom agissant pour le compte de la SEP.

Enfin, en cinquième lieu, les appelantes reprochent une violation des dispositions de l'article L. 221-13 du Code de commerce.

Toutefois, dans la mesure où le tribunal arbitral a retenu que la SEP avait un caractère civil, l'article L. 221-13 du Code de commerce relatif aux sociétés en nom collectif n'a pas lieu de s'appliquer.

Il n'y a donc pas violation d'une quelconque règle d'ordre public pour non-application de l'article L. 221-13 du Code de commerce.

En conséquence, la sentence arbitrale du 17 juillet 2018 sera partiellement annulée c'est-à-dire uniquement en ce qui concerne la condamnation solidaire des associés non-retrayants.

Sur la condamnation des appelants associés de la SEP

L'arbitre ayant reçu mission de statuer en amiable composition, après annulation, la cour statue aussi en amiable composition.

[...]

Sur l'exequatur

Par application des dispositions de l'article 1527 alinéa 2 du Code de procédure civile, le présent arrêt confère l'exequatur aux dispositions de la sentence arbitrale du 18 juillet 2018 qui ne sont pas annulées.

– **Aix-en-Provence, Chambre 3-4, 25 novembre 2021, n° 18/13726, *Sarl Du Languedoc Roussillon, IPA c. Clea***

Clauses compromissoires – Référé – Procédure – En la forme des référés – Notions – Article 1449 CPC – Mesures provisoires ou conservatoires – Article 145 CPC – Décision provisoire

Il sera rappelé que la procédure « en la forme des référés », telle qu'applicable alors, suit le régime de la procédure de référé mais saisit la juridiction au fond, et que la juridiction ainsi saisie rend des décisions au principal, et non au provisoire comme en matière de référé.

Comme le reconnaît la société, les conventions qui la lient avec la partie adverse contiennent toutes une clause compromissoire.

L'article 1449 du Code de procédure civile prévoit que l'existence d'une convention d'arbitrage ne fait pas obstacle, tant que le tribunal arbitral n'est pas constitué, à ce qu'une partie saisisse une juridiction de l'État aux fins d'obtenir une mesure d'instruction ou une mesure provisoire ou conservatoire.

Sous réserve des dispositions régissant les saisies conservatoires et les sûretés judiciaires, la demande est portée devant le président du tribunal judiciaire ou de commerce, qui statue sur les mesures d'instruction dans les conditions prévues à l'article 145 et, en cas d'urgence, sur les mesures provisoires ou conservatoires sollicitées par les parties à la convention d'arbitrage.

La clause compromissoire n'exclut pas, tant que le tribunal arbitral n'est pas constitué, la faculté de saisir le juge des référés aux fins de mesures provisoires ou conservatoires.

Selon l'article 484 du même code, l'ordonnance de référé est une décision provisoire, et le juge des référés n'est pas saisi du principal.

Comme l'indique la décision querellée, l'article 492-1 du code précité, applicable alors, prévoyait qu'*« à moins qu'il en soit disposé autrement, lorsqu'il est prévu que le juge statue comme en matière de référé ou en la forme des référés, la demande est formée, instruite et jugée dans les conditions suivantes :*

1° Il est fait application des articles 485 à 487 et 490 ;

2° Le juge exerce les pouvoirs dont dispose la juridiction au fond et statue par une ordonnance ayant l'autorité de la chose jugée relativement aux contestations qu'elle tranche ;

3° L'ordonnance est exécutoire à titre provisoire, à moins que le juge en décide autrement. »

Il ressort de ce qui précède que le président du tribunal de commerce ne pouvait être saisi qu'en référé, et non en la forme des référés, au vu de laquelle la décision n'est pas de même nature que celle d'une ordonnance de référé.

Aussi, faute pour la société d'établir que sa demande pouvait être présentée « en la forme des référés », il convient de confirmer le jugement en ce qu'il a déclaré la demande irrecevable.

– Versailles, 12e chambre, 25 novembre 2021, *SAS À c. Emirates Advanced Investments Group*

Clause compromissoire – Référé – Validité – Applicabilité – Référé provision – Urgence – Absence de péril –

Sur la compétence du juge des référés en présence d'une clause compromissoire

[...]

Aux termes de l'article 1449 du Code de procédure civile : « *L'existence d'une convention d'arbitrage ne fait pas obstacle, tant que le tribunal arbitral n'est pas constitué, à ce qu'une partie saisisse une juridiction de l'État aux fins d'obtenir une mesure d'instruction ou une mesure provisoire ou conservatoire. Sous réserve des dispositions régissant les saisies conservatoires et les sûretés judiciaires, la demande est portée devant le président du tribunal judiciaire ou de commerce, qui statue sur les mesures d'instruction dans les conditions prévues à l'article 145 et, en cas d'urgence, sur les mesures provisoires ou conservatoires sollicitées par les parties à la convention d'arbitrage* ».

Il résulte de ce second alinéa qu'en présence d'une convention d'arbitrage, la compétence du juge des référés pour prononcer une mesure provisoire ou conservatoire est expressément subordonnée à la condition de l'urgence, confortant ainsi la jurisprudence antérieure au décret n° 2011-48 du 13 janvier 2011, qui, si elle admettait le référé-provision, le réservait aux cas d'urgence afin de ne pas empiéter sur la compétence arbitrale.

En l'espèce, le contrat liant les parties comportait, en son article 14, une clause d'arbitrage aux termes de laquelle « *tous les litiges auxquels le contrat pourra donner lieu au sujet de sa validité, de son interprétation, de son exécution et de sa résiliation, seront résolus par voie d'arbitrage* ».

Cette clause n'est pas manifestement inapplicable au présent litige, qui porte sur l'exécution du contrat, les intimées concluant d'ailleurs à son applicabilité.

Or, l'urgence n'a jamais été invoquée par ces dernières et elle n'est nullement caractérisée, l'action ayant pour objet le paiement de cotisations et de factures de marchandises pour lesquelles le risque de non-recouvrement est inexistant.

La cour relève en effet que les intimées n'ont jamais fait état d'une quelconque fragilité économique et financière de la débitrice, qui aurait justifié une action urgente, et il résulte de la saisie-attribution qu'elles ont fait pratiquer le 7 mai 2021 que les comptes de la société en demande, qui exploite désormais un magasin sous une autre enseigne, étaient créditeurs d'une somme de plus de 650 000 euros.

La demande reconventionnelle tendant à ce qu'une des sociétés intimées soit condamnée à lui remettre l'historique de sa comptabilité et de la gestion des paies sur la période 2017-2020 ne revêt pas davantage de caractère d'urgence et ce, d'autant moins que l'injonction en ce sens prononcée par le premier juge a été exécutée par l'ouverture d'un accès au logiciel en cause le 11 janvier 2021, ainsi que les intimées en justifient.

En l'absence d'urgence, il n'y a donc pas lieu à référé.

– **Paris, Pôle 1 – Chambre 8, 26 novembre 2021, n° 21/05934,** ***Domalane c. ITM Entreprises***

Arbitrage interne – Arbitrage ICC – Sentence arbitrale – Signature – Date – Délibéré – Collégialité – Ordre du jour – Pouvoir juridictionnel – Audience – Principe du contradictoire – Moyen tardif – Ordre public – Mission – Égalité des armes – Procès équitable – Règlement ICC – Calendrier – Déroulement – Règle procédurale – Modification – Grief

Sur le moyen d'annulation tiré du défaut de signature et de datation de la sentence arbitrale (1492-6° Code de procédure civile)

15 – Il résulte de l'article 1480 du Code de procédure civile, applicable en l'espèce, s'agissant d'une sentence arbitrale interne, que « *la sentence arbitrale est rendue à la majorité des voix. Elle est signée par tous les arbitres. Si une minorité d'entre eux refuse de la signer, la sentence en fait mention et celle-ci produit le même type que si elle avait été signée par tous les arbitres.* ».

16 – Aux termes de l'article 1481, 4° du même code « *la sentence arbitrale contient l'indication de sa date* ».

17 – En application de l'article 1492, 6° du Code de procédure civile, applicable à l'arbitrage interne uniquement, le recours en annulation est ouvert contre une sentence arbitrale si elle n'indique pas la date à laquelle elle est rendue et/ou ne comporte pas la ou les signatures requises. Il est constant que la signature de la sentence par les trois arbitres fait présumer que ceux-ci ont délibéré et prononcé la sentence à la majorité (Cass. 1re civ., 1er avril 2015).

[...]

19 – La sentence comporte donc toutes les signatures requises par l'article 1492, 6° du Code de procédure civile, aucune disposition ne prévoyant l'obligation pour tous les arbitres d'apposer simultanément leur signature sur la sentence sur la même page.

20 – Le fait que les arbitres aient signé séparément les pages 51 à 51 ter ne signifie pas que lesdits arbitres auraient signé trois sentences différentes, alors que la numérotation de la sentence de la page 1 à la page 51 ter démontre qu'il s'agit d'une sentence unique et que la date et la signature séparée de chacun des arbitres, sur des feuillets distincts mais faisant partie intrinsèque de la sentence, concerne bien une seule et même sentence, collationnée de la page 1 à la page 51 ter.

21 – Il ne permet pas plus de faire douter du respect de la collégialité, ni de ce que la sentence a été prise à la majorité des voix dès lors que ces feuillets ont été collationnés avec l'original unique de la sentence, qu'aucune forme (écrite ou orale) n'est imposée par le droit français pour l'organisation du délibéré, et qu'aucune instruction précise n'avait été établie par la CCI à cette date pour procéder à la signature en tenant compte des contraintes sanitaires récentes, une note n'ayant été établie par la CCI que le 9 avril 2020.

[...]

Sur le moyen d'annulation tiré du non-respect de la contradiction du fait de la modification in extremis de l'ordre du jour par le tribunal arbitral (1492-4° Code de procédure civile)

– Sur la recevabilité du grief allégué au soutien du moyen tiré d'une méconnaissance du principe de la contradiction

[...]

26 – Aux termes de l'article 1466 du Code de procédure civile « *la partie qui, en connaissance de cause et sans motif légitime, s'abstient d'invoquer en temps utile une irrégularité devant le tribunal arbitral est réputée avoir renoncé à s'en prévaloir* ».

[...]

– Sur le moyen d'annulation tiré de la contrariété de la sentence à l'ordre public du fait de la modification in extremis de l'ordre du jour par le tribunal arbitral (1492-5° Code de procédure civile)

[...]

49 – Il résulte de l'article 1492, 5° du Code de procédure civile applicable en arbitrage interne que le recours en annulation est ouvert si la sentence est contraire à l'ordre public.

Le contrôle exercé par la cour ne porte que sur la solution donnée au litige, l'annulation n'étant encourue que dans la mesure où cette solution heurte l'ordre public.

50 – L'égalité des armes, qui constitue un élément du procès équitable protégé par l'ordre public, implique l'obligation d'offrir à chaque partie une possibilité raisonnable de présenter sa cause – y compris les preuves – dans des conditions qui ne la placent pas dans une situation substantiellement désavantageuse par rapport à son adversaire.

[...]

53 – Le règlement CCI, choisi par les parties, permet en outre au tribunal arbitral de gérer la procédure dans un souci d'efficacité, dans le respect du contradictoire, et d'adopter les mesures procédurales qu'il juge appropriées. En l'espèce, comme rappelé ci-dessus, les parties ont pu débattre contradictoirement des choix procéduraux et les réserves invoquées ont fait l'objet d'un débat devant le tribunal arbitral, qui n'a fait qu'user de son pouvoir de gérer la procédure.

54 – Ce moyen d'annulation sera par conséquent rejeté.

– Sur le moyen d'annulation tiré du non-respect par l'arbitre de sa mission (1492-3° Code de procédure civile)

[...]

57 – Aux termes de l'article 1492, 3° du Code de procédure civile, le recours en annulation est ouvert si le tribunal arbitral a statué sans se conformer à la mission qui lui avait été confiée. La mission des arbitres, définie par la convention d'arbitrage, est délimitée principalement par l'objet du litige, tel qu'il est déterminé par les prétentions des parties sans s'attacher uniquement à l'énoncé des questions dans l'acte de mission.

58 – Le tribunal arbitral s'écarte de sa mission s'il ne respecte pas les règles procédurales qui ont été arrêtées par les parties. Cependant, cet écart, en ce qu'il porte sur une règle procédurale, ne saurait emporter l'annulation de la sentence que s'il est établi qu'il a pu causer à une partie un grief ou qu'il a eu une incidence

sur l'issue du litige et si l'irrégularité procédurale avait été soulevée préalablement devant le tribunal arbitral.

– Paris, Pôle 5 – Chambre 16, 30 novembre 2021, n° 20/10166, *Boralex Energie France c. Innovent*

Sentence arbitrale – TBI – Interprétation – Tribunal arbitral – Compétence – Investisseur – Notion

Après avoir relevé l'abandon, postérieurement à l'annulation partielle de la sentence sur la compétence, de certaines demandes dans l'instance au fond qui s'est poursuivie, la cour d'appel a retenu justement que l'intérêt d'une partie à invoquer l'incompétence du tribunal arbitral n'était pas remis en cause par l'effet de circonstances postérieures à la date d'introduction de son recours.

6. Le moyen n'est donc pas fondé.

[...]

Vu l'article 1520, 1°, du Code de procédure civile :

8. Selon ce texte, le recours en annulation n'est ouvert que si le tribunal arbitral s'est déclaré à tort compétent ou incompétent.

9. Pour annuler la sentence, l'arrêt relève, d'abord, que l'article XI du TBI prévoit que peut être soumis à l'arbitrage « *tout différend survenant entre un investisseur d'une Partie contractante et l'autre Partie contractante concernant l'exécution par celles-ci des obligations établies dans le présent Accord* » et que, selon l'article I du même traité, le terme investisseur désigne « *les personnes physiques qui ont la nationalité d'une des Parties contractantes en vertu de leur loi nationale et qui réalisent l'investissement sur le territoire de l'autre Partie contractante* » et le terme investissements, « *tout type d'actifs, investis par des investisseurs d'une Partie contractante sur le territoire de l'autre Partie contractante* ». Il retient, ensuite, qu'en ne vérifiant pas que la condition de nationalité des investisseurs était remplie au jour où les investissements étaient réalisés en 2001, le tribunal s'est déclaré à tort compétent pour connaître de toutes les demandes.

10. En statuant ainsi, la cour d'appel, qui a ajouté au traité une condition qu'il ne prévoit pas, a violé le texte susvisé.

– Cass. 1re civ., 1er décembre 2021, n° 20-16.714, F-D, *X c. République bolivarienne du Vénézuela*, Paris (pôle 5, chambre 16) 3 juin 2020 Cassation, voir le commentaire de François de Bérard dans ce numéro.

Arbitrage interne – Tierce opposition – Juridiction compétente – Irrecevabilité – Obligation de ne pas se contredire – Définition – Acceptation – Demande en justice – Comportement procédural – Fin de non-recevoir – Tribunal arbitral – Compétence – Contrôle étendu – Clause compromissoire – Opposabilité – Contrat de travail – Définition – Conseil des prud'hommes – Compétence exclusive – Clause réputée non écrite – Absence d'écrit – Charge de la preuve – Activité – Contrat de consultant – Qualification – Litige – Champ d'application – Principe du contradictoire – Définition – Égalité des armes – Moyen tardif – Renonciation

L'article 1501 du Code de procédure civile admet la possibilité pour les tiers de former tierce opposition, à l'encontre des sentences arbitrales qui leur porteraient préjudice, devant « *la juridiction qui eût été compétente à défaut d'arbitrage* ».

La juridiction qui eut été compétente à défaut d'arbitrage n'est ni le tribunal arbitral par hypothèse puisque ce tiers n'y est pas partie, ni le juge de l'annulation de la sentence arbitrale saisi dans le cadre d'une clause d'arbitrage mais le juge qui aurait été compétent pour juger le litige, en l'absence d'une telle clause.

Il y a donc lieu de déclarer la tierce opposition de la société irrecevable.

Sur l'irrecevabilité du recours en annulation

[...]

Le principe selon lequel nul ne peut se contredire au détriment d'autrui sanctionne une attitude procédurale consistant au cours d'une même instance à adopter des positions contraires ou incompatibles entre elles dans des conditions qui induisent son adversaire en erreur sur ses intentions, ou dans le cadre d'instance différente lorsqu'il y a identité de parties et de cause.

[...]

Le fait qu'il ait formé des demandes au titre de la procédure abusive et sur le fondement de l'article 700 du Code de procédure civile, ne peut dans ces circonstances, être interprété comme l'acceptation par ce dernier de la compétence arbitrale.

Il résulte de ces constatations que le comportement procédural de M. A ne caractérise pas un changement de position de celui-ci ayant pu induire en erreur la société sur ses intentions.

En conséquence la fin de non-recevoir tirée du principe de l'interdiction de se contredire au détriment d'autrui, doit être rejetée.

Sur le moyen d'annulation de la sentence tiré ce que le tribunal arbitral s'est déclaré à tort compétent (article 1492-1° du Code de procédure civile)

[...]

Selon l'article 1492 1°, du Code de procédure civile, le recours en annulation est ouvert si le tribunal s'est déclaré à tort compétent ou incompétent.

Le juge de l'annulation contrôle la décision du tribunal arbitral sur sa compétence, qu'il se soit déclaré compétent ou incompétent, en recherchant tous les éléments de droit ou de fait permettant d'apprécier la portée de la convention d'arbitrage.

Sur l'opposabilité de la clause compromissoire

Le conseil de prud'hommes étant seul compétent en application des dispositions des articles L. 1411-1 et suivants du Code du travail, pour connaître des différends qui peuvent s'élever à l'occasion du contrat de travail, toute clause compromissoire inscrite dans un contrat de travail est réputée non écrite.

En l'absence d'écrit ou d'apparence de contrat, c'est à celui qui se prévaut d'un contrat de travail d'en établir la réalité. L'existence d'une relation de travail ne dépend ni de la volonté exprimée par les parties ni de la dénomination qu'elles ont donnée à leur convention mais des conditions de fait dans lesquelles est exercée l'activité du travailleur. En effet, pour qu'un contrat soit qualifié de contrat de travail, il est nécessaire que le salarié accepte de fournir une prestation de travail au profit d'une autre personne en se plaçant dans un état de subordination juridique vis-à-vis de cette dernière. Le lien de subordination se caractérise par l'accomplissement d'une prestation de travail sous l'autorité d'un employeur qui a le pouvoir de donner des ordres et des directives, d'en contrôler l'exécution et de sanctionner les manquements de son subordonné et ce dans le cadre d'une organisation dirigée.

[...]

Dès lors, comme retenu par l'arbitre, il y a lieu de constater que le litige porte sur l'exécution du contrat de consultant et non sur l'exécution d'un contrat de travail de sorte que le moyen tiré de l'inopposabilité de la clause compromissoire est rejeté.

Sur le champ d'application de la clause compromissoire

Le contrat de consultant prévoit en son article 5 que « *les différends qui viendraient se produire à propos de la validité, de l'interprétation, de l'exécution ou de l'inexécution, de l'interruption ou de la résiliation du présent contrat, seront soumis à l'arbitrage conformément au règlement d'arbitrage du CMAP (Paris) auquel les parties déclarent adhérer* ».

[...]

Dès lors que la généralité des termes de la clause compromissoire traduit la volonté des parties de soumettre à l'arbitrage tous les litiges découlant du contrat de consultant, sans s'arrêter à la qualification contractuelle ou délictuelle de l'action engagée, il y a lieu de retenir que l'arbitre était compétent.

Le grief tiré de l'incompétence de l'arbitre doit en conséquence être rejeté.

Sur le moyen d'annulation de la sentence tiré ce que le tribunal arbitral a statué en violation du contradictoire (article 1492-4° du Code de procédure civile)

[...]

Le principe de la contradiction permet d'assurer la loyauté des débats et le caractère équitable du procès. Il interdit qu'une décision soit rendue sans que chaque partie ait été en mesure de faire valoir ses prétentions de fait et de droit, de connaître les prétentions de son adversaire et de les discuter.

L'égalité des armes qui représente un élément du procès équitable protégé par l'ordre public, implique l'obligation d'offrir à chaque partie une possibilité raisonnable de présenter sa cause, dans des conditions qui ne la placent pas dans une situation de net désavantage par rapport à son adversaire.

L'article 1466 du Code de procédure civile dispose que la partie qui en connaissance de cause et sans motif légitime s'abstient d'invoquer en temps utile une irrégularité devant le tribunal arbitral est réputée avoir renoncé à s'en prévaloir.

[...]

Au regard de ces éléments, M. A est réputé avoir renoncé à se prévaloir ultérieurement des irrégularités précitées qu'il s'est en connaissance de cause abstenu d'invoquer devant l'arbitre.

Le grief tiré du défaut de respect du principe de la contradiction et de l'égalité des armes sera rejeté.

– Paris, Pôle 5 – Chambre 16, 7 décembre 2021, n° 19/03844, *X c. Sarl France Oxygene (Région Nord)*

Sentence arbitrale – Exécution – Droit de retrait litigieux – Incidence – Notion – Exéquatur – Pouvoir du juge – Principe du contradictoire – Notion – Moyen tardif – Renonciation – Attitude d'une partie – Ordre public international – Égalité des armes – Fraude

43-L'exercice du droit de retrait litigieux est susceptible d'affecter indirectement l'exécution de la sentence en ce qu'il affecte directement le montant de la créance fixée par celle-ci.

44-Ce faisant, l'examen du moyen tiré de l'exercice du droit litigieux ne constitue pas un grief pouvant conduire le juge à remettre en cause le fond du litige et à réviser la sentence et qui, pour ce seul motif, échapperait au juge du contrôle de l'exequatur.

45-Pour autant, l'exercice du droit de retrait litigieux devant le juge du contrôle de l'exéquatur, n'a pas pour effet de modifier et d'étendre les pouvoirs de ce juge au-delà des cas prévus par la loi.

46-A cet égard, il convient de rappeler que dans le cadre de ce contrôle, en application de l'article 1525 du Code civil, la « cour d'appel ne peut refuser la reconnaissance ou l'exequatur de la sentence arbitrale que dans les cas prévus à l'article 1520 »

47-Au terme de l'article 1520 précité, le recours en annulation n'est ouvert que si : 1° Le tribunal arbitral s'est déclaré à tort compétent ou incompétent ; ou 2° Le tribunal arbitral a été irrégulièrement constitué ; – 3° Le tribunal arbitral a statué sans se conformer à la mission qui lui avait été confiée ; ou 4° Le principe de la contradiction n'a pas été respecté ; ou 5° La reconnaissance ou l'exécution de la sentence est contraire à l'ordre public international.

48-Il ressort de ces dispositions que ne figure pas dans les cas de refus possibles de l'exequatur l'exercice d'un droit au retrait litigieux.

49-Dans ces conditions, cette demande, impropre à faire obstacle à une telle exequatur sera rejetée, sans préjudice du débat qui pourrait naître à l'occasion de l'exécution forcée de cette sentence devant le juge compétent.

Sur le moyen tiré de la violation du principe du contradictoire

56-Il résulte de l'article 1520, 4° du Code de procédure civile que le recours en annulation est ouvert si le principe de la contradiction n'a pas été respecté.

57-Le principe de la contradiction exige seulement que les parties aient pu faire connaître leurs prétentions de fait et de droit et discuter celles de leur adversaire de telle sorte que rien de ce qui a servi à fonder la décision des arbitres n'ait échappé à leur débat contradictoire.

Sur la recevabilité de ce moyen ;

58-Aux termes de l'article 1466 du Code de procédure civile « *La partie qui, en connaissance de cause et sans motif légitime, s'abstient d'invoquer en temps utile une irrégularité devant le tribunal arbitral est réputée avoir renoncé à s'en prévaloir* ».

[...] de sorte qu'il ne peut lui être opposé une renonciation présumée à se prévaloir du non-respect du principe de la contradiction « en connaissance de cause ».

Sur le bien-fondé de ce moyen ;

[...]

74-Ayant choisi délibérément de se désintéresser de la poursuite de l'instance arbitrale, la partie n'est pas fondée à soutenir qu'elle n'a pas été en mesure de faire valoir ses prétentions de fait et de droit, de connaître les prétentions de son adversaire et de les discuter.

75-Le moyen tiré du non-respect du principe du contradictoire sera en conséquence rejeté.

Sur le moyen d'annulation tiré de la contrariété à l'ordre public international

[...]

Sur le non-respect de l'égalité des armes ;

80-L'égalité des armes, qui constitue un élément du procès équitable protégé par l'ordre public international, implique l'obligation d'offrir à chaque partie une possibilité raisonnable de présenter sa cause y compris les preuves dans des conditions qui ne la placent pas dans une situation substantiellement désavantageuse par rapport à son adversaire.

81-Le principe d'égalité des armes relève de l'ordre public international de protection, de sorte qu'il est loisible à une partie de renoncer à son bénéfice.

[...]

87-Consciente de cette situation, la partie n'a pas pour autant, alors qu'elle avait connaissance de l'instance arbitrale, fait connaître au tribunal une quelconque difficulté pour suivre cette instance ou même sollicité en raison de la situation politique et militaire interne, une suspension de cette instance afin de lui permettre de s'y consacrer, ayant fait le choix de s'en désintéresser.

88-Ce faisant, la partie n'est pas fondée à se prévaloir d'une méconnaissance du principe de l'égalité des armes alors qu'ayant délibérément choisi de ne pas suivre l'instance arbitrale, elle ne s'est jamais prévalue de telles difficultés devant le tribunal arbitral, sans pouvoir raisonnablement soutenir avoir été dans l'impossibilité matérielle de le faire savoir audit tribunal et à tout le moins solliciter une suspension de l'instance.

89-Ce moyen sera en conséquence rejeté.

Sur l'allégation de fraude

[...]

91-Cependant, d'une part, il n'est justifié ni même allégué d'aucune production devant les arbitres de pièces frauduleuses, de faux documents ou témoignages et le seul fait de soutenir qu'une cession de créance ait pu intervenir avant la procédure arbitrale et n'être signifiée au débiteur cédé que postérieurement, n'est pas de nature à caractériser une telle fraude à l'arbitrage.

92-D'autre part, si une partie soutient que cette manœuvre l'a privée de se prévaloir en 2001 de son droit au retrait litigieux, il n'est pas justifié que l'exercice de ce droit de retrait était applicable alors que le contrat initial était régi par le droit suisse, qui ne connaît pas ce mécanisme, de sorte qu'aucune fraude à la loi française, qui n'était pas applicable à la cession de créance, ne peut être caractérisée.

93-Ce moyen sera en conséquence rejeté.

– Paris, Chambre commerciale internationale, pôle 5 – chambre 16, 7 décembre 2021, n° 18/10217 et 18/10220, *République démocratique du Congo c. FG Hémisphère Associates* (deux arrêts)

Clause compromissoire – Principe de compétence compétence – Article 1449 CPC – Mesure d'instruction – Mesure provisoire ou conservatoire – Urgence – Péril – Navire – Chambre arbitrale maritime de Paris – Saisie conservatoire – Sûretés judiciaires – Astreinte

Ce contrat comportait une clause compromissoire en son article 18, précisant que « *les parties conviennent de soumettre à l'arbitrage l'ensemble des différends, de quelque nature que ce soit, pouvant naître du présent contrat. Les litiges seront résolus selon le règlement d'arbitrage de la chambre arbitrale maritime de Paris par un ou trois arbitres nommés conformément à ce règlement* ».

Aux termes des dispositions de l'article 1449 du Code de procédure civile, l'existence d'une convention d'arbitrage ne fait pas obstacle, tant que le tribunal arbitral n'est pas constitué, à ce qu'une partie saisisse une juridiction de l'État aux fins d'obtenir une mesure d'instruction ou une mesure provisoire ou conservatoire.

Sous réserve des dispositions régissant les saisies conservatoires et les sûretés judiciaires, la demande est portée devant le président du (Décr. n° 2019-966 du 18 sept. 2019, article 8, en vigueur le 1er janv. 2020) tribunal judiciaire [ancienne rédaction tribunal de grande instance] ou de commerce, qui statue sur les mesures d'instruction dans les conditions prévues à l'article 145 et, en cas d'urgence, sur les mesures provisoires ou conservatoires sollicitées par les parties à la convention d'arbitrage.

Le premier juge était saisi d'une demande de condamnation à titre provisionnel correspondant aux loyers échus depuis 2018. La partie sollicitait également l'enlèvement du navire sous astreinte.

Dès lors le juge des référés devait, en présence d'une convention d'arbitrage, vérifier sa compétence et la réalisation de la condition d'urgence requise par les dispositions de l'article 1449 du Code de procédure civile.

Si l'urgence requise par cette disposition peut être constituée par l'ancienneté de la créance, son montant et le péril pesant sur son recouvrement, la partie ne justifie, ni en première instance, ni en appel, d'un péril pesant sur le recouvrement de la créance réclamée d'autant qu'il n'est pas contesté que dès le 2 avril 2019 la Sarl remettait au conseil de la partie un chèque à l'ordre de la Carpa, la créance étant contestée pour le surplus.

La partie ne justifie pas plus que devant le premier juge d'une urgence à voir enlever le navire, étant observé que celui-ci a quitté le chantier le 27 février 2020.

En conséquence c'est à juste titre que le juge des référés, constatant l'absence d'urgence, s'est déclaré incompétent pour statuer sur les demandes.

– **Fort-de-France, Chambre civile, 7 décembre 2021, 21/00183,** ***Carenantilles Compagnie de Transport Maritime Deher c. T.m. DEHER, Frères Deher, Generali iard,***

Compétence – Fin de non-recevoir – Clause compromissoire – Désignation d'arbitre – Constitution du Tribunal – Juge d'appui – Désignation – Choix des parties – Tribunal judiciaire – Tribunal de commerce – Président de juridiction

Sur la compétence et/ou la fin de non-recevoir

36 – Il convient de relever que si en application des articles 1454 et 1459 du Code de procédure civile, le président du tribunal de commerce peut connaître en qualité de juge d'appui, d'un différend « *lié à la constitution du tribunal arbitral* » dès lors que la convention d'arbitrage le prévoit expressément, la compétence de ce dernier est limitée à la connaissance de ces différends.

37 – À cet égard, l'article 1459 du Code de procédure civile évoque la « compétence » du juge d'appui.

38 – En l'espèce, si la clause compromissoire insérée à l'article 11 du contrat de franchise prévoit expressément qu'à défaut de désignation de son arbitre par une partie, cette désignation pourra résulter d'une ordonnance du président du tribunal

de commerce de Paris, en ce compris le différend quant à la désignation du président du tribunal arbitral, cette clause n'a pas pour effet de conférer compétence à ce juge pour statuer sur des différends autres que ceux liés à la constitution du tribunal arbitral, et notamment un différend portant sur le délai d'arbitrage.

39 – En conséquence, le président du tribunal de commerce de Paris s'est à bon droit déclaré incompétent au profit du président du tribunal judiciaire de Paris, pour statuer sur cette demande de telle sorte que 'le jugement' sera confirmé.

– Paris, Chambre commerciale internationale, Pôle 5 – chambre 16, 14 décembre 2021, n° 21/17792, *Fadis c. CSF* (voir TC Paris, Ord., 29 septembre 2021, n° 2021034991, *CSF c. Fadis* reproduite ci-dessus)

Recours en annulation – Compétence – Étendue du pouvoir juridictionnel – Contrôle plein – TBI Interprétation – Volonté des parties – Offre permanente – État signataire – Investisseur – Règlement CNUDCI – Arbitrage – Notification – Instance arbitrale – Constitution – Moyen tardif – Nouveaux arguments – Renonciation – Mission – Étendue – Ordre public international – Contrôle du juge de l'annulation – Conception française – Valeurs et principes – Égalité des parties Désignation des arbitres – Principe

41-Selon l'article 1520, 1°, du Code de procédure civile, le recours en annulation est ouvert si le tribunal s'est déclaré à tort compétent ou incompétent.

[...]

43-Dans le cadre d'un recours en annulation fondé sur l'article 1520, 1° du Code de procédure civile, il appartient au juge de l'annulation de contrôler la décision du tribunal arbitral sur sa compétence, qu'il se soit déclaré compétent ou incompétent, en recherchant tous les éléments de droit ou de fait permettant d'apprécier la portée de la convention d'arbitrage.

44-Lorsque la convention d'arbitrage résulte d'un Traité bilatéral d'investissements, la compétence du tribunal arbitral et l'étendue de son pouvoir juridictionnel dépendent de ce traité qui l'investit.

45 – Il convient dès lors d'apprécier la volonté commune des parties de recourir à l'arbitrage au regard de l'ensemble des dispositions du traité de sorte que le tribunal arbitral n'est compétent pour connaître d'un litige que s'il entre dans le champ d'application du traité et qu'il est satisfait à l'ensemble de ses conditions d'application, sans faire nécessairement dépendre la compétence du tribunal arbitral de la seule forme des notifications matérialisant ce consentement.

46-En l'espèce, le consentement de la République de l'Équateur à l'arbitrage trouve sa source dans l'offre permanente d'arbitrage à laquelle il a consenti en concluant le TBI conclu en 1996 dont l'article 11 stipule que : « *1. Tout différend relatif à un investissement survenant entre une des Parties Contractantes et un investisseur de l'autre Partie Contractante concernant des questions régies par le présent Accord sera notifié par écrit, accompagné d'une description détaillée, par l'investisseur à la Partie Contractante qui reçoit l'investissement. Dans la mesure du possible, les parties s'efforceront de régler ces différends par un accord à l'amiable 2. Si le différend n'a pas pu être réglé à l'amiable dans un délai de six mois à compter de la date de la notification écrite visée au paragraphe 1, le différend sera soumis au choix de l'investisseur : Au Tribunal Arbitral « ad hoc » établi par le Règlement d'Arbitrage de la Commission des Nations Unies pour le Droit Commercial International, ou Au Centre*

International pour le Règlement des Différends Relatifs aux Investissements (CIRDI), créé par la « Convention pour le règlement des différends relatifs aux investissements entre États et ressortissants d'autres États », ouvert à signature à Washington le 18 mars 1965, lorsque chaque État partie au présent Accord y a adhéré. 3. L'arbitrage sera fondé sur : Les dispositions du présent Accord. Le droit national de la Partie Contractante sur le territoire duquel l'investissement a été réalisé, y compris les règles relatives aux conflits de Lois. Les règles et principes du Droit International généralement admis. 4. Les sentences arbitrales seront définitives et obligatoires pour les parties au différend. Chaque Partie Contractante s'engage à exécuter les sentences conformément à son droit national ».

47 – Il appartenait ainsi à l'État, les conditions d'application du traité étant réunies, d'adopter une attitude procédurale permettant de garantir la mise en œuvre de la procédure arbitrale à laquelle elle avait consentie.

48-S'agissant des investisseurs, il n'est pas contesté que le consentement à l'arbitrage des investisseurs devait résulter, conformément à l'article 3 du règlement CNUDCI auquel le TBI se réfère, d'une notification d'arbitrage adressée au défendeur dont l'article 3.3 indique qu'elle doit contenir notamment les informations suivantes « *b) Les noms et coordonnées des parties ; e) Une brève description du litige et, le cas échéant, une estimation de la somme sur laquelle il porte ;* ».

[...]

51-Il ressort à cet égard de l'article 3.2 du règlement CNUDCI, que la procédure arbitrale est seulement « *réputée commencer à la date à laquelle la notification d'arbitrage est reçue par le défendeur* », ce qui laisse donc la possibilité pour celui qui émet une telle notification, censée manifester son propre consentement, de préciser, voire de rectifier celle-ci dès lors que cette rectification s'inscrit dans une démarche permettant de garantir une mise en œuvre efficace de la procédure arbitrale.

52-Tel était le cas en l'espèce dès lors que par ce courrier, les investisseurs ont entendu clarifier la portée de leur démarche pour s'inscrire dans le processus prévu par le TBI.

53-L'Etat ne peut dès lors exciper de la seule première notification pour considérer que la procédure arbitrale avait commencé dès celle-ci et qu'elle était figée dans son périmètre *ratione personae et materiae*.

[...]

55-En outre, il résulte de l'article 3.3 précité que la notification d'arbitrage doit seulement contenir « *e) Une brève description du litige et, le cas échéant, une estimation de la somme sur laquelle il porte* » Ce qui laisse en tout état de cause aux parties la possibilité de préciser par la suite leurs prétentions et moyens, même lorsque l'envoi est une requête d'arbitrage.

56-Ainsi, sauf à lui imputer, une attitude contraire au principe d'efficacité qui doit guider tout État ayant consenti une offre permanente d'arbitrage, l'État devait, compte tenu des circonstances de l'espèce, afin au surplus de s'inscrire dans un processus de négociation préalable, considérer la notification du 1er juillet 2015 comme une notification de différend.

[...]

66-Au regard de l'ensemble de ces éléments, dont il ne résulte pas l'existence de différends distincts alors que les mêmes faits sont à l'origine du litige et seront soumis au fond à l'appréciation du tribunal afin de savoir s'ils permettent de caractériser une violation du TBI, le tribunal s'est à juste titre déclaré compétent pour statuer sur le litige.

67-Ce moyen d'annulation sera en conséquence rejeté.

2) Sur le moyen d'annulation tiré de l'irrégularité de la constitution du tribunal arbitral (article 1520 2° du Code de procédure civile).

** Sur la renonciation au moyen*

[...]

70-Aux termes de l'article 1466 du même code, la partie qui, en connaissance de cause et sans motif légitime, s'abstient d'invoquer en temps utile une irrégularité devant le tribunal arbitral est réputée avoir renoncé à s'en prévaloir.

71-Si lorsque la compétence a été débattue devant les arbitres, les parties ne sont pas privées du droit d'invoquer sur cette même question, devant le juge de l'annulation, de nouveaux moyens et arguments et à faire état, à cet effet, de nouveaux éléments de preuve, elles ne peuvent sans encourir l'irrecevabilité précitée, invoquer et articuler de nouvelles irrégularités au soutien d'autres moyens d'annulation que celui tiré de l'incompétence dès lors qu'ils ne sont pas nécessairement impliqués par ce dernier.

[...]

74-Force est de constater qu'elle n'a alors émis aucune contestation à cette date alors qu'elle avait tous les éléments pour le faire.

75-En outre, la contestation portant sur la compétence du tribunal arbitral, qui ne trouvait pas sa source dans le caractère pathologique de la convention d'arbitrage, n'impliquait donc pas nécessairement celle portant sur la constitution irrégulière de ce même tribunal arbitral qui n'est pas ici une conséquence indissociable de cette convention, puisqu'en l'espèce il avait été reproché au tribunal d'avoir statué au-delà de son champ de compétence matériel sur des demandes alléguées comme non couvertes par le consentement des parties à l'arbitrage, moyen dissociable de celui portant sur la régularité de désignation de l'un des arbitres par l'une des parties.

76-I1 convient dès lors de considérer que, faute de l'avoir invoqué en temps utile et alors qu'elle a agi en connaissance de cause, la partie est réputée avoir renoncé à se prévaloir de la constitution irrégulière du tribunal arbitral.

77-Ce moyen sera en conséquence déclaré irrecevable.

3) Sur le moyen d'annulation tiré du non-respect par le tribunal arbitral de sa mission (article 1520 3° du Code de procédure civile)

[...]

82-Selon l'article 1520, 3°, du Code de procédure civile, le recours en annulation est ouvert si le tribunal a statué sans se conformer à la mission qui lui avait été confiée.

83-La mission des arbitres, définie par la convention d'arbitrage, est délimitée principalement par l'objet du litige, tel qu'il est déterminé par les prétentions des parties sans s'attacher uniquement à l'énoncé des questions dans l'acte de mission, ou a fortiori dans la requête d'arbitrage.

84-En l'espèce, il convient de relever d'une part, que seule la compétence du tribunal arbitral ayant été tranchée au terme de la sentence du 21 décembre 2018, il ne peut être imputé au tribunal une violation de sa mission alors que les prétentions des parties sur le fond n'avaient pas encore été formulées.

85-D'autre part, il convient de rappeler que le tribunal arbitral est investi en l'espèce par la convention d'arbitrage résultant du TBI qui prévoit qu'il peut lui être soumis « *Tout différend relatif à un investissement survenant entre une des Parties Contractantes et un investisseur de l'autre Partie Contractante concernant des questions régies par le présent Accord* » de sorte que le tribunal peut statuer sur toutes les demandes qui lui sont soumises sans s'attacher à l'énoncé des questions litigieuses visées dans la notification intervenue le 1er juillet 2015 dont au surplus il a été considéré qu'elle constituait une simple notification de différend, insusceptible de figer dès ce stade la mission des arbitres.

86-En conséquence, ce moyen sera rejeté.

4) Sur le moyen d'annulation tiré de la violation par la sentence de l'ordre public international (article 1520 5° du Code de procédure civile).

[...]

89 – Il résulte de l'article 1520, 5° du Code de procédure civile que le recours en annulation est ouvert si la reconnaissance ou l'exécution de la sentence est contraire à l'ordre public international.

90-L'ordre public international au regard duquel s'effectue le contrôle du juge de l'annulation s'entend de la conception qu'en a l'ordre juridique français, c'est-à-dire des valeurs et des principes dont celui-ci ne saurait souffrir la méconnaissance même dans un contexte international.

91-Le contrôle exercé par le juge de l'annulation pour la défense de l'ordre public international s'attache seulement à examiner si l'exécution des dispositions prises par le tribunal arbitral heurte les principes et valeurs compris dans l'ordre public international.

92-Le principe d'ordre public de l'égalité des parties dans la désignation des arbitres suppose la possibilité pour chaque partie de pouvoir participer de manière égale à la constitution d'un tribunal arbitral.

[...]

94-Quand bien même la notification d'arbitrage est intervenue postérieurement, il ne peut être déduit aucune atteinte au principe d'égalité précité, ce d'autant que la désignation par la société de « son » arbitre a également été faite antérieurement à cette notification d'arbitrage.

95-Ce moyen sera en conséquence également rejeté.

– **Paris, Chambre commerciale internationale, Pôle 5 – chambre 16, 14 décembre 2021, n° 19/12417, *République de l'Équateur c. Mantenimientos, Ayuda A La Explotacion Y Servicios – Maessa***

France | France

Règlements amiables des litiges 2021

Priscille PEDONE
Avocat

Contrat d'architecte – Conseil de l'ordre des architectes – Clause de conciliation – Obligatoire préalable – Définition – Fin de non-recevoir – Intervention à tout moment – Champ – Non régularisable – Droit de la construction – Garantie décennale – Article 1792 CC – Article 1231 (ex 1147) CC – Responsabilité contractuelle – Effet relatif – Tardiveté – Intention dilatoire – Connaissance de la clause – Procédure d'urgence – Référé – Procédure conservatoire – Référé expertise

Sur la fin de non-recevoir de l'action pour non-respect de la clause contractuelle de saisine préalable pour avis du conseil de l'ordre des architectes :

L'article 14 du contrat d'architecte stipule qu'« *en cas de différend portant sur le respect des clauses du présent contrat, les parties conviennent de saisir pour avis le conseil régional de l'ordre des architectes dont relève l'architecte, avant toute procédure judiciaire, sauf conservatoire. Cette saisine intervient à l'initiative de la partie la plus diligente* ».

Cette clause convenue entre les parties institue une procédure préalable de consultation. Le défaut de respect de ladite clause est une fin de non-recevoir de l'action en justice sur le fond qui n'est pas régularisable en cours d'instance. Elle s'impose au juge si une partie l'invoque tant à titre principal qu'à titre reconventionnel. Dès lors, si elle est retenue, elle interdit au juge d'examiner le fond sans qu'il soit nécessaire de justifier d'un grief. Elle peut être soulevée à tout moment sauf à devoir verser des dommages et intérêts en cas d'exception d'irrecevabilité soulevée tardivement en application de l'article 123 du Code de procédure civile.

La seule limite du caractère opérant de cette clause est l'existence d'un dommage décennal, ce qui implique l'existence d'une réception d'un ouvrage. Il appartient dès lors au juge même d'office de rechercher si l'action n'est pas fondée sur l'article 1792 et suivants du Code civil instaurant une présomption légale de responsabilité objective rendant la clause inapplicable. En revanche, la clause s'applique lorsque l'action en justice est fondée sur la responsabilité contractuelle de droit commun (1147 ancien du Code civil devenu 1231 et suivant du Code civil).

[...]

Or, il ne suffit pas d'invoquer le fondement juridique des articles 1792 et suivants du Code civil pour rendre la clause contractuelle de saisine préalable pour avis du CROA inapplicable.

En conséquence, seule la responsabilité de droit commun étant mobilisable, ladite clause s'applique. En ne l'ayant pas mise en œuvre, les demandes ne peuvent qu'être irrecevables à l'encontre de l'architecte.

[...]

Cette cause d'irrecevabilité ne peut qu'être propre à Monsieur B et la société B Architectes. Elle ne peut pas être invoquée au profit d'autres constructeurs qui doivent être déboutés de leur demande de ce chef.

Sur la demande subsidiaire de dommages et intérêts pour exception d'irrecevabilité soulevée tardivement de manière dilatoire :

Selon l'article 123 du Code de procédure civile, « *les fins de non-recevoir peuvent être proposées en tout état de cause, sauf possibilité pour le juge de condamner à des dommages et intérêts, ceux qui se seraient abstenus, dans une intention dilatoire, de les soulever plus tôt* ».

Pour autant, les appelants signataires du contrat d'architecte ne peuvent faire grief à l'adversaire de ne pas leur avoir rappelé une clause claire du contrat dont ils ne peuvent qu'avoir eu dûment connaissance.

Par ailleurs, cette clause n'est expressément pas applicable durant les procédures conservatoires comme le référé expertise. Les appelants ne peuvent dès lors pas faire grief à l'architecte de ne pas l'avoir revendiqué à ce moment-là.

Enfin, le fait de n'en faire état qu'au troisième jeu de conclusions devant la première instance ne saurait être qualifié de tardif d'autant qu'il leur appartient de démontrer que l'architecte et sa société ont agi dans une intention dilatoire alors que l'objectif de cette fin de non-recevoir dont ils n'ont pas attendu de la soulever à hauteur d'appel avait justement pour but de mettre fin au litige sans examen au fond.

– Lyon, 5 janvier 2021, n° 18-05946, *époux A c. B. Architecte*

Conseil régional de l'ordre des architectes – Clause de conciliation – Recevabilité – Fin de non-recevoir – Cour de renvoi – Délai pour la soulever – Autorité de la chose jugée – Triple identité – Validité – Procédure – Obligatoire et préalable – Non régularisable – Opposabilité – Contrats – Cahier des clauses générales – Cahier des clauses particulières – Sémantique – Contrats séparés – Parties – Connaissance de la clause – Confusion – Preuve – Irrecevable

Bien que les demandeurs ne le formulent pas expressément ainsi, la réponse à la fin de non-recevoir soulevée par la partie adverse tirée de l'irrecevabilité de leurs demandes en raison de la méconnaissance de l'article G.10 du contrat de maîtrise d'œuvre revient à s'interroger sur l'autorité de la chose jugée attachée au jugement déféré.

[...]

En outre, conformément aux dispositions de l'article 1355 du Code civil, l'application du principe de l'autorité de la chose jugée des décisions de justice suppose que la chose demandée soit la même, que la demande soit fondée sur la même cause, que la demande soit entre les mêmes parties et formées par elles et contre elles en la même qualité.

La mise en œuvre du principe de l'autorité de la chose jugée suppose ainsi la constatation préalable d'une triple identité, à savoir, une identité d'objet, une identité de cause et une identité de parties.

[...]

Il sera au surplus ajouté qu'il apparaîtrait pour le moins paradoxal d'appliquer le principe de l'autorité de la chose jugée alors que la décision qui le consacrerait n'aurait pas eu à examiner une telle fin de non-recevoir, ce qui est le cas en l'espèce puisque, jusqu'à présent, la défenderesse n'invoquait pas la violation d'une clause de conciliation préalable et obligatoire prévue dans le contrat de maîtrise d'œuvre et, par voie de conséquence, l'irrecevabilité des demandes des maîtres d'ouvrage dirigées contre elle.

[...]

Bien-fondé de ce moyen :

La fin de non-recevoir tirée du défaut de mise en œuvre d'une clause contractuelle qui institue une procédure, obligatoire et préalable à la saisine du juge, favorisant une solution par le recours à un tiers, revêt un caractère obligatoire lorsque le différend porte sur les manquements allégués d'un architecte à ses obligations contractuelles. Dès lors, l'absence de saisine du conseil régional de l'ordre des architectes dont relève l'architecte préalablement à la saisine de l'autorité judiciaire rend irrecevables les maîtres d'ouvrage en leur action dirigée contre ce maître d'œuvre.

En outre, une telle clause n'est pas susceptible d'être régularisée par la mise en œuvre de la clause en cours d'instance.

Toutefois, en l'espèce, le contrat signé intitulé « cahier des clauses particulières » ne précise pas en préambule qu'il est constitué dudit cahier ainsi que du cahier des clauses générales, mais indique seulement, en préambule, ce qui suit « *ce contrat [donc le cahier des clauses particulières] se réfère au cahier des clauses générales* ». Le verbe « se référer » n'est pas synonyme des verbes « être constitué de », « faire partie de », « inclure » mais des verbes « citer », « avoir recours à », « renvoyer », ce qui revêt un sens bien différent. Le verbe « se référer » ne signifie donc pas que ces deux documents, à savoir le cahier des clauses particulières et le cahier des clauses générales, forment un tout indissociable et complémentaire. En outre, la pièce précitée ne comporte pas plus de mention expresse stipulant que le cahier des clauses générales qui contient l'article G.10 invoqué par l'architecte, est annexé à ce contrat signé entre les parties ni n'indique explicitement que le contrat d'architecte est constitué du « présent cahier des clauses particulières » et du « cahier des clauses générales » qui forment un tout indissociable et complémentaire et qui constituent ensemble le contrat d'architecte liant les parties.

Le document signé par les parties ne mentionne pas non plus que les maîtres d'ouvrage déclarent avoir pris connaissance d'un autre document qui aurait été annexé au « présent contrat » signé entre les parties et qui, avec lui, formerait un tout indissociable.

De plus, les stipulations de ce document intitulé « cahier des clauses particulières » signé par les parties ne sont pas claires voire sont confuses. En effet, l'article 3 du cahier des clauses particulières stipule que « *le maître d'ouvrage charge l'architecte, qui accepte, de la maîtrise d'œuvre de l'opération définie, aux conditions du présent cahier des clauses générales, les clauses contraires y dérogeant expressément étant indiquées à l'article 6 ci-dessous* ». L'article 6 en question intitulé « *clauses dérogeant expressément aux dispositions du présent cahier des clauses générales* » stipule « *sans objet* ».

De ces stipulations, il apparaît que, alors que le préambule de ce document précise qu'il constitue le cahier des clauses particulières, les stipulations de ce document indiquent que le « présent » document représente le « cahier des clauses générales ». De telles mentions, incompatibles, sont de nature à créer la confusion chez les cocontractants du maître d'œuvre qui ont pu légitimement croire que ce même document constituait à lui seul le cahier des clauses particulières et le cahier des clauses générales, donc que les obligations du cahier des clauses générales et celles du cahier des clauses particulières étaient contenues sous ce même document. Or, le contrat qu'ils ont signé ne contenait pas la clause G.10 invoquée de sorte que les demandeurs ont pu légitimement croire que leur action en justice n'était pas subordonnée à une procédure, obligatoire et préalable à la saisine du juge, à savoir la saisine préalable du Conseil régional de l'ordre des architectes.

Il découle de ce qui précède que la clause invoquée n'apparaît pas opposable.

Par voie de conséquence, la fin de non-recevoir soulevé par l'architecte n'est pas fondée.

– Versailles, 11 janvier 2021, n° 19-05934, *A c. GS Constructions*

Contrat d'architecte – Clause de conciliation – Définition – Champ – Fin de non-recevoir – Obligatoire et préalable – Suspension – Prescription – Opposabilité – Tiers à la clause – Action directe – Article 1792 CC – Article 1134 CC – Fondement – Recours subrogatoire – Assureur

Sur la clause de conciliation préalable et sur la recevabilité des demandes formées :

Il résulte des articles 122 et 124 du Code de procédure civile que les fins de non-recevoir ne sont pas limitativement énumérées. La clause licite d'un contrat instituant une procédure de conciliation obligatoire et préalable à la saisine du juge, dont la mise en œuvre suspend jusqu'à son issue le cours de la prescription, constitue une fin de non-recevoir qui s'impose au juge si les parties l'invoquent.

En l'espèce, le contrat d'architecte régularisé entre la SCCV et A en janvier 2004 stipule qu'« *en cas de litige portant sur l'exécution du présent contrat, les parties conviennent de saisir pour avis le Conseil régional de l'Ordre des Architectes dont relève l'architecte, avant toute procédure judiciaire* ».

Cependant, le demandeur recherche la responsabilité de M. au titre de la garantie décennale. Ce dernier ne peut donc lui opposer cette clause de conciliation préalable alors qu'il est constant que la clause de saisine préalable à toute action judiciaire en cas de litige sur l'exécution du contrat du Conseil de l'Ordre des Architectes, ne peut s'appliquer que sur les obligations des parties au regard des dispositions de l'article 1134 ancien du Code civil et n'a pas vocation à s'appliquer quand la responsabilité de l'architecte est recherchée sur le fondement de l'article 1792 du Code civil.

La partie, en qualité d'assureur, ne peut davantage opposer cette clause de conciliation préalable, alors que la saisine préalable par les maîtres de l'ouvrage du Conseil de l'Ordre des Architectes prévue dans un contrat les liant à l'architecte n'est pas une condition de recevabilité de l'action directe engagée par eux contre l'assureur de celui-ci.

De même, l'assureur dommages-ouvrage, exerce, par son recours subrogatoire, l'action de la SCCV, son assurée dans les droits de laquelle elle est subrogée à l'encontre de la mutuelle et de A au titre de la responsabilité décennale des constructeurs, de sorte que la clause de conciliation préalable ne peut davantage lui être opposée.

En conséquence, il y a lieu de déclarer recevables les demandes indemnitaires formées ainsi que le recours subrogatoire.

– Lyon, 12 janvier 2021, n° 18-07057, *Bertrand c. Compagnie d'assurance Smabtp et a.*

Clause de conciliation – Conciliation conventionnelle – Définition – Article 1528 CPC – Procédure participative – Validité – Tiers – Impartialité – Partie

En vertu de l'article 1530 du Code de procédure civile, la conciliation s'entend comme un processus structurel par lequel des parties tentent de parvenir à un accord avec l'aide d'un tiers choisi par elles. Or l'article 59-1 des statuts ne prévoit pas le recours à un tiers mais confie la mission de conciliation au conseil d'administration de la cave lequel a pour mission d'assurer la gestion de la coopérative et son bon fonctionnement.

Si les parties peuvent convenir de différentes modalités de conciliation, l'article 1528 du Code de procédure civile les inscrit dans le cadre d'un recours à un médiateur ou à un conciliateur de justice, donc un tiers, ou encore dans le cadre d'une procédure participative, de leurs avocats. Quelles que soient les modalités retenues, la conciliation conventionnelle suppose que le tiers choisi accomplisse sa mission avec impartialité, ce qui exclut de considérer le conseil d'administration de la société comme un tiers.

C'est donc à tort que les premiers juges ont retenu l'irrecevabilité de l'action en se fondant sur l'article 59-1 des statuts.

– Nîmes, 13 janvier 2021, n° 18-03002, *S.C.A. Société Coopérative Vinicole Cave de Cairanne c. Les Avocats*

Contrat d'agence commerciale – Clause de conciliation – Définition – Rédaction – Tentative de conciliation – Mise en œuvre – Clause satisfaite

Sur la fin de non-recevoir soulevée :

L'appelante, au visa de l'article 122 du Code de procédure civile, soulève l'irrecevabilité de l'action engagée, au profit de la mise en œuvre du processus conventionnel de tentative de conciliation amiable par application de l'article 14 du contrat.

[...]

L'article 14 du contrat d'agent commercial stipule que « *tout différend ou conflit ayant son origine dans l'exécution ou l'interprétation du présent contrat fera l'objet d'une tentative de conciliation amiable. À défaut de résolution amiable, le litige sera porté devant le tribunal compétent de Grasse* ».

Les parties par leurs courriers respectifs ont proposé d'entrer en discussion ; même si aucune des parties n'y a donné suite, il y a lieu de retenir que la clause a été satisfaite, celle-ci ne faisant obligation aux parties que d'une tentative de conciliation, sans prévoir de modalités particulières de mise en œuvre.

Le jugement qui a écarté ce moyen est confirmé de ce chef.

– Aix-en-Provence, Chambre 3-1, 14 janvier 2021, n° 18-16090, *Laboratoires Arkopharma c. A*

Contrat de travail – Juridiction – Clause de conciliation – Lien de subordination – Prud'hommes – Compétence

L'article 11 du contrat de collaboration signé par les parties stipule : « *En cas de difficulté venant à se produire dans le cadre du présent contrat, il est prévu avant toute procédure qui serait alors de la compétence des Tribunaux Civils, une tentative de conciliation. Elle sera confiée à deux masseurs kinésithérapeutes désignés chacun par l'une des parties* ».

[…]

Par ailleurs, la demande tendant à la reconnaissance d'un contrat de travail, à l'encontre de laquelle la société a développé divers moyens, sans que de quelconques autres demandes au titre du contrat de collaboration ne soient formulées de la part des parties, relève sans conteste de la juridiction prud'homale, seule compétente pour déterminer, au vu des pièces produites, s'il existait notamment un lien de subordination entre les parties.

Il convient donc d'infirmer le jugement entrepris.

– Aix-en-Provence, Chambre 4-1, 15 janvier 2021, n° 20/05612, *Phocéanne Sud c. X*

Contrat de travail – Clause compromissoire – Prud'hommes – Ordre public – Procédure amiable

2 – Sur la compétence du conseil de prud'hommes de Boulogne-Billancourt :

Le contrat de travail conclu stipule que tout différend qui pourrait naître entre les parties à raison de la validité du contrat ou à l'occasion de son interprétation, de son exécution ou de sa fin sera soumis à l'appréciation d'un tribunal arbitral.

Le contrat de travail de droit local conclu stipule que tout différend ou litige pouvant survenir à l'occasion de l'interprétation ou de l'exécution du contrat, doit être réglé à l'amiable entre les parties sauf en cas de faute grave, à défaut, le litige sera soumis à la juridiction territorialement compétente.

L'objet du litige est déterminé par les prétentions respectives des parties.

Les demandes soumises au conseil de prud'hommes, exclusivement dirigées contre une société, exigeant de déterminer au préalable qui, de celle-ci ou de la société signataire du premier contrat, est le véritable employeur du salarié, le conseil de prud'hommes était dès lors tenu de trancher cette question de fond dont dépendait la détermination de la compétence de la juridiction française. Il convient en conséquence de confirmer le jugement entrepris en ce qu'il a déclaré la société irrecevable en son exception d'incompétence au profit du tribunal arbitral.

– Versailles, 20 janvier 2021, n° 18-02160, *A c. CFAO*

Clause de médiation – Fin de non-recevoir – À tout moment – Procédure – Parties – Rédaction claire – Responsabilité délictuelle – Manquements contractuels

En rappelant la clause figurant dans le cahier des clauses générales du contrat de maîtrise d'œuvre signé en 2005 concernant le recours à une médiation en cas de litige « *avant toute procédure judiciaire* », en indiquant que le moyen soulevé était une fin de non-recevoir et non une exception de procédure pouvant donc être soulevée en tout état de cause, en estimant que, compte tenu du contexte de l'affaire, la partie n'était pas fautive pour l'avoir invoquée tardivement, en déclarant en conséquence irrecevables les demandes formées par le maître de l'ouvrage à l'encontre de cette société d'architecture et en déboutant la SCI de sa demande de dommages-intérêts formée contre elle, le premier juge a fait une juste analyse des faits de la cause, appliqué à l'espèce les règles de droit qui s'imposaient et pertinemment répondu aux moyens des parties pour la plupart repris en appel.

À ces justes motifs que la cour adopte, il convient seulement d'ajouter : Que le maître d'ouvrage, ayant à ses côtés un assistant à la maîtrise d'ouvrage, ne pouvait se méprendre sur la portée de la clause litigieuse, rédigée dans des termes particulièrement clairs. Que contrairement à ce qu'il indique, cette clause n'était nullement imprécise, puisqu'elle portait sur tout « *litige portant sur l'exécution du présent contrat* » sans aucune exclusion, définissait les modalités d'exercice de la médiation, précisait que cette mesure devait intervenir « *avant toute procédure judiciaire* », et que « *toutes les contestations se rapportant au présent contrat, qui n'auront pas été réglées à l'amiable, seront soumises au tribunal de grande instance d'Aix-en-Provence* ». Qu'en conséquence, pour échapper à l'application de ladite clause contractuelle s'imposant aux parties, le maître de l'ouvrage n'est nullement fondé à se prévaloir des règles de la responsabilité délictuelle, alors même qu'il invoque plusieurs manquements contractuels du maître d'œuvre, que si le maître de l'ouvrage invoque une mauvaise foi manifeste d'une partie qui aurait été pour lui à l'origine d'un préjudice dont il demande réparation, il n'établit nullement que le comportement de ce maître d'œuvre est directement à l'origine d'un préjudice, a fortiori pour un tel montant. En conséquence, la décision déférée doit être ici confirmée, en partie pour d'autres motifs.

– Aix-en-Provence, 28 janvier 2021, n° 17-06194, *SCI Parc A c. Carta et a.*

Référé – Contrat – Bonne foi – Consentement – Contrôle du Juge – Protocole transactionnel – Définition – Validité – Concessions réciproques – Exécution forcée – Compétence judiciaire – Mesures conservatoires – Difficulté sérieuse – Définition – Force – Homologation

Sur la demande d'exécution forcée du protocole d'accord transactionnel :

Attendu qu'aux termes de l'article 835 du Code de procédure civile, le président du tribunal judiciaire ou le juge du contentieux de la protection, dans les limites de sa compétence, peuvent toujours, même en présence d'une contestation sérieuse, prescrire en référé les mesures conservatoires ou de remise en état qui s'imposent soit pour prévenir un dommage imminent soit pour faire cesser un trouble manifestement illicite : dans les cas ou l'existence de l'obligation n'est pas sérieusement contestable, ils peuvent accorder une provision au créancier ou ordonner l'exécution de l'obligation même s'il s'agit d'une obligation de faire. Qu'une difficulté est sérieuse lorsque la question peut donner lieu à plusieurs réponses d'égale pertinence ou lorsqu'elle implique un examen approfondi des dispositions applicables. À l'inverse, ne pose pas de difficulté sérieuse une question dont la réponse s'impose avec évidence ou n'exige qu'un examen sommaire ou rapide des textes en cause.

Attendu qu'un protocole d'accord transactionnel s'analyse comme un contrat nommé au sens de l'article 1105 du Code civil. Qu'à ce titre, il relève tant du droit commun des contrats que des dispositions spécifiques des articles 2044 à 2052 du Code civil, réformées par l'ordonnance du 10 février 2016 et la loi de ratification du 20 avril 2018. Qu'en vertu des dispositions combinées des articles 1103 et 1104 du même code, il a force obligatoire à condition d'avoir été négocié, formé et exécuté de bonne foi ; qu'il n'est revêtu de la force exécutoire que s'il a été homologué par une décision de Justice ou reçu par un notaire.

Attendu que la validité d'un protocole d'accord transactionnel, même exécuté partiellement, peut être affectée par un vice du consentement, tel que l'erreur, le dol ou la violence. Qu'aux termes de l'article 2044 du Code civil, il doit contenir des concessions réciproques sans qu'il soit nécessaire, en application de l'article 1168, qu'elles soient équivalentes. Que l'article 1169 dispose néanmoins qu'elles ne doivent pas être illusoires ou dérisoires.

– Aix-en-Provence, 28 janvier 2021, 20/01490, *X c. Y*

Règlement amiable – Accord – Homologation – Juge compétent – Détermination – Non contradictoire – Procédure – Contrôle du juge – Ordre public et bonnes mœurs

Selon les dispositions de l'article 1565 du Code de procédure civile, l'accord auquel sont parvenues les parties à une médiation, une conciliation ou une procédure participative peut être soumis, aux fins de le rendre exécutoire, à l'homologation du juge compétent pour connaître du contentieux dans la matière considérée. Le juge à qui est soumis l'accord ne peut en modifier les termes.

Selon l'article 1566 dudit code, le juge statue sur la requête qui lui est présentée sans débat, à moins qu'il n'estime nécessaire d'entendre les parties. S'il est fait droit à la requête, tout intéressé peut en référer au juge qui a rendu la décision.

Selon l'article 1567, les dispositions des articles 1565 et 1566 sont applicables à la transaction conclue sans qu'il ait été recouru à une médiation, une conciliation ou une procédure participative. Le juge est alors saisi par la partie la plus diligente ou l'ensemble des parties à la transaction. La dérogation au principe fondamental de la contradiction ne peut se justifier que par autorisation de la loi ou par autorisation du juge.

Selon l'article 58 du Code de procédure civile, la requête est l'acte par lequel le demandeur saisit la juridiction sans que son adversaire en ait été préalablement informé. En cas d'autorisation de la loi, le requérant est fondé à agir par voie de requête sans avoir à démontrer qu'il est nécessaire d'emprunter cette voie procédurale comme tel est le cas en l'espèce puisque la procédure rappelée ci-dessus, applicable à la procédure sur requête aux fins d'homologation, autorise expressément une partie à saisir le juge des requêtes, le recours au débat contradictoire étant par ailleurs toujours possible conformément aux dispositions prévues par les articles 496 alinéa 2 et 1566 du Code de procédure civile, s'agissant d'une requête déposée par l'une des parties à la transaction à l'insu de l'autre. Il n'y a donc pas lieu de procéder, comme l'a fait le premier juge, à l'examen des circonstances exigeant que la mesure réclamée ne soit pas prise contradictoirement, au sens de l'article 493 du Code de procédure civile, qui ne s'applique pas à la présente procédure.

Le juge de la requête et le juge de la rétractation sont cependant tenus de vérifier que les conditions prévues par la loi pour ordonner la mesure sollicitée sont réunies. Il est constant que sur une demande tendant à conférer force exécutoire à une transaction, le contrôle du juge ne peut porter que sur la nature de la convention qui lui est soumise et sur sa conformité à l'ordre public et aux bonnes mœurs.

Ainsi, si le juge a la faculté de rétracter l'ordonnance, c'est en vertu d'un simple contrôle de la régularité formelle de la transaction. Son contrôle ne peut porter sur la validité de l'acte, lequel n'est susceptible d'être annulé que par le juge du fond.

– Paris, Pôle 1, Chambre 8, 29 janvier 2021, 20/07621, *X c. Y*

Conseil Départemental de l'Ordre des Médecins – Clause de conciliation – Contrat de travail – Champ – Procédure prud'homale

– *Sur la fin de non-recevoir :*

Une partie soulève une fin de non-recevoir tirée du non-respect de la clause de conciliation préalable insérée dans le contrat de travail en son article 11 stipulant « *qu'en cas de difficultés d'interprétation et d'exécution du présent contrat, les parties s'engagent avant toute action contentieuse, à soumettre leur différend à deux conciliateurs, l'un choisi par la Résidence, l'autre par Monsieur le Docteur A, parmi les membres du Conseil Départemental de l'Ordre des Médecins. Ceux-ci s'efforceront de concilier les parties et d'amener une solution amiable, et ce dans un délai maximum de deux mois à compter de la désignation du premier conciliateur. À l'issue de ce délai, les parties reprendront leur liberté d'action* ».

Cependant la cour constate que ladite clause vise uniquement l'interprétation et l'exécution du contrat de travail et non pas la « résiliation » du contrat de travail quelle que soit l'origine et qu'ainsi celle-ci n'est pas opposable à Monsieur A dans sa demande de qualification de la rupture du contrat de travail à l'initiative du salarié à raison des faits que celui-ci reproche à son employeur, pour laquelle aux termes de l'article L. 1451-1 du Code du travail, l'affaire est directement portée devant le bureau de jugement qui statue sur le fond dans un délai d'un mois suivant sa saisine.

– Amiens, 3 février 2021, n° 19-01982, *A c. Orpéa*

Expert-comptable – Code déontologique – Clause de conciliation – Lettre de mission obligatoire – Signature – Application – Inopposabilité

Et cette lettre n'est complétée ni accompagnée d'aucun document permettant de démontrer que celle-ci a été soumise à l'approbation et à la signature de la partie adverse. Ainsi même si l'élaboration d'une lettre de mission est obligatoire conformément au code déontologique des experts-comptables il n'est pas établi en l'espèce qu'elle a été soumise à la signature des parties.

[...]

Aussi répétant que cette lettre de mission n'est pas opposable à la partie adverse, il ne peut en tirer la constatation d'aucun manquement à l'une de ses clauses.

– Reims, 9 février 2021, n° 19-01644, *C Propre Nettoyage c. Dardoise Jeunot Expertise Conseil*

Clause de conciliation – Contrat – Documents liés – Connaissance – Conseil de l'Ordre des architectes – Préalable et obligatoire – Irrecevabilité – Opposabilité – Effet relatif – Assureur

Il convient de constater que ce cahier des clauses générales constitue la partie 2 du contrat liant les parties, dont la partie 1 constituée par le cahier des clauses particulières a été signée et paraphée par Mme A. Cette première partie du contrat comporte un préambule en italique qui mentionne que : « *le contrat qui lie le maître d'ouvrage et l'architecte est constitué par le présent Cahier des Clauses Particulières pour travaux sur existants et par le Cahier des Clauses Générales pour travaux sur existants de l'Ordre des architectes du 1er juin 2004 annexé, dont les parties déclarent avoir pris connaissance. Ces deux documents dont les articles commencent respectivement par les lettres P et G sont complémentaires et indispensables.* »

Ces stipulations contractuelles claires et précises rendent opposables à Mme A le cahier des clauses générales pour travaux sur existants qui fait partie intégrante du contrat, nonobstant le fait qu'il n'ait été revêtu ni du paraphe ni de la signature du maître de l'ouvrage, Mme A ayant expressément reconnu en avoir eu connaissance.

La clause G10 prévoit qu'en cas de différends portant sur le respect de clauses du contrat, les parties conviennent de saisir pour avis le Conseil de l'Ordre des architectes dont relève l'architecte, avant toute procédure judiciaire, sauf conservatoire, cette saisine devant intervenir sur l'initiative de la partie la plus diligente.

En l'espèce, le différend opposant les parties porte incontestablement sur le respect des clauses du contrat puisqu'il concerne l'étendue de la mission dévolue à l'architecte, de sorte qu'il appartenait à Mme A de saisir le Conseil de l'Ordre des architectes avant d'appeler en garantie la société A. Sa demande est dès lors irrecevable.

Le jugement entrepris sera donc infirmé en tant qu'il a déclaré l'appel en garantie dirigé contre la société recevable.

Toutefois, ce préalable de conciliation ne constitue pas une condition de recevabilité de l'action directe engagée contre l'assureur, de sorte que la demande dirigée contre l'assureur est recevable.

– Colmar, 25 février 2021, n° 19-01286, *Architecture Avenir c. A*

Arbitrage du bâtonnier – Procédure obligatoire – Ordre public – Clause de conciliation – Tentative de conciliation – Fin de non-recevoir – Non régularisable – Loi dans le temps – Irrecevabilité

Sur la fin de non-recevoir tirée du non-respect de la clause instaurant un préalable de conciliation :

L'article 26 de statuts de la SCM datant de 2008 était rédigé de la façon suivante : « *En cas de litige, les parties conviennent, préalablement à toute instance judiciaire, de soumettre leur différend à un conciliateur désigné qui sera missionné par M. Le Bâtonnier de l'Ordre des Avocats. Il pourra être saisi sans forme ni frais* ».

Les dispositions issues de la loi du 12 mai 2009 instaurent une procédure dérogatoire du droit commun imposant l'arbitrage du bâtonnier, seul compétent en premier ressort pour connaître de tous les différends entre avocats relatifs à leur exercice professionnel, y compris ceux nés de leur qualité d'associés d'une société de moyens. La loi de 2009 étant applicable immédiatement à tous les litiges dont aucune juridiction n'était encore saisie à la date de la publication du décret du 11 décembre 2009, l'article 26 des statuts doit être interprété comme imposant une procédure de conciliation préalable à la saisine du bâtonnier en qualité d'arbître, celui-ci ayant dorénavant le pouvoir de trancher les litiges relevant auparavant de la compétence des juridictions de droit commun.

À la stipulation conventionnelle sus-reproduite, dont la validité n'est pas remise en cause par les dispositions législatives et réglementaires postérieures, s'ajoutent les dispositions d'ordre public réglementant la profession d'avocat. Ainsi, l'article 21 de la loi du 31 décembre 1971 énonce que « *tout différend entre avocats à l'occasion de leur exercice professionnel est, en l'absence de conciliation, soumis à l'arbitrage du bâtonnier* ». De même, l'article 179-1 du décret du 27 novembre 1991 impose l'obligation de procéder à une tentative de conciliation avant de saisir le bâtonnier en qualité d'arbitre en ces termes : « *En cas de différend entre avocats à l'occasion de leur exercice professionnel et à défaut de conciliation, le bâtonnier du barreau auprès duquel les avocats intéressés sont inscrits est saisi par l'une ou l'autre des parties.* »

Il s'ensuit que la saisine du bâtonnier dans les formes de l'article 142 du décret doit être précédée de l'organisation d'une tentative de conciliation préalable dont le défaut rend irrecevable la demande d'arbitrage soumise au bâtonnier, aucune régularisation en cours d'instance n'étant possible.

[...]

La fin de non-recevoir d'irrecevabilité de la demande d'arbitrage faute de mise en œuvre de la procédure de conciliation obligatoire préalable, soulevée par l'appelant devant la cour, sera en conséquence accueillie. Il y a lieu dès lors d'infirmer la décision et de déclarer la saisine du bâtonnier irrecevable.

– Rennes, 2 mars 2021, n° 20-01977, *A c. B*

Contrat d'architecte – Clause de conciliation – Tiers – Inopposabilité

Ainsi que l'a retenu le tribunal, l'action dirigée contre l'assureur sur le fondement de la garantie contractuelle due par la société A au titre des désordres liés aux infiltrations affectant les menuiseries est recevable, car elle ne peut se prévaloir de la clause de conciliation préalable des conditions générales du contrat d'architecte souscrit.

– Rennes, 1re Chambre, 2 mars 2021, n° 19-01354, *Tryba Industrie c. A et a.*

Règlement des différends – Arbitrage du bâtonnier – Délai – Nullité – Covid – Prorogation des délais – Convocation – Calendrier de procédure – Procédure orale – Audience obligatoire – Principe du contradictoire – Absence – Sanction – Annulation – Clause de conciliation – Obligatoire et préalable – Fin de non-recevoir – Modalités – Tout moment – Dilatoire

Le bâtonnier statue en matière de règlement de différend entre avocats à l'occasion de leur exercice professionnel, il doit rendre la décision dans le délai de 4 mois à compter de sa saisine. À l'issue de ce délai, éventuellement prorogé de 4 mois par décision motivée, le bâtonnier est dessaisi de plein droit et la décision qu'il peut rendre postérieurement se trouve entachée de nullité.

[...]

Ayant été saisi par requête le 19 novembre 2019, réceptionnée le 20 mars 2020, il devait rendre sa décision le 20 mars 2020 au plus tard, délai reporté par application de l'ordonnance n° 2020-306 du 25 mars 2020 relative à la prorogation des délais échus pendant la période d'urgence sanitaire et à l'adaptation des procédures pendant cette même période au 23 juillet 2020. La décision a en conséquence été rendue dans le délai imparti.

Sur la nullité de la décision rendue par le bâtonnier de l'ordre des avocats à raison du défaut de convocation des parties à une audience :

La procédure prévue par les articles 179-1 et suivants du décret 91-1197 du 27 novembre 1991 est une procédure orale obéissant aux règles de la procédure civile.

À cet égard conformément aux dispositions du décret relatives au différend entre avocats, les règles prévues aux articles 142 à 148 et 150 à 152 sont applicables.

L'article 144 prévoit que dès l'enregistrement de la requête, le bâtonnier saisi, fixe les délais dans lesquels les parties seront tenues de produire leurs observations, ainsi que toutes pièces utiles à l'instruction du litige, qu'il arrête la date à laquelle il entendra leurs observations orales, que les parties peuvent à tous les stades de la procédure être assistées par un confrère, que les avocats des parties sont rendus destinataires de la copie de toute correspondance adressée aux parties par le bâtonnier dans le cadre de la procédure, que le bâtonnier convoque les parties par lettre recommandée avec demande d'avis de réception adressée au moins huit jours avant la date de l'audience et que la copie de la lettre de saisine est jointe à la convocation du défendeur.

La décision déférée ayant été rendue sans débats et sans aucune référence à la convocation des parties ou à l'organisation en période de crise sanitaire à une procédure sans audience à laquelle les parties auraient pu consentir, il convient de l'annuler pour défaut de respect de la procédure ci-dessus rappelée, notamment en ce qui concerne la tenue d'une audience et le respect du principe du contradictoire.

[...]

Sur la fin de non-recevoir soulevée du chef du défaut de préalable obligatoire de conciliation :

Il sera préalablement rappelé que le non-respect d'une clause ou d'un texte instituant une procédure, obligatoire et préalable à la saisine du juge, favorisant une solution alternative de règlement des différends constitue une situation donnant lieu à une fin de non-recevoir au sens de l'article 122 du Code de procédure civile. Elle peut être soulevée en tout état de cause sauf condamnation à dommages-intérêts de ceux qui se seraient abstenus, dans une intention dilatoire, de la soulever plus tôt.

[...]

Toutefois, le défaut de mise en œuvre de cette procédure préalable de conciliation dont les modalités ne sont pas définies n'est pas une cause d'irrecevabilité de la saisine du bâtonnier régi par les dispositions de l'article 142 précité mais affecte la procédure préalable à cette saisine. En considération de ce vice autre que l'irrégularité de la saisine et au regard de l'annulation de la décision déférée, la Cour est tenue de statuer sur l'entier litige.

– Nancy, 3 mars 2021, n° 20-00979, *X C. KPMG*

Clause de conciliation – Clause de médiation – Chambre des notaires – Contrat de bail – Préalable obligatoire – Absence de mise en œuvre – Inapplicable

Le bail consenti en 2012 prévoit expressément une clause intitulée « *Conciliation Médiation* » rédigée dans les termes suivants : « *En cas de litige, les parties conviennent, préalablement à toute instance judiciaire, de soumettre leur différend au conciliateur, qui sera missionné par le président de la Chambre des Notaires* ».

Cette clause figurant dans le contrat établi par les parties constitue le fruit d'un accord et elle est donc susceptible de constituer un préalable obligatoire avant la saisine du juge.

Il convient cependant de constater que cette clause faute de contenir les conditions particulières de sa mise en œuvre ne constitue pas une procédure de conciliation obligatoire préalable à la saisine du juge faute notamment de préciser quelle chambre des notaires aurait dû être saisie, selon quelles modalités de prise en charge des frais, outre l'étendue du champ d'application de cette clause qui n'est aucunement définie et pas davantage la durée de la conciliation médiation.

Il convient en conséquence de considérer ainsi que l'a décidé le premier juge, qu'il n'y a pas lieu de prononcer la nullité de l'assignation et que la SARL était bien recevable en sa demande.

– Aix-en-Provence, Chambre 1-8, 4 mars 2021, n° 19-01729, *Grepi c. Jolie Il Était Une Fois*

Conseil régional de l'ordre des architectes – Clause de conciliation – Recevabilité – Fin de non-recevoir – Validité – Procédure – Obligatoire et préalable – Contrats – Caractère indissociable et complémentaire – Conditions générales – Conditions particulières – Contrats séparés – Parties – Connaissance de la clause – Irrecevable

Comme le jugement attaqué l'a retenu par des motifs pertinents mais dont il n'a toutefois pas tiré les conséquences dans son dispositif « *il résulte du préambule du contrat d'architecte pour travaux sur existants « signé par le maître de l'ouvrage et l'architecte le 24 septembre 2008 que le contrat qui lie le maître de l'ouvrage et l'architecte est constitué par le présent cahier des clauses particulières pour travaux sur existants et par le cahier des clauses générales pour travaux sur existants de l'ordre des architectes du 1er octobre 2002 annexé dont les parties déclarent avoir pris connaissance. Ces deux documents dont les articles commencent respectivement par les lettres P et G sont complémentaires et indissociables. L'article G10 du cahier des conditions générales dispose qu'en cas de différend portant sur le respect des clauses du présent contrat, les parties conviennent de saisir pour avis le conseil régional de l'ordre des architectes dont relève l'architecte avant toute procédure judiciaire, sauf conservatoire. Mme A a signé et paraphé sur toutes les pages le contrat d'architecte contenant la clause précitée ne peut légitiment soutenir avoir ignoré l'existence et le contenu du cahier des clauses générales auquel il renvoie, qui est annexé et dont elle a déclaré avoir pris connaissance. La formulation de cette clause qui constitue la loi des parties au sens de l'article 1134 du Code civil traduit la volonté non équivoque des parties de ne pas considérer l'avis du conseil de l'ordre comme une simple formalité, mais comme un préalable obligatoire à toute action en justice dans le but de tenter de désamorcer le litige, de parvenir à un règlement amiable du conflit et de ne saisir la juridiction compétente qu'à défaut d'y être parvenu. De ce fait, elle exclut par sa nature même toute possibilité de régularisation après la date de l'introduction de l'instance qui lui fait perdre son objet en la privant de toute efficacité et la vidant de toute portée pratique* ».

Comme la cour l'avait déjà retenu dans son arrêt du 13 juin 2013 statuant sur l'appel contre l'ordonnance de référé du 28 août 2012, « *La clause de conciliation préalable à toute action judiciaire prévue dans le contrat du maître d'œuvre oblige le maître de l'ouvrage qui recherche la responsabilité contractuelle de son architecte à s'y conformer en saisissant l'autorité de conciliation avant l'introduction du procès. À défaut, son action doit être déclarée irrecevable, aucune régularisation postérieure à l'introduction de l'instance n'étant envisageable. Le contrat d'architecte stipule dans son préambule que « le contrat qui lie le maître de l'ouvrage et l'architecte est constitué par le présent « cahier des clauses particulières pour travaux sur existants » et par le « cahier des clauses générales pour travaux sur existants » de l'Ordre des architectes du 1er octobre 2002 annexé dont les parties déclarent avoir pris connaissance. Ces deux documents dont les articles commencent respectivement par les lettres P et G sont complémentaires et indissociables ». A, qui a signé et paraphé sur toutes ses pages le contrat d'architecte contenant la clause précitée, ne peut raisonnablement soutenir avoir ignoré l'existence et le contenu du cahier des clauses générales auquel il renvoie, qui lui est annexé et dont elle a déclaré avoir pris connaissance. Ainsi M. C justifiait avoir donné connaissance ou avoir communiqué le cahier des clauses générales litigieux au maître de l'ouvrage lors de la signature du contrat de maîtrise d'œuvre. Le cahier des clauses générales pour travaux sur existants de l'Ordre des architectes du 1er octobre 2002 prévoit qu'en cas de différend sur le respect des clauses du contrat, les parties conviennent de saisir pour avis le conseil régional de l'Ordre des architectes dont relève l'architecte, avant toute procédure judiciaire, sauf conservatoire. Or, il n'est pas contesté que A n'a pas procédé à cette saisine pour avis, préalablement à l'introduction de l'instance des 2 et 4 mai 2012* ».

La cour ne peut que procéder aux mêmes constatations sur les pièces produites dans la présente instance et en tirer les mêmes conclusions quant à l'irrecevabilité des demandes.

– Montpellier, 4 mars 2021, n° 16-00708, *Mutuelles des Architectes Français (MAF) c. A*

Conseil régional de l'ordre des architectes – Clause de conciliation – Étendue – Champ – Obligatoire et préalable – Sémantique – Assurance – Tiers à la clause – Opposabilité

Sur la fin de non-recevoir prise du non-respect de la clause de conciliation préalable :

[...]

Sur le premier point, la clause litigieuse constitue l'avant-dernier paragraphe du contrat d'architecte. Elle est rédigée comme suit : « *En cas de litige portant sur l'exécution du présent contrat, les parties conviennent de saisir pour avis le Conseil régional de l'ordre des architectes dont relève l'architecte avant toute procédure judiciaire. Le dernier paragraphe stipule : À défaut d'un règlement amiable, le litige opposant les parties sera du ressort des juridictions civiles territorialement compétentes* ».

Il n'est pas fait état de la résiliation par une partie mais de l'hypothèse d'un litige portant sur l'exécution du contrat.

Or, la partie motive son recours par le fait que l'autre a commis des fautes contractuelles.

Sur le second point, le caractère obligatoire de la saisine préalable se déduit des termes des deux clauses précitées qui sont indissociables. À défaut, il aurait été écrit que les parties pouvaient saisir le Conseil régional avant de saisir le juge.

Le jugement est donc confirmé en ce qu'il a déclaré la demande irrecevable contre M. B, celle-ci restant recevable à l'égard de son assureur.

– Rennes, 4 mars 2021, n° 18-08053, *Les papeteries c. B*

Contrat d'architecte – Clause de conciliation – Moyen nouveau – Tardiveté – Irrecevabilité – Contrat – Signature – Charge de la preuve – Action irrecevable

5. D'une part, la partie n'ayant pas soutenu devant les juges du fond que la clause de saisine de l'ordre des architectes avant toute procédure judiciaire, n'était pas applicable dans le cas d'une action ayant pour objet la recherche de responsabilité de l'architecte, le moyen est, de ce chef, nouveau, mélangé de fait et de droit et, partant, irrecevable.

6. D'autre part, la cour d'appel a relevé que les conditions particulières du contrat de maîtrise d'œuvre renvoyaient à un cahier des clauses générales contenant la clause de saisine de l'ordre des architectes et que A avait signé les conditions particulières du contrat.

7. Sans inverser la charge de la preuve et par des motifs qui suffisent à établir que le cahier des clauses générales produit aux débats correspondait à celui annexé au contrat, la cour d'appel, qui a pu en déduire que la clause de saisine préalable de l'ordre des architectes était opposable à A, de sorte que les demandes

de celle-ci contre B étaient irrecevables en l'absence d'accomplissement de cette démarche, a légalement justifié sa décision de ce chef.

– Cass. civ. 3e, 4 mars 2021, n° 19-24.176, F-D, *B c. Mutuelle des architectes français et a,* (Montpellier, 3 octobre 2019), Cassation partielle

Arbitrage interne – Sentence arbitrale – Appel – INTERBEV (Association Nationale Interprofessionnelle du Bétail et des Viandes) – Procédure de conciliation – Préalable et obligatoire Volonté des parties – Qualité à agir – Mandataire ad hoc – Saisine de l'institution

Selon l'article 1489 du Code de procédure civile, « *la sentence n'est pas susceptible d'appel sauf volonté contraire des parties* ».

L'appelant n'a pas fourni les statuts d'Interbev mais seulement l'accord professionnel du 24 mars 2016. Toutefois, il ressort du dispositif de la sentence que la voie de l'appel est ouverte.

[...]

Ce même accord prévoit aux termes du § III « Règlement des litiges » qu'en cas de litige, les parties ou la partie la plus diligente saisit la commission de conciliation en région territorialement compétente aux fins d'organiser une procédure de conciliation conformément aux règles prévues par les statuts d'Interbev et qu'en cas d'échec de la procédure de conciliation, la partie la plus diligente peut saisir la commission nationale interprofessionnelle des litiges afin d'engager une procédure d'arbitrage, conformément aux règles prévues par les statuts d'Interbev.

[...]

En l'absence de copie de l'acte de saisine adressée à l'Earl et dès lors que les courriers se réfèrent toujours dans le coupon d'acceptation ou refus de conciliation à « la conciliation demandée », il est retenu que la demande de conciliation a été introduite par une personne qui n'avait pas qualité à agir, n'étant pas partie au contrat de vente du cheptel. En tout état de cause, à supposer même, que la société ait régularisé la saisine de la commission régionale, le dernier courrier adressé par Interbev évoquant la saisine de la commission régionale avait pour destinataire M. Ac, qui n'avait pas qualité de vendeur, le cheptel vendu ayant appartenu à l'Earl.

En conséquence, la commission régionale interprofessionnelle n'a pas été valablement saisie d'une demande de conciliation entre l'acheteur et le vendeur de la vente du cheptel de l'Earl en septembre 2016, alors que cette procédure était un préalable obligatoire à l'arbitrage.

En outre, s'agissant de la saisine du tribunal arbitral, il ressort de la sentence que « *M. Ac ayant refusé la conciliation, le 4 septembre 2018 Interbev Nouvelle-Aquitaine a averti par courrier RAR les parties de la soumission du litige à la commission nationale d'arbitrage* ».

Alors que les dispositions de l'Accord interprofessionnel (III, règlement des litiges) prévoient qu'en cas d'échec de la procédure de conciliation, la partie la plus diligente peut saisir la commission nationale interprofessionnelle des litiges afin d'engager une procédure d'arbitrage, ni la sentence ni les pièces produites par les appelants ne démontrent que l'Earl est intervenue en ce sens. Si le courrier adressé le 9 octobre 2018 par le secrétaire du tribunal arbitral à M. Ac relatif « *à la préparation de la convention d'arbitrage* » comportait en annexe un courrier de réclamation adressé par l'Earl manifestement à Interbev concernant la vente du cheptel par l'Earl de A, il ne comprenait aucun courrier de saisine de la commission nationale.

De surcroît, en application de l'article 32 du Code de procédure civile qui dispose qu'est irrecevable toute prétention émise par ou contre une personne dépourvue du droit d'agir, le tribunal arbitral a statué sur la demande de l'Earl prise en la personne de son représentant légal à l'encontre du liquidateur amiable de l'Earl de A, société en liquidation. Or, à la date à laquelle le tribunal arbitral a été saisi, l'Earl de M était radiée du registre du commerce et des sociétés depuis le 5 juillet 2018, de sorte qu'elle n'avait plus d'existence juridique (2e civ, 23 septembre 2010, pourvoi n° 09-70.355) et ne pouvait être attraite devant le tribunal arbitral sans qu'un mandataire ad hoc ne lui soit préalablement désigné pour la représenter.

En conséquence, la demande à l'encontre du liquidateur amiable de l'Earl de A est irrecevable. Il s'ensuit que la sentence doit être annulée.

– **Paris, Pôle 5, Chambre 16, chambre commerciale internationale, 16 mars 2021, n° 19-03195,** *X mandataire ad hoc de l'EARL de A et a. c. La Ferme de Beaujoly*

Garantie de passif – Clause de conciliation – Obligatoire préalable – Consentement – Omission de statuer – Irrecevabilité

Il s'agissait par conséquent d'une action entrant dans la définition large de la garantie de passif stipulée à l'acte de réitération de la garantie d'actif et de passif telle que citée par l'arrêt.

La Cour a déclaré cette action irrecevable au motif qu'il existait, dans cet acte, une clause de conciliation obligatoire préalable à toute contestation qui s'élèverait concernant l'interprétation et/ou l'exécution de sorte que les parties se devaient de la mettre en œuvre avant toute procédure judiciaire.

Cette clause s'appliquait ainsi indépendamment de l'allégation de dol formée à l'encontre des cédants.

La requête déposée, sous couvert d'une prétendue omission de statuer, tend à modifier le fond de la décision. Par suite, elle doit être rejetée.

– **Agen, 17 mars 2021, n° 20-00955,** *Financière Dr et Forme & O c. A*

Clause de conciliation – Définition – Aménagement amiable – Sémantique – Mise en œuvre – Conciliateur – Institution – Tiers – Rôle passif

« Si malgré les soins apportés à notre mission, un litige venait à opposer les parties à la présente, celles-ci s'engagent à rechercher en premier lieu un arrangement amiable, puis en second lieu d'informer la commission Arbitrage de la chambre des Indépendants du Patrimoine. (...) Ce n'est qu'en cas d'échec de cet arrangement amiable que l'affaire serait alors portée devant les tribunaux compétents. »

L'intimée fait valoir qu'une procédure ne pouvait être diligentée contre elle qu'en cas d'échec de la procédure de conciliation obligatoire, argumentation retenue par le premier juge pour déclarer l'action des époux A irrecevable.

Mais sauf à priver les mots de leur sens, la recherche d'un arrangement amiable entre deux parties et la simple information donnée à une commission d'arbitrage et de discipline, ne sauraient être assimilées à une procédure de conciliation obligatoire sous l'égide d'un conciliateur, dont l'absence de mise en œuvre constitue une fin de non-recevoir qui s'impose au juge.

C'est à tort que l'intimée soutient que la clause litigieuse désigne bien un conciliateur à savoir la CNCGP, alors que celle-ci n'a qu'un rôle passif qui se limite à être tenue informée.

– Grenoble, 23 mars 2021, n° 19-00852, *A c. Axyalis Patrimoine*

Tentative préalable – Clause de conciliation – Définition – Préalable obligatoire – Formulation – Sémantique – Sanction – Comité Arbitral de la Fédération des Industries Mécaniques (F.I.M.)

Sur l'exigence d'une tentative préalable de conciliation :

La stipulation invoquée par l'appelante est rédigée comme suit : « *Les parties conviennent de faire leur possible pour régler tout différend à l'amiable : il est rappelé que le Comité Arbitral de la Fédération des Industries Mécaniques (F.I.M.) est compétent* ».

Les termes ainsi employés dans des dispositions contractuelles ne constituent pas un préalable obligatoire de conciliation permettant d'opposer une fin de non-recevoir à l'action en paiement initiale.

Il n'y a pas lieu d'y faire droit.

– Nîmes, 31 mars 2021, n° 19-00840, *Service Technique Industriel du Caoutchouc Distribution c. Phenix Technologie*

Règlement amiable – Conseil régional de l'ordre des architectes – Clause de règlement amiable – Fin de non-recevoir – Préalable obligatoire – Mise en œuvre – Irrecevabilité – Non régularisable

Après avoir rappelé les dispositions de l'article 122 du Code de procédure civile, puis relevé : – que les parties peuvent convenir d'instaurer un préalable à la saisine du juge, notamment en instituant une tentative de règlement amiable en cas de litige entre elles ;

– qu'en l'espèce, le contrat de maîtrise d'œuvre conclu entre les parties le 3 janvier 2013 stipulait au point 7.2 en cas de litige portant sur l'exécution du présent contrat, les parties conviennent expressément de saisir pour avis le conseil régional de l'ordre des architectes avant toute procédure judiciaire sauf conservatoire. À défaut de règlement amiable, le litige opposant les parties sera du ressort des juridictions civiles ;

– que les parties s'opposaient sur l'exécution du contrat, le maître d'ouvrage ayant résilié le contrat ;

– que la clause précitée n'avait pas été mise en œuvre par les parties préalablement à la saisine du juge, puis estimé que le défaut de la mise en œuvre de cette clause constituait une fin de non-recevoir privant une partie du droit d'agir en justice, le premier juge a fait une juste analyse des faits de la cause et appliqué à l'espèce les règles de droit qui s'imposaient.

À ces justes motifs que la cour adopte, il convient seulement d'ajouter :

– que la production par l'appelant d'un avis du Conseil Régional de l'Ordre des Architectes de la région Provence-Alpes-Côte d'Azur, datant du 19 juillet 2016 est postérieur à l'action introduite par assignation du 17 juin 2016,

– que la fin de non-recevoir tirée du défaut de mise en œuvre de la clause de conciliation obligatoire, préalablement à une action en justice, ne peut être régularisée par la mise en œuvre de la clause en cours d'instance.

En conséquence, le jugement déféré doit être confirmé en toutes ses dispositions, sauf à ajouter que les demandes sont irrecevables.

– Aix-en-Provence, 1er avril 2021, n° 18-07175, *X c. SCI Azur*

Contrat d'architecte – Clause de conciliation – Qualité – Parties – Tiers – Opposabilité – Conseil régional de l'Ordre des architectes – Champ contractuel – Application – Article 1792 CC – Garantie de parfait achèvement

L'article G.10 Litiges de la convention invoquée par les maîtres d'œuvre stipule que : « *En cas de différend portant sur le respect des clauses du présent contrat, les parties conviennent de saisir pour avis le Conseil régional de l'Ordre des architectes dont relève l'architecte, avant toute procédure judiciaire, sauf conservatoire. Cette saisine intervient sur l'initiative de la partie la plus diligente* ».

En ce qui concerne une des défenderesses, la saisine préalable pour avis du Conseil régional de l'Ordre des Architectes ne pouvait se réaliser matériellement puisqu'elle ne dépend pas de cet ordre, n'ayant pas la qualité d'architecte et n'étant donc pas inscrite à l'Ordre des architectes.

Ainsi, il ne pouvait y avoir de saisine préalable auprès d'un Ordre des architectes pour évoquer le litige pendant avec la société I.

La fin de non-recevoir sera dès lors rejetée à l'égard de la société.

Pour la société A, la présente instance a pour objet de statuer sur l'origine des désordres survenus dans l'immeuble litigieux, d'examiner notamment leurs causes, de déterminer les responsabilités respectives des intervenants au chantier, de fixer les préjudices éventuels, soit, de trancher aussi un différend portant sur le respect des clauses du contrat de maîtrise d'œuvre.

Les SCI font valoir que cette clause ne s'applique pas aux garanties légales dues par les maîtres d'œuvre. Toutefois, il a été jugé plus haut que les désordres du rez-de-chaussée ne relèvent d'aucune garantie légale en l'absence de réception de l'ouvrage à la date de leur apparition tandis que les infiltrations du sous-sol ne relèvent pas non plus de l'article 1792 du code civil mais de la garantie de parfait achèvement due exclusivement par le constructeur.

Or, en s'abstenant de saisir préalablement l'ordre des architectes dont dépend la société A, même après le dépôt du rapport d'expertise, les SCI maîtres d'ouvrage ont manqué à leur obligation de respecter les stipulations contractuelles auxquelles elles étaient tenues en vertu des dispositions de l'article 1134 du code civil dans sa version applicable à la cause.

En conséquence, il convient d'accueillir la fin de non-recevoir soulevée à l'égard des maîtres d'ouvrage mais aussi des appels en garantie des sociétés cotraitants de la société A, soumis à la même convention.

– Saint-Denis (Réunion), Chambre civile, 2 avril 2021, n° 18-00126, *Impulsion Ingénierie c. Ingénierie Concept Réunion et a.*

Règlement amiable – Clause de médiation – Définition – Critères – Obligatoire et préalable – Mise en œuvre – Absence – Inapplicabilité – Modalité choisie – Respect

Sur la recevabilité de la demande : le recours préalable à la médiation :

[...]

La saisine du juge, sans avoir préalablement mis en œuvre la clause préalable de médiation stipulée est sanctionnée par une fin de non-recevoir.

La clause doit être écrite et prévoir les modalités de mise en œuvre de la médiation.

Elle doit ainsi indiquer de manière expresse que le recours à la médiation est un préalable obligatoire à la saisine du juge.

La clause doit prévoir tous les détails, et notamment le nom du médiateur ou, à défaut, les critères permettant sa désignation.

Elle doit prévoir le déroulement de la procédure : les délais pour saisir le médiateur, la durée maximale de la médiation et les éventuelles causes de prorogation, les modalités de constatation de l'accord ou de l'échec de la médiation.

En l'espèce, l'article 6 du protocole du 6 avril 2019 énonce : « *Pendant la durée du Protocole, les parties conviennent de s'efforcer de régler à l'amiable, tout différent qui viendrait à naître entre elles quant à la validité, l'interprétation, l'exécution ou de défaut d'exécution du Protocole, et s'engagent à saisir, préalablement à tout litige, leur avocat respectif à savoir Me pour le bailleur et Me pour le preneur. Toutefois, et pour le cas où une solution amiable n'aurait pu être trouvée dans le délai d'un mois suivant la saisine de leur avocat, les parties retrouveront leur liberté aux fins de saisine du tribunal de commerce, lequel sera seul compétent pour connaître de leurs litiges* ».

Ainsi que l'a retenu à bon droit le premier juge, la clause invoquée ne prévoit en aucun cas la désignation d'un médiateur, ni les modalités de sa désignation, de sorte qu'elle n'est pas une clause de médiation.

En revanche, cette clause s'impose aux parties et M. C devait donc s'efforcer de régler à l'amiable tout litige ayant trait au protocole.

[...]

Dès lors c'est à juste titre que le premier juge a considéré que le délai d'un mois pour trouver une solution amiable avait été respecté et qu'ainsi au jour de la délivrance des assignations les parties avaient retrouvé leur liberté de saisir le tribunal de commerce.

En outre, c'est par une motivation pertinente que la cour adopte expressément, que le premier juge a considéré que la clause était en tout état de cause inapplicable dans la mesure où désormais chacun des administrateurs avait son propre avocat.

– Chambéry, Chambre civile – 1re section, 6 avril 2021, n° 20-00908, *AJ UP c. X*

Médiation judiciaire – Procédure – Juge des référés – Pouvoirs – Nomination – Contrôle – Délai – Provision – Procédure – Homologation – Médiation conventionnelle – Taxation – Sursis à statuer

Aux termes de l'article 131-1 du Code de procédure civile, le juge saisi d'un litige peut, après avoir recueilli l'accord des parties, désigner une tierce personne afin d'entendre les parties et de confronter leurs points de vue pour leur permettre de trouver une solution au conflit qui les oppose.

Ce pouvoir appartient également au juge des référés, en cours d'instance.

[...]

Il est rappelé qu'en application des articles 131-2, 131-9 et 131-10 du Code de procédure civile, la médiation ne dessaisit pas le magistrat, qui dans le cadre du contrôle de la mesure peut être saisi de toute difficulté et mettre fin à la mission du médiateur à la demande de ce dernier et/ou des parties, ou s'il estime que les circonstances l'imposent.

Le médiateur est désigné pour trois mois, durée qui peut être renouvelée une fois à la demande du médiateur. Le délai commencera à courir à compter de la première réunion de médiation. Il appartient au médiateur ayant accepté la mission de convoquer les parties dans les meilleurs délais.

À l'expiration de sa mission, le médiateur devra informer le conseiller/la cour de l'accord intervenu entre les parties ou du non-aboutissement de la mesure.

En cas d'accord, les parties pourront saisir le conseiller/la cour d'une demande d'homologation de cet accord par voie judiciaire.

Si dans le cadre de la médiation judiciaire d'une durée maximale de six mois, les parties ne sont pas parvenues à un accord, elles peuvent convenir de poursuivre les discussions dans le cadre d'une médiation conventionnelle régie par les articles 1531 à 1535 du Code de procédure civile, pour une durée et suivant des modalités financières qui seront, cette fois, librement convenues entre les parties et le médiateur.

[...]

Au terme de sa mission, le médiateur devra présenter au magistrat une demande de taxation du montant final de ses honoraires.

Il est sursis à statuer jusqu'à la fin de la mesure de médiation judiciaire.

– **Reims, Chambre civile, 1re section, 13 avril 2021, n° 21-00329,** ***SCEA du Domaine d'Orbais c. Commune d'Orbais l'Abbaye***

Médiation judiciaire – Procédure – Juge des référés – Pouvoirs – Nomination – Contrôle – Délai – Provision – Procédure – Homologation – Médiation conventionnelle – Taxation – Sursis à statuer

Aux termes de l'article 131-1 du Code de procédure civile, le juge saisi d'un litige peut, après avoir recueilli l'accord des parties, désigner une tierce personne afin d'entendre les parties et de confronter leurs points de vue pour leur permettre de trouver une solution au conflit qui les oppose.

Ce pouvoir appartient également au juge des référés, en cours d'instance.

[...]

Il est rappelé qu'en application des articles 131-2, 131-9 et 131-10 du Code de procédure civile, la médiation ne dessaisit pas le magistrat, qui dans le cadre du contrôle de la mesure peut être saisi de toute difficulté et mettre fin à la mission du médiateur à la demande de ce dernier et/ou des parties, ou s'il estime que les circonstances l'imposent.

Le médiateur est désigné pour trois mois, durée qui peut être renouvelée une fois à la demande du médiateur. Le délai commencera à courir à compter de la première réunion de médiation. Il appartient au médiateur ayant accepté la mission de convoquer les parties dans les meilleurs délais.

À l'expiration de sa mission, le médiateur devra informer le conseiller/la cour de l'accord intervenu entre les parties ou du non-aboutissement de la mesure.

En cas d'accord, les parties pourront saisir le conseiller/la cour d'une demande d'homologation de cet accord par voie judiciaire.

Si dans le cadre de la médiation judiciaire d'une durée maximale de six mois, les parties ne sont pas parvenues à un accord, elles peuvent convenir de poursuivre les discussions dans le cadre d'une médiation conventionnelle régie par les articles 1531 à 1535 du Code de procédure civile, pour une durée et suivant des modalités financières qui seront, cette fois, librement convenues entre les parties et le médiateur.

[...]

Au terme de sa mission, le médiateur devra présenter au magistrat une demande de taxation du montant final de ses honoraires.

Il est sursis à statuer jusqu'à la fin de la mesure de médiation judiciaire.

– **Reims, Chambre civile, 1re section, 13 avril 2021, n° 21-00321, *Alpimho c. BJC Terrassement***

Médiation judiciaire – Procédure – Juge des référés – Pouvoirs – Nomination – Contrôle – Délai – Provision – Procédure – Homologation – Médiation conventionnelle – Taxation – Sursis à statuer

Aux termes de l'article 131-1 du Code de procédure civile, le juge saisi d'un litige peut, après avoir recueilli l'accord des parties, désigner une tierce personne afin d'entendre les parties et de confronter leurs points de vue pour leur permettre de trouver une solution au conflit qui les oppose.

Ce pouvoir appartient également au juge des référés, en cours d'instance.

[...]

Il est rappelé qu'en application des articles 131-2, 131-9 et 131-10 du Code de procédure civile, la médiation ne dessaisit pas le magistrat, qui dans le cadre du contrôle de la mesure peut être saisi de toute difficulté et mettre fin à la mission du médiateur à la demande de ce dernier et/ou des parties, ou s'il estime que les circonstances l'imposent.

Le médiateur est désigné pour trois mois, durée qui peut être renouvelée une fois à la demande du médiateur. Le délai commencera à courir à compter de la première réunion de médiation. Il appartient au médiateur ayant accepté la mission de convoquer les parties dans les meilleurs délais.

À l'expiration de sa mission, le médiateur devra informer le conseiller/la cour de l'accord intervenu entre les parties ou du non-aboutissement de la mesure.

En cas d'accord, les parties pourront saisir le conseiller/la cour d'une demande d'homologation de cet accord par voie judiciaire.

Si dans le cadre de la médiation judiciaire d'une durée maximale de six mois, les parties ne sont pas parvenues à un accord, elles peuvent convenir de poursuivre les discussions dans le cadre d'une médiation conventionnelle régie par les articles 1531 à 1535 du Code de procédure civile, pour une durée et suivant des modalités financières qui seront, cette fois, librement convenues entre les parties et le médiateur.

[...]

Au terme de sa mission, le médiateur devra présenter au magistrat une demande de taxation du montant final de ses honoraires.

Il est sursis à statuer jusqu'à la fin de la mesure de médiation judiciaire.

– Reims, Chambre civile, 1re section, 13 avril 2021, n° 20-01623, *Nomine Metha c. Agrogaz France*

Contrat d'architecte – Clause de conciliation – Conseil régional de l'ordre des architectes – Fin de non-recevoir – Champ – Application – Connaissance – Article 1792 CC

Sur l'irrecevabilité des demandes en l'absence de saisine préalable du conseil régional des architectes :

[...]

Le contrat d'architecte conclu le 4 décembre 2007, contient une clause « litiges » qui stipule qu'en cas de différend portant sur le respect des clauses du contrat, les parties conviennent de saisir pour avis le conseil régional de l'ordre des architectes dont relève l'architecte avant toute procédure judiciaire, sauf conservatoire.

[...]

Dans les rapports des maîtres d'ouvrage avec l'architecte, cette clause n'a vocation à s'appliquer qu'aux obligations contractuelles des parties au regard des dispositions de l'article 1134 du Code civil dans sa rédaction applicable au litige, mais n'est pas applicable dès lors que la responsabilité de l'architecte est recherchée sur le fondement de l'article 1792 du même code, à raison de désordres survenus postérieurement à la réception, ce qui est le cas en l'espèce. En conséquence, les demandes sont recevables.

– Rennes, 4e Chambre, 15 avril 2021, n° 19-00790, *SAMCV Mutuelle des Architectes Français et a c. X et a.*

Clause de conciliation – Conseil régional de l'ordre des architectes – Fin de non-recevoir – Signature – Inopposabilité

La société ne démontre pas que les conditions générales qui contiennent la clause de conciliation préalable ont été transmises à Mme A et qu'elle les a approuvées.

Cette clause lui est donc inopposable. Le jugement est confirmé pour avoir rejeté la fin de non-recevoir.

– Rennes, 4e Chambre, 15 avril 2021, n° 19-01159, *A c. Atelier d'architecture Frances*

Contrat de bail – Clause de médiation – Référé – Premier président – Violation manifeste – Principe fondamental – Question de fond – Procédure – Compétence

Doit donc être considéré comme « moyen sérieux d'annulation ou de réformation » au sens de l'article précité, le moyen qui, en violation manifeste d'un principe fondamental de procédure, ou d'une règle de droit, serait retenu par la cour d'appel comme moyen d'infirmation de la décision de première instance sans contestation sérieuse sur le fond.

En l'espèce, le premier juge a estimé en premier lieu que la clause de médiation contenue au bail n'était pas impérative entre les parties. Cette clause est rédigée comme suit : « *Les parties sont informées qu'en cas de litige entre elles ou avec un tiers, elles pourront, préalablement à toute instance judiciaire, le soumettre à un médiateur qui sera désigné et missionné par le Centre de médiation notariale dont elles trouveront toutes les coordonnées et renseignements utiles sur le site.* »

Dès lors que le premier juge a retenu sa compétence de la lecture et non de l'interprétation de la clause ci-dessus, le moyen soulevé tendant à considérer que le juge des référés a excédé ses prérogatives, apparaît être un moyen qui sera nécessairement discuté et raisonnablement apprécié par la cour d'appel saisie au fond, sans qu'il puisse être considéré, en l'état par le conseiller désigné par le Premier président, que ce moyen entraînera inéluctablement infirmation de la décision.

– Douai, référé du Premier président, Ordonnance, 19 avril 2021, n° 21-00058, *A c. X*

Clause de conciliation – Fin de non-recevoir – Conseil de l'ordre des architectes – Action directe – Assurance – Tiers à la clause – Obligatoire et préalable – Inapplicabilité – Effet relatif

Or, il est de jurisprudence assurée que la saisine préalable, par le maître de l'ouvrage, du conseil de l'ordre des architectes prévues au contrat le liant à l'architecte, n'est pas une condition de recevabilité de l'action directe engagée par lui contre l'assureur de celui-ci (Cass. 3e civ., 10 novembre 2016, P n° 15-25449).

Le maître de l'ouvrage, est donc recevable à agir contre l'assureur sans avoir préalablement saisi le Conseil de l'ordre des architectes.

Quant à la société qui n'a jamais été liée par un contrat d'architecte, elle ne peut donc se voir opposer la clause instituant une procédure de conciliation obligatoire et préalable à la saisine du juge, laquelle ne peut porter que sur les obligations des parties au contrat d'architecte.

Le jugement sera ainsi confirmé en ce qu'il a rejeté cette fin de non-recevoir.

– Poitiers, 4 mai 2021, n° 19-01860, *Re Marine et M&H Épicerie c. Axa et a.*

Contrat d'architecte – Clause de conciliation – Obligatoire et préalable – Fin de non-recevoir – Irrecevabilité – Assurance – Tiers à la clause – Inopposabilité – Étendue – Article 1134 CC – Article 1792 CC

Sur sa recevabilité :

Le contrat d'architecte contient la clause suivante : « *En cas de différend portant sur le respect des clauses du présent contrat, les parties conviennent de saisir pour avis le conseil régional de l'ordre des architectes dont relève l'architecte avant toute procédure judiciaire sauf conservatoire. Cette saisine intervient à l'initiative de la partie la plus diligente* ».

Cette clause contractuelle qui institue une procédure, obligatoire et préalable à la saisine du juge, favorisant une solution du litige par le recours à un tiers, n'a pas été mise en œuvre avant d'assigner devant le juge du fond.

Elle ne peut porter que sur les obligations des parties au regard de l'article 1134 du Code civil et n'a pas vocation à s'appliquer lorsque la responsabilité de l'architecte est recherchée sur le fondement de la garantie légale des constructeurs de l'article 1792 du même code.

Elle doit recevoir application en l'espèce dès lors que la responsabilité de l'architecte est recherchée et ne peut l'être que sur le fondement de la responsabilité contractuelle de droit commun de l'article 1147 du Code civil pour manquement à ses obligations avant toute réception de l'ouvrage puisque le contrat a été résilié par les maîtres d'ouvrage alors que l'opération de construction était au stade des terrassements.

Elle rend l'action irrecevable vis-à-vis de l'architecte.

Cette action reste parfaitement recevable à l'encontre de l'assureur de l'architecte au regard des dispositions de l'article L 124-3 du Code des assurances, la saisine préalable par les maîtres d'ouvrage de l'ordre des architectes imposée par le contrat de maîtrise d'œuvre n'étant pas une condition de recevabilité de l'action directe engagée par eux contre l'assureur de celui-ci.

– **Toulouse, 10 mai 2021, n° 17-04951,** ***A c. F. Privat Architecte et a.***

Clause de règlement amiable – Fin de non-recevoir – Définition – Obligation préalable – Absence de mise en œuvre – Contrat d'édition – Règlement amiable – Société des gens de lettres – Adhérent – Syndicat national de l'édition – Attitude des parties

La cour rappelle que la clause contractuelle prévoyant une tentative de règlement amiable, non assortie de conditions particulières de mise en œuvre, ne constitue pas une procédure de conciliation obligatoire préalable à la saisine du juge, dont le non-respect caractérise une fin de non-recevoir.

En l'espèce, il résulte de l'article 15 du contrat d'édition litigieux, que les parties se sont engagées, avant de recourir aux tribunaux compétents, à soumettre leur litige à la Société des gens de lettres, sans en préciser les modalités, et notamment le délai au terme duquel en l'absence d'accord la tentative de règlement amiable sera réputée infructueuse, l'action en justice ne pouvant être différée de manière indéterminée, de sorte que la clause litigieuse ne constitue pas une procédure de conciliation obligatoire préalable à la saisine du juge dont le non-respect caractérise une fin de non-recevoir. Dès lors, l'action ne peut pas être jugée irrecevable de ce chef.

Au surplus, il résulte des pièces versées, et ainsi que l'a retenu le tribunal, que par courrier du 9 juin 2016 la société a indiqué que la Société des gens de lettres ne pouvait pas mettre en œuvre cette mesure de médiation car M. A n'en était pas un adhérent, mais qu'elle entendait cependant respecter la mesure de médiation contractuelle, qui pourrait avoir lieu sous l'égide du syndicat national de l'édition ; puis par courrier du 25 juillet 2016, elle a réitéré sa proposition de médiation, M. A ne produisant, de son côté, aucune pièce établissant qu'il aurait répondu à ces propositions, de sorte que la clause de résolution amiable a été respectée, et que la fin de non-recevoir opposée doit être rejetée.

– Paris, Pôle 5, Chambre 1, 11 mai 2021, n° 19-00977, *A c. Bernard Giovanangeli Éditeur*

Clause de conciliation – Qualification – Préalable et obligatoire – Contrat de travail – Facultative Inapplicabilité – Prud'hommes – Champ – Procédure de conciliation prud'homale – Préliminaire et obligatoire – Licenciement – Action contentieuse – Action disciplinaire

Sur la procédure de conciliation conventionnelle :

Le contrat signé entre les parties prévoit en son article 8 : « [...] *En cas de difficultés soulevées soit par l'exécution, soit par l'interprétation ou la cessation du présent contrat, les parties s'engagent, préalablement à toute action contentieuse, à soumettre leur différend à deux conciliateurs, l'un choisi par le docteur A parmi les membres du conseil départemental de l'ordre, l'autre par le directeur de l'établissement. Ceux-ci s'efforceront de trouver une solution amiable dans un délai maximum de trois mois, à compter de la désignation du premier conciliateur* ».

Cette clause prévoit que, préalablement à toute action contentieuse, les parties doivent soumettre leur différend à deux conciliateurs, il s'agit d'une clause de conciliation préalable et obligatoire.

Il est de jurisprudence constante que l'existence d'une clause du contrat de travail qui institue une procédure de conciliation préalable en cas de litige survenant à l'occasion du contrat n'empêche pas les parties de saisir directement le juge prud'homal de leur différend, en raison de l'existence en matière prud'homale d'une procédure de conciliation préliminaire et obligatoire.

Il en résulte que la saisine du conseil de prud'hommes par le salarié est recevable nonobstant l'absence de saisine des deux conciliateurs prévue à l'article 8 du contrat.

La décision de l'employeur d'engager une procédure de licenciement à l'encontre d'un de ses salariés n'est pas une action contentieuse mais une action disciplinaire. Il en résulte que l'association n'était pas tenue de saisir les conciliateurs avant d'engager la procédure de licenciement.

– Montpellier, 12 mai 2021, n° 16-00604, *A c. Association pour Adultes et Jeunes Handicapés de l'Aude (APAJH11)*

Conseil régional de l'ordre des architectes – Clause de conciliation – Champ – Recevabilité – Fin de non-recevoir – Clause facultative – Déséquilibre

En l'espèce, la clause litigieuse prévoit qu'en cas de différend portant sur le respect des clauses du présent contrat, les parties conviennent de saisir le conseil régional de l'ordre des architectes dont relève l'architecte, avant toute procédure judiciaire, sauf conservatoire. Le conseil régional peut, soit émettre un avis sur l'objet du différend, soit organiser une procédure de règlement amiable.

En matière de recouvrement d'honoraires, la saisine du conseil régional est facultative.

Il résulte de l'examen de cette clause qu'en matière de recouvrement d'honoraires, tant le maître de l'ouvrage que l'architecte sont dispensés du préalable obligatoire de la saisine de l'ordre des architectes.

En effet, cette clause est applicable aux deux parties qui peuvent, l'une et l'autre, prétendre engager une action en contestation ou en recouvrement des honoraires.

Dans cette mesure, c'est à bon droit que le tribunal a estimé que la clause était exempte d'un quelconque déséquilibre significatif au profit de l'architecte et a déclaré recevable la demande en paiement.

– Pau, 2e Chambre, Section 1, 17 mai 2021, n° 20-01027, *Despre Architectes c. Le Roman des Aventures*

Contrat – Conditions générales – Clause de médiation – Imprécise – Volonté des parties – Référé – Urgence – Provision – Article 873 CPC – Critère – Recevabilité – Obligatoire et préalable – Fin de non-recevoir – Conditions – Doutes sérieux sur les capacités financières

Le contrat comporte la mention : « *Les parties conviennent qu'en cas de litige les opposant au présent contrat, et à défaut de toute médiation, le tribunal compétent serait le tribunal de commerce de Salon de Provence* ». Les conditions générales de vente stipulent en leur article 6-2 « Compétence juridictionnelle » « *En vue de trouver ensemble une solution à tout litige qui surviendrait dans l'exécution du présent contrat, les parties conviennent de se réunir dans les huit (8) jours de survenance de l'événement à l'initiative de la partie la plus diligente. Si au terme d'un délai de quinze (15) jours, les parties n'arrivaient pas à se mettre d'accord sur un compromis ou une solution, tout litige relatif à la naissance, l'exécution, l'interprétation du présent contrat sera de la compétence exclusive des tribunaux de Salon de Provence* ».

S'il est vrai que le contrat ne comporte pas une clause de médiation précise en ses modalités, il s'infère de ces deux documents contractuels que la volonté des parties, qui ne souffre pas d'interprétation, est de tenter une conciliation préalable en cas de litige les opposant. Les conditions générales de vente ne sauraient être écartées alors qu'elles sont communiquées par la société à son client, avec chacune des factures dont le montant est réclamé, et que la société elle-même s'en prévaut dans sa lettre de mise en demeure du 2 juin 2020, en indiquant qu'à défaut de règlement sous huit jours, la société aura « *à supporter, outre les intérêts de retard, la clause pénale* », le contrat ne comportant lui-même aucune disposition relative à une clause pénale, ou à des pénalités de retard.

La clause instituant une procédure de médiation ou de conciliation préalable à la saisine du juge constitue une fin de non-recevoir qui s'impose au juge si une partie l'invoque.

Une telle clause de règlement amiable des différends ne fait pas obstacle à la saisine immédiate du juge des référés sur le fondement de l'article 873 alinéa 2 du Code de procédure civile et ne prive pas ce dernier d'allouer une provision au créancier si l'urgence justifie de passer outre le processus de règlement amiable du conflit.

Tel n'est pas le cas en l'espèce, la société ne faisant pas état, ni ne justifiant d'une situation d'urgence et aucun élément versé au dossier n'autorisant à nourrir des doutes sérieux sur les capacités financières de la partie adverse à respecter son obligation de régler les sommes qui seront retenues comme étant dues.

En conséquence, il y a lieu de déclarer l'action irrecevable et d'infirmer en toutes ses dispositions l'ordonnance attaquée.

– Aix-en-Provence, Chambre 3-1, 20 mai 2021, n° 20-08736, *Pompeani Francois Carrières Travaux Publics c. MC Expertise*

Tribunal arbitral – Traité bilatéral d'investissement – Compétence – Contrôle plein – Volonté commune – Arbitre – Pouvoir juridictionnel – Clause compromissoire – Offre de compromettre – Offre permanente – Offre indépendante et autonome – Champ d'application du Traité – Condition d'application – Investissement – Licéité – Gravité – Répartition des pouvoirs – Absence de pouvoir de juger au fond du juge de l'annulation – Révision – Validité de l'opération – Champ de l'offre d'arbitrage – CNUDCI – Clause préalable de conciliation – Recevabilité – Cas d'ouverture du recours – Fraude – Corruption – Clause préalable de conciliation – Période de réflexion (« *cooling off period* ») – Exception d'incompétence – Recevabilité – Cas d'ouverture du recours en annulation – Moyen tardif – Nouveaux moyens – Siège de l'arbitrage – Loi de la procédure – Motivation – Pertinence – Révision au fond – Clause CFL (compensation pour pertes) – War Clause – Standard FPS (protection pleine et entière) – Motivation – Obligation positive de protection et sécurité pleine et entière – Ordre public international – Droit international coutumier – Garantie bancaire – Conception française – Heurte de manière manifeste, effective et concrète – Principes et valeurs – Allégations – Moyen tardif – Indices – Corruption d'agent public étranger – Définition – Absence de poursuite pénale – Faisceau d'indices graves et concordants

[...]

1-2 Sur l'incompétence du Tribunal arbitral pour statuer sur les demandes à défaut de respect par cette dernière des conditions au consentement de l'État de Libye à l'arbitrage prévues à l'article 8 du TBI :

54 – En l'espèce, l'article 8 de l'Accord entre la République turque et la Grande Jamahiriya arabe libyenne populaire et socialiste concernant l'encouragement et la protection réciproques des investissements du 25 novembre 2009, intitulé « *Règlement des différends entre une Partie contractante et les investisseurs de l'autre Partie contractante* » stipule : « *1. En cas de différends surgissant entre l'une des Parties contractantes et un investisseur de l'autre Partie contractante concernant un investissement de ce dernier, l'investisseur notifie par écrit et de manière détaillée la Partie contractante sur le territoire de laquelle l'investissement a été réalisé. Dans la mesure du possible, l'investisseur et la Partie contractante concernée s'efforcent de régler ces différends par voie de consultations et de négociations, menées de bonne foi. 2. Si le différend ne peut être réglé de cette manière dans les quatre-vingt-dix jours qui suivent la date de la notification écrite mentionnée au paragraphe 1 ci-dessus, le différend peut être soumis, si l'investisseur le décide, au tribunal compétent de la Partie contractante sur le territoire de laquelle l'investissement a été réalisé ou à l'arbitrage international, soit* (...) ».

55 – Cependant, le grief tiré du non-respect d'une clause préalable de conciliation et notamment de la période de réflexion (« cooling off period ») qu'elle prévoit ne constitue pas une exception d'incompétence mais une question relative

à la recevabilité des demandes, qui n'entre pas dans les cas d'ouverture du recours en annulation énumérés par l'article 1520 du Code de procédure civile.

56 – Ce grief sera en conséquence rejeté.

[...]

2 – Sur le moyen subsidiaire d'annulation tiré du manquement par le Tribunal Arbitral à la mission qui lui a été confiée (Article 1520,3° du Code de procédure civile) :

[...]

Sur le grief tiré du non-respect par le tribunal de ses pouvoirs juridictionnels :

126 – Cependant, le fait que le tribunal arbitral ait statué au fond sur les demandes de la société suffit à caractériser qu'il a considéré que ces demandes étaient recevables et que ce faisant, les conditions résultant de la clause de conciliation préalable ont été satisfaites, étant observé qu'au § 342 de sa sentence, il a énoncé que « *compte tenu du fait qu'aucun accord n'a été conclu entre les parties au cours de la période de 90 jours, la société était en droit d'exercer son droit d'engager une procédure d'arbitrage en vertu de l'article 8 du TBI* ».

127 – Ce grief sera en conséquence rejeté.

– Paris, Pôle 5 – Chambre 16, chambre commerciale internationale, 25 mai 2021, n° 18-27648, *État de Libye c. Cengiz Insaat Sanayi Ve Ticaret A.S.*[1]

Clause de conciliation – Obligatoire et préalable – Saisine du Tribunal – Faculté – Rédaction – Fin de non-recevoir – Invitation

Il en résulte que la saisine de la juridiction de première instance était antérieure à la tentative de conciliation prévue contractuellement.

Toutefois, la clause invoquée ne prévoit qu'une faculté de saisine du Président de l'Ordre. Elle n'institue pas une procédure de conciliation préalable et obligatoire à la saisine du juge de sorte que son défaut de mise en œuvre ne peut pas constituer une fin de non-recevoir.

– Colmar, 1re Chambre civile – Section A, 31 mai 2021, n° 19-01003, *Société Fiduciaire Du Bas-Rhin c. A*

Clause de mediation – Consommateur – L. 612-4 du code de la consommation – Inopposabilité

Attendu que l'article L. 612-4 du code de la consommation dispose qu'« *est interdite toute clause ou convention obligeant le consommateur, en cas de litige, à recourir obligatoirement à une médiation préalablement à la saisine du juge* ».

En conséquence, le tribunal déclarera non écrite la clause de l'article 7 « litiges » du contrat de vente conclu entre les parties et déboutera la société de sa demande en irrecevabilité des demandes de Madame A.

– T. com. Chalon-sur-Saône, 7 juin 2021, n° 2020001991, *X c. Celtic Horse's Paradise*

1. Pour les aspects « arbitrage » de l'arrêt, voir le Panorama des Cahiers de l'arbitrage/Paris Journal of International Arbitration, 2020-4.

Tribunal de commerce – Conciliation préalable – Facultative – Absence d'une partie

Devant le Tribunal de commerce, la conciliation préalable n'est pas obligatoire. En l'absence de la société à l'audience du juge chargé d'instruire l'affaire, il n'a pas été possible de l'entendre sur la mise en place par le juge chargé d'instruire l'affaire d'une conciliation. En conséquence, la demande est recevable.

– TC Créteil, 2e Chambre, 8 juin 2021, 2020F00375, *ACOF c. Cabinet Cherifi*

Contrat d'architecte – Conseil régional de l'ordre des architectes – Clause de conciliation – Obligatoire et préalable – Fin de non-recevoir – Médiation – Conciliation – Définition – Article L. 612-4 du Code de la consommation – Inapplicabilité – Préalable contractuel obligatoire de conciliation – Irrecevabilité

Le contrat souscrit stipule en son article 14 : « *En cas de différend portant sur le respect des clauses du présent contrat, les parties conviennent de saisir pour avis le conseil régional de l'Ordre des architectes dont relève l'architecte, avant toute procédure judiciaire, sauf conservatoire. Cette saisine intervient sur l'initiative de la partie la plus diligente* ».

Cette clause institue une procédure de conciliation obligatoire et préalable à la saisine du juge et constitue une fin de non-recevoir.

Les époux X invoquent l'article L. 612-4 du Code de la consommation qui dispose : « *Est interdite toute clause ou convention obligeant le consommateur, en cas de litige, à recourir obligatoirement à une médiation préalablement à la saisine du juge* ».

Cet argument ne peut être retenu.

En effet, la clause en litige n'institue pas une médiation, définie à l'article 131-1 du Code de procédure civile, mais une conciliation.

Par conséquent, dès lors qu'il est constant qu'avant d'assigner M. A en responsabilité contractuelle devant le tribunal de grande instance d'Agen par acte du 2 septembre 2016, les époux X n'ont pas respecté le préalable contractuel obligatoire de conciliation, leur action à l'encontre de celui-ci doit être déclarée irrecevable.

– Agen, 9 juin 2021, 19/00784, *X c. Y*

Volonté des parties – Fin de non-recevoir – À tout moment – Contrat d'architecte – Conseil de l'Ordre des Architectes – Avis – Clause de saisie obligatoire et préalable – Règlement du Conseil – Procédure de règlement amiable

En droit

Selon les dispositions de l'article 1103 du Code civil, « *les contrats légalement formés tiennent lieu de loi à ceux qui les ont faits* ».

L'article 122 du Code de procédure civile dispose : « *Constitue une fin de non-recevoir tout moyen qui tend à faire déclarer l'adversaire irrecevable en sa demande, sans examen au fond, pour défaut de droit d'agir, tel le défaut de qualité, le défaut d'intérêt, la prescription, le délai préfix, la chose jugée* ».

Au regard des dispositions de l'article 123 dudit Code, « *Les fins de non-recevoir peuvent être proposées en tout état de cause, à moins qu'il en soit disposé autrement et sauf la possibilité pour le juge de condamner à des dommages-intérêts ceux qui se seraient abstenus, dans une intention dilatoire, de les soulever plus tôt* ».

En l'espèce, les parties ont signé un contrat d'architecte, le 27 avril 2010, définissant la mission du maître d'œuvre dans le cadre du projet de construction d'un immeuble à Montlebon. La partie défenderesse soulève, à titre principal, l'irrecevabilité de la procédure, en se fondant sur l'article 5.2 du contrat précité.

Selon cet article : « *En cas de litige portant sur l'exécution du présent contrat, les parties conviennent de saisir, pour avis, le conseil régional de l'ordre des architectes dont relève l'architecte avant toute procédure judiciaire, sauf conservatoire* ».

Force est de constater que ce contrat s'impose aux parties en tant que loi commune, et qu'aux termes de l'article précité, toute procédure judiciaire devait être précédée d'une saisie du Conseil de l'Ordre des Architectes.

Or, la partie demanderesse a porté le présent litige, de manière prématurée, devant le Tribunal Judiciaire, qui s'est déclaré incompétent au profit du Tribunal de céans, alors qu'existait une clause de saisie obligatoire et préalable du Conseil de l'ordre des Architectes.

Le règlement intérieur de l'Ordre des architectes dispose en son article 70 traitant du « *différend entre un architecte et un maître d'ouvrage non consommateur ou un fiers* » que « *Lorsque le contrat comporte une clause de saisine du Conseil régional, il est tenu d'émettre un avis ou d'organiser une procédure de règlement amiable, dans un délai de 4 mois à compter de la demande (ce délai étant renouvelable une fois). Il est tenu d'initier la procédure auprès des parties dans un délai de 2 mois à compter de la demande* ».

Cette demande pouvant s'entendre aussi bien d'un simple avis que d'une procédure de règlement amiable, le Tribunal dira bien-fondée la demande de la défenderesse et déclarera irrecevable la demande.

– T. com. Besançon, 9 juin 2021, n° 2020002710, *IBS c. Idea Concept Architecture*

Tentative de règlement amiable – Procédure de conciliation – Obligaoire préalable – Définition – Tentative – Mise en œuvre – Fin de non recevoir – Urgence

L'article 122 du Code de procédure civile dispose : « *Constitue une fin de non-recevoir tout moyen qui tend à faire déclarer l'adversaire irrecevable en sa demande, sans examen au fond, pour défaut de droit d'agir, tel le défaut de qualité, le défaut d'intérêt, la prescription, le délai préfix, la chose jugée*». Il a été jugé que la clause contractuelle prévoyant une tentative de règlement amiable, non assortie de conditions particulières de mise en œuvre, ne constitue pas une procédure de conciliation obligatoire préalable à la saisine du juge, dont le non-respect caractérise une fin de non-recevoir s'imposant à celui-ci.

L'urgence des demandes n'est pas contestable puisque l'arrêté des comptes 2019 de l'association en dépend ; d'autre part, la clause de conciliation préalable, citée ci-dessus, ne comporte aucune condition particulière de mise en œuvre.

En conséquence, nous dirons que la clause de conciliation préalable n'est pas de nature à rendre irrecevables les présentes demandes.

– T. com. Nanterre, 10 juin 2021, référé, n° 2021R00182, *Solidarité Patrimoine c. Association Jeanne de Lestonnac*

Clause de conciliation – Ordre public international – Ordre juridique français – Valeurs et principes – Violation manifeste, effective et concrète – Applicabilité – Recours en annulation – Ouverture – Égalité des parties – Principe de la contradiction – Égalité des armes – Procès équitable – Expertise contradictoire – Règlement de la Cour Internationale d'Arbitrage de la Chambre de Commerce Internationale (CCI) – Article 25.4 Règlement CCI

• *Sur le grief tiré de la violation de la clause de conciliation stipulée à l'article 20 du contrat pour l'exécution des travaux de réparation :*

[...]

38-Le tribunal arbitral a écarté la mise en œuvre de cette clause, en rappelant la nécessité d'interpréter strictement les clauses de conciliation préalable en raison de la restriction qu'elles imposent au droit fondamental d'accès au juge. Il a estimé que la rédaction ne prévoit pas clairement comment les paragraphes s'articulent ni la fonction exacte que remplit l'intervention du Bureau Veritas (§157).

39-Sous couvert d'une violation de l'ordre public international et du principe d'exécution des contrats de bonne foi, la partie reproche au tribunal d'avoir procédé à une interprétation de la clause de conciliation nonobstant son caractère clair et précis et d'en avoir écarté son application, invitant ce faisant la cour d'appel à une révision au fond de la sentence partielle, ce qui est prohibé, même à l'occasion de l'examen d'un moyen tiré de la méconnaissance de l'ordre public international.

40-Il convient dès lors de rejeter ce grief.

• *Sur le grief tiré du non respect du principe d'égalité des armes :*

[...]

43-En vertu de l'article 1510 du Code de procédure civile, le tribunal arbitral doit garantir l'égalité des parties et le principe de la contradiction. L'égalité des armes est un élément du procès équitable protégé par l'ordre public international et qui implique l'obligation d'offrir à chaque partie une possibilité raisonnable de présenter sa cause – y compris les preuves – dans des conditions qui ne la placent pas dans une situation substantiellement désavantageuse par rapport à son adversaire.

[...]

45-L'examen de ce grief par le juge de l'annulation suppose que la Cour se prononce sur le bien-fondé de la décision du tribunal arbitral relativement à la mise en œuvre de la clause de conciliation, ce qui revient à solliciter la révision de la sentence partielle sur ce point, ce qui est prohibé.

[...]

47-Toutefois, la sentence partielle entreprise ne tranche que la question de la recevabilité de l'action engagée, au regard notamment de la mise en œuvre de la clause de conciliation, sans se prononcer sur les éléments de preuve de nature à fonder les demandes. Dans le cadre de l'interprétation de cette clause de conciliation, le tribunal arbitral a retenu qu'une partie n'a pas fait suite aux propositions de l'autre de soumettre le différend au Bureau Veritas comme le prévoit la clause litigieuse.

48-Par ailleurs, la demanderesse ne prétend ni ne démontre avoir sollicité du tribunal arbitral l'organisation d'une expertise contradictoire, tel que permis par l'article 25.4 du règlement de la Cour Internationale d'Arbitrage de la Chambre de Commerce Internationale (CCI), selon lequel « *le tribunal arbitral peut, après avoir consulté les parties, nommer un ou plusieurs experts, définir leurs missions et recevoir leurs rapports. Si l'une des parties le demande, celles-ci doivent avoir la possibilité d'interroger lors d'une audience tout expert ainsi nommé* ».

49-Il s'infère de ce qui précède que le grief n'est pas fondé et doit être rejeté.

– Paris, Chambre commerciale internationale, Pôle 5, Chambre 16, 9 juin 2021, n° 20/01304, *C.M.R.T c. Sofema*[2]

Conseil régional de l'ordre des architectes – Avis – Clause de conciliation – Étendue – Champ – Article 1134 CC – Article 1792 CC – Obligatoire et préalable – Irrecevabilité – Non régularisable – Assurance – Tiers à la clause – Opposabilité

Sur la recevabilité de l'action des époux A à l'encontre de l'architecte et de son assureur :

La clause qui stipule qu'« *en cas de litige portant sur le respect des clauses du présent contrat, les parties conviennent de saisir pour avis le conseil régional de l'ordre des architectes dont relève l'architecte, avant toute procédure judiciaire, sauf conservatoire* », institue une procédure de conciliation, obligatoire et préalable à la saisine du juge.

Le moyen tiré du défaut de mise en œuvre de cette clause constitue une fin de non-recevoir, et la situation donnant lieu à celle-ci n'est pas susceptible d'être régularisée par la mise en œuvre de la clause en cours d'instance. (Cass. 3e civ., 16 novembre 2017, n° 16-24. 642, *Bull.* 2017, III, n° 24).

Toutefois, la clause de saisine de l'ordre des architectes préalablement à toute action judiciaire en cas de litige sur l'exécution du contrat ne porte que sur les obligations des parties au regard de l'article 1134 du Code civil, et n'a pas vocation à s'appliquer lorsque la responsabilité de l'architecte est recherchée sur le fondement de l'article 1792 du Code civil. (Cass. 3e civ., 23 mai 2007, n° 06-15.668, *Bull.* 2007, III, n° 80).

Le contrat d'architecte liant les époux A à Madame C comporte une clause selon laquelle « *en cas de litige portant sur le respect des clauses du présent contrat, les parties conviennent de saisir pour avis le conseil régional de l'ordre des architectes dont relève l'architecte, avant toute procédure judiciaire, sauf conservatoire* ».

La lecture littérale de cette clause, qui ne nécessite aucune interprétation, l'identifie immédiatement comme une clause de conciliation.

Par ailleurs, les époux A, qui ne citent aucun texte légal dans leurs écritures, ne viennent à aucun moment se prévaloir de ce que les ouvrages seraient affectés de dommages en compromettant la solidité ou bien, l'affectant dans un

2. Pour les aspects « arbitrage » de l'arrêt, voir le Panorama des Cahiers de l'arbitrage/Paris Journal of International Arbitration, 2020-4.

de ses éléments constitutifs ou l'un de ses éléments d'équipement, les rendraient impropres à leur destination. En outre, les appelants viennent indiquer qu'il n'y avait jamais eu de réception des travaux, excluant par là même toute mobilisation de la garantie décennale.

Au surplus, ils ne se prévalent d'aucune réception expresse ou tacite des ouvrages, et un examen attentif de leurs pièces, et en particulier de l'expertise judiciaire, ne permet pas de caractériser la moindre réception.

Dès lors, l'action des époux A ne peut être fondée sur la responsabilité décennale. C'est dès lors à bon droit que l'architecte et son assureur en déduisent que l'action des époux A se fonde sur la responsabilité contractuelle de droit commun des constructeurs. Il est constant que les époux A n'ont pas justifié de l'accomplissement de la formalité contractuelle préalable de saisine du conseil régional de l'ordre des architectes.

Il conviendra donc de déclarer irrecevable l'action des époux A à l'encontre de Madame C, et l'ordonnance sera confirmée de ce chef.

La saisine préalable par le maître de l'ouvrage de l'ordre des architectes pour conciliation, prévue au contrat la liant à l'architecte, n'est pas une condition de la recevabilité de l'action directe engagée contre l'assureur de celui-ci (Cass. 3e civ., 18 novembre 2013, n° 12-18.439, *Bull.* 2013, III, n° 169).

L'action des époux A engagée à l'encontre de l'assurance est donc recevable. Il conviendra donc de rejeter le moyen d'irrecevabilité opposée par celle-ci, et l'ordonnance sera confirmée de ce chef.

– Reims, 22 juin 2021, n° 20/01812, *X c. Y*

Clause de conciliation – Conseil Régional de l'Ordre des experts comptables – Obligatoire et préalable – Prescription – Suspension – Fin de non-recevoir – Irrecevabilité

Le Tribunal observe l'article 18 « Différends » des Conditions Générales d'Intervention de la lettre de mission de la société défenderesse constatant que cette dernière est légalement formée et acceptée de la société demanderesse, le 25 novembre 2013. Ledit article stipule que « *les litiges qui pourraient éventuellement survenir entre la société et son Client seront portés, avant toute action judiciaire devant le Président du Conseil Régional de l'Ordre des experts comptables aux fins de conciliation* ».

Le Tribunal dira que ledit article de la lettre de mission instituant une procédure de conciliation obligatoire et préalable à la saisine du juge, dont la mise en œuvre suspend jusqu'à son issue le cours de la prescription, constitue une fin de non-recevoir qui s'impose si une des parties l'invoque.

En l'espèce, ladite clause se limitait à imposer à la société demanderesse de porter l'action devant le Président du Conseil Régional de l'Ordre avant toute action judiciaire indépendamment de la position qui pourrait être prise sur sa saisine, ce que n'a pas fait la société.

En conséquence, le Tribunal : – Dira la demande de la société à l'égard de la société défenderesse à titre de dommages et intérêts irrecevable.

– T. com. Bordeaux, 29 juin 2021, n° 2020F00163, *Teza c. Compta Expert Laval et KPMG*

Clause de conciliation – Contrat d'architecte – Conseil régional de l'Ordre des architectes – Fin de non-recevoir – Champ – Garantie décennale – Obligations contractuelles

L'article 12 du contrat de maîtrise d'œuvre de 2002 liant M. et Mme A à l'architecte X stipule en son troisième alinéa que « *en cas de litige portant sur l'exécution du présent contrat, les parties conviennent de saisir pour avis le Conseil régional de l'Ordre des architectes dont relève l'architecte, avant toute procédure judiciaire. À défaut d'un règlement amiable, le litige opposant les parties sera du ressort des Juridictions Civiles territorialement compétentes* ».

Il résulte des dispositions des articles 122 du Code de procédure civile et 1103 du Code civil, anciennement article 1134 avant l'entrée en vigueur de l'ordonnance n° 2016-131 du 10 février 2016, que l'absence de saisine du conseil régional de l'ordre des architectes, préalablement à l'introduction d'une action en justice, constitue une fin de non-recevoir.

En l'espèce, il résulte des termes mêmes de cette clause contractuelle d'abord qu'elle concerne uniquement tout litige portant sur l'exécution de ce contrat et ensuite qu'elle ne s'applique donc pas à un litige fondé sur la garantie décennale du maître d'œuvre.

Aux termes de leurs conclusions, les demandes se fondent sur cette garantie décennale pour ce qui concerne des désordres affectant : [...] Elles se fondent sur cette garantie contractuelle pour ce qui concerne des désordres [...].

En conséquence, d'une part il convient de confirmer le jugement attaqué en ce qu'il a rejeté la fin de non-recevoir tirée du moyen tiré du non-respect de la clause de saisine préalable du conseil régional de l'ordre des architectes, et a statué, dans son dispositif, sur les demandes de M. et Mme A fondées sur cette garantie décennale.

– Montpellier, 3e chambre civile, 1er juillet 2021, n° 16/00889, ***MAF c. A***

Clause de conciliation – Champ – Architecture – Opposabilité

Or, s'agissant de la peinture des retours d'escalier de service, M. A est en droit d'opposer la clause de conciliation préalable, de sorte que la demande en garantie à son encontre est irrecevable.

En revanche, la demande est recevable à l'égard de l'assureur, ce dernier ne pouvant opposer la clause laquelle ne s'applique qu'à l'égard de l'architecte.

– Douai, chambre 1, section 2, 8 juillet 2021, n° 19/00568, ***Syndicat des copropriétaires de la résidence Les Jardins du Bail c. A et a.***

Conseil Régional de l'Ordre des experts comptables – Clause de conciliation – Préalable obligatoire – Faculté – Inopposabilité – Recevabilité

« *Les litiges qui pourraient éventuellement survenir entre le membre de l'Ordre et son client pourront être portés, avant toute action en justice, devant le Président du Conseil Régional de l'Ordre compétent aux fins de conciliation.* »

Cette clause ne prévoyant qu'une simple faculté, elle ne peut constituer un préalable obligatoire à la saisine de la juridiction judiciaire.

En second lieu, l'appelante soulève également une fin de non-recevoir de l'action en paiement en invoquant les dispositions de l'article 159 du décret n° 2012-432 du 30 mars 2012 relatif à l'exercice de l'activité d'expertise comptable dont les termes sont les suivants : « *En cas de contestation par le client ou adhérent des conditions d'exercice de la mission ou de différend sur les honoraires, les personnes mentionnées à l'article 141 (les experts-comptables) s'efforcent de faire accepter la conciliation ou l'arbitrage du président du conseil régional de l'Ordre avant toute action en justice. La même obligation pèse sur l'expert-comptable qui succède à un confrère dans les conditions prévues à l'article 164* ».

Tout comme les dispositions de la lettre de mission, ce texte n'ouvre qu'une simple faculté et ne déroge pas à la compétence de la juridiction de droit commun pour connaître d'une demande en recouvrement d'honoraires formée par un expert-comptable à l'encontre de son client et ne peut faire obstacle au droit qu'à toute personne d'agir en justice.

Le jugement qui a déclaré recevables les demandes présentées par l'expert-comptable doit être confirmé.

– Agen, Chambre civile, Section commerciale, 18 août 2021, n° 19/00732, *Cc2rails c. Morereau Conseil*

Clause de conciliation – Contrat d'architecte – Référé – Conditions – Provision – Conseil régional de l'ordre des architectes – Préalable obligatoire – Inopposable – Demande provisionnelle – Recevabilité

L'article 873 alinéa 2 du Code de procédure civile dispose que le président du tribunal de commerce peut, dans les cas où l'existence de l'obligation n'est pas sérieusement contestable, accorder une provision au créancier, ou ordonner l'exécution de l'obligation même s'il s'agit d'une obligation de faire.

Sur la recevabilité de la demande :

La société appelante se prévaut de l'article XXIII du contrat de maîtrise d'œuvre qui prévoit une clause de conciliation préalable en ces termes : « *En cas de litige, la partie qui s'estime lésée adressera une lettre de mise en demeure avec accusé de réception à l'autre contractant. Et, préalablement à toute procédure judiciaire, les parties s'engagent à saisir le conseil régional de l'ordre des architectes dont relève le maître d'œuvre. À défaut de résolution amiable, les tribunaux compétents seront ceux dépendant de la cour d'appel de Paris* ».

[...]

Il apparaît qu'une telle clause de conciliation préalable obligatoire ne peut s'appliquer à une action en paiement de sommes provisionnelles sur le fondement de l'article 873 du Code de procédure civile en raison de son caractère provisoire.

La demande, nonobstant l'absence de saisine du conseil régional de l'ordre des architectes préalablement à l'introduction de l'instance devant le juge des référés, est donc recevable.

– Paris, Pôle 1, Chambre 3, 8 septembre 2021, n° 20/17883, *Riboutté Cadet c. Zoomfactor Architectes et a.*

Secteur automobile – Chartre – Membres – Clause de médiation – Obligatoire et préalable – Fin de non-recevoir – Irrecevabilité

La société appelante est membre de la fédération nationale de l'automobile tandis que l'intimée est membre de l'Alliance nationale des experts en automobile. Une charte de bonnes pratiques experts automobiles/réparateurs a été signée le 28 janvier 2014 entre la Fédération Nationale de l'artisanat automobile (FNAA) et l'Alliance nationale des experts en automobile. L'article 8 de ladite Charte stipule : « *En cas de litige, les experts et les réparateurs membres des organisations signataires doivent obligatoirement, avant toute action judiciaire, faire application de la procédure de médiation dont les modalités sont précisées ci-après* ».

L'appelante ne justifie d'aucune tentative de résolution amiable du litige et de désignation d'un médiateur avant l'assignation devant le tribunal de commerce d'Antibes. L'absence de nomination de conciliateurs régionaux avant l'assignation n'est établie par aucun élément et ne saurait justifier l'absence de tentative de conciliation. La clause contractuelle instituant une médiation obligatoire et préalable à la saisine du juge, constitue une fin de non-recevoir qui s'impose au juge. En conséquence, c'est à juste titre que les premiers juges ont déclaré la demande irrecevable.

– Aix-en-Provence, Chambre 3-2, 9 septembre 2021, n° 17/20799, *Carrosserie Automobile Qualité c. BME Expertises 06*

Clause de conciliation – Régler à l'amiable – Obligatoire préalable – Fin de non-recevoir – Rédaction – Mise en œuvre – Faculté – Inopposabilité

1. Sur la fin de non-recevoir tirée du défaut de conciliation préalable :

[...]

L'article 13 du contrat stipulant que « *préalablement à toute action en justice* », « *les parties s'efforceront de régler à l'amiable* » leur « *différend à l'occasion de l'interprétation ou de l'exécution du présent contrat* » et instituant une procédure de conciliation obligatoire préalable à la saisine du juge dont le non-respect caractérise la fin de non-recevoir.

Néanmoins, en n'étant assortie d'aucune condition particulière pour sa mise en œuvre, cette clause ne constitue pas une procédure de conciliation obligatoire préalable à la saisine du juge, de sorte que la société n'était pas tenue d'y déférer avant de mettre en demeure puis de saisir la juridiction dont le jugement sera confirmé en ce qu'il a écarté cette fin de non-recevoir.

– Paris, Pôle 5, Chambre 11, 17 septembre 2021, n° 19/10836, *Calytis c. Testing Training & Consulting*

Acte notarié – Président de la Chambre des Notaires – Clause de médiation – Commandement de payer – Saisie – Fin de non-recevoir – Inopposabilité – Mesure d'exécution forcée

L'appelante rappelle qu'aux termes de l'acte notarié du 30 octobre 2019 fondant les poursuites les parties ont convenu « *en cas de litige* [...], *préalablement à toute instance judiciaire, de soumettre leur différend au conciliateur qui sera missionné par le Président de la Chambre des Notaires* », clause intitulée

« *conciliation médiation* » dont il n'est pas discuté qu'elle n'a pas été mise en œuvre préalablement aux poursuites.

Toutefois, il résulte des dispositions des articles 1103, anciennement 1134 du Code civil et 122 du Code de procédure civile qu'une clause imposant ou permettant une conciliation préalablement à la présentation d'une demande en justice relative aux droits et obligations contractuels des parties ne peut, en l'absence de stipulation expresse en ce sens, faire obstacle à l'accomplissement d'une mesure d'exécution forcée.

Or, la clause litigieuse qui stipule qu'une conciliation ou une médiation doit obligatoirement être mise en œuvre préalablement à l'engagement d'une instance judiciaire, n'a pas prévu expressément son application à l'occasion de la mise en œuvre d'une mesure d'exécution forcée, de sorte qu'elle ne pouvait faire obstacle à la délivrance d'un commandement de payer valant saisie immobilière et à l'assignation de l'appelante à l'audience d'orientation.

Il s'en suit la confirmation du rejet de la fin de non-recevoir soulevée par la société saisie.

– Aix-en-Provence, Chambre 1-9, 23 septembre 2021, n° 20/11666, *SCI Bruguet c. BNP Paribas Personal Finance, Hoist Finance AB et Le Trésor Public SIP de Valbonne*

Contrat de bail – Clause de médiation – Rédaction – Fin de non-recevoir – Loi n° 89-462 du 6 juillet 1989 dans sa rédaction issue de la loi n° 2014-366 du 24 mars 2014 – Saisine préalable de la commission départementale de conciliation – Champ – Étendue – Recevabilité

Le premier juge a exactement énoncé que la clause d'un contrat instituant une clause de conciliation obligatoire et préalable à la saisine du juge constitue une fin de non-recevoir qui s'impose au juge si les parties l'invoquent.

La clause de « conciliation-médiation » stipulée en page 15 du bail énonce qu'en cas de litige entre les parties, l'une d'elle devra, préalablement à toute instance judiciaire, soumettre leur différend à la Commission départementale de conciliation, conformément à l'article 18 de la loi n° 89-462 du 6 juillet 1989 modifiée par la loi n° 2014-366 du 24 mars 2014.

Cette clause ne précise pas pour quel type de litige elle impose la saisine préalable de la commission.

Toutefois, la référence à l'article 18 de la loi n° 89-462 du 6 juillet 1989 dans sa rédaction issue de la loi n° 2014-366 du 24 mars 2014, lequel porte sur le montant maximum de l'évolution des loyers et prévoit qu'en cas de litige relatif à cette évolution la saisine préalable de la commission départementale de conciliation est obligatoire, à l'exclusion de toute référence à l'article 20 de cette même loi lequel fixe la compétence générale de ladite commission, implique que le préalable de saisine de la commission est limité à un litige relevant de l'article 18 de la loi n° 89-462 du 6 juillet 1989.

Ainsi, la demande en paiement ayant trait aux réparations et dégradations locatives, le jugement sera infirmé et la demande en paiement sera déclarée recevable.

– Douai, Chambre 8, Section 4, 14 octobre 2021, n° 20/01480, *SCI la Gayette c. X*

Clause de conciliation – Rédaction – Tentative de résoudre – Agir en justice – Non contraignant

4. Après avoir reproduit la clause litigieuse dont les termes se bornaient à inviter les parties à « *coopérer avec diligence et bonne foi en vue de trouver une solution à leur différend* [...] *dans un délai de 45 jours à compter de la naissance de ce différend* », l'arrêt retient que cette clause, qui n'imposait pas le recours préalable à un médiateur, conciliateur ou arbitre, ne faisait que rappeler l'obligation générale d'exécuter de bonne foi les contrats et de tenter une résolution amiable des litiges. En l'état de ces seuls motifs, dont il résulte qu'en raison de son caractère non contraignant, cette clause ne pouvait faire obstacle au droit qu'a toute personne d'agir en justice, la cour d'appel a justifié sa décision et le moyen, qui critique des motifs surabondants, est inopérant.

– Cass. com., 20 octobre 2021, n° 20-13.819, *X c. K et a. contre Rennes (1re chambre) 28 janvier 2020, Rejet*

Conditions générales – Clause de médiation – Mise en œuvre – Invitation

Sur la demande au titre de la violation d'une clause de médiation :

Attendu qu'une partie fait valoir que le §11 des conditions générales de vente et de prestations de services, annexées au devis signé le 11 septembre 2018, institue une procédure de médiation préalable obligatoire à la saisine d'une juridiction.

Attendu que dans son courriel du 21 juillet 2019, la demanderesse propose à la partie adverse de s'adjoindre le service d'un médiateur ou avocat pour pourvoir engager une conciliation, conforme à l'esprit du §11 des conditions générales de vente.

Le tribunal déboutera la partie de sa demande au titre de la violation de la clause de médiation préalable.

– T. com. Paris, 27 octobre 2021, n° 2021009566, *Ora enseigne Mister Clean c. X*

Clause de conciliation – Préalable – Contrat d'architecte – Fin de non-recevoir – Étendue – Responsabilité contractuelle – Article 1792 CC – Responsabilité contractuelle – Opposabilité – Conseil régional de l'ordre des Architectes – Préalable obligatoire – Assureur

La recevabilité de l'action engagée sur le fondement des articles 1792 et suivants du Code civil n'est plus remise en cause à hauteur d'appel, de sorte que le jugement déféré devra être confirmé sur ce point.

C'est par ailleurs de manière pertinente que le premier juge a écarté la fin de non-recevoir tirée de la clause de conciliation préalable stipulée au contrat d'architecte, dès lors que celle-ci ne concerne que les litiges fondés sur la responsabilité contractuelle.

[...]

A) sur les demandes en tant qu'elles sont formées à l'encontre de la société architecte :

[...]

La clause litigieuse, figurant au paragraphe G10 du contrat, est libellée de la manière suivante : « *En cas de litige portant sur le respect des clauses du présent contrat, les parties conviennent de saisir pour avis le conseil régional de l'ordre des architectes dont relève l'architecte, avant toute procédure judiciaire, sauf conservatoire. Cette saisine intervient sur l'initiative de la partie la plus diligente* ».

Cette stipulation exige donc la saisine préalable du conseil régional de l'ordre préalablement à l'introduction de toute action judiciaire au fond. Elle s'analyse dès lors incontestablement en un préalable obligatoire de conciliation. Par ailleurs, la société ne peut sérieusement prétendre que cette clause ne serait pas applicable à l'objet du présent litige, alors qu'entendant mettre en jeu la responsabilité contractuelle de l'architecte, c'est bien le respect des clauses du contrat d'architecte que l'appelante vise à mettre en cause.

La société n'ayant pas mis en œuvre la procédure de conciliation préalable avant d'agir judiciairement au fond, les demandes formées à l'encontre de l'architecte et de son assureur sur le fondement contractuel devront être déclarées irrecevables.

– Dijon, 1re chambre civile, 9 novembre 2021, n° 19/01892, *BDR et Les Allouettes c. Didier Jacques Architecte D.P.L.G., Mutuelle Architectes Français, et Thevenet fils*

Clause de conciliation – Obligatoire – Fin de non-recevoir – Champ – Étendu

Sur la fin de non-recevoir pour défaut de la mise en œuvre de la clause de conciliation obligatoire :

Nous relevons que la défenderesse soulève l'irrecevabilité des demandes pour défaut de mise en œuvre de la clause de conciliation prévue à l'article 14 des conditions générales de ventes du contrat liant les parties.

Nous retenons que le cas d'espèce n'est pas concerné par cette clause de conciliation, la demande visant à obtenir le respect par la défenderesse de ses obligations contractuelles.

En conséquence, nous écarterons la fin de non-recevoir soulevée et dirons recevable la demande.

– T. com. Paris, 12 novembre 2021, n° 2021032970, *Metro Optic c. Compagnie de Phalsbourg*

Contrat d'architecte – Avis – Conseil régional de l'ordre des architectes – Clause de conciliation – Qualification – Obligatoire et préalable – Fin de non-recevoir – Cahier des clauses générales et particulières – Signature – Connaissance – Article L 124-3 du Code des assurances – Tiers lésé – Action directe – Assureur – Responsabilité civile

L'article G10 du cahier des clauses générales du contrat d'architecte conclu stipule qu'en cas de litige portant sur le respect des clauses du contrat, les parties conviennent de saisir pour avis le conseil régional de l'ordre des architectes dont relève l'architecte, avant toute procédure judiciaire, sauf conservatoire.

Cette clause, qui institue une procédure de conciliation, obligatoire et préalable à la saisine du juge, constitue une fin de non-recevoir relevant des dispositions de l'article 122 du Code de procédure civile.

La société appelante ne saurait valablement soutenir que la clause G10 lui est inopposable, alors qu'elle a signé le 18 décembre 2009 le cahier des clauses particulières du contrat d'architecte, précisant bien en son § 2 que la mission de maîtrise d'œuvre est définie dans « *le cahier des clauses générales annexé au présent CCP* ».

L'ensemble des dispositions du cahier des conditions particulières et du cahier des clauses générales lui sont donc opposables, même en l'absence de signature et de paraphe de ce cahier des clauses générales.

Peu importe également que l'article G10 prévoit que la saisine du conseil régional de l'ordre des architectes intervient sur l'initiative de la partie la plus diligente. Dès lors que la société était à l'origine de l'action contre son architecte, il lui appartenait de mettre en œuvre la clause litigieuse, sous peine d'irrecevabilité de ses demandes.

Le jugement doit donc être confirmé en ce qu'il a jugé que cette fin de non-recevoir pouvait être invoquée en tout état de cause et en ce que l'appelante, n'ayant pas cherché à appliquer ce préalable de conciliation avant de saisir le tribunal de Grenoble, devait voir ses demandes déclarées irrecevables.

En revanche, il résulte des dispositions de l'article L 124-3 du Code des assurances que le tiers lésé dispose d'un droit d'action directe à l'encontre de l'assureur garantissant la responsabilité civile de la personne responsable.

Dès lors, la saisine préalable de l'ordre des architectes n'est pas une condition de recevabilité de l'action directe engagée contre l'assureur de l'architecte et le jugement sera infirmé en ce qu'il a déclaré irrecevables les demandes de la société à l'encontre de l'assureur.

Il y a donc lieu d'apprécier les désordres invoqués, ainsi que l'éventuelle responsabilité de l'architecte, la société en charge de la pose du carrelage n'étant plus dans la cause.

– Grenoble, 16 novembre 2021, n° 19/04846, *Dromedis anciennement Établissements Roudaut c. X*

Clause de conciliation – Préalable obligatoire – Fin de non-recevoir – À tout moment – Procédure d'appel – Contrat d'architecte – Rédaction – Responsabilité contractuelle – Clause d'arbitrage – Centre de médiation et d'arbitrage de Paris – Faculté – Champ – Tiers – Inapplication

Il ressort de l'article 123 du Code de procédure civile que les fins de non-recevoir peuvent être soulevées en tout état de cause, sauf exception.

Le moyen tiré du non-respect d'une clause de conciliation préalable obligatoire et préalable à la saisine du juge peut être proposé pour la première fois en cause d'appel.

Cette clause est pleinement opposable lorsque la responsabilité contractuelle de l'architecte est recherchée, à condition que son libellé soit dénué d'équivoque quant à la volonté des parties d'en faire un préalable obligatoire à l'introduction de l'instance.

Une des parties, dont la responsabilité contractuelle est recherchée, se prévaut d'une clause insérée au contrat conclu le 22 février 2011 selon laquelle : « *si les parties ou l'une d'elle n'ont pas le statut de commerçant, elles s'engagent, avant toute procédure judiciaire, à examiner ensemble, avec le centre de médiation et d'arbitrage de Paris, la possibilité de soumettre le litige à l'arbitrage, à condition que le litige n'implique aucun tiers* ».

Cette clause ne saurait constituer une fin de non-recevoir, puisqu'il s'agit simplement pour les parties d'examiner ensemble « la possibilité » de soumettre le litige à l'arbitrage, vocabulaire qui traduit l'existence d'une simple faculté et non d'une obligation de saisine préalable.

Par ailleurs, le litige opposant en l'espèce le maître de l'ouvrage à l'architecte implique également des tiers, en l'occurrence les constructeurs défaillants et leurs assureurs, si bien que la clause n'était pas applicable quant à son champ.

Il y a enfin lieu de relever que les époux A justifient avoir saisi l'ordre des architectes d'Ile-de-France aux fins de conciliation, mais que les parties concernées, et notamment l'architecte, n'ont pas pu se rendre disponibles pour participer à la mesure.

Cette fin de non-recevoir ne peut donc qu'être rejetée.

– Rouen, 17 novembre 2021, n° 20/00377, *X c. Y*

Contrat de bail – Clause de médiation – Centre de médiation notariale – Fin de non-recevoir – Sémantique – Clause résolutoire – Faculté – Évidence – Juge des référés

Le bail indique que « *les parties sont informées qu'en cas de litige entre elles ou un tiers, elles pourront, préalablement à toute instance judiciaire, le soumettre à un médiateur qui sera désigné et missionné par le centre de médiation notariale dont elles trouveront toutes les coordonnées et renseignements utiles sur le site http://www.mediation.notaires.fr* ».

Cette disposition constitue un énoncé qui ne requiert aucune interprétation du juge pour constater qu'il n'ouvre qu'une simple possibilité de règlement du litige alternative à la voie judiciaire et ne fait pas obstacle à la mise en œuvre par le bailleur des dispositions de la clause résolutoire.

Cette constatation relève de l'évidence sur laquelle le juge des référés a compétence pour statuer.

– Douai, Chambre 2, Section 1, 18 novembre 2021, n° 21/00689, *Maison Landemaine Lille c. X*

Arbitrage interne – Centre de Médiation et d'Arbitrage de Paris – Règlements d'arbitrage et de médiation – Sentence arbitrale – Sentence partielle – Recours en annulation – Clause compromissoire – Clause de médiation – Compétence – Obligatoire – Mise en œuvre – Fin de non-recevoir – Application – Médiation antérieure – nouveau différend – Tribunal arbitral – Mission – Annulation

Règle applicable

L'article 1492, 1° et 3° du Code de procédure civile dispose que le recours en annulation est ouvert si le tribunal arbitral s'est déclaré à tort compétent ou incompétent ou s'il a statué sans se conformer à la mission qui lui avait été confiée.

Réponse de la cour

L'article 12 du protocole prévoit que « *les différends qui viendraient à se produire à propos de la validité, de l'interprétation, de l'exécution ou de l'inexécution du présent accord seront soumis au règlement de médiation et en cas d'échec au règlement d'arbitrage du CMAP auquel les parties déclarent adhérer* ».

Il résulte de ces stipulations que les parties ont entendu conférer au préalable de la médiation un caractère obligatoire, le recours à l'arbitrage ne pouvant avoir lieu qu'en cas d'échec de la médiation, la médiation et l'arbitrage ne pouvant de surcroît être organisés que dans le cadre des règlements du Centre de Médiation et d'Arbitrage de Paris.

Il est constant qu'une médiation a été initiée et qu'à la suite de l'échec de cette médiation, une sentence définitive a été prononcée.

Il est également constant qu'aucune médiation n'est intervenue en application du règlement de médiation visé par l'article 12 avant la saisine du tribunal arbitral ayant prononcé la sentence partielle, objet du recours.

Or, cet article 12 prévoit la mise en œuvre d'une médiation pour « *les différends qui viendraient à se produire* », ce dont il faut déduire que le préalable de la médiation s'impose pour tous les différends successifs entre les parties.

Dès lors, la saisine le 25 mars 2009 du Centre de médiation et d'arbitrage de Paris à propos du premier différend qui a conduit, en l'absence de succès de la médiation, à la sentence du 16 octobre 2014 ne dispensait pas les parties de recourir à une nouvelle médiation avant de solliciter, le 13 mars 2017, un nouvel arbitrage.

La sentence partielle a d'ailleurs elle-même énoncé que « *la clause de médiation n'épuise pas ses effets de par sa première mise en œuvre* », qu'« *elle a vocation à jouer de manière générale dès lors qu'un litige, au besoin nouveau, survient et entre dans son champ d'application* » et qu'« *en l'espèce, le litige soumis au tribunal entre parfaitement dans le périmètre de la clause de médiation* ».

[...]

Toutefois, s'il est vrai, d'une manière générale, qu'une clause d'un contrat instituant une procédure de médiation obligatoire et préalable constitue une fin de non-recevoir, il n'en demeure pas moins qu'en l'espèce, le tribunal arbitral s'est déclaré compétent, alors pourtant que les demandeurs au recours en annulation ont soutenu devant lui qu'une médiation préalable et obligatoire s'imposait en vertu de l'article 12 du protocole, qu'il a lui-même relevé que le litige relevait du champ d'application de la clause de médiation et qu'il a de surcroît invité les parties à mettre en œuvre une procédure de médiation parallèle à la procédure d'arbitrage.

Or, le tribunal arbitral ne pouvait pas se reconnaître compétent, alors que la procédure de médiation préalable prévue par l'article 12 du protocole n'avait pas été mise en œuvre.

Le non-respect de la clause de médiation n'est donc pas en l'espèce une fin de non-recevoir ne relevant pas de l'appréciation de la cour d'appel mais constitue une circonstance de l'espèce qui doit être prise en compte pour apprécier la violation de l'article 1492, 1° du Code de procédure civile.

La sentence partielle doit donc être annulée en application de l'article 1492, 1° du Code de procédure civile. L'annulation de la sentence étant prononcée en raison de l'incompétence du tribunal arbitral, la cour doit s'abstenir de statuer au fond et les parties doivent être renvoyées à mieux se pourvoir sans qu'il y ait lieu à désigner la juridiction devant être saisie.

– Paris, Pôle 5, Chambre 16, 23 novembre 2021, n° 18/22099, *X c. HD Holding*

Clause de médiation – Obligatoire et préalable – Fin de non-recevoir – Rédaction – Référé – Référé-provision – Urgence – Volonté des parties

Il est constant qu'une clause d'un contrat instituant une procédure de médiation obligatoire et préalable à la saisine du juge constitue une fin de non-recevoir qui s'impose au juge si les parties l'invoquent.

La clause litigieuse résulte de l'article 31 du contrat des parties ainsi rédigé : « *Les différends nés entre les parties à l'occasion notamment de l'exécution, de l'application ou de l'interprétation du contrat et qui n'auront pas pu faire l'objet d'un règlement amiable seront résolus par une procédure de médiation, sans préjudice pour l'une ou l'autre des parties d'avoir recours à des procédures d'urgence destinées à la sauvegarde de leurs droits* ».

Il résulte sans ambiguïté possible de cette rédaction que les parties sont convenues d'écarter l'obligation de rechercher une solution amiable préalablement à toute saisine du juge en cas de « *recours à des procédures d'urgence destinées à la sauvegarde de leurs droits* ».

Or en droit français, ces procédures dites d'urgence visant à la préservation des droits d'une partie répondent précisément à la définition de la procédure de référé ouverte devant le juge du tribunal de commerce selon les termes des articles 872 et 873 du Code de procédure civile.

L'essence même de la procédure de référé, notamment s'agissant du référé-provision, est de permettre à une partie d'obtenir plus rapidement qu'en saisissant le juge du fond, un paiement provisoire confortant ses droits, en l'absence de toute contestation sérieuse.

En conséquence, par application des prévisions contractuelles, l'action en référé-provision sera déclarée recevable.

– Versailles, 14e chambre, 25 novembre 2021, n° 21/01194, *Thello c. Gate Gourmet Italia*

Médiation – Transaction – Définition – Écrit – Condition de preuve – Commencement de preuve par écrit – Force obligatoire – Autorité de la chose jugé – Homologation – Erreur de droit – Lésion – Requête – Non contradictoire – Pouvoirs du juge

L'article 1362 du Code civil dispose que constitue un commencement de preuve par écrit tout écrit qui, émanant de celui qui conteste un acte ou de celui qu'il représente, rend vraisemblable ce qui est allégué. L'article 2044 du Code civil dispose que la transaction est un contrat par lequel les parties, par des concessions réciproques, terminent une contestation née, ou préviennent une contestation à naître. Ce contrat doit être rédigé par écrit.

Aux termes de l'article 2052 du Code civil, les transactions ont, entre les parties, l'autorité de la chose jugée en dernier ressort. Elles ne peuvent être attaquées pour cause d'erreur de droit, ni pour cause de lésion.

Conformément aux dispositions de l'article 1565 du Code de procédure civile, l'accord auquel sont parvenues les parties à une médiation, une conciliation ou une procédure participative peut être soumis, aux fins de le rendre exécutoire, à l'homologation du juge compétent pour connaître du contentieux dans la matière considérée. Le juge à qui est soumis l'accord ne peut en modifier les termes.

En vertu de l'article 1566 du Code de procédure civile, le juge statue sur la requête qui lui est présentée sans débat, à moins qu'il n'estime nécessaire d'entendre les parties.

S'il est fait droit à la requête, tout intéressé peut en référer au juge qui a rendu la décision.

[...]

En matière de transaction, l'écrit n'est pas exigé comme une condition de validité mais comme une condition de preuve.

En outre, un écrit non signé est à tout le moins constitutif d'un commencement de preuve. [...]

Si la transaction met en principe fin au litige, c'est sous réserve de son exécution et ne peut ainsi être opposée par l'une des parties que si celle-ci en a respecté les conditions.

– Caen, 30 novembre 2021, n° 21/00294, *X c. Maurouard*

Clause de conciliation – Contrat d'architecte – Conseil Régional de l'Ordre des Architectes – Avis – Fin de non-recevoir – Définition – Champ – Article 1792 CC – Inopposabilité – Action directe – Assureur – Inapplicabilité

Sur la fin de non-recevoir pour défaut de mise en œuvre de la clause de conciliation du contrat d'architecte :

Les premiers juges ont retenu que la clause n'avait pas vocation à s'appliquer puisque l'action en responsabilité était fondée sur l'article 1792 du Code civil et que l'assureur ne pouvait s'en prévaloir dans le cadre de l'action directe dirigée contre elle.

[...]

Selon l'article 122 du Code de procédure civile, constitue une fin de non-recevoir tout moyen qui tend à faire déclarer l'adversaire irrecevable en sa demande, sans examen au fond, pour défaut de droit d'agir, tel le défaut de qualité, le défaut d'intérêt, la prescription, le délai préfix, la chose jugée.

Une clause d'un contrat d'architecte qui institue une procédure de conciliation obligatoire et préalable à la saisine du juge constitue une fin de non-recevoir.

En l'espèce, l'article 5-2 du contrat d'architecte conclu prévoit que « *en cas de litige portant sur l'exécution du présent contrat, les parties conviennent de saisir pour avis le Conseil Régional de l'Ordre des Architectes dont relève l'architecte, avant toute procédure judiciaire* ».

Cependant, la clause de saisine de l'ordre des architectes préalablement à toute action judiciaire en cas de litige sur l'exécution du contrat n'a pas vocation à s'appliquer lorsque la responsabilité de l'architecte est recherchée sur le fondement de l'article 1792 du Code civil.

L'action dirigée contre l'architecte étant fondée à titre principal sur l'article 1792 du Code civil, la clause n'est pas applicable, le fait que celui-ci soutienne qu'il n'y a pas de désordre décennal étant manifestement inopérant dans le cadre de l'examen de la fin de non-recevoir.

En ce qui concerne l'assureur, les premiers juges ont retenu à bon droit que la saisine préalable, par le maître d'ouvrage, de l'ordre des architectes prévue au contrat le liant à l'architecte, n'est pas une condition de recevabilité de l'action directe engagée contre l'assureur de celui-ci.

En conséquence, le jugement sera confirmé en ce qu'il a retenu que la fin de non-recevoir pour défaut de saisine préalable du conseil régional de l'ordre des architectes ne pouvait être opposée.

– **Paris, Pôle 4, Chambre 6, 10 décembre 2021, n° 19/10371,** ***Les 3 Caryatides c. SMABTP, Cabinet d'Architecture Alibert 164 et MAF***

Tables de jurisprudence 2020-2021 | 2020-2021 Table of Cases

Bertrand ROBERT
Avocat

Priscille PEDONE
Avocat

Ces tables reprennent l'ensemble des décisions citées dans les *Cahiers de l'Arbitrage* parus en 2020-2021.

This tables covers all the cases contained in the 2020-2021's *Cahiers de l'Arbitrage/ Paris Journal of International Arbitration.*

Les numéros renvoient aux pages et aux numéros de revue

2014

CIRDI / ICSID

Serafín García Armas et Karina García Gruber c. République bolivarienne du Venezuela, CPA n° 2013-3, décision sur la juridiction, 15 décembre 2014 ; opinion dissidente de l'arbitre Rodriguo Oreamuno Blanco, 15 décembre 2014 .... 2020.3.551

2017

Allemagne/Germany

LG Dortmund, Urteil v. 13.09.2017– 8 O 30/16 .... 2020.1.121

BGH, Beschluss v. 11.10.2017 – I ZB 12/17 .... 2020.1.122

OLG Saarbrücken, Urteil v. 23.11.2017 – 4 U 44/16 .... 2020.1.123

Autriche / Austria

OGH, Beschluss v. 07.09.2017 – 18 ONc 1/17t 2020.1.127

OGH, Beschluss v. 21.12.2017 – 6 Ob 178/17w 2020.1.128

OGH, Beschluss v. 21.12.2017 – 6 Ob 104/17p 2020.1.129

CIRDI / ICSID

Mohamed Abdel Raouf Bahgat c. République arabe d'Égypte, CPA n° 2017-07, décision sur la juridiction, 30 novembre 2017 .... 2020.3.551

France

CA Paris, Pôle 1, Ch. 1, n° 15/01040, 25 avril 2017, *République bolivarienne du Venezuela c. Serafín García Armas et Karina García Gruber* 2020.3.551

2018

Allemagne / Germany

BGH – Beschluss v. 9.05.2018 – I ZB 53/17 .... 2020.1.125

OLG Frankfurt am Main, Beschluss v. 06.06. 2018 – 26 Sch 3/18 .... 2020.1.125

BGH, Beschluss v. 07.06.2018 – I ZB 70/17 .... 2020.1.126

Autriche / Austria

OGH, Beschluss v. 06.02.2018 – 18 ONc 4/17h 2020.1.130

OGH, Beschluss v. 13.02.2018 – 5 Ob 188/17h 2020.1.131

OGH, Beschluss v. 28.02.2018 – 6Ob 14/18d 2020.1.131

OGH, Beschluss v. 20.03.2018 – 18 OCg1/17x 2020.1.132

OGH, Beschluss v. 17.04.2018 – 18 Onc 2/18s 2020.1.132

CIRDI / ICSID

Dawood Rawat c. République de Maurice, CPA n° 2016-20, sentence sur la juridiction, 6 avril 2018 .... 2020.3.551

David R. Aven et al. c. République du Costa Rica, n° UNCT/15/3, sentence finale, 18 septembre 2018 .... 2020.3.551

Italie / Italy

Court of Brescia, 5 April 2018, *Wave s.r.l. in liquidazione v International Chamber of Commerce* 2020.4.999

Court of Appeal of Milan, 19 November 2018, *GE Wind Energy Gmbh and GE International Inc. Italian Branch v. Wind Energy Racalmuto s.r.l.* 2020.4.1001

2019

Angleterre & Pays de Galles / England & Wales

Minister of Finance (Inc) and another v International Petroleum Investment Company and another [2019] EWCA Civ 2080 (26 November 2019).................................... 2020.3.631

Autriche / Austria

OGH, Beschluss v. 15.05.2019 – 18 OCg 1/19 z 2020.4.875

OGH, Beschluss v. 19.11.2019 – 3 Ob 13/19m.. 2020.4.877

Belgique / Belgium

Cour de cassation, C.17.0558.N, 3 octobre 2019, « *Raad Voor Arbitrage vzw / J.V., G.V., V&W Construct bvba* » 2020.3.653

Cour de cassation (1re chambre), C.19.0048.N, 7 novembre 2019, « *Servagri nv / ESC Belgium s.p.r.l.u.* » 2020.3.649

Tribunal de première instance francophone de Bruxelles (4e chambre), 18/1312/A, 20 décembre 2019, « *La République du Kazakhstan / A.S., G.S., la société de droit étranger A., la société de droit étranger T.* ».. 2020.3.650

Canada

Li v. Rao, 2019 BCCA 264, July 26, 2019 .... 2020.1.135

International Air Transport Association v. Instrubel, N.V., 2019 SCC 61, December 11, 2019 .... 2020.1.136

The Russia Federation v. Luxtona Limited, 2019 ONSC 7558, December 13, 2019 .... 2020.1.137
2020.1.138

CIRDI / ICSID

Anglo American PLC c. République bolivarienne du Venezuela, CIRDI n° ARB(AF)/14/1, sentence, 18 janvier 2019 .... 2020.3.586

United Utilities (Tallinn) B.V. et Aktsiaselts Tallinna Vesi c. République d'Estonie, CIRDI n° ARB/14/24, sentence, 21 juin 2019 .... 2020.3.569

Michael Ballantine et Lisa Ballantine c. République dominicaine, CPA n° 2016-17, sentence finale, 3 septembre 2019 ; opinion dissidente partielle de l'arbitre Marney Cheek, 3 septembre 2019 .... 2020.3.551
2020.3.591

CMC Muratori Cementisti CMC Di Ravenna SOC. Coop., CMC Muratori Cementisti CMC Di Ravenna SOC. Coop. A.R.L. Maputo Branch and CMC Africa, and CMC Africa Austral, LDA c. *République du Mozambique,* CIRDI n° ARB/17/23, sentence, 24 octobre 2019 .... 2020.3.586

Oded Besserglik c. République du Mozambique, CIRDI n° ARB(AF)/14/2, sentence du 28 octobre 2019 .... 2020.3.540

Enrique Heemsen et Jorge Heemsen c. République bolivarienne du Venezuela, CPA n° 2017-18, sentence sur la juridiction, 29 octobre 2019 .... 2020.3.551

Magyar Farming Company Ltd, Kintyre Kft and Inicia Zrt c. Hongrie, CIRDI n° ARB/17/27, sentence, 13 novembre 2019 .... 2020.3.591

Manuel García Armas et al. c. *République bolivarienne du Venezuela*, CPA n° 2016-8, sentence sur la juridiction, 13 décembre 2019 .... 2020.3.551

Fédération de Russie – CEI / Russian Federation – CIS

Supreme Court of the Russian Federation, 17 September 2019, Case No. 4-KG19-36, *Kurjanov V.V. (Russia) v. JSC Arbita (Russia)* 2020.3.713

Commercial court of the Moscow circuit, 20 June 2019, Case No. A41-107668/2018, *Dow AgroSciences GmbH (Germany) v. LLC Semena Chernozem'ja (Russia)* 2020.3.716

Commercial court of the Moscow circuit, 24 July 2019, Case No. A40-84581/2019, *Uzbekiston havo jullari (Uzbekistan) v. BB Energy (GULF) DMCC (UAE)* 2020.3.715

France

Cass. 1re civ., 13 février 2019, n° A 17-25.851, *République bolivarienne du Venezuela c. Serafín García Armas et Karina García Gruber*, Cour d'appel de Paris (Pôle 1, Chambre 1), n° 15/01040, 25 avril 2017 .... 2020.3.551

CA Paris, pôle 1, 1re ch., arrêt du 28 mai 2019, n° 16-11182, *Sté Alstom Transport SA et Sté Alstom Network UK Limited c/ Sté Alexander Brothers Limited* 2020.2.289

CA Paris, 24 septembre 2019, n° 18/14721 .... 2020.2.315

CA Paris, Pôle 1, Ch. 2, 31 octobre 2019, n° 19/05913 .... 2020.1.95

T. com. Caen, 13 novembre 2019, n° 2018007027, *ITM alimentaire Ouest c. Cacobene* 2020.1.147

CA Bordeaux, 18 novembre 2019, n° 17-07157, *Z c. Y* 2020.1.147

CA Grenoble, 19 novembre 2019, n° 17-05589, *Z c. Axyalis Patrimoine* 2020.1.148

CA Aix-en-Provence, 29 novembre 2019, n° 19-00505, *La Tournerie Hôtel et a. c. BTSG2* 2020.1.148

Cass. 1re civ., 4 décembre 2019, n° 18-15848, F-D, *Z c. X* 2020.1.150

Cass. 1re civ., 4 décembre 2019, n° 18-23395, F-D, *Federal State Unitary Enterprise Russian Satellite Communications Company (RSCC) c.* Orion Satellite Communications INC 2020.1.150

Cass. 1re civ., 4 décembre 2019, n° 18-23176, F-D, *Priosma Limited c. Cat* (contre arrêt CA Paris, Pôle 1, Chambre 1, rendu le 29 mai 2018, Rejet) 2020.1.151

Cass. 1re civ., 4 décembre 2019, n° 18-26809, F-D, *Thermador groupe et a. c. Diffusion Equipements Loisirs et a.* contre l'arrêt de CA Rennes, 3e chambre commerciale, rendu le 2 octobre 2018, Cassation partielle)........ 2020.1.151

CA Montpellier, 11 décembre 2019, n° 19-01166, *Z c. Y*........ 2020.1.151

Cass. 2e civ., 12 décembre 2019, n° 18-24493, F-D, *Cabinet Patrick Desbordes c. Conti et Sceg* (contre l'ordonnance rendue le 13 septembre 2018 par le premier président de la cour d'appel de Paris, Pôle 2, Chambre 6, Rejet)........ 2020.1.152

CA Versailles, 12 décembre 2019, n° 18-05673, *X c. Z*........ 2020.1.153

CA Paris, Pôle 1, Chambre 1, 12 décembre 2019, n° 19-00058, *République du Mali c. Planor Afrique*........ 2020.1.153

CA Nîmes, 16 décembre 2019, n° 19-02187, *IPA c. Clea*........ 2020.1.154

T. com. Draguignan, 17 décembre 2019, n° 2017006028, *Fre-Co-Sud c. Grande Galerie de Fréjus Place*........ 2020.1.154

CA Paris, Pôle 1, Chambre 1, 17 décembre 2019, n° 17-23073, *Galeries Lafayette et a. c. BNP Paribas Personal Finance*........ 2020.1.155

CA Paris, Pôle 5, Chambre 5, 19 décembre 2019, n° 17/14452, *E-LOGIK c. MY American Market*........ 2020.1.156

Singapour / Singapore

BWF v BWG [2019] SGHC 81........ 2020.4.1009

BNA v BNB and another [2019] SGCA 84........ 2020.4.1011

XS v BXT [2019] SGHC(I) 10........ 2020.4.1013

ST Group Co Ltd and others v Sanum Investments Limited and another appeal [2019] SGCA 65........ 2020.4.1014

Sun Travels & Tours Pvt Ltd v Hilton International Manage (Maldives) Pvt Ltd [2019] SGCA 10........ 2020.4.1015

Ng Tze Chew Diana v Aikco Construction Pte Ltd and another matter [2019] SGHC 258........ 2020.4.1017

Rex International Holding Ltd and another v Gulf Hibiscus Ltd [2019] SGCA 5........ 2020.4.1023

Suisse / Switzerland

Tribunal fédéral (1re Cour de droit civil), 6 juin 2019 (4A_146/2019)........ 2020.2.379

Tribunal fédéral (1re Cour de droit civil), 17 juin 2019 (4A_66/2019)........ 2020.2.381

Tribunal fédéral (1re Cour de droit civil), 19 juin 2019 (4A_628/2018)........ 2020.2.383

Tribunal fédéral (1re Cour de droit civil), 25 juin 2019 (4A_494/2018)........ 2020.2.385

Tribunal fédéral (1re Cour de droit civil), 4 juillet 2019 (4A_462/2018)........ 2020.2.388

Tribunal fédéral (1re Cour de droit civil), 9 juillet 2019 (4A_234/2019) 2020.2.390

Tribunal fédéral (1re Cour de droit civil), 29 juillet 2019 (4A_248/2019) 2020.2.390

Tribunal fédéral (1re Cour de droit civil), 31 juillet 2019 (4A_74/2019) 2020.2.393

Tribunal fédéral (1re Cour de droit civil), 4 septembre 2019 (4A_272/2019) 2020.2.394

Tribunal fédéral (1re Cour de droit civil), 24 septembre 2019 .... 2020.2.395

Tribunal fédéral (1re Cour de droit civil), 16 octobre 2019 (4A_264/2019) 2020.2.396

Tribunal fédéral (1re Cour de droit civil), 16 octobre 2019 (4A_292/2019) 2020.2.398

Tribunal fédéral (1re Cour de droit civil), 17 octobre 2019 (4A_268/2019) 2020.2.399

Tribunal fédéral (1re Cour de droit civil), 28 octobre 2019 (4A_413/2019) 2020.2.402

Tribunal fédéral (2e Cour de droit civil), 5 novembre 2019 (5A_1019/2018) 2020.2.407

Tribunal fédéral (1re Cour de droit civil), 13 novembre 2019 .... 2020.2.409

2020

Allemagne / Germany

BGH, Beschluss v. 20.02.2020 – I ZB 45/19 .... 2020.4.871

BGH, Beschluss v. 23.07.2020 – I ZB 88/19 .... 2020.4.872

OLG Frankfurt am Main 13.07.2020 26 SCH 18 19 .... 2020.4.873

BayObLG, Beschluss v. 18.08.2020 – 1 Sch 93/20 .... 2020.4.874

Angleterre & Pays de Galles / England & Wales

Kabab-Ji SAL (Lebanon) v Kout Food Group (Kuwait) [2020] EWCA Civ 6 (20 January 2020) 2020.1.61

A Company v X and others [2020] EWHC 809 (TCC) 2020.1.79

Filatona Trading Ltd v Navigator Equities Ltd [2020] EWCA Civ 109 (6 February 2020)... 2020.3.633

Micula & Others v Romania [2020] UKSC 5 (19 February 2020) 2020.3.634

Carpatsky Petroleum Corporation v PJSC Ukrnafta [2020] EWHC 769 (Comm) (31 March 2020) 2020.3.637

Petrochemical Logistics Ltd and another v PSB Alpha AG and another [2020] EWHC 975 (Comm) (27 April 2020) 2020.3.639

Daewoo Shipbuilding And Marine Engineering Company Ltd v Songa Offshore Equinox Ltd & Anor [2020] EWHC 2353 (TCC) (1st September 2020) 2020.3.641

Enka Insaat Ve Sanayi AS (Respondent) v OOO Insurance Company Chubb (Appellant) [2020] UKSC 38 (9 October 2020) 2020.3.643

UK Supreme Court, 27 November 2020, [2020] UKSC 4, *Halliburton v Chubb*....... 2020.1.501

Autriche / Austria

OGH, Beschluss v. 15.01.2020 – 18 OCg 9/19a 2020.4.878

OHG, Beschluss v. 10.06.2020 – 18 ONc 3/19i 2020.4.879

OGH, Beschluss v. 18.06.2020 – 18 OCg 4/20t 2020.4.879

OGH, Beschluss v. 23.07.2020 – 18 ONc 3/20s 2020.4.880

Belgique / Belgium

Cour d'appel de Bruxelles (9e chambre), RG 2019/KR/33 et 34, 17 janvier 2020, *« Banque M.I., société de droit iranien / scrl Society for Worldwide Inerbank Financial Telecommunication ("SWIFT") E.I.H. AG, société de droit allemand / SWIFT »* 2020.3.648

Tribunal de première instance néerlandophone de Bruxelles (4e chambre), 9 mars 2020, *« NV. I.E.C v. A.B. SA »* (décision en langue néerlandaise) 2020.3.654

Cour de cassation (1re chambre), C.20.0175.F, 24 septembre 2020, *« L.D.H. / S.M. et C.L. »* 2020.3.647

Canada

Sokolov v. The World Anti-Doping Agency, 2020 ONSC 704, February 11, 2020 .... 2020.1.138

Metso Minerals Canada Inc. c. Arcelormittal exploitation minière Canada, 2020 QCCS 1103, March 10, 2020 .... 2020.1.139

79411 USA Inc. c. Mondofix Inc., 2020 QCCS 1104, March 24, 2020 .... 2020.1.140

Uber Technologies Inc., Uber Canada, Inc., Uber B.V. and Rasier Operations v. Heller, 2020 SCC 16, June 26, 2020 .... 2020.1.141

Corner Brook Pulp and Paper Limited c. Valmet Ltd., 2020 QCCS 2136, July 13, 2020 .... 2020.1.142

The United Mexican States v. Burr, 2020 ONSC 2376, July 20, 2020 .... 2020.1.143

Geophysical Service Incorporated v. Canada (Attorney General), 2020 FC 984, October 20, 2020 .... 2020.4.883

Sunlodges Ltd. v. The United Republic of Tanzania, 2020 ONSC 8201, November 10, 2020 .... 2020.4.884

Bakaris v. Southern Sky, 2020 ONSC 7306, November 26, 2020 .... 2020.4.885

CIRDI / ICSID

Theodoros Adamakopoulos et al. c. Chypre, CIRDI n° ARB/15/49, décision sur la compétence et opinion dissidente de M. Marcelo G. Kohen, 7 février 2020 .... 2020.3.602

Thomas Gosling et al. c. République de Maurice, CIRDI n° ARB/16/32, sentence, 18 février 2020 .... 2020.3.569

Strabag SE, Raiffeisen Centrobank AG, Syrena Immobilien Holding AG c. République de Pologne, CIRDI ADHOC/15/1, décision partielle sur la compétence, 4 mars 2020 .... 2020.3.586

Raymond Charles Eyre et Montrose Developments (Private) Limited c. République socialiste démocratique du Sri Lanka, CIRDI n° ARB/16/25, sentence, 5 mars 2020 .... 2020.3.569

Hydro Energy 1 S.A.R.L. and Hydroxana Sweeden AB c. Royaume d'Espagne, CIRDI n° ARB/15/42, décision sur la juridiction, la responsabilité et directives sur la détermination du montant de la réparation, 9 mars 2020 .... 2020.3.591

Daniel W. Kappes et Kappes, Cassiday & Associés c. République du Guatemala, CIRDI n° ARB/18/43, décision sur les objections préliminaires du défendeur, 13 mars 2020 .... 2020.3.569

Itisaluna Iraq LLC et al. c. République d'Iraq, CIRDI n° ARB/17/10, sentence, 3 avril 2020 .... 2020.3.533

Lotus Holding Anonim Şirketi c. Turkmenistan, CIRDI n° ARB/17/30, sentence, 6 avril 2020 .... 2020.3.569

A.M.F. Aircraftleasing Meier & Fischer GmbH & Co. KG, Hamburg (Germany) c. République tchèque, CPA n° 2017-15, sentence finale, 11 mai 2020........ 2020.3.591

Eiser Infrastructure Limited et Energía Solar Luxembourg S.àr.l. c. Royaume d'Espagne, CIRDI n° ARB/13/36, décision du comité *ad hoc*, 11 juin 2020 .... 2020.3.622

Strabag SE c. Libye, CIRDI n° ARB(AF)/15/1, sentence, 29 juin 2020........ 2020.3.569

Michael Anthony Lee-Chin c. République dominicaine, CIRDI n° UNCT/18/3, sentence partielle sur la compétence, 15 juillet 2020 .... 2020.3.569

Orascom TMT Investments S.à r.l. c. République algérienne démocratique et populaire, CIRDI n° ARB/12/35, décision sur l'annulation, 17 septembre 2020........ 2020.3.569

Fédération de Russie – CEI / Russian Federation – CIS

Supreme Court of the Russian Federation, 12 March 2020, Case No. A27-5147/2019, *LLC OLIMP-GRUPP (Russia) v. LLC VostokJenergoChermet (Russia)* 2020.3.711

Commercial Court of the Moscow circuit, 18 March 2020, Case No. A41-94316/2019, *LLC TD HIMMED (Russia) v. LLC REAFARM (Russia)* 2020.3.712

Supreme Court of the Russian Federation, 28 April 2020, No. 4-KG20-14, *CJSC Bank VTB (Armenia) v. Bagdasarov M.I. (Armenia)* 2020.3.717

Commercial Court of the Moscow circuit, 6 July 2020, Case No. A40-149566/2019, *LLC Instar Logistics (Russia) v. Nabors Drilling International Limited* 2020.3.713

France

CA Pau, 7 janvier 2020, n° 18-01797, *BTI Victoria et a c. X* 2020.1.156

CA Paris, Chambre commerciale internationale, Pôle 5, Chambre 16, 7 janvier 2020, n° 19-07260, *République Démocratique du Congo c. Divine Inspiration Group (PTY)* 2020.1.158

CA Toulouse, 8 janvier 2020, n° 18-01609, *Airbus c. East Sino Holdings Limited*.... 2020.1.159

CA Bastia, 15 janvier 2020, n° 18-00080, *Z c. X* 2020.1.159

Cass. 1re civ., 15 janvier 2020, n° 18-18088, F-D, *Legal Department du Ministère de la Justice de la République d'Irak c. Fincantieri Cantieri Navali Italiani et Finmeccanica*, contre l'arrêt CA Paris, pôle 1, chambre 1, rendu le 16 janvier 2018, Rejet 2020.1.160

Cass. 1re civ., 15 janvier 2020, 18-20.102, F-D, *Fiacre La BâtieHoffman, c. X*, contre l'arrêt CA Versailles, 1re chambre, 1re section, rendu le 25 mai 2018, Cassation partielle 2020.1.161

CA Versailles, 16 janvier 2020, n° 19-04609, *Z c. Y* 2020.1.161

CA Paris, Pôle 5, Chambre 9, 16 janvier 2020, n° 18-14278, *Alpha Petrovision Holding AG APV c. Brouard-Daude, en qualité de mandataire judiciaire de Ipsa Holding* 2020.1.164

CA Aix-en-Provence, 16 janvier 2020, n° 19-06759, *Rn Patri One, Patri Invest, Patri.cap, Patri.dev, Patri.eco c. HSO 31 et HBC 31* 2020.1.164

T. com. Versailles, 17 janvier 2020, n° 2017F00894, *Groupe Pallas c. X* 2020.1.165

CA Poitiers, 21 janvier 2020, n° 19-01458, *Masson Marine c. Association Hermione – Lafayette* 2020.1.166

Cass. 1re civ., 22 janvier 2020, n° 19-10036, F-D, *X c. Commune de Saint-Yrieix la-Perche*, contre l'arrêt CA Poitiers, 1re chambre, rendu le 13 novembre 2018, Cassation 2020.1.167

CA Pau, 28 janvier 2020, n° 18-02350, *Banque Pouyanne c. Y* 2020.1.167

CA Aix-en-Provence, 30 janvier 2020, n° 17-08916, *Z c. Bnp Paribas Personal Finance* 2020.1.168

CA Aix-en-Provence, 6 février 2020, n° 19-14154, *Airbus Helicopters c. Pan Industrias* 2020.1.168

CA Amiens chambre économique, 6 février 2020, n° 19-01633, *L'embarcadère c. Au bord de l'eau* 2020.1.169

CA Poitiers, 11 février 2020, n° 19/01756, *Géant Casino c. Sas Brunet* 2020.1.170

CA Paris, Pôle 1, Chambre 3, 12 février 2020, n° 19-04488, *Z c. Coopérative d'Habitation La Sécurité* 2020.1.172

CA Nancy, 19 février 2020, n° 19-03323, *SDT Financière c. Y* 2020.1.172

CA Paris, Chambre commerciale internationale, Pôle 5, Chambre 16, 25 février 2020, n°s 19-07575, 19/15816, 19/15817, 19/15818 et 19/15819, *Dommo Energia c. Enauta Energia, SA, anciennement Queiroz Galvao Exploraçao e Produçao et Barra Energia Do Brazil Petróleo E Gás Ltda* (cinq arrêts) 2020.1.173

CA Paris, Pôle 1, Chambre 1, 25 février 2020, n 17-18001, *C D Limited c. UZUC SA* ... 2020.1.175

Cass. com., 26 février 2020, n° 18-15381, F-D, *OOCL France, OOCL UK Ltd, c. Compagnie nouvelle de manutentions portuaires (CNMP), Compagnie nouvelle de manutentions et de transport (CNMT), et Hapag Lloyd AG, et CP Ships UK Ltd,* contre l'arrêt CA Rouen, Chambre civile et commerciale, rendu le 27 avril 2017, Cassation partielle 2020.1.177

CA Paris, Pôle 1, Chambre 2, 27 février 2020, n° 19-16470, *Ecomar c. Les Hauts de Rivière Roche* 2020.1.177

CA Paris, Pôle 1, Chambre 1, 3 mars 2020, n° 18-05766, *Ekyog et Francis Alexander Investments Inc c. SCI Elo* 2020.1.179

Cass. 1re civ., 4 mars 2020, FS P+B, 18-22.019, *Antrix Corporation Limited c. Devas Multimedia Private Limited*, contre l'arrêt CA Paris, pôle 1, chambre 1, rendu le 27 mars 2018 .... 2020.1.180

CA Montpellier, 5 mars 2020, n° 15-08584, *Les Marinas Del Sol c. Fontes et Y* 2020.1.181

CA Bordeaux, 2e Chambre civ., 5 mars 2020, n° 17/03250, *Z c. SCA de la Madrouques* 2020.2.325

Cass. 1re civ., 11 mars 2020, n° 18/26789, FS-PB, *OPH de la communauté urbaine du Mans c. Mancelle d'HLM*, contre arrêt rendu par la Cour d'Angers, Chambre A civile, 19 septembre 2018, rejet 2020.2.326

CA Versailles, 12e chambre, 12 mars 2020, n° 19-07463, *X Y c. The Stanley Works Limited* 2020.1.185

CA Paris, Pôle 4, Chambre 6, 13 mars 2020, n° 18/21768, *Architecture Olivier Chopin c. Y* 2020.2.327

CA Versailles, 3[e] chambre, 19 mars 2020, n° 18/08571, *Z c. Groupama Gan Assurance* 2020.2.327

CA Nîmes, chambre civile, 2[e] chambre, section B, 6 avril 2020, n° 19/03756, *X c. Synlab Provence* 2020.1.187
2020.2.328

Cass. 1re civ., 13 mai 2020, n° 18/25966, F-P+B, *Kimmolux c. Boulangerie Neuhauser* contre l'arrêt rendu par la Cour d'appel de Colmar, 1re Chambre, Section A, 21 novembre 2018, cassation 2020.2.329

CA Lyon, 1re Chambre civile, 14 mai 2020, n° 17/06968, *Z c. Y* 2020.2.329

CA Aix-en-Provence, Chambre 1-2, 14 mai 2020, n° 19/08772, *Discount c. La Ville de Nice* 2020.2.330

CA Paris, Pôle 1, Chambre 3, 20 mai 2020, n° 19/18891, *Discount c. La Ville de Nice* 2020.2.331

CA Montpellier, 22 mai 2020, n° 19/05838, *Subway international c. X*.................... 2020.2.332

CA Paris, Pôle 1, Chambre 1, 2 juin 2020, n° 17/18900, *Z c. Subway International*...... 2020.2.332

CA Paris, Pôle 1, Chambre 1, 2 juin 2020, n° 17/17373, *Société générale de surveillance c. Z*.................... 2020.2.334

CA Paris, Pôle 5, Chambre 16, 3 juin 2020, n° 19/03588, *République bolivarienne de Venezuela c. Z*.................... 2020.2.337 2020.3.551

CA Paris, Pôle 5, Chambre 16, 3 juin 2020, n° 19/072621, *TCM FR c. NGSC*........ 2020.2.340

CA Bordeaux, 4e Chambre civile, 11 juin 2020, n° 17/06155, *La Ferme du Gat c. Norea*.................... 2020.2.347

CA Paris, Pôle 5, Chambre 4, 17 juin 2020, n° 18/16996, *Z c. GB 2000 International*.................... 2020.2.348

CA Colmar, 22 juin 2020, n° 18/02745, *Centre européen d'arbitrage et de médiation c. Intersnack Knaber Geback*.................... 2020.2.349

CA Paris, 23 juin 2020, n° 17/22943, Kabab-Ji S.A.L. (Liban) c/ Kout Food Group (Koweït). Kabab-Ji S.A.L v Kout Food Group.................... 2020.1.61 2020.2.350

CA Paris, Pôle 1, Chambre 1, 23 juin 2020, n° 18/09652, *Z c. Quarks*.................. 2020.2.354

Cass. 1re civ., 24 juin 2020, n° 19-12701, F-D, *Clemessy Services c. Kem One* contre l'arrêt rendu par la Cour d'appel d'Aix-en-Provence, Chambre 3-3, 24 janvier 2019, rejet.................... 2020.2.355

CA Montpellier, 24 juin 2020, n° 20/00028, *I2A intelligence artificielle applications c. Y*.................... 2020.2.355

CA Besançon, 30 juin 2020, n° 18/02102, *A c. B*.................... 2020.2.355

CA Paris, Pôle 1, chambre 1, 30 juin 2020, n° 17/22515, *Sheikh Faisal Bin Fayyadh Al Gobain c. Crédit Foncier de France et LGT Bank*.................... 2020.2.356

CA Paris, Pôle 1, Chambre 1, 30 juin 2020, n° 17/22494, *Souflet Negoce c. Egyptian International Factory For Splitting*.................... 2020.2.358

CA Paris, Pôle 5, Chambre 16, 30 juin 2020, n° 19/199729, *Z c. Axon Entreprise Inc*.................... 2020.2.359

T. com. Versailles, Ord., 1er juillet 2020, 2020R00082, *Don Carlos c. BHI*............. 2020.2.362

T. com. Paris, Ord., 2 juillet 2020, 2020017456, *Artelia Ville & Transport c. Crédit Industriel et Commercial et c.*.................... 2020.2.362

Cass. 2e civ., 2 juillet 2020, n° 19-16326, F-D, *Crédit logement c. Z*, contre l'arrêt rendu par la Cour d'appel de Grenoble, 12 mars 2019, infirmation.................... 2020.2.363

CA Paris, Pôle 5, Chambre 9, 2 juillet 2020, RG 19/21120, *Closaf c. X*.................. 2020.2.363

T. com. Nanterre, Ord., 3 juillet 2020, 2013F01765, *SDE Matelec Sal Amchit Ghorfine c. Bollore Logistics*.................... 2020.2.364

T. com. Paris, 8 juillet 2020, 2019036900, *MJ Synergie, Mandataires Judiciaires, agissant dans l'intérêt collectif des créanciers de la SAS Geryan c. ITM Restauration*.................. 2020.2.366

T. com. Paris, 8 juillet 2020, 2020022118, *Atos International c. NSC Global Ltd*.... 2020.2.367

CA Aix-en-Provence, Chambre 3-2, 9 juillet 2020, 17/00486, *X c. Euro Batiment*... 2020.2.367

CA Rennes, 2e Chambre, 10 juillet 2020, n° 16/09622, *Aelis Patrimoine c. Northwestern Manetary Institute*.................. 2020.2.368

CA Pau, 2e Chambre, section 1, 20 juillet 2020, n° 18/04056, *CQFDD c. Crédit coopératif*.................. 2020.2.369

T. com. Chalon-sur-Saône, Ord. 3 août 2020, n° 2020001694, *Ares c. Dsa Construction*.................. 2020.3.660

CA Rennes, 1er août 2020, n° 19-04270, *X et GM Développement c. Y et XO Conseil*... 2020.3.661

CA Colmar, 1re Chambre civile – Section A, 31 août 2020, n° 20-00455, *Defranceschi c. Domaine Rolly Gassmann et Gauthier SARL Materiels et Articles de Cave*........... 2020.3.662

T. com. Evry, 1er septembre 2020, 2e Chambre, n° 2019F00344, *Serfa c. Rabot Dutilleul Construction*.................. 2020.3.662

T. com. Nanterre, Ord., 4 septembre 2020, n° 2020R00628, *Société Du Grand Théatre des Champs Élysées c. Chubb European Group SE*.................. 2020.3.662

CA Paris, Pôle 5, Chambre 4, 9 septembre 2020, n° 19-00485, *Cegedim c. Iqvia Opérations France*.................. 2020.3.663

T. com. Reims, 9 septembre 2020, n° 2020002751, *X c. Y*.................. 2020.3.663

T. com. Nanterre, 10 septembre 2020, n° 2018F01172, *SDE des Tubes d'acier et d'aluminium de Côte d'Ivoire c. KDI Export et c.*.................. 2020.3.663

CA Rennes, 3e Chambre commerciale, 11 septembre 2020, n° 17-07714, *X c. CDPO et Cooperl Arc Atlantique*.................. 2020.3.666

CA Rennes, 3e Chambre commerciale, 11 septembre 2020, n° 20-00855, *GM Développement c. Réseau Herviaux Mobilité*.................. 2020.3.668

CA Paris, Pôle 5, Chambre 16, 15 septembre 2020, n° 19-09058, *Samwell International Holdings limited c. Airbus Helicopters*.................. 2020.3.669

CA Paris, Pôle 5, Chambre 16, 15 septembre 2020, n° 19-09580, *Sharmel c. Mirato*.... 2020.3.672

CA Paris, Pôle 1, Chambre 1, 15 septembre 2020, n° 18-01360, *A c. Subway international BV*.................. 2020.3.673

T. com. Lille, 22 septembre 2020, n° 2019002545SAS, *Potentiel c. Rabot Dutilleul Construction*.................. 2020.3.675

CA Toulouse, 2e Chambre, 23 septembre 2020, n° 18-04848, *X c. Clinique de Montberon et ADSPS*.................. 2020.3.676

CA Rennes, 2e Chambre, 25 septembre 2020, n° 19-04142, *Matière c. Zwahlen & Mayr et c.*.................. 2020.3.677

CA Angers, Chambre A, Civile, 29 septembre 2020, n° 18-00104, *SDMA exercant sous l'enseigne Maisons Socoren c. X* 2020.3.678

Cass. 1re civ., 30 septembre 2020, n° 19-15728, *ETF c. Matissa*, CA Paris, pôle 2, chambre 5, 26 février 2019, F-D, Renvoi 2020.3.678

T. com. Paris, 1re Chambre, 13 octobre 2020, n° 2017005123, *Monsieur le Ministre de l'Économie et des Finances et a. c. Subway International BV et Subway Realty of France EURL* 2020.3.679

CA Aix-en-Provence, Chambre 3-4, 15 octobre 2020, n° 17-11777, *Bâtiment Concept Services c. X* 2020.3.680

CA Paris, Pôle 5, Chambre 16, chambre commerciale internationale, 20 octobre 2020, n° 19-05231, *Senelec c. Itoc* 2020.3.681

CA Paris, Pôle 1, Chambre 1, 20 octobre 2020, n° 18-07943, *Flashbird Limited c. Compagnie de Sécurité Privée et Industrielle – CSP1* 2020.3.685

CA Rennes, 3e Chambre commerciale, 20 octobre 2020, n° 20/00843 et n° 20/00963, *X, Thermador Groupe et a. c. Diffusion Équipements Loisirs D.E.L. et a.* 2020.3.689

CA Paris, Pôle 1, Chambre 1, 27 octobre 2020, n° 20/09005, *SCI Fredema c. La Dame de Cœur* 2020.3.689

T. com. Versailles, 28 octobre 2020, n° 2020R00128, *Emoceg Montage Construction Électrique et Gaz c. Flowserve Sihi* 2020.3.691

CA Pau, 5 novembre 2020, n° 20/01175, *La Tagliatella c. Tagli'apau* 2020.3.691

CA Aix-en-Provence, Chambre 3-1, 5 novembre 2020, n° 19/12813, *Menton 107 et a c. BTSG7 et a.* 2020.3.695

CA Orléans, 5 novembre 2020, n° 19/03278, *Hydro construction c. Vergnet et Villa ès qualités de mandataire judiciaire* 2020.3.695

CA Nancy, 9 novembre 2020, n° 19/03570, *A c. De Cleuvra* 2020.3.698

CA Paris, Pôle 1, Chambre 1, 10 novembre 2020, n° 18/19033, *Kraydon Ltd c. Chambre de Commerce Internationale de Paris CCI* 2020.3.698

CA Dijon, 2e chambre civile, 12 novembre 2020, n° 18/00617, *X c. BMRA* 2020.3.699

Cass. com., 12 novembre 2020, n° 19-18849, F-P+B, *IPSA Holding, CBF associés, agissant en qualité de commissaire à l'exécution du plan de sauvegarde de la société IPSA, et a. c. Alpha Petrovision Holding* contre Paris (pôle 1, chambre 1) 14 mai 2019, Rejet 2020.3.701

T. com. Toulouse, Ord. 12 novembre 2020, n° 2020R00068, *X c. Navallon Groupe* 2020.3.702

CA Paris, Pôle 1, Chambre 8, 13 novembre 2020, n° 20/10471, *Atos International c. NSC Global LTD* 2020.3.702

CA Montpellier, 2e chambre civile, 19 novembre 2020, n° 19/04956, *X c. Sander Participation* 2020.3.703

Aix-en-Provence, Chambre 3-4, 19 novembre 2020, n° 19/19951, *X c. Datacet*...... 2020.3.704

Besançon, 1re Chambre civile, 19 novembre 2020, n° 20/00357, *SCI La Vallée c. Aa A*........ 2020.3.705

Besançon, 1re Chambre civile, 19 novembre 2020, n° 20/00529, *Concept Machine c. Firac*........ 2020.3.705

Colmar, 2e Chambre civile, 20 novembre 2020, n° 2 A, n° 18/04377, *Thales Architectures c. X*........ 2020.3.706

Poitiers, 24 novembre 2020, n° 18/01230, *X c. S.A. SPBI* et *Simpson Marine Limited*........ 2020.3.706

Paris, Pôle 1, Chambre 1, 24 novembre 2020, n° 18/06448, *Bouygues Bâtiment Île-de-France c. Comsa Instalaciones y Sistemas Industriales SL anciennement EMTE Mechanical Engineering SL*........ 2020.3.707

Agen, Chambre civile, section commerciale, 25 novembre 2020, n° 18/00934, *Financière Dr et Forme & O c. X*........ 2020.3.708

T. com. Toulouse, Ord, 26 novembre 2020, n° 2020R00235, *Ed Master c. Paprec Sud-Ouest*........ 2020.3.709

Inde / India

Supreme Court of India, *Vijay Karia and Ors. vs. Prysmian Cavi E Sistemi SRL & Ors.*, 2020 SCC Online SC 177........ 2020.2.271

Italie / Italy

Court of Milan, 8 January 2020, No. 34972/2018, *RCD Europe Limited and Waaree Industries Private Limited v. Targa S.p.A., Immogar S.p.A. et al.*........ 2020.2.371

Italian Court of Cassation, 22 January 2020, No. 1439, *T.G. v. Edilco Immobiliare Group S.r.l.*........ 2020.2.373

Italian Court of Cassation, 25 February 2020, No. 4956, *C.R.F. v. Fallimento (omissis) S.r.l. in liquidazione*........ 2020.2.375

Court of Appeal of Genoa, 9 July 2020, no. 649, *Ferruccio Rossi v Ferretti S.p.A*........ 2020.4.997

Court of Milan, 26 November 2020, No. 7692, *Istituto San Giorgio s.r.l. v Omnia Fondazione Onlus*........ 2020.4.1004

Singapour / Singapore

BWG v BWF [2020] SGCA 36........ 2020.4.1009

AnAn Group (Singapore) Pte. Ltd. v VTB Bank (Public Joint Stock Co.) [2020] SGCA 33........ 2020.4.1010

China Machine New Energy Corp v Jaguar Energy Guatemala LLC and another [2020] SGCA 12 .... 2020.4.1019

CEB v CEC and another matter [2020] SGHC(I) 11 .... 2020.4.1021

CBP v CBS [2020] SGHC 23 .... 2020.4.1022

BXH v BXI [2019] SGHC 141 / *BXH v BXI* [2020] SGCA 28 .... 2020.4.1025

Suisse / Switzerland

Tribunal fédéral (1re Cour de droit civil), 6 janvier 2020 (4A_287/2019).......... 2020.2.412

Tribunal fédéral (1re Cour de droit civil), 6 janvier 2020 (4A_342/2019).......... 2020.2.417

Tribunal fédéral (1re Cour du droit civil), 16 mars 2020 (4A_536/2018).......... 2020.2.419

Tribunal fédéral (1re Cour de droit civil), 17 mars 2020 (4A_597/2019).......... 2020.2.422

Tribunal fédéral (1re Cour de droit civil), 17 avril 2020 (4A_12/2019) 2020.2.423

Tribunal fédéral (1re Cour de droit civil), 21 avril 2020 (4A_422/2019) 2020.2.427

Tribunal fédéral (1re Cour de droit civil), 29 avril 2020 (4A_548/2019 ; 4A_550/2019) 2020.2.428

Tribunal fédéral (1re Cour de droit civil), 30 avril 2020 (4A_160/2020) 2020.2.431

Tribunal fédéral (1re Cour de droit civil), 20 mai 2020 (4A_114/2020) 2020.2.432

Tribunal fédéral (1re Cour de droit civil), 18 juin 2020 (4A_70/2020) 2020.2.433

Tribunal fédéral (1re Cour de droit civil), 18 juin 2020 (4A_93/2020) 2020.2.435

Tribunal fédéral (1re Cour de droit civil), 24 juillet 2020 (4A_300/2020) 2020.4.1027

Tribunal fédéral (1re Cour de droit civil), 29 juillet 2020 (4A_462/2019) 2020.4.1029

Tribunal fédéral (1re Cour de droit civil), 5 août 2020 (4A_202/2020) 2020.4.1034

Tribunal fédéral (1re Cour de droit civil), 17 août 2020 (4A_486/2019) 2020.4.1035

Tribunal fédéral (1re Cour de droit civil), 25 août 2020 (4A_248/2019 et 4A_398/2019) 2020.4.1041

Tribunal fédéral (1re Cour de droit civil), 26 août 2020 (4A_290/2020) 2020.4.1050

Tribunal fédéral (1re Cour de droit civil), 27 août 2020 (4A_36/2020) 2020.4.1051

Tribunal fédéral (1re Cour de droit civil), 17 septembre 2020 (4A_618/2019) 2020.4.1052

Tribunal fédéral (1re Cour de droit civil), 18 septembre 2020 (4A_324/2020) 2020.4.1055

Tribunal fédéral (1re Cour de droit civil), 30 septembre 2020 (4A_62/2020) 2020.4.1057

Tribunal fédéral (1re Cour de droit civil), 1er octobre 2020 (4A_156/2020).......... 2020.4.1058

Tribunal fédéral (1re Cour de droit civil), 4 novembre 2020 (4A_416/2020).......... 2020.4.1061

Tribunal fédéral (1re Cour de droit civil), 13 novembre 2020 (4A_124/2020).......... 2020.4.1063

Tribunal fédéral (1re Cour de droit civil), 1er décembre 2020 (4A_198/2020) 2020.4.1065

Tribunal fédéral (1re Cour de droit civil), 1er décembre 2020 (4A_444/2020) 2020.4.1067

Tribunal fédéral (1re Cour de droit civil), 10 décembre 2020 (4A_384/2020) 2020.4.1068

Tribunal fédéral (1re Cour de droit civil), 16 décembre 2020 (4A_244/2020) 2020.4.1070

Tribunal fédéral (1re Cour de droit civil), 22 décembre 2020 (4A_318/2020) 2020.4.1072

Tribunal fédéral (1re Cour de droit civil), 29 décembre 2020 (4A_478/2020) 2020.4.1083

2021

Canada

Lululemon athletica canada inc. v. Industrial Color Productions Inc, 2021 BCSC 15, January 6, 2021 .... 2020.4.886

United Mexican States v. Burr, 2021 ONCA 64, February 2, 2021 .... 2020.4.887

Razar Contracting Services Ltd. v. Evoqua Water, 2021 MBQB 69, March 30, 2021 .... 2020.4.887

Kore Meals LLC v. Freshii Development LLC, 2021 ONSC 2896, April 19, 2021 ...... 2020.4.888

China Yantai Friction Co. Ltd. v. Novalex Inc., 2021 ONSC 3571, May 13, 2021 .... 2020.4.889

The Russian Federation v. Luxtona Limited, 2021 ONSC 4604, June 30, 2021 .... 2020.4.890

CEDH / ECHR

Beg v. Italy, Nr. 53/1211, 20 May 2021 .... 2020.4.845
2020.4.1006

États-Unis / USA

Setty v. Shrinivas Sugandhalaya LLP, 986 F.3d 1139, 2021 U.S. App. LEXIS 1490 ... 2020.3.509

France

Nîmes, 6 janvier 2021, n° 20-02583, *A Projets Ingenierie Actions (CPIA) Delepine c. Edit Environnement* 2020.4.893

Rouen, Chambre de la proximité, 7 janvier 2021, n° 20-01665, *21.D. c. Entreprise Générale Leon Grosse* 2020.4.893

Paris, Pôle 3, Chambre 5, 12 janvier 2021, n° 17-07290, *Seitur Agencia de viajes y turismo (Compania Limit Ada) c. CW Travel Holdings Nv (Carlson Wagon Lit Travel)* 2020.4.895

Paris, Pôle 5 – Chambre 16, n° 19-12417, *République d'Équateur c. Mentenimientos Ayuda a la Explotacion y Servicios Maessa* 2020.4.897

Cass. 1re civ., 13 janvier 2021, n° 19-22.932, F-P+I, *Egyptian General Petroleum Corporation (EGPC) c société National Gas Company (NATGAS)*, Paris (pôle 1, chambre 1), 21 mai 2019, Rejet 2020.4.897

CA Versailles, 14 janvier 2021, n° 19-06572, *SNPC c. Commisimpex*........ 2020.4.898

CA Grenoble, 14 janvier 2021, n° 18-04332, *Wistar Enterprises Limited c. Top Bagage International*........ 2020.4.900

CA Paris, Pôle 3, Chambre 5, 19 janvier 2021, n° 18-04465, *Rotana Jet Limited c. Hop!* 2020.4.901

CA Versailles, 20 janvier 2021, n° 18-02160, *A c. CFAO*........ 2020.4.902

CA Rouen, 21 janvier 2021, n° 16-05847, *A c. Image Passion*........ 2020.4.903

CA Versailles, 21 janvier 2021, n° 19-02675, *Rohlig france c. SDE Vinci Construction Grands Projets – Jordan, XLIC SE et Corporate Solutions Assurance*........ 2020.4.904

CA Paris, Pôle 3 – Chambre 5, 26 janvier 2021, n° 18-05543, *Grant Thornton c. X* 2020.4.905

CA Paris, Pôle 5 – Chambre 16, chambre commerciale international, 26 janvier 2021, n° 19-18582, *X c. URECO*........ 2020.4.906

Cass. 1re civ., 27 janvier 2021, n° 19-25.683, F-D, *Scor SE c. Mutuelle Mieux-Être (MME)*, Paris (pôle 1, chambre 1), 15 octobre 2019, Rejet........ 2020.4.907

CA Paris, Pôle 1, Chambre 3, 27 janvier 2021, n° 19-20160, *A c. Socorest*........ 2020.4.907

T. com. Toulouse, 28 janvier 2021, n° 2017J00144, *A c. Airbus*........ 2020.4.908

CA Paris, Pôle 5 – Chambre 16, chambre commerciale internationale, 2 février 2021, n° 20-01789, *Tok Tokkie Company (TTC) c. Monster Energy Limited*........ 2020.4.909

T. com. Nanterre, 2 février 2021, n° 2019F01623, *SDE Oman Pro (Offshore) c. SDE ODC F. et a.* 2020.4.910

Cass. 1re civ., 3 février 2021, n° 19-10.669, FP-P+I, *Commissions Import Export (Commisimpex) c. République du Congo et procureur général près la cour d'appel de Paris, contre l'arrêt rendu le 6 septembre 2018 par la cour d'appel de Paris (pôle 4, chambre 8), Rejet*........ 2020.4.911

CA Rennes, 9 février 2021, n° 20-03714, *BCB International LTD c. Redcore*........ 2020.4.912

CA Paris, Pôle 5 – Chambre 16, chambre commerciale internationale, 16 février 2021, n° 18-16695, *Grenwich c. Indémia*........ 2020.4.914

CA Rouen, 18 février 2021, n° 20-01507, n° 20-01607 et n° 20-01610, *A c. Cauchoise Presse Publicité Soc* (trois arrêts) 2020.4.917

CA Rennes, 19 février 2021, n° 20-05735, *X c. Faiensol et a.* 2020.4.918

CA Poitiers, 23 février 2021, n° 20-01534, *A c. Baicuianu-Cirjaliu*........ 2020.4.919

CA Paris, Pôle 5 – Chambre 16, chambre commerciale internationale, 23 février 2021, n° 18-03068, *Libyan Emirates Oil Refining Company c. National Oil Corporation*........ 2020.4.920

CA Rennes, 2 mars 2021, n° 20-01977, *A c. B*........ 2020.4.923

CA Nancy, 3 mars 2021, n° 20-00979, *X C. KPMG*.. 2020.4.924

CA Paris, Pôle 3, Chambre 5, 2 mars 2021, n° 18-16891, *Lebanese Media Holding Limited, PAC et a. c. Lebanese Broadcasting Corporation-International SAL, LBCI*........ 2020.4.925

CA Paris, Pôle 5, Chambre 16, chambre commerciale internationale, 9 mars, n° 17-10664 et n° 19-04410, *B C X of Ukraine – Ukravtodor, agence étatique des routes de l'Ukraine agissant poursuites et diligences du Ministère de la Justice c. Todini Costruzioni Generali* (deux arrêts).. 2020.4.929

CA Versailles, 9 mars 2021, n° 19-05333, *Gan Yael Crèche et Jardin d'enfants c. A* 2020.4.935

CA Paris, Pôle 5, Chambre 16, chambre commerciale internationale, 16 mars 2021, n° 19-03195, *X mandataire ad hoc de l'EARL de A et a. c. La Ferme de Beaujoly* 2020.4.937

Cass. 1re civ., 17 mars 2021, n° 20-14.360, F-P, *A c. AA*, (Versailles, 28 janvier 2020), Cassation.. 2020.4.939

CA Colmar, 22 mars 2021, n° 18-03474, *D2AT Developpement de l'agro-alimentaire du terroir c. SHDA*.. 2020.4.939

CA Paris, Pôle 5, Chambre 16, chambre commerciale internationale, 23 mars 2021, n° 18-14817, *Projet Pilote Garoubé c. CCI*.. 2020.4.940

CA Paris, Pôle 5, Chambre 16, Chambre commerciale internationale, 23 mars 2021, n° 18-05756, *État de Libye c. DS Construction* 2020.4.944

CA Paris, Pôle 5, Chambre 16, Chambre commerciale internationale, 30 mars 2021, n° 19-04161, *Fédération de Russie c. Joint Stock Company « State Savings Bank of Ukraine » (Jsc Oschadbank)* 2020.4.950

Tribunal judiciaire de Paris, 31 mars 2021, n° 19/00795 .... 2020.4.857

Cass. 1re civ., 31 mars 2021, n° 19-11.551, FS-P, *Rusoro Mining Limited c. République bolivarienne du Venezuela,* Cassation Paris (pôle 1, chambre 1), 29 janvier 2019 .... 2020.4.955

CA Paris, Pôle 4, Chambre 13, 31 mars 2021, n° 18-08337, *SCI Chripimarc c. G*... 2020.4.957

Tribunal judiciaire Paris, 31 mars 2021, n° 19/00795, *S c. G*................................ 2020.4.958

CA Paris, Pôle 5, Chambre 16, chambre commerciale internationale, 6 avril 2021, n° 20-13048, *GBO Gesellschaft Für Betriebsorganisation MBH c. CA. Finance*........ 2020.4.963

CA Montpellier, Chambre commerciale, 6 avril 2021, n° 18-03887, *X c. Y* 2020.4.964

T. com., Melun, 12 avril 2021, n° 019F00143, *Christophe Ancel es qualité Liquidateur de Sutra International et Causidor c. Ingenieria Franco Espanola Omega*................. 2020.4.965

CA Paris, Pôle 5, Chambre 16, Chambre commerciale internationale, 13 avril 2021, n° 18-09809, *Republique de Guinée c. A.D. – Trade Belgium S.P.R.L.*..................... 2020.4.965

CA Paris, Pôle 5, Chambre 16, chambre commerciale internationale, 13 avril 2021, n° 18-27764, *Brezillon c. Eurocoustique*.. 2020.4.969

CA Paris, Pôle 5, Chambre 16, Chambre commerciale internationale, 13 avril 2021, n° 18-17862, *Ferrovial Agroman c. A*... 2020.4.971

CA Aix-en-Provence, Chambre 3-4, 15 avril 2021, n° 18-07428, *Nikaiadis II c. A...* 2020.4.974

Tribunal judiciaire Paris, 16 avril 2021, n° 21-50115, *G. L c. ICC et a.* 2020.4.975

CA Agen, 3 mai 2021, n° 18-00153, *Financière Auxgane c. Gmba Essonne et a* 2020.4.977

CA Nîmes, 6 mai 2021, n° 19-03172, *Favarel et Associés c. Cap Niel* 2020.4.977

T. com. Reims, 11 mai 2021, n° 2020004974, *A c. GFA Saintot-Novel* 2020.4.979

CA Paris, Pôle 5, Chambre 16, Chambre commerciale internationale, 11 mai 2021, n° 18-07442, n° 18-07552 et n° 18-19907, *Karizma Enerji Gaz Petrol Madencilik Mermer Insaat Ormancilik Sanayi Ve, Ticaret anonim sirkety et Cevikler Enerji Madencilik Mermer Turizm Insaat Sa Limited c. Turchrome Krom Madencilik Sanayi Ve Dis Ticaret Anonim* (trois arrêts) 2020.4.979

T. com. Belfort, 18 mai 2021, n° 2021000236, *Johnson Controls Industries c. Kelvion Phe GmbH* 2020.4.982

CA Paris, Pôle 5 – Chambre 16, chambre commerciale internationale, 25 mai 2021, n° 18-27648, *État de Libye c. Cengiz Insaat Sanayi Ve Ticaret A.S.* 2020.4.983

CA Paris, Pôle 5, Chambre 16, chambre commerciale internationale, 25 mai 2021, n° 18-20625, *Delta Dragon Import c. Byd Auto Industry Co* 2020.4.990

CA Paris, Pôle 5, Chambre 16, chambre commerciale internationale, 25 mai 2021, n° 18-18708, *République Gabonaise et Commune de Libreville c. Webcor ITP Limited & Grand Marché de Libreville* 2020.4.993

Cass. 1re civ., 26 mai 2021, n° 19-20.410, *International Exhibits Holding Aps et a c. The Ministry of Culture of the Republic of Iraq, et a.* contre Paris (pôle 1, chambre 1) 28 mai 2019, F-D, Rejet 2020.4.995

CA Paris, Pôle 5, Chambre 16, chambre commerciale internationale, 27 mai 2021, n° 19-08675, *DHL Freight c. Legrand* 2020.4.996

CA Paris (Pôle 5, Ch. 16), 8 juin 2021, n° 19/02245 .... 2020.4.809

CA Paris, Chambre internationale, 22 juin 2021, n° 21/07623, *Société Saad Buzwair Automotive co (SBA) c/ M. G.* 2020.4.831 2020.4.857

Italie / Italy

Court of Cassation, United Chambers, 30 March 2021, No. 8776, *A.T.I. CIME s.r.l. and S.T.I.M s.r.l. v Orion società cooperativa a r.l.* 2020.4.1005

Court of Appeal of Brescia, 28 April 2021, *Wave s.r.l. in liquidazione v International Chamber of Commerce* 2020.4.999

Court of Appeal of Milan, 8 June 2021, *Wind Energy Racalmuto s.r.l. v GE Wind Energy Gmbh and GE International Inc. Italian Branch* 2020.4.1001

Suisse / Switzerland

Tribunal fédéral (1re Cour de droit civil), 5 janvier 2021 (4A_476/2020).................. 2020.4.1083

Tribunal fédéral (1re Cour de droit civil), 6 janvier 2021 (4A_346/2020).................. 2020.4.1086

Tribunal fédéral (1re Cour de droit civil), 27 janvier 2021 (4A_600/2020)................ 2020.4.1090

Tribunal fédéral (1re Cour de droit civil), 10 février 2021 (4A_430/2020) 2020.4.1093

Tribunal fédéral (1re Cour de droit civil), 15 février 2021 (4A_660/2020) 2020.4.1096

Tribunal fédéral (1re Cour de droit civil), 15 mars 2021 (4A_438/2020)..................... 2020.4.1097

Tribunal fédéral (1re Cour de droit civil), 15 mars 2021 (4A_626/2020)..................... 2020.4.1098

Tribunal fédéral (1re Cour de droit civil), 1er avril 2021 (4A_332/2020)...................... 2020.4.1100

Tribunal fédéral (1re Cour de droit civil), 7 mai 2021 (4A_27/2021) 2020.4.1102

Tribunal fédéral (1re Cour de droit civil), 17 mai 2021 (4A_666/2020) 2020.4.1102

Tribunal fédéral (1re Cour de droit civil), 17 mai 2021 (4A_667/2020) 2020.4.1104

Tribunal fédéral (1re Cour de droit civil), 17 mai 2021 (4A_668/2020) 2020.4.1106

Index 2020-2021

Bertrand ROBERT
Avocat

Priscille PEDONE
Avocat

Les chiffres renvoient aux numéros de page / References are to page numbers

A

Abus de droit / de procédure : 155, 158, 181, 355, 356, 359, 423, 432, 433, 469, 637, 641, 1102

Accès à la justice : 147, 332, 359, 691, 911

Acte de mission : 334, 354, 929, 965

Action de groupe : 141

Action délictuelle : 128, 151, 164, 165, 366, 371, 658, 908
v. Rupture des relations commerciales

Action directe : 904

Action récursoire : 177

Allemagne
jurisprudence : 121-127, 871-874

Amiable composition : 181, 681, 707, 969

Angleterre et Pays de Galles
jurisprudence : 61, 79, 501, 614, 631-646

Anti-suit injonction : 135, 643, 958

Appel : 355, 649, 672, 699, 937
appel-nullité : 172, 893, 963
déclaration d'appel : 153

Application de la loi dans le temps : 166, 181, 702, 923

Arbitrabilité : 121, 373, 702, 705

Arbitrage
ad hoc : 179, 712, 944
caractère économique : 185, 347
caractère international : 347, 897
notion : 122, 125

Arbitrage du bâtonnier : 151, 161, 923, 924

Arbitrage en matière de sport
v. Tribunal arbitral du sport

Arbitre
amiable compositeur : 181, 681, 707, 969
collégialité / majorité : 905, 917
constitution du tribunal : 161, 364, 398, 657, 963, 1100
contrat d' – : 831, 857, 958, 975
démission : 412
désignation / nomination : 122, 125, 130, 132, 170, 181, 364, 664, 666, 698, 699, 703, 879, 940, 944, 963
d'urgence : 362, 648, 655
fonction juridictionnelle : 159, 469, 880, 893, 929, 983
jura novit curia : 1093
listes d'arbitres : 809
mission : 158, 170, 327, 350, 354, 359, 669, 673, 681, 685, 707, 886, 925, 965, 971, 979
ordonnance de procédure : 897, 940
pouvoirs : 469, 874, 880
récusation : 402, 880, 990, 1072
remplacement : 1100
rémunération : 349, 666, 940
responsabilité : 349, 831, 857, 958
v. Compétence-compétence
v. Indépendance et impartialité
v. Instance arbitrale

Autorité de la chose jugée : 177, 181, 363, 394, 419, 650, 656, 661, 893, 1001, 1083

Autriche
jurisprudence : 127-133, 875-881

Avocat
décès : 879
devoir d'information et de conseil : 156, 957, 977
mission : 152
responsabilité professionnelle : 156, 706, 957, 977
v. Arbitrage du Bâtonnier

B

Belgique
jurisprudence : 647-654
Bonne foi : 168, 337, 354, 356, 359, 396, 433, 925, 929, 1035, 1055, 1090

C

Canada
jurisprudence : 135-145, 883-891
Chambre arbitrale du sport : 809
Chambre de commerce internationale : 340, 940
procédure accélérée : 453
Règlement d'arbitrage 2021 : 453
responsabilité : 940
CIRDI
v. Investissements internationaux
CJUE : 315
Clause attributive de compétence : 150, 181, 664, 680, 982
Clause compromissoire
acceptation : 151, 166, 329
activité professionnelle : 166, 662, 702
autonomie : 61, 131, 150, 181, 227, 332, 350, 673, 685, 691, 925, 929
conditions générales : 141, 166, 675, 678, 705, 887
connaissance de la clause : 151, 329, 705, 996
consentement à l'arbitrage : 1063, 1090
contrat-cadre : 123
étendue / champ d'application : 121, 123, 138, 164, 175, 329, 334, 348, 363, 373, 375, 637, 656, 662, 664, 689, 885, 904, 907, 908, 920, 939, 975
extension : 61, 169, 350, 395, 509, 925, 995
forme : 347, 887
implication dans l'exécution du contrat : 350, 364, 657, 925, 995
interprétation : 154, 181, 371, 373, 417, 423, 685, 885, 1004, 1063
listes d'arbitres : 809
loi applicable : 61, 142, 417, 509, 643, 669, 685, 897, 925, 1011
non-signataires : 325, 509, 633, 925, 963, 995
notion / définition : 170, 329, 903, 977
nullité et inapplicabilité manifeste : 150, 151, 159, 170, 355, 702, 903, 982, 996
opposabilité : 325, 355, 363, 364, 656, 705, 907
pathologique : 154, 156, 175, 179, 181, 347, 663, 675, 680, 702
renonciation : 704
signature : 161
transmission : 350
validité : 159, 164, 166, 172, 181, 329, 332, 334, 348, 359, 367, 417, 660, 673, 685, 689, 699, 704, 904, 925, 975, 997
Clause pénale : 965
CNUDCI
Convention sur les accords de règlement issus de la médiation : 105
loi type : 65, 191
règlement d'arbitrage : 334, 337, 673, 983
Code civil français
article 2061 : 166, 689, 702, 705
Code de procédure civile français
article 12 : 148
article 48 : 705
article 76 : 706
article 81 : 678
article 145 : 177, 181
article 524 : 148, 483
article 1009-1 : 483
article 1442 : 169, 170, 181
article 1448 : 151, 159, 164, 169, 177, 187, 328, 332, 355, 364, 367, 660, 664, 673, 675, 678, 680, 689, 691, 939
article 1449 : 148, 187, 328, 362, 367, 660, 691, 702, 977
article 1450 : 666
article 1452 : 161, 666
article 1454 : 170
article 1455 : 170
article 1456 : 173
article 1460 : 172
article 1463 : 161
article 1465 : 159, 164, 168
article 1466 : 175, 483, 673
article 1482 : 181
article 1483 : 181
article 1484 : 177
article 1499 : 695
article 1509 : 669, 944
article 1511 : 669
article 1520 : 332
article 1526 : 757
article 1843-4 : 154
Compétence *ratione temporis* : 412, 950, 955
Compétence-compétence : 141, 142, 147, 159, 164, 168-170, 177, 187, 227, 328, 329, 348, 350, 355, 395, 399, 402, 417, 423, 643, 657, 673, 675, 678, 691, 903, 939, 950, 982
Compromis : 327, 935
Conciliation : 15, 151, 168, 366, 369
clause préalable obligatoire : 147, 148, 150, 153, 154, 165, 167, 325-327, 330, 363, 368, 676, 698, 706, 708, 923, 924, 937, 983
conciliateur de justice : 366, 658
conditions de forme de la clause : 368
Concurrence : 121
déloyale : 151
Conditions générales de vente : 141, 166, 675, 678, 705, 887
Confidentialité : 139, 900
Conflit d'intérêts
v. indépendance et impartialité
Connaissement : 363, 657
Contradictoire (*principe du –*) : 125, 126, 128, 332, 334, 340, 350, 354, 358, 381, 383, 393, 402, 419, 423, 427, 428, 433, 669, 699, 872, 874, 878, 880, 895, 901, 907, 914, 924, 979, 982, 1001, 1005, 1006, 1029, 1035, 1041, 1057, 1058, 1065, 1068, 1093, 1097, 1104
Contrat
avenant : 675
d'adhésion : 662, 679

d'agence commerciale : 131, 168, 181, 912
d'arbitre : 831, 857, 958, 975
d'assurance : 227, 904
de bail : 647, 689
de cession : 329, 363, 656, 659
de distribution : 181, 348
de franchise : 332, 673, 679, 691, 907
de maître d'œuvre : 327
de prêt : 167, 168, 331
de sous-traitance : 367, 662
distinct : 939
d'organisation de l'arbitrage : 975
effet relatif : 355
expiré : 912
groupe de – : 150, 151, 664
imprévision : 385
liés : 169
multi-partite : 123
novation : 168
pacta sunt servanda : 385, 433, 1086, 1096
pacte d'associés / d'actionnaires : 151, 153
principe de bonne foi dans l'exécution : 168
renouvellement implicite : 664

Convention d'arbitrage
v. Clause compromissoire

Convention de l'OCDE sur la lutte contre la corruption du 17 décembre 1997 : 993

Convention de New York : 181, 407, 706, 737

Convention d'entraide judiciaire : 737

Convention européenne des droits de l'homme : 332, 390, 399, 695, 809, 845, 975, 1006, 1035, 1041, 1083, 1090

Corruption : 289, 356, 669, 983, 993

Coûts / frais : 141, 332, 340, 412, 649, 691, 1027
frais irrépétibles : 152, 431
non-paiement de l'avance sur frais : 1034, 1058, 1067
répartition : 349
requête en garantie des frais de la procédure : 889
v. Honoraires

Covid-19 : 880, 924

D

Délai : 175, 757
caractère raisonnable : 979
computation : 172, 666
de l'arbitrage : 673, 969
de procédure : 128, 1106
de recours : 396, 1005, 1013
prescription : 161, 167, 177, 325, 955, 964
prorogation : 924, 969
sursis à statuer : 161, 631, 689, 885, 888, 1023
suspension / interruption : 893, 964, 1098
v. Moyens (tardifs)

Déni de justice : 160, 334, 359, 963, 975, 1083

Dilatoire : 483, 666, 924

Discounted Cash Flow : 727

Dommages-intérêts : 11, 128, 181, 356, 666
perte de change : 957
perte de gains : 727
punitifs : 175, 716

Droit des assurances : 227, 904

Droit des sociétés
actionnaires : 131
contrat de cession : 367, 656, 659, 668
groupe de sociétés : 569, 995
pacte d'associés / d'actionnaires : 151, 153
statuts : 129, 656

Droit d'être entendu
v. Contradictoire (principe du –)

Droit du sport
v. Tribunal arbitral du sport, Chambre arbitrale du sport

Droit européen : 340, 602
Règlement n° 44/2001 : 347, 831, 857, 939, 958
Règlement n° 1215/2012 : 958, 999

Droit fiscal : 993

Droit maritime : 364, 657

Droit public : 167
marchés publics : 247

Droit social : 702, 902, 903, 917, 935

E

Égalité des armes : 669, 681, 872, 911, 979
v. Contradictoire (pincipe du –)

Égalité des parties : 128, 349, 393, 469, 1104
v. Contradictoire (pincipe du –)

Embargo : 160, 965

Enrichissement sans cause : 128

Estoppel : 180, 337, 509, 637, 691, 711, 929, 971

États-Unis
jurisprudence : 509

Exception d'incompétence : 367, 659, 910, 983

Excès de pouvoir : 154, 172, 681, 703, 963

Exécution provisoire : 154, 355, 483, 677, 757

Exequatur : 407, 650, 677, 699, 701, 873, 889, 905, 935, 997
étendue du contrôle judiciaire : 139, 877, 971

Expert : 79, 154, 161, 175, 422, 901

F

Faits nouveaux : 137, 890, 1051

FIDIC : 929

Fin de non-recevoir : 329-331, 337, 367-369, 659, 676, 708, 918, 923, 924, 944

Financement par des tiers : 449, 883

Forclusion : 340, 695

Forum non conveniens : 888

France
jurisprudence : 95, 147-188, 289, 315, 325-369, 655-709, 809, 831, 857, 893-996

Fraude : 334, 359, 650, 979, 983
procédurale : 925, 929, 971, 983

G

Garanties bancaires : 362

H

Honoraires : 349, 666
de résultat : 152, 332
v. Coûts / frais

I

IBA
Lignes directrices sur les conflits d'intérêts dans l'arbitrage international : 920
Règles sur l'administration de la preuve : 359
Impartialité et indépendance : 151, 412, 698, 809, 914, 1072, 1100
doute raisonnable : 173, 895, 901, 914, 920, 925
faits notoires : 155, 173, 990
liens entre les arbitres et les conseils des parties : 155, 398, 449, 883, 895, 1006
obligation de révélation : 15, 173, 501, 831, 845, 895, 920, 975, 990
In limine litis : 329
Inde : 271
Infra petita
v. Recours en annulation
Insolvabilité / Impécuniosité : 332, 375, 691, 879
Instance arbitrale : 170
acte de mission : 334, 354, 929, 965
bifurcation : 1001
célérité : 334
demande d'arbitrage : 130
durée de la mission du tribunal arbitral : 161
lieu de tenue de l'audience : 958
loyauté procédurale : 79, 170, 354
mesures d'organisation : 349
ordonnance de procédure : 897, 940
suspension / interruption : 132, 161
visioconférence : 453, 880, 888
Institution arbitrale : 180, 347, 349, 364, 657, 698
avance sur la provision pour frais : 1034, 1058, 1067
contrat d'organisation de l'arbitrage : 975, 999
pouvoirs de la Cour : 975
pouvoirs du secrétariat : 175
règlement : 669
responsabilité : 698
Intérêt à agir : 337, 569, 944
Investissements internationaux : 449, 531-628, 634, 890
ALENA : 143, 883, 887
arbitre d'urgence : 95
clause de la nation la plus favorisée : 779, 944
clause relative à une révolution ou un conflit armé : 779, 983
compétence & recevabilité : 337, 533, 569
consentement : 533
Convention de Vienne sur le droit des traités : 337, 944, 950
corruption : 983
double hatting : 622
droit de l'Union européenne : 602
exécution de la sentence : 634
expropriation : 591, 779
immunité : 884, 911
indépendance et impartialité : 883
investissement (notion) : 315, 983
investisseur (notion) : 569
nationalité de l'investisseur : 337, 551
protection des individus binationaux : 551
TBI : 449, 779, 950, 955, 983
Traité sur la Charte de l'énergie : 315
treaty claims / contract claims : 596
Irak
jurisprudence : 160
Iran : 340
Italie : 247
jurisprudence : 371-377, 997-1008

J

Juge
conseiller de la mise en état : 153, 483, 757, 914, 918
d'appui : 161, 170, 172, 181, 664, 703, 871, 879, 880, 963, 975, 978
de l'execution : 677
erreur d'interprétation : 148, 355
évolution jurisprudentielle : 911
excès de pouvoir : 154, 172, 681, 703, 963
v. Compétence-compétence, Exequatur, Recours en annulation et *Référé*

K

Koweit
jurisprudence : 160

L

Langue : 381, 432, 679, 702, 879, 912, 1029, 1102
Lieu d'arbitrage
v. Siège
Loyauté : 79, 170, 354

M

MARD : 15
Médiation : 15, 663
clause préalable obligatoire : 156, 168, 331, 678
Convention de Singapour : 105
médiation judiciaire : 170
Mesures d'instruction *in futurum* : 367, 660
Mesures provisoires et conservatoires : 148, 161, 177, 181, 189, 328, 648, 695, 883, 893, 919
pouvoirs de l'autorité judiciaire : 362, 655, 912
Moyens : 173
nouveaux : 179, 325, 334, 929, 950, 983
reconventionnels : 354
rectification des demandes : 641
rédaction des demandes : 172
retrait des demandes : 691
tardifs : 179, 180, 329, 340, 359, 673, 681, 695, 699, 914, 944, 950, 979, 983, 990, 993
v. In limine litis

N

Notaire : 325

O

OHADA : 15, 737

Ordre public : 132, 160, 289, 332, 650, 701, 711, 716, 737, 902, 903, 925, 997, 1035, 1102
conception française de l'arbitrage international : 158, 340, 356, 359, 669, 906, 920, 929, 965
de procédure : 394, 419, 423, 872, 877, 878, 979, 1029, 1061, 1083, 1106
interne : 672, 701
lois de police : 181, 340, 906, 965, 993
matériel : 385, 390, 422, 433, 1041, 1055, 1058, 1086, 1090, 1093, 1096
violation flagrante, effective et concrète : 175, 334, 340, 356, 925, 929, 965, 971, 983, 993

P

Parties
activité professionnelle : 166, 662, 702
attitude / comportement : 156, 168, 175, 328, 334, 356, 359, 673, 676, 704, 706, 885, 908
consommateurs : 131, 167, 678
égalité : 349
impécuniosité : 332, 375, 691, 879
intention : 181, 334, 925, 929, 983
multiples : 142, 453, 975
non-comparantes : 328, 673
non-signataires : 325, 509, 633, 925, 963, 995
particulier : 159
parties faibles : 131, 141, 325, 679
personne de droit public : 326
personne morale : 935
qualité à agir : 666, 937
représentant légal : 125
société civile immobilière : 705
v. Contradictoire (pincipe du-), Tiers, Volonté des Parties

Perte de chance : 156

Pièces
v. Preuve

Porte-fort : 907

Portugal
jurisprudence : 227

Prescription : 161, 167, 177, 325, 955, 964

Preuve : 348, 669, 1097
administration / appréciation : 393, 912, 1029, 1104
charge : 906, 911, 1052
preuves nouvelles : 137, 890, 1051

Procédures collectives : 123, 147, 148, 164, 373, 672, 695, 701, 713, 925, 965, 1009, 1010
déclaration de créance : 348

Procédures multiples : 142

Procédures parallèles : 631

Q

Question préjudicielle : 315

R

Recours en annulation : 483
annulation partielle : 383, 886, 901, 920, 971, 1025
caractère suspensif du recours : 893
constitution du tribunal : 161, 364, 398, 657, 963, 1100
effet cassatoire du recours : 383, 388, 1052, 1055
infra / ultra petita : 132, 925, 971, 1001, 1065, 1070, 1093
mission de l'arbitre : 158, 170, 327, 350, 354, 359, 669, 673, 681, 685, 707, 886, 925, 965, 971, 979
notion / étendue du contrôle : 143, 158, 350, 359, 379, 423, 685, 893, 897, 906, 909, 920, 925, 929, 944, 950, 955, 969, 974, 983, 1035, 1041, 1050
recevabilité : 137, 379, 390, 394, 395, 402, 406, 412, 431, 432, 631, 649, 670, 809, 914, 955, 971, 983, 1027, 1051, 1065, 1083
renvoi au tribunal arbitral : 127, 388
révision au fond : 155, 158, 175, 340, 350, 359, 681, 707, 914, 925, 979, 983
v. Compétence-compétence, Contradictoire (principe du –), Délai et *Ordre public*

Recours en révision : 422, 1051, 1072

Référé : 95, 330, 709, 907, 919, 977
compétence : 362, 648, 655, 660, 662, 691, 702, 912
contestation sérieuse : 177
dommage imminent : 148, 702
trouble manifestement illicite : 702
v. Urgence

Renonciation : 704, 901, 911
à l'appel / au droit de demander l'annulation : 886, 1070, 1093

Res judicata : 177, 181, 363, 394, 419, 650, 656, 661, 893, 1001, 1083

Rupture des relations commerciales : 996

Russie : 890
jurisprudence : 711-718

S

Saisie : 136, 363, 639, 677, 757, 893, 911, 917

Sanctions internationales : 340, 713

Sentence arbitrale
confidentialité : 139, 900
contradiction de motifs : 359, 653, 1001
d'accord parties : 181
définition / notion : 122, 897
délai / date : 161, 971
dispositif : 173, 179, 668
erreur de droit : 641, 914
exécution provisoire : 136, 483, 917
infra / ultra petita : 132, 925, 971, 1001, 1065, 1070, 1093
lieu : 971
mentions obligatoires : 971
mission de l'arbitre : 158, 170, 327, 350, 354, 359, 669, 673, 681, 685, 707, 886, 925, 965, 971, 979
motivation : 158, 354, 359, 433, 435, 653, 895, 979, 1052, 1086
notification / signifcation : 332, 396, 893
omission de statuer : 126
partielle / prémininaire : 887, 890, 893, 929, 1001, 1027
rectification : 673, 940
sentences successives : 453
signature : 905, 917
v. Arbitre, Exequatur et *Recours en annulation*

Siège de l'arbitrage : 340, 350, 654, 679, 711, 831, 857, 914, 944, 971, 979, 983, 997, 1014

Singapour
jurisprudence : 1009-1025

Suisse
jurisprudence : 379-436, 1027-1106
Loi fédérale sur le droit international privé : 379, 388, 1050, 1051

Surprise : 383, 925, 929, 979, 1068, 1093

Sursis à statuer : 161, 631, 689, 885, 888, 1023

T

Témoins : 125, 681, 871, 979
subordination : 872

Tiers : 61, 363, 366, 395, 658, 661, 895, 907, 908, 995
financement par des – : 449, 883
intervention forcée : 142, 963
intervention volontaire : 908

Titre exécutoire : 326, 677, 893

Tribunal arbitral
v. Arbitre

Tribunal arbitral du sport : 138, 379, 385, 390, 394, 399, 402, 412, 419, 422, 427, 428, 431, 433, 1029, 1034, 1035, 1041, 1057, 1061, 1065, 1068, 1072, 1083, 1096-1098, 1102, 1104, 1106

U

Ultra petita
v. Recours en annulation

Urgence : 95, 148, 177, 189, 328, 362, 367, 655, 660, 691, 695, 893, 907, 919

V

Volonté des parties : 121, 131, 148, 150, 154, 159, 170, 325, 663, 664, 676, 680, 893, 944

A

Abuse of process : 155, 158, 181, 355, 356, 359, 423, 432, 433, 469, 637, 641, 1102

Access to justice : 147, 332, 359, 691, 911

Actions to review : 422, 1051, 1072

Actions to set aside : 483
- admissibility : 137, 379, 390, 394, 395, 402, 406, 412, 431, 432, 631, 649, 670, 809, 914, 955, 971, 983, 1027, 1051, 1065, 1083
- arbitrator's mission : 158, 170, 327, 350, 354, 359, 669, 673, 681, 685, 707, 886, 925, 965, 971, 979
- constitution of the tribunal : 161, 364, 398, 657, 963, 1100
- *infra / ultra petita* : 132, 925, 971, 1001, 1065, 1070, 1093
- notion / extent of the judge's review : 143, 158, 350, 359, 379, 423, 685, 893, 897, 906, 909, 920, 925, 929, 944, 950, 955, 969, 974, 983, 1035, 1041, 1050
- nullifying effect of the action : 383, 388, 1052, 1055
- order to remand to the arbitration tribunal : 127, 388
- partial annulment : 383, 886, 901, 920, 971, 1025
- review of the arbitral tribunal's decision on the merits : 155, 158, 175, 340, 350, 359, 681, 707, 914, 925, 979, 983
- suspensory effect : 893
- *see Kompetenz-kompetenz, Public policy and Time-limit*

ADR : 15

Amicable composition : 181, 681, 707, 969

Anti-suit injunction : 135, 643, 958

Appeal : 355, 649, 672, 699, 937
- notice of appeal : 153

Arbitrability : 121, 373, 702, 705

Arbitral institution : 180, 347, 349, 364, 657, 698
- advance on costs : 1034, 1058, 1067
- contractual relationship with the parties : 975, 999
- Court's powers : 975
- liability : 698
- rules : 669
- Secretariat's powers : 175

Arbitration
- *ad hoc* : 179, 712, 944
- concept : 122, 125
- economic nature : 185, 347
- international nature : 347, 897

Arbitration by the Bâtonnier (President of the Bar) : 151, 161, 923, 924

Arbitration clause
- acceptance : 151, 166, 329
- autonomy : 61, 131, 150, 181, 227, 332, 350, 673, 685, 691, 925, 929
- binding nature : 325, 355, 363, 364, 656, 705, 907
- characterization : 170, 329, 903, 977
- extension : 61, 169, 350, 395, 509, 925, 995
- formal requirements : 347, 887
- framework agreement : 123
- general terms & conditions : 141, 166, 675, 678, 705, 887
- governing law : 61, 142, 417, 509, 643, 669, 685, 897, 925, 1011
- interpretation : 154, 181, 371, 373, 417, 423, 685, 885, 1004, 1063
- involvement in the contract's enforcement : 350, 364, 657, 925, 995
- knowledge of the clause : 151, 329, 705, 996
- lists of arbitrators : 809
- manifestly void or inapplicable : 150, 151, 159, 170, 355, 702, 903, 982, 996
- non-signatories : 325, 509, 633, 925, 963, 995
- party's consent : 1063, 1090
- pathological : 154, 156, 175, 179, 181, 347, 663, 675, 680, 702
- professional activity : 166, 662, 702
- scope : 121, 123, 138, 164, 175, 329, 334, 348, 363, 373, 375, 637, 656, 662, 664, 689, 885, 904, 907, 908, 920, 939, 975
- signing : 161
- transfer : 350
- validity : 159, 164, 166, 172, 181, 329, 332, 334, 348, 359, 367, 417, 660, 673, 685, 689, 699, 704, 904, 925, 975, 997
- waiver : 704

Arbitration procedure : 170
- bifurcation : 1001
- celerity : 334
- duration of the tribunal's mandate : 161
- good faith in the conduct of the proceedings : 79, 170, 354
- hearing venue : 958
- organisation measures : 349
- procedural order : 897, 940
- request for arbitration : 130
- suspension / interruption : 132, 161
- terms of reference : 334, 354, 929, 965
- virtual hearings : 453, 880, 888

Arbitrator
- amicable compositeur : 181, 681, 707, 969
- appointment : 122, 125, 130, 132, 170, 181, 364, 664, 666, 698, 699, 703, 879, 940, 944, 963
- arbitrator's contract : 831, 857, 958, 975
- challenge : 402, 880, 990, 1072
- collegiality / majority : 905, 917
- constitution of the tribunal : 161, 364, 398, 657, 963, 1100
- emergency arbitrator : 362, 648, 655
- fees : 349, 666, 940
- *jura novit curia* : 1093
- jurisdictional nature : 159, 469, 880, 893, 929, 983
- lists of arbitrators : 809
- mission : 158, 170, 327, 350, 354, 359, 669, 673, 681, 685, 707, 886, 925, 965, 971, 979
- powers : 469, 874, 880
- procedural order : 897, 940
- replacement : 1100
- resignation : 412
- responsibility : 349, 831, 857, 958
- *see Arbitration procedure*
- *see Impartiality and independence*
- *see Kompetenz-kompetenz*

Arguments : 173
- amendment of claims : 641

counterclaims : 354
formal requirements : 172
new – : 179, 325, 334, 929, 950, 983
raised untimely : 179, 180, 329, 340, 359, 673, 681, 695, 699, 914, 944, 950, 979, 983, 990, 993
withdrawal of claims : 691
see In limine litis

Austria
case law : 127-133, 875-881

Award
arbitrator's mission : 158, 170, 327, 350, 354, 359, 669, 673, 681, 685, 707, 886, 925, 965, 971, 979
by consent : 181
compulsory mentions : 971
confidentiality : 139, 900
contradiction in the reasoning : 359, 653, 1001
correction : 673, 940
definition / notion : 122, 897
dispositive section : 173, 179, 668
error of law : 641, 914
infra / ultra petita : 132, 925, 971, 1001, 1065, 1070, 1093
legal reasoning : 158, 354, 359, 433, 435, 653, 895, 979, 1052, 1086
notification : 332, 396, 893
omission to rule : 126
partial / interim award : 887, 890, 893, 929, 1001, 1027
place of submission of the award : 971
provisional enforcement : 136, 483, 917
signature : 905, 917
succession of awards : 453
time-limit / date : 161, 971
see Arbitrator, Exaquatur and Actions to set aside

B

Bank Guarantees : 362

Belgium
case law : 647-654

Bill of lading : 363, 657

C

Canada : 135-145, 883-891

Class action : 141

Competition law : 121

Conciliation : 15, 151, 168, 366, 369
formal requirements of the clause : 368
mandatory conciliation clause : 147, 148, 150, 153, 154, 165, 167, 325-327, 330, 363, 368, 676, 698, 706, 708, 923, 924, 937, 983

Confidentiality : 139, 900

Conflict of interests
see impartiality and independence

Contract
arbitration procedure organization agreement : 975
arbitrator's – : 831, 857, 958, 975
commercial agent : 131, 168, 181, 912
distinct – : 939
distribution agreement : 181, 348
expired – : 912
franchise agreement : 332, 673, 679, 691, 907
frustration : 385
group of – : 150, 151, 664
implied renewal : 664
insurance agreement : 227, 904
linked agreements : 169
loan agreement : 167, 168, 331
multi-parties : 123
novation : 168
of adhesion : 662, 679
pacta sunt servanda : 385, 433, 1086, 1096
prime contractor argreement : 327
principle of good faith in the execution : 168
privity : 355
purchase agreement : 329, 363, 656, 659
rental agreement : 647, 689
rider : 675
shareholders' agreement : 151, 153
subcontractor : 367, 662

Corporate law
articles of incorporation : 129, 656
group of companies : 569, 995
purchase agreement : 367, 656, 659, 668
shareholders : 131
shareholders' agreement : 151, 153

Corruption : 289, 356, 669, 983, 993

Costs : 141, 332, 340, 412, 649, 691, 1027
expenses and other costs : 152, 431
failure to pay the advance on costs : 1034, 1058, 1067
parties' bearing of the costs : 349
security for costs : 889
see Fees

Counsel / lawyer
demise : 879
duty to provide information and advice : 156, 957, 977
mission : 152
professional liability : 156, 706, 957, 977

Court of arbitration for sports : 138, 379, 385, 390, 394, 399, 402, 412, 419, 422, 427, 428, 431, 433, 1029, 1034, 1035, 1041, 1057, 1061, 1065, 1068, 1072, 1083, 1096-1098, 1102, 1104, 1106

Covid-19 : 880, 924

D

Damages : 11, 128, 181, 356, 666
loss of chance : 957
loss of profits : 727
punitive : 175, 716

Defense of lack of jurisdiction : 367, 659, 910, 983

Denial of justice : 160, 334, 359, 963, 975, 1083

Dilatory tactics : 483, 666, 924

Discounted Cash Flow method : 727

Due process / adversarial proceedings : 125, 126, 128, 332, 334, 340, 350, 354, 358, 381, 383, 393, 402, 419, 423, 427, 428, 433, 669, 699, 872, 874, 878, 880, 895, 901, 907, 914, 924, 979, 982, 1001, 1005, 1006, 1029, 1035, 1041, 1057, 1058, 1065, 1068, 1093, 1097, 1104

E

Embargo : 160, 965

Emergency : 95, 148, 177, 189, 328, 362, 367, 655, 660, 691, 695, 893, 907, 919

Emergency proceedings (State court) : 95, 330, 709, 907, 919, 977
- imminent damages : 148, 702
- jurisdiction : 362, 648, 655, 660, 662, 691, 702, 912
- manifestly illegal nuisance : 702
- serious ground for challenge (Article 808 French Code of Civil Procedure) : 177

Enforcement order : 326, 677, 893

England and Wales
- case law : 61, 79, 501, 614, 631-646

Estoppel : 180, 337, 509, 637, 691, 711, 929, 971

European Convention on Human Rights : 332, 390, 399, 695, 809, 845, 975, 1006, 1035, 1041, 1083, 1090

European Court of Justice : 315

European Union law : 340, 602
- Regulation n°44/2001 : 347, 831, 857, 939, 958
- Regulation n°1215/2012 : 958, 999

Evidence : 348, 669, 1097
- assessment : 393, 912, 1029, 1104
- burden of proof : 906, 911, 1052
- new – : 137, 890, 1051

Excess of powers : 154, 172, 681, 703, 963

Exequatur : 407, 650, 677, 699, 701, 873, 889, 905, 935, 997
- extent of the judicial review : 139, 877, 971

Exhibits
- *see Evidence*

Expert : 79, 154, 161, 175, 422, 901

F

Facts (new –) : 137, 890, 1051

Fees : 349, 666
- contingency fees : 152, 332
- *see Costs / fees*

FIDIC : 929

Forum non conveniens : 888

France
- case law : 95, 147-188, 289, 315, 325-369, 655-709, 809, 831, 857, 893-996

Fraud : 334, 359, 650, 979, 983
- procedural fraud : 925, 929, 971, 983

French Civil Code
- article 2061 : 166, 689, 702, 705

French Code of Civil Procedure
- article 12 : 148
- article 48 : 705
- article 76 : 706
- article 81 : 678
- article 145 : 177, 181
- article 524 : 148, 483
- article 1009-1 : 483
- article 1442 : 169, 170, 181
- article 1448 : 151, 159, 164, 169, 177, 187, 328, 332, 355, 364, 367, 660, 664, 673, 675, 678, 680, 689, 691, 939
- article 1449 : 148, 187, 328, 362, 367, 660, 691, 702, 977
- article 1450 : 666
- article 1452 : 161, 666
- article 1454 : 170
- article 1455 : 170
- article 1456 : 173
- article 1460 : 172
- article 1463 : 161
- article 1465 : 159, 164, 168
- article 1466 : 175, 483, 673
- article 1482 : 181
- article 1483 : 181
- article 1484 : 177
- article 1499 : 695
- article 1509 : 669, 944
- article 1511 : 669
- article 1520 : 332
- article 1526 : 757
- article 1843-4 : 154

G

General terms of sale : 141, 166, 675, 678, 705, 887

Germany & Austria
- case law : 121-127, 871-874

Good faith : 168, 337, 354, 356, 359, 396, 433, 925, 929, 1035, 1055, 1090

I

IBA
- Guidelines on Conflict of Interest in International Arbitration : 920
- Rules of Evidence : 359

ICSID
- *see International investments*

Impartiality and independence : 151, 412, 698, 809, 914, 1072, 1100
- notorious facts : 155, 173, 990
- obligation to disclose : 15, 173, 501, 831, 845, 895, 920, 975, 990
- reasonable doubt : 173, 895, 901, 914, 920, 925
- relation between the arbitrators or the parties' counsel : 155, 398, 449, 883, 895, 1006

Impecuniosity of a party : 332, 375, 691, 879

In limine litis : 329

India : 271

Infra petita
- *see Actions to set aside*

Insolvency : 123, 147, 148, 164, 373, 672, 695, 701, 713, 925, 965, 1009, 1010
- declaration of claim : 348

Insurance law : 227, 904

Intention of the parties : 121, 131, 148, 150, 154, 159, 170, 325, 663, 664, 676, 680, 893, 944

Interest in bringing legal action : 337, 569, 944

Interim measures : 148, 161, 177, 181, 189, 328, 648, 695, 883, 893, 919
- powers of judicial authority : 362, 655, 912

International chamber of commerce : 340, 940
- 2021 ICC Rules of arbitration : 453
- expedited procedure : 453
- liability : 940

International investments : 449, 531-628, 634, 890
- BIT : 449, 779, 950, 955, 983
- consent : 533
- corruption : 983
- double hatting : 622
- emergency arbitrator : 95
- Energy Charter Treaty : 315
- enforcement of the award : 634
- EU law : 602
- expropriation : 591, 779
- immunity : 884, 911
- independence and impartiality : 883
- investment (notion) : 315, 983
- investor (notion) : 569
- investor's nationality : 337, 551
- jurisdiction & admissibility : 337, 533, 569
- most favoured nation clause : 779, 944
- NAFTA : 143, 883, 887
- protection of dual nationals : 551
- revolution or armed conflict clause : 779, 983
- treaty claims / contract claims : 596
- Vienna Convention on the Law of Treaties : 337, 944, 950

Iran : 340

Iraq
- case law : 160

Italy : 247
- case law : 371-377, 997-1008

J

Judge
- acting in support of arbitration : 161, 170, 172, 181, 664, 703, 871, 879, 880, 963, 975, 978
- changes in case law : 911
- enforcement judge : 677
- excess of powers : 154, 172, 681, 703, 963
- misintrepretation : 148, 355
- pre-trial judge : 153, 483, 757, 914, 918
- *see Kompetenz-kompetenz, Enforcement, Actions to set aside and Emergency proceedings (State court)*

Jurisdiction clause : 150, 181, 664, 680, 982

K

Kompetenz-kompetenz : 141, 142, 147, 159, 164, 168-170, 177, 187, 227, 328, 329, 348, 350, 355, 395, 399, 402, 417, 423, 643, 657, 673, 675, 678, 691, 903, 939, 950, 982

Kuweit
- case law : 160

L

Labour law : 702, 902, 903, 917, 935

Language : 381, 432, 679, 702, 879, 912, 1029, 1102

Liquidated damages clause : 965

Loss of an opportunity : 156

Loyalty : 79, 170, 354

M

Maritime law : 364, 657

Mediation : 15, 663
- judicially ordered mediation : 170
- mandatory mediation clause : 156, 168, 331, 678
- Singapore Convention : 105

Multiple proceedeings : 142

Mutal Legal Assistance Convention : 737

N

New York Convention : 181, 407, 706, 737

Notary (France) : 325

O

OECD Convention on Combating Bribery of Foreign Public Officials in International Business Transactions (17 December 1997) : 993

OHADA : 15, 737

P

Parallel proceedings : 631

Parties
- behaviour : 156, 168, 175, 328, 334, 356, 359, 673, 676, 704, 706, 885, 908
- consumer : 131, 167, 678
- equality : 349
- failure to appear before the court : 328, 673
- impecuniousity : 332, 375, 691, 879
- intention : 181, 334, 925, 929, 983
- legal person : 935
- legal representative : 125
- *locus standi* : 666, 937
- multi-parties : 142, 453, 975
- non-signatories : 325, 509, 633, 925, 963, 995
- private individual : 159
- professionnal activity : 166, 662, 702
- public entity : 326
- weaker parties : 131, 141, 325, 679
- *see Due process, Third party*

Place of arbitration
- *see Seat of arbitration and Actions to set aside*

Portugal
- case law : 227

Prescription : 161, 167, 177, 325, 955, 964

Priority preliminary ruling : 315

Provisional execution : 154, 355, 483, 677, 757

Public law : 167
- public procurement : 247

Public policy : 132, 160, 289, 332, 650, 701, 711, 716, 737, 902, 903, 925, 997, 1035, 1102
- flagrancy, effectiveness and concreteness of the violation : 175, 334, 340, 356, 925, 929, 965, 971, 983, 993
- French conception of international arbitration : 158, 340, 356, 359, 669, 906, 920, 929, 965
- internal / domestic : 672, 701
- lois de police : 181, 340, 906, 965, 993
- procedural – : 394, 419, 423, 872, 877, 878, 979, 1029, 1061, 1083, 1106

substantive – : 385, 390, 422, 433, 1041, 1055, 1058, 1086, 1090, 1093, 1096

R

Ratione temporis jurisdiction : 412, 950, 955

Res judicata : 177, 181, 363, 394, 419, 650, 656, 661, 893, 1001, 1083

Russia : 890
 case law : 711-718

S

Sanctions (international) : 340, 713

Seat (arbitral –) : 340, 350, 654, 679, 711, 831, 857, 914, 944, 971, 979, 983, 997, 1014

Seizure / Freezing order : 136, 363, 639, 677, 757, 893, 911, 917

Singapore
 case law : 1009-1025

Sports arbitration
 see Court of arbitration for sports

Sports Arbitration Chamber (France) : 809

Stay of proceedings : 161, 631, 689, 885, 888, 1023

Surprise : 383, 925, 929, 979, 1068, 1093

Switzerland : 379-436, 1027-1106
 Federal Act on Private International Law : 379, 388, 1050, 1051

T

Tax law : 993

Termination (sudden) of business relations : 996

Terms of reference : 334, 354, 929, 965

Third party : 61, 363, 366, 395, 658, 661, 895, 907, 908, 995
 compulsory joinder : 142, 963
 third party funding : 449, 883
 voluntary joinder : 908

Time-limit : 175, 757
 arbitration time-limit : 673, 969
 calculation of time-limits : 172, 666
 extension : 924, 969
 prescription : 161, 167, 177, 325, 955, 964
 proceedural time-limit : 128, 1106
 reasonableness : 979
 stay of proceedings : 161, 631, 689, 885, 888, 1023
 suspension / interruption : 893, 964, 1098
 see Arguments (raised untimely)

Tort action : 128, 151, 164, 165, 366, 371, 658, 908
 see Termination (sudden) of business relations

Tribunal (arbitral –)
 see Arbitrator

U

Ultra petita
 see Actions to set aside

UNCITRAL
 Convention on International Settlement Agreements resulting from Mediation : 105
 model law : 65, 191
 Rules of arbitration : 334, 337, 673, 983

Unfair competition : 151

United States of America
 case law : 509

Unjust enrichment : 128

W

Waiver : 704, 901, 911
 appeal / action to set aside : 886, 1070, 1093

Witnesses : 125, 681, 871, 979

Événement | Event

Sous la direction de Priscille PEDONE

Sorbonne Arbitrage: a legal scientific pilgrimage

Kamalia MEHTIYEVA
Professor of law
Paris-Est Créteil University

The Grand Salon of Sorbonne University in Paris is one of the academic world's most emblematic and historical places. This symbolic lieu for the scientific community served, on 14 February 2022, as a venue for the celebration of a birth. Law professors, practitioners and students, brought together by a common passion for arbitration, totaling two hundred participants, gathered in the Grand Salon, with as many attending remotely, to inaugurate the newly-born *Sorbonne Arbitrage* initiative.

It all began when Professor Thomas Clay, initiator of the project, realised that the Sorbonne law school counts among the highest number of international arbitration specialists in the world: Farhad Ameli, Hervé Ascencio, Mathias Audit, Laurent Aynès, Sylvain Bollée, Loïc Cadiet, Philippe Delebecque, Liliane Larribère, Remy Libchaber, Daniel Mainguy, Pierre Mayer and Philippe Stoffel-Munck, to name but a few.

And yet, in spite of this unique concentration of arbitration specialists in one University, the link between their respective activities and Sorbonne law school has not always been clear. Their academic and professional pursuits remain scattered, when it is, on the contrary, necessary to promote synergies.

From an assessment of the need to the implementation of the initiative, Professor Clay did what it took to create a new "label" – *Sorbonne Arbitrage*. Owing to the oft-decried inertia of the French university system, this took a good deal of battling established mindsets, compounded by a crippling lack of funds. Summarising the predicament of scholars in France and abroad, Professor Clay declared: "Universities suffer from overly restrictive frameworks that end up breaking initiatives. Old patterns are excessively cumbersome, forcing one to go through national bodies and either create new degrees or partnerships".

One can only deplore the irony that such restrictions are being imposed on scholars, in a place of freedom *par excellence*, the University, when they simply seek to cultivate and share ideas, knowledge and research. Hence *Sorbonne Arbitrage* appears as an oasis of academic freedom in an increasingly gridlocked university environment.

As emphasized by University President Professor Christine Neau-Leduc during her inaugural address, such flexible initiatives are testament to the Sorbonne tradition of academic excellence and commitment to interdisciplinarity. These characteristics are of great benefit to the eighteen thousand students of the Sorbonne Law School, as pointed out by Faculty Director Agnes Roblot-Troisier, who also reminded the audience of the University's status as Europe's largest centre for studies in social sciences.

However, despite its impressive assets, the University sometimes lacks the means to accompany students beyond its doors. *Sorbonne Arbitrage*, in the words of Professor Neau-Leduc, is conceived to be a bridge between the University and the law in practice and to narrow the gap between the legal profession and academia.

From this perspective, the *Sorbonne Arbitrage* initiative could not have been both more daring and necessary. At a time when the head of the French State advocates that universities must become "more effective in professional training", their role in France has never been more in question.

In midst of a crisis, a new institution is being built, which may, if it fulfils and even exceeds its goals, perhaps give an example of how the University crisis may be resolved.

Whatever *Sorbonne Arbitrage*'s contribution to wider educational and societal goals may be, the combination of theory and practice is in its DNA, as shown at the very first event organized by *Sorbonne Arbitrage*, which brought together a professor and a practitioner. Professor Daniel Mainguy, from Paris 1 Panthéon-Sorbonne and Jalal El-Ahdab, partner at Bird & Bird, introduced their newly released and rethought presentation of arbitration: *Arbitration Law: Theory and Practice* (original title in French *Droit de l'arbitrage: théorie et pratique*, LexisNexis, 2021).

The question remains: what is *Sorbonne Arbitrage*?

With so many legal minds gathered in one room, how can one escape a common legal exercise which we teach our students from the very first day of their legal studies? To identify, to define, and finally to ... categorize.

Without any false modesty, lawyers are masters of the art of definition. But those who master an art know its limits. Is definition always possible? Does definition always lead to understanding? Do we not sometimes fall into our own trap when we attempt to define? Therefore, should not the temptation to define be resisted in favour of allowing *Sorbonne Arbitrage* to define itself?

To define

Old labels rarely fit new ideas, and emerging concepts often deserve their own categories. Yet, legal minds still feel the irresistible urge to define. Professor Clay proved no exception and baptized *Sorbonne Arbitrage* an "unidentified university object". Lawyers do not lack humour but even an admittedly amusing definition can fail to satisfy.

One is prone to forget Albert Camus' famous prophecy: naming things badly only adds to the misfortune of the world (*"Mal nommer les choses c'est ajouter au malheur du monde")*.

Reductive simplicity harms the prospect of full self-realisation which sometimes can only be achieved through self-definition.

To self-define

Self-definition, on the contrary, rescues lawyers from the spell of constant categorization and would allow the newly-created *Sorbonne Arbitrage* freely to develop its essence.

After all, a parent's first duty under the law is twofold : to declare the birth of the newborn and to name their offspring. Both have been fulfilled by Professor Clay in his role as the *pater* of *Sorbonne Arbitrage*.

Professor Thomas Clay named the newborn and named it well. Against all odds, since international arbitration forms a multicultural and multilingual community, the new legal initiative bears a French name.

However, once legal parental duties have been duly fulfilled, parents have a limited say as to the future of their child. What matters most is a simple parental blessing of longevity and prosperity, which Professor Clay has a fittingly given to *Sorbonne Arbitrage*, wishing it to continue bringing together lawyers passionate about arbitration, even a hundred-and-fifty years from now.

What will the trajectory of *Sorbonne Arbitrage* be, on its path of self-definition? One can only hope it will tend towards greater enrichment and greater academic freedom since, as Professor Clay has stated, *Sorbonne Arbitrage* is a federation where everyone leads and everyone has the same level of responsibility to bring up the newborn. It is a pure example of participatory democracy, leaving room for imagination, where inventiveness is rewarded.

The chosen method of governance shapes the essence of the thing governed and contributes to its self-definition: participatory democracy will be implemented through discussions over newly published books and articles, conferences, feedback from arbitrators on non-confidential cases, organising moots, webinars, discussing new doctoral theses in the field of arbitration and inventing other formats such as "one day, one judgment" (*"un jour, un arrêt"*) to discuss the most recent French or foreign caselaw.

Through these initiatives, *Sorbonne Arbitrage* will live and define itself. More lively than a think tank, more diverse than a school of thought, *Sorbonne Arbitrage* will be a scientific pilgrimage. It will also be a scientific umbrella which covers a cohesive gathering of intellects and serves as a shelter for independent and irreductible spirits.

And on this path of scientific pilgrimage and self-definition, *Sorbonne Arbitrage* will reassert the place of Paris as world center for international arbitration.

Administration / Management

Les Cahiers de l'Arbitrage • The Paris Journal of International Arbitration
Revue éditée par Lextenso
La Grande Arche La Défense – 1, Parvis de La Défense – 92044 Paris – La Défense Cedex
Tél. : 01 40 93 40 00 – Fax : 01 41 08 12 39
P-DG, Directeur de la publication : Bruno Vergé
Directrice générale déléguée : Emmanuelle Filiberti
Assistante d'édition : Sylvie Mauzen
sylvie.mauzen@lextenso.fr
ISSN : 2107-5387
Revue trimestrielle – Dépôt légal : à parution

Abonnement / Subscription
Tél. : 01 40 93 40 40 – Fax : 01 41 09 92 10
abonnements@lextenso.fr
Tarif France 2022 : 458,93 € TTC (435 € HT)
Tarif Étranger 2022 : 500 €
Prix au numéro France : 128,71 € TTC (122 € HT)
Prix au numéro Étranger : 140,30 €

Imprimé en France. - Dupliprint Mayenne, 733, rue Saint Léonard, 53101 Mayenne CEDEX

N° 2972647N - Dépôt légal : à parution

Imprimé sur des papiers produits en Pologne (couverture, 0 % de fibres recyclées) et en Allemagne (intérieur, 100 % de fibres recyclées), issus de forêts gérées durablement ; impact gaz à effet de serre pour un exemplaire : 428 g éq. CO_2